WINCHESTER STUDIES

General editor: Martin Biddle

====

4

THE ANGLO-SAXON MINSTERS OF WINCHESTER

PART III

PROPERTY AND PIETY IN EARLY MEDIEVAL WINCHESTER

DOCUMENTS RELATING TO THE TOPOGRAPHY OF THE ANGLO-SAXON AND NORMAN CITY AND ITS MINSTERS

WINCHESTER STUDIES 4.iii
THE ANGLO-SAXON MINSTERS
OF WINCHESTER

═══

PROPERTY AND PIETY IN EARLY MEDIEVAL WINCHESTER

DOCUMENTS RELATING TO THE
TOPOGRAPHY OF THE ANGLO-SAXON AND
NORMAN CITY AND ITS MINSTERS

ALEXANDER R. RUMBLE

CLARENDON PRESS · OXFORD
2002

OXFORD

UNIVERSITY PRESS

Great Clarendon Street, Oxford OX2 6DP

Oxford University Press is a department of the University of Oxford.
It furthers the University's objective of excellence in research, scholarship,
and education by publishing worldwide in

Oxford New York

Auckland Bangkok Buenos Aires Cape Town Chennai
Dar es Salaam Delhi Hong Kong Istanbul Karachi Kolkata
Kuala Lumpur Madrid Melbourne Mexico City Mumbai Nairobi
São Paulo Shanghai Singapore Taipei Tokyo Toronto

Oxford is a registered trade mark of Oxford University Press
in the UK and in certain other countries

Published in the United States
by Oxford University Press Inc., New York

© Oxford University Press 2002

The moral rights of the author have been asserted
Database right Oxford University Press (maker)

First published 2002

British Library Cataloguing in Publication Data

Data available

Library of Congress Cataloging in Publication Data

Data applied for

ISBN 0-19-813413-4

1 3 5 7 9 10 8 6 4 2

Typeset in Bembo
by Joshua Associates Ltd., Oxford
Printed in Great Britain
on acid-free paper by
St Edmundsbury Press
Bury St Edmunds, Suffolk

IN MEMORY OF
DOROTHEA OSCHINSKY
and
JOHN McN. DODGSON

GENERAL EDITOR'S PREFACE

THIS is the first time that the Anglo-Saxon and Norman charters of a single city have been brought together in one volume. The interest of these documents goes far beyond urban history and topography. They include the New Minster refoundation charter of 966 (Document **IV**), the first modern edition and translation of one of the central documents of the English Benedictine reform of the tenth century; a reconstruction of what seems to have been the tenth-century refoundation confirmation of the properties of Old Minster (Document **V**); and the key documents relating to what may have been the original seventh-century endowment of Old Minster, the so-called 'beneficial hidation of Chilcomb' (Documents **XXX–XXXII**).

When Roger Quirk began his study of the architecture and topography of the Anglo-Saxon minsters in Winchester in the 1950s, modern editions of the documents edited, translated, and annotated in this volume were not available. Many had been published by J. M. Kemble from 1839 to 1845 and by W. de G. Birch between 1885 and 1899, but with the exception of Documents **I** and **XXIX** and the work of G. B. Grundy on Hampshire charters (including the bounds of Document **XXII**) no attempt had then yet been made to set them in their historical or topographical context or to solve the bounds of the properties which some describe in detail. In other words, this material had not been used as a whole in the study of Winchester as an emerging urban centre and the greatest monastic community of Anglo-Saxon England.

Winchester was no different in this from any other English city. G. B. Grundy had studied the rural charters of the pre-conquest period county by county and had attempted to solve their bounds, but no such work had been done on urban charters. The practice of studying Anglo-Saxon charters in groups by archive (in essence, by recipient), understandable as it is, may have deflected attention from the importance for urban studies of dealing with the charters of a single place as a group. No study comparable to the present volume yet exists for any other English town, and it is doubtful whether it would be possible for more than a handful—Canterbury, London, Rochester, Worcester, and York are the most obvious.

Early in the planning of Winchester Studies it became obvious that for Winchester such a compilation was both possible and essential. In 1984 the Delegates of the University Press agreed to the addition of this volume to the series of Studies already approved, Alex Rumble, who had been on the staff of the Winchester Research Unit, having already agreed to take it on. Dr Rumble's London doctoral thesis of 1980 had been devoted to the Old Minster's *Codex Wintoniensis*, the single most important source of the documents edited here. When his study of the Old Minster archive is published as a volume in the British Academy's series of Anglo-Saxon Charters, alongside Sean Miller's recent study of the New Minster charters in the same series, Winchester will have almost all the relevant material available from the perspectives of both place and archive or recipient.

The present volume forms part of Winchester Studies 4, a series of three volumes devoted to the history, archaeology and architecture of the Anglo-Saxon minsters of Winchester (WS 4.i), to the cult of St Swithun (WS 4.ii), and to the evidence of the Anglo-Saxon and Norman charters (WS 4.iii). Important as the documents presented here are for the general topography of the city and its immediate surroundings, their significance for the history, topography, and religious development of the three great minsters cannot be over-estimated.

The documents which reflect the original endowment of *Old Minster* in the seventh century (Documents **XXX–XXXII**) and confirm its estates and privileges at the time of the Benedictine reform in the later tenth century (Document **V**) have already been mentioned. Document **II** reveals information about the northern boundary of the precinct of Old Minster as it may have been in the seventh century; Documents **VI**, **VII**, and **VIII** reveal changes in that precinct in the tenth; and Documents **XIII** and **XV** cast light on the reversion to the cathedral priory in *c*.1110 of the land alienated in 901–3 to form part of the site of New Minster.

The measurements and boundaries of the site provided for the building of *New Minster* in the centre of the city in *c*.901–3 are laid out in Document **II**; its supposed original endowment defined in Document **III**; and its refoundation described in detail in Document **IV**, one of the principal witnesses to the Benedictine reform of the 960s, as already noted. Documents **VI** and **VII** detail the extension of the New Minster precinct in the later tenth century. Documents **X**, **XI**, **XIV**, and **XVII** deal with the surrender of part of the site of New Minster for William the Conqueror's enlargement of the old royal palace and the building of his new hall. The relocation of New Minster from the centre of the city to a new site at Hyde outside North Gate is dealt with in Documents **XII**, **XIII**, **XV**, **XVI**, and **XVII**, which also reveal important information about the site and rights of New Minster before its move to Hyde.

The *Nunnaminster*, the third of the three minsters, was probably founded on a property of Queen Ealhswith, wife of King Alfred, the bounds of which are set out in Document **I**, before the queen's death in 902. Documents **VI** and **VII** deal with adjustments in the boundary of that site in the aftermath of the Benedictine reform in the later tenth century.

The Winchester Excavations Committee, under whose aegis this volume has been produced as part of their investigation of the Anglo-Saxon Minsters of Winchester, is thus doubly pleased to welcome the appearance of Alex Rumble's *Property and Piety* as Part iii of the fourth volume of Winchester Studies.

MARTIN BIDDLE

Hertford College, Oxford. Translation of St. Æthelwold, 2001

AUTHOR'S PREFACE

MANY winters have passed since Martin Biddle first invited me to prepare an edition of relevant early medieval charters as an appendix to Winchester Studies 4.i, the volume containing the published results of the extensive excavation of the Old and New Minsters. I was at that time, in 1976–77, working in the city at the Winchester Research Unit, as a research assistant under Derek Keene on the Social and Economic History of Medieval Winchester, funded by the Social Science Research Council. Quite soon after I began work on the edition it became clear that the results of my labours on the charters would be better published in separate covers, for ease of reference and accessibility. With hindsight, the inclusion of translations, commentaries, and extensive annotation, as well as the texts themselves, in the present book has shown the separation of archaeology and documents in this way to have been a wise decision for reasons of economy too. I have, however, always tried to place the texts within their topographical context, and have made reference to the results of archaeological excavation wherever relevant. The close association of documents, archaeology, and hagiographical texts for the early medieval history of Winchester is reflected in the fact that the final version of Winchester Studies 4 will include all these categories of evidence within its three parts.

Most of the work done for the present book has been accomplished since I moved north from Winchester in 1981 to teach palaeography at the Victoria University of Manchester. I am grateful for funding which I received before then from the Robert Kiln Trust. Study leave jointly financed by the British Humanities Research Board and the University of Manchester allowed me to work in the session 1995–96 particularly on documents **IV** and **V** within the context of a wider study of the diplomas of King Edgar.

I am grateful to Professor Martin Biddle for his patience, help, and support as General Editor; to Professor Simon Keynes, both for generously reading and commenting on the whole book and for his sympathetic encouragement; and to Dr Derek Keene for his example of scholarly dedication to the history of Winchester, as also to him and to Professor Judith Green for answering my query about twelfth-century gelds. I am indebted to Professor Michael Lapidge both for his helpful criticism of an early stage of my work on document **IV** and for reading through the Latin texts in proof and suggesting important improvements to both edition and translation in a number of places. Further valuable comments by Professor Lapidge are included in the Addenda.

I am thankful to Dr Sean Miller for allowing me access to his work on the New Minster charters prior to its publication in the British Academy series. I should note however that both his edition and the two volumes on the Abingdon archive edited by Dr Susan Kelly in the same series appeared in print too late for their commentaries to be fully taken into account in the present work.

The production of this volume began in the age of the typewriter and finished in that of computer typesetting. I am grateful to June and David Lloyd who first word-processed the bulk of my typed (and handwritten) editions, translations, and notes. I pay tribute to the skill of Anne Joshua in converting my final and much expanded text on disk to the desired page-format worthy of the Winchester Studies series and for her patience in dealing with the problems entailed in presenting Anglo-Saxon and early medieval manuscript conventions in modern print.

This book is dedicated to two remarkable scholars and teachers, both now alas deceased, late respectively of the University of Liverpool and University College London, who initiated me in the palaeography and significance of Anglo-Saxon charters and inspired me to study them further as texts of importance to a whole range of academic disciplines.

ALEXANDER R. RUMBLE

Manchester, New Year's Day 2002

CONTENTS

List of plates   xiii

List of figures   xv

List of abbreviations   xvii

I. INTRODUCTION

1. CRITERIA FOR THE INCLUSION OF DOCUMENTS IN THE
PRESENT VOLUME   1

2. THE MANUSCRIPT SOURCES   1

    General character   1

    List of manuscripts   5

3. THE AUTHENTICITY OF THE DOCUMENTS   14

    Typology   14

    Degrees of authenticity   16

    Monastic propaganda   17

4. THE DOCUMENTS AS EVIDENCE FOR HISTORICAL
TOPOGRAPHY   19

    Chronological survey   23

    Recurrent references to topographical features of the Anglo-Saxon and Norman city   28

    Street-names   29

    Topography outside the city   29

5. THE DOCUMENTS AS A REFLECTION OF THE HISTORY OF
THE CITY *c*.900–*c*.1150   29

    Winchester as a royal city   30

    Winchester as an ecclesiastical centre   31

    Winchester as a national and regional centre   35

II. DOCUMENTS RELATING TO THE TOPOGRAPHY OF ANGLO-SAXON AND NORMAN WINCHESTER AND ITS MINSTERS

1. EDITORIAL PRINCIPLES   37

2. LIST OF DOCUMENTS   38

III. DOCUMENTS I–XXXIII: TEXT, TRANSLATION AND NOTES

1. **I–XVII** Anglo-Saxon and early medieval documents relevant to the sites and foundations in Winchester of the three minsters and Hyde Abbey   45

2. **XVIII–XXIX** Anglo-Saxon documents relevant to the topography of the city of Winchester   183

3. **XXX–XXXII** Late Anglo-Saxon and early medieval documents relating to the beneficial hidation of the estate of Chilcomb, Hants   223

4. **XXXIII** Papal letter concerning the reform of the Old Minster   233

Latin word-list   239

Old English word-list   243

Index of biblical references   245

Index of persons named in the documents   246

Index of places named in the documents   249

Index of references to Anglo-Saxon charters   251

ADDENDA   253

LIST OF PLATES

All plates are reproduced by permission of the British Library Board

Frontispiece   BL, Cotton MS. Vesp. A. viii, fo. 2^v [**IV**, minature]

(*After p. 40*)

I. BL, Cotton MS. Vesp. A. viii, fo. 19^v [**IV**, text]

II. BL, Add. MS. 15350, fo. 8^r, top [**VIII(i)** and **(ii)**]

III. BL, Add. MS. 15350, fo. 8^v : *a*, top [**VI**]; *b*, foot [**VII**]

IV. BL, Add. MS. 29436, fo. 10^v [**XXIX**]

V. BL, Add. MS. 15350, fo. 8^r, foot [**II**]

In approximate chronological order of scribes

LIST OF FIGURES

Drawn by Technical Graphics Department, OUP

1. Places and areas in or near Winchester to which the pre-1066 documents relate   2

2. Places and areas in or near Winchester to which the early Norman documents relate   3

3. Settlements mentioned in the documents (distinguishing those with Winchester tenements)   20

4. The south-east corner of Winchester *c.*963–1066   24

5. The south-east corner of Winchester *c.*1110   26

6. Winchester *c.*1148   27

7. The bounds of Ealhswith's *haga* in **I** (*a.* 5 December 902)   49

8. The bounds of the New Minster in **II** (A.D. ?901)   55

9. The bounds of Hyde Moors in **IX** (A.D. 983)   153

10. The bounds of Easton, Hants, in **XXII** (A.D. 961)   194

11. The bounds of Ælfswith's tenement in **XXVI** (A.D. 996)   208

12. The bounds of Queen Ælfgifu Emma's tenement in **XXVIII** (A.D. 1012)   216

13. Chilcomb, Hants, and its eleventh-century dependencies   227

Figs. 1, 2, 4–6, and 13 are adapted from Winchester Studies 1,
Figs. 25, 26, 9 (*c.*963–1066), 9 (*c.*110), 27, and 6, respectively.

LIST OF ABBREVIATIONS

a.	*ante*
Add. MS.	Additional Manuscript
Ælfric *Vita S. Æthelwoldi*	'Ælfric's *Vita S. Æthelwoldi* ', Appendix A in Michael Lapidge and Michael Winterbottom (ed.), *Wulfstan of Winchester, Life of St Æthelwold* (Oxford Medieval Texts, Oxford, 1991, repr. 1996)
Anglia Sacra	H. Wharton (ed.), *Anglia sacra sive collectio historiarum* (2 vols., London, 1691)
ArchJ	*Archaeological Journal*
ASC [A, B, etc.]	The Anglo-Saxon Chronicle (different versions), see Whitelock *EHD* 1
AS Ch	A. J. Robertson (ed.), *Anglo-Saxon Charters* (Cambridge, 1939)
ASE	*Anglo-Saxon England* (Cambridge, 1972–)
Asser	Asser's *Life of King Alfred*, trans. in Keynes and Lapidge
AS Wills	Dorothy Whitelock (ed.), *Anglo-Saxon Wills* (Cambridge, 1930)
AS Writs	F. E. Harmer (ed.), *Anglo-Saxon Writs* (Manchester, 1952)
Bates *Regesta*	David Bates (ed.), *Regesta regum Anglo-Normannorum: The Acta of William I (1066–1087)* (Oxford, 1998)
BCS	Walter de Gray Birch (ed.), *Cartularium Saxonicum* (3 vols. and index, London, 1885–99)
Birch *Ancient Manuscript*	Walter de Gray Birch (ed.), *An Ancient Manuscript* (HRS, London and Winchester, 1889)
BL	British Library, London
Bod	Bodleian Library, Oxford
BR	The Rule of St. Benedict, ed. and trans. in *RB 1980*
Brooks 'Micheldever Forgery'	N. P. Brooks, 'The Oldest Document in the College Archives? The Micheldever Forgery', in R. D. Custance (ed.), *Winchester College: 6th Centenary Essays* (Oxford, 1982), 189–222, plus 6 pp. maps
BSV	Robert Weber (ed.), *Biblia sacra iuxta vulgatam versionem* (2nd edn., Stuttgart, 1975)
BT	T. Northcote Toller, *An Anglo-Saxon Dictionary based on the Manuscript Collections of the late Joseph Bosworth* (Oxford, 1898, repr 1973)
BT *Addenda*	Alistair Campbell, *Enlarged Addenda and Corrigenda* to BT *Suppl.* (Oxford, 1972, repr. 1973)
BT *Suppl.*	T. Northcote Toller, *Supplement* to BT (Oxford, 1921, repr. 1973)
c.	*circa*
Cal Chart R	*Calendar of Charter Rolls* (6 vols., PRO, London, 1903–27)

Cal Inq Misc	*Calendar of Inquisitions Miscellaneous* (in progress, PRO, London, 1916–)
Cal Pat R	*Calendar of Patent Rolls* (in progress, PRO, London, 1891–)
Campbell	A. Campbell, *Old English Grammar* (Oxford, 1959)
Campbell *Rochester*	A. Campbell (ed.), *Charters of Rochester* (Anglo-Saxon Charters 1, Oxford, 1973)
CBA	Council for British Archaeology
CCCC	Corpus Christi College, Cambridge
CCSL	Corpus Christianorum, series latina
Chart Antiq	Chartae Antiquae Rolls (C 52) in PRO
Chart R	Charter Rolls (C 53) in PRO
Codex Wintoniensis	BL, Add. MS. 15350, the *Codex Wintoniensis*, the earliest surviving cartulary of Winchester cathedral priory
Conf R	Confirmation Rolls (C 56) in PRO
Councils	D. Whitelock, M. Brett and C. N. L. Brooke (ed.), *Councils & Synods with other Documents relating to the English Church*, i, *A.D. 871–1204* (Oxford, 1981)
CSEL	Corpus scriptorum ecclesiasticorum latinorum
Curia Regis R	*Curia Regis Rolls* (in progress, PRO, London, 1923–)
CW + number	References to individual documents copied into the *Codex Wintoniensis*, numbered according to the descriptive list in Rumble 1980, vol. ii
d.	died
Davis	G. R. C. Davis, *Medieval Cartularies of Great Britain: a Short Catalogue* (London, 1958)
DB, i	Great Domesday Book
DB + *county abbreviation*	Great and Little Domesday Book (translation and printed text), quoted by section number from the Phillimore county volumes (gen. ed. John Morris, Chichester, 1974–86)
DBS	P. H. Reaney, *A Dictionary of British Surnames* (2nd edn., with corrections and additions by R. M. Wilson, London 1974, repr. 1983)
Drögereit 'Königskanzlei'	Richard Drögereit, 'Gab es eine angelsächsische Königskanzlei?', *Archiv für Urkundenforschung* 13 (1935), 337–436
Du Cange	C. Du Cange, *Glossarium mediae et infimae latinitatis* (Niort, 1883–7)
Earle	John Earle (ed.), *A Handbook to the Land-Charters and other Saxonic Documents* (Oxford, 1888)
EHD	*English Historical Documents*
EHR	*English Historical Review*
EPN	A. H. Smith, *English Place-Name Elements* (2 vols., EPNS 25–6, Cambridge, 1956)
EPNS	English Place-Name Society

ex.	*exeunte*/end (for dating of manuscripts following small Roman numeral indicating century)
fem.	feminine grammatical gender
Finberg	H. P. R. Finberg, *The Early Charters of Wessex* (Leicester, 1964)
fo(s).	folio(s)
France	J. H. Round (ed.), *Calendar of Documents preserved in France*, i, *918–1206* (PRO, London, 1899)
Gesta Pontificum	N. E. S. A. Hamilton (ed.), *Willelmi Malmesbiriensis monachi de gestis pontificum Anglorum libri quinque* (RS 52, London, 1870)
Gesta Regum	William Stubbs (ed.), *Willelmi Malmesbiriensis monachi de gestis regum Anglorum libri quinque* (2 vols., RS 90, London, 1887–9)
Goodman *Chartulary*	A. W. Goodman (ed.), *Chartulary of Winchester Cathedral* (Winchester, 1927)
Goodman *Goodbegot*	A. W. Goodman, *The Manor of Goodbegot in the City of Winchester* (Winchester, 1923)
Green	Judith A. Green, *The Government of England under Henry I* (Cambridge Studies in Medieval Life and Thought, 4th ser. 3, Cambridge, 1986)
Gretsch *Intellectual Foundations*	Mechthild Gretsch, *The Intellectual Foundations of the English Benedictine Reform* (Cambridge Studies in Anglo-Saxon England 25, Cambridge, 1999)
Grierson 'Grimbald'	Philip Grierson, 'Grimbald of St. Bertin's', *EHR* 55 (1940), 529–61
Harl. MS.	Harleian Manuscript
Harmer *SEHD*	F. E. Harmer (ed.), *Select English Historical Documents of the Ninth and Tenth Centuries* (Cambridge, 1914)
Hart *ECEE*	C. R. Hart, *The Early Charters of Eastern England* (Leicester, 1966)
Hart *ECNE*	C. R. Hart, *The Early Charters of Northern England and the North Midlands* (Leicester, 1975)
HBC	E. B. Fryde, D. E. Greenway, S. Porter, and I. Roy (ed.), *Handbook of British Chronology* (Royal Historical Society, 3rd edn., London, 1986)
Hill and Rumble *Defence of Wessex*	David Hill and Alexander R. Rumble (ed.), *The Defence of Wessex: the Burghal Hidage and Anglo-Saxon Fortifications* (Manchester and New York, 1996)
HRH	David Knowles, C. N. L. Brooke, and Vera C. M. London (ed.), *The Heads of Religious Houses, England and Wales 940–1216* (Cambridge, 1972)
HRO	Hampshire Record Office, Winchester
HRS	Hampshire Record Society
in.	*ineunte*/beginning (for dating of manuscripts following small Roman numeral indicating century)

Initia Consuetudinis Benedictinae	K. Hellinger (ed.), *Initia consuetudinis Benedictinae: consuetudines saeculi octavi et noni* (Corpus consuetudinum monasticarum 1, Siegburg, 1963)
Jaffé	P. Jaffé, *Regesta Pontificum Romanorum ad annum 1198*, ed. W. Wattenbach, S. Loewenfeld, F. Kaltenbrunner, and P. Ewald (2 vols., Leipzig, 1885–8)
JEH	*Journal of Ecclesiastical History*
JEPNS	*Journal of the English Place-Name Society*
John 'Church of Winchester'	Eric John, 'The Church of Winchester and the Tenth-Century Reformation', *Bulletin of the John Ryland's Library* 47 (1965), 404–28
John *Orbis Britanniae*	Eric John, *Orbis Britanniae and Other Studies* (Leicester, 1966)
KCD	John M. Kemble (ed.), *Codex diplomaticus ævi Saxonici* (6 vols., London, 1839–48)
Ker *Catalogue*	N. R. Ker, *Catalogue of Manuscripts Containing Anglo-Saxon* (Oxford, 1957)
Keynes *Atlas*	Simon Keynes, *An Atlas of Attestations in Anglo-Saxon Charters c.670–1066* (Department of Anglo-Saxon, Norse, and Celtic, University of Cambridge, Cambridge, 1995)
Keynes *Diplomas*	Simon Keynes, *The Diplomas of King Æthelred 'the Unready': a Study in their Use as Historical Evidence* (Cambridge Studies in Medieval Life and Thought, 3rd ser. 13, Cambridge, 1980)
Keynes *Liber Vitae*	Simon Keynes (ed.), *The Liber Vitae of the New Minster and Hyde Abbey, Winchester: British Library Stowe 944 together with Leaves from British Library Cotton Vespasian A. viii and British Library Cotton Titus D. xxvii*, (Early English Manuscripts in Facsimile 26, Copenhagen, 1996)
Keynes 1994	Simon Keynes, 'The West Saxon Charters of King Æthelwulf and his Sons', *EHR* 109 (1994), 1109–49
Keynes and Lapidge	Simon Keynes and Michael Lapidge (trans.), *Alfred the Great: Asser's Life of King Alfred and other Contemporary Sources* (Harmondsworth, 1983)
'King Edgar's Establishment of Monasteries'	'An Account of King Edgar's Establishment of Monasteries', *c.*970 × 984 (*Councils* 33)
Knowles and Hadcock	David Knowles and R. Neville Hadcock, *Medieval Religious Houses, England & Wales* (London, 1971)
Lapidge 'Æthelwold as Scholar'	Michael Lapidge, 'Æthelwold as Scholar and Teacher', in B. Yorke (ed.), *Bishop Æthelwold: His Career and Influence* (Woodbridge, 1988), 89–117
Lapidge 'Hermeneutic Style'	Michael Lapidge, 'The Hermeneutic Style in Tenth-Century Anglo-Latin Literature', *ASE* 4 (1975), 67–111; quoted from reprint in *idem*, *Anglo-Latin Literature 900–1066* (London and Rio Grande, 1993), 105–49
Lat.	Latin
Latham	R. E. Latham, *Revised Medieval Latin Word-List from British and Irish Sources* (London, 1965, repr. 1973)
Le Neve *Lincoln Diocese 1066–1300*	John Le Neve, *Fasti ecclesiae Anglicanae 1066–1300*, iii, *Lincoln Diocese* (compiled by Diana E. Greenway, London, 1977)

Le Neve *Monastic Cathedrals 1066–1300*	John Le Neve, *Fasti ecclesiae Anglicanae 1066–1300*, ii, *Monastic Cathedrals* (compiled by Diana E. Greenway, London, 1971)
Le Neve *St. Paul's London 1066–1300*	John Le Neve, *Fasti ecclesiae Anglicanae 1066–1300*, i, *St. Paul's London* (compiled by Diana E. Greenway, London, 1968)
Lewis and Short	Charlton T. Lewis and Charles Short, *A Latin Dictionary founded on Andrews' Edition of Freund's Latin Dictionary* (Oxford, 1879, repr. 1969)
LH	E. Edwards (ed.), *Liber monasterii de Hyda* (RS 45, London, 1866)
Liber (abbatiae) de Hyda	MS. of the chronicle-cartulary of Hyde Abbey, in the possession of the Earl of Macclesfield, Shirburn Castle
Liber Diurnus	Th. E. Ab Sickel (ed.), *Liber Diurnus Romanorum pontificum* (Vienna, 1889)
Loyd	L. C. Loyd, *The Origins of Some Anglo-Norman Families* (Harleian Soc. 103, Leeds, 1951)
LVH	Walter de Gray Birch (ed.), *Liber Vitae: Register and Martyrology of New Minster and Hyde Abbey, Winchester* (HRS 5, London and Winchester, 1892)
masc.	masculine grammatical gender
med.	*mediante*/middle (for dating of manuscripts following small Roman numeral indicating century)
Miller 1998	Sean Michael Miller, 'An Analysis of the Anglo-Saxon Charters of the New Minster, Winchester' (unpublished, Cambridge Ph. D thesis, 1998)
Miller *New Minster*	Sean Michael Miller (ed.), *Charters of the New Minster, Winchester* (Anglo-Saxon Charters 9, Oxford, 2001)
MLat.	Medieval Latin
Monasticon	William Dugdale, *Monasticon Anglicanum* (ed. J. Caley, H. Ellis, and B. Bandinel, 6 vols. in 8 parts, London, 1817–30)
Monasticon 1st edn.	Roger Dodsworth and William Dugdale, *Monasticon Anglicanum* (3 vols., London, 1655–73)
MS(S).	manuscript(s)
n(n).	note(s) *or* noun(s)
neut.	neuter grammatical gender
New Pal Soc.	*New Palaeographical Society*, 1st ser. (London, 1903–12)
Num Chron	*Numismatic Chronicle*
O'Donovan i	M. A. O'Donovan, 'An Interim Revision of Episcopal Dates for the Province of Canterbury, 850–950, Part I', *ASE* 1 (1972), 23–44
O'Donovan ii	M. A. O'Donovan, 'An Interim Revision of Episcopal dates for the Province of Canterbury, 850–950, Part II', *ASE* 2 (1973), 91–113
O'Donovan *Sherborne*	M. A. O'Donovan (ed.), *Charters of Sherborne* (Anglo-Saxon Charters 3, Oxford, 1988)
OE	Old English

OFr	Old French
OG	Old German
OS	Ordnance Survey
O. S. Facs	W. B. Sanders, *Facsimiles of Anglo-Saxon Manuscripts* (3 vols., Ordnance Survey, Southampton, 1878–84)
Pal. Soc.	*Palaeographical Society*, 1st and 2nd ser. (London, 1873–94)
Pat R	Patent Rolls (C 66) in PRO
PBA	*Proceedings of the British Academy*
Pierquin *Recueil*	Hubert Pierquin (ed.), *Recueil général des chartes anglo-saxonnes: Les Saxons en Angleterre, 604–1061* (Paris, 1912)
Pl(s)	Plate(s)
pl.	plural
PN + *county abbreviation*	county volumes of the EPNS
PNDB	Olof von Feilitzen, *The Pre-Conquest Personal Names of Domesday Book*, (Nomina Germanica 3, Uppsala, 1937)
PRO	Public Record Office, London
Proc Hants FC	*Proceedings of the Hampshire Field Club*
Quirk *NM*	R. N. Quirk, 'Winchester New Minster and its Tenth-Century Tower', *Journal of the British Archaeological Society*, 3rd ser. 24 (1961), 16–54
Quirk *OM*	R. N. Quirk, 'Winchester Cathedral in the Tenth Century', *ArchJ* 114 (1957), 28–68
r	recto (of manuscript folio)
RB 1980	Timothy Fry *et al.* (ed.), *RB 1980: The Rule of S. Benedict in Latin and English with Notes* (Collegeville, Minnesota, 1981)
RC	*Regularis Concordia*, text ed. T. Symons and S. Spath, in K. Hallinger (ed.), *Consuetudinarum saeculi x/xi/xii monumenta non-Cluniacensia* (Corpus consuetudinum monasticarum 7.3, Siegburg, 1984), 61–147; translation taken from Thomas Symons (ed. and trans.), *Regularis Concordia Anglicae nationis monachorum sanctimonialiumque* (Nelson Medieval Classics, London, etc, 1953), with chapter-numbers which differ from those in the 1984 edition shown in square brackets
Rec Comm	Record Commission
Regesta	H. W. C. Davis, R. H. C. Davis, H. A. Cronne, and C. Johnson (ed.), *Regesta regum Anglo-Normannorum* (4 vols., Oxford, 1913–69)
Reg Pontissara	Register of Bishop John of Pontoise in HRO
Reg Pontissara	C. Deedes (ed.), *Registrum Johannis de Pontissara episcopi Wyntoniensis* (Canterbury and York Society 19 (1915) and 30 (1924))
RS	Rolls Series
Rumble 1980	Alexander R. Rumble, 'The Structure and Reliability of the *Codex Wintoniensis* (British Museum Add. MS. 15350: the Cartulary of

	Winchester Cathedral Priory)', (unpublished, London Ph. D. thesis, 1980)
Rumble 1982	Alexander R. Rumble, 'The Purposes of the *Codex Wintoniensis*', in R. Allen Brown (ed.), *Proceedings of the Battle Conference on Anglo-Norman Studies IV: 1981* (Woodbridge, 1982), 153–66, 224–32
Rymer's Foedera	T. D. Hardy (ed.), *Rymer's Foedera: Syllabus, in English, with Index* (3 vols., PRO, London, 1869–85)
Rymer's Foedera (1816– edn)	Adam Clarke, J. Caley, J. Bayley, F. Holbrooke, and J. W. Clarke (ed.), *Foedera, conventiones, litterae, etc.; or Rymer's Foedera, 1066–1383* (4 vols., PRO, London, 1816–69)
s. + small roman numeral	*saeculo*, from Lat. *saeculum* 'century' (for dating of manuscripts)
S	see Sawyer
s.a.	*sub anno*
SASLC: Trial Version	Frederick M. Biggs, Thomas D. Hill, and Paul E. Szarmach (ed.), with Karen Hammond, *Sources of Anglo-Saxon Literary Culture: A Trial Version* (Binghamton, 1990)
Sawyer	P. H. Sawyer, *Anglo-Saxon Charters: an Annotated List and Bibliography* (Royal Historical Society, London, 1968)
Sawyer (Kelly)	Revised edn. of preceding by S. E. Kelly (privately circulated, 1994)
Sawyer *Burton*	P. H. Sawyer (ed.), *Charters of Burton Abbey* (Anglo-Saxon Charters 2, Oxford, 1979)
SC	F. Madan, H. H. E. Craster, *et al.* (ed.), *A Summary Catalogue of Western Manuscripts in the Bodleian Library at Oxford* (6 vols. and index, Oxford, 1895–1953)
sg.	singular
s.n.	*sub nomine*
Spelman *Concilia*	Sir Henry Spelman, *Concilia, decreta, leges, constitutiones in re ecclesiarum orbis Britannici* (2 vols., London, 1639–64)
Stevenson *Chron. Abingdon*	Joseph Stevenson (ed.), *Chronicon monasterii de Abingdon* (2 vols., RS 2, London, 1858)
s.v.	*sub verbo* or *sub voce*
TA	Tithe Awards in HRO
Tengvik	Gösta Tengvik, *Old English Bynames* (Nomina Germanica 4, Uppsala, 1935)
Thorpe	Benjamin Thorpe (ed.), *Diplomatarium Anglicum ævi Saxonici* (London, 1865)
Thorpe *ASC*	Benjamin Thorpe (ed.), *The Anglo-Saxon Chronicle according to the Several Original Authorities*, i, *Original Texts* (RS 23, London, 1861)
TRE	*Tempore regis Edwardi*
TRW	*Tempore regis Willelmi*

v	verso (of manuscript folio)
v.	*vide*
VCH + *county abbreviation*	volumes of the Victoria History of the Counties of England
VEPN	David Parsons and Tania Styles, with Carole Hough, *The Vocabulary of English Place-Names (á–box)* (Nottingham, 1997)
WAM	*Wiltshire Archaeological and Natural History Magazine*
WCL	Winchester Cathedral Library and Archives
WCM	Winchester College Muniments
Whitelock *EHD*	Dorothy Whitelock (ed.), *English Historical Documents*, i, *c.500–1042* (London, 1955)
Wilkins *Concilia*	David Wilkins (ed.), *Concilia Magnae Britanniae et Hiberniae A.D. 446–1717* (4 vols., London, 1737)
Williams 'Princeps Merciorum gentis'	A. Williams, '*Princeps Merciorum gentis*: the Family, Career and Connections of Ælfhere, Ealdorman of Mercia, 956–83', *ASE* 10 (1982), 143–72
Winchester ann.	*Annales monasterii de Wintonia (A.D. 519–1277)*, in Henry Richards Luard (ed.), *Annales monastici*, ii (RS 36, 1865), 1–125
WS	Winchester Studies
WS 1	Frank Barlow, Martin Biddle, Olof von Feilitzen, and D. J. Keene (ed. Martin Biddle), *Winchester in the Early Middle Ages: an Edition and Discussion of the Winton Domesday* (Winchester Studies 1, Oxford, 1976)
WS 2.i and ii	Derek Keene, with a contribution by Alexander R. Rumble, *Survey of Medieval Winchester* (2 vols., Winchester Studies 2, Oxford, 1985)
Wulfstan *Vita S. Æthelwoldi*	Michael Lapidge and Michael Winterbottom (ed. and trans.), *Wulfstan of Winchester, Life of St Æthelwold* (Oxford Medieval Texts, Oxford, 1991, repr. 1996)

I. INTRODUCTION

1. CRITERIA FOR INCLUSION OF DOCUMENTS IN THE PRESENT VOLUME

THE documents presented in this volume relate either to the ownership of land and property rights in early medieval Winchester, or to the foundation or reform of each of the three minsters there. They represent one of the largest groups of surviving early medieval documents concerning the topography of an Anglo-Saxon city.[1] Most are the product of royal bounty towards favoured individuals, the minsters or other churches. Their creation and survival reflect the twin influences of the desirability of ownership of property rights within and around the city of Winchester and the wish to express and maintain Christian piety through its ecclesiastical institutions. Both the definition of property boundaries and the powerful presence of the minsters had major and lasting effects on the life and layout of the city.

The evidentiary value of the content of the documents here collected covers a broad range of modern academic interest, including the study of national history; urban and rural historical topography; medieval Latin; Old and Middle English; onomastics; and Anglo-Saxon and Norman palaeography and diplomatic. Each of the texts is accompanied by a new translation into Modern English and is fully annotated. All of the pre-conquest documents will eventually be edited again, but not translated, in the new British Academy corpus of Anglo-Saxon charters, but within diverse volumes and mostly in the company of other documents from the archives of the three Winchester minsters, many of which do not concern the city itself but deal with estates elsewhere in England.

2. THE MANUSCRIPT SOURCES

General Character

The edition is based on texts contained in 49 manuscripts. Of these, 40 may be associated with Anglo-Saxon or medieval archives as follows:

- 5 come from the Old Minster / Winchester Cathedral (nos. 3–4, 16, and 47–8 in the list, below). These consist of three cartularies, one chronicle, and one episcopal register
- 6 come from the New Minster / Hyde Abbey (nos. 7–8, 12, 15, 46, and 49). These comprise two cartularies, one chronicle-cartulary (the *Liber de Hyda*), one necrology (the *Liber Vitae*), the refoundation codex, and one forged single-sheet diploma
- 1 from Nunnaminster (13, a prayer-book)
- 2 from Abingdon Abbey, Berks. (5 and 6, both cartularies)
- 1 from Glastonbury Abbey, Somerset (45, a cartulary)

---

[1] Rivalled only by those for Canterbury, London, Worcester, and York. See Sawyer, index, s. nn. For York, see also D. W. Rollason, with D. Gore and G. Fellows-Jensen, *Sources for York History to AD 1100* (The Archaeology of York, vol. 1, York, 1998).

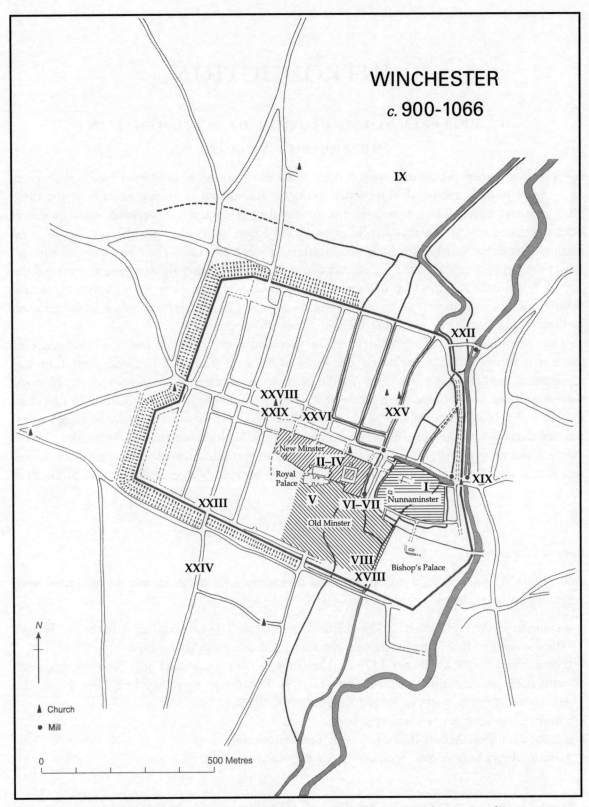

WINCHESTER
c. 900-1066

IX

XXII

XXVIII
XXIX   XXVI   XXV

New Minster
II–IV

Royal
Palace

XXIII   V   VI–VII

Old Minster

Nunnaminster

I   XIX

Bishop's Palace

VIII
XXIV   XVIII

N

▲ Church

● Mill

0   500 Metres

Fig. 1. Places and areas in or near Winchester to which the pre-1066 documents relate.

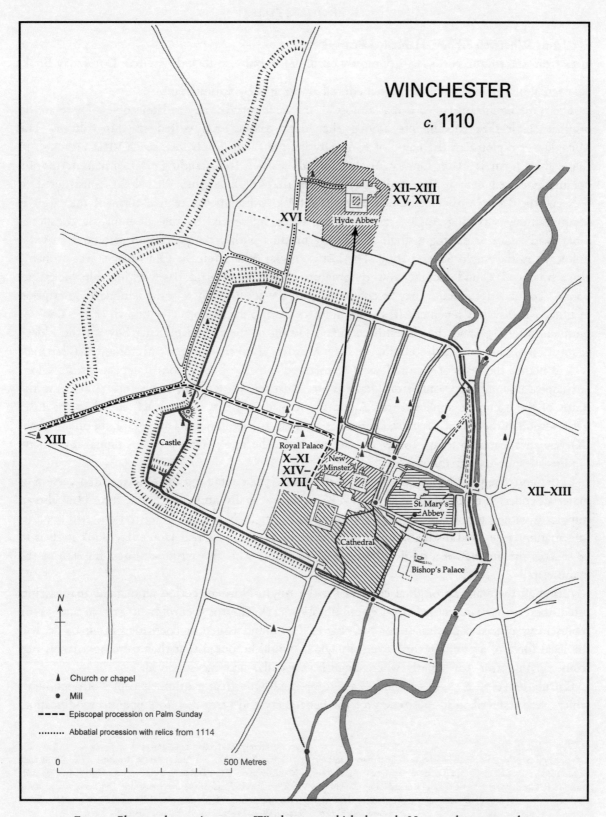

FIG. 2. Places and areas in or near Winchester to which the early Norman documents relate.

- 1 from Wherwell Abbey, Hants (9, a cartulary)
- 24 from the royal records (17–40, mostly enrolments, but also including Great Domesday Book)

The remaining manuscripts are post-medieval transcripts by antiquarians.

The most significant factor is that almost all the texts survive only as later copies. There are no original single-sheet documents among the Anglo-Saxon texts edited in this volume. The Micheldever diploma in the name of King Edward the Elder (49, below, see **XVIII**), although in single-sheet form, is a later forgery. Accordingly, the earliest free-standing original manuscript of a document edited here is the small codex of the mid tenth century (8, below), constructed to preserve the New Minster refoundation charter (**IV**). Although the textual form of the latter is unique among surviving Anglo-Saxon charters, being influenced by that of monastic consuetudinaries, the idea of placing a single diplomatic product within the protection of a book was not unknown in the Anglo-Saxon period. The lost exemplar of **V** from the Old Minster was probably also a small codex,[1] and documents were sometimes copied onto blank pages within valuable gospel books.[2] To the latter practice may be compared both the addition *c.*900 of the boundary-description of Queen Ealhswith's tenement (**I**) to the ninth-century prayer-book later known as the Book of Nunnaminster (13), and the eleventh-century addition of the record of King Edward the Elder's acquisition of land on which to build the New Minster (**II**) to that church's necrology or *Liber Vitae* (15). Whether the texts of **I** and **II** were transcribed into the books from independent, now-lost, fair-copied documents or only from drafts is not, however, known. The same uncertainty as to the status of the exemplar applies to the Anglo-Norman documents (**X** and **XI**) added to the *Liber Vitae*, although the use of a *signum*, claimed as William the Conqueror's autograph, in one of them (**X**) was an apparent attempt to get the document in the book treated as an original diplomatic product, despite its physical context.[3]

In the post-conquest period, Great Domesday Book (32), containing the official edited version of materials collected in the Domesday Survey, is not only a legally-authentic public record but also an important witness to the Anglo-Saxon contribution to Anglo-Norman administration.[4] Although its information is the final distillation of a huge number of returns, Great Domesday Book itself is to be seen as the product of a single editor's skill, an editor who also wrote all but a fraction of the manuscript.[5]

Although there are no original charters for the Anglo-Norman period among the manuscripts listed, there is one later sealed royal exemplification (31). The royal enrolments (17–30 and 33–9), representing official copies made for the king of documents issued or confirmed in his name, had the legal force of a public record, even though it should be noted that they were not always free from copying error, particularly where English vernacular text was involved.[6]

Cartularies (3–7, 9, 12, 45–6, and 48) are to be used with great caution, as copies of documents which were transcribed in most cases for the beneficiary and were therefore open to modification,

[1] See below, p. 100.

[2] See Francis Wormald, 'The Sherborne "Chartulary"', in D. J. Gordon (ed.), *Fritz Saxl 1890–1948* (London, 1957), 101–19, at 106–7; also C. R. Cheney, 'Service-Books and Records: The Case of the Domesday Monachorum', *Bulletin of the Institute of Historical Research* 56 (1983), 7–15.   [3] See below, pp. 156–7.

[4] See V. H. Galbraith, *Domesday Book: Its Place in Adminis-* *trative History* (Oxford, 1974), 27–32.

[5] For his work, see Alexander R. Rumble, 'The Domesday Manuscripts: Scribes and Scriptoria', in J. C. Holt (ed.), *Domesday Studies: Papers Read at the Novocentenary Conference of the Royal Historical Society and the Institute of British Geographers, Winchester, 1986* (Woodbridge, 1987), 79–99, especially 82–6.

[6] For an example, see below, p. 213, n. 5.

but which are also liable to contain errors of copying, particularly where the sources were already several centuries old when transcribed. Episcopal registers (e.g. 47) contain both documents received and documents issued, and may thus represent text copied from either drafts or originals.

Medieval works of history which quote documentary materials, sometimes in a modified form, may remove the text even further from what was first issued. Thomas Rudborne thus interpolated sections into the presentation of one Old Minster dipoma (**V, xiv**) in his *Historia maior Wintoniensis* (16),[7] while the compiler of the *Liber de Hyda* (46) usually inserted Latin and Middle English translations of Old English boundary-clauses.[8]

The copies made by antiquarians of the early modern period (see 1–2, 10–11, 14, and 41–4) were intended to be accurate but their makers, like their medieval predecessors, were often let down by errors of technique or by an insufficient familiarity with the scripts encountered.

It will be seen from the above that the texts retrieved from the surviving manuscripts should always be treated with caution. Nearly all of them are copies, rather than original documents. Even 8, the New Minster refoundation codex, contains errors made during copying from a draft.[9] A careful reading of the textual notes given *passim* in the present volume is thus to be recommended, especially as, where errors are repeated, they can sometimes give an indication of characteristic misreadings encountered in the work of a particular copyist.

List of Manuscripts

The following is a list of the manuscripts used for the edition of the documents in the present volume, with brief notes on the most important ones which have a Winchester origin or close connection. Note that there is also some evidence of further manuscripts, now-lost, associated with **XIII, XIV, XXIX,** and **XXXIII**.[10]

CAMBRIDGE, Corpus Christi College (CCCC)

1. MS. 110 (a Parkerian transcript of Winchester texts, s.xvi. med.; itself later copied in 44, below):
   V (part)

2. MS. 350, pp. 43–5 (a Parkerian transcript from 16, below; s.xvi med.):
   V

LONDON, British Library (BL)

3. Add. MS. 15350 (the *Codex Wintoniensis*, the earliest surviving cartulary of Winchester cathedral priory; Davis 1042; see Rumble 1980, Rumble 1982; and Pls. II, III, and V); s.xii[1]–xiv[2]
   II, V–VIII, XIX, XX, XXII, XXIII, XXV, XXVI, XXVIII, XXX, and **XXXI**

A study of the codicology of this very important Winchester cathedral MS. (containing i + 119 + i fos.) indicates that a core primary group of quires was added to at various dates from the mid

---

[7] Below, **V, xiv**, nn. *ww, e-f,* and *h.*
[8] For example, in **IX**. On the Middle English versions, see Matti Rissanen, 'Middle English Translations of Old English Charters in the *Liber Monasterii de Hyda*: A case of Historical Error Analysis', in Dieter Kastovsky and Aleksander Szwedek

(ed.), *Linguistics Across Historical and Geographical Boundaries: In Honour of Jacek Fisiak on the Occasion of his Fiftieth Birthday*, 2 vols. (Berlin, 1986), i, 591–603.
[9] See below, **IV**, nn. *f-g, j, o-p, r-s, w, z,* and *ff.*
[10] See below, the respective bibliographies to these documents.

twelfth century to the second half of the fourteenth. The main and earliest part, *Cod. Wint. I* (fos. 9–11^v, 13^v–67^r, 67^v–110^v) was a lavishly-written and decorated book of transcripts of Anglo-Saxon documents thought to record the pre-conquest endowment of Winchester Cathedral, which was made in 1129 × 1139 with the intention of obtaining a royal restoration of lands lost in and after 1066. *Cod. Wint. II*, folios and material added at more than one time in the twelfth century, consisted of transcripts of various documents omitted from *Cod. Wint. I*. One distinct group amongst them relates to Anglo-Saxon grants of tenements within Winchester and may be contemporary with Survey II of the city (1148).[11] *Cod. Wint. III* consists of thirteenth and fourteenth-century additions of folios and documents to the cartulary.

Some of the rubrics in *Cod. Wint. I* and *II* are copied from contemporary endorsements on the exemplars, others are copied from later endorsements. Of the latter type, a group of either bilingual (English and Latin) or Latin endorsements may reflect a rearrangement of the cathedral archive in the early twelfth century.[12] The rubrics to the various sections of **V** were probably existing headings within the late tenth-/early eleventh-century codex which it is postulated constituted the exemplar.[13]

The work of sixteen text-scribes is distinguishable in the *Codex Wintoniensis*. The present edition includes documents copied by five of the sixteen. The five may be distinguished as follows:

Scribe *a* copied the text of **V, i–viii**, as well as **XIX, XX, XXII, XXIII**, and **XXV**. He wrote a fine, regular, Latin bookscript (protogothic *textualis formata*) which is large, round, and generally upright in appearance.[14] In the context of surviving Winchester cathedral manuscripts,[15] it may reasonably be dated to the second quarter of the twelfth century. The same scribe also wrote a large section of the text of a Winchester cathedral manuscript containing Jerome on Isaiah, wherein scribe *b* (below) also had a part.[16] In the *Codex Wintoniensis*, scribe *a* began each Latin document with a *diminuendo*, the first line, after a decorated initial, being in a display script of mixed square and rustic capitals and uncials and the second line being in rustic capitals, before the minuscule of the third and subsequent lines. He reserved a different, more angular, duct of script, together with some special letter-forms, for English vernacular material (see below). In Latin, the following letter-forms are characteristic of his work:

a   has a back which is thick and upright, with serifs at head and foot, and a belly which is finely curved with a mixture of thick and thin lines;

d   is always straight-backed;

ę   has a closed spur in the shape of a pointed oval;

g   has a very upright back to its head, which often has a 'chin', and its descender is scythe-shaped and always open;

E   (rustic) has a stem which is not intersected by the letter's middle bar;

Q   sits with its tail on the line;

W   is formed from two intersecting *V*s.

There are ligatures of *c* + *t* and *s* + *t*. In the former, the letters are linked by a backward curl

---

[11] For Survey II, see WS I, 18–28, 69–141.

[12] These rubrics are discussed in more detail in Rumble 1980, i, 217–22.   [13] See below, p. 100.

[14] See Rumble 1982, Pl. I.

[15] Listed Rumble 1980, i, 47 n. 2.

[16] WCL, MS. 5, fos. 137–147^v and 159–224^v.

which starts at the joint of the stem and the bar of the *t*; in *s* + *t*, the back of *s* is only very rarely met by a leftward continuation of the bar of *t*.

The ampersand is used as the abbreviation for *et*, while the final syllable *-bus* is represented by -b₃ and the conjunction *-que* by q;

Scribe *a* seems at first to have been unfamiliar with writing English vernacular text and to have had to learn its special insular letter-forms during his work of transcribing documents into Quire I of *Cod. Wint. I*, the present second quire of the MS.,[17] perhaps taking a document in Anglo-Saxon minuscule from the cathedral archive as his guide. Significantly, however, for the identification of his work, he chose not to use the insular form of *a*, but employed the caroline minuscule shape for the letter in English as well as in Latin text. He did, however, use the following differentiated letter-forms in writing English text: round-backed *d*; insular *f, g* (which has a hook-shaped descender), *h, r*, and often *s* (long), also *æ, þ, ð, p*, and *y*. The latter is dotted and has a clubbed left-turning serif at the top of its right minim. Many descenders are curved to the left. Rustic capitals are used as well as *Đ* and enlarged forms of *æ, þ, ð*, and *p*. As regards vernacular orthography, the most noticeable feature of his work is the great confusion over the relative values of *æ* and *e*.[18]

Although in the main a faithful copyist of the text according to his ability, scribe *a* did sometimes alter the status of witnesses, e.g. from *minister* to *dux*, apparently to give greater uniformity to the columns of subscriptions on the page rather than in any effort to deceive.[19]

Scribe *b* acted as the corrector and rubricator of most of scribe *a*'s work in *Cod. Wint. I* and was responsible for writing the rubrics of **XXII** and **XXV**.[20] Later, he began *Cod. Wint. II* in continuation of the earlier cartulary and this work included the copying of both the text and the rubrics of **VI–VIII**, **XXVI**, and **XXVIII**. Different grades of his hand occur in the *Codex Wintoniensis*, being more or less formal according to the type of text being copied, with his least formal grade being reserved for the copying of twelfth-century writ-charters and for corrections.[21] In general, however, he wrote a good mid twelfth-century bookscript (protogothic *textualis formata* or *media*; see Pls. II and III), somewhat less monumental than that of scribe *a*. In Latin text, the following letter-forms are characteristic:

a (caroline) in initial position sometimes rises higher than minims;

d has either an upright or a rounded back;

g is round-headed, and its descender is open and hook-shaped;

A (rustic) is usually triangular;

E (rustic) has a central bar which intersects the stem; an enlarged version of minuscule *e* also occurs, with a protruding tongue;

M (rustic) has an inward-curving first leg;

Q usually has a tail which descends below the baseline;

S is tall with well-rounded curves.

---

[17] On fo. 14ʳ, he was inconsistent over the use of either caroline or insular *f* and *s*. On fo. 14ᵛ, he added descenders to letters *f* and *þ*. He then returned to modify some letters *f, s*, and *þ* which he had already written up to this point (e.g. fo. 10ᵛ *þ*, fos. 13ᵛ and 14ᵛ *f* and *s*).   [18] See Rumble 1980, i, 250.

[19] See Keynes *Diplomas*, 234–5, 239, and 245.

[20] He was also the rubricator of WCL, MS. 5. Eleven lines of text were written by him in the same MS. (on fo. 305ʳ).

[21] Three grades of his script (*b1, b2*, and *b3*) are distinguished in Rumble 1980, i, 309–15.

In English text, scribe *b* used insular letter-forms of *a*, *d*, *f*, *g* (with an s-shaped descender), *r*, *s* (long or low, but sometimes caroline or round), and *y* (not always dotted); also *æ*, *þ*, *ð*, *p*, *Æ*, and *Ð*.

In Latin, the ampersand is usually used for *et*, but the tironian nota also occurs. The abbreviation for *-bus* is either b: or b[9] and that for *-que* is q:

In copying documents into the *Codex*, scribe *b* sometimes omitted witnesses in order to save space, and occasionally (like scribe *a*, above) altered their status,[22] but appears to have copied the main text in full.

Scribe *c* copied the text of almost half of **V** (**V, ix–xiv**), and also the rubrics to the whole of it. He probably did this to complete work left unfinished by scribe *a*.[23] He wrote a handsome mid twelfth-century bookscript (protogothic *textualis formata*) in copying these documents, but also had a more heavily-abbreviated documentary version. This latter script he used in copying a writ-charter of Henry II into the *Codex*,[24] as well as in writing two surviving original documents datable to 1153 × 1171 and 1158 respectively.[25] Both of the originals were drawn up for Henry of Blois, one as bishop of Winchester and the other as dean of St. Martin's le Grand in London.[26] This suggests that he was an episcopal clerk in the personal service of Bishop Henry. There are some similarities to the script of the contemporary *Liber Wintoniensis*,[27] but also enough differences to discount an identity of scribe.[28] Besides his frequent use of clubbed left-curling descenders, the letters most characteristic of his script are as follows:

a   often has a high back;

d   has either an upright or a round back;

ę   often has a long, oblique, hairline descender;

g   has either an open or a closed descender;

E   (rustic) has a centre-bar which only sometimes intersects the stem; there is also an enlarged version of minuscule *e* in which the tongue is sometimes protruded and clubbed;

G   is uncial, i.e. 6–shaped;

M   (uncial) sometimes has its first two feet turned towards each other, while its third foot has a descender which curves to the left and is clubbed;

Q   sometimes has its bowl completed above the baseline while its tail is bracket-shaped;

W   is made up of two overlapping rustic capital letters *V*, but sometimes seems more exotic when one of the ascending stems is broken.

Apart from names, all the text which scribe *c* wrote in the *Codex* was in Latin. In English names the letters *Æ* (sometimes replaced by *Ę*), *Ð*, and *Þ* are found. He used both the ampersand and the tironian nota for *et*. For the abbreviation of *-bus* he used b; and for that of *-que* he used q;

---

[22] See below, **XXVI**, nn. *g* and 34–6; and Keynes *Diplomas*, 255 (S 889).

[23] See below, pp. 99–100.

[24] *CW* 13, a grant (? December 1154) to Winchester Cathedral of the manors of East Meon, Hants, and Wargrave, Berks., together with eight extra days for St. Giles's Fair.

[25] WCM, Muniments, 10629 [Hamble, drawer 5a]; and London, Westminster Abbey Muniments, 13247. For their texts, see M. J. Franklin (ed.), *English Episcopal Acta VIII:*

Winchester 1070–1204 (Oxford, 1993), nos. 52 and 76.

[26] For his episcopate, see Franklin, ibid. xxxv–xlix; on his decanate of St. Martin's, see Lena Voss, *Heinrich von Blois, Bischof von Winchester (1129–71)* (Historische Studien 210, Berlin, 1932), 100–7.

[27] See T. J. Brown, 'The Manuscript and the Handwriting', WS 1, Appendix II, 520–2 and Pls. I–III.

[28] The scribes differ in their treatment of the following letters: *ę*, *g*, *E* (enlarged minuscule), *Q*, and *W*.

Scribe *g* copied two vernacular documents relating to Chilcomb (**XXX** and **XXXI**) on to an additional folio associated with *Cod. Wint. II*, using a modified mid twelfth-century bookscript (protogothic *textualis*). He employed the same script at the end of *Cod. Wint. II* to copy S 1428, the alleged letter of Eadwine, child-master of the New Minster.[29] He used the following insular letter-forms: *a* (occasionally), *d, f, g, r, s* (long and low), and *y* (dotted, straight-limbed), as well as *æ, þ, ð,* and *p; Æ , þ,* and *Đ*. Besides the use of long, leftward-curving descenders and of wedged ascenders and minims, the following letters are characteristic:

d   (round-backed) often has a transverse hairline at the top of the ascender;
g   has a wide, sickle-shaped descender;
A   is triangular; this also affects the shape of *Æ*;
M   has serifs on its feet;
N   is an enlarged version of minuscule *n*;
T   has a serif at the foot of its stem;
U   has a descender.

The tironian nota for *and* has a long, oblique descender which sometimes has a serif to the right.

Scribe *m* copied **II** as part of *Cod. Wint. III*. He used a distinctive, but rather untidy script which he had apparently developed for the transcription of vernacular texts (see Plate V). It was a modified version of the mid thirteenth-century gothic textura which he used for copying Latin texts in two other surviving Winchester cathedral MSS, one of them a religious miscellany[30] and the other a cartulary (4, below) in which this vernacular script also appears. In it he used insular forms of the following letters: *a* (only very occasionally, normally caroline), *d, f* (usually long, but sometimes caroline), *g* (almost always, but sometimes caroline), *h, r, s* (long); also *æ, þ, ð, p,* and *Æ*. Ascenders tend to be notched. The following letters are most characteristic:

d   (round-backed) has a very long ascender;
g   consists of a straight bar with a hook-shaped descender coming from its mid point;
h   has its right foot facing right but below the baseline;
p   has an open-topped head;
x   has a long, trailing left foot

A ligature of caroline *s* + *t* is used. The letter *i* is often distinguished by a long hairline stroke. In copying **II** into the *Codex Wintoniensis*, scribe *m* omitted seventeen subscriptions because of lack of available space.[31]

4. Add. MS. 29436 (cartulary, etc., of Winchester cathedral priory; Davis 1043; see Pl. IV); s.xiii–xv:
   XXIX
The thirteenth-century scribe who copied this and several other documents, both Latin and English, on fos. 10–38 and 42 is identifiable as scribe *m* of the *Codex Wintoniensis* (3, above).

---

[29] *CW* 232, *AS Writs* 113, Miller *New Minster* 34.
[30] Bod, MS. Laud Misc. 368, fos. 8–73ᵛ and 88–164.

[31] See below, **II**, where the missing subscriptions are supplied from the *Liber de Hyda*.

5. Cotton MS. Claud. B. vi (chronicle-cartulary of Abingdon Abbey, a revision of 6, below; Davis 4);
   s.xiii²:
   XXI

6. Cotton MS. Claud. C. ix, fos. 105–203 (chronicle-cartulary of Abingdon Abbey, cf. 5, above;
   Davis 3); s.xii med.:
   XXI

7. Cotton MS. Domitian xiv, fos. 22–237 (cartulary of Hyde Abbey, cf. 12, below; Davis 1047);
   s.xiii²-xv:
   IX, **XIII** and **XV**

8. Cotton MS. Vesp. A. viii (the New Minster refoundation charter, etc.: Davis 1049; see
   Frontispiece, and Pl. I); s.x²-xiv:
   IV and **XVI**
   A small codex of the mid tenth century, constructed for the preservation of **IV**, but expanded by
   the addition of material in the twelfth and fourteenth centuries.[32]

9. Egerton MS. 2104A (cartulary of Wherwell Abbey: Davis 1031); s.xiv–xv:
   XXVII

10. Harl. MS. 84 (transcript of 17, below, when it was kept in the Tower of London); s.xvi:
    XIV

11. Harl. MS. 358, fos. 27–70 (copy of Sir John Prise's register of monastic documents *temp.* Henry
    VIII, on which see S. E. Kelly (ed.), *Charters of St Augustine's Abbey, Canterbury and Minster-in-
    Thanet* (Anglo-Saxon Charters 4, Oxford, 1995), lix–lx); s.xvi¹:
    V (part), **XXXIII**

12. Harl. MS. 1761 (cartulary of Hyde Abbey, a revision of 7, above, now incomplete; Davis 1048);
    s.xiv ex.–xv med.:
    III, **IX**, **XV**, **XVII**, and **XXXIII**
    All of the above documents were entered by the earlier scribe of the cartulary, who used a
    gothic cursive anglicana script but with frequent secretary *a*. He also wrote the table of contents
    at fos. 3ᵛ–8ᵛ, covering fos. 23–170. A different scribe wrote an index on fos. 10–13ᵛ and the
    'Annals of Hyde' on fos. 14–22, as well as continuing the cartulary, in the early fifteenth century.

13. Harl. MS. 2965 (the Book of Nunnaminster; Ker *Catalogue* 237; see Birch *Ancient Manuscript*, and
    Michelle P. Brown, *The Book of Cerne: Prayer, Patronage and Power in Ninth-Century England*
    (London, Toronto, and Buffalo, 1996), 137, 168–71, and 175); s. ix¹ with this addition of s.ix/x:
    I
    A prayer-book of Mercian type, thought to have belonged to Ealhswith, wife of King Alfred.
    Mainly written in Anglo-Saxon hybrid and cursive minuscules, but with **I** added in a precursor
    of Anglo-Saxon square minuscule.[33]

---

[32] See below, pp. 69–72.   [33] See below, p. 46.

14. Lansdowne MS. 717 (John Stow's extracts from 46, below, written in August 1572); s.xvi²:
    II and **XVIII**

15. Stowe MS. 944 (the New Minster *Liber Vitae*, etc.; Davis 1050; Ker *Catalogue* 274; see *LVH* and
    Keynes *Liber Vitae*); s.xi¹-xvi¹:
    II and **X–XI**
    The necrology of the New Minster whose main text was written in 1031 by the monk Ælfsige.
    The text of **II** was an early addition in the first half of the eleventh century. **X** and **XI** were
    added after the Norman Conquest by a scribe whose work appears also in other New Minster
    MSS.[34]

LONDON, Lambeth Palace

16. MS. 183 (Thomas Rudborne, *Historia maior Wintoniensis*; see *Anglia Sacra*, i, 179–286, and
    Antonia Gransden, *Historical Writing in England II: c. 1307 to the Early Sixteenth Century* (London,
    1982), 394–8 and 493–4); s.xv:
    V, xiv
    An early but incomplete MS. of Rudborne's partly-legendary history of the monastic
    community at Winchester Cathedral which was completed in 1454.

LONDON, Public Record Office (PRO)

17. Chart Antiq (C52) 23, document Y (cf. 10, above); s.xiii:
    XIV

18. Chart R 44 Henry III (C53/50); s.xiii med.:
    XXVII

19. Chart R 54 Henry III (C53/59); s.xiii med.:
    XIV

20. Chart R 10 Edward II (C53/103), cf. 41, below; s.xiv¹:
    XII, XIII, and **XXIX**

21. Chart R 4 Edward III (C53/117); s.xiv¹:
    XIII and **XIV**

22. Chart R 9 Edward III (C53/122); s.xiv¹:
    XXIX

23. Chart R 4 Richard II (C53/158); s.xiv²:
    XXIX

24. Chart R 1 Henry IV, part 2 (C53/169); s.xiv/xv:
    XXIX

[34] See below, p. 157.

25. Chart R 2 Henry V, part 1 (C53/183); s.xv[1]:
    XXIX

26. Conf R 4 Henry VII, part 2 (C56/20); s.xv[2]:
    XXIX (twice)

27. Conf R 2 Henry VIII, part 2 (C56/34); s.xvi[1]:
    XXIX

28. Conf R 2 Henry VIII, part 3 (C56/35); s.xvi[1];
    XXIX

29. Conf R 2 Henry VIII, part 7 (C56/39); s.xvi[1]:
    XXVII

30. Curia Regis R 18 Henry III (KB 26/115B); s.xiii[1]:
    XVII (part)

31. DL 10/291 (sealed exemplification, 15 Edward III, of inspeximus dated 9 Edward III); s.xiv med.:
    XXIX

32. E 31/2 (Great Domesday Book);[35] s.xi[2]:
    XXXII

33. E 32/267 (forest proceedings, 29 Edward III); s.xiv med.:
    XXIX

34. Pat R 41 Edward III, part 1 (C66/275); s.xiv[2]:
    XXVII

35. Pat R 2 Henry VI, part 2 (C66/413); s.xv[1]:
    XXIX

36. Pat R 9 Henry VI, part 1 (C66/429); s.xv[1]:
    XXVII

37. Pat R 2 Edward IV, part 6 (C66/504); s.xv[2]:
    XXIX (twice)

38. Pat R 16 Edward IV, part 2 (C66/539); s.xv[2]:
    XIII and **XIV**

39. Pat R 22 Edward IV, part 1 (C66/549); s.xv[2]:
    XXVII

OSLO (Norway) and LONDON, The Schøyen Collection

40. MS. 1354 (inspeximus 44 Henry III of a now-lost diploma of King Æthelred II); s. xiii med.:
    XXVII

---

[35] See above, nn. 4 and 5.

OXFORD, Bodleian Library (Bod)

41. Dodsworth MS. 24 (SC 4166; transcript from 20, above, by Roger Dodsworth); s.xvii med.:
    XXIX

42. Eng. hist. c. 242 (Sir Henry Spelman's transcripts for his *Concilia*); s. xvii[1]:
    IV

43. James MS. 10 (SC 3847; notebook on ecclesiastical history by Richard James, Cotton Librarian); s.xviii[1]:
    IV (part)

44. Jones MS. 4 (SC 8911; copy of 1, above, owned by the Rev. Henry Jones d. *c.*1707); s.xvii[1] :
    V (part)

45. Wood MS. empt. 1 (SC 8589; the *Secretum abbatis*, mainly a fair copy (*c.*1340–2) of a Glastonbury Abbey cartulary now at Longleat (Davis 434), with additions and omissions; Davis 435, see Aelred Watkin (ed.), *The Great Chartulary of Glastonbury*, i (Somerset Record Soc. 59, 1947), x–xii); s.xiv med.:
    XXIV

SHIRBURN CASTLE, Oxfordshire; MSS. of the earl of Macclesfield

46. *Liber (abbatiae) de Hyda* [*ex* Bod, MS. Film 184] (chronicle-cartulary of Hyde Abbey; Davis 1051; see *LH* (including frontispiece), and Keynes *Liber Vitae*, 44–5; and 14, above); s.xiv/xv:
    II, IV, IX, and **XVIII**

Although there are some illuminated foliate borders and initials in its earlier part, this, the sole surviving MS. of the partly legendary *Liber*, is unfinished, lacking some decorated initials and rubrics and breaking off in the middle of a chapter. Its scribe used a distinctive gothic bookscript for Latin text whose overall formality is modified by rather delicate looped ascenders on *b, d, h,* and *l.* It may be classed as a fere-textura and there is a notable lack of influence from gothic cursive secretary. Minims have a bulging middle and a rounded serif at their base. As in some types of textura, the letter *g* has an open descender. The letter *r* is short. Long *s* is frequent in initial and medial positions, with round *s* usual in final position. There is biting of *b, d,* and *p* with a following *a, e,* or *o.*

Old English boundaries are written in an attempt at insular minuscule script, with differentiated forms of *a, d, f, g* (which is 5-shaped), *r,* and *s* (long, and low), also *æ, þ, ð, p,* and *y* (undotted). There is an occasional ligature of *r + t.* In contrast, the Middle English versions of the bounds are written in a modified version of the script used for Latin in which the letters *k, w, y* (dotted), and yogh occur.

WINCHESTER, Hampshire Record Office (HRO)

47. Reg. Pontissara (register of John of Pontoise, bishop of Winchester, 1282–1304; see *Reg Pontissara*); s.xiii/xiv:
    XIII and **XXXIII**

WINCHESTER, Winchester Cathedral Library and Archives (WCL)

48. W52/74 ('St Swithun's cartulary' of Winchester cathedral priory; Davis 1044; see Goodman *Chartulary*, especially pp. xx–xxv and Pls. 1–6); s.xiii[ex.]–xiv:

   V (part), **XII, XXIX**, and **XXXIII** (twice)

   The MS. is now bound in three volumes. It was originally arranged as 43 quires of which only 23 survive. Of the above documents, all except the second copy of **XXXIII** were copied by the scribe of fos. 1–6 of Quire I of the cartulary. The remaining document was copied into Quire XIV by a different scribe in the first half of the fourteenth century. Both scribes used gothic cursive anglicana script.

WINCHESTER, Winchester College Muniments (WCM)

49. 12090 [Cabinet 7, drawer 2, no.1] (S 360 MS. 1, claiming to be a diploma of King Edward the Elder; see *O. S. Facs.*, ii, Winchester College 1; and Brooks 'Micheldever Forgery'); s.xi[1]:

   XVIII

   A forged single-sheet written in an imitation of square Anglo-Saxon minuscule script.

3. THE AUTHENTICITY OF THE DOCUMENTS

Before using any document as an historical source it is essential to establish the degree of its authenticity and its probable date. Its formulae and witnesses need to be compared with those in other texts coming from the same period and region. Accordingly, each document included in this volume has been assessed in the respective commentaries against the established norms of its specific diplomatic type. Because of the nature of the collection made for the volume, the documents come from a number of different Anglo-Saxon and medieval archives. They have survived in various forms and states of preservation, and most, but not all, have been found to be genuine. Before a summary analysis of their authenticity, they are considered below in relation to their typology.

Typology

The texts include the following diplomatic categories:

i. Anglo-Saxon royal diplomas and related texts: III, VI, IX, XXII, XXIV, XXVI, and XXVIII

These diplomas claim to date from the reign of King Edward the Elder (899–924) to that of Æthelred II (978–1016). As with other documents of this type, they record royal grants of privileged landholding or 'bookland' to favoured individuals or churches.[1] Composed in formulaic Latin (apart from any vernacular boundary-clauses or endorsements), the diplomas listed above represent the work of several draftsmen, some known, distinguished through their preference for a particular range of vocabulary and formulae.[2]

---

[1] For the general nature of Anglo-Saxon diplomas, see F. M. Stenton, *The Latin Diplomas of the Anglo-Saxon Period* (Oxford, 1955); and Keynes *Diplomas*, 28–39.

[2] For 10th-cent. draftsmen, see Richard Drögereit, 'Gab es eine angelsächsische Königskanzlei?', *Archiv für Urkundenforschung* 13 (1935), 335–436.

IV–V

These two documents relating to the tenth-century Benedictine Reform are especially distinctive. **IV** is part monastic consuetudinary and part diploma; it is a record of the New Minster's refoundation but no part of the endowment is named. In contrast, **V** is a record of the Old Minster's refoundation with particular reference to its endowment; it is constructed from a series of modified diplomas concerning particular estates. In places within **IV** and **V**, echoes are found of the work of the draftsmen known to present-day commentators as 'Æthelstan A' and 'Edgar A'.[3] In addition, certain formulations connect parts of these texts with diplomas from the '*Orthodoxorum*' group.[4]

ii. Anglo-Saxon royal writs: XXIX–XXX

These two examples of short vernacular letters, addressed specifically and in highly formulaic Old English phraseology, come from the reigns of King Æthelred II and Edward the Confessor. Usually complementary to the diploma, such writs were used to inform local officials, and often also a local assembly, of the king's grant of rights over the estates involved.[5]

iii. Old English memoranda

This group of texts comprises vernacular declarations, without any specific addressee(s), made to record a state of affairs or an agreement. Such documents were sometimes authenticated by being issued in chirograph form,[6] and were capable of recording a variety of information, some of which is represented by the examples included here:

• the description of estate-boundaries: either rural, **IX** and **XXII** (both subsumed within Latin diplomas); or urban, **I** (a separate text), and **XXVI** and **XXVIII** (both within Latin diplomas)
• the record of an acquisition or exchange of land: **II**, **VII**, and **VIII** (the last being bilingual where the Latin version has apparently been translated from the Old English one).[7]
• a list of places dependent on an estate-centre, e.g. Chilcomb, Hants, in **XXXI**

iv. Old English declarations of grant: XIX–XX

In internal form both these documents take that of a general declaration by the royal donor,[8] of a grant which is supplementary to that in an earlier diploma.

Each of this pair of texts records a grant by King Eadred (946–55) to the same beneficiary, the thegn Æthelgeard, of a tenement in Winchester. Each was later subsumed into an earlier Latin diploma granted to Æthelgeard by Eadred's predecessor, King Edmund, which has only survived as a cartulary-copy in the *Codex Wintoniensis*, and the former external form of neither is discernible. The vernacular texts may have been endorsed on the original diplomas or have been attached to them in some way, and then have been moved into the body of the diploma by the cartulary-maker. Alternatively, the vernacular texts may already have been included in the main text of the respective diplomas, if these had both been rewritten as apographs at some point before this part of the

[3] For 'Æthelstan A', see Drögereit, 'Angelsächsische Königs-kanzlei', 361–9; and below **IV**, n. 81, and **V**, nn. 114, 164–5, and 167. For 'Edgar A', see Drögereit, ibid. 394–400; Keynes *Diplomas*, 70–6; and below, **IV**, nn. 13, 16, 65, 114–15, and 122, and **V**, nn. 159–61, 163–4, and 167.
[4] For this group of diplomas (S 658, 673, 786, 788, 812, and 876), see E. John, 'Some Latin Charters of the Tenth-Century Reformation', in John *Orbis Britanniae*, 181–209; Keynes *Diplomas*, 98–101; and S. E. Kelly (ed.), *Charters of Abingdon Abbey* (Anglo-Saxon Charters 7–8, Oxford, 2000), lxxxiv–cxv. See below, **IV**, nn. 16 and 69; **V**, nn. 23 and 69.
[5] For a full discussion of such documents, see *AS Writs*, 1–118.
[6] **VII**, below, was a triple chirograph, and **VIII** one in quadruplicate.
[7] See below **VIII(ii)**, nn. 4 and 14.
[8] For some comparable non-royal documents, see S 1418–19, and 1496; Miller *New Minster* 14, 16, and 21.

cartulary was made (in 1129 × 1139).[9] They may have been drafted at the New Minster, with which Æthelgeard had an association and whence some comparable texts survive.[10]

v. Norman royal documents

- **X, XII**, and **XIV–XVII**. These royal writs, comprising short Latin letters with specific addressees, were issued in the names of William I, Henry I, and Henry II.[11]
- **XIII**. This royal confirmation of an agreement was made with Henry I as mediator. Written in Latin, it described the arrangements for the liturgical procession at Winchester on Palm Sundays.
- **XXXII**. An entry from Great Domesday Book, the final edited version of returns from the Domesday Survey of 1086.[12]

vi. an abbatial charter: XI

This charter in the name of Abbot Riwallon of the New Minster (1077–88) is in the form of a general declaration, corroborated by witnesses.

vii. a papal letter: XXXIII

This (now incomplete) letter in the name of a pope called John is probably to be attributed to John XII (955–64).[13] It contains some formulae from the *Liber Diurnus*.[14]

Degrees of authenticity

The documents are listed below according to the variant degree of their authenticity. For fuller discussion, reference should be made to the commentaries which precede the edition and translation of each of the individual documents.

i. genuine documents: These take the following forms:
- an original record (uniquely) in the form of a codex and splendidly written in gold ink: **IV**, the New Minster refoundation charter;
- an original record written into a space in a religious book, probably copied from a draft: **I**, the boundary of Ealhswith's *haga*;
- a cartulary copy of an original record on a single-sheet of parchment: **II, VI–XV, XVII, XXI–XXVIII**, and **XXX–XXXIII**.
- a cartulary copy of an apparently authentic record of a subsidiary grant added to an existing record on a single-sheet of parchment: **XIX–XX**.

ii. an interpolated individual document: XXIX

A new clause has been added at the end of the pre-existing text of a writ, in an attempt to extend privileges to an estate additional to that to which it relates.

iii. forged documents: These take the following forms:
- a forgery in single-sheet state and in an imitative script: **XVIII**, the Micheldever diploma in the name of Edward the Elder;

---

[9] See above, p. 6.
[10] For Æthelgeard, see below, **XIX**, n. 2.
[11] For the most recent analysis of the diplomatic of the Latin writs of William I, see Bates *Regesta*, 52–62. For an analysis of those of Henry I, see *Regesta*, II, xxvii–xxviii.

[12] See V. H. Galbraith, *The Making of Domesday Book* (Oxford, 1961), especially 189–204.
[13] See Dom Thomas Symons, 'Notes on the Life and Work of St Dunstan, II', *Downside Review* n.s. 80 (1962), 355–66, at 357–8.
[14] See below, **XXXIII**, nn. 4, 6, 17, and 20–1.

- a copy of a (?single-sheet) forgery: **III**, a foundation-charter in the name of Edward the Elder; and **XVI**, a writ-charter in the name of Henry I.

All three of these documents come from the New Minster / Hyde Abbey and share some aspects of formulation; the draftsman (or draftsmen) who constructed **III** and **XVI** in the twelfth century appears (or appear) to have used the pre-existing forgery **XVIII** as one of their sources.[15]

iv. a conflated or edited series of pre-existing documents

Fourteen diplomas in the name of King Edgar appear to have been conflated in the late tenth or early eleventh century to make a unitary text (**V**), which purported to restore the endowment of the Old Minster to its ancient state. What was constructed was in essence a mini–cartulary, containing edited and cross-referred versions of the diplomas. Some of the diplomas may already have been interpolated. Thus, references to previous royal grants of an estate occur only in **V, i–vi, viii,** and **xiii** but are comparable with those found in other documents in the Old Minster archive, particularly relating to the ancient cathedral estates of Alresford (Hants),[16] Chilcomb (Hants),[17] Downton (Wilts.),[18] and Taunton (Somerset).[19] This may point to a consistent campaign of interpolation of 'historical' passages into such documents in the archive at some date before the construction of **V**, possibly not long before, as two apparently genuine diplomas of King Æthelred II contain such passages.[20]

V, xiv, the last of the constituent sections of **V**, may represent a modified version of an 'Æthelwoldian' text whose original purpose was to record the constitutional changes at the Old Minster resulting from the Benedictine Reform.

Monastic propaganda

Charters emanating from the context of the tenth-century Benedictine Reform were both memorial and political in function. They included philosophical and often outspoken statements of the monastic position. As such, tests for their authenticity are somewhat different from those which can be applied to more regular diplomatic products issued by the king. Their interrelationship with other texts that were important in the Reform period may sometimes speak in their favour, however.[21] Extended passages of criticism or praise are included in **IV** and **V** in order to propagate and perpetuate a highly critical view of the shortcomings of the secular clergy as opposed to the regular. These passages demonstrate the use of royal documents (i.e. those issued in the monarch's name) as a vehicle for the promotion of the monastic cause. There is an explicit contrast made between monastic humility and clerical pride, and the list of monastic virtues in **IV, xii** can be placed against the list of clerical vices in **V, xiv**. If we remember that the New Minster refoundation-charter was intended to be read out aloud during the course of the year as a reminder to the monks of the New Minster of what was expected of them, then chapter **IV, xii** may be seen as an especially important summary of the ideals of the monastic life:

---

[15] See below, pp. 58–9, 178–9 and 184.

[16] S 242, 284, and 375; *CW* 51, 54, and 50; *BCS* 102, 398, and 623.

[17] S 325 and 376 (MS. 1), and **XXX**; *CW* 236, BL Harl. Ch. 43 C. 1, and *CW* 14; *BCS* 493 and 620, and *AS Writs* 107.

[18] S 275, 375, 393, 540 (MS. 1), and 891; *CW* 41, 50, 42, BL Cotton Ch. viii. 11, and *CW* 44; *BCS* 391, 623, 690, 862, and

KCD 698.

[19] S 310–11, 443 (MS. 1), 521, and 806; *CW* 128, 117, BL Cotton Ch. viii. 17, and *CW* 57–8; *BCS* 475–6, 727, 831, and 1219–20.

[20] S 835 and 891; *CW* 222 and 44; and *KCD* 622 and 698.

[21] Cf. Eric John, 'Some Latin Charters of the Tenth-Century Reformation', in John *Orbis Britanniae*, 181–209.

WHAT SORT OF MONKS ARE TO DWELL IN THIS MONASTERY, AND IN WHAT WAY.

Let regular monks therefore, not seculars, dwelling in the aforementioned monastery in company with Christ, conform to the practices of a rule.

While worshipping, let the spiritual fathers copy the example of the Holy Fathers, doing nothing except what the common rule of the monastery or the precept of the Elders shall have mentioned.

Removed therefore from worldly displays, let them guard **purity** with full exertion of body and of mind.

Striving in devotion to **humility**, strengthening the body with the vigour of **frugality**, let them be restrained by an eager mind.

Let them blush with shame—under perpetual interdict—at being made table-companions of the citizens within the city.

Let charitable people who dwell in the city employ permitted foods in the refectory, rejecting, like melancholy, the showy and lascivious delights of the worldly.

Let them not eat outside the refectory, unless they are ill and confined to the infirmary; and let them only eat those things which are permitted.

Let them entertain most warily guests of a sacred, or of the highest, rank, if reason requires it, and well-ordered pilgrims coming from far-distant lands, at the abbot's table in the refectory.

Let seemly kindness be shown to laymen in the guest-house;

And let none of the monks be allowed to eat or drink with them, in accordance with the decrees of the Fathers;

Moreover let [laymen] not be brought into the refectory to eat or drink.

Let the poor be supported, like Christ, with great jubilation of heart.

Within **IV**, this chapter echoes in part the description, in **IV, ii**, of Adam's happy existence before the expulsion from Paradise, but in the specific context of the reform of the Old and New Minsters in 964 it may more tellingly be contrasted with the account of the pre-reform cathedral clergy from **V, xiv**. This was also intended to be remembered in perpetuity, but as a list of things to be avoided by those who professed their faith as monks:

Undoubtedly, the canons, disfigured by every blemish of vices, exalted with **vain glory**, putrefying with the malice of **envy**, blinded by the blemishes of **avarice**, taking pleasure in the fires of **wantonness**, entirely devoted to **gluttony**, subject to the earthly king not to the bishop, were wont to feast themselves by ancient custom in modern time on the food of the aforementioned land. Since indeed, following drunkenness with **murder**, and embracing their wives in an unseemly manner with an excessive and uncommon **lust**, very few wished to visit God's church, and rarely, they did not deign to keep the canonical hours.

As in a similar passage in Wulfstan's 'Life of St. Æthelwold',[22] the canons are condemned chiefly because they were not celibate and did not follow the monastic liturgical ritual.[23] However, as secular clergy, they had not sworn to follow the monastic way of life, and only someone writing from an obsessively rigid monkish perspective would castigate them for not living according to monastic norms. The passages were written (**IV, xii** by Æthelwold; and **V, xiv** by him or by one of his followers) with the aims of justifying both the introduction of the monks and the expulsion of

---

[22] Wulfstan *Vita S. Æthelwoldi*, cap. 16 (trans. Lapidge and Winterbottom, 31): 'there were in the Old Minster . . . cathedral canons involved in wicked and scandalous behaviour, victims of pride, insolence and riotous living to such a degree that some did not think to celebrate mass in due order. They married wives illicitly, divorced them, and took others; they were constantly given to gourmandizing and drunkenness'.

[23] Reference to married cathedral canons is also made in the '*Altitonantis*' diploma from Worcester: S 731, *BCS* 1135 ('A. D. 964'; ?12th cent.). On this diploma, see Patrick Wormald, 'Oswaldslow: an Immunity?', in Nicholas Brooks and Catherine Cubitt (ed.), *St Oswald of Worcester: Life and Influence* (London and New York, 1996), 117–28, especially 120–2, and references there cited.

their secular predecessors. They belong more naturally to the genre of religious propaganda rather than that of historical record, but their inclusion within royal diplomas has succeeded, as intended, in giving longevity to their sentiments.

4. THE DOCUMENTS AS EVIDENCE FOR HISTORICAL TOPOGRAPHY

Most of the documents edited in the present volume refer to particular aspects of the physical environment of early medieval Winchester. Certain of the city's walls, gates, streets, tenements, watercourses, mills, monastic precincts, suburbs, and churches of varying sizes and importance, are mentioned in them, as well as the Norman royal palace and the castle; see Figs. 1 and 2. A few documents relate to the ownership or taxation of estates around or adjacent to the city, such as those of Chilcomb (see Fig. 13) and Easton (see Fig. 10), or to Winchester tenements belonging to rural estates (see Fig. 3). In each case, however, these are fundamentally bound up with the contemporary or future life and history of the city.

- **I–VIII** and **XXXIII** concern the south-eastern quarter of the city and the three minsters therein before A.D. 1000.
- **IX–XVII** relate to the history of the south-eastern quarter after 1066 and of Hyde, whither the New Minster community moved *temp.* Henry I.
- **XVIII–XXIX** concern property before 1066 in various locations within the city or in the suburbs.
- **XXX–XXXII** concern the estate of Chilcomb in the late tenth and eleventh centuries.

We may note that although references to topography may seem often to be accurate even within forged documents, questions of date are to be approached with due reference to the criticism of the full text as contained in the respective commentaries.

Alterations to the physical environment recorded in these documents are seen to follow directly from changes in royal policy or ecclesiastical life and thought and some remain today as physical manifestations of such early medieval changes. It is discernible from the documents too that the citizens of Winchester at the time felt the consequences both of new royal and religious policies and of topographical reorganisations within the city. When public buildings, such as the three minsters, the royal palace, the castle, or Hyde Abbey, were built or extended, some lesser inhabitants of the city or suburbs would have been forced to move from their dwellings,[1] while other more wealthy ones were pressurised to exchange one piece of land for another or for money.[2] Even the religious communities themselves were sometimes forced by royal or episcopal command to compromise and to end disagreement over property or privileges.[3] At such times, streets could be closed or cleared and watercourses diverted with the consequent destruction of houses and buildings, and the ruin of mills.[4]

---

[1] The need for such removal was recognised by King Edgar in **VI**: *dissipatis secularium domunculis* 'when the small houses of the secular have been demolished'.

[2] See below, **VIII**.
[3] See below, **VII** and **XIII**.
[4] See below, **VII**.

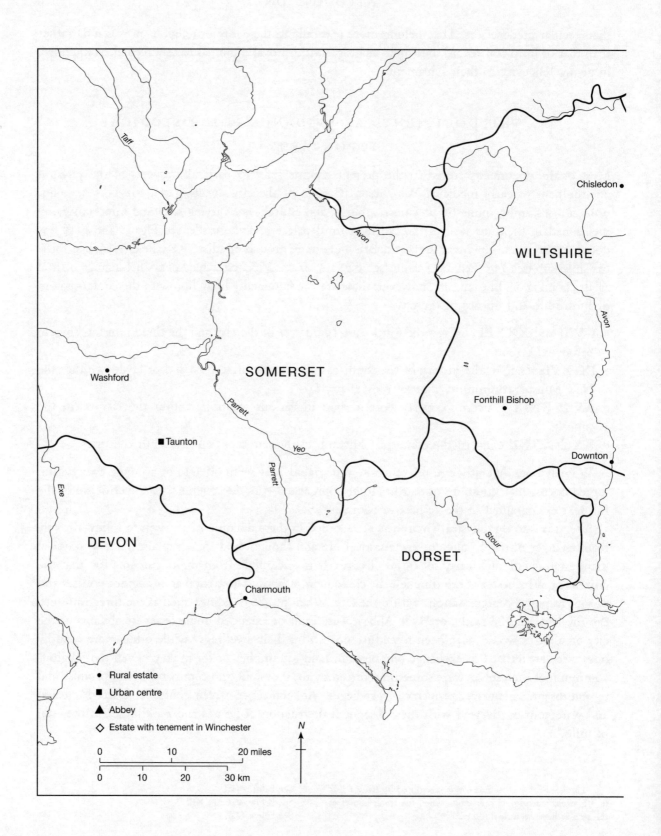

WILTSHIRE

Chisledon •

SOMERSET

Washford •

Fonthill Bishop •

Downton •

■ Taunton

DEVON

DORSET

Charmouth •

● Rural estate
■ Urban centre
▲ Abbey
◇ Estate with tenement in Winchester

N

| 0 | 10 | 20 miles |
| 0 | 10 | 20 | 30 km |

Taff

Parrett

Yeo

Parrett

Exe

Stour

Avon

Avon

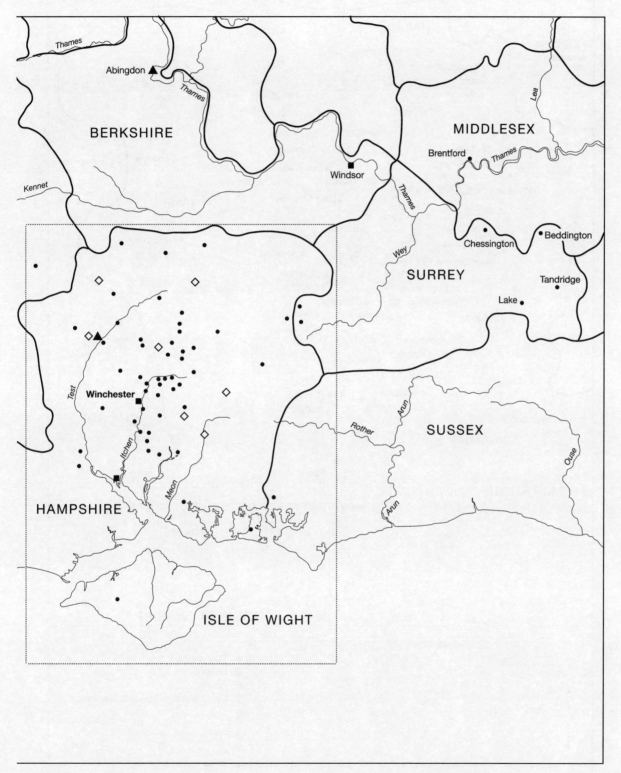

Fig. 3. Settlements mentioned in the documents (distinguishing those with Winchester tenements)

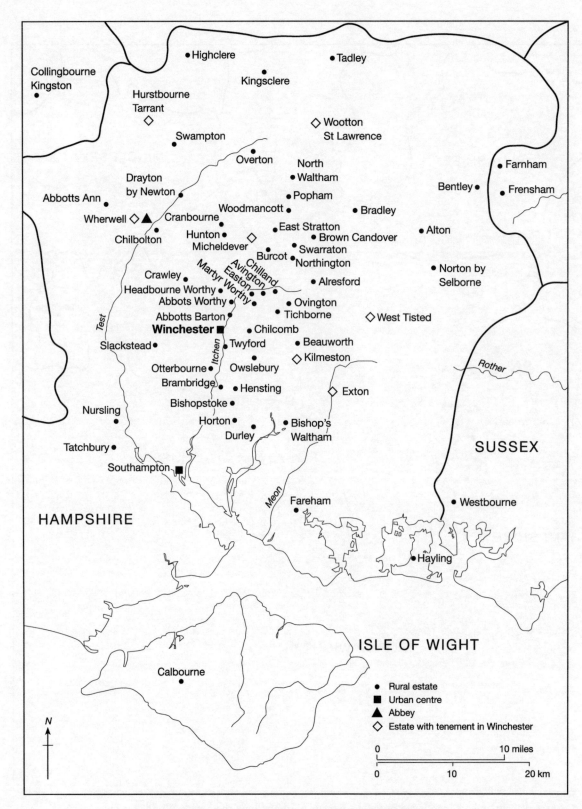

Collingbourne
Kingston

Highclere

Tadley

Hurstbourne
Tarrant ◇

Kingsclere

Swampton

◇ Wootton
St Lawrence

Overton

North
Waltham

Farnham

Drayton
by Newton

Popham

Bentley

Frensham

Abbotts Ann

Woodmancott

Bradley

Wherwell ◇ ▲ Cranbourne

East Stratton

Alton

Chilbolton

Hunton
Micheldever ◇

Brown Candover

Swarraton

Burcot
Chilland
Avington
Easton

Northington

Crawley

Martyr Worthy

Alresford

Norton by
Selborne

Headbourne Worthy

Test

Abbots Worthy

Ovington
Tichborne

Abbotts Barton

Winchester ■

Chilcomb

◇ West Tisted

Slackstead

Itchen

Twyford

Beauworth

Otterbourne

Owslebury

◇ Kilmeston

Rother

Brambridge

Hensling

Bishopstoke

Horton

Meon

◇ Exton

Nursling

Durley

Bishop's
Waltham

Tatchbury

Southampton ■

SUSSEX

Fareham

Westbourne

HAMPSHIRE

Hayling

ISLE OF WIGHT

Calbourne

N

• Rural estate
■ Urban centre
▲ Abbey
◇ Estate with tenement in Winchester

0   10 miles

0   10   20 km

FIG. 3 (detail). Settlements nearest to Winchester.

Chronological survey

The early medieval history of the city has been extensively discussed by Martin Biddle and Derek Keene in the first volume of Winchester Studies, mainly using the evidence of Surveys I and II, but also making reference to earlier editions of many of the documents in the present volume.[5] All that will be attempted here is a short summary of the main developments from the early tenth to the early twelfth centuries.

c. 900

The New Minster and Nunnaminster were founded *temp.* Edward the Elder in the ancient episcopal city of Wessex which had recently been revived as a royal centre of government. It seems to have been newly refortified as part of a defensive system of strongholds against the Vikings and to have been given a new street layout.[6] The evidence of **I** and **II**, from this period, relates only to a part of the south-eastern quarter of the city. However, it indicates that to the north of the cathedral stood a group of lesser churches (the 'wound' church, St. Andrew's, and St. Gregory's) and domestic ecclesiastical buildings (a stone dormitory and a refectory), in close proximity to a rectilinear pattern of streets. To the east of the cathedral lay part at least of its cemetery. Further north-east lay a large urban tenement or *haga*, at this time belonging to Queen Ealhswith, but possibly preserving boundaries from an earlier period, through which a number of water-channels flowed north-south and were dammed in places to drive water-mills. Some minor route-ways crossed the channels by means of fords. There was a market in the later High Street (Broadway) and the south-eastern side of the city was fortified by means of a 'city-hedge', associated with the king.

Unfortunately, the evidence of **XVIII**, in the name of Edward the Elder, which refers both to an urban mill appurtenant to Micheldever and to the southern wall of the city, cannot be used for this period as it is a forgery of the early eleventh century.

temp. Eadred (946–955)

XIX and **XX** record the acquisition at this time of urban property by one particular owner of rural estates in Hampshire, the thegn called Æthelgeard. His probable purpose was to obtain not only permanently available accommodation within a fortified centre but also privileged access to the city's market for the produce of his country estates. It is probable that an increasing demand for property in Winchester and other economically-viable fortified boroughs in the tenth and eleventh centuries led to the gradual subdivision of the earlier large burghal plots and consequently to a greater variety of size of urban tenement covered by the OE term *haga*. **XIX** refers both to an urban mill and to the east gate of the city.

temp. Edgar (959–75) and Edward the Martyr (975–8)

IV-VIII indicate some of the physical effects on the city stemming from religious changes due to the Benedictine Reform, of which Winchester was a major centre in England, due to the influence of Bishop Æthelwold.[7] The most dramatic and long-lasting physical symbol of the enforcement of monastic celibacy and exclusivism was the construction of separate precincts to contain the church

---

[5] See WS 1; in particular, chap. 2 'General Topography' and chap. 3 'Public Buildings'.

[6] Ibid. 450–2; cf. Rumble and Hill *Defence of Wessex*, 225.

[7] See Barbara Yorke (ed.), *Bishop Æthelwold: His Career and Influence* (Woodbridge, 1988, reprinted 1997).

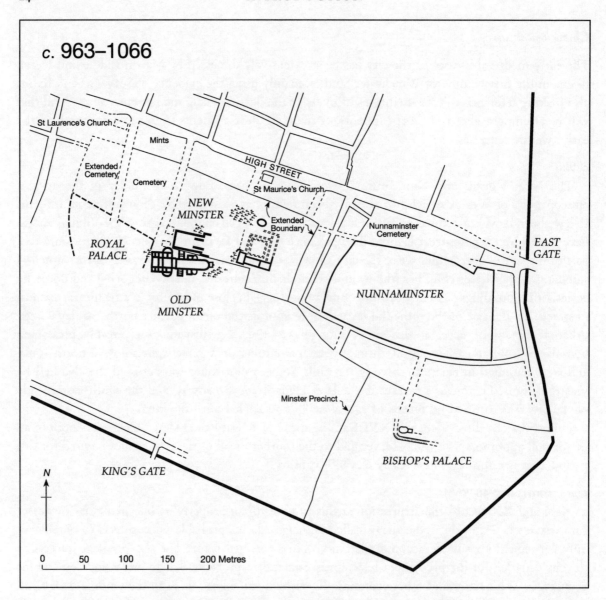

FIG. 4. The south-east corner of Winchester *c*.963–1066.

and domestic buildings of each of the three minsters, in accordance with the Rule of St. Benedict (*BR* 66. 6–7):

Monasterium autem, si possit fieri, ita debet constitui ut omnia necessaria, id est aqua, molendinum, hortum, vel artes diversas intra monasterium exerceantur,
    ut non sit necessitas monachis vagandi foris, quia omnino non expedit animabus eorum.

The monastery should, if possible, be so constructed that within it all necessities, such as water, mill and garden are contained, and the various crafts are practiced.
    Then there will be no need for the monks to roam outside, because this is not at all good for their souls.

In accordance with this injunction, King Edgar ordered each of the minsters to be surrounded with a 'space' (*spacium*), where the members of their communities might be 'removed from the bustle of the citizens' (*á ciuium tumultu remoti*).[8] The construction of the precincts, marked by walls or hedges,[9] caused the stopping or diversion of watercourses, the closure of streets, the demolition of houses, and the ruin of some established mills.[10] It also involved the exchange of land and property both between the three minsters and between the Old Minster and the family of one of their lay benefactors.[11] At the same time, Wolvesey became an episcopal precinct, enclosed by its own northern wall, by the city wall to the east and south, and by the precinct of the Old Minster and a watercourse, perhaps that mentioned in **VIII**, to the west.

VIII and **XXIII** refer to the south wall of the city. **XXI** and **XXIII**, both dated 961, refer to tenements in Winchester belonging to rural estates.

temp. Æthelred II (978–1016)

XXIV–XXVIII refer in total to forty tenements within the city and another in the southern suburb. Those benefitting from grants of such tenements ranged from the queen to the bishop of Sherborne, the Old Minster, Wherwell Abbey, and an important thegn called Æthelweard. **XXVI** and **XXVIII** provide further references to the city's market in the later High Street and **XXV** and **XXVI** show that by this time some of the side-streets to the north and north-east of it were occupied by groups of specialist manufacturers.[12] **XXVIII** indicates that small churches had begun to be founded on burghal plots.

IX relates to the meadowland just outside the city to the north, later known as Hyde Moors.

temp. William I (1066–87)

X and **XI** record that the royal palace was built, or extended, at this time on to the site of part of the New Minster cemetery.[13] This was after the destruction by fire of the monastery's domestic buildings in 1064 or 1065.[14] The action probably represented a reoccupation by the king of ancient royal land given by Edward the Elder in 901 after he himself had been granted it by the West Saxon *witan*.[15]

temp. Henry I (1100–35)

The relocation of the New Minster to Hyde *c*.1110 constituted a major upheaval both in the south-eastern quarter of the city and in the northern suburb.[16] In the city, land formerly occupied by the New Minster's church, chapels, houses, and mills passed to the cathedral.[17]

The north gate of the city is mentioned in **XII**, and the west gate, as well as the castle and its gate, in **XIII**. The western suburb appears to have reached as far as the church of St. James. It also included a church dedicated to St. Valery. Further development of the eastern suburb was encouraged by the king's grant of an increase in the duration of St. Giles's Fair, held on the eastern hill since 1096.[18]

---

[8] See below, **VI**. Cf. *a secularibus . . . pompis remoti* 'removed . . . from worldly displays' (**IV, xii**) with reference to the New Minster and *ab huius uitę curis remoti* 'removed from the cares of this life' (**V, xiv**) with reference to the Old Minster.

[9] See below, **VI**: *spacium omne muris uel sepibus complexum* 'the whole space, encompassed by walls or hedges'.

[10] See below, **VI** and **VII**.   [11] See below, **VII** and **VIII**.

[12] See below, p. 29.

[13] See WS 1, 292–5.

[14] On the date, see ibid. 293, n. 1.

[15] See below **II**, n. 14.

[16] Compare Figs. 2 and 6.

[17] See below, **XIII–XV**.

[18] See below, **XII** and **XIII**. For the fair, see WS 1, 286–8.

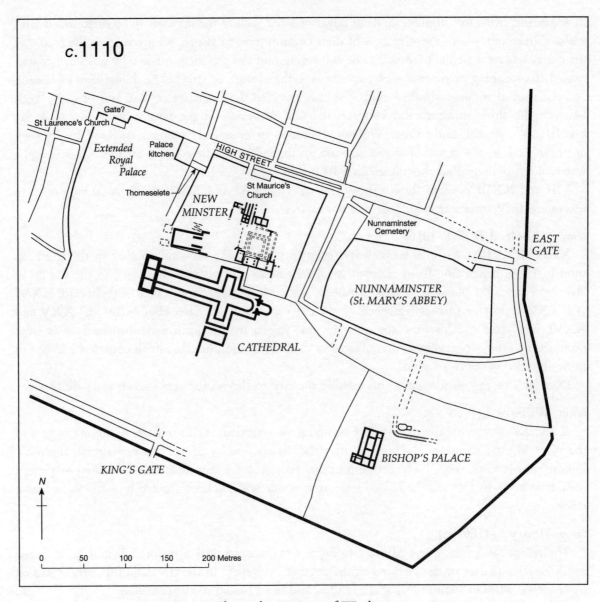

FIG. 5. The south-east corner of Winchester *c*.1110.

temp. **Henry II** (1154–89)

XVII provides a reference to the *aula regis* 'the royal hall', presumably still meaning, in this particular context, residual rights in the old royal palace-site, whose buildings were destroyed in the early 1140s, rather than the king's new residence within the castle.[19]

[19] Cf. WS 1, 296–305, and 326.

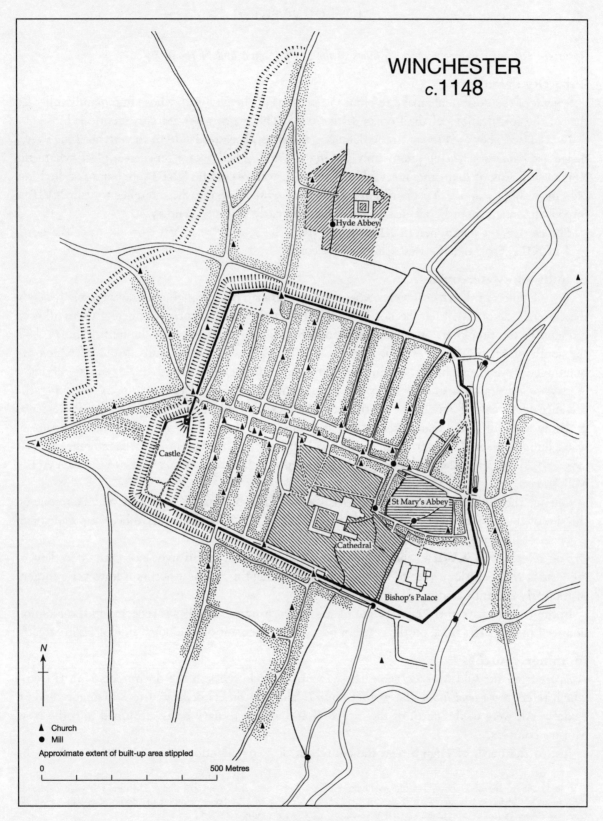

WINCHESTER
*c.*1148

Hyde Abbey

Castle

St Mary's Abbey

Cathedral

Bishop's Palace

N

▲ Church
● Mill
Approximate extent of built-up area stippled

0   500 Metres

Fɪɢ. 6. Winchester *c.*1148.

Recurrent references to topographical features of the Anglo-Saxon and Norman city

i. the city defences

Several of the documents make reference to sections of the city wall, whose line mainly followed that of the fortifications of the Roman settlement.[20] The major gates are also mentioned.

I (*a.* 5 December 902) refers to the defences in the south-eastern side of the city as 'king's city-hedge' (*oð cyninges burghege*), presumably signifying a living hedge or a fence at a place where the Roman wall was, at that time, not visible. The south wall occurs in **XXIII** (961) and is called 'the old city-wall' (*to þan ealdan portpealle*) in **VIII** (975 × 978). However, the reference to it in **XVIII**, a forged diploma, cannot be taken as earlier than the early eleventh century.

The east gate is mentioned in **XIX** (946 × 955), the south gate in **VII** (?970 × 975), the north gate in **XII** (1110), and the west gate in **XIII** (1114).

ii. mills and watercourses

Side-channels of the river Itchen, some of them artificial, run through (and now mostly beneath) the eastern side of city.[21] To the north of High Street the presence of a number of them allowed residents of the Brooks area to specialise in industrial pursuits from at least the tenth century.[22] To the south of High Street the same flow of water was used to drive mills, some of which are mentioned or inferred in the documents. Thus the OE compound term *mylengear*, signifying a 'transverse stream-dam or weir',[23] occurs three times in **I** (*a.* 5 December 902), implying the presence of three different mills on the boundary of Ealhswith's tenement.[24] One of these was probably the mill of Nunnaminster which, according to **VII**, was later ruined by the diversion of water into the New Minster by Bishop Æthelwold in ?970 × 975. The subsequent reference in **VIII** (975 × 978) to a stream which passes through the south wall of the city may refer to the later Abbey Mill Stream.

Outside the walls, the mention in **XIX** (946 × 955) of a mill outside East Gate may be to one on the site of the modern City Mill, while Costic's mill in **XXII** (961) may have been a precursor of Durngate Mill, further to the north.

The reference in **XVIII** to the southernmost mill within the wall may be to an antecedent of Floodstock Mill, a little further to the north. The document in which it occurs is however a forgery of the early eleventh century.

In the western part of the city the use of subterranean water supplies is reflected in the mention of a well in **XXVIII** (1012) on the rear boundary of a tenement on the north side of High Street.[25]

iii. minor churches[26]

Apart from the Old Minster, the earliest mention of churches in the documents is in **II** (?901) which refers to *þa pindcirican* 'the wound-church' and two others dedicated to St. Gregory and St. Andrew. All were to the north of the cathedral and appear to have been subsumed into the New Minster complex.

Just to the north of High Street, the church of St. Peter mentioned in **XXVIII** (1012) can be

[20] Cf. WS 1, 272–7.

[21] Ibid. 282–5. See also above, Fig. 1; and John Crook, 'Winchester's Cleansing Streams, Parts I and II', *Winchester Cathedral Record* 53 (1984), 26–34, and 54 (1985), 14–24.

[22] See WS 2.i, 63–4, and 287; also WS 2.ii, **435**.

[23] BT *Suppl.*, 644.

[24] See below, **I**, nn. 4, 6, and 9. The third reference, to 'the old mill-yair', may however reflect the disuse of one of these mills by the early 10th cent.

[25] See below, **XXVIII**, n. 18.

[26] See WS 1, 329–35.

identified with that later known as St. Peter in the Fleshambles. It appears to have begun life as a place of worship (*basilica*) founded by the port-reeve Æthelwine.

In the eastern suburb the church of St. Giles is mentioned in **XII** (1110).

In the western suburb the church of St. James appears in **XIII** (1114), while that of St. Valery is implied by a street-name.

Street-names[27]

Three of the Anglo-Saxon documents contain the earliest recorded Winchester street-names.[28] These are of a type that reflects the activity carried on in the streets concerned. The main west-east route through the city (later High Street) is shown to have already contained a market by the early tenth century from its designation as *seo ceapstræt* in **I** (*on þa ceap stræt*), although the use of the definite article may show that this was not yet a fixed name, but rather a description. By 996, however, the definite article was dropped in **XXVI** (*andlang cypstræte*), by which date it was, in this document at least, treated as a name.

In the late tenth century some of the streets to the north of High Street were designated by the occupation of their residents. Thus by 990 (**XXV**) the activities of tanners gave rise to *Tænnerestret* (= Lower Brook Street), while the butchers and shield-makers are referred to respectively in *flæsmangere stræt* (= Parchment Street) and *scyldpyrhtana stræt* (= part of St. George's Street) in 996 (**XXVI**).

In the post-conquest period, document **XIII** shows that the dedication of a church in honour of the continental St. Valery, which is referred to in Survey I of *c.*1110,[29] had been transferred by 1114 to a street (later Sussex Street) in the western suburb leading towards Hyde.

Topography outside the city

Besides the above features within Winchester, the partly conterminous rural estate of Easton is delimited in **XXII**, its bounds including reference to the following man-made features: a fortified site (*burh*) on the river Itchen near Avington; heathen burials; a mill just outside the city to the north-east; and a trench (*furh*), probably for drainage or channeling of the river Itchen near King's Worthy. The area of Hyde Moors, on or adjacent to which Hyde Abbey was later built, was divided off from this estate of Easton by the reign of Æthelred II and its measurements are given in **IX**.

5. THE DOCUMENTS AS A REFLECTION OF THE HISTORY OF THE CITY *c.*900–*c.*1150

Because of the twin bias of their intrinsic purposes and of the haphazard nature of manuscript survival, the documents can only give a very incomplete and slanted account in relation to the full history of churches and property in Anglo-Saxon and Norman Winchester. However, they do reflect some of the more general aspects of the nature of the city in the early medieval period as

[27] Cf. ibid. 233–5. For later medieval street-names in the city, see WS 2.i, 54–6.

[28] Note that 'the middle street' in **I** and 'the north street', 'the east street', and 'the south street' in **II** are descriptive phrases relevant only to the immediate context of particular pieces of land, rather than true street-names, and are here disregarded.

[29] See WS 1, **I, 107**, n. 7.

revealed by other surviving sources such as the Anglo-Saxon Chronicle, saints' lives, the *Liber Wintoniensis*, and the archaeological record.

Winchester as a royal city

The period covered by the documents was one in which royal power was very strong in Winchester, after the city's refortification in the late ninth century and before the citizens' rights to govern themselves evolved in the later twelfth century.[1]

Of the two West Saxon dioceses co-existing since 705,[2] the kings in the earlier ninth century had apparently favoured Sherborne, west of Selwood, over Winchester to its east, but the mid-century expansion of their power over Kent and Sussex gave heightened importance to the strategic position of Winchester in the centre of southern England.[3] In 860, the year in which Kent and Sussex were united with Wessex under King Æthelbeorht, the city suffered attack from viking marauders.[4] Whether it was extensively damaged at that time, giving the necessity for reconstruction, is not known, but Winchester appears from its street-plan to have been revived in the latter years of the century as a major fortified site.[5] Although the sole reference to the city *temp.* Alfred is to captured vikings being brought in 896 to the king there (who sentenced them to be hanged),[6] Winchester was included in the Burghal Hidage (*temp.* Edward the Elder) as a fortification rated at the highest assessment of 2400 hides.[7] It has been suggested that the royal court may have settled there towards the end of Alfred's reign.[8] At least from this time, it probably took some political, administrative, and economic functions away from the exposed coastal trading-centre and royal vill of Southampton.[9] Although the latter remained of importance both to the West Saxon economy and to shrieval government, Winchester began to advance to national significance.

In this context, the foundation of the New Minster by King Edward the Elder and his advisers (the acquisition of whose site is recorded in **II**) may be seen as a political action, underlining the king's power in the refortified borough as against that of the bishop who had previously been the most prominent figure in the area. In subsequent reigns, although the bishop or some of the leading citizens may have been at times out of favour with the king, due to dynastic politics,[10] the city remained of crucial importance to the southern part of the kingdom, first of the Anglo-Saxons and later of England.

The appointment of the monk Æthelwold as bishop of Winchester was a significant political act of King Edgar in 963 and an essential precursor to the reform of the Old and New Minsters in the following year.[11] The expulsion of the secular clergy was of great national importance, and their forcible ejection may be contrasted with the favour shown to the monks. Partly by means of the removal of secular dwellings from the land used for the three new monastic precincts, the

---

[1] See WS 1, 449–508; and WS 2.i, 69–70.

[2] Bertram Colgrave and R. A. B. Mynors (ed.), *Bede's Ecclesiastical History of the English People* (Oxford, 1969), 514–15.

[3] Barbara A. E. Yorke, 'The Bishops of Winchester, the Kings of Wessex and the Development of Winchester in the Ninth and Early Tenth Centuries', *Proc Hants F C* 40 (1984), 61–70, at 64 and 67.

[4] *ASC* [A], s.a. See Barbara Yorke, *Wessex in the Early Middle Ages* (London and New York, 1995), 97–8.

[5] See Martin Biddle, 'The Study of Winchester: Archaeology and History in a British Town', *PBA* 69 (1983), 93–135, at 121–3.

[6] *ASC* [A], s.a.

[7] Hill and Rumble *Defence of Wessex*, 225.

[8] Keynes *Liber Vitae*, 16.

[9] Martin Biddle, 'The Study of Winchester', 120–3; and Barbara A. E. Yorke, 'Bishops of Winchester', 66–7.

[10] Bishop Frithestan may have been out of favour with King Æthelstan 924–8, due to apparent support in the city for the position of King Ælfweard before the latter's death in August 924; see Keynes *Liber Vitae*, 19–22.

[11] *ASC* [A], s.a. 964. Nunnaminster appears to have been reformed at about the same time; see WS 1, 322.

south-east quarter of Winchester became dedicated solely to ecclesiastical purposes.[12] The settlement by King Edgar of a subsequent dispute over urban property between the three minsters, recorded in **VII**, reflects his special position as protector of the monastic life in England, referred to both in the *Regularis Concordia* and in the New Minster refoundation charter (**IV**).[13]

The removal *c*.1110 of the New Minster to Hyde (partly to land recorded in **IX** as meadow in the late tenth century) represented a virtual admission that the building of the new foundation so close to the cathedral had been a royal error in the reign of Edward the Elder which, according to **XIII**, required royal mediation by Henry I to put right. This removal eased, but did not end, the almost continuous rivalry between the two minsters since the New Minster's construction, no doubt to the relief of the kings who owed protection to both communities.

In the eleventh century and for the greater part of the twelfth, Winchester was the site of an important royal treasury.[14] In the reign of the Norman kings of England, it was one of three cities distinguished as the site of an annual royal crown-wearing.[15] The data in Surveys I and II, recorded in the *Liber Wintonienis*,[16] reveal the economic prosperity and sophistication that early medieval Winchester had gained from two centuries of close connection with the kings of England.

The city formed an essential base for those conducting business on behalf of the king.[17] In this respect it probably took over some of the functions of the more exposed shire-town of Southampton in the later Anglo-Saxon period. The following royal officials are referred to specifically in the documents in this volume:

- **the port-reeve**. Æthelwine, named in **XXVIII** (1012) as the founder of the church (of St. Peter in the Fleshambles) within the tenement part of which was later called Godbegot, is the earliest named eleventh-century reeve of Winchester.[18] His connection with the tenement may be indicative of a royal administrative use of it before King Æthelred gave it to his wife. Some continuing association of the locality with royal officialdom is suggested by the fact that the later reeve Æthelwold gave property next to Godbegot to his parents *TRE*.[19]
- **sheriffs of Hampshire**. Hugh the sheriff (?de Port), named as a witness to **XI**, was elsewhere called the *vicarius* of the city.[20] Hugh de Port's son Henry, who occurs in **XII–XIV**, had been sheriff 1101–?1106.[21] William of Pont de l'Arche is addressed specifically as sheriff in **XII** and is probably addressed in that capacity also in **XV**.
- **the collectors**. Mentioned (but not named) in **XV**, these were appointees of the king charged with the collection of geld and other royal dues in the county.[22]

Winchester as an ecclesiastical centre

i. The diocese and minsters before the mid tenth century

The see of the West Saxons had migrated to Winchester in *c*.660 from Dorchester-on-Thames on the border with Mercia. The cathedral (later called the Old Minster) seems to have been constructed

---

[12] Cf. below, **IV–VIII**.
[13] *RC*, cap. 3; and below, **IV, xvi**.
[14] WS 1, 291, 295, and 304–5.
[15] Ibid. 296. For the suggestion that Winchester may already have been the venue of a crown-wearing *TRE*, see ibid. 290. See further, Martin Biddle, 'Seasonal Festivals and Residence: Winchester, Westminster and Gloucester in the Tenth to Twelfth Centuries', *Anglo-Norman Studies* 8 (1986), 51–72.

[16] Edited and translated WS 1, 33–141.
[17] Cf. ibid. 387–92.
[18] For the known 11th- and 12th-cent. reeves, see ibid. 424–5.
[19] Ibid. 38 (**I, 23**).
[20] *Regesta* i, no. 379. On him, see below, **XI** n. 7.
[21] He is also included as a witness to **XVI**, below, but that is a later forgery.
[22] See WS 1, 425.

just south of the site of the Roman forum.[23] According to Bede, the relics of Birinus, the first bishop of the West Saxons, were moved hither in c.690.[24] In 705 the diocese was split in two on the death of Bishop Hædde; the area west of Selwood was given to Aldhelm, abbot of Malmesbury, with a see at Sherborne, while Wessex east of Selwood was made the responsibility of Bishop Daniel, with a see at Winchester.[25] This twofold division was still the case at the beginning of the reign of Edward the Elder, but by its end in 924 had become a fivefold one, with additional bishops in charge of newly-created dioceses at Crediton, Ramsbury, and Wells.[26]

The great size of the original diocese, and its extent even when halved in 705, ensured that the early endowment of the cathedral community was widely spread through south and south-western England. According to medieval Winchester tradition, ownership of the estates of Chilcomb, Alresford and (Headbourne) Worthy, Hants, and Downton, Wilts., dated from the foundation of the church in the mid seventh century.[27] Estates in the Isle of Wight are said to have been granted by King Ine in the late seventh century,[28] and Queen Frithugyth apparently gave Taunton, Somerset, before 737.[29] Before the middle of the tenth century, a number of other estates, many of them large, were acquired in Hampshire, Wiltshire, Surrey, Berkshire, and the Isle of Wight.[30] By that time, however, their profits may have been appropriated to individual prebends, rather than to a communal chest.[31]

By contrast, the New Minster's landed endowment, dating only from the early tenth century, was much smaller, both in the number and size of estates. By the time of the Benedictine Reform, however, it included lands in Hampshire, Wiltshire, and Berkshire.[32] The extensive estate of Micheldever, Hants, belonged to the New Minster by at least the first half of the eleventh century, when the single-sheet diploma containing **XVIII** was fabricated, but the diploma's claim that it was part of the original endowment is not independently supported.[33]

The early endowment of Nunnaminster seems to have been very small, with at least one estate in Hampshire and possibly another in Wiltshire.[34]

Members of the communities of secular priests at the Old and New Minsters probably occur among the witnesses to **II**, and in other documents from the reign of Edward the Elder.[35] It has been

---

[23] Ibid. 306–7.

[24] Bertram Colgrave and R. A. B. Mynors (ed.), *Bede's Ecclesiastical History of the English People* (Oxford, 1969), 232–3; see further, WS 4.i.

[25] Colgrave and Mynors (ed.), *Bede's Ecclesiastical History*, 514–15.

[26] A fivefold division of the West Saxon sees during the reign of Edward the Elder is recorded in the so-called 'Plegmund narrative' (*Councils* 35(i) = Sawyer (Kelly) 1451a) which bears the date 905 but was composed in the mid or late 10th century. For a translation and discussion, see Alexander R. Rumble, 'Edward the Elder and the Churches of Winchester and Wessex' in N. J. Higham and D. H. Hill (ed.), *Edward the Elder* (London and N. York, 2001), 230–47, at 238–44. The episcopal lists in CCCC, MS. 183 record the division by 934 × 937 or 939; see R. I. Page, 'Anglo-Saxon Episcopal Lists, Part III', *Nottingham Medieval Studies* 10 (1966), 2–24, at 8–12; and Mildred Budny, *Insular, Anglo-Saxon, and Early Anglo-Norman Manuscript Art at Corpus Christi College, Cambridge: An Illustrated Catalogue* (2 vols, Kalamazoo, 1997), i, 163.

[27] See *Winchester ann.*, s.a. 639; and the cathedral benefactors' lists in *Reg Pontissara*, 609–10 and in John Leland, *De rebus*

Britannicis collectanea (2nd edn., London, 1770), vol. 1, part ii, 428–30. Cf. below, **V, i–iii, v**, and **xiv**.

[28] *Winchester ann.*, s.a. 683 (Brading and Yaverland). According to **V, i**, below, the estate of Calbourne, also in the Isle of Wight, was an appurtenance of Downton, Wilts., from the time of the Old Minster's foundation.

[29] *Winchester ann.*, s.a. 721. Cf. S 254(i), *CW* 119, *BCS* 158.

[30] See *Winchester ann.*, passim; and the benefactors' lists (see above, n. 27). Cf. below, **V**.

[31] *ECW*, 225–6, and 239–41.

[32] For the New Minster endowment, see Miller *New Minster*, liii–lxii.

[33] Ibid. lv. Cf. Brooks 'Micheldever Forgery', 216–18.

[34] Of eight estates held *TRE*, only Leckford (Hants) and All Cannings (Wilts.) are recorded in surviving documents as being acquired before 955. See *DB* i, 43[v], 59[v], and 68[r] (*DB Hants* 14: 1–6; *DB Berks*. 14: 1; and *DB Wilts*. 14: 1–2); S 526, *BCS* 824 and S 1419, *BCS* 825–7; and Osbert of Clare's 'Life of St. Edburga', cap. 6: Susan J. Ridyard, *The Royal Saints of Anglo-Saxon England* (Cambridge, 1988), 33, 270.

[35] E.g. in S 385, *CW* 126a, *AS Ch* 20: a lease from the Old Minster ?908.

suggested that some of them may have acted as scribes for the royal administration in the early tenth century.[36] The community at Nunnaminster, amongst whom Edward the Elder's daughter (St.) Eadburh was lodged, appears to have consisted of aristocratic and politically-astute females.[37] Such worldly ecclesiastics contrasted with the monastic ideals propagated in the reign of Edgar but it is likely that some of their secular connections and activities brought material benefit to their churches, two of which were in their infancy.

ii. The reign of Edgar and after

The power of the bishop and the prestige of the Old Minster, although they had received a setback in the early tenth century from both the foundation of the New Minster and the second division of the diocese, were revived under (St.) Æthelwold and his successor (St.) Ælfheah. The reform of the two male Benedictine minsters which took place in 964 is recorded (by the reformers, in texts such as **IV** and **V, xiv**) as a process by which the secular canons, priests, or clerks were ejected from the churches and the practice of monastic humility was thus enabled to overcome the clerical sin of pride.[38] Estates appear to have been put on a communal footing at this time.[39] Some new grants were soon attracted to the Old Minster from pious lay supporters of the reforms.[40]

No specific ejection is recorded at Nunnaminster at this time but Æthelwold is said to have 'established flocks of nuns' there under one Æthelthryth.[41]

The many pupils of Æthelwold who appear as witnesses to **IV** attest also to the political ascendancy of the monastic faction by 966.[42] Monks (and nuns) were already by then part of a powerful ecclesiastical network, one which proved strong enough to weather the attacks of their enemies after the death of King Edgar.[43] This network was also a scholastic one which made use of hermeneutic Latin vocabulary and a sophisticated literary style for the delectation of its members.[44] In addition, Æthelwold and his pupils, such as Ælfric, seem to have deliberately limited and refined their wording of vernacular texts, translations, and glosses in order to establish an 'official' Old English prose vocabulary; this Winchester vocabulary appears as a dominant feature of the manuscripts which survive from late Anglo-Saxon England.[45]

The tenth-century reform also altered the role of the bishop of Winchester within his church. Æthelwold's successors as bishop were to be monks elected by the community of the Old Minster and were assigned added responsibilities for the safeguarding of the monastic life.[46] The construction of the monastic precincts also meant that the bishop's own residence had to be moved to Wolvesey and thus become separate from that of his community.[47]

[36] Keynes 1994, 1146–7.

[37] Ridyard, *Royal Saints*, 102–3.

[38] See below, **IV, viii**; and **V, xiv**.

[39] See below, **V, xiv**; cf. **IV, xvii** and **xxi**. At the Old Minster, at least, this may in part have been a restoration of an earlier arrangement. In 877, Bishop Tunbeorht had granted 5 hides at Nursling, Hants, to the refectory of his cathedral community (*familia*): S 1277, *CW* 219, *BCS* 544.

[40] Ælfgifu (?the divorced wife of King Eadwig) bequeathed Princes Risborough, Bucks., and the reversion of Berkhampstead, Herts., and Mongewell, Oxon., in 966 × 975: S 1484, *CW* 187, *AS Wills* 8. None of these were, however, held by the Old Minster by 1066: Rumble 1980, ii, 183–4. Ælfwaru, widow of Leofwine (and ?sister of the above Ælfgifu; cf. S 1484) granted Alverstoke, Exton, and East Woodhay, Hants, at about the same time, according to the benefactors' lists (see above, n. 27):

Rumble 1980, ibid.

[41] Wulfstan *Vita S. Æthelwoldi*, cap. 22 (eds. Lapidge and Winterbottom, 36–9).

[42] See below, **IV**, nn. 135, 146–9.

[43] See Whitelock *EHD* 236 (*Vita Oswaldi*); and D. J. V. Fisher, 'The Anti-Monastic Reaction in the Reign of Edward the Martyr', *Cambridge Historical Journal* 10 (1952), 254–70.

[44] See Lapidge 'Hermeneutic Style'. Cf. below, Latin Word-List, *passim*.

[45] See Helmut Gneuss, 'The Origin of Standard Old English and Æthelwold's School at Winchester', *ASE* 1 (1972), 63–83, especially 73–83; Walter Hofstetter, 'Winchester and the Standardization of Old English Vocabulary', *ASE* 17 (1988), 139–61; and Gretsch *Intellectual Foundations, passim*. Cf. below, **V, iii**, n. 61.

[46] See below, **V, xiv**, and **XXXIII**; and *RC*, cap. 9.

[47] *WS* 1, 323–4.

The beginnings of a shift in power over secular affairs within and around the city are indicated by the creation of ecclesiastical liberties from the late tenth or early eleventh century onwards, out of the devolution of royal rights and responsibilities. Their appearance and expansion is evidence of the gradual waning of the king's influence in the area by the mid twelfth century at the latest. There was fierce defence by the holders of such legal and economic privileges against loss or encroachment in the post-conquest period.[48] There were also attempts to gain extra privileges through deceit: **XVI** was forged in the mid twelfth century in an attempt to show that Hyde Abbey had been given exclusive rights over Hyde Street by Henry I.

The areas within the city which were accorded special privileges from the reign of Edgar comprised the three monastic precincts and the episcopal enclosure at Wolvesey. To the north of High Street, the liberty of Godbegot was also later acquired by the Old Minster, having developed within a tenement granted by King Æthelred II to his wife Emma.[49] Outside the city, the Old Minster acquired from the same king confirmation of a beneficial hidation for its ancient estate of Chilcomb.[50] In the late eleventh century the bishop obtained the right to hold the annual St. Giles's Fair, a very successful commercial event whose extent was considerably expanded in the early twelfth century as part of exchanges made with the New Minster under royal mediation.[51]

The New Minster was able to acquire control of the hundred of Micheldever in the first half of the eleventh century, with jurisdiction over its estates near the city, its rights perhaps coming from those of a previous royal capital manor.[52] Some of the rights of Hyde Abbey referred to in **XIII** stem from those of the New Minster, others arose out of bargaining with the bishop for the site previously occupied by the monastery within the city. In the mid twelfth century the community of Hyde obtained royal confirmation of fiscal and other rights over its new location (including those of sanctuary in the abbey-church).[53]

Episcopal power reached new heights in the reign of King Stephen (1135–54), when his brother Henry of Blois was both bishop of Winchester and papal legate.[54] Some cathedral estates which had been lost in or since 1066 were retrieved in 1136 through his influence.[55] He also made two unsuccessful attempts to promote the diocese of Winchester to the status of an archbishopric.[56]

---

[48] As witnessed particularly by the number of royal confirmations relating to the liberty of Godbegot; see below, **XXIX**.

[49] See below, **XXVIII** and **XXIX**; and WS 2.ii, **50–6**.

[50] The late Anglo-Saxon and *TRW* extent and privileges of Chilcomb are detailed below in **XXX–XXXII**.

[51] See below, **XII** and **XIII**. For the fair, see WS 1, 286–8; and WS 2.ii, 1091–1133.

[52] See below, **XVIII**; and Brooks 'Micheldever Forgery', 216–18.

[53] See below, **XVII**.

[54] See WS 1, 490–3; Lena Voss, *Heinrich von Blois, Bischof von Winchester (1129–71)* (Historische Studien 210, Berlin, 1932), 41–53; H. Tilmann, *Die päpstlichen Legaten in England bis zur Beendigung der Legation Gualas (1218)* (Bonn, 1926), 41–50; M. J. Franklin (ed.), *English Episcopal Acta VIII: Winchester 1070–1204* (Oxford, 1993), xxxv–xlix; and Nicholas Riall, *Henry of Blois, Bishop of Winchester: A Patron of the Twelfth-Century Renaissance* (Hampshire Papers 5, Winchester, 1994), 4–6.

[55] *Cod. Wint. I*, the earliest part of the *Codex Wintoniensis* (see above, pp. 5–9), was compiled at the beginning of his episcopate to provide a manageable record of title for the Anglo-Saxon endowment of the cathedral which could be referred to as evidence for the retrieval of lost estates; see Rumble 1982, 162–4. For King Stephen's restoration in 1136 of East Meon, Hants; Wargrave, Berks.; Bradford, Crowcombe, Hele, and Norton Fitzwarren, Somerset, see *Regesta* iii, nos. 945–9; *CW* 2–4, 7, and 10.

[56] *Winchester ann.*, s.a. 1143; WS 1, 320 (with dates 1144–5 and 1148–50); A. Morey and C. N. L. Brooke, *Gilbert Foliot and his Letters* (Cambridge, 1965), 91, 158–9 (with dates 1143 and 1149–50); Marjorie Chibnall (ed.), *Johannis Saresberiensis Historia pontificalis, John of Salisbury's Memoirs of the Papal Court* (London, 1956), 78–80; W. J. Millor, H. E. Butler, and C. N. L. Brooke (ed.), *The Letters of John of Salisbury* (London, 1955), i, 254; and William Stubbs (ed.), *Radulphi de Diceto Opera historica, The Historical Works of Master Ralph de Diceto, Dean of London* (Rolls Series 68, London, 1876), i, 255.

These attempts at metropolitan status explain the presence in *Cod. Wint. II* (mid 12th-cent.; see above, pp. 7–8) of two Anglo-Saxon documents relating to the episcopacy : *BCS* 53 and *Councils* 35(i) = Sawyer (Kelly) 1428a and 1451a; *CW* 213–14. For the second of these two, see above, n. 26.

However, although he is remembered now as a patron of the arts, he was also blamed for the destruction in 1141 of buildings and treasures at Hyde and at St. Mary's Abbey (the former Nunnaminster) during the civil war between King Stephen and the Empress Matilda.[57]

iii. other churches and clerics

Within the city some smaller churches are also mentioned. In the early tenth century, the 'wound' church, St. Andrew's church, and St. Gregory's occur in **II**, of which the latter at least appears to have been adjacent to the cathedral. By the early eleventh century the church of St. Peter (in the Fleshambles) lay slightly to the north of High Street.[58] Reference is also made in the early twelfth century to the suburban churches of St. James, St. Valery, and St. Giles.[59]

The two priests Wulfhun and Wulfsige, mentioned respectively in **XIX** (by 946 × 955) and **XXVI** (996), may have been in charge of urban churches,[60] but those in **II** (?901) were probably members of the Old Minster's pre-reform secular clergy.

It is uncertain what influence was wielded by the external churches which held property within Winchester, such as the abbeys of Abingdon, Glastonbury, and Wherwell.[61] They may have founded urban churches or merely have been content to use the city as an outlet for the produce of rural estates.

Winchester as a national and regional centre

The city's function in the early medieval period as a focus for ecclesiastical, political, and economic business meant that its permanent population was of mixed status, trade, and regional origin. Nobles and their servants, pilgrims, merchants, and officials from upcountry or abroad swelled its size at different seasons of the year. The fact that some of its tenements were held as appurtenances of rural estates also ensured a variety of long-term external links within its economic sphere of influence. The documents record such links with the Hampshire estates of Exton, Hurstbourne Tarrant, Kilmeston, West Tisted, and Wootton St. Lawrence.[62]

In 966, the citizens were characterized in **IV, xii** as beings of secular levity whose company at table is prohibited to the monks of the New Minster. In 975 × 978, however, they (the *burhwaru*), or more probably their representatives, were allowed to act as witnesses to the agreement recorded in **VIII(i)**, in company with the communities of the three minsters. In **XXIX** they were addressed by Edward the Confessor as the *burhmen*.[63] Both these compounds are reminders of the citizens as people living within a fortified centre.

The documents also give us the names of some of earliest known tenement-holders in the city, before those named in the two surveys in the *Liber Wintoniensis*. The close association with the royal court, firstly of Wessex and later of England, is exemplified by the ownership of property in

[57] See T. S. R. Boase, *English Art 1100–1216* (Oxford, 1953), 169–80; also Riall, *Henry of Blois*, 19–26. For his influence on sculpture at Winchester, see Yoshio Kusaba, ' Henry of Blois, Winchester, and the 12th-Century Renaissance', in John Crook (ed.), *Winchester Cathedral: Nine Hundred Years 1093–1993* (Chichester, 1993), 69–79. For the damage to Hyde, St. Mary's, and other parts of the city (including the royal palace), see WS 1, 297–8.

[58] See below, **XXVIII**, nn. 9, 13, and 20.

[59] See below, **XII** and **XIII** (nn. 17 and 20).

[60] Cf. the 12th-cent. priests in Surveys I and II; see WS 1, 394–6.

[61] See below, **XXI, XXIV**, and **XXVII**.

[62] See below, **XIX–XXI, XXIII**, and **XXV**. Cf. WS 1, 384 (Table 28), which however omits reference to Exton and Wootton St. Lawrence. Note also the mill associated with Micheldever, Hants, in a diploma forged in the first half of the 11th century: **XVIII**, below.

[63] For the burgesses in the 12th century, see WS 1, 423.

Winchester by two queens. At some time before her death on 5 December 902, Ealhswith, the widow of King Alfred, owned the urban estate or *haga* delimited in **I**. Ælfgifu Emma, queen successively of Æthelred II and Cnut, and mother of Edward the Confessor, was granted in 1012 the tenement delimited by the boundary-clause of **XXVIII**. Lower in the court hierarchy there is the thegn Æthelgeard, a witness to royal diplomas between 932 and 958 and a benefactor of the New Minster, who was given two city tenements in the reign of King Eadred.[64] Conan the moneylender (a tenement-holder by *c.*1137) is the sole named representative of the mercantile class, but pursued a trade that may have been vital to many members of the later royal court.[65] The names of the lesser inhabitants do not appear in the documents concerning the city collected here. Nevertheless, there is no doubt that the lives of many of them would have been touched in some respect by the provisions or changes the documents record.

[64] See below, **XIX** and **XX**. On Æthelgeard, see below, **XIX**, n. 2.

[65] He held the tenement which had earlier been granted by **XXIV**, below; see ibid. n. 4.

II. DOCUMENTS RELATING TO THE TOPOGRAPHY OF ANGLO-SAXON AND NORMAN WINCHESTER AND ITS MINSTERS

I. EDITORIAL PRINCIPLES

THE texts of documents **I–XXXII** have been taken from manuscripts of widely varying dates and origin, and the fairly conservative method of editing them here adopted preserves significant differences in the surviving record. The orthography of the manuscripts has been followed and all Anglo-Saxon letters (including wynn) are retained. The letters i and j, u and v are shown as in the manuscript; as are æ, ae and ę; th, ð, and þ; and uu, w, and wynn. Except in a few instances where it obstructs the sense, the medieval punctuation has in general been retained, having been found to be more consistent and systematic than is generally recognized by most modern editors;[1] medial points are, however, not distinguished from low points. However, in relation to document **XXXIII**, whose text has been taken from a sixteenth-century printed book, this now being the earliest surviving version, some of the punctuation and orthography has been standardized. In all the documents, the usage of capital letters and word-division has been modernized and paragraphing has been standardized.

The text of each document is preceded by a brief summary of its content; by a commentary discussing its manuscript context, diplomatic phrasing, and historical significance; and by a bibliography of known manuscripts, facsimiles, previous editions, and translations. The siglum A is used only for the manuscript of an original document; other sigla are assigned to manuscript copies in alphabetical order of date, a fresh series being used for each individual document.

Each document is edited from what appears to be the best surviving manuscript (or, in the case of **XXXIII**, the earliest printed version), with collation to other early manuscripts. Where any words are missing from a base manuscript and they have been supplied from another, they are printed in italic type. Standard abbreviations have been silently extended, except for þ = 'that' and the tironian nota (7) used for 'and' in the vernacular, both of which symbols represent words which have variant spellings in Old English and early Middle English. A few ambiguous abbreviations (mostly post-conquest name-forms) have either been extended in italic type or left unextended with an

---

[1] For a strong case made in favour of retaining manuscript punctuation in Old English texts, see Bruce Mitchell, 'The Dangers of Disguise: Old English Texts in Modern Punctuation', *Review of English Studies* ns 31 (1980), 385–413. The punctuation of an early manuscript was retained by Malcolm Godden (ed.),

Ælfric's Catholic Homilies, the Second Series: Text (Early English Text Society, suppl. ser 5, 1979), and (but in a regularized form) by Celia and Kenneth Sisam (ed.), *The Salisbury Psalter edited from Salisbury Cathedral MS. 150* (Early English Text Society 242, 1959).

apostrophe. Editorial emendation or addition lacking manuscript authority is indicated by the use of square brackets. However, scribal errors of grammar or those due to misreading of letter-forms in an exemplar have been corrected without the use of brackets in the case of documents whose texts are taken from manuscripts which are later copies; here the manuscript reading is given in a lettered footnote. Such scribal errors have been retained in the case of **IV**, the New Minster re-foundation codex, but have been pointed out in a lettered footnote; they have also been kept in **XVI**, a forgery with several possibly significant copying errors.. Interlined text has been indicated by the use of caret-marks ` ´ and unless otherwise stated all such interlineations are the work of the scribe of the text.

Each text is printed facing a new translation into Modern English. This translation aims to be intelligible to the modern reader while, it is hoped, not losing too much of the flavour of documentary prose. It is intended to be a guide to the text rather than a replacement for it. Anglo-Saxon personal names in the translation and commentary are mostly standardized to an ideal (late West Saxon) form, resulting in spellings of name-elements such as Ælf- -beorht, and -weald. The exceptions to this treatment are the following: the names Æthelwold, Alfred, Edgar, Edmund, Edward, Oswald, and Swithun; and the element -red for -ræd. A set of numbered factual notes has been supplied to each text and translation, to identify places and individuals, to explain allusions, and to point out quotations from, or parallels in, other texts. Where Latin or Old English text is quoted in these factual notes it has been supplied with a Modern English translation; when a printed source for such a translation is not stated the translation is my own and this has been placed within square brackets.

2. LIST OF DOCUMENTS

I–XVII *Anglo-Saxon and early medieval documents relevant to the sites and foundations in Winchester of the three minsters and Hyde Abbey*

I. *a.* 5 December 902, boundary of Ealhswith's tenement at Winchester. *English.* S 1560

II. A.D. ?901, acquisition by King Edward the Elder of land on which to build the New Minster. *English* with *Latin.* S 1443

III. 'A.D. 903', alleged endowment of the New Minster by King Edward the Elder; granting the hundred of Micheldever with East Stratton, Burcot, Popham, Woodmancott, Brown Candover, Cranbourne, Drayton by Newton, Swarraton, Northington, Norton by Selborne, Slackstead and Tatchbury (all in Hants); the manors of Abbotts Ann (Hants), Collingbourne Kingston (Wilts.), and Chisledon (Wilts.); with fiscal exemptions for the estate of Durley (Hants), and for the site of the monastery. *Latin.* S 370

IV. A.D. 966, refoundation charter of the New Minster granted by King Edgar. *Latin.* S 745

V. 'A.D. 964 × 975', confirmation of the endowment and privileges of the Old Minster by King Edgar, concerning estates at Charmouth (Dorset); Alresford, Beauworth, Bentley, Bishopstoke, Bishop's Waltham, Bradley, Chilcomb, Chilland, Crawley, Easton, Fareham, Hensting, Highclere, Horton, Hunton, North Waltham, Otterbourne, Overton, Ovington, Owslebury, Tadley, Tichborne, Twyford, and [Headbourne or Martyr] Worthy, (Hants); Calbourne (Isle of Wight); Taunton and Washford (Somerset);

Beddington, *Cyslesdun* [?Chessington], Farnham, Frensham, Lake, and Tandridge (Surrey); and Downton and Fonthill Bishop (Wilts.). Also providing for the government of relations between the bishop and the recently re-established monks at the Old Minster, whose food is to be supplied from the estate of Chilcomb (Hants); and confirming the beneficial hidation of the latter estate. *Latin* with *English*. S 821, 817, 825, 814, 819, 824, 826, 823, 815, 822, 816, 827, and 818

VI. A.D. 984 [?for 970], establishment of the precincts of the three minsters by King Edgar. *Latin*. S 807

VII. A.D. ?970 × 975, adjustment of the boundaries and property of the three minsters by King Edgar. *English*. S 1449

VIII. A.D. 975 × 978, exchange between Bishop Æthelwold and the community at the Old Minster and Ælfwine, son of Ælfsige and Æthelhild, of 12 hides of land *æt Mordune* [unidentified], for 2 acres of land and a stream in Winchester. (i) *English*, (ii) *Latin*. S 1376

IX. A.D. 983, grant by King Æthelred II to Bishop Æthelgar [of Selsey], of meadow-land to the north of Winchester. *Latin* with *English*. S 845

X. A.D. 1072 × 1086, grant by King William I to the New Minster, of the church of Alton (Hants), with its tithes, rents, and 5 hides of land, and of the church of Kingsclere (Hants), with its tithes, rents, and 4 hides and 1 yardland of land; in exchange for the site of the New Minster cemetery. *Latin*. *Regesta* i, 37; Bates *Regesta* 344

XI. A.D. 1082 × 1087, grant in alms to the poor and to pilgrims by Abbot Riwallon of the New Minster, of the estate of Alton (Hants), which King William I had granted in exchange for the site of the New Minster cemetery. *Latin*.

XII. Windsor (Berks.) [29 May 1110], confirmation of grant by King Henry I to the Old Minster and to Bishop William Giffard of Winchester, of a fair for eight days at the church of St. Giles on the eastern hill of Winchester and of all royal profits in the city during the same period; i.e. for the three days which King William II had granted them, and for five extra days now granted in exchange for the land of the bishopric recently given for the new site of the New Minster outside the north gate of the city. *Latin*. *Regesta* ii, 947

XIII. Westbourne (Sussex), 13 September 1114, declaration by King Henry I of the agreement between Bishop William [Giffard] of Winchester and Abbot Geoffrey of the New Minster, concerning the removal of the monastery to Hyde, the grant of Worthy [Abbotts Barton, Hants] and the settlement of their dispute about arrangements for the annual Palm Sunday procession; also referring to the grant by the king to the bishop of five extra days for St. Giles's Fair. *Latin*. *Regesta* ii, 1070

XIV. Windsor (Berks.) [?2 February 1116], confirmation by King Henry I to Hyde Abbey, of the churches of Kingsclere and Alton (Hants), with 5 hides of land at Alton, as granted to them by King William I in exchange for the land in Winchester on which he built his hall; the said property to be held free of geld, murder-fine, pleas, and plaints, like the land in Winchester on which the king's house stands. *Latin*. *Regesta* ii, 1126

XV. Windsor (Berks.) [?2 February 1116], writ of King Henry I to William of Pont de l'Arche and the collectors of Winchester, ordering that the land of Hyde and that taken in exchange by the abbey of Winchester should be as free from gelds and other plaints as was the land where the abbey used to stand and as are the king's own house and the men who dwell in it, and particularly in regard to the geld of 400 marks and all other gelds. *Latin. Regesta* ii, 1886

XVI. 'A.D. 1107 × 1118', alleged grant by King Henry I to the New Minster, of the 'liberty' of the street outside the north gate of the city of Winchester. *Latin. Regesta* ii, 1125

XVII. A.D. 1154 × 1171, confirmation by King Henry II to Hyde Abbey of the land of Hyde given by King Henry I and the land of Worthy [Abbotts Barton, Hants] given in exchange by Bishop William [Giffard]; to be held as quit and as freely as the abbot and monks used to hold their church and cemetery within the city. Also confirming rights of sanctuary and burial at the abbey church and such freedom of the said lands from service as the king has with regard to his own hall within the city. *Latin.*

XVIII–XXIX *Anglo-Saxon documents relevant to the topography of the city of Winchester*
[those marked here with an asterisk are extracts only]

XVIII.* 'A.D. 900', a reference to the southernmost mill in Winchester, pertaining to the 100–hide estate of Micheldever (Hants). *English.* S 360

XIX.* A.D. 946 × 955, grant by King Eadred to his thegn Æthelgeard, of a mill at the east gate and a tenement formerly held by Wulfhun the priest, both of which are to be held as appurtenances of the [12–hide] estate at Exton (Hants). *English.* S 463

XX.* A.D. 946 × 955, grant by King Eadred to his thegn Æthelgeard, of the tenement in Winchester pertaining to the 7–hide estate at West Tisted (Hants). *English.* S 488

XXI.* A.D. 961, a reference to 13 tenements in Winchester pertaining to the 50–hide estate at Hurstbourne Tarrant (Hants). *Latin.* S 689

XXII. A.D. 961, grant by King Edgar to Bishop Beorhthelm [of Winchester], of the 7½-hide estate at Easton (Hants). *Latin* with *English.* S 695

XXIII.* A.D. 961, a reference to a tenement within the south wall at Winchester, pertaining to the 10–hide estate at Kilmeston (Hants). *English.* S 693a

XXIV. A.D. 988, grant by King Æthelred II to Bishop Æthelsige [of Sherborne], and Æthelmær, *miles*, of a tenement in Winchester which Eadgeard had held. *Latin.* S 871

XXV.* A.D. 990, a reference to 9 tenements in Tanner Street, Winchester, pertaining to the 15–hide estate at Wootton St. Lawrence (Hants). *English.* S 874

XXVI. A.D. 996, restoration by King Æthelred II to the Old Minster, of a tenement in Winchester bequeathed to them by the lady Ælfswith, and grant of half a fish-weir with adjacent ground at Brentford (Middx.). *Latin* with *English.* S 889

XXVII.* *c.* A.D. 1002, a reference to 29 tenements in Winchester pertaining to Wherwell Abbey. *Latin* and *English.* S 904

XXVIII. A.D. 1012, grant by King Æthelred II to his queen Ælfgifu, of a tenement in Winchester. *Latin* with *English.* S 925

XXIX. A.D. 1052 × 1053, confirmation by King Edward the Confessor to the Old Minster, of his mother's bequest of the tenement in Winchester called Ælfric's Godbegot; and of the 10–hide estate at Hayling (Hants). *English.* S 1153

uel uerbis uel factis ...
sctatis studio hono
rauerint ·

QVALES ET QVALI
TER MONACHI IN
HOC MONASTERIO
CONUERSENTUR ·

Regulares igitur mona
chi non seculares in pre
fato xp̄o comite degen
tes monasterio regulę
mozib; obtemperent ·
Patres uenerati spitales
scōrum patrum imi

BL, Cotton MS. Vesp. A. viii, fo. 19ᵛ (s.xˀ), the New Minster refoundation charter (**IV**),
the first scribe: part of caps **xi** and **xii** (see pp. 71–2 and 85).

BL, Add. MS. 15350, fo. 8ʳ, top. The *Codex Wintoniensis*, documents **VIII** (**i**) and (**ii**), written by scribe *b* (s.xii med.; see pp. 7–8 and 145–8). [reduced]

BL, Add. MS. 15350, fo. 8ᵛ. The *Codex Wintoniensis*, two documents written by scribe *b*
(s.xii med.; see pp. 7–8). *a* (at top) **VI** (pp.137-9), *b* (at foot) **VII** (pp.141-3)
[*c*.395 x 275 mm.]

ind indan seanoche· butan he con hic fond side hic gebete·

⸿ Carta Sci Edwardi Regis· De Godebiete·

Eadpard cing gret stigand· b· 7 Godpine eorl· 7 ealle þa burh men on pincestre freondlice· 7 ic kyðe eop þ ic habbe geunnen þ se cypðe stande þe min moder be cped criste 7 sce petre· 7 sce spiðine 7 þan hipede in to ealdan mynstre· þ is se haga þe man hat ælfpuces gode begeaton· þene ic pille þ hi habban eal spa freo pið ealle þa þing þe to me belimpoð· eal spa he hire æfter mines fæder gife on handan stod· 7 non minra prnerpa name socne nabbe uppon þa þe þer on uppon sittað· ne nanmann on nanan þingan· butan se hiped· 7 þa þe hi heom to prnepan settað· 7 ge þe tene hida æt helinge stande al þa hi hi hem bicyað·

⸿ Carta Willelmi Regis Senioris· De libertate Ecclie·

Willm kyng gret palchelm· b· 7 hugan de porto 7 eadpard scipge pefan· 7 odan· 7 æþelfi· 7 saulf· 7 ælfsi æt hæccan· 7 cole· 7 eadpic 7 ealle hir þegnas on hamtun scyre· 7 on piltun scyre freondlice· 7 ic kyðe eop þ ic pille þ sce peter 7 palchelm· b· beon ealra þare lagena peorðe þe pas ælpine bisop on eadperdes dæge kyngef· spa full 7 spa he hi betst ahte· Nu for þig bidde ic eop 7 festlice beode þ ge ne la tan for me ne for nanan oþran men þ ge ne kyðan þ sce petre· for þan ic nelle ge þolian þ ænig man sce petre ne palkelme· b· ænige oþre lage beode·

⸿ Carta eiusdem Regis De libertate Ecclie·

BL, Add. MS. 29436, fo. 10ᵛ (s. xiii med.). Winchester cathedral cartulary at top, document **XXIX**, written by the same scribe as in Pl. V. (see pp. 9 and 22) (*c*.250 x 180 mm.]

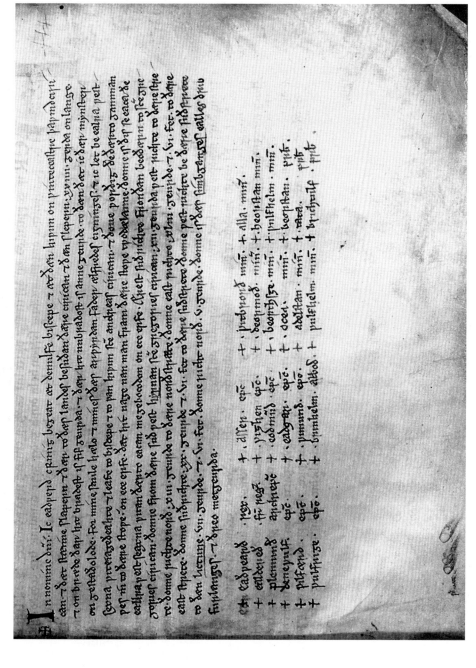

BL, Add. MS. 15350, fo. 8ʳ, foot. The *Codex Wintoniensis*, document **II**, written by scribe *m* (s. xiii med.; see pp. 9, 52–6, and Pl. IV). [reduced]

XXX–XXXII *Late Anglo-Saxon and early medieval documents relating to the beneficial hidation of the estate of Chilcomb, Hants*

    XXX. A.D. 984 × 1001, confirmation by King Æthelred II to Bishop Ælfheah [II, of Winchester] of the beneficial hidation of Chilcomb, as first granted by his forefathers and previously confirmed by King Alfred. *English.* S 946

    XXXI. *a.* A.D. 1086. List of lands [in Hants] belonging to Chilcomb. *English.* S 1820

    XXXII. A.D. 1086. The Domesday Book entry for the estate of Chilcomb. *Latin.*

XXXIII *Papal letter concerning the reform of the Old Minster*

    XXXIII. A.D. ?963. Letter of Pope John [XII] to King Edgar, giving approval to the replacement of the secular canons of the Old Minster by monks and to new arrangements for the election of the bishop. *Latin.* Jaffé 3753

III. DOCUMENTS I–XXXIII:
TEXT, TRANSLATION, AND NOTES

I–XVII

ANGLO-SAXON AND EARLY MEDIEVAL DOCUMENTS RELEVANT TO THE SITES AND FOUNDATIONS IN WINCHESTER OF THE THREE MINSTERS AND HYDE ABBEY

I

Before 5 December 902, boundary of Ealhswith's tenement at Winchester

English

S 1560, Finberg 177, Ker *Catalogue* 237

THIS text records the outer limits of a tenement (*haga*) in Winchester which, it states, Ealhswith 'has' (*hæfð*, present tense); thus its composition is to be dated before the death of Ealhswith [King Alfred's consort] on 5 December 902.[1] The tenement lay between 'the market street' (High Street) to the north and 'the middle street' (subsequently disused) to the south, and between the most westerly watercourse south of High Street to the west and an intra-mural route to the east (see Fig. 7). This area of land was apparently that later given by Ealhswith for the foundation of Nunnaminster and was afterwards occupied by the monastic buildings as well as by properties in the street, now known as Colebrook Street, which had developed outside the monastic precinct of Nunnaminster (later called St. Mary's Abbey) by 1148.[2] The description of the boundary of this *haga* proceeds clockwise from point to point and is important for its reference to several topographical features which have since disappeared; for instance, some of the watercourses mentioned, with their mills and fords, were probably affected by the establishment of the three monastic precincts in the reign of King Edgar.[3] Pauline Stafford has suggested that the territorial unit could have been

---

[1] See below, **I**, n. 2.

[2] See WS 1, 321–3 and Fig. 19; cf. WS 2.ii, Fig. 94 (*c.*1300). Also WS 4.i, (forthcoming), Part XI. Ealhswith probably received the support of her son Edward the Elder, whose daughter (St.) Eadburh was placed in the Nunnaminster community; see Susan J. Ridyard, *The Royal Saints of Anglo-*

Saxon England: a Study of West Saxon and East Anglian Cults (Cambridge Studies in Medieval Life and Thought, 4th ser. 9, Cambridge, 1988), 16–17, 32.

[3] See below, **VI–VII**. Note that the present interpretation of the boundary differs from that by F. J. Baigent in Birch *Ancient Manuscript*, after p. 32, which proceeds anti-clockwise and also

Ealhswith's dower when she married King Alfred in 868.[4] While this is impossible to prove, it is true that the unit of land could have existed for some time before Ealhswith's death in 902, and may even have existed, in someone else's ownership, prior to 868. It may thus give a picture of part of the city before its redevelopment *c.* 880. The apparently rather informal nature of the eastern defence, 'king's city-hedge' may support this view.[5]

There is no reason to doubt the authenticity of the text. The boundary describes a complete circuit and is recorded in the form of a general declaration phrased in an acceptable Old English syntax.

The record has survived only because it was entered in a blank space in the ninth-century prayer-book of Mercian origin, later known as the Book of Nunnaminster, which may have belonged to Ealhswith who herself came from Mercia.[6] The script used for **I** is a transitional one, a precursor of the tenth-century 'reformed' or Anglo-Saxon square minuscule.[7] As mentioned above, the boundary-description was composed before Ealhswith's death in 902. It may have been copied into the prayer-book by the first scribe of the Parker manuscript of the Anglo-Saxon Chronicle.[8] Malcolm Parkes has suggested that it, like some of the other surviving early examples of the reformed script, was written by a member of the community at Nunnaminster.[9] If, however, the prayer-book had indeed formerly belonged to Ealhswith, even if it later belonged to Nunnaminster (which is not proven), the scribe of the additional text need not have been based in the nunnery. David Dumville has suggested that **I** may have been written at the Old Minster and this is a real possibility, although it should be remembered that, even if written by a priest attached to the (unreformed) Old Minster, the actual place of writing need not have been the church itself or its buildings as secular clerks were not usually confined to a precinct in the way that monks were.[10]

---

takes in a strip of land along the Itchen to the N. of City Mill; see map, ibid.

[4] In discussion at the Alfred the Great Conference, South-ampton, September 1999. For the marriage, see Asser, cap. 29: Keynes and Lapidge, 77.

[5] See below, **I**, n. 8.

[6] BL, Harl. MS. 2965; see E. A. Lowe, *Codices Latini Antiquiores* (Oxford, 1934–72), ii, 199, and Ker *Catalogue* 237. For its relationship to other Mercian manuscripts and prayer-books of s.ix[1], see Michelle P. Brown, *The Book of Cerne: Prayer, Patronage and Power in Ninth-Century England* (London, Toronto, and Buffalo, 1996), esp. pp. 137, 168–71, 175. For further discussion of its prayers, see Barbara Raw, 'Alfredian Piety: the Book of Nunnaminster', in Jane Roberts, Janet L. Nelson, and Malcolm Godden (ed.), *Alfred the Wise: Studies in Honour of Janet Bately on the Occasion of her Sixty-Fifth Birthday* (Cambridge, 1997), 145–53.

[7] See David N. Dumville, 'English Square Minuscule Script:

the Background and Early Phases', *ASE* 16 (1987), 147–79, at 163–4; and *idem, Wessex and England from Alfred to Edgar: Six Essays on Political, Cultural and Ecclesiastical Reform* (Woodbridge, 1992), 83–97. Also M. B. Parkes, 'The Palaeography of the Parker Manuscript of the *Chronicle*, Laws and Sedulius, and Histori-ography at Winchester in the Late Ninth and Tenth Centuries', *ASE* 5 (1976), 149–71, and *idem*, 'A Fragment of an Early-Tenth-Century Anglo-Saxon Manuscript', *ASE* 12 (1983), 129–40.

[8] CCCC, MS. 173, fos. 1–16[r]. See Parkes, 'A Fragment', 131–2; cf. Ker *Catalogue*, lix, and Parkes, 'Parker Manuscript', 158, n. 3. Note that although Dumville does not believe it to be the same hand, he would date both to the 910s; see *Wessex and England from Alfred to Edgar*, 83, 95.

[9] Parkes, 'A Fragment', 132.

[10] 'English Square Minuscule Script', 164, n. 89. Cf. below, **IV**, **xii**; also **VI** and **VII** for the later monastic precincts at Winchester.

MS.:   B. BL, Harl. MS. 2965, fo. 40ᵛ (s.ix/x)

Facsimiles: *ASE* 12 (1983), Pl. III*b*; David N. Dumville, *Wessex and England from Alfred to Edgar: Six Essays on Political, Cultural, and Ecclesiastical Reform* (Woodbridge, 1992), Pl. II; Michelle P. Brown, *The Book of Cerne: Prayer, Patronage and Power in Ninth-Century England* (London, Toronto, and Buffalo, 1996), Fig. 13

Edited: *BCS* 630
              Birch, *Ancient Manuscript*, 96; with translation and map, 32–3

Printed from the manuscript

þæs hagan gemære þe Ealhspið[1] hæfð[2] æt Þintan ceastre lið up of þæm forda[a][3] on þone pestmestan mylengear[4] pestepeardne[5] þæt east on þone ealdan pelig 7 þonan up andlanges[b] þæs eastran mylengeares[6] þæt norð on þa ceap stræt[7] ~

The boundary of the tenement which Ealhswith[1] has[2] at Winchester runs up from the ford[3] on to the western side of[5] the westernmost mill-yair,[4] then east to the old willow and thence up along the eastern mill-yair,[6] then north to the market street;[7] then there east along the market

---

[a] *The alternative dative sg. of* ford *'a ford, crossing place'; see BT, s.v.*   [b] *The adverbial form of the preposition* andlang *'along'; see BT Suppl. and BT Addenda, s.v. (ex inf. the late Professor J. McN. Dodgson).*

---

[1] Ealhswith the wife of King Alfred, whom she married in 869 according to Asser, cap. 29: Keynes and Lapidge, 77.

[2] *hæfð*. The use here of the present indicative tense indicates a date for the composition of this text before Ealhswith's death on 5 December 902: see the entry in the *Mercian Register* translated in Whitelock *EHD* 1, and her obit in Bod, Junius MS. 27, fo. 7ᵛ and in BL, Cotton MS. Galba A. xviii, fo. 14ʳ.

[3] *up of þæm forda*. The boundary began at the ford (also below at n. 13) at the SW. corner of the tenement, where the 'the middle street' (see n. 12) crossed a watercourse which ran south from High Street (see n. 7) to drive the mill referred to below in n. 4. This may have been the watercourse (?fed from the Lower Brook) which Bishop Æthelwold later diverted to the New Minster; see below, **VII**, n. 17. The ford probably took the highway across shallow water south of 'the westernmost mill-yair' (see n. 4). It is unlikely to have been identical with *(la) Forda*, discussed WS 1, 237 and WS 2.ii, **485**, which seems to have been further north.

[4] *mylengear*. The term 'mill-yair' denotes a transverse stream-dam or weir; cf. P. Rahtz and D. Bullough, 'The Parts of an Anglo-Saxon Mill', *ASE* 6 (1977), 15–37, at 25–6, and 32. The compound *mylen-gear* (BT Suppl., 644) has as its second element OE **gear*, 'a yair, an enclosure or dam made in a river or other water for catching fish'; see *EPN* i, 197. The connection with fishing may not be relevant in the present compound, but was known later in Winchester; see WS 2.ii, **977**, for a reference in 1575 to the 'jarre with the fish beds' at a location (near Durn Gate Mill, ibid. **972**) which in 1490 had been described as a weir called *Fissherbede*. Two other examples of the compound *mylen-gear* occur in surviving Anglo-Saxon records. One (*on ðone ealdan mylier þær þa pelegas standað*) is in the bounds described in BL, Cotton MS. Augustus ii. 63 (S 495 (1)), an original diploma which recorded the grant in 944 by King Edmund to Bishop

Ælfric [of Hereford; see Hart *ECNE* 2] of land in Northants. The other (*on ðone mulen ger þonan andlang ðære mylen dic*) is in the boundary of Padworth, Berks., which survives in a 13th-cent. copy of a diploma granted in 956 by King Eadwig to his man Eadric: *BCS* 984 (S 620), *PNBerks* iii, 645–6.

'The westernmost mill-yair' was apparently a weir built across the watercourse referred to above in n. 3 and probably served to control its water for the powering of a mill slightly to the east of where the Postern Mill later stood (see WS 1, Fig. 8 and WS 2.ii, **555–6**). This mill was possibly that referred to below in **VII** (see ibid. n. 19) as having later been ruined by Bishop Æthelwold's diversion of its water to the New Minster. For other mill-yairs, further east within the city, see below, nn. 6 and 9.

[5] *pestepeardne* is an adjective in the masc. sg. accusative case agreeing with *mylengear* and specifying the western end of the mill-yair so that the edifice and the water of the ford (see nn. 3 and 13) are included within the tenement. This is the opposite of the usage of *westeweardne* (and *easteweardne*) advanced in A. R. Rumble, 'The Merstham (Surrey) Charter-Bounds, A.D. 947', *JEPNS* 3 (1970–71), 6–31, at pp. 9–10, with reference to S 528. The usage in the present text is more likely to be the correct one, however, and the Merstham boundary should be taken to have altered its line at points 6, 12, 13, and 16 at some time since 947.

[6] The boundary proceeded on to, and apparently along, 'the westernmost mill-yair' (see n. 4) and continued eastwards to 'the old willow' which stood to the west of 'the eastern mill-yair'. The latter was another transverse weir, but built across the next watercourse to the east of that on which the 'westernmost' one stood. The boundary then crossed this second watercourse by means of 'the eastern mill-yair'.

[7] Northwards from the eastern end of 'the eastern mill-yair' (see n. 6) to 'the market-street', i.e. High Street, towards its eastern end. See WS 1, 234, s.n. *(In) Magno Vico*, and ibid. 278; see also below, **XXVII**, n. 12 and **XXVIII**, n. 16. The route was probably that marked by the later boundary wall which runs N.-S. behind the Guildhall.

þonne þær east andlanges[c] þære ceap stræte oð cyninges burghege[8] on þone ealdan mylengear[9] þæt þær 7langes[c] þæs ealdan mylegeares oð hit sticað on þæm ifihtan æsce[10] þæt þær suð ofer þa tƿifealdan fordas[11] on þa stræt midde[12] þæt þær eft ƿest andlanges[d] strẹte 7 ofer þone ford[13] þæt hit sticaþ eft on þæm ƿestemestan mylengeare .,[14]

[c] *See p. 47, n. b*   [d] *Altered from* andlangæs

---

[8] Eastwards along 'the market-street' (see n. 7) to the urban defence called 'king's city-hedge' near East Gate; see WS 1, 273. The absence of a definite article might suggest that 'king's city-hedge' was an established place-name at the time that the present text was composed, and hence that the feature was already of some age. The point appears to have been at the NE. corner of the tenement. The significance of the use of *hecg* here, rather than *weall*, may reflect the non-use of the remains of the Roman wall as the city defence here. However, as the later defences follow the precise line of this part of the Roman wall, *hecg* may refer to a timber palisade (or even a live hedge) on top of the covered foundations of the wall.

[9] The adjective *eald* may here mean 'former, disused'; cf. *EPN* i, 8, s.v. *ald*. 'The old mill-yair' seems to have been a weir near, but within, the city's eastern defences (see n. 8), and may have been one which had been made obsolete by their construction if, for example, that had necessitated the draining of a side-channel of the R. Itchen which had driven a mill here. Alternatively, it may have been affected by the building of the city bridge, attributed to St. Swithun (d. 863: Keynes 1994, 1129–30); see WS 1, 271–2, and WS 4.ii (forthcoming).

[10] The boundary proceeded on to and (?SW.) along 'the old mill-yair' (see n. 9) as far as 'the ivy-covered ash' which seems to have been adjacent to it (?at its western end). The word *sticað* is from OE *stician* which literally means 'to stick, stab, pierce'. BT, s.v., sect. III, gives a meaning 'to run, lie' in relation to the course of a boundary, but the significance of the verb in the present text, and also in some of the examples quoted by BT, ibid., seems to be closer to the literal meaning, describing the figurative action by which the line of the boundary 'strikes' a particular

street as far as king's city-hedge,[8] on to the old mill-yair,[9] then there along the old mill-yair until it strikes the ivy-covered ash,[10] then there south over the double fords[11] to the middle street,[12] then there west again along the street and over the ford,[13] so that it strikes again the westernmost mill-yair.[14]

named feature. It occurs again (*sticaþ*) in relation to 'the westernmost mill-yair' at the end of the boundary (see n. 14).

[11] *fordas*. The use of the plural form here implies that there was more than one 'double ford' to the south of 'the ivy-covered ash' (see n. 10), between it and 'the middle street' (see n. 12). The fords were presumably across watercourses which had been channelled W.-E. (or E.-W.) within the city. The line of the boundary here is the earliest written evidence to imply a N.-S. route within the eastern city-defences to the south of High Street; cf. the later Colebrook St East and the tenement to the south described in 1148 as being *ubi callis regis solebat esse* (WS 1, **II, 716**).

[12] *on þa stræt midde*. The former E.-W. street midway between High Street and the southern wall of the city. It was probably on the line now followed by the north wall of the Wolvesey enclosure and the passage leading to Water Close (cf. WS 1, 235). It may have fallen into disuse as a public route when the monastic precincts were created in the reign of Edgar (cf. below, **VI** and **VII**) but survived as the path from the cathedral into the precinct of the bishop's palace at Wolvesey. Further west this may have been 'the south street' referred to below in **II**, n. 20.

[13] *ofer þone ford*. To and over the same ford mentioned above in n. 3. The bounds do not mention the N.-S. watercourse (Abbey Mill Stream) which now runs immediately to the west of the Wolvesey enclosure, suggesting that, if it then existed, it may have been in a culvert under the street. It may however be recorded further south in 975 × 978; see below, **VIII**, n. 11.

[14] The boundary-circuit was completed by 'striking' (cf. n. 10) 'the westernmost mill-yair'. Since the ford had already been crossed (see n. 13), this final point must again have been at the western end of the mill-yair (cf. nn. 4 and 5).

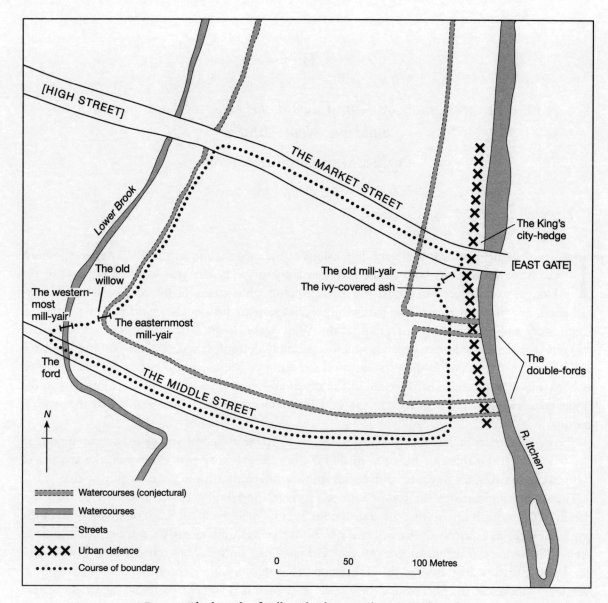

[HIGH STREET]

THE MARKET STREET

Lower Brook

The King's
city-hedge

[EAST GATE]

The old
willow

The old mill-yair

The ivy-covered ash

The western-
most
mill-yair

The easternmost
mill-yair

The
double-fords

The
ford

THE MIDDLE STREET

N

R. Itchen

Watercourses (conjectural)

Watercourses

Streets

✕✕✕ Urban defence

Course of boundary

0   50   100 Metres

FIG. 7. The bounds of Ealhswith's *haga* in **I** (*a.* 5 December 902).

II

A.D. ?901, acquisition by King Edward the Elder of land on which to build the New Minster

English, with Latin invocation

S 1443, Finberg 33, *CW* 23

Tʜɪs document records the exact dimensions of the original site within Winchester on which the New Minster was built in the early tenth century. The site was acquired by Edward the Elder as two distinct (but apparently adjacent) plots which are to be located to the north of the cathedral, one of them received as part of an exchange with Bishop Denewulf and the cathedral community and the other by the grant of the West Saxon *witan*. The involvement of the *witan* suggests that the second piece of land, which is precisely delimited, was in some sense public land, either because it belonged to the adjacent royal residence or because it had not before been granted as bookland. It is possible that the line of the north and west sides of the plot acquired from the cathedral preserved the boundaries of the Old Minster's enclosure as first granted in the seventh century.[1]

The outside limits of date for the transactions, fixed by the episcopal witnesses and the donor, are 899 × 908. A reasonable case has been made for the year 901 (see below); however, the absence of Grimbald of St. Bertin's from the witness-list implies a date after his death on 8 July of that year.[2]

The diplomatic form of the text is that of a general declaration before witnesses of the exact details of the acquisitions, so that the transactions became matters of public record. Nearly all of the witnesses recur in other documents claiming to be of the late ninth or early tenth centuries, some of them of better diplomatic status than others.[3] The episcopal subscriptions reflect Edward the Elder's royal power at this time. Besides the archbishop of Canterbury, they consist of the two bishops of Wessex (Winchester and Sherborne), three bishops of Mercia (Lichfield, Hereford, and Dorchester), and the bishops of London, Rochester, and the South Saxons (Selsey). It is probable that this witness-list (or the memorandum that lay behind it, see below) was later used by those who forged S 360 (see below, **XVIII**) and **III**, but it itself appears to be genuine. The absence of ealdormen (*duces*) is paralleled in S 363, 380, 1285, and 1287, of this period. Several of the remaining witnesses were probably members of the cathedral community.[4] Simon Keynes has suggested that the witness-list of **II** is based on 'the same, or a very similar memorandum' also used for the (much shorter) witness-lists in S 365–6, both dated 901, the latter at Southampton. If so, this would date the acquisition of land for the New Minster to that year.[5]

---

[1] See WS 4.i (forthcoming). For the two plots see Fig. 8, respectively: (i) land between B–H and K–L, and (ii) land within a line B–C–D–E–F–G–H.

[2] See Grierson, 'Grimbald', 554. Cf. WS 1, 313.

[3] See below, **II**, nn. 24–61.

[4] See Keynes *Liber Vitae*, 105, and cf. Keynes 1994, 1146.

[5] Keynes *Liber Vitae*, ibid.

None of the four surviving MSS. contains a complete text of the document. The earliest text, that in MS. B (the New Minster *Liber Vitae*) is acephalous, due to the loss of a folio. That in MS. C (the *Codex Wintoniensis;* an addition made in the mid thirteenth century by scribe *m*)[6] has undergone some linguistic modernization and also lacks seventeen subscriptions present in B. The text in D (the *Liber de Hyda*) is a chronicler's paraphrase. While it is possible that all these three MSS. had the same, now-lost, exemplar, it is perhaps more likely that both the cathedral and the New Minster had separate copies of the record, and there may have been another in the royal archive. From the scribal errors in MS. C we can at least say that its exemplar was written in insular minuscule script.[7] The fourth MS. (E) is an extract from D, made by the antiquary John Stow in 1572.

[6] See above, p. 9. This scribe also copied **XXIX**, below, into another Winchester cathedral cartulary, BL, Add. MS. 29436; see Pl. IV.

[7] See below, **II**, nn. *a, d, u, cc,* and *ff.*

MSS.:   B. BL, Stowe MS. 944, fo. 57[rv] (s.xi[1]; incomplete)
               C. BL, Add. MS. 15350, fo. 8[r] (s.xiii med.; incomplete)
               D. Earl of Macclesfield, Shirburn Castle, *Liber (abbatiae) de Hyda*, fo. 12[v] (s.xiv/xv; incomplete)
               E. BL, Lansdowne MS. 717, fo. 29[rv] (s. xvi[2]), from D

Facsimiles: Keynes, *Liber Vitae*, from B
               See below, Pl. V, from C

Edited: *KCD* 1087, from C
               Thorpe, 156–8, with translation, from C
               LH, 80–1, from D
               BCS 605, from C; ibid. 1338, from B
               LVH, 155–8, from B; ibid. 155–7 n., with translation, from C
               Harmer *SEHD* 16, with translation, p. 59, from C
               Miller *New Minster* 2, from B and C

Main text printed from C collated to B; witness-list printed from B collated to C. D is but a short and muddled notice (in Latin) of the transaction, with Latin and Middle English bounds added. E is an extract from D.

+ In nomine Domini . Ic Eadperd[1] cynig[a] begeat æt Denulfe[2] biscepe ⁊ æt ðæn hipun[3] on Þinteceastre þa pindcirican[4] . ⁊ ðæt stænne[b] slapern[5] ⁊ ðærto ðæs landes be suðan ðære cirican ⁊ ðæn slepern . xxiiii . gerda[6] on lange . ⁊ on bræde ðar hit bradest is fif geurda . ⁊ ðær hit unbradost is anne geurde .[7] to ðæn ðæt ic ðær mynster[8] on gestaðolode . for mine saule hælo ⁊ mines ðæs arpyrðan[c] fader Ælfredes[9] cyninges[d] . ⁊ ic let be ealra Þest Sexna pitena[e] geðeahte ⁊ leafe to biscepe ⁊ to þan hipun sancte Andreas cirican[10] . ⁊ ðone porðig[11] ðe ðærto geunnan[f] þes into ðære stope[12] ⫶ on ece erfe[13] . ðæt hit nage nan man fram ðære stope to dælanne[g] .

a crinig C, *a scribal misreading of the exemplar's letter* y *as insular minuscule* r; *cf. nn.* d *and* u. Cynig *would be an intermediate form between standard West Saxon* cyning *and late West Saxon* cyng; *v. Campbell §474. The text in B does not begin until n.* m, *below*
b *Second minim of first* n *of* stænne *marked in error as letter* i *in C*
c arpyrdan C   *d* cigninges C, *with the exemplar's letter* y *misread as* i *followed by insular minuscule* g; *cf. nn.* a *and* u
e þiteia C   *f* gannnan C   *g* tþodælanne C, *a copying error influenced by the preceding word*

---

[1] Edward the Elder, king of the Anglo-Saxons, 899–924. His widow Eadgifu witnessed the New Minster refoundation-charter in 966; see below, **IV**, n. 132.

[2] Bishop of Winchester, 878 × 879–908. Denewulf subscribes *c.* 901 × 904: O'Donovan i, 29; ii, 109. Also referred to in **III** (n. 4).

[3] *æt ðæn hipun.* That is, the bishop's *familia* of secular clergy associated with the cathedral. Members of it are probably represented amongst the subscriptions below, from Beornstan, priest (see below, n. 44), to the end. Cf. **III**, n. 5.

[4] *þa pindcirican.* The significance of the compound *pindcirice* is not clear but it may describe a church constructed of wattle. It may refer to the *breve monasteriolum* said to have been given by King Alfred to Grimbald; see below, n. 9. The legendary first church at Glastonbury, associated with Joseph of Arimathea, was also said to have been partly built of twisted wattle (*uirgis torquatis*); this passage, however, is from a later interpolation into William of Malmesbury's 12th-cent. account; see John Scott, *The Early History of Glastonbury: An Edition, Translation and Study of William of Malmesbury's De antiquitate Glastonie ecclesie* (Woodbridge, 1981), cap. 1 (pp. 44–5), and p. 186, n. 14.

[5] *ðæt stænne slapern.* This was presumably the dormitory later said to have been given by King Alfred to Grimbald; see below, n. 9. It is perhaps stated specifically to be made of stone in contrast to the 'wound' church.

[6] *gerda.* The Anglo-Saxon 'yard' (OE *gyrd*, Lat. *virga* or *virgata*) was equivalent to a rod, 5½ modern yards. The measurement also occurs in **IX** and **XXVIII**, q.v., and in the Burghal Hidage Calculation; see David Hill and Alexander R. Rumble (ed.), *The*

+ In the name of the Lord. I, King Edward,[1] acquired from Bishop Denewulf[2] and from the community[3] in Winchester the 'wound' church[4] and the stone dormitory[5] and thereto, of the land to the south of the church and the dormitory, [a piece] 24 'yards'[6] in length and 5 'yards' broad at its broadest and one 'yard' at its narrowest,[7] so that I might found a monastery[8] thereon for the salvation of my soul and of that of my venerable father King Alfred.[9] And I gave up to the bishop and the community, with the advice and permission of all the West Saxon counsellors, St. Andrew's church[10] and the enclosure[11] which was given thereto, unto the cathedral[12] in perpetual inheritance,[13] so that no one may alienate it from the cathedral.

Defence of Wessex: the Burghal Hidage and Anglo-Saxon Fortifications (Manchester and New York, 1996), 30, 71. Cf. below, n. 22.

[7] Quirk *NM*, 52 and n. 1, inserts here 'ab occidente monasterii 12 virgas longitudinis, "on the west of the monastery 12 rods in length"', on the authority of MS. D, assuming that a corresponding OE phrase was omitted from MS. C by the copyist. However, this part of MS. D is only a Latin and Middle English paraphrase of those sections of the text which contain measurements, and the '12 rods' are those mentioned below, due west of the SW. corner of St. Gregory's church.

[8] The New Minster.

[9] King Alfred (871–99) is said in *LH* (51) to have bought for Grimbald of St. Bertin's land at Winchester for a chapel and a dormitory and to have intended to build a monastery there for him but to have died before he could do so; the (?12th-cent.) *Vita secunda* of Grimbald also refers to King Alfred's planning of the New Minster, but the (?10th-cent.) *Vita prima* refers only to a *breve monasteriolum*, given to Grimbald by King Alfred until a bishopric should become vacant for him; see Grierson, 'Grimbald', 533–4, 556, n. 1, and cf. below, **III**, n. 3.

[10] *sancte Andreas cirican.* St. Andrew's, Gar Street, is the only church in the city which is known to have had this dedication, but is not necessarily the one referred to here; see WS 2.ii, 628–9.

[11] *ðone porðig.* OE *worðig* (*EPN* ii, 275–6) could refer here either to an enclosed piece of land within the city or to a whole estate outside it. If the latter, there is nothing to connect it with the cathedral estates of Headbourne Worthy and Martyr Worthy.

[12] *into ðære stope.* OE *stōw* (*EPN* ii, 159–61) is here used in its specialized sense of 'holy place' referring, as is shown by the rest of this passage, to the cathedral. Cf. S 1285 (*BCS* 599; an episcopal lease of A.D. 902) which is dated *on þære mæran stope on Þintanceastre.*

[13] *on ece yrfe.* This is a standard phrase to describe the perpetuity of tenure in bookland, used most often in the vernacular endorsements to Latin diplomas of the tenth and eleventh centuries (cf. the rubric to **XXII**, at n. *a*). See also following note.

Ðonne is ðis se eaca ðe eallra Ƿest Seaxna pitan ðærto eacan me gebocodon on ece erfe[14]. Ærest suðrichte from[h] ðan beodærn[j] [15] to sancte Gregories cirican[16]. ðonne from ðære suð pest hyrnan[k] sancte Gregories cirican . xii . geurda pestrichte to ðære strete[17]. ðonne richte norð . xiii . geurde to ðære norð stræte[18]. ðonne eastrichte . xliii . geurde . 7 . vi . fet[l] to ðære east strete[19]. ðonne suðrichte . xx . geurde [.] 7 . vi . fet to ðære suð strete[20]. ðonne pestrichte[m] be ðære suð strete[n] to ðæm[o] lictune[p] [21]. vii . geurde[q] . 7 . vi . fet . ðonne richt[r] norð . v . geurde[s] .

Ðonne[t] is ðæs ymbgang[u] ealles ðriu[v] furlanges[w] . 7 [.] ðreo metgeurda[x] [22].

+ [.] Eadpeard[y] [23] . rex .

+ [.] Æðelpearð[z] [24] . frater regis .

+ [.] Plegmund[aa] [25] [.] archiepiscopus [.]

+ [.] Denepulf[26] . episcopus .

Moreover, this is the addition which the counsellors of all the West Saxons granted me by diploma as an augmentation thereto in perpetual inheritance.[14] First due south from the refectory[15] to St. Gregory's church,[16] then from the south-west corner of St. Gregory's church 12 'yards' due west to the street,[17] then due north 13 'yards' to the north street,[18] then due east 43 'yards' and 6 feet to the east street,[19] then due south 20 'yards' and 6 feet to the south street, [20] then due west by the south street to the cemetery[21] 7 'yards' and 6 feet, then due north 5 'yards'.

Furthermore, the total circumference of this is 3 furlongs and 3 measured 'yards'.[22]

+ Edward,[23] king

+ Æthelweard,[24] the king's brother

+ Plegmund,[25] archbishop

+ Denewulf,[26] bishop

---

[h] fron C   [j] beoðærn C   [k] hyrnan *underlined* C
[l] *Point after* fet C   [m] pestryhte B, *which begins here*
[n] stræte B   [o] ðæm, ðæn C   [p] lictune
underlined C   [q] gerda B   [r] ryhte B
[s] gerda B   [t] donne B   [u] ymbganges B; simb-
ganges (*underlined*) C, *with the exemplar's letter* y *misread as* si; *cf.
nn.* a *and* d   [v] ðreo B, driu C   [w] furlang B
[x] metgerda B   [y] Eaðpearð C. *Neither this nor any other of
the subscriptions in B are punctuated. Ear* (*erased*) *beneath the signum
crucis* C   [z] Ealdereð C   [aa] Plemunð C

---

[14] *ðe eallra Ƿest Seaxna pitan . . . me gebocodon on ece yrfe*. The permission and witness of the West Saxon counsellors would be needed before King Edward could grant any land as bookland (cf. above, n. 13), since such a grant curtailed customary dues and inheritance. According to **III** (q.v.), a post-conquest forgery, land was bought back from neighbouring persons holding property by right of inheritance. It may be, however, that this second piece of land was part of the royal residence and was thus thought of as held by the king in trust for his successors on the throne. In this context it is interesting that William I recovered possession of part of the New Minster site *c.* 1070 for the extension of the royal palace; see WS 1, 292–4, 316; WS 2.ii, 573–5 and Fig. 65; cf. below, **X–XI**, and **XIV**.

[15] *from ðan beodærn*. NW. of the cathedral. Presumably part of the same institution as the 'wound church' and the 'stone dormitory'; see above, nn. 4 and 5. See A on Fig. 8.

[16] *to sancte Gregories cirican*. NW. of the cathedral. For a possible reference to this church *c.*1000, see C.H. Turner, 'The Churches at Winchester in the Early Eleventh Century', *Journal of Theological Studies* 17 (1916), 65–8, at 67. See WS 4.i, and Fig. AG. See below, B on Fig. 8.

[17] *to ðære strete*. A street (later destroyed) running S.–N. Fig. 8, C–D.

[18] *to ðære norð stræte*. To the 'back street' (later destroyed) running W.–E.; the line from D to E on Fig. 8. Note that 'the north street' (and 'the east street', 'the south street', below) are descriptive phrases rather than street-names. Their directional terms are only relative to this specific plot of land.

[19] *to ðære east strete*. To a street (later destroyed) running N.–S. Fig. 8, E–F. Cf. preceding note.

[20] *to ðære suð strete*. To a street (later destroyed) running E.-W. Fig. 8, F–G. Possibly the extension westwards of 'the middle street' mentioned above in **I**, n. 12. Cf. above, n. 18.

[21] *to ðæm lictune*. The cathedral cemetery to the E. of the church; see WS 4.i.

[22] *metgeurda*. OE *met-gyrd* means literally a 'measured yard', that is, a standard rod's length (cf. BT, s.v. *met-gird*). It also occurs below in **VII** (see ibid. n. 24). This third paragraph, giving the total circumference (*ymbgang ealles*), was no doubt the result of a final measuring process separate from those dealing with the two constituent pieces of land and this may explain the use of the compound word here but not earlier in the text (cf. n. 6). The word *ymbgang* is also used in the Burghal Hidage Calculation; see reference cited above in n. 6.   [23] As above, n. 1.

[24] Æthelweard died on 16 October 922 according to John of Worcester; see R.R. Darlington and P. McGurk (ed.), *The Chronicle of John of Worcester*, II, *The Annals from 450 to 1066* (Oxford, 1995), 382–3; but in 920 (four years before Edward the Elder) according to *Gesta Regum*, 141. He subscribes as *filius regis* 900 × 909 (cf. also S 1605 and 354 (*BCS* 565), both 9th-cent. charters), but is called *frater regis* in S 375–6, 377 (MS. 1), 378, and 383 (all dated A.D. 909); *BCS* 623, 620, 625, 624, and 628; see Keynes, *Atlas*, Tables XXII and XXXV.

[25] Plegmund was archbishop of Canterbury 890–2 August 923: O'Donovan i, 26, 31. Like the other witnesses, he is also in **III**, whose witness-list was taken from that in **II**.

[26] As above, n. 2.

+ [.] Ƿilferð*ᵇᵇ 27* . episcopus .   + Wilfrith,[27] bishop

+ [.] Ƿulfsige*ᶜᶜ 28* . episcopus . *ᵈᵈ*   + Wulfsige,[28] bishop

+ . Asser[29] . episcopus [.]   + Asser,[29] bishop

+ . Ƿighelm*ᵉᵉ 30* . episcopus .   + Wighelm,[30] bishop

+ . Ceolmund*ff 31* . episcopus .   + Ceolmund,[31] bishop

+ . Eadgar[32] . episcopus .   + Edgar,[32] bishop

+ . Ƿimund[33] . episcopus .   + Wigmund,[33] bishop

+ . Byrnhelm[34] . abbud .*ᵍᵍ*   + Beornhelm,[34] abbot

+ . Ƿihtbrord*ʰʰ 35* [.] minister .   + Wihtbrord,[35] thegn

+ . Deormod*ʲʲ 36* . minister .   + Deormod,[36] thegn

+ . Beorhtsige*ᵏᵏ 37* . minister .   + Beorhtsige,[37] thegn

+ . Ocea[38] . minister .   + Ocea,[38] thegn

+ [.] Æðelstan*ˡˡ 39* . minister .   + Æthelstan,[39] thegn

+ [.] Ƿulfhelm[40] . minister .*ᵐᵐ*   + Wulfhelm,[40] thegn

+ . Alla[41] . minister .   + Alla,[41] thegn

+ [.] Beornstan*ⁿⁿ 42* [.] minister .   + Beornstan,[42] thegn

+ . Ƿulfhelm[43] . minister .   + Wulfhelm,[43] thegn

+ . Beornstan*ᵒᵒ 44* . presbiter .   + Beornstan,[44] priest

+ . Tata[45] . presbiter [.]   + Tata,[45] priest

ᵇᵇ Ƿilfærd C   *ᶜᶜ* Ƿulfrige C, *with insular minuscule low s in the exemplar misread as insular minuscule* r   *ᵈᵈ First column of subscriptions ends here* C   *ᵉᵉ* Ƿighen C   *ff* Eodmund C, *with Ce- in the exemplar misread as insular minuscule high e followed by o, and the following letters -ol- misread as -d-*   *ᵍᵍ* Brinhelm . abbod C; *the second column of subscriptions ends here* C   *ʰʰ* Ƿitbrorð C   *ʲʲ* Deormoð C   *ᵏᵏ* Beorhtisige B; Beorthsge C   *ˡˡ* Adelstan C   *ᵐᵐ Third column of subscriptions ends here* C   *ⁿⁿ* Heorstan C   *ᵒᵒ* Beorstan B

---

[27] Wilfrith was either the bishop of Lichfield (889 × 900–903 × 915) or that of Dorchester-on-Thames (893 × 900–903 × 909): O'Donovan i, 27–8; ii, 94. Both Wilfrith and Wigmund (see below, n. 33) occur in charters of Edward the Elder in the company of bishops from Wessex and Mercia and may be assigned alternately to either Lichfield or Dorchester.

[28] Wulfsige was bishop of London 897 × 900–909 × 926; he subscribes 900 × 909: O'Donovan i, 28; ii, 97; and Keynes *Atlas*, Table XXXIII.

[29] Asser was bishop of Sherborne (890 × 896) × 900–909 or 908. He subscribes ?900 × 904: O'Donovan i, 29; ii, 104; and Keynes *Atlas*, Table XXXIII. On him, see Keynes and Lapidge, *passim*.

[30] Wighelm was bishop of Selsey ? × 900–c.909 or 909 × 925: O'Donovan i, 29; ii, 101–2.

[31] Ceolmund was bishop of Rochester 893 × 900–909 × 926. He subscribes 900 × 909: O'Donovan i, 29; ii, 100; and Keynes *Atlas*, Table XXXIII.

[32] Edgar was bishop of Hereford 888 × 900–930 × 931: O'Donovan i, 27, 41.   [33] As above, n. 27.

[34] Beornhelm, abbot, also subscribes in S 366, *BCS* 598 (A.D. 901). He has been wrongly described in the surviving text of S 365, *BCS* 597 (A.D. 901) as a bishop and in that of S 1286, *BCS*

611 (A.D. 904) as an ealdorman. He was probably the abbot who took the 'alms of the West Saxons and of King Alfred' to Rome in 890 and may have been head of a Kentish monastery; see Keynes *Liber Vitae*, 105, and *ASC* [A], s.a.

[35] Wihtbrord subscribes as first or second thegn A.D. 900 × 909; see Keynes *Atlas*, Table XXXV. In S 345, *BCS* 550 (A.D. 882) he subscribes as fourth thegn. He was probably the beneficiary of S 364, *BCS* 588, a grant of 10 hides at Fovant, Wilts., in 901.

[36] Deormod subscribes as first, second or third thegn A.D. ?878 × 909, fifth in S 345, *BCS* 550 (A.D. 882), and as *cellerarius* in S 348, *BCS* 567 (A.D. 892); see Keynes *Atlas*, Tables XXI and XXXV. He was probably the beneficiary of S 355, *BCS* 581 (A.D. 892 × 899), an exchange of lands in Berkshire.

[37] Beorhtsige subscribes 898× 903: Keynes *Atlas*, ibid.

[38] (Apart from in **III**, below) Ocea subscribes 892× 901: Keynes *Atlas*, ibid.

[39] Æthelstan subscribes ?878 × 904: Keynes *Atlas*, ibid. Possibly the beneficiary of S 345, *BCS* 550 (A.D. 882), an exchange of lands in Somerset.

[40] Wulfhelm (1) subscribes 900× 909: Keynes *Atlas*, Table XXXV.

[41] Alla subscribes 900 × 903: Keynes *Atlas*, ibid.

[42] Beornstan subscribes 892 × 903: Keynes *Atlas*, Tables XXI and XXXV. In S 348, *BCS* 567 (A.D. 892) he subscribes as *miles*.

[43] Wulfhelm (2) subscribes 900× 909: Keynes *Atlas*, Table XXXV.

[44] Beornstan, a priest (of the cathedral), subscribes 900× 909; see Keynes *Atlas*, Table XXXIV, and Keynes 1994, 1146.

[45] Tata, a priest (of the cathedral), subscribes 900 × 909 and may have been the Tata, *fasallus*, who was the beneficiary of S 369, *BCS* 601, a grant of land in Berks. in 903. See Keynes, *Atlas*, ibid., and Keynes 1994, ibid.

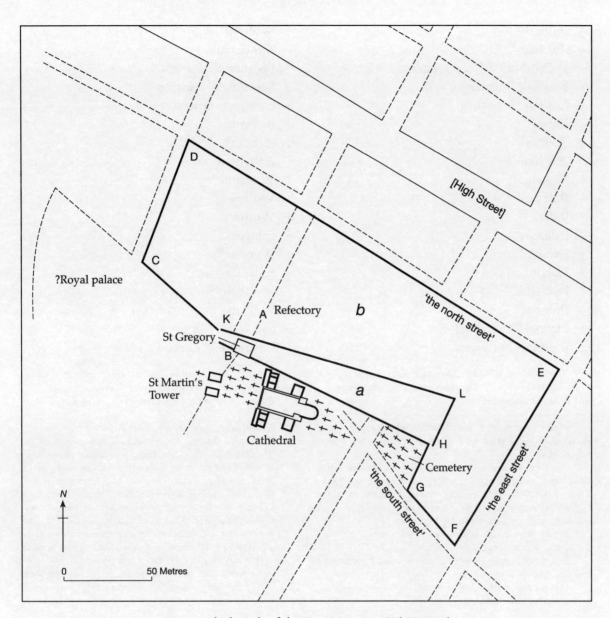

FIG. 8. The bounds of the New Minster in **II** (A.D. ?901).

+ Þulfred[pp][46]	+ Wulfred[46]
+ Æðelstan[47]	+ Æthelstan[47]
+ [.] Beorhtulf[qq][48] . presbiter .[rr]	+ Beorhtwulf,[48] priest
+ Beornulf[49] diaconus	+ Beornwulf,[49] deacon
+ Eadstan[50] diaconus	+ Eadstan,[50] deacon
+ Eadulf[51]	+ Eadwulf[51]
+ Ælfstan[52]	+ Ælfstan[52]
+ Æðelstan[53]	+ Æthelstan[53]
+ Þighelm[54]	+ Wighelm[54]
+ Þulfstan[55]	+ Wulfstan[55]
+ Þulfric[56]	+ Wulfric[56]
+ Ealhstan[57]	+ Ealhstan[57]
+ Þynsige[58]	+ Wynsige[58]
+ Eadulf[59]	+ Eadwulf[59]
+ Þulfhelm[60]	+ Wulfhelm[60]
+ Þulfsige[61]	+ Wulfsige[61]
[+ E]adpold[62] presbiter	+ Eadweald,[62] priest
[+ Þ]ulfnoð[63] presbiter	+ Wulfnoth,[63] priest

[pp] *This and the following subscription do not appear in* C
[qq] Brichtulf C   [rr] *The fourth column of subscriptions, and with it the text, ends here* C

---

[46] (Apart from in **III**, below) Wulfred subscribes 900 × 902. He is designated a priest in S 365–6, *BCS* 597–8. See Keynes *Atlas*, ibid.

[47] Æthelstan subscribes ?878 × 909, usually as *presbiter,* but as *sacerdos* in S 350, *BCS* 576 (A.D. 898). See Keynes *Atlas*, Tables XX and XXXIV. He is probably to be identified with the Mercian priest recruited by King Alfred; see Keynes 1994, 1146; and Asser, cap. 77: Keynes and Lapidge, 93.

[48] (Apart from in **III**, below) Beorhtwulf, priest, subscribes 900 × 901: Keynes *Atlas*, Table XXXIV.

[49] Beornwulf, deacon, subscribes 900 × *c*.909: Keynes *Atlas*, ibid. In S 385, *BCS* 622 (*c*.909) he is called *minister.*

[50] (Apart from in **III**, below) Eadstan, deacon, subscribes 900 × 902: Keynes *Atlas*, ibid.

[51] Eadwulf (1) subscribes 900 × *c*.909 and is variously designated *minister, presbiter,* and *clericus*: Keynes *Atlas*, ibid.

[52] Ælfstan (1), a priest, subscribes 900 × *c*.909: Keynes *Atlas*, ibid.

[53] Æthelstan (2), a priest, subscribes as preceding.

[54] Wighelm, a deacon, subscribes like Ælfstan, above, n. 52.

[55] Wulfstan (1), a priest, subscribes like Ælfstan, above, n. 52.

[56] Wulfric (1), a priest, subscribes like Ælfstan, above, n. 52.

[57] Ealhstan, a priest, subscribes 900 × 909: Keynes *Atlas*, ibid.

[58] Wynsige (2), a clerk, subscribes like Ælfstan, above, n. 52.

[59] Eadwulf (2), a clerk, subscribes like Ælfstan, above, n. 52.

[60] Wulfhelm, a clerk, subscribes like Ælfstan, above, n. 52.

[61] Wulfsige (1), a clerk, subscribes like Ælfstan, above, n. 52.

[62] (Apart from in **III**, below) Eadweald, priest, does not occur in any other surviving witness-list of this period.

[63] (Apart from in **III**, below) Wulfnoth, priest, does not occur in any other surviving witness-list of this period.

III

'A.D. 903', alleged endowment of the New Minster by King Edward the Elder; granting the hundred of Micheldever with East Stratton, Burcot, Popham, Woodmancott, Brown Candover, Cranbourne, Drayton by Newton, Swarraton, Northington, Norton by Selborne, Slackstead and Tatchbury, all in Hants; the manors of Abbotts Ann, Hants, and Collingbourne Kingston and Chisledon, both Wilts.; with fiscal exemptions for the estate of Durley, Hants, and for the site of the monastery

Latin

S 370, Finberg 36

THE present diploma purports to be the record of the original endowment of the New Minster by Edward the Elder after its foundation by him in alleged fulfilment of his dead father's wish.[1] The date 903 appears to follow the (incorrect) later Anglo-Saxon historical tradition of that year as the date of the dedication of the New Minster.[2] The rural estates named, several of them with churches, were in Hampshire and Wiltshire. Most of the Hampshire ones were later part of the abbot's hundred of Micheldever; of these, Durley was transferred to the bishop in 1114 as part of an exchange.[3] Drayton was restored to the New Minster by King Cnut in 1019, having apparently been alienated.[4] Not all of the Hampshire estates were named in Domesday Book, some of them probably being included under the entry for Micheldever.[5] Tatchbury was not acquired until 1066, according to Domesday Book.[6] The places claimed therefore were together held by the New Minster only between 1066 and 1114, a fact which supports the suggestion made below that the document was a product of the early twelfth century.

As Professor N. P. Brooks has noted, this forged diploma has many formulae in common with S 360 and 648, both also in favour of the New Minster.[7] S 360 claims to be the record of a grant by King Edward the Elder in 900 of the hundred of Micheldever, the bounds of whose constituent parts it describes in detail, although Brooks has demonstrated it to be a forgery of the eleventh century.[8] S 648 claims to record a grant by King Eadwig in 957 of an estate at Heighton, Sussex.[9] All three documents include the same anachronistic clause of notification (... *ego* ... *cunctis gentis nostre*

---

[1] See above, **II**, n. 9, and below, **III**, n. 3.

[2] According to *ASC* [F], s.a. 903, the New Minster was dedicated after the death of Grimbald but in the same year. The annal date appears to be two years late in this and other versions of *ASC* [A, B, C, D], an error which was followed by the *Vita Prima* (s. x²) and most later sources for the life of Grimbald; see Grierson 'Grimbald', 554, 538–40, and Thorpe *ASC*, s.a.

[3] See below, **XIII**, n. 11.

[4] S 956 (*LH*, 324–6).

[5] See below, **III**, nn. 14, 20–1, 23, and 29.

[6] Ibid. n. 24.

[7] Brooks 'Micheldever Forgery', 193–4.

[8] Ibid. 193–5, 215–16. For an edition of S 360, see ibid. 219–22.

[9] *BCS* 1000.

fidelibus innotesco quod . . . pro salute anime mee . . . benigne confero) of a sort not found in genuine Anglo-Saxon diplomas before the mid 990s.[10] Besides this, there is virtual identity of verbal invocation, immunity and reservation, corroboration clause, prohibition, and anathema between the three documents. The occasion of the production of S 648 is not at present known. S 360 and **III** are more directly associated however, having the same donor. They also share the same dating-formula (with the same erroneous indiction but different A.D. dates) and the same witness-list (closely related to that in **II**, above); the description of Micheldever (*quendam fundum quem indigene Myceldefer appellant*) is also identical. The presence of certain non-formulaic historical allusions in **III**, but not in S 360, suggests, however, that **III** is secondary to the latter document. These interpolations refer to the New Minster as having been founded by Edward the Elder as the 'executor' of his father's wish; to Edward's purchase of six 'furlongs' of land to the north of the Old Minster, from Bishop Denewulf and the 'canons' of the Old Minster as well as from others living nearby, at the price of one mancus of gold per foot; to the building and naming of the New Minster and its dedication in 903 in honour of the Holy Trinity, the Virgin Mary, and St. Peter.[11] Another interpolation refers to a 'coronation' of King Alfred.[12]

If **III** is indeed secondary to S 360 it is unlikely to have been constructed earlier than the eleventh century.[13] Although some of its wording has been influenced by that of the late-tenth-century account of the early history of the New Minster in the *Liber Vitae*,[14] the present document is probably later than 1066, in which year Tatchbury was acquired, as noted above. It may have been in existence by 1125 and have been used by William of Malmesbury as one of the sources of the *Gesta Pontificum*;[15] alternatively, it shares a common source with the latter. It may also have been used by the author of the *Vita Secunda* of Grimbald, probably in the second quarter of the twelfth century.[16] More certainly, it was used by the compiler of the *Liber de Hyda* in the late fourteenth or early fifteenth century.[17] The details of hidage of the various estates named do not tally very well with either the *TRE* or the *TRW* hidages of Domesday Book and may perhaps have been taken from a variety of different sources, as the bounds in S 360 earlier had been.[18] It may be suggested that **III** was constructed not long after the move of the New Minster to Hyde in 1110; it is probably significant that **XVI**, below, an alleged grant by Henry I, was also based on S 360.[19] The specific reference in **III** to the exemption of the site of the New Minster from worldly or secular service (apart from the Three Burdens) would also fit this period when the right of freedom from geld and other plaints for the new site of the abbey at Hyde was being settled.[20] Also at this time, the lack of a detailed primary foundation-charter may have caused concern and it may have been decided to safeguard the interests of the abbey by constructing one, including not only what was thought to have been the original endowment but also some extra information safeguarding rights over churches. That it was intended to complement the New Minster refoundation charter (**IV**, below), which dealt with the monastic constitution and which had been splendidly written in gold in the

[10] Keynes *Diplomas*, 111–12.

[11] The first two of these interpolations probably formed a source for similar statements in *LH*; see below, **III**, nn. 3 and 6.

[12] See below, **III**, n. 11.

[13] Brooks 'Micheldever Forgery', 193–4.

[14] See below, **III**, n. 6.

[15] See below, **III**, n. 6 and Grierson 'Grimbald', 536.

[16] Ibid. 536, 538.

[17] See below, **III**, nn. 3 and 6.

[18] Brooks 'Micheldever Forgery', 215.

[19] See below, p. 178.

[20] See below, **XIV** and **XV**. Note, however, that the formula *in puram et perpetuam elemosinam* is not recorded in a genuine document until *c.* 1160; see below, **III**, n. 28. It could possibly be a later interpolation into **III**.

latter part of the tenth century, may be surmised from the fact that **III** refers to itself as *in aureis literis scriptis* (hence Birch's name for it as 'the Golden Charter').[21] It may be noted that **XVI**, with which it shares source-material, survives written in gold ink on extra leaves added to the codex containing **IV**.[22]

The only surviving text of **III** is a late medieval cartulary copy whose scribe has modernized its Latin, sometimes under the influence of French spelling conventions.[23] The forms of the place-names may also have been modernized by him, but alternatively could have been extracted, like the hidages mentioned above, by the draftsman of the exemplar from various post-conquest sources. The updating of the royal style in the superscription from *rex Anglorum* (as in S 360 and 648) to *rex Anglie* was more probably the work of the cartularist.[24] Some misreadings in the cartulary text, of both Latin words and some OE names, suggest that the cartularist's exemplar was written in some form of insular minuscule script.[25] If so, that exemplar may have taken the form of a single-sheet forgery imitative of the external appearance of S 360 (itself written in an imitative square Anglo-Saxon minuscule script),[26] with which document, as noted above, the present text shares several formulae.

[21] *BCS* 602.
[22] See below, p. 178.
[23] See below, **III**, nn. *q* and *t*.
[24] Ibid. n. 10.
[25] Ibid. nn. *k, p, w, y, z, cc, ff,* and *gg*.
[26] See Brooks 'Micheldever Forgery', 192–3.

MS.:   B. BL, Harl.MS. 1761, fo. 47[rv] (s.xiv ex.)

Edited: *Monasticon*, ii, 437–8 (no. 4)
           KCD 336
           BCS 602
           LVH, 214–17
           Miller *New Minster* 6

Printed from the manuscript

Omnip`o'tencia[a] diuine magestatis vbique presidente et sine fine cuncta gubernante[.] Ego Edwardus[1] ipso largitante[b] primus post mortem patris mei Alfredi[2] ad regalis solii fastigium sublimatus patris[c] voti non segnis exsecutor[3] ad officinas monasterii construendas quoddam terre spacium tres acras et tres virgatas quod ling`u'a[d] Anglorum sex furlang' in aquilonari parte Veteris Monasterii a Denulfo[4] ipsius ciuitatis episcopo et canonicis[5] illius ecclesie seu a quibuslibet circummanentibus iure hereditatis reddemi vnoquoque pede mancham auri[6] contuli moxque in arduam monasterii strutturam super tres acras et tres virgatas totam mentis diligenciam inpendi et edificaui et ad distringcionem Vetusti Monasterii Nouum Monasterium appellari feci predictam autem ecclesiam in honore summe Trinitatis genetricisque Christi Marie atque apostoli Petri[7] benediccione

The omnipotence of divine majesty presides everywhere and governs all things without end. I, Edward,[1] as divine majesty grants, the first after the death of my father Alfred[2] to be raised to the highest point of royal dominion, a not inactive executor of a father's wish,[3] acquired for the purpose of erecting monastic buildings a certain space of land, 3 acres and 3 yardlands, which in the tongue of the English is 6 'furlongs', to the north of the Old Minster, from Denewulf,[4] bishop of that city, and from the canons[5] of that church, and also from each of those dwelling nearby by right of inheritance, and I gave a mancus of gold for every foot;[6] and soon afterwards I applied the whole attention of [my] mind to the laborious erection of a monastery on the 3 acres and 3 yardlands. And I have built it, and I have caused it to be called the New Minster in distinction to the Old Minster and, moreover, I have caused the aforesaid church to be dedicated in honour of the Highest Trinity and of Mary, the mother of Christ, and of the apostle Peter,[7] with the

---

[a] Carta Edwardi primi fundatoris abbatie de Hyda *rubric; this document is no. xliii in the Micheldever section of* B. *The sixth letter of the first word is a corrector's insertion* [b] largitante *is probably a copying error for* largiente *which occurs in* S 360, *and in* XVI, *below. There may be confusion here, however, with the MLat verb* largitor *(Latham 12th cent.)* [c] patre' *MS* [d] *A corrector's insertion*

[1] Edward the Elder, 899–924.
[2] Alfred, king of the West Saxons, 871–, of the Anglo-Saxons *c.* 880–99. See Simon Keynes, 'Rulers of the English, *c.* 450–1066', in Michael Lapidge, John Blair, Simon Keynes, and Donald Scragg (ed.), *The Blackwell Encyclopaedia of Anglo-Saxon England* (Oxford, 1999), Appendix, pp. 500–20, at 513–14.
[3] *patris voti non segnis exsecutor.* See II, n. 9. Cf. *LH,* 51: . . . *Alfredus, ante mortem imminentem, terram pro capella et dormitorio emit, et filio suo Edwardo pro testamento legavit, ut monasterium a patre per plurima annorum curricula præcogitatum, complere et fundare non tepesceret.* In *LH,* 82, Edward is called *rex gloriosus, non segnis executor sanctæ monitionis,* equivalent to the phrase in the present document. The spelling *exsecutor* used in III for *executor* echoes others with *exs-* for *ex-* found much earlier in IV; see below, 72.
[4] Denewulf, bishop of Winchester; see above, II, n. 2.
[5] *canonicis.* The pre-Reform secular clergy of the cathedral; ibid. n. 3.
[6] *quoddam terre spacium . . . a . . . episcopo et canonicis illius ecclesie seu a quibuslibet circummanentibus iure hereditatis reddemi vnoquoque pede mancham auri.* This section was probably based on the opening part of the late-10th-cent. account of the foundation (Keynes *Liber Vitae* 1; *LVH,* 4):

EADVVARDUS . . . dicitur a pontifice huiuscę diocesis petisse .

quo sibi mutua uicissitudine . tantum terrae proprii iuris annueret . quatinus monasterium regalibus usibus haud indecens stabiliri quiret.
Cuius benignissimi regis talibus uotis presul uetusti monasterii libentissime assensum tribuens . insuper reciproca uice non modicam pretiosissimi metalli quantitatum percipiens . redemit deuotissimus princeps uniuscuiusque passus istius loci summam ab illo . seu a quibuslibet circummanentibus iure hereditatis . uno purgatissimi mancuso auri .

This section of III became a source for *LH,* 80: *emitque Deo amabilis princeps capellam et dormitorium quod pater suus fabricare jussit, et insuper terram reliquam a supradicto præsule [Denewulf], seu a quibuslibet circummanentibus, jure hæreditatis redemit; scilicet passus uniuscujusque istius loci emit uno mancuso purgatissimi auri.* Cf. also, with reference to King Alfred as the alleged founder of the New Minster, *Gesta Pontificum,* 173: . . . *suffitiens terræ spatium ab episcopo et canonicis temporis mercatus, ad unumquemque pedem mancam auri publico pondere pensitavit.* The mancus (about 4.5 gr.) was established by the late 8th cent. as the normal unit of weight in England for measuring gold. It seems to have been the equivalent of 30 silver pence. By the end of the reign of Cnut (1016–35) its use appears to have been replaced by that of the mark. See Pamela Nightingale, 'The Ora, the Mark, and the Mancus: Weight-Standards and the Coinage in Eleventh-Century England: Part 2', *Num Chron* 144 (1984), 234–48, especially 236–8.
[7] *in honore summe Trinitatis genetricisque Christi Marie atque apostoli Petri.* For the varied dedication of the New Minster, see Miller *New Minster,* introduction, n. 8; cf. WS 1, 313, n. 8. The

pontificali[8] deuotissime feci dedicari et anno incarnacionis dominice . dcccc . iii°. indiccione . iiii^to .[9] ego Edwardus rex Anglie[10] et fundator primus N`o´ui^d Monasterii Þ[i]ntonie cunctis gentis nostre fidelibus innotesco quod pro anima patris mei Alfredi regis tocius Anglie primi coronati[11] et pro salute anime mee liberalissimus tantam eidem ecclesie benigne confero opum prediorum ornamentorumque copiam ditissimorum monasteriorum equare videretur opulenciam eidem ecclesie do quendam fundum quem indigene Myceldefer[12] appellant cum suo hundredo et appendicibus habens centum cassatos et ecclesiam vtrumque villam de Strattone[13] cum nouem hidis Burcote[14] cum . iiii . hidis et dimidia^e Popham[15] cum . viii . hidis et dimidia Woedemanecote[16] cum . x . hidis Candeuerre[17] cum . x . hidis et ecclesia^f

greatest devotion and with papal blessing.[8] And in the year of the Lord's Incarnation 903, in the fourth indiction,[9] I, Edward, king of England[10] and the first founder of the New Minster at Winchester, make it known to all the faithful of our people that, for the soul of Alfred my father, the first to be crowned[11] king of the whole of England, and for the salvation of my soul, I, a most bountiful person, freely give to the same church so much wealth of resources in estates and jewels as will be seen to equal the opulence of the richest monasteries. I give to the same church a certain estate which the natives call Micheldever[12] with its hundred and [its] dependencies, having 100 hides and a church, as well as the estate of Stratton[13] with 9 hides, Burcot[14] with 4½ hides, Popham[15] with 8½ hides, Woodmancott[16] with 10 hides, Candover[17] with 10 hides and a church,

---

^d A corrector's insertion   ^e dimidia' MS., presumably standing for dimidiam and wrongly taken to refer to the following estate   ^f Corrected from ecclesie

---

earliest dedication in a genuine diploma is to St. Peter alone (S 374, BCS 604), but in a lease datable to 925 × 933 it was to St. Saviour (S 1417, BCS 648). The late-10th-cent. account of the foundation has the Holy Trinity and St. Mary (Keynes Liber Vitae 1; LVH, 3). LH, 83, also includes St. Paul. The forged S 360 (see above, p. 57) refers to the Holy Trinity alone; cf. below, **XVI**, n. 4.

[8] benediccione pontificali. There is no independent evidence for any papal involvement in the foundation of the New Minster. Neither LVH nor LH refers to the claim made here.

[9] In error for the sixth indiction, if the A.D. date is 903. The same error occurs in the forged S 360; it is repeated in the main dating clause, below (cf. below, n. 33).

[10] rex Anglie. This royal style is anachronistic before the reign of John (1199–1216); see Pierre Chaplais, English Royal Documents: King John–Henry VI, 1199–1461 (Oxford, 1971), 13. It may be however that the scribe of the present MS. (s.xiv ex.) has extended an abbreviated form rex Angl' (for rex Anglorum, an acceptable style for Edward the Elder), in accordance with his own contemporary practice.

[11] Alfredi regis tocius Anglie primi coronati. Possibly an oblique reference to the story of Alfred's boyhood visit to Rome in 853, when he was said to have been received by Pope Leo IV in a ceremony (?of confirmation) misinterpreted, after Alfred's eventual accession, as one of royal consecration. See Thorpe ASC[A,G] s.a. 853, [B,C] s.a. 854; The Chronicle of Æthelweard, ed. A. Campbell (London, 1962), 32; Asser, cap. 8; Keynes and Lapidge, 69, 232; and Janet L. Nelson, 'The Problem of King Alfred's Royal Anointing', JEH 18 (1967), 145–63. Nelson questions the occurrence of the journey in 853, but suggests that this story of papal consecration was propagated by Alfred

himself: ibid. 158–63. On the other hand, corroborative evidence for Alfred's journey in 853 may exist in a North Italian confraternity book; see Simon Keynes, 'Anglo-Saxon Entries in the "Liber Vitae" of Brescia', in Jane Roberts and Janet L. Nelson, with Malcolm Godden (ed.), Alfred the Wise: Studies in Honour of Janet Bately on the Occasion of her Sixty-Fifth Birthday (Cambridge, 1997), 99–119, especially 107–9 and 112–13.

[12] Myceldefer . . . cum suo hundredo. On the origin of the hundred of Micheldever, Hants, perhaps only a part of an older administrative unit centred on the 9th-cent. royal vill there, see Brooks 'Micheldever Forgery', 216–17; see also ibid. Map 6. The New Minster held 106 hides at Micheldever TRE: DB, i, fo. 42^v (DB Hants 6: 16). Cranbourne, Drayton, Stratton, Popham, and other unnamed dependencies were counted in the 106 hides: ibid.

[13] East Stratton, Hants, was included within the boundary of Myceldefer in S 360; see Brooks 'Micheldever Forgery', 199 and ibid. Map 1. It was described as part of the manor of Micheldever TRW: DB, i, fo. 42^v (DB Hants 6: 16).

[14] Burcot, Hants (in East Stratton parish), is not named in DB, but is within the area of Myceldefer as shown in Brooks 'Micheldever Forgery', Map 1.

[15] Popham, Hants, had the same relationship to Micheldever as that given for East Stratton in n. 13, above.

[16] Woodmancott, Hants, was described as part of the manor of Brown Candover TRW: DB, i, fo. 42^r (DB Hants 6: 13). It does not, however, appear to have been included in the estate of Kendefer described in S 360; see Brooks 'Micheldever Forgery', 212–14 and Map 5.

[17] The New Minster held 20 hides at Brown Candover, Hants, TRE: DB, i, fo. 42^r (DB Hants 6: 13). An estate there, consisting of a narrow strip of land along the eastern boundary of the parish, was described under the name Kendefer in S 360; see Brooks 'Micheldever Forgery', 212–14 and Map 5.

Cramborne[18] cum . viii . hidis et capella Draitone[19] iuxta Niuuetone cum . iiii . hidis Swerwetone[20] cum . iii . hidis et vna virgata et dimidia Northametone[21] cum . vi . hidis Nortone[22] iuxta Seleborne cum . iii . hidis Slastede[23] et Tachburi[24] cum vna hida et dimidia libera et consuetudine regia[.] Manerium quod dicitur Anna[25] . xv . hidas cassatos[g] habens et ecclesiam[.][h] Manerium quod [dicitur] Colengaburnan[26] habens . l . cassatos et appendicibus suis cum ecclesia[.][h] Manerium quod vocatur[j] Ceoseldene[27] [habens] . xl . cassatos[k] et ecclesiam[.][l] eidem ecclesie Noui Monasterii[m] in Þintonia a me Edwardo rege fundate[n] do et concedo in puram et perpetuam elemosinam[28] et preteria[o] totam

Cranbourne[18] with 8 hides and a chapel, Drayton[19] by Newton with 4 hides, Swarraton[20] with 3 hides and 1½ yardlands, Northington[21] with 6 hides, Norton[22] by Selborne with 3 hides, Slackstead[23] and Tatchbury[24] with 1½ hides and free from customary royal dues; the manor which is called Ann,[25] having 15 hides and a church; the manor which is called Collingbourne,[26] having 50 hides and its dependencies, with a church; the manor which is called Chisledon,[27] having 40 hides and a church. And, besides, I give and grant in pure and perpetual alms,[28] to the same church of the New Minster in Winchester, founded by me

---

[g] Sic MS., although hida and cassatus both mean 'a hide (of land)'
[h] As above, n. f   [j] kalatur cancelled and vocatur inserted overline by a corrector   [k] cassator' MS.; a scribal misreading of the exemplar's insular minuscule low s as insular minuscule r. Cf. below, n. z   [l] As n. f   [m] Monasterio MS.
[n] fundata MS.   [o] A spelling for preterea

[18] An estate at Cranbourne, Hants (in Wonston parish), was described in S 360; see Brooks 'Micheldever Forgery', 203–6 and Map 2. It was listed as part of the manor of Micheldever TRW: DB, i, fo. 42[v] (DB Hants 6: 16).

[19] Drayton (lost) was on the R. Test to the north of Bransbury, Hants. It is here designated 'by Newton', in reference to Newton Stacey, to distinguish it from another Drayton, near Sparkford, on the R. Itchen to the south of Winchester. One hide at Drayton seems to have been the subject of a lease by the New Minster to one Wulfmær before 995 × 1006; cf. S 1420, AS Ch 70. 5 hides here were restored to the New Minster in 1019 by King Cnut, having been acquired by a layman through deception: S 956; LH, 324–6; Whitelock EHD 132. It was listed as part of the manor of Micheldever TRW: DB, i, fo. 42[v] (DB Hants 6: 16). Its inclusion probably accounts for the assessment of Micheldever at 106 hides TRE: ibid.

[20] Swarraton, Hants, is not named in DB. It is excluded from the area of Myceldefer as shown in Brooks 'Micheldever Forgery', Map 1.

[21] Northington, Hants, is not named in DB, but is within the area of Myceldefer as shown in Brooks 'Micheldever Forgery', Map 1.

[22] Norton by Selborne, Hants, was not associated with the New Minster TRE or TRW: DB, i, fos. 46[r], 47[r] (DB Hants 23: 55 and 29: 12).

[23] The manor of Slackstead, in Farley Chamberlayne parish, Hants, is not named in DB. It seems to have formerly been called Rige leage, the bounds of which are included in S 360; see Brooks 'Micheldever Forgery', 210–12 and Map 4.

[24] Half a hide at Tatchbury, Hants, to the west of Southampton, was given to the New Minster in 1066 by Eadsige the

sheriff of Hampshire: DB, i, fo. 43[r] (DB Hants 6: 10). According to DB, ibid. it did not pay geld.

[25] 15 hides at Abbotts Ann, Hants, are the subject of an apparently genuine diploma, dated 901, in the name of Edward the Elder and in favour of the New Minster: S 365, BCS 597. The reversion of an estate (?of personal bookland or loanland) there was bequeathed to the New Minster by Bishop Ælfsige of Winchester in 955 × 956: S 1491, AS Wills 4. The New Minster held an estate at Abbotts Ann (15 hides TRE, 8 hides TRW) in 1066 and 1086: DB, i, fo. 43[r] (DB Hants 16: 11).

[26] An estate (50 hides TRE) at Collingbourne Kingston, Wilts., was held by the New Minster in 1066 and 1086: DB, i, fo. 67[r] (DB Wilts. 10: 2). The 10 hides AT COLINGBURNE which are the subject of a forged diploma of Edward the Elder to the thegn Wulfgar, dated 921, apparently represented the manor (later called Aughton) within Collingbourne Kingston which Wulfgar bequeathed to his daughter Æffe with reversion to the New Minster in 931 × 939: S 379 and 1533, BCS 635, AS Ch 26; see D. J. Bonney, 'Two Tenth-Century Wiltshire Charters Concerning Lands at Avon and Collingbourne', WAM 64 (1969), 56–64, especially 60–4.

[27] Chisledon, Wilts., was in the possession of the New Minster in 925 × 933 when it was leased to the thegn Alfred: S 1417, BCS 648. It appears in the 9th cent. to have been in the possession of the Old Minster and of Kings Æthelwulf and Alfred, and to have been the subject of an exchange between Edward the Elder and the Old Minster in 900: S 354, 359, and 1507; BCS 565 and 594, Harmer SEHD 11. S 366, BCS 598 claims to record the grant of 50 hides at Chisledon to the New Minster in 901, but is of doubtful authenticity. The New Minster held an estate there (40 hides TRE) in 1066 and 1086: DB, i, fo. 67[v] (DB Wilts. 10: 5).

[28] in puram et perpetuam elemosinam. This formula is anachronistic here. It also occurs in another New Minster forgery, claiming to be a grant by King Edgar of estates in Sussex and Wiltshire: S 746, BCS 1191. The earliest reference to it in a genuine document so far found is c. 1160; see R. E. Latham and D. R. Howlett (ed.), Dictionary of Medieval Latin, i, A-L (Oxford, 1975–97), 761, s.v. elemosina. KCD 1335 (=S 1016), also quoted ibid., is a 14th-cent. forgery from Winchester Cathedral.

terram de Durlea[29] et illam in qua abatiam fundaui ab omni seruicio mundano[p] et ceculari[q] negocio semper sint libere exceptis tribus causis hoc est expedicione et arcis pontis constructione[.][30]

Huic autem libertati et donacioni fautores ac consiliarii mei fuerunt duces et magnates qui me ad hanc largitatem incitauerunt qui etiam omnes vnanimiter concesserunt vt donacio ista firma in eternum permaneat[r] et in aureis literis scriptis[31] neque a quolibet seu superiore vel inferiore comutetur set gloriosum maneat inuiolabile et quisquis violare presumsserit[s] excommunicetur a sosietate[t] dei et sanctorum[.] Celebrata est igitur hec regalis institucio et donacio in pago qui dicitur[u] Hamtone[32] . anno dominice incarnacionis . dcccc . iii . indiccione quarta[.][33] sub testimonio et autoritate[v] gentis nostre principum quorum vocabula[w] hic cerenuntur[.][x]

+ Ego Eadpeard[y] [34] rex
+ Ego Plegmund[35] bisce*op*
+ Ego Aðelpeard filius regis[36]
+ Ego Denulf[37] bisce*op*

---

[p] *mundana MS.; a scribal misreading of insular minuscule* a *as* o. Cf. n. w   [q] *A spelling for* seculari, *due to the influence of French. Cf. n. t*   [r] permanet *MS., but cf. S 360 (Brooks 'Micheldever Forgery', 219) and* **XVI**   [s] *Sic MS.*   [t] *A spelling for* societate, *as in n.* q   [u] *Corrected from* datur   [v] *A spelling for* auctoritate   [w] vocabulo *MS.; a misreading as in n.* p   [x] *A spelling for* cernuntur   [y] Eudpeard *MS., with scribal misreading of (?open-topped) insular minuscule* a *in the exemplar as* u

---

[29] An estate at Durley, Hants, formed a detached part of the 100 hides at Micheldever in S 360, where its bounds are described; see Brooks 'Micheldever Forgery', 208–10 and Map 3. It was not named as a New Minster estate in DB but was probably included under the Micheldever entry (*DB*, i, fo. 42[v]; *DB Hants* 6: 16). The single virgate held by Edmund son of Payne from the king (*DB*, i, fo. 50[v]; *DB Hants* 69: 51) was no doubt a separate entity at the same place, since the bounds of Durley in S 360 do not include the whole of the parish; see Brooks 'Micheldever Forgery', 210. In 1114 the New Minster's estate at Durley was granted to the bishop of Winchester as part of the exchange concerning the move to Hyde; see below, **XIII**, n. 11.

[30] *ab omni seruicio mundano et ceculari negocio sint libere exceptis tribus causis.* Cf. the statements regarding freedom from service, geld, etc., in relation to the New Minster site; see below, **X**, n. 7; **XIII**, n. 12; **XIV**, n. 9; and **XV**, nn. 6 and 7.

[31] *in aureis literis scriptis.* See above, p. 59.

King Edward, that the whole estate of Durley[29] and that land on which I founded the abbey, should always be free from all worldly service and secular affairs except for the Three Burdens, namely, military service and the building of fortifications and bridges.[30]

My supporters and advisers with regard to this freedom and donation were the ealdormen and magnates who urged me on to this liberality, and who all unanimously granted that this donation should remain constant for all time and that it should be written in golden letters[31] and that it should not be changed by anyone, whether of the higher or the lower rank, but that it should continue as a glorious and inviolable thing and that whoever should presume to violate it shall be excommunicated from the fellowship of God and the saints. This royal foundation and donation has therefore been pronounced in the district which is called Southampton,[32] in the year of the Lord's Incarnation 903, in the fourth indiction,[33] under the witness and authority of the leading men of our people whose names are here distinguished.

+ I, Edward,[34] king
+ I, Plegmund,[35] bishop
+ I, Æthelweard, king's son[36]
+ I, Denewulf,[37] bishop

---

[32] *Hamtone.* This place-name spelling is probably a modernized version of *Hamtun* in the exemplar. The latter form is that in S 360; see Brooks 'Micheldever Forgery', 221. On this and other name-forms for Southampton, see Alexander R. Rumble, 'HAMTVN *alias* HAMWIC (Saxon Southampton): the Place-Name Traditions and their Significance', in Philip Holdsworth, *Excavations at Melbourne Street, Southampton, 1971–6*, (CBA, Research Report 33; Southampton Archaeological Research Committee, Research Report 1; London, 1980), 7–20.

[33] *indiccione quarta.* As above, n. 9. The occurrence of two dating-clauses in the same diploma is an irregular feature.

[34] As above, n. 1.

[35] Like those of the other witnesses, Plegmund's name has been taken from the witness-list in **II**, above.

[36] *Aðelpeard filius regis.* See **II**, n. 24, where he is more correctly described as *frater regis*. The designation *filius regis* here (as in S 360) is the Latin equivalent to OE *ætheling*, 'a king's son'; see David N. Dumville, 'The Ætheling: a Study in Anglo-Saxon Constitutional History', *ASE* 8 (1979), 1–33, especially 11.

[37] As above, **II**, n. 26.

+ Ego Ƿiferd[38] bisceop

+ Ego Ƿulfsige[39] bisceop

+ Ego Asser[z][40] bisceop

+ Ego Ƿ[i]ghelm[aa][41] bisceop

+ Ego Ceolmund[42] bisceop

+ Ego Eadgar[43] bisceop

+ Ego Ƿimund[44] bisceop

+ Ego Beornelm[45] abbas[bb]

+ Ƿihtbrord[46] minister

+ Deormod[47] minister

+ Beorhtsie[48] minister

+ Ocea[49] minister

+ Adelstan[50] minister

+ Ƿulfhelm[51] minister

+ Alla[52] minister

+ Beornstan[53] minister

+ Ƿulfhelm[54] minister

+ Beornstan[55] minister

+ Tata[56] minister

+ Ƿulf[r]ed[cc][57] minister[dd]

Aðelstan[58]

Beorhtulf[59] presbiter

Beornulf[60] diaconus[ee]

Eadstan[61] diaconus[ee]

Eadulf[62]

Ælfstan[ff][63]

Æðelstan[gg][64]

Ƿighelm[65]

Ƿulfstan[66]

Ƿulfric[67]

Ealhstan[68]

Ƿyns[i]ge[69]

Eadulf[70]

Ƿulfhelm[71]

Ƿulfs[i]ge[hh][72]

+ I, Wilfrith,[38] bishop

+ I, Wulfsige,[39] bishop

+ I, Asser,[40] bishop

+ I, Wighelm,[41] bishop

+ I, Ceolmund,[42] bishop

+ I, Edgar,[43] bishop

+ I, Wigmund,[44] bishop

+ I, Beornhelm,[45] abbot

+ Wihtbrord,[46] thegn

+ Deormod,[47] thegn

+ Beorhtsige,[48] thegn

+ Ocea,[49] thegn

+ Æthelstan,[50] thegn

+ Wulfhelm,[51] thegn

+ Alla,[52] thegn

+ Beornstan,[53] thegn

+ Wulfhelm,[54] thegn

+ Beornstan,[55] thegn

+ Tata,[56] thegn

+ Wulfred,[57] thegn

Æthelstan[58]

Beorhtwulf,[59] priest

Beornwulf,[60] deacon

Eadstan,[61] deacon

Eadwulf[62]

Ælfstan[63]

Æthelstan[64]

Wighelm[65]

Wulfstan[66]

Wulfric[67]

Ealhstan[68]

Wynsige[69]

Eadwulf[70]

Wulfhelm[71]

Wulfsige[72]

---

[z] Arrer *MS.*, *with scribal misreading of insular minuscule low s as insular minuscule r; cf. n. k*   [aa] Ƿghelm, *altered from* Ƿa- *MS.* [bb] abb' *MS.*, *which could also stand for OE* abbod. *The first column of subscriptions ends here*   [cc] Ƿulfed *MS.*, *with scribal error probably caused by the proximity of insular minuscule* f *and insular minuscule* r *in the exemplar*   [dd] *Second column of subscriptions ends here*   [ee] diac' *MS.*, *which could also stand for OE* diacon [ff] Celfstan *MS.*, *with scribal misreading of* Æ *in the exemplar as* Ce; *cf. following*   [gg] Ceðelstan *MS.*, *a misreading as preceding* [hh] *Third column of subscriptions ends here*

[38-54] As above, **II**, nn. 27–43.

[55] Beornstan is wrongly designated here as *minister* rather than as a priest; see **II**, n. 44.

[56] Tata is wrongly designated here as *minister* rather than as a priest; see **II**, n. 45.

[57] Wulfred is wrongly designated here as *minister* rather than as a priest; see **II**, n. 46.

[58-72] See **II**, nn. 47–61, respectively.

IV

A.D. 966, refoundation charter of the New Minster granted by King Edgar
Latin

S 745, Finberg 100

THE New Minster refoundation charter is one of the most important surviving contemporary records of the Benedictine Reform of the reign of Edgar. Its uncompromising assertion of the divinely ordained rights of the monks of the New Minster against those of their secular predecessors is almost certainly the work of Bishop Æthelwold, in the first years of his episcopate. There is no reason to doubt the date 966 which the document carries as being that of the publication of the text. This is in complete accord both with the composition of the witness-list and with the sentiments expressed throughout the body of the document. It is likely that the date 964 under which the refoundation of the New Minster is noted in the Anglo-Saxon Chronicle (A and F) marks only the beginning of a prolonged dispute between the monks and the secular canons, each with their own supporters. The year 966 may have seen the apparent end of the dispute and a victory for the monks, but the fact that such a monumental and affirmative royal document as the present one was deemed necessary does perhaps suggest that the monks still feared a future attempt by the canons to regain their position, as indeed was to happen elsewhere on the death of Edgar in 975.[1] The monastic party evidently appreciated fully the symbolic value of their victory at the New Minster, the church which served the inhabitants of the important city of Winchester and in which Kings Alfred, Edward the Elder, and Eadwig lay buried.[2] The opportunity seems to have been taken by them to publicise the refoundation of the monastery, and to have this confirmed by King Edgar, at a major gathering of the royal court, presumably in the city. This included, besides his wife and children, Edgar's grandmother (the widow of Edward the Elder the founder of the New Minster) as well as the two archbishops, ten bishops, five abbots, six ealdormen, and eight leading thegns.[3] It is probable that the written record of the occasion, in the form of MS. A, was deliberately written in luxurious fashion because it was intended to be kept on the altar.[4] There is internal provision for its public reading to the New Minster community during the year.[5]

While there is no way of giving an exact date to the completion of the writing of MS. A in its extravagant final form, its witness-list is unlikely to have been copied intact much later than 971 (after which the ætheling Edmund, described as *clito legitimus*, was dead).[6] Differences in page-ruling

---

[1] See D. J. V. Fisher, 'The Anti-Monastic Reaction in the Reign of Edward the Martyr', *Cambridge Historical Journal* 10 (1952), 254–70. For fuller treatment of the political context in Mercia, see Ann Williams, '*Princeps Merciorum gentis*: The Family, Career and Connections of Ælfhere, Ealdorman of Mercia, 956–83', *ASE* 10 (1982), 143–72, especially 158–70.

[2] See WS 1, 314.

[3] See below, **IV**, nn. 125–30, 132–4, 136–49, and 151–64.

[4] As suggested by Francis Wormald, 'Late Anglo-Saxon Art: Some Questions and Suggestions', in M. Meiss (ed.), *Acts of the 20th International Congress of the History of Art*, New York, 1961 (4 vols, Princeton, 1963), i, *Romanesque and Gothic Art*, 19–26, at 24–5.

[5] See below, **IV, xxii.**

[6] Ibid. n. 128.

and size of script between the main body of the text and the witness-list (see below) might suggest that the main part of the text was actually written into MS. A before the assembly recorded in the witness-list took place, after which the names of those present were added. There is, however, no specific cause to think that the preliminary miniature in MS. A, well-known to art historians as the earliest example of the so-called 'Winchester-style' of decoration, is any later in date than the witness-list and it is likely that it was added to the *codex* as soon as the written record was complete.[7]

The internal structure of the text is elaborate and its wording reflects a taste for the learned latinity that was fostered by the monastic reformers.[8] It was suggested by Francis Wormald in 1963 that Bishop Æthelwold was its 'creator', a suggestion which has been supported by subsequent comparative textual analyses by Dorothy Whitelock and Michael Lapidge.[9] **IV** may be seen as an exhibition, to his pupils and colleagues, of Æthelwold's powers of composition as well as of his belief in the fundamental rights of the monastic cause. There are certainly passages that are similar in tone and content to those in other works associated with Æthelwold—the slightly later *Regularis Concordia*,[10] and the vernacular tract on 'King Edgar's Establishment of monasteries'.[11] There are also various traits, most of them probably deliberatively imitative of Aldhelm's style, which are characteristic of Æthelwold's Latin prose:[12]

(a) numerous grecisms, as may be seen from the many examples taken from **IV** which are included in the Latin Word-List, below (e.g. *arcisterium* 'monastery', *brauium* 'reward', *cataclismas* 'the Flood', *macrobius* ?'long-lived one', *policrates* 'very mighty', *singrapha* 'document', *thema* 'theme', and *zabulus* 'the Devil').

(b) the use of rhymed prose, as in the following examples, the first of which is also patterned:
   IV, ii: *Fruebatur . . . tripudio . et . . . consortio / Non . . . inbecillitas . nec . . . anxietas / Non . . . superbię . sed . . . mirifice / Non . . . gloria . sed . . . memoria / Non . . . profectu . sed . . . amplexu / Non . . . infestus . sed . . . patientissimus / Non . . . deiciebat . sed . . . florebat / Non . . . cupidus . sed . . . largissimus / Non . . . edulio . sed . . . cibario / Non . . . nefaria . sed . . . premia /*
   IV, ix: *Nec inde euulsi . . . sed . . . conglutinati . . . perusti . . . priuati . . . anxii . . . compediti . . . perculsi . . . confusi . . . semoti . . .*
   IV, xiii: *eruditi . . . ocupati . . . letissimi . . . promtissimi . . . sincerissimi . . . fixi . . . decorati . . .*

(c) the use of alliteration. Here, this is only occasional, but the following phrases alliterating on the letter *c* may be noted:

---

[7] For discussions of this miniature, see Wormald, 'Late Anglo-Saxon Art', 23–6; J. J. G. Alexander, 'The Benedictional of St Aethelwold and Anglo-Saxon Illumination of the Reform Period', in David Parsons (ed.), *Tenth-Century Studies: Essays in Commemoration of the Millennium of the Council of Winchester and 'Regularis Concordia'* (London and Chichester, 1975), 169–83 (179–80); E. Temple, *Anglo-Saxon Manuscripts 900–1066* (London, 1976), no. 16; Robert Deshman, *The Benedictional of Æthelwold* (Studies in Manuscript Illumination 9, Princeton, 1995), 196–7, 226, and 232–3; Thomas H. Ohlgren, *Insular and Anglo-Saxon Illuminated Manuscripts: an Iconographic Catalogue c.A.D. 625 to 1100* (New York and London, 1986) 94; Keynes *Liber Vitae*, 26; and Richard Gameson, *The Role of Art in the Late Anglo-Saxon Church* (Oxford, 1995), 6–7.   [8] See Lapidge 'Hermeneutic Style'.
[9] See Wormald, 'Late Anglo-Saxon Art', 25; Dorothy White-

lock, 'The Authorship of the Account of King Edgar's Establishment of Monasteries', in J. L. Rosier (ed.), *Philological Essays: Studies in Old and Middle English Language and Literature in Honour of Herbert Dean Meritt* (The Hague, 1970), 125–36, at 131; and Lapidge 'Æthelwold as Scholar', 95–6.
[10] For parallels in *RC*, see below, **IV**, nn. 11, 44, 47, 50, 52–3, 58, 62, 69, 76–7, 83, 85, 88, 91, 96–8, and 121.
[11] For parallels in 'King Edgar's Establishment of Monasteries', see below, **IV**, nn. 37, 47, 50, 111, and 119. For a discussion of the purpose and style of this text, see Gretsch *Intellectual Foundations*, 121–4.
[12] See Lapidge 'Æthelwold as Scholar', 95–101; also Lapidge 'Hermeneutic Style', 126–8; and Wulfstan *Vita S. Æthelwoldi*, pp. lxxxix–xc. For the influence of Aldhelm on Æthelwold, see also Gretsch *Intellectual Foundations*, 125–30.

IV, iv: *contemnentes conditorem . a cunctis insequuntur creatis*
IV, vi: *Christi sanctorumque eius celo collocatus contubernio coronatus*
IV, xi: *creator cunctitenens clementer . . . lucupletet*

(d) the use of interlaced word-order or 'envelope patterns' in which nouns and their adjectives are divided by intervening words or phrases. This was a style favoured by Aldhelm and apparently copied by Æthelwold.[13] It occurs quite frequently in **IV** and in at least the following four ways:

  (i) the noun and adjective are separated by a noun or noun phrase in the genitive case:
  IV, prol.: *Omnipotens totius machinae conditor* and *aeternis baratri incendiis*
  IV, i: *lucidas cęlorum sedes*
  IV, v: *perpetuis baratri incendiis*
  IV, vi (heading): *de beniuolo regis meditamine*
  IV, vii: *e diuersis nostri regminis coenobiis* and *uariis uitiorum neuis*
  IV, xii: *pompaticas lasciuasque secularium delicias*
  IV, witness-list (Dunstan): *largifluam beniuoli regis donationem*
  Sometimes a clause contains a string of such occurrences:
  IV, i: *Euacuata namque polorum sede / et eliminata tumidi fastus spurcitia / summus totius bonitatis arbiter / lucidas cęlorum sedes / . . . formatis . . . diuersarum rerum speciebus /*
  IV, xix: *tranquillum uitę presentis excursum / longeuam instantis temporis uitam / futuram ęternae beatitudinis talionem / Sufficientem uictualium ubertatem / interminabile prosperitatis augm⟨en⟩tum / copiosum uirtutum omnium iuuamen /*

  (ii) the noun and adjective are separated by a verb, often in present participle form:
  IV, prol.: *libero utens arbitrio* and *contumaci arrogans fastu*
  IV, iv: *a cunctis insequuntur creatis*
  IV, v: *bonis insudantes operibus*
  IV, xv: *subtili protegens tutamine / robusto prelians triumpho*
  IV, xvi: *fortissimo roborans munimine* and *uisibiles expugnans aduersarios*
  IV, xx: *perpetua possideat miseria*

  (iii) there is a combination of types (i) and (ii) in **IV, xv**: *aerias demonum expugnans uersutias*

  (iv) pairs of nouns and adjectives are sometimes interlaced:
  IV, xv: *abbas . . . armis succinctus spiritalibus* and *a rabida hostium persecutione inuisibilium*

The document, whose practical purpose was to confirm the monks in their possession of the New Minster and its property while giving them guidance in the keeping of the Benedictine Rule, is of great interest in both internal and external form. Its text consists of three intertwined groups of material, each stemming from different roots. While both a series of conventional Anglo-Saxon diplomatic formulae and also statements of Benedictine monastic regulations and practice (see below) occur, the main theme of the document is an elaborate theological argument. Explicit parallels are intended to be drawn between the ejection of the secular canons and firstly the Fall of

---

[13] See Gretsch *Intellectual Foundations*, 127–8; also Andy Orchard, *The Poetic Art of Aldhelm* (Cambridge Studies in   Anglo-Saxon England 8, Cambridge, 1994), 10. Cf. **V**; see below, pp. 101–2.

the Lucifer and his Angels[14] and secondly the Fall of Adam and his ejection from Paradise,[15] all three acts of expulsion being presented as God's punishment for sins of disobedience committed through pride while in a position of privilege relative to Him. In contrast, the humility and obedience of the monastic life is described in a way that invites comparison with Adam's ordered existence whilst in Paradise,[16] before he succumbed to the plot laid by the Devil.[17] The events of 964–6 are thus given an eternal significance in a very powerful use of the hexaemeral tradition which directly or indirectly influenced the Anglo-Saxons of this period through the biblical commentaries of earlier writers such as Ambrose, Augustine of Hippo, Gregory the Great, Bede, and Alcuin.[18] The prose *Hexaemeron* of Ælfric, who had been educated at the Old Minster, came directly from this monastic exegetical context.[19] It is very probable, however, that only an ecclesiastic of the status of Bishop Æthelwold or Archbishop Dunstan would have dared to use such religious themes in this way to underpin the monastic cause. Given the location of the New Minster, adjacent to the cathedral at Winchester, the similarities to other writings attributed to Æthelwold, and the wording of his subscription,[20] it is much more likely to have been Æthelwold than Dunstan who was responsible for the composition of the present text.

Some of the diplomatic formulae used in **IV**[21] are also found in original diplomas of King Edgar written by the scribe known as 'Edgar A',[22] one of which (S 690) was in favour of Abingdon Abbey while Æthelwold was abbot there. It has been suggested that Æthelwold drafted another of these diplomas (S 687)[23] and it is possible that he also drafted the remainder, thus explaining the similarities between them and the present text. There are also similarities of wording to **V**, below, associated with the re-establishment of the Old Minster, Æthelwold's cathedral church, but which was probably composed later than **IV**.[24] Some textual features that are used in **IV** also appear in diplomas of the so-called '*Orthodoxorum*' group but it is likely that this coincidence is due either to a common source or to the use of **IV** itself as a model for parts of the text of documents in that group.[25]

Some passages in **IV** reflect a familiarity with the Benedictine Rule[26] and with certain acts of the synod of Aachen that modified it in 816.[27] However, the draftsman of **IV** (?Æthelwold) prefers the

---

[14] Compare below, **IV, prol.** with **IV, ix.**

[15] Compare below, **IV, iii–iv** with **IV, ix.**

[16] Compare below, **IV, xii** with **IV, ii.**

[17] See below, **IV, iii.**

[18] Ambrose, *Hexaemeron* (ed. Karl Schenkl, CSEL 32.1 (Vienna, 1897), 3–261) and *De paradiso* (ibid. 265–336), see also 'Ambrose as Theologian', in F. Homes Dudden, *The Life and Times of St. Ambrose*, (Oxford, 1935), 555–677; Augustine, *De Genesi ad litteram* (ed. Joseph Zycha, CSEL 28.1 (Vienna, 1894), 3–435), also *De civitate Dei* (eds. Bernard Dombart and Alphonse Kalb, CCSL 47–8 (Turnhout, 1955)), cf. below, **IV**, nn. 6, 9, 14–15; Gregory the Great, *Moralia in Iob* (ed. Mark Adriaen, CCSL 143, 143A and B (Turnhout, 1979–85), cf. below, **IV**, n.15); Bede, *Commentarius in Genesim* (ed. Ch. W. Jones, CCSL 118A (Turnhout, 1987)); and Alcuin, *Quaestiones in Genesim* (ed. J. P. Migne, *Patrologia Latina* 100 (Paris, 1863), 516–66). For an important survey of the hexaemeral tradition, see Frank Egleston Robbins, *The Hexaemeral Literature: a Study of the Greek and Latin Commentaries on Genesis* (Chicago, 1912).

[19] See S. J. Crawford (ed.), *Exameron Anglice or The Old English Hexameron*, Bibliothek der angelsächsischen Prosa 10 (Hamburg, 1921). For a brief introduction to Ælfric's life and works, see Jonathan Wilcox (ed.), *Ælfric's Prefaces*, Durham Medieval Texts

9 (Durham, 1994), 1–64. Interest in hexaemeral material is of course evident in the Old English poetry, particularly 'Genesis A', 'Genesis B', and 'Christ and Satan'; see Malcolm Godden, 'Biblical Literature: The Old Testament', in Malcolm Godden and Michael Lapidge (ed.), *The Cambridge Companion ito Old English Literature* (Cambridge, 1991), 206–26, especially 206–16.

[20] In which he refers to his pupils; see below, **IV, witness-list.**

[21] Diplomatic clauses in **IV**, may be discerned as follows: pictorial invocation (chrismon) and verbal invocation (**prol.**); superscription (**vi**); exposition (**vi–vii**); dispositive section (**viii**); immunity clause and appurtenances (**xvii**); reservation clause (**xxi**); prohibition clause (**xviii**); sanctions (**ix, x, xx**, and the final clause of **witness-list**); blessings (**xi** and **xix**); date; and witness-list. The rubric is also formulaic, see below, **IV**, n. 1.

[22] See below, **IV**, nn. 13, 16, 65, 115, 122, and 125; also above, p. 15. S 690 and 703 (*BCS* 1066 and 1082) have the same proem, using the theme of the Creation and the Fall of Man.

[23] See Lapidge 'Æthelwold as Scholar', 94–5.

[24] See below, pp. 101, 103.

[25] See below, **IV**, nn. 16 and 69.

[26] Ibid. nn. 58, 63, 69, 76–7, 83–6, 88, 91, 94, 97, 105, 118, and 120.

[27] Ibid. nn. 83, and 89–90

practice subsequently laid down by Benedict of Aniane in 818 / ?819 to that of the said synod in relation to the entertainment of ecclesiastical and noble guests at table.[28] Another influence of monastic texts on **IV** is the division into numbered chapters and the wording of the chapter-headings; there are echoes here in particular of the *Memoriale qualiter*, the late-eighth-century text apparently popularized by Benedict of Aniane, a new manuscript of which was later copied at Abingdon.[29] As noted above, there are also connections with the *Regularis Concordia* (of which the *Memoriale qualiter* was an important source), from England itself.

The text of **IV** in MS. A appears originally to have constituted a small parchment book (*c*.220 × 160 mm.) containing at least 32 folios,[30] and splendidly written throughout in gold ink. Other folios (34–43), of thicker parchment, were added to the original codex in the twelfth and fourteenth centuries so that the manuscript now contains ii + 43 + i.[31] There is a seventeenth-century table of contents on fo. 1^v.

The present binding is a modern (British Museum) style but there are some signs of a previous one, apparently with wooden boards, indicated by a grained offlay on the rear sides of what appear to be former pastedowns, now bound respectively before the (?original) flyleaf in front of fo. 1, and after fo. 43 of the volume as it now exists. That these boards were covered in some form of metal, affixed to them by nails, is suggested by a series of small holes with discolouration around them which may be seen around the external edges of each of the former pastedowns and the flyleaf, mentioned above, as well as on the later medieval fo. 43. The original collation is now difficult to retrieve, due not only to the tightness of the modern binding, but also to the loss of some folios after fo. 29, as is suggested by loss of text after the heading to **IV, xxii**. The number of lost folios may be four, since there is an early modern (?s. xvi) note *summa xlviij* on the second of the two pastedowns mentioned above. If this is a note of the foliation, and if the two pastedowns were still performing their original function and were not counted, then at that time there were still 48 folios in the manuscript, that is the currently ink-foliated 1–43 plus the unfoliated original flyleaf plus four other folios. Since, as noted above, fo. 43 bears similar nail-marks to the original pastedowns, it is probable that nothing is missing after it, but rather that all the folios have been lost internally after fo. 29.

The following description is concerned primarily with the original Anglo-Saxon codex (surviving as fos. 1–33) containing the text of **IV**. Palaeographical details of the texts on the added folios will be found in the discussion of **XVI**, below.

Apart from fos. 2^{rv}, 3^r, and 13^r which are not ruled, and fos. 3^v and 13^v which are, ruling occurs on the recto side only of leaves, apparently having been done after folding of the sheet. Ruling is in hard point, with two pairs of vertical bounding lines and either horizontal lines ruled only within a small framed area (fos. 3^v, 4^r), or 16 (fos. 5–12), 14 (fos. 13–29), or 15 horizontal rulings (fos. 30–3). The text throughout is arranged in single column in accordance with the above ruling; initial capital letters to clauses are offset, being placed within the left pair of vertical bounding lines.

After the present fo. 2^r which is blank (apart from a British Museum stamp), the beginning of the document is marked by some pages of decoration and majuscules. On fo. 2^v appears a full-page

[28] Ibid. **IV, xii**, and n. 87.
[29] Ibid. n. 75.
[30] For (?four) folios lost after fo. 29, see below.

[31] These additional folios contain texts of S 746 (twice; a spurious diploma of King Edgar granting to the New Minster lands in Sussex and Wiltshire), and of **XVI**, below.

illuminated miniature which shows in its lower register King Edgar, crowned[32] and bearded, flanked by the Virgin Mary and St. Peter the patron saints of the New Minster, who stand here as the king's intercessors; Edgar humbly offers up a book, presumably the refoundation codex, to Christ in the upper register, who is seated in majesty immediately above the king and is holding the Book of Life, within a gold mandorla supported by four flying angels.[33] It is probable that Edgar is here pictured as the 'vicar of Christ', the role accorded to him in one section of the text (**IV, vii**). The whole scene is contained within a 'Winchester-Style' frame made of two illuminated rectangles intertwined with acanthus leaves, while the parchment on this page has been stained to give a purple (now pink) background. Fo. 3[r] contains a piece of Latin verse, written in gold uncial letters, whose composition, it has been suggested, mirrors that of the miniature on the opposite side of the opening.[34] The verse reads:

SIC CELSO RESIDET SOLIO QUI CONDIDIT ASTRA
   REX VENERANS EADGAR PRONUS ADORAT EUM

THUS HE WHO FASHIONED THE STARS SITS ON A LOFTY THRONE;
   KING EDGAR, INCLINED IN REVERENCE, WORSHIPS HIM.

This represents an elegiac distich whose first word (*sic*) links it to the painting opposite. The first line is a hexameter describing Christ as shown in heavenly majesty, while the second line is a pentameter describing Edgar's terrestrial attitude. The verse is thought to be the only surviving example of Æthelwold's Latin poetry.[35] Its language has been said to suggest a familiarity with the poetry of Prudentius, and perhaps that of Vergil, Sedulius, and Avitus.[36]

It may be remarked that the whole scene depicted in the miniature is reminiscent of a passage in the (later) *Regularis Concordia*, with which Æthelwold was also involved: 'the bishops, abbots and abbesses were not slow in raising their hands to heaven in hearty thanksgiving to the throne above'.[37]

---

[32] Edgar is shown wearing the so-called 'lily crown'. A royal crown, rather than a diadem, first appears on coins in the reign of Æthelstan; see C. E. Blunt, 'The Coinage of Æthelstan, 924–939, a Survey', *British Numismatic Journal* 42 (1974), 57, 65–6. The same king is shown wearing a rather angular crown in the presentation miniature on fo. 1[v] of CCCC, MS. 183 (934 × 939); see Mildred Budny, *Insular, Anglo-Saxon, and Early Anglo-Norman Manuscript Art at Corpus Christi College, Cambridge* (2 vols., Kalamazoo, 1997), i, p. 176, and ii, Plate IV. A crown is first mentioned in the coronation liturgy in the second Anglo-Saxon *ordo* (?late 9th / early 10th cent.), whose revised 'B' version contains a coronation oath and is possibly to be connected with the consecration of Edgar *c.* 960; see Janet L. Nelson, 'The Second English *Ordo*', in *Politics and Ritual in Early Medieval Europe* (London and Ronceverte, 1986), 361–74, especially 369–72. Note, however, that the Benedictional of Archbishop Robert, containing the 'B' version, is dated to 'not before the second quarter of the eleventh century' by David N. Dumville, *Liturgy and the Ecclesiastical History of Late Anglo-Saxon England* (Woodbridge, 1992), 87. For the significance of the king's crown as a symbol of 'his virtuous acts of rulership in this life which will enable him to win the crown of eternal rulership with the heavenly monarch', see Robert Deshman, 'Benedictus Monarcha et

Monachus: Early Medieval Ruler Theology and the Anglo-Saxon Reform', *Frühmittelalterliche Studien* 22 (1988), 204–40, at 226. For the effect of crown symbolism on word-usage at Winchester at this time, see Gretsch *Intellectual Foundations*, 98–104 and 297–304.

[33] See Frontispiece. For discussions of the iconography and date of the miniature, see above, n. 7. The intercessory role of St. Peter and the Virgin Mary was developed by Deshman, *Benedictional of Æthelwold*, 196–7.

[34] See E. C. Teviotdale, 'Latin Verse Inscriptions in Anglo-Saxon Art', *Gesta* 35 (1996), 99–110, at 101.

[35] Lapidge 'Æthelwold as Scholar', 96. See also Gretsch *Intellectual Foundations*, 309–10, who suggests that *rex* could refer both to Christ and to Edgar in order to 'point up in a subtle way the dual notion of Christ as king and of the king as *imago Christi*.'   [36] Lapidge, 'Æthelwold as Scholar', 96, n. 53.

[37] . . . *non tantum episcopi, uerum etiam abbates ac abbatissae . . . erectis ad aethera palmis inmensas celsithrono grates uoti compotes referre non distulerunt.* Cf. Aldhelm, *De virginitate* (prose) 1 (ed. Rudolf Ehwald, Monumenta Germaniae Historica, Auctores Antiquissimi 15 (Berlin, 1919), 229): *erectis ad aethera palmis immensas Christo pro sospitate vestra gratulabundus impendere grates curavi.*

Fo. 3ᵛ contains, within a gold, green, and dark blue rectangular frame and on a light blue ground, the text of the rubric to **IV**, written in gold mixed square capital and uncial letters.

Fo. 4ʳ (on the opposite side of the opening to 3ᵛ) contains, within a similar frame but on an uncoloured ground, a green-panelled gold chrismon followed by the first four words of the text of **IV** (*Omnipotens totius machinae conditor*), written in gold square capitals, including a letter *H* with decorative cross-bar.

Fos. 4v-33v contain the rest of the refoundation charter, written throughout in gold. After the prologue, the document is subdivided into chapters and these are numbered, roman numerals being placed in the left margin opposite the first line of the opening words of each chapter. The first word of each chapter begins with a large initial letter. Within chapters there is some subdivision by means of paragraphos marks in the left margins, and also by the offsetting of the first word of clauses by placing initial letters within the left pair of vertical bounding lines. In the witness-list (fos. 30v-32v) there are *signa crucis* against names, only a few of which have been completed in gold, the remainder being indicated in outline either in ordinary ink or in drypoint.

The twenty-two chapter-headings and the initial letters to clauses are in uncial script, while the remainder of the writing is in English Caroline minuscule of the Abingdon and Winchester type designated Style I by T. A. M. Bishop.[38] The latter suggested it was written by an Abingdon scribe,[39] but as Simon Keynes has noted, it is equally possible, in view of Æthelwold's role as draftsman of the text, that the manuscript was written at the Old Minster, recently filled with monks from Abingdon.[40]

There is a reduction in the size of the writing at fo. 30ʳ, where the witness-list begins, and this reduced size continues to the end of the document, including the sanction on on fo. 33ʳᵛ. The change in size is aided by an increase in the number of ruled horizontal lines from 14 to 15 on the rectos of fos. 30–33. These changes might suggest that the dating-clause, witness-list and final sanction were added to the manuscript at a slightly later date than the main text, after a confirmation of the contents by the king and his counsellors. The later loss of folios at this point, i.e. after fo. 29 (see above), appears to be coincidental.

One scribe was responsible for writing the text as far the last quarter of the witness-list, when he was replaced by another whose hand admits some insular minuscule letter-forms. The first scribe[41] uses a decorative form of spurred *e*, a letter *t* in which the crossbar is occasionally a little below the top of the vertical stroke, and sometimes, but not always, uses ligatures of *c* + *t* (*doctrinis* fo. 13ʳ, line 1), *r* + *t* (*exortatus* fo. 12ᵛ, foot), and *s* + *t* (in *iustissime* fo. 11ᵛ, line 10, but not in *mastigia* fo. 18ʳ, line 10). In vernacular name-forms within the witness-list he avoided the use of *þ*, making use of *ð* instead. He uses the ampersand for *et* within words in initial, medial or final position (*eternum* fo. 11ᵛ, line 8; *pietate* fo. 4ᵛ, line 1; *fugaret* fo. 10ʳ, line 8). For the abbreviation of *-que* he uses [q.] and for *-bus* he uses either [b.] or (fos. 15ʳ, 19ᵛ) [b;]. His overline abbreviation symbol for *-us* often resembles a reversed *c* (*eius* and *primus* fo. 30ʳ, line 11).

Punctuation is by the *punctus simplex*, high at the end of chapters and clauses but elsewhere low. It is occasionally absent.

Besides some scribal interlineations and corrections in gold ink (*tristiˋtiˊa* fo. 7ʳ; *ASˋCˊENDERET* fo. 8ʳ; *cruciˋaˊtus* fo. 28ʳ; *hˋuˊius* and ˋinibiˊ fo. 30ʳ; *concors* fo. 22ᵛ, corrected from *consors*), there are also

---

[38] *English Caroline Minuscule* (Oxford, 1971), xxi–ii.   [40] Keynes *Liber Vitae*, 28.
[39] Ibid. xxi, n. 1.   [41] See Plate I.

corrections in a reddish ink (*r`e´pleta* fo. 10ᵛ; *uariis* fo. 14r, corrected from *uicariis*). Some errors remain, however, particularly due to accidental omission of the overline abbreviation-mark (*MOCHOS* fo. 24ᵛ, for *MONACHOS* ; *augmtum* fo. 27ʳ, for *augmentum*; and *omium* fo. 30ʳ, for *omnium*). The form *in ciuitatę* fo. 20ᵛ, for *in ciuitate*, is also presumably due to the copyist's lack of concentration rather than to a grammatical error in the draft.

Word division is very irregular. Some errors occur (*superbiatur gente* fo. 6ʳ, for *superbia turgente*; and *qua esuo* fo. 10ʳ, for *quae suo*).

Peculiarities of orthography include the use of -*ncx* for -*nx* (*coniuncx* in **IV, witness-list**), and *exs*- for *ex*- (*exsecutura* **IV, i**, *exstra* **IV, xii**, and *exstraneam* **IV, xiv**).[42] The letters *ae* and *e* and spurred *e* are all found in use for the classical diphthong *ae* (*aeternis* fo. 5ʳ, *eternis* fo. 25ᵛ, and *ęternae* fo. 27ʳ). The word *ecclesia* is spelt with a similar variation between *ae, e* and *ę* and normally here with a single -*c*- (*aeclesiae* fo. 31ʳ, *aeclesie* fo. 17ᵛ, *ęclesiae* fos. 14ᵛ and 15ᵛ, *ęclesię* fos. 30ᵛ and 31ʳᵛ). Insular Latin -*ss*- for -*s*- occurs in *parssimoniae* fo. 20ʳ.

The second scribe writes only on fos. 32ᵛ–33ᵛ, adding the names of the last ten witnesses and the final sanction. He began his work with the name of Ealdorman Æthelwine. (The whole column of *Ego*s on fo. 32v appears to be by the first scribe however.) The hand of the second scribe is characterized by the occasional use of insular minuscule forms for *a* and *f* within names, and the use of þ as well as ð. There are wedged ascenders on *b, d, h, l*, and þ The letter *g* has a closed descender (*priuilegio regis* fo. 33ʳ). There is no reason to think that the second scribe was not a contemporary of the first.[43]

As noted above, the codex was added to in the twelfth and fourteenth centuries. It was evidently in Hyde Abbey at the date of MS. B, below. After the dissolution of the monasteries it eventually found its way into the library of Sir Robert Cotton, explaining its modern location in the British Library.

MS. B, the *Liber (abbatiae) de Hyda* includes a text of **IV** copied from A, which is complete apart from the non-addition of decorated initials at the beginning of chapters and clauses. MS. C is Sir Henry Spelman's transcript, preparatory to the edition in his *Concilia* (1639–64) from B, which MS. he then owned.[44]

The text in MS. D is an extract containing only **IV, vi**, copied from by Richard James from A, after it had reached the Cottonian Library. James classicized spellings, giving forms such as *admonuit* for *ammonuit*, *ædificans* for *edificans*, *cælo* for *celo*, *præmia* for *premia*, and *regiminis* for *regminis*.

The earliest printed edition, that of John Selden (1623) omitted the preliminary distich, the prologue, and caps. i–v, which he considered irrelevant to the document's purpose.[45]

---

[42] Cf. *exsecutor* for *executor* in **III**, above (q.v., n. 3).

[43] Note, however, that Keynes *Liber Vitae*, 27, n. 112, regards only the final sanction to be by a second scribe, whom he dates to the late 10th cent.   [44] See Keynes ibid. 74.

[45] *Eadmeri monachi Cantuariensis Historiæ Novorum . . .*, 154:

Præfatione ad illius æui morem satis turgidâ (quæ aliquot paginas occupat nec tamen ad rem omnino facit) hic prætermissa . . . ['The preceding matter has here been omitted, which, in the custom of that period (is) extremely inflated, occupying several pages but not doing anything in relation to the matter . . .'].

MSS.:   A. BL, Cotton MS. Vesp. A. viii, fos. 3^v–33^v (s. x^2)

               B. Earl of Macclesfield, Shirburn Castle, *Liber (abbatiae) de Hyda*, fos. 27^r–29^v (s.xiv/xv), from A

               C. Bod, Eng. hist. c. 242, fos. 76^r–83^v (s. xvii^1), from B

               D. Bod, James MS. 10, pp. 14–15 (s. xviii^1; incomplete), from A

Facsimiles: *Pal. Soc.*, 1st series, iv, Pls. 46–7; from A (fos. 2^v, and 11^v)

               Keynes *Liber Vitae*, Pls. I–IV; from A (fos. 2^v, 3^{rv}, and 4^r)

               See also Frontispiece, and below, Pl. I; from A (fos. 2^v and 19^v)

Edited: John Selden (ed.), *Eadmeri monachi Cantuariensis historiæ novorum siue sui sæculi libri vi* (London, 1623), 154–60, from A (incomplete)

               Spelman *Concilia*, i, 435–42, from B

               M. Alford, *Fides regia Anglicana sive annales ecclesiæ Anglicanæ*, iii (Liège, 1663), 343–7, from Spelman

               Wilkins *Concilia*, i, 240–4, from Spelman

               Monasticon, ii, 439–41 (no. 7), from A

               KCD 527, from A

               LH, 192–202, from B collated to A

               BCS 1190, from A

               LVH, 232–46, from A

               Councils, i, 119–33 (no. 31), from A collated to B

               Miller *New Minster* 23, from A collated with B

Printed from A

[a][1] + EADGAR[2] REX HOC PRIUILEGIUM NOUO EDIDIT MONASTERIO AC OMNIPOTENTI DOMINO EIUSQUE GENITRICI MARIĘ [b] EIUS LAUDANS MAGNALIA CONCESSIT .[c]

[3] ☧ OMNIPOTENS TOTIVS MACHINAE CONDITOR[d] ineffabili pietate uniuersa mirifice moderatur quę condidit .

Qui coaeterno uidelicet uerbo quaedam ex nichilo[4] edidit . quaedam ex informi subtilis artifex propagauit materia .[5]

Angelica quippe creatura ut informis materia . nullis rebus existentibus diuinitus formata . luculento resplenduit uultu .

Male pro dolor libero utens arbitrio .[6] contumaci

[1]+ KING EDGAR[2] PROMULGATED THIS PRIVILEGE FOR THE NEW MINSTER AND GRANTED IT TO THE ALMIGHTY LORD AND HIS MOTHER MARY, PRAISING HIS GREAT WORKS.

[3] ☧ THE ALMIGHTY CREATOR OF THE WHOLE SCHEME OF THINGS guides marvellously with ineffable love everything which He has created.

He, through the co-eternal Word, so to speak, formed certain things 'out of nothing'[4] and, like a fine craftsman, created certain other things out of shapeless matter.[5]

An angelic creation indeed, as shapeless matter given shape by divine influence when no [other] things existed, it was resplendent with a bright countenance.

Alas, making bad use of its free will,[6] assuming

---

[a] *The text given here begins at fo. 3ᵛ in A. It is preceded there by a full-page illuminated miniature (fo. 2ᵛ) showing King Edgar offering up the refoundation codex to Christ who is seated in majesty. See further, above, Frontispiece and p. 70. Facing the miniature, on fo. 3ʳ, is written the following explanatory elegiac distich, on which see above, ibid.:* SIC CELSO RESIDET SOLIO QUI CONDIDIT ASTRA | REX VENERANS EADGAR PRONUS ADORAT EUM | THUS HE WHO FASHIONED THE STARS SITS ON A LOFTY THRONE; | KING EDGAR, INCLINED IN REVERENCE, WORSHIPS HIM.   [b] MARIÆ, *in error,* Councils, *i, 121*
[c] + EADGAR . . . CONCESSIT *written on a light blue ground within an illuminated rectangle on fo. 3ᵛ*   [d] ☧...CONDITOR *written within an illuminated rectangle on fo. 4ʳ. The words* OMNIPOTENS . . . CONDITOR *are in square capital letters, unlike the other majuscule letters in the text, which are uncials.*

---

[1] **IV, rubric.** The introductory rubric states the name of the donor, those of the beneficiaries, and the nature of the grant. The same three elements are found in the short descriptive vernacular endorsements on royal diplomas of the period.

[2] *EADGAR.* Born 943, the son of King Edmund; king of Mercia 957–9, of England 959–75. For his education by Bishop Æthelwold, see below, nn. 134 and 135.

[3] **IV, prologue.** After a pictorial invocation in the form of a chrismon, and a general statement of God's power, the prologue describes how God created Lucifer and his fellow angels and how sin first came into existence through their pride and arrogant disobedience, causing their Fall into Hell. Unlike subsequent sections of the present document, the prologue is not numbered as a chapter, possibly to emphasize the occurrence of the events it describes in a period before the existence of Man. Although not fully described in canonical books of the Bible (but cf. Isa. 14: 12–15, Rev. 12: 9, and 2 Pet. 2: 4), the story of the creation and Fall of the Angels is drawn from hexaemeral material which ultimately goes back to Jewish attempts to square the references in Isa. 14: 12–15 with the non-mention of angels in Gen. 1–3. For example, the 2nd cent. B.C. apocalyptic book of Jubilees (2: 2) inserts angels into the narrative of the Creation; see

O. S. Wintermute (trans.), 'Jubilees', in James H. Charlesworth (ed.), *The Old Testament Pseudepigrapha* (2 vols, London, 1983–5), ii, 35–142, at 55. Elsewhere, some other apocalyptic texts (such as the late 1st cent. A.D. Slavonic 2 Enoch (29: 4–5); trans F. I. Anderson in Charlesworth (ed.), *Old Testament Pseudepigrapha,* i, 91–221, at 148) or non-biblical ones (such as the Koran, suras 2, 7, 15, 17–18, 20, and 38; trans. E. H. Palmer (Oxford, 1938)) refer to the Fall of Lucifer / Satan and his colleagues; see refs. given by M. D. Johnson in Charlesworth (ed.), *Old Testament Pseudepigrapha,* ii, 262n. For Anglo-Saxon knowledge of Jubilees, see *SASLC: Trial Version,* 25.

[4] *ex nichilo.* Cf. 2 Macc. 7: 28 (*BSV,* ii, 1494) *peto nate aspicias in caelum et terram et ad omnia quae in eis sunt et intellegas quia ex nihilo fecit illa Deus et hominum genus* 'I beseech thee, my son, look upon heaven and earth, and all that is in them: and consider that God made them out of nothing, and mankind also.'

[5] *ex informi . . . materia.* Cf. Wisd. 11: 18 (*BSV,* ii, 1015) *omnipotens manus tua quae creauit orbem terrarum ex materia invisa* 'thy almighty hand, which made the world of matter without form'.

[6] *libero . . . arbitrio.* Lucifer was given primal freedom in the same way that Adam was later. Both exercised it badly through disobedience to the Creator. The doctrine of Adam's primal freedom and of Man's free will (to sin or not) was fully developed by Augustine of Hippo in the late 4th–early 5th cents.; see Henry Bettenson, *The Later Christian Fathers: a Selection from the Writings of the Fathers from St. Cyril of Jerusalem to St. Leo the Great* (London, 1970), 24–7, 195, and 206–8. Cf. Augustine, *De Genesi ad litteram* 7: 26 (ed. Joseph Zycha, CSEL 28.1 (Vienna, 1894), 224: *Natura quippe hominis ex deo est, non iniquitas, qua se ipse inuoluit male utendo libero arbitrio* ['Man's substance indeed, not his wickedness, came from God, because he involved himself in badly exercising free will'].

arrogans fastu .[7] creatori uniuersitatis famu-
lari dedignans . semetipsum creatori
equiperans . aeternis baratri incendiis cum
suis complicibus demersus . iugi merito
cruciatur miseria .[8]

Hoc itaque themate totius sceleris peccatum
exorsum est .[9]

I [.][10] QUARE HOMINEM CONDIDIT ET
QUID EI COMMISIT .

Euacuata namque polorum sede . et eliminata
tumidi fastus spurcitia .[11] summus totius
bonitatis arbiter lucidas cęlorum sedes non
sine cultore passus torpere[e] . formatis ex
informi materia diuersarum rerum
speciebus . hominem tandem ex limo
conditum . uitę spiraculo ad sui formauit[12]
similitudinem .

Cui uniuersa totius cosmi superficie condita[13]
subiciens . seipsum suosque posteros sibi
subiecit . quatenus eius exsecutura posteritas
angelorum suppleret numerum celorum sedibus[14] superbia turgente[f] detrusum .

---

[e] torpore, *in error*, Councils, *i, 121*   [f] superbiatur gente
MS. *This erroneous word-division was subsequently corrected by a much
later scribe*

---

[7] *contumaci arrogans fastu.* Cf. below, **IV, ix** and n. 62, *fastu
superbientes arrogantię*, applied to the canons ejected from the
New Minster.

[8] *aeternis . . . miseria.* Cf. below, n. 65.

[9] *totius sceleris peccatum exorsum est.* Cf. Ecclus. 10: 15 (*BSV*, ii,
1041) *quoniam initium peccati omnis superbia* 'for pride is the
beginning of all sin'. Cf. Augustine, *De Genesi ad litteram* 11: 14
(ed. Joseph Zycha, CSEL 28.1 (Vienna, 1894), 346): . . . *nonnulli
enim dicunt ipsum ei fuisse casum a supernis sedibus, quod inuiderit
homini facto ad imaginem dei. porro autem inuidia sequitur superbiam,
non praecedit* . . . ['. . . for many people say that he (Lucifer) fell
from the heavenly dwellings because he envied Man being made
in God's image, but on the contrary envy followed pride, it did
not precede it']. For Gregory the Great's doctrine on the nature
of pride, see below, n. 15.

[10] **IV, i.** This chapter describes God's creation of Man,
intended with his descendants eventually to replace the fallen
angels as inhabitants of Heaven.

[11] *eliminata . . . spurcitia.* Cf. below, **IV, vi** (*agens Christo faciente
in terris quod ipse iuste egit in celis . extricans uidelicet domini cultura
criminum spurcitias*) and **IV, x** (*uitiorum spurcitias expurgans*), in
reference to the canons ejected from the New Minster and
elsewhere. See also below, **V, ii** *pro . . . detestandis spurcitiis inde
eliminatos* and **V, xiv** *eliminata immundorum spurcicia*, in reference

---

with stubborn arrogance,[7] disdaining to serve
the Creator of the Universe, placing itself
equal to the Creator, it plunged into the
eternal fires of the Abyss with its confederates, and is deservedly tormented with perpetual misery.[8]

The sin of all wickedness also arose from this
same theme.[9]

i.[10] WHY HE CREATED MAN AND WHAT
HE ENTRUSTED TO HIM.

When indeed the abode of Heaven had been
emptied, and the filth of swollen pride had
been put out of doors,[11] the Supreme Judge of
All Goodness did not allow the bright dwellings of Heaven to remain still without an
inhabitant; having shaped diverse species of
beings from shapeless matter, He at length
shaped Man out of clay, created with the
breath of life in His own likeness.[12]

Subjecting all created things on the surface of
the whole universe[13] to Man, He subjected
Man and his progeny to Himself, until his
descendants to come should make good the
number of angels driven out, full of pride,
from the dwellings of Heaven.[14]

---

to the canons of the Old Minster; and *eliminatis clericorum neniis et
spurcis lasciviis* in S 731, *BCS* 1135, referring to the secular clergy
at Worcester Cathedral. The words *eiectisque neglegentium clericorum spurcitiis* are also used in *RC*, cap. 2, in relation to the
general replacement of secular clergy by monks in the English
monasteries. Cf. also *eliminata omni spurcitia*, used by Bede in
referring to the conversion of the Pantheon at Rome into a
Christian church (Santa Maria Rotunda) by Pope Boniface IV in
609; see B. Colgrave and R. A. B. Mynors (ed.), *Bede's Ecclesiastical
History of the English People* (Oxford, 1969), 148 (ii. 4).

[12] *hominem . . . ex limo conditum. uitę spiraculo . . . formauit.* Cf.
Gen. 2: 7 (*BSV*, i, 6) *formavit igitur Dominus Deus hominem de limo
terrae et inspiravit in faciem eius spiraculum vitae* . . . 'And the Lord
God formed man of the slime of the earth: and breathed into his
face the breath of life . . .'. Portions of the clay from which God
made Adam were reputed to be among relics at Christ Church,
Canterbury and at Tynemouth priory in the medieval period; see
I. G. Thomas, 'The Cult of Saints' Relics in Medieval England'
(unpublished, London Ph. D. thesis, 1975), 342, 348, 356. Cf. also
below, **IX**, n. 1.

[13] *totius cosmi superficie condita.* A related phrase, *totius cosmi
fabricae conditor*, is used in S 690 and 703, royal diplomas written
by 'Edgar A'; see above, pp. 15 and 68.

[14] *quatenus eius exsecutura posteritas angelorum suppleret numerum*

II [.]¹⁵ QUALITER IN PARADISO SINE CRIM-
   INE CONUERSATUS SIT .

Qui paradisiacae uoluptatis amenitate locatus .¹⁶
   nullius rei patiebatur dispendium . sed ei
   totius mundi ad uotum subpeditabat facultas .

Totius namque bonitatis ubertate fruenti . nulla
   ei res infesta resistebat .

Quippe altithrono deuote obsequenti . creatura
   cuncta famulabatur subiecta .

Fruebatur letabundus creatoris tripudio . et
   angelorum alacriter utebatur consortio [.]

Non eum corporalis debilitabat inbecillitas . nec
   animi affligebat anxietas .

Non typo leuis raptabatur superbię . sed suo se
   coniungens auctori . humilis pollebat mirifice .

Non eum inanis tumidum uexabat gloria . sed
   deuotum creatoris magnificabat memoria .

Non inuidia eum alieno torquebat profectu . sed
   caritatis iugiter letabatur amplexu .

Non ira cruciabatur infestus . sed caritatis
   tranquillitate leniebatur patientissimus .

Non eum tristi'ti'a merore deiciebat . sed gaudii
   spiritalis spe pollente florebat .

ii.¹⁵ IN WHAT WAY HE SHOULD HAVE
   LIVED IN PARADISE WITHOUT
   REPROACH.

Man, having been placed in the delight of
paradisiac beauty,¹⁶ endured the lack of no
thing, but the abundance of the whole world
supplied everything he required..

While indeed he enjoyed the copiousness of all
goodness, no hostile thing opposed him.

Indeed, while he submitted faithfully to the
High-throned One, all Creation waited subject upon him.

Full of gladness he enjoyed the Creator's jubilation, and happily received the fellowship of
the angels.

Bodily weakness did not disable him, nor did
anxiety of mind weaken him.

He was not ravaged by the vanity of petty pride,
but, uniting with his Maker, he flourished
marvellously in humility.

Vainglory did not make him swollen with pride,
but memory of the Creator made him more
devoted.

Envy did not torture him with its hostile effect,
but he was made joyful in perpetuity by the
embrace of charity.

He was not tormented, disturbed by anger, but,
most patient, was soothed by the calmness of
affection.

Sadness did not cast him down with lamentation, but he flourished in the potent hope of
spiritual joy.

celorum sedibus. For this notion, see Augustine, *De civitate Dei* 22: 1 (ed. Bernard Dombart and Alphonse Kalb, CCSL 48 (Turnhout, 1955), 807). Cf. below, n. 21.

¹⁵ **IV, ii**. This chapter describes Man's happy existence in Paradise before his expulsion. Cf. Augustine, *De Genesi ad litteram* 11: 18 (ed. Joseph Zycha, CSEL 28.1 (Vienna, 1894), 351): *quanto magis ergo et ampliore modo beatus erat homo in paradiso ante peccatum. quamuis incertus futuri sui casus* . . . ['indeed how much more and to what greater extent was Man blessed in Paradise before sin, since he was ignorant of his coming Fall . . .']. A parallel is here intended with the life of the monks described below in **IV, xii**. The text between *Fruebatur* and *premia* is in rhyming half-lines and is perhaps the earliest surviving example of rhyming Latin prose from Anglo-Saxon England; see Lapidge 'Æthelwold as Scholar', 95. Cf. above, p. 66. Specific contrasts are made in this chapter between vices (*adversa*) and virtues (*uirtutes*), e.g. pride / humility, envy / charity, avarice / generosity, and luxury / continence. The order here of the seven cardinal vices (vanity, envy, anger, sadness (*tristitia*), avarice, gluttony, and luxury) is the same as that used in his treatment of them as subdivisions of pride (*superbia*) by Gregory, *Moralia in Iob* 31: 45 (ed. Mark Adriaen, CCSL 143B (Turnhout, 1985), 1610). Gregory reduced the number of vices from eight (of Evagrius and Cassian) to seven by a process of amalgamation; see Owen Chadwick, *John Cassian* (2nd edn., Cambridge, 1968), 94–5.

¹⁶ *paradisiacae uoluptatis amenitate locatus.* Cf. Gen. 2: 8 and 15 (*BSV*, i, 6) *plantaverat autem Dominus Deus paradisum voluptatis a principio in quo posuit hominem quem formaverat* 'And the Lord God had planted a paradise of pleasure from the beginning: wherein he placed man whom he had formed', and *tulit ergo Dominus Deus hominem et posuit eum in paradiso voluptatis* . . . 'And the Lord God took man, and put him into the paradise of pleasure'. A related phrase, *paradisiace iocunditatis amenite*, is used in S 690 and 703, written by 'Edgar A'; see above, pp. 15, 68. Cf. also *paradisiacae amenitatis iocunditate* in diplomas of the 'Orthodoxorum' group (S 658, 673, 786, 788, 812, and 876); see above, p. 15, and cf. below, n. 69.

Non auaritia nimium incitabatur cupidus . sed
dapsilitatis studio exercebatur largissimus .

Non illicito massicus[17] delectabatur edulio . sed
parcitate contentus licito utebatur cibario .[18]

Non luxuria eum stimulabat nefaria . sed con-
tinentia competens constringebat ad premia .

Omnium policrates[19] uirtutum cunctis carens
aduersis . omnibus florens prosperis . rite
pollebat ingenuus .

III [.][20] QUOMODO CELUM SINE MORTE
CONSCENDERE CONFIDEBAT ET
DIABOLUS INUIDUS NE AS'C'EN-
DERET IMPEDIEBAT .

Qui prole ad numerum patrata superbientium
angelorum .[21] uniuersa comitante prosapia
sine loeto . gustato ligni uetiti fructu .[22]
ethereos aeterne beatitudinis suggestus . triuiatim cum Domino regnans conscendere
macrobius[23] confidebat .

Inuidus igitur hoc animaduertens Zabulus .
nimia perculsus inuidia rimari callide uersu-
tus coeperat . quibus insidiis ne ad tantam
inmunis conscenderet gloriam . subdolus
deciperet .

Pro nichilo forte ducens concessa . illicita
nimium allubescendo laudans . mulierem[24]
ammodum fragilem pellexit .

He was not incited by avarice to be exceedingly
greedy, but, most liberal, was driven on by
the eagerness for generosity.

The man-like creature[17] was not seduced by
illicit food, but, content with parsimony,
enjoyed permitted fare.[18]

Abominable wantonness did not arouse him, but
an appropriate continence constrained him
for its own rewards.

Very mighty[19] in all virtues, lacking all vices,
flourishing with all good fortune, he was
rightly able to be noble.

iii.[20] HOW HE TRUSTED THAT HE
WOULD ASCEND INTO HEAVEN
WITHOUT DEATH AND HOW THE
ENVIOUS DEVIL HINDERED [HIM]
LEST HE SHOULD ASCEND.

He, the long-lived one,[23] was assured that, when
his progeny had attained the number of the
pride-filled angels[21] [and] his universal family
was accompanying him without death, the
fruit of the forbidden tree having been
tasted,[22] he would ascend to the ethereal
heights of eternal bliss, ruling far and wide
with the Lord.

The envious Devil, therefore, perceiving this,
impelled by excessive envy, shrewdly clever,
began to investigate by what devices he might
cunningly beguile [him] so that he might not
ascend stainless to such great glory.

Treating these bounties as if they were nothing,
praising illicit things with too much delight,
he enticed a very weak woman.[24]

[17] *Massicus*. The 'man-like creature', i.e. Adam, from *mas*[2] +
-icus (ex inf. D. R. Howlett).

[18] *illicito . . . edulio . . . licito . . . cibario*. Adam was at this time
forbidden to eat the fruit of the Tree of Knowledge; see Gen. 2:
17, and below, n. 22. Cf. the limitations on the monks' diet in
IV, xii, below.

[19] *policrates*. A rare grecism, meaning 'very mighty'. See
Lapidge 'Hermeneutic style', 89, and *idem* 'Æthelwold as
Scholar', 95–6, 98, where the use of the word (to denote God)
is noted as occurring in a letter, which may have been written by
Bishop Æthelwold, preserved in BL, Cotton MS. Tiberius A. xv
and printed by W. Stubbs (ed.), *Memorials of St. Dunstan,
Archbishop of Canterbury* (Rolls Series 63, London, 1874), 361–2.

[20] **IV, iii**. This chapter describes the temptation and Fall of
Man, at the instigation of the envious Devil. Cf. Gen. 3: 1–6.

[21] *prole ad numerum patrata superbientium angelorum*. See above,
n. 14.

[22] *gustato ligni uetitu fructu*. Once the number of Adam's
progeny had equalled that of the expelled angels, he himself
would be allowed to taste the fruit of the Tree of Knowledge

and ascend to Heaven. Cf. above, n. 18. In the Greek text
(Apocalypse of Moses) of the 1st cent. A.D. 'Life of Adam and
Eve', cap. 37, Adam's soul, on his bodily death, is allowed to
ascend to the third heaven until the Day of Judgement; see trans.
by M. D. Johnson in James H. Charlesworth (ed.), *The Old
Testament Pseudepigrapha*, ii (London, 1985), 249–95, at 291. For
Anglo-Saxon knowledge of the Latin text of the 'Life', see
SASLC: Trial Version, 23–4. See Addendum.

[23] *macrobius*. 'The long-lived one', a rare grecism (?a coinage
from μακρός + βίος). See Lapidge 'Hermeneutic style', 89, and
idem 'Æthelwold as Scholar', 96.

[24] *mulierem*. Eve.

Quae sui detrimenti minime contenta . uirum muliebriter uictum . blande suasionibus delinitum . exili heu malo gustato sibi similem faciens perdidit .

IIII .[25] QUOMODO IN HAC MISERIA OMNIBUS PRIUATI UIRTUTIBUS DEICIUNTUR TANDEMQUE CATACLISMATE DEMUNTUR .

Vtrique tandem prefatis priuati donariis . paradisi eliminati metis impresentis uitae erumna miserrimi deiciuntur .

Contemnentes conditorem . a cunctis insequuntur creatis .

Uita desiit . mors inoleuit .

Uirtutum caterua recedente . uitiorum cumulus successit .

Succedente nepotum prosapia . successit cumulata criminum collegio . uniuersi cum suis sceleribus cataclismate demti tandem octo utriusque sexus[26] reseruatis tabescendo deficiunt .

Uitiis copiose surgentibus conditor se hominem fecisse indoluit .

Postremo misericors mortalibus ut pollicitus est succurrit .[27]

V .[28] QUOMODO CHRISTUS NATUS SUA NOS PASSIONE REDEMIT AC CELOS CONSCENDERE FECIT .

Stella emicuit matutina .[29] quae suo[g] radio mundi tenebras fugaret .

Fausta resplenduit Maria cuius utero uirginali .

She, not content with her own ruin, destroyed the man, conquered by the ways of a woman and flattered with seductive exhortations, making him like herself, alas, when the meagre apple had been tasted.

iv.[25] HOW THEY WERE CAST DOWN IN THIS MISERY, DEPRIVED OF ALL VIRTUES, AND AT LENGTH TAKEN OFF BY THE FLOOD.

At length, both of them, bereft of the aforementioned bounties, are banished from the bounds of Paradise and cast down, most wretched, into the distresses of this present life.

Disdaining the Creator, they are followed by all created things.

Life desisted, death implanted [itself].

The crowd of virtues withdrawing, a heap of vices took their place.

When a stock of offspring succeeded, it succeeded with an increased company of evil deeds; all, except for eight of both sexes,[26] having at length been removed with their sins by the Flood, they declined through decay.

When vices arose in great abundance, the Creator grieved that He had made Man.

Merciful in the end, He came to the aid of mortals, as He had promised.[27]

v.[28] HOW CHRIST, HAVING BEEN BORN, REDEEMED US WITH HIS PASSION AND MADE HIS ASCENT INTO HEAVEN.

The morning-star[29] appeared which with its beam would put the shadows of the world to flight.

Blessed Mary was resplendent, from whose virginal womb Christ having been ineffably

---

[g] qua esuo *MS.*

[25] **IV, iv.** The condition of Man after the Expulsion from Paradise is here described; at first totally sinful, then gradually improving after the Flood, but still in need of reform. Cf. Gen. 4–8.

[26] *octo utriusque sexus.* That is, Noah and his wife and their three sons and their wives; see Gen. 7: 13, and 8: 18.

[27] *misericors . . . ut pollicitus est.* Cf. Deut. 4: 31 'Because the Lord thy God is a merciful God: he will not leave thee, nor altogether destroy thee, nor forget the covenant [cf. Gen. 9: 9–17], by which he swore to thy fathers'.

[28] **IV, v.** This chapter recounts the birth, death, Resurrection,

and Ascension of Christ as the Redeemer of Man's sin (cf. 1 Cor. 15: 21–2, and Rom. 5: 9–21), and how true Christians will ascend to Heaven while the evil will be punished in Hell.

[29] *Stella matutina.* With reference to Rev. 22: 16 (*BSV*, ii, 1905) *ego Iesus . . . sum . . . stella splendida et matutina* 'I Jesus . . . am . . . the bright and morning star.'

Christus ineffabiliter editus . peccatorum tenebras mediator clementissimus demsit .

Uiguit Christus uirtutibus plenus . incanduit Iudea ingenti rancore r`e'pleta[h] .[30]

Carnem suscipiens pro nobis pati uoluit .

Quod eius permissu infelix audacter compleuit Iudea .

Ligno quippe perditum . ligni scandens gabulum genus redemit humanum .[31]

Uniuersas namque hominum demon nationes ludificando insultans . iure ut mandati transgressorem possidens . morte multabat perpetua .

Surgens uero a mortuis ultorem tropheo crucis deuicit . predam de perfidi leonis ore tulit .[32] secumque super ethera uehens . supernis angelorum coetibus consociauit . ut cum eo communi contubernio fruentes . bonitate perspicui . uirtutum omnium ubertate referti . expertes peccati . omni contagione priuati . sine fine post diem iudicii restauratis corporibus exultantes regnarent .[33]

Hanc precipuam sine dubio gloriam . credentibus qui Trinitatis ueraeque Unitatis fidem bonis insudantes operibus sectantur pollicitus . non credentibus supplicium minatus eternum . perpetuis baratri incendiis iustissime spopondit.

VI [.][34] DE BENIUOLO REGIS MEDITAMINE .

HINC EGO EADGAR diuina fauente gratia totius Albionis basileus[35] rimari magnopere

begotten, a most merciful Mediator, He removed the shadows of [our] sins.

Christ flourished full of virtues; Judea blazed, filled with huge rancour.[30]

Assuming flesh, He wished to suffer for us.

Which [wish] unhappy Judea audaciously fulfilled with His permission.

He redeemed the human race, which had been destroyed by a tree, by mounting the Cross made of a tree.[31]

For indeed the Devil, abusing all the nations of men with deceit, holding them as of right, as one might hold the infringer of an injunction, was punishing them with perpetual death.

But rising up from the dead He conquered the punisher with the sign of the Cross. He took the booty from the mouth of the treacherous lion,[32] and carrying it with Him above the ether, He shared it with a celestial company of angels, so that they might reign forever with Him after the Day of Judgement, delighting in a common dwelling, manifest in goodness, filled with an abundance of all virtues, free from sin, bereft of all contamination, exulting in restored bodies.[33]

He promised this particular glory without doubt to those believers who pursue the faith of the Trinity and the True Unity, sweating over good works; He threatened unbelievers with an eternal penalty, very rightly promising them to the perpetual fires of the Abyss.

vi.[34] CONCERNING THE KING'S BENEVOLENT DESIGN.

HENCE, I, EDGAR, king of all Albion while the divine grace favours,[35] had begun earnestly to investigate what works I might engage in

---

[h] e inserted from above in reddish-brown ink

---

[30] *incanduit Iudea ingenti rancore r`e'pleta.* The latter part of Herod the Great's reign as client king of Judea, 37 B.C. to 4 A.D., was marked by a succession of plots against his rule; see Bruce M. Metzger and Michael D. Coogan (ed.), *The Oxford Companion to the Bible* (New York and Oxford, 1993), 281–2.

[31] *Ligno . . . humanum.* The Cross of the Crucifixion is here taken to have been prefigured by the Tree of Knowledge in Paradise; cf. above, nn. 18 and 22.

[32] *de . . . leonis ore tulit.* Cf. Ps. 21: 22 (*BSV,* i, 794–5), *Salva me ex ore leonis* 'Save me from the lion's mouth'. In his Harrowing of Hell, Christ saved the righteous who had died before his Crucifixion and took them to Heaven.

[33] *secumque super ethera uehens . . . sine fine post diem iudicii*

restauratis corporibus exultantes regnarent. Cf. Matt. 25: 46 (*BSV,* ii, 1567) *ibunt . . . iusti . . . in uitam aeternam* 'the just [shall go], into life everlasting'.

[34] **IV, vi**. Here King Edgar explains his hope for eternal salvation through the doing of good works on earth.

[35] *EADGAR diuina fauente gratia totius Albionis basileus.* A very similar royal style (which includes the grecism *basileus* 'ruler, king') occurs in **V, iv**, *diuina fauente clementia tocius Albionis basileus.* For Edgar, see above, n. 2; and below, n. 126.

coeperam quid operum studio exercerem .[36]
ut ad tantam gloriam perueniens Christi
sanctorumque eius celo collocatus contubernio coronatus fruerer . tantamque inferni
miseriam deuitarem .

Instigante etenim Domini clementia occurrit
animo . ut ipse criminibus cessarem
cunctis .[37] adque[j] bonis operibus insistens
forma factus gregi[38] quosque nostri regminis
gubernamine degentes[39] lucri facerem .

Quosdam igitur suasionibus inuitans ad premia .
quosdam terroribus conpellens ad gloriam .
bona edificans . mala ut Domino faciente
potui dissipaui .

Scriptum quippe per Hieremiam memini
prophetam .

Ecce constitui te super gentes et super regna ut
euellas et destruas et disperdas et dissipes et
edifices et plantes .[40]

Talibus igitur exortatus doctrinis quibus nos
Dominus   per   prophetam   clementer
ammonuit . agens Christo faciente in terris
quod ipse iuste egit in celis . extricans
uidelicet Domini cultura criminum
spurcitias .[41] uirtutum semina sedulus agricola inserui .[42]

with zeal,[36] so that, attaining such great glory,
placed in the Heaven of Christ and His saints,
furnished with a crown, I might delight in the
common dwelling, and might avoid the great
misery of Hell.

And indeed it occurs to me, at the Lord's kindly
inspiration, that I myself should cease from
all evil deeds[37] and, pursuing good works,
having been made into a model for the
flock,[38] I should bring about the conversion
of everyone dwelling within the governance
of our kingdom.[39]

Attracting certain people to rewards therefore
by exhortations, driving others on to glory by
terrible threats, building up good things, I
have destroyed bad things, so far as I have
been able, at the Lord's doing.

I am mindful indeed of that which was written
by the prophet Jeremiah:

'Lo, I have set thee this day over the nations, and
over kingdoms, to root up, and to pull down,
and to waste, and to destroy, and to build, and
to plant.'[40]

Exhorted therefore by such teachings by which
the Lord has kindly admonished us through
the Prophet, effecting on earth at Christ's
doing what He himself has justly effected in
Heaven, namely, clearing the filth[41] of evil
deeds from the Lord's ploughland, as a
diligent farmer, I have inserted the seeds of
virtues.[42]

---

[j] *MS. error for* atque

---

[36] *rimari magnopere coeperam quid operum studio exercerem.* Cf.
RC, cap. I, *quibus sanctorum operum meritis in feruidum perfectionis
ardorem accendi ualeret, studiose percunctari sollicitus cepit* 'he began
carefully and earnestly to consider by what holy and deserving
works it [the spark of faith] could be made to burn with the
brilliance and ardour of perfection'.

[37] *ut ipse criminibus cessarem cunctis.* Cf. 'King Edgar's Establishment of Monasteries', 149, *Eadgar cyning . . . geornlice angan to
smeagenne ærest þinga hu he his agen lif gerihtlæcan meahte mid rihtre
æfestnesse* 'King Edgar . . . began eagerly to inquire first of all how
he could rectify his own life with true piety'.

[38] *gregi.* Cf. below, n. 98, for another reference by the king to
his 'flock', but there meaning the monks, rather than all his
Christian subjects.

[39] *quosque nostri regminis gubernamine degentes.* King Edgar may
here have been referring in particular to the inhabitants of the
Danelaw, both Scandinavian immigrants and native English, who
were either still pagan or who had lost their Christian faith
through lack of clergy in the area. Bishop Æthelwold's refoundation of ruined churches in the Danelaw during the latter part of
Edgar's reign was intended to help restore the area to its former
level of Christianity.

[40] *Ecce . . . plantes.* Jer. I: 10 (*BSV*, ii, 1167).

[41] *agens . . . spurcitias.* See above, n. 11.

[42] *Domini cultura . . . semina sedulus agricola inserui.* Cf. the use
of *cultores* and *Christi cultura* in **IV, viii** and **xviii**; see below, nn.
57 and 110; also the farming metaphors used below in **V, i,** in
describing the growth of Christianity in Wessex. See Addendum.

VII .[43] QUA RATIONE CLERICOS[44] ELIMI-
NANS MONACHOS COLLOCAUIT .

Timens ne eternam incurrerem miseriam si
adepta potestate non facerem quod ipse qui
operatur omnia quae in celo uult et in terra
suis exemplis iustus examinator innotuit .[45]
uitiosorum cuneos canonicorum . e diuersis
nostri regminis coenobiis Christi uicarius[46]
eliminaui .[47]

Quod nullis mihi intercessionibus prodesse
poterant . sed potius ut beatus ait Gregorius
iusti uindictam iudicis prouocarent[48] qui
uariis[k] uitiorum neuis contaminati . non
agentes quę Deus iubendo uolebat . omnia
quę nolebat rebelles faciebant auidus inqui-
sitor aduertens . gratos Domino monachorum
cuneos qui pro nobis incunctanter intercederent .[49] nostri iuris monasteriis deuotus
hilariter collocaui .[50]

vii.[43] BY WHAT MANNER, [AFTER] EXPEL-
LING THE CLERKS,[44] HE INSTALLED
THE MONKS.

Fearing lest I should incur eternal misery if I, on
the acquisition of power, should not do what
He wishes who Himself administers everything in Heaven and [who] has become
known on earth as a Righteous Judge from
His warning punishments,[45] I, the vicar of
Christ,[46] have expelled the crowds of
depraved canons from the various monasteries of our kingdom.[47]

Because they had been of no benefit to me with
their intercessory prayers, but rather, as the
blessed Gregory said, they had 'provoked the
vengeance of the Just Judge',[48] they who were
contaminated with diverse blemishes of vices
were not performing the things which God
wished in his commandments, and were
rebelliously doing all things which God did
not wish, I, a keen investigator, turning my
attention to these matters, have joyously
installed,[50] in the monasteries within our
jurisdiction, throngs of monks pleasing to
the Lord, who might intercede unhesitatingly
for us.[49]

---

[k] uicariis, -ic- *subpuncted for omission in reddish-brown ink*

---

[43] **IV, vii**. This chapter recounts how King Edgar expelled
the secular clergy from monasteries in England. Cf. 'King Edgar's
Establishment of Monasteries'; see below, n. 47.

[44] *CLERICOS*. Note the use of the word *clericus* (here, and
below, **IV, viii**) as the equivalent of *canonicus*; cf. Finberg, 241
n. 1. A similar usage is found in *RC*, cap. 2; in **V, ii** and **xiv**,
below; in S 731 (cf. above, n. 11); and in Ælfric *Vita S. Æthelwoldi*
(see below, n. 60).

[45] *in terra suis exemplis . . . innotuit*. Cf. IV Edgar, prol. and cap.
1 (*c*.963) which explains the pestilence recently suffered by the
king's people as merited *mid synnum 7 mid oferhyrnysse Godes
beboda* 'by sins and by contempt of God's commands'; see
Councils 28 (pp. 105–6). The pestilence was probably that
recorded in *ASC* [A], s.a. 962.

[46] *Christi uicarius*. The same title, applied here to King Edgar,
is later used to refer to the abbot of the New Minster; see below,
n. 97. Edgar is probably portrayed as the 'vicar of Christ' in the
miniature on fo. 2ᵛ; see above, p. 70.

[47] *uitiosorum cuneos canonicorum . . . eliminaui*. Cf. *RC*, cap. 2,
eiectisque neglegentium clericorum spurcitiis; 'King Edgar's Establishment of Monasteries',149–50, *began georne mynstera wide geond his
cynerice to rihtlæcynne . . . Halige stowa he geclænsode fram ealra
manna fulnessum, no þæt an on Wesseaxna rice, ac eacswylce on
Myrcena lande. Witodlice he adref [cano]nicas þe on þæm foresædum
gyltum ofer[fle]de genihtsumedon* ' . . . he began zealously to set
monasteries in order widely throughout his kingdom . . . He
cleansed holy places from all men's foulnesses, not only in the
kingdom of the West Saxons, but in the land of the Mercians

also. Assuredly he drove out canons who abounded in the
aforementioned sins'; and *ASC* [A], s.a. 964 (in relation to the
Old and New Minsters and the abbeys of Chertsey and Milton
Abbas), where the canons are referred to as *preostas*.

[48] *ut beatus ait Gregorius iusti uindictam iudicis prouocarent*. Cf.
uindictam iusti iudicii ['the vengeance of just judgement'] in Mark
Adriaen (ed.), *S. Gregorii Magni, Moralia in Iob, libri xxiii–xxv*,
CCSL 143B, p. 1252 (book 25, cap. 10, line 62); Miller 1998, 98.

[49] *pro nobis . . . intercederent*. Cf. the various liturgical items to
be said for the king and queen mentioned in *RC*, caps. 17, 19, 21,
24, etc.; cf. also below, n. 59.

[50] *monachorum cuneos . . . collocaui*. Cf. 'King Edgar's Establishment of Monasteries', 150, *on þam fyrmestum stowum [e]alles his
andwealdes munecas gestapolode to weorþfulre þenunge Hælendes
Cristes* 'he established monks in the foremost places of all his
dominion for the glorious service of the Saviour Christ'; and *RC*,
cap. 2, *non solum monachus uerum etiam sanctimonialis . . . ad dei
famulatum ubique per tantam sui regni amplitudinem deuotissime
constituit* 'placing in their stead for the service of God, throughout the length and breadth of his dominions, not only monks
but also nuns'.

VIII .[51] QUOD SANCTI SPIRITUS GRATIA COMPUNCTUS[52] ABBATEM ET MONACHOS IN NOUO CONSTITUIT MONASTERIO .

Hac itaque ratione sancti spiritus actactus flamine[53] locum Domini mundans Uuintaniensis ęclesiae[1] Noui Monasterii arcisterium nostro saluatori eiusque genitrici semper uirgini Mariae et omnibus apostolis cum caeteris sanctis dicatum restauraui .[54]

Sciens scriptum . consentientes et facientes pari constringuntur pena .[55] rebelliones omnipotentis uoluntati obuiantes possessionem Domini usurpare non sustinens clericos[56] lasciuientes repuli . ac ueros Dei cultores[57] monachico gradu[58] fungentes . qui pro nostris nostrorumque inibi quiescentium excessibus sedulo intercederent[59] seruitio . quo eorum intercessionibus nostri regminis status uigeret munitus . abbatem[60] Christo cooperante eligens altithrono subiectus illic deuote ordinaui .

[1] ęcclesiae, in error, Councils, i, 125

[51] **IV, viii.** This chapter refers specifically to the refoundation of the New Minster by King Edgar.

[52] *SANCTI SPIRITUS GRATIA COMPUNCTUS*. This phrase occurs also in the Tavistock foundation-charter of 981: S 839, *KCD* 679. Cf. *RC*, caps. 2 and 4, *domini conpunctus gratia* and *Christi conpunctus gratia*; and below, **V, xiv** (disposition), *Christi compunctus spiramine*.

[53] *sancti spiritus actactus flamine*. Cf. *RC*, cap. 1, *respectu diuino attactus*; also below, **V, iv**, *superni moderatoris instinctu attactus*; and **V, xiii**, *sancti spiritus carismate partim attactus*. Cf. below, **V**, n. 184. See Addendum.

[54] *Noui Monasterii arcisterium . . . restaurari*. See *ASC* [A], s.a. 964.

[55] *consentientes . . . pena*. Cf. Rom. 1: 32 (*BSV*, ii, 1751): *qui cum iustitiam Dei cognovissent non intellexerunt quoniam qui talia agunt digni sunt morte non solum qui ea faciunt sed et consentiunt facientibus* 'Who, having known the justice of God, did not understand that they who do such things, are worthy of death; and not only they that do them, but they also that consent to them that do them'.

[56] *clericos*. See above, n. 44, and below, n. 60.

[57] *ueros Dei cultores*. There may be a play on the meanings of *cultor* here, either as 'worshipper' or as 'cultivator' (cf. above, n. 42), but note that *catholicæ fidei cultoribus* is also used below in **XXXIII**, the papal letter relating to the refoundation of the Old Minster.

[58] *monachico gradu*. Cf. *RC*, cap. 8, *gradus ille regularis in quo praecipitur ut nihil agat monachus nisi quod communis monasterii*

viii.[51] WHEREFORE, GOADED ON BY LOVE OF THE HOLY GHOST,[52] HE ESTABLISHED AN ABBOT AND MONKS IN THE NEW MINSTER.

For this reason therefore, having been touched by the spirit of the Holy Ghost,[53] cleansing the Lord's abode, I have re-established the monastery of the New Minster of the church of Winchester,[54] dedicated to Our Saviour and to His mother Mary, the Perpetual Virgin, and to all the Apostles, with other saints.

Being acquainted with the writing, 'those who consent to things and those who do them are equally fettered in punishment',[55] not supporting rebels who oppose the will of the Almighty in usurping the Lord's property, I have driven away the wanton clerks,[56] and I, subject to the High-throned One, choosing an abbot[60] with Christ's help, have faithfully appointed thither true worshippers[57] of God, observing the monkish degree [of humility],[58] who might intercede[59] for our sins, and for those of our people lying at rest there, by zealous service, [so that], fortified by their intercessions, the condition of our kingdom might thrive.

regula vel maiorum cohortantur exempla, diligentissime custodiatur 'that degree of humility, set forth in the Rule, which ordains *that a monk should do nothing beyond that which the common rule of the monastery and the example of the elders exhort*, be most carefully fulfilled', where *nihil . . . exempla* is quoting the eighth degree of humility defined in *BR*, cap. 7.55. Cf. also below, n. 77.

[59] *pro nostris . . . intercederent*. See above, n. 49.

[60] *abbatem*. Abbot Æthelgar; see below, nn. 149 and 135. Cf. *ASC* [A], s.a. 964, where he is named; Wulfstan *Vita S. Æthelwoldi*, cap. 20 (ed. Lapidge and Winterbottom, 36–7), *antistes Ætheluuoldus . . . annuente rege Eadgaro, canonicos de Nouo expulit Monasterio, illucque monachos introduxit regulariter conuersantes, ordinans illis abbatem discipulum suum Æthelgaru[m] . . .* 'Bishop Æthelwold . . . with the permission of King Edgar drove the canons from the New Minster, introducing there monks living according to the Rule and ordaining as their abbot his pupil Æthelgar'; and Ælfric *Vita S. Æthelwoldi*, cap. 16 (ed. Lapidge and Winterbottom, 76), *Ætheluuoldus . . . annuente rege Eadgaro, expulit clericos de Nouo Monasterio, ordinans ibi Æthelgarum discipulum suum abbatem, et sub eo monachos regulariter conuersantes*. It is noteworthy that Ælfric used *clericus* as the equivalent of Wulfstan's *canonicus*; cf. above, n. 44.

Hoc subnixe efflagitans deposco . ut quod in suis egi . hoc agat in mihi ab ipso conlatis . scilicet aduersarios nostros deiciens amicos sublimando prouehat . ut inimicos sanctę Dei ęclesiae[m] deprimens . amicos eius monachos uidelicet beatificans iustificaui .

VIIII .[61] DE ILLORUM ANATHEMATE QUI MONACHIS INSIDIANTUR .

Si autem qualibet ocasione diabolo instigante contigeret ut fastu superbientes arrogantię[62] deiecti canonici monachorum gregem quem ego uenerans cum pastore[63] in Dei constitui possessione . deicere insidiando uoluerint . agatur de eis et de omnibus qui quolibet munere cecati[64] iuuamen eis impenderint . quod actum est de angelis superbientibus et de protoplasto diaboli fraude seducto . ut paradisi uidelicet limitibus sublimibus`que´ regni celorum sedilibus eiecti . cum his qui Domini famulatum aspernentes contemserunt barathri incendiis detrusi iugi crucientur miseria .

Nec inde euulsi se glorientur euasisse tormenta sed cum Iuda Christi proditore eiusque complicibus Acharonte conglutinati . frigore stridentes . feruore perusti . letitia priuati . merore anxii . catenis igneis compediti . lictorum metu perculsi . scelerum memoria

Humbly requesting this, I beseech that what I have done for His people, He do for those collected together by Himself under me, namely that, in casting down our enemies, He should elevate our friends with advancement, just as I, suppressing the enemies of the Holy Church of God, have blessedly advanced His friends, namely the monks.

ix.[61] CONCERNING THE ANATHEMA ON THOSE WHO PLOT AGAINST THE MONKS.

If moreover it should happen on any occasion, at the Devil's instigation, that, glorying in the arrogance of presumption,[62] the cast-down canons should wish to plot to cast down the flock of monks which I have respectfully established with a shepherd[63] in God's property, let it be done with them, and with everyone who might give them aid, blinded by some kind of bribe,[64] as happened with the proud angels and with the first man seduced by the Devil's trick, namely that, having been expelled from the bounds of Paradise and from the sublime seats of the kingdom of Heaven, they shall be thrust down into the fires of the Abyss with these [other] disdainful ones who have spurned the Lord's service, and be tormented with perpetual misery.

Nor pulled out from there to boast that they have evaded the torments, but, rather, they shall be joined together in the Underworld with Judas, the betrayer of Christ, and his confederates, shrieking with cold, scorched with heat, deprived of joy, troubled by lamentation, fettered by fiery shackles, smitten by dread of the attendants, perplexed by the memory of crimes, removed from the

---

[m] æcclesiae, *in error, ibid.*

[61] **IV, ix**. This chapter prohibits anyone from helping the ejected canons against the monks; cf. below, n. 131. The canons are compared specifically to the fallen angels, who were expelled from Heaven and consigned to Hell (see above, **IV, prologue**), and to the first man, who was expelled from Paradise (see above, **IV, iii–iv**).

[62] *fastu . . . arrogantię*. Cf. *fastu arrogantiae* in Benedict of Aniane's preface to the supplement to the Gregorian Sacramentary; see Jean Deshusses (ed.), *Le Sacramentaire Grégorien: Ses Principes Formes d'Après les Plus Anciens Manuscrits*, i, *Le Sacramentaire, Le Supplément d'Aniane*, Spicilegium Friburgense 16 (1971), 352, line 31. Cf. also above, n. 7; and *RC*, caps. 6 and 8, *arrogantiae fastu inopinate seducti* and *contempto arrogantiae fastu*. See Addendum.

[63] *pastore*. Cf. the references to the abbot as shepherd in *BR*, cap. 2. 7–9, 39, and in cap. 27. See also below, n. 98.

[64] *munere cecati*. Cf. Exod. 23:8 (*BSV*, i, 108) . . . *munera, quae excaecant etiam prudentes* ' . . . bribes which even blind the wise'; Deut. 16: 19 (*BSV*, i, 258) . . . *munera excaecant oculos sapientium* ' . . . gifts blind the eyes of the wise'; and Ecclus. 20: 31 (*BSV*, ii, 1054) *xenia et dona excaecant oculos iudicum* 'Presents and gifts blind the eyes of judges . . .'.

confusi . totius bonitatis recordatione semoti .
eterno lugubres punientur cruciatu .[65]

X [.][66]   ITEM   DE   ANATHEMATE INSIDIANTIUM .

Qui autem iam predictos Noui Uintaniensis
aeclesie Cenobii monachos uel quoslibet
eiusdem ordinis nostro regmine degentes . e
monasteriis que uitiorum spurcitias expurgans[67] Iesu Christo Domino nostro uicto
demone adquisiui eliminare presumens
uoluerit anathema sit . et eadem maledictione
qua Cain parricida qui fratrem suum Abel
stimulante inuidia liuidus interemit mastigia
addictus est .[68] sine termino teneatur
obnoxius . atque in Dei persecutione con-
tinuo perseuerans in hac uita nullum dignitatis adquirat honorem . nec in futuro sine
miseria umquam persistat . sed eum Annaniae
et Saphirę[69] una Stix[70] porrigene" heiulantem
crucians complectatur .

XI .[71] DE BENEDICTIONE MONACHOS UENERANTIUM .

Quicumque pretitulatos monachos bonis quibuslibet locupletans ditare uoluerit . creator
cunctitenens clementer eos eorumque

recollection of all goodness, mourning, they
shall be punished with eternal torment.[65]

x.[66] ALSO CONCERNING THE ANATHEMA ON THOSE WHO PLOT.

Let him moreover be cursed who, with presumption, should wish to expel the aforesaid
monks of the New Minster of the church of
Winchester, or any of the same order dwelling in our kingdom, from the monasteries
which I have acquired, cleansing the filth of
vices,[67] through Our Lord Jesus Christ, the
Devil having been defeated; and let him be
held punishable without end by the same
curse by which Cain is adjudged a parricide
who, spiteful with the goading on of envy,
killed his brother Abel with a club,[68] and,
persisting in God's continuous persecution,
let him acquire no honour of merit in this
life, nor let him ever persist in the future
without misery, but, together with the scurf
of Ananias and Sapphira,[69] let the tormenting
Styx[70] embrace him, bewailing.

xi.[71] CONCERNING THE BLESSING ON THOSE WHO RESPECT THE MONKS.

Whoever should wish to enrich the aforementioned monks, making them rich with
all good things, may the Creator, mercifully
controlling all things, make them and their

" porrigene, *first* e *erased and replaced by* i

[65] *paradisi . . . limitibus sublimibus`que' . . . eiecti . . . barathri
incendiis . . . iugi crucientur miseria . . . cum Iuda Christi proditore
eiusque complicibus Acharonte conglutinati . . . eterno lugubres
punientur cruciatu.* Cf. below, **V, i,** *paradysi ianuis eliminatus. eternis
barathri incendiis iugiter ustulatus. Acharonte . . . suffocatus. cum Iuda
Christi proditore eiusque complicibus . . . iugi`que' miseria . . . puniatur
iudicio . . .;* also above, **IV, prologue,** *aeternis . . . miseria.* Cf. too
the phrase *eternis barathri incendiis lugubris iugiter cum Iuda Christi
proditore eiusque complicibus puniatur* which may have been
'devised and popularized' by the scribe usually denoted as
'Edgar A' (see above, p. 15), the first occurrence of which is in
S 683, *BCS* 1054, dated 960 and in favour of Bishop Beorhthelm
of Winchester; see Keynes *Diplomas,* 72–3. Other diplomas
written by 'Edgar A' which contain the phrase are S 690 (A.D.
961, in favour of Abingdon Abbey), 706, 717, *BCS* 1066, 1083,
1101. For the suggestion that S 687, also written by 'Edgar A',
was drafted by Æthelwold in 960, see Lapidge 'Æthelwold as
Scholar', 94–5. See also below, nn. 114–15, and 122.

[66] **IV, x.** The curse of Cain is invoked against anyone plotting
to expel the monks from the New Minster (cf. below, n. 131), or
from any of the other reformed monasteries in England.

[67] *uitiorum spurcitias expurgans.* See above, n. 11.

[68] *eadem maledictione qua Cain . . . addictus est.* See Gen. 4:
11–16.

[69] *Annaniae et Saphirę.* See Acts 5: 1–11. The story of the
sudden death of Ananias and his wife Saphira is elsewhere
quoted as a warning to those engaged in fraud or deceit; see
BR, cap. 57. 4–6; and *RC,* cap. 104 [69]. The couple are also
referred to in the anathemas of diplomas belonging to the
'Orthodoxorum' group (S 658, 673, 786, 788, and 812); see
above, p. 15, and cf. above, n. 16. They earlier occur in a
group of documents from the reign of King Edmund with close
diplomatic links: S 487, *CW* 76, *BCS* 787 (A.D. 943); S 471, *BCS*
761 (A.D. 940 ? for 943); S 492, *BCS* 782 (A.D. 943); and S 486,
CW 91, *BCS* 788 (A.D. 943).

[70] *Stix.* The Styx, the river of the Underworld in classical
mythology.

[71] **IV, xi.** Those who support the monks are here promised
both earthly and eternal blessings.

progeniem totius ubertate prosperitatis hic et in futuro seculo ditando locupletet .

Scriptis decenter eorum in libro uite[72] nomini-bus cum Christo portionem in celorum habitaculis habeant qui monachos suos quos nostris congregatos[73] temporibus possidet uel uerbis . uel factis . sanctitatis studio honorauerint .

XII .[74] QUALES ET QUALITER MONACHI IN HOC MONASTERIO CONUER-SENTUR .[75]

Regulares igitur monachi non seculares in pre-fato Christo comite degentes monasterio[76] regulę moribus obtemperent .

Patres uenerates° spiritales sanctorum patrum imitentur exempla . nil agentes nisi quod communis monasterii regula uel maiorum demonstrauerit norma .[77]

A secularibus igitur pompis remoti .[78] toto nisu corporis custodiant et animae castitatem .

Humilitatis[79] studio pollentes . corpus parssimo-niae uigore munientes . alacri constringant animo .

descendants rich, enriching [them] with a copiousness of prosperity now and in a future age.

Let those who shall have honoured, either in words or in deeds, with devotion to holiness, His monks whom He possesses, collected as a flock[73] in our times, have a share with Christ in the dwellings of Heaven, their names fitly having been written in the Book of Life.[72]

xii.[74] WHAT SORT OF MONKS ARE TO DWELL IN THIS MONASTERY, AND IN WHAT WAY.[75]

Let regular monks therefore, not seculars, dwell-ing in the aforementioned monastery[76] in company with Christ, conform to the prac-tices of a rule.

While worshipping, let the spiritual fathers copy the example of the Holy Fathers, doing nothing except what the common rule of the monastery or the precept of the Elders shall have mentioned.[77]

Removed therefore from worldly displays,[78] let them guard purity with full exertion of body and of mind.

Striving in devotion to humility,[79] strengthening the body with the vigour of frugality, let them be restrained by an eager mind.

° *MS. error for* uenerantes

---

[72] *libro uite*. The Book of Life; see Rev. 20: 12 and 15, and 21: 27. It is also referred to in the sanctions of **V, i** and **xiv**, below.

[73] *monachos . . . congregatos*. Cf. below, n. 98.

[74] **IV, xii**. This chapter sets out the main characteristics of the monastic life to be led in the New Minster. Cf. the description of Man's life in Paradise, above, **IV, ii**. Cf. also below, **V, xiv**, n. 206.

[75] *. . . QUALITER . . . IN HOC MONASTERIO CON-UERSENTUR*. This part of the chapter-heading seems to echo a particular variant (using a passive verb) of one of the various titles of the (late 8th cent.) Continental monastic text, known for short as *Memoriale qualiter*, apparently popularized by Benedict of Aniane. The title in MSS. *E, Q*, and *S* of this text reads: *Memoriale qualiter in monasterio conversari debemus*. See D. C. Morgand (ed.), *Memoriale qualiter*, in *Initia Consuetudinis Benedictinae*, 177–282, esp. 179–80, 211, 224–5, 229. Of these MSS., CCCC MS. 57, fos. 33ʳ–37ʳ (= MS. *E*), written *c*.1000, has an 11th-cent. Abingdon provenance; see Mildred Budny, *Insular, Anglo-Saxon, and Early Norman Manuscript Art at Corpus Christi College, Cambridge: An Illustrated Catalogue* (2 vols., Medieval Institute, Kalamazoo, Michigan, 1997) 25. It is probable that there was an earlier MS., now lost, of *Memoriale qualiter* at Abingdon (or Winchester) with which Æthelwold was familiar. For the possibility that the

(mixed) text of *BR* which CCCC, MS. 57 also contains was copied for use at Abingdon, see Gretsch *Intellectual Foundations*, 252–4.

[76] *in prefato . . . degentes monasterio*. Cf. *BR*, cap. 5. 12, *in coenobiis degentes*, and *RC*, cap. 95 [63], *in monasterio degens*.

[77] *nil agentes . . . norma*. Referring to the eighth grade of humility; see *BR*, cap. 7. 55, *nihil agat monachus, nisi quod communis monasterii regula uel maiorum cohortantur exempla* 'a monk does only what is endorsed by the common rule of the monastery and the example set by his superiors'. This was also quoted by *RC*, cap. 8; see above, n. 58. Cf. below, n. 79. See also below, **V, xiv**, n. 242.

[78] *A secularibus . . . pompis remoti*. Cf. below, **V, xiv**, *ab huius uitę curis remoti*, with reference to the monks of the Old Minster; and **VI** (disposition), *á ciuium tumultu remoti*, with reference to all three monastic communities at Winchester. The word *pompis* is abl. pl. of *pompa*, borrowed into Latin from Greek πομπή 'solemn procession, public display'; see Lewis and Short, 1394; cf. below, n. 80.

[79] *Humilitatis*. See above, n. 77. See Addendum.

Ciuium conuiuae intra urbem perpetuo inter-
dictu fieri erubescant .

In ciuitaeᵖ degentes in refectorio pompaticas⁸⁰
lasciuasque secularium delicias ut melanco-
liam⁸¹ aporiantes .⁸² licitis caritatiui utantur
cibariis .

Exstra refectorium autem minime . nisi domo
infirmorum egroti decubuerint .⁸³ edentes
licite quae iussi fuerint .⁸⁴

Sacri summique ordinis hospites si ratio exigerit .
et peregrini ordinati⁸⁵ longo terrarum spatio
uenientes . ad abbatis mensam⁸⁶ in refectorio
cautissime inuitentur .⁸⁷

Laicis in hospitio condecens exhibeatur humanitas .⁸⁸

Et monachorum quispiam manducandi uel

Let them blush with shame—under perpetual
interdict—at being made table-companions of
the citizens within the city.

Let charitable people who dwell in the city
employ permitted foods in the refectory,
rejecting,⁸² like melancholy,⁸¹ the showy⁸⁰
and lascivious delights of the worldly.

Let them not eat outside the refectory, unless
they are ill and confined to the infirmary;⁸³
and let them only eat those things which are
permitted.⁸⁴

Let them entertain most warily guests of a
sacred, or of the highest, rank, if reason
requires it, and well-ordered pilgrims⁸⁵
coming from far-distant lands, at the abbot's
table⁸⁶ in the refectory.⁸⁷

Let seemly kindness be shown to laymen in the
guest-house;⁸⁸

And let none of the monks be allowed to eat or

ᵖ MS. error for ciuitate

⁸⁰ pompaticas. A grecism; see Lapidge 'Hermeneutic style', 89,
and idem 'Æthelwold as Scholar', 95. Derived from pompa; cf.
above, n. 78. See Addendum.

⁸¹ melancoliam. A grecism; cf. Lapidge, as above, n. 80. Also
used below in V, vi and xi. It occurs in the proem Flebilia fortiter
detestanda, favoured by the draftsman 'Æthelstan A' and adapted
in the reign of Edgar; see below, V, xi, n. 160. 'Melancholy' was
one of the seven cardinal vices and is referred to by the
alternative Latin word tristitia 'sadness' in IV, ii; see above, n. 15.

⁸² aporiantes. From the grecism aporiari 'to be in uncertainty,
to doubt' but here requiring a more positive act of denial, hence
'rejecting'. It is used in a similar way in V, vi, below.

⁸³ Exstra refectorium . . . nisi domo infirmorum egroti decubuerint.
Cf. RC, cap. 95 [63], extra refectorium nec ipse abbas nec fratrum
quispiam nisi causa infirmitatis manducet uel bibat 'neither the abbot
himself nor any of the brethren shall eat or drink outside the
refectory except in the case of sickness'. This clarification of BR,
caps. 53 and 56, was in accordance with the decree of the synod
of Aachen in 816; see J. Semmler (ed.), Synodi primae Aquisgranensis decreta authentica, canon 25, in Initia consuetudinis Benedictinae, 464–5. The domus infirmorum of the New Minster may be
the claustral building found east of the church in 1970; see WS
1, 315.

⁸⁴ edentes liciter quae iussi fuerint. For the permitted monastic
diet, see BR, cap. 39. Cf. the limitations placed on Adam's diet in
Paradise; see above, IV, ii, and n. 18.

⁸⁵ peregrini ordinati. Cf. BR, cap. 56. 1, Mensa abbatis cum
hospitibus et peregrinis sit semper 'The abbot's table must always be
with guests and travelers', and RC, cap. 95 [63], superuenientibus
peregrinis pauperibus abbas cum fratribus quos elegerit secundum
regulae preceptum mandati exibeat obsequium . . . Profiscentibus uero
peregrinis secundum quod loci suppetit facultas eis inpendantur uictualium solacium 'when poor strangers arrive, the abbot and such of
the brethren as he shall choose shall render to them the service

of the Maundy in accordance with the ordinance of the Rule . . .
For the rest, wayfarers shall on their departure be provided with
a supply of victuals according to the means of the house'. The
strictures against nearly all laymen (cf. below, nn. 87 and 90)
eating in the refectory indicates that the pilgrims referred to
here as ordinati are ecclesiastics only. For the use of ordinatus to
describe the abbot of the New Minster, see below, n. 150.

⁸⁶ abbatis mensam. For arrangements regarding the abbot's
table, see BR, cap. 56.

⁸⁷ Sacri summique ordinis hospites . . . in refectorio . . . inuitentur.
This was an exception to the decree of the synod of Aachen in
816, quoted below, n. 90, and in accordance with the rule of
Benedict of Aniane, 818/?819; see J. Semmler (ed.), Regula Sancti
Benedicti abbatis Anianensis sive collectio capitularis, in Initia
consuetudinis Benedictinae, 522, canon 21 . . . ipse [abbas] cum
episcopis, abbatibus, canonicis, nobilibus . . . sumat ['the abbot himself
should dine with bishops, abbots, canons, nobles . . .']. Abbot
Ælfric in his instructions to the monks of Eynsham (c.1005)
allows only for the entertainment of the king and his sons; see
H. Nocent (ed.), Aelfrici abbatis epistula ad monachos Egnesham-
nenses directa, cap. 64, in K. Hallinger (ed.), Consuetudinum saeculi
x/xi/xii monumenta non-Cluniacensia, Corpus consuetudinum
monasticarum 7.3 (Siegburg, 1984), p. 179; also Christopher
A. Jones, Ælfric's Letter to the Monks of Eynsham (Cambridge
Studies in Anglo-Saxon England 24, Cambridge, 1998), pp. 140–
1 (and, for the date, pp. 5–12).

⁸⁸ in hospitio . . . humanitas. Cf. RC, cap. 95 [63], Omnia igitur
humanitas officia in ospitio pater ipse . . . uel fratrum quilibet
deuotissime prebeat 'Wherefore . . . the father himself, no less
than each of the brethren, shall be most zealous in providing
every kind service in the guesthouse'; and BR, cap. 53, De
hospitibus suscipiendis 'The reception of guests'.

bibendi cum eis secundum patrum decreta licentiam non habeat .[89]

In refectorio autem edendi causa uel bibendi non introducantur .[90]

Pauperes ut Christus ingenti cordis suscipiantur tripudio.[91]

XIII [.][92] DE ABBATUM ELECTIONE [.]

Diuinarum studio scripturarum luculentissime eruditi . orationum frequentia assidue ocupati. caritatis amplexu letissimi . fidei exercitio promtissimi . spe prouehente sincerissimi . pace concorditer fixi . omniumque uirtutum flore decorati . ad finem usque coeptum tantę bonitatis initium Christo iuuante perducentes . eadem gloriosi fruantur libertate . quam beatus patronus BENEDICTUS[93] omnibus regulę precepto subiectis instituit .

Scilicet ut post abbatis obitum tunc temporis regentis . abbatem ex eadem ordinent congregatione . quem sibi omnis concors[q] congregatio siue pars quamuis minima congregationis sulubriori[r] elegerit consilio .[94]

drink with them, in accordance with the decrees of the Fathers;[89]

Moreover let [laymen] not be brought into the refectory to eat or drink.[90]

Let the poor be supported, like Christ, with great jubilation of heart.[91]

xiii.[92] CONCERNING THE CHOOSING OF ABBOTS.

Let the glorious [monks], most splendidly learned in study of divine writings, constantly busy with a great number of prayers, most happy in the embrace of charity, most ready in the exercise of faith, most sincere with exalting hope, attached amicably to peace, adorned with the flower of all virtues, carrying through right to the end the beginning of so great goodness begun with Christ's help, enjoy the same freedom which the blessed patron BENEDICT[93] established for everyone subject to the command of the Rule:

namely, that, after the death of the abbot then ruling, they may appoint an abbot from the same community, whom the whole united community, or even a small part of the community, shall have chosen for itself by wholesome deliberation.[94]

---

[q] consors, *first s erased and replaced by c*   [r] *MS. error for* salubriori; *cf. n. 94*

---

[89] *monachorum quispiam . . . licentiam non habeat.* Referring to the decree of the synod of Aachen in 816, canon 25 *Ut abbas uel quispiam fratrum ad portam monasterii cum hospitibus non reficiat* ['That neither the abbot nor any of the brothers should eat with guests at the gate of the monastery']; see J. Semmler (ed.), *Synodi primae Aquisgranensis decreta authentica*, in *Initia consuetudinis Benedictinae*, 464–5.

[90] *In refectorio . . . non introducantur.* Referring to the decree of the synod of Aachen in 816, canon 14 *Ut laici in refectorium causa manducandi uel bibendi non ducantur* ['That laymen should not be brought into the refectory to eat or drink']; see J. Semmler, ibid. 476. For exceptions to this decree, see above, n. 87. Cf. below, **V, xiv**, n. 244.

[91] *Pauperes ut Christus . . . suscipiantur tripudio.* This alludes to Matt. 25: 35–45; as does *BR*, cap. 53. 15, *Pauperum et peregrinorum maxime susceptioni cura sollicite exhibeatur, quia in ipsis magis Christus suscipitur . . .*; 'Great care and concern are to be shown in receiving poor pilgrims, because in them more particularly Christ is received . . .' and *RC*, cap. 94 [62], *Mandatum . . . pauperibus summa cum diligentia prebeatur, in quibus Christus adoretur qui et suscipitur. Sint igitur in unoquoque monasterio singula*

loca ad hoc constituta, ubi pauperum fiat susceptio 'The Maundy . . . shall be administered with the greatest care to the poor, in whom Christ shall be adored Who is received in them. Therefore let there be a place set apart for the reception of the poor . . .'.

[92] **IV, xiii.** This chapter first describes the virtues that the monks should possess and then says how the abbot should be chosen.

[93] *BENEDICTUS.* St. Benedict of Nursia, *c.*480–*c.*550, the author of the Benedictine Rule.

[94] *quem . . . consilio.* Quoting *BR*, cap. 64. 1, but with *sulubriori* (see n. *r*) here for the more usual *saniore*. Most MSS. of the Benedictine Rule have *saniore, saniori,* or *seniore,* but one, now in Verona, Biblioteca Capitolare, MS. LII (s.viii/ix), has *salubriore.* John *Orbis Britanniae,* 187, calls the present clause 'the first provision for a disputed election found in English sources'. For other references in diplomas to the election of abbots, see S 792, *BCS* 1297 (the spurious Thorney foundation-charter, A.D. 973); S 876, *Councils* 39 (the Abingdon confirmation-charter, A.D. 993); and S 911, *KCD* 714 (the Eynsham foundation-charter, A.D. 1005). For the choosing of a monastic bishop, see *RC*, cap. 9; also below, **V, xiv**, nn. 240–1, and **XXXIII**.

XIIII [.]⁹⁵ QUALITER REX ABBATEM ET
MONACHOS UENERANTES
MUNIAT .

Reges itaque quicumque nostri fuerint
successores nullam exstraneam personam ius
tirannidis super monachos exercentem
imponant .⁹⁶ ne forte Deus eos damnans . et
regno deponat et uita .

Electum uero a fratribus Christi uicarium⁹⁷
dignanter suscipiant . eumque caritatis igne
succensi locupletando uenerentur .

Iuuamen in qua`n´tum indiguerit . Christi
amore conpuncti alacriter impendant .

Mutuo namque confortati iuuamine . in nullo a
regulę preceptis discordantes . Domini
gregem non mercennarii sed pastores
fidissimi . luporum rictibus eximentes intre-
pidi defendant .⁹⁸

XV .⁹⁹ QUALITER ABBAS ET MONACHI
REGEM A DEMONUM TEMPTA-
TIONE ERIPIANT .

Abbas autem armis succinctus . spiritalibus .
monachorum cuneo hinc inde uallatus .

xiv.⁹⁵ IN WHAT WAY THE KING SHOULD
DEFEND THE ABBOT AND THE
WORSHIPPING MONKS.

Whichever kings therefore shall be our successors, let them impose no extraneous personage exercising the rule of a tyrant over
the monks,⁹⁶ lest perchance God, condemning
them, should take away both kingdom and
life.

Let them indeed worthily support the vicar of
Christ⁹⁷ chosen by the brothers and, set alight
with the fire of charity, sustain him with
generous gifts.

Goaded on by love of Christ, let them eagerly
give as much help as shall be needed.

And indeed, comforted by reciprocal help,
dissenting in no respect from the commands
of the Rule, not as hirelings but as most
faithful shepherds let them, intrepid, defend
the Lord's flock, delivering it from the jaws of
wolves.⁹⁸

xv.⁹⁹ IN WHAT WAY THE ABBOT AND
MONKS SHOULD SNATCH THE
KING FROM THE TEMPTATION OF
DEVILS.

Moreover, let the abbot, girded with spiritual
arms, defended on all sides by a troop of

---

⁹⁵ **IV, xiv**. The king's successors are here enjoined to protect the independence of the abbot and monks.

⁹⁶ *nullam exstraneam personam ius tirannidis . . . imponant*. No lay official or lord is to have power over the monks, who are to be under the direct protection of the king. Cf. *RC*, cap. 10, which forbids *secularium prioratus* and offers royal protection to the monks and nuns in England; also S 876 (Abingdon; see above, n. 94), . . . *nec extraneorum quispiam tyrannica fretus contumacia in predicto monasterio ius arripiens exerceat potestatis . . .*; see further the discussion by John *Orbis Britanniae*, 154–80. For *ius tirannidis*, see also below, **IV, xviii**. The word *tirannidis* (a grecism derived from τύραννος) has a Greek genitive ending (*ex inf.* Michael Lapidge).

⁹⁷ *Christi uicarium*. Referring here to the abbot of the New Minster. Cf. *RC*, cap. 95 [63], where someone in the office of abbot is described as *aeterni Christi uicarius* in ministering to the poor, and ibid. cap. 104 [69] where abbots and abbesses are said to be *uicarii* of Christ. In *BR*, caps. 2. 2 and 63. 13, the abbot is said to be *uices Christi*. Cf. also above, **IV, vii**, where King Edgar is also described as *Christi uicarius*.

⁹⁸ *Domini gregem . . . defendant*. The contrast made here between hirelings (*mercennarii*) and the kings as faithful shep-herds is a development of that made in relation to Christ as the Good Shepherd in John 10: 11–13. Cf. *RC*, cap. 3, where King Edgar is likened to a shepherd in his protection of the monks, *Regali utique functus officio ueluti pastorum pastor sollicitus a rabidis perfidorum rectibus, uti hiantibus luporum faucibus, oues quas domini largiente gratia studiosus collegerat muniendo eripuit* 'Thus, in

fulfilment of his royal office, even as the Good Shepherd, he carefully rescued and defended from the savage open mouths of the wicked—as it were the gaping jaws of wolves—those sheep which by God's grace he had diligently gathered together'. See also below, n. 104; and cf. above, n. 38. Elsewhere it is the abbots, following *BR*, cap. 27. 8, rather than the king, who are more usually described in this way. In his poem which prefaces the Benedictional of St. Æthelwold (BL, Add. MS. 49598, fos. 4v–5r), Godeman describes Bishop Æthelwold as protecting his lambs (*agni*) from the Devil, as being in charge of a flock (*grex*) from which no small lamb (*ouilis agniculus paruus*) has been lost, and as saying to God that he has prevented the 'fierce gluttonous wolf' (*lupus audax . . . lurcon*) from taking any away; see Lapidge 'Hermeneutic style', 106. In 'King Edgar's Establishment of Monasteries', 153, abbesses are said to be 'shepherds on God's behalf' (*Gode to hyrdum*). Cf. the use of the words *congregatos* and *gregem* in reference to the monks, above, **IV, xi**, and below, **IV, xvi**; and the use of *pastor* for the abbot in **IV, ix**, and for the bishop in **XXXIII**. Cf. also below, **V, xiv**, n. 212.

⁹⁹ **IV, xv**. The king is to be protected from unearthly enemies by the abbot and the monks.

carismatum celestium rore perfusus .[100] aerias demonum expugnans uersutias . regem omnemque sui regminis clerum . Christo cuius uirtute dimicant iuuante . a rabida hostium persecutione inuisibilium . sollerter spiritus gladio[101] defendens . fidei scuto[102] subtili protegens tutamine . robusto prelians triumpho miles eripiat inperterritus .

XVI .[103] QUALITER REX ABBATEM ET MOCHOS[s] AB HOMINUM PERSE-CUTIONE DEFENDAT .

Rex itidem terrenus cęlestis castra regis fortissimo roborans munimine . armis secularibus uisibiles expugnans aduersarios . hostiumque rabiem seuientium adnihilando deiciens . conditoris sui pascua gregemque sollicita inexpugnabilis tueatur custodia .[104] quatinus ad uitae brauium perueniens . eternis tripudians fruatur bonis . quae nec oculus uidere aliquatenus potuit humanus . nec in hominis cor ullatenus ascendit . quę preparauit Deus diligentibus se .[105]

XVII .[106] DE MONASTICĘ[t] POSSESSIONIS LIBERTATE [.]

Sint prefati monasterii rura omnisque monachorum possessio in rebus magnis uel modicis . internis uel externis . in urbanis uel suburbanis . prediis .[107] campis . pratis . pascuis . siluis . molendinis . riuulorum

monks, drenched with the dew of celestial gifts,[100] conquering the phantom-like tricks of devils, skilfully defending with a sword of the spirit,[101] protecting with the subtle shield of faith[102] as a defence, fighting in hardy triumph as an undaunted soldier, snatch the king and all the clergy of his kingdom from the rabid persecution of invisible enemies, with the help of Christ, through whose power they contend.

xvi.[103] IN WHAT WAY THE KING SHOULD DEFEND THE ABBOT AND THE MONKS FROM THE PERSECUTION OF MEN.

In like manner, let the earthly king, strengthening the camp of the Celestial King with the strongest fortification, conquering visible adversaries with worldly arms and bringing the frenzy of barbarous enemies to nought, by casting them down, protect his Creator's pastures and flock with careful watch,[104] inconquerable, so that, coming to the reward for life, he, rejoicing, might enjoy eternal blessings which neither any human eye has been able to see nor to which the heart of man has risen in any respect, which God has prepared for those who love Him.[105]

xvii.[106] CONCERNING THE FREEDOM OF MONASTIC PROPERTY.

Let the lands of the aforementioned monastery and all the property of the monks in great or modest matters, domestic or external, in city or suburban estates,[107] fields, meadows, pastures, woods, mills, [and] watercourses, be

---

[s] MS. error for MONACHOS   [t] The spur of Ę has been added in pinkish ink

---

[100] carismatum . . . perfusus. Cf. carismatis . . . perfusi, below, **V, v.**

[101] spiritus gladio. With reference to Ephes. 6: 17 (BSV, ii, 1815) gladium spiritus quod est verbum Dei '. . . the sword of the Spirit (which is the word of God)'.

[102] fidei scuto. With reference to Ephes. 6: 16 (BSV, ibid.) scutum fidei in quo possitis omnia tela nequissimi ignea extinguere ' . . . the shield of faith, wherewith you may be able to extinguish all the fiery darts of the most wicked one'.

[103] **IV, xvi.** The king is to defend the abbot and the monks from earthly enemies.

[104] gregemque . . . tueatur custodia. Cf. above, n. 98.

[105] quae . . . se. With reference to 1 Cor. 2: 9 (BSV, ii, 1771) quod oculus non vidit nec auris audivit nec in cor hominis ascendit quae praeparauit Deus his, qui diligunt illum 'That eye hath not seen, nor

ear heard, neither hath it entered into the heart of man, what things God hath prepared for them that love him'. This is also quoted partially in BR, cap. 4. 77. Cf. below, **VI**, n. 1.

[106] **IV, xvii.** This chapter states that all the lands, property, and appurtenances of the monks of the New Minster are to be held as bookland (eterna libertate). They are to be subject however, like most estates of bookland, to the obligation of the Three Burdens; see below, **IV, xxi.**

[107] urbanis uel suburbanis . prediis. Cf. the New Minster's property in Winchester referred to in **VII**, below.

cursibus eterna libertate[108] in Christi nomine eiusque genitricis ditata .

XVIII .[109] QUOD NULLUS SECULARIUM MONASTERII POSSESSIONEM INLICITE USURPET .

Secularium quispiam ausu temerario ius tirannidis non in Christi cultura[110] presumtuosus exerceat .[111]

Non minuat instigante diabolo . quod sancti spiritus instinctu tam a me quam a predecessoribus meis necnon a catholicis utriusque sexus hominibus largiflua concessum est dapsilitate [.]

XVIIII[u] [.][112] DE BENEDICTIONE AUGENTIUM .

Augenti tribuat rerum cunctarum opifex tranquillum uitę presentis excursum . longeuam instantis temporis uitam . futuram ęternae[v] beatitudinis talionem [.]

Sufficientem uictualium ubertatem interminabile prosperitatis augmtum[w] . copiosum uirtutum omnium iuuamen .

XX [.][113] DE MALEDICTIONE MINUENTIUM [.]

Minuentem . perpetua possideat miseria .

In Domini manens persecutione . eius genitricis sanctorumque omnium incurrat offensam .

Presentis uitę aduersitas illi semper eueniat .

Nulla ei bonitatis accidat prosperitas .

enriched with eternal freedom[108] in the name of Christ and of His Mother.

xviii.[109] THAT NO SECULAR PERSON SHOULD UNLAWFULLY ENCROACH ON THE MONASTERY'S PROPERTY.

Let no secular person, presuming with an imprudent attempt, exercise the rule of a tyrant[111] in Christ's ploughland.[110]

Let him not, at the Devil's instigation, diminish what has been granted, at the inspiration of the Holy Ghost, with generous bounty both by me and by my predecessors, as well as by orthodox people of both sexes.

xix.[112] CONCERNING THE BLESSING ON THOSE WHO INCREASE [THE MONASTERY'S PROPERTY].

Let the Maker of All Things bestow on him who increases [the monastery's property] a quiet end to the present life, a life of great age for the present time, a future reward of eternal bliss;

a sufficient abundance of provisions, an endless enlargement of prosperity, the copious assistance of all virtues.

xx.[113] CONCERNING THE CURSE ON THOSE WHO DIMINISH [THE MONASTERY'S PROPERTY].

Let perpetual misery overwhelm him who diminishes [the monastery's property].

Remaining in the Lord's persecution, let him incur the hatred of His Mother and all the saints.

Let misfortune always befall him in this present life.

Let no prosperity of goodness fall to him.

---

[u] XVIII, *in error*, Councils, *i, 129*   [v] æternae, *in error, ibid.*   [w] *MS. error for* augmentum

---

[108] *eterna libertate*. See above, n. 106. The tenure is similarly described, below, **IV, xxi**.

[109] **IV, xviii**. This chapter takes the form of a clause of prohibition forbidding the alienation of the New Minster's property to laymen.

[110] *in Christi cultura*. Cf. *Domini cultura* in **IV, vi**; see above, n. 42.

[111] *Secularium quispiam . . . ius tirannidis non . . . exerceat*. Cf. 'King Edgar's Establishment of Monasteries', 153, which enjoins the abbesses *þæt heora nan ne gedyrstlæce þæt hi Godes landare naþor ne heora magum ne woroldricum mid ungesceade sellen, ne for sceatte ne lyffetunge* 'that none of them presume senselessly to give God's estates either to their kinsfolk or to secular great persons, neither

for money nor for flattery'. For *ius tirannidis*, see above, n. 96. Cf. below, **V, ii**, n. 41; **V, iii**, n. 61; and **V, xiv**, n. 247.

[112] **IV, xix**. Those who augment the present privilege are to be eternally blessed.

[113] **IV, xx**. This chapter, in the form of an anathema with saving clause, threatens eternal punishment to those who diminish the present privilege unless they make amends.

Omnia eius peculia inimici uastantes diripiant .
In futuro autem eterni miserrimum cum ędis in
sinistra positum[114] damnent cruci`a´tus . si
non satisfactione emendauerit congrua .[115]
quod in Domini usurpans detraxit censura .

XXI .[116] QUIBUS MODIS SECULARIBUS
OPTEMPERENT ET QUOD
NULLIUS REATUS HOC
DOMINI PRIUILEGIUM MIN-
UERE UALEAT .

Tribus tantummodo causis secularibus obtemperent preceptis . rata uidelicet expeditione .[x]
pontis arcisue constructione . alias ęterna
ditati glorientur libertate .[117]

Reatus quippiam si incitante demone seductus
uel abbas uel fratrum aliquis fragiliter quod
absit contraxerit . iustitia purgante secundum
regulę preceptum[118] abolitus damnetur .
maneatque prefatę munificentię libertas altithrono per nostram humilitatem oblata ad
monachorum usus gratuite sibi famulantium
inuiolabilis ęterna libertate iocunda . quia
Deus qui hanc priuilegii largifluam donationem locumque cum uniuersa monachorum
familia ruraque omnia sacro subiecta coeno-
bio possidet . numquam reatum commisit .
nec ullo umquam tempore committet .[119]

[x] *The point is in reddish-brown ink*

---

[114] *cum ędis in sinistra positum.* With reference to Matt. 15: 31–
43 (esp. 32–3), the sorting of the sheep from the goats at the Last
Judgement. Note that S 687, a diploma written by 'Edgar A' (see
above, p. 15) and perhaps drafted by Æthelwold (see above, n. 65)
uses a quotation from Matt. 15: 41 in its sanction.

[115] *si non satisfactione emendauerit congrua.* Cf. S 690, 707, and
717 (diplomas written by 'Edgar A'; see above, p. 15) which have
the following saving clause, *si non satisfactione emendauerit congrua
quod contra nostrum deliquid decretum.*

[116] **IV, xxi.** This chapter strictly limits the liability of the
monks with regard to secular obligations, punishment, or
forfeiture for crime.

[117] *ęterna . . . libertate.* Cf. above, **IV, xvii.**

[118] *secundum regulę preceptum.* See *BR,* caps. 23–8, where
various forms of punishment are prescribed, including excommunication, beating, and expulsion.

[119] *Reatus quippiam . . . uel abbas uel fratrum aliquis . . . quia Deus . . .
numquam reatum commisit . nec ullo umquam tempore committet.* Cf. S
782, BCS 1270 (A.D. 971, in favour of Bishop Æthelwold), *pro*

Let ravaging enemies plunder all his property.
In the future, moreover, let eternal torments
condemn him, placed most wretchedly on the
left hand side with the goats,[114] unless he
should make amends with a suitable reparation[115] for what, encroaching, he has taken
away from the Lord's property.

xxi.[116] IN WHAT WAYS THESE [GIFTS]
SHOULD BE SUBJECT TO SECULAR
[OBLIGATIONS]; AND THAT NO
MAN'S GUILT SHOULD HAVE THE
POWER TO DIMINISH THIS, THE
LORD'S PRIVILEGE.

Let these [gifts] be subject to secular commands
only in respect of the Three Burdens, namely,
established military-service and the building
of bridges or fortifications; otherwise, let
them glory, enriched by eternal freedom.[117]

If either the abbot or any one of the brothers,
seduced by the Devil's urging, should weakly
commit some sort of crime, which heavens
forbid!, let him be condemned, destroyed by
cleansing justice, according to the command
of the Rule,[118] but let the freedom of the
aforementioned donation remain inviolable,
delightful in eternal freedom, bestowed by
the High-throned One through our humility,
for the use of the monks voluntarily serving
Him, because God, who owns this abundant
donation of privilege as well as the place with
the whole family of monks and all the lands
which have been made subject to the holy
monastery, has never committed any offence,
nor will He ever commit one at any time.[119]

*nullius altioris vel inferioris gradus hominis reatu rus præfatum a domini
qui nunquam reatum commisit possessione privetur* ['the aforesaid
estate should not be taken out of the possession of the Lord,
who never committed any offence, on account of the offence of
any man of higher or lower rank']; and 'King Edgar's Establishment of Monasteries', 153–4, *Gif heora hwilc, mid deofles costnunge
beswicen, for Gode oþþe for worulde gyltig biþ, ne gladige on þæt noþer ne
cyning ne worulrica, swilce him gerymed sy 7 antimber geseald þæt he God
bereafige, þe þa æhta ah, 7 nænne gylt næfre ne geworhte,* 'If any one of
them, led astray by the temptation of the devil, be convicted of
crime against the church or the state, let neither king nor secular

Sit igitur prefata libertas eterna . quia Deus
libertatis possessor eternus est .

[XXII .][120] QUOTIES ET QUARE IN ANNI
                CIRCULO[121] HOC FRATRIBUS
                LEGATUR PRIUILEGIUM [.][γ]

                    *   *   *   *   *

[122]Anno incarnationis dominicę . dcccclxvi .
scripta est h`u´ius priuilegii singrapha[123] his
testibus consentientibus quorum inferius
nomina ordinatim caraxantur [.][124]
[125]+ EGO EADGAR .[126] diuina largiente gratia

Let therefore the aforementioned freedom be
eternal, because God is the Eternal Possessor
of freedom.

xxii.[120] HOW MANY TIMES, AND WHY,
THIS DOCUMENT SHOULD BE
READ TO THE BROTHERS IN THE
COURSE OF THE YEAR.[121]

                    *   *   *   *   *

[122]The document[123] of this privilege was written
in the year of the Lord's Incarnation 966, with
these witnesses in agreement whose names
are written[124] below.

[125]+ I, EDGAR,[126] king of the English while the

γ *The text of this chapter, and possibly of subsequent ones, has been
lost, being contained on a leaf or leaves now missing from A after fo. 29.
This part was apparently already lacking by the 14th cent. as it is also
omitted in B. The third MS. (C) contains only chapter VI*

---

lord be glad of it, as if the way were cleared and a reason given for
him to rob God, who owns those possessions, and who never
committed any crime'. On the probability of Æthelwold's authorship of all three passages, see D. Whitelock, 'The Authorship of the
Account of King Edgar's Establishment of Monasteries', in J. L.
Rosier (ed.), *Philological Essays: Studies in Old and Middle English
Literature in Honour of Herbert Dean Meritt* (The Hague and Paris,
1970), 125–36, esp. 130–3. Whitelock, ibid. 132, notes that S 792,
BCS 1297, the forged foundation-charter of Thorney Abbey,
contains a similar clause and was probably based on a copy of S
782; see also C. R. Hart, *The Early Charters of Eastern England*
(Leicester, 1966), 165–86.

[120] **IV, xxii.** This chapter, apart from the heading, is missing;
see note γ. The missing text seems to have included an attempt
to ensure that the provisions and privileges recorded in the
present document would be familiar to all the monks of the
New Minster. Cf. *BR*, cap. 66. 8, *Hanc autem regulam sepius
uolumus in congregatione legi, ne quis fratrum se de ignorantia excuset*
'We wish this rule to be read often in the community, so that
none of the brothers can offer the excuse of ignorance'.

[121] *IN ANNI CIRCULO.* Cf. *RC*, title to caps. 15–38 [14–28],
. . . *ORDO QVALITER DIVRNIS SIVE NOCTVRNIS HORIS
REGVLARIS MOS A MONACHIS PER ANNI CIRCVLVM
OBSERVARI CONVENIAT* 'THE ORDER IN WHICH THE
CUSTOMS OF THE REGULAR LIFE OUGHT TO BE
OBSERVED BY MONKS DAY AND NIGHT THROUGH-
OUT THE YEAR'. The words *anni circulus* are an ancient
formula, found for example in the preface to the Hadrianum
(. . . *HIC SACRAMENTORUM DE CIRCULO ANNI EXPO-
SITO* . . .); see Jean Deshusses (ed.), *Le Sacramentaire Grégorien*, i
(as above, n. 62), 86; and in other sacramentaries quoted *RC*, eds.
Symons and Spath, p. 80 n.

[122] **IV, dating clause.** This dating clause has similarities to
those in diplomas written by 'Edgar A' (see above, n. 65).
However, it is even closer to those in S 737, 754, 757–9, and
773 (*BCS* 1189, 1200, 1221–2, 1224, and 1234; A.D. 966–9,
nearly all from the Abingdon or the Old Minster archives). An

extended version occurs in the Pershore refoundation charter of
A.D. 972 (S 786, *BCS* 1282), and thus also in the interpolated
Worcester diploma (S 788, *BCS* 1284) which is based on it. Cf.
also S 876, *KCD* 684 (A.D. 996, to Abingdon).

[123] *singrapha.* A grecism; for other 10th-century instances of
the word, see John *Orbis Britanniae*, 182–3; and O'Donovan
Sherborne Charters, 30.

[124] *caraxantur.* A grecism, ultimately from χαράσσω; see
M. Herren, 'Insular Latin *c(h)araxare (craxare)* and its Derivatives',
Peritia 1 (1982), 273–80. For the use in Æthelwold's attestation to
S 739, Sawyer *Burton Charters* 21 (bearing the date 966 but
possibly written in the reign of Æthelred) of an alternative
preterite form *karessi* from the same Greek verb, see Lapidge
'Æthelwold as Scholar', 90, 93–4.

[125] **IV, witness-list.** The datable subscriptions are in agreement with the date 966; see John *Orbis Britanniae*, 271–5. The
subscriptions of the king's two sons, his wife, and his grandmother are sandwiched between those of the two archbishops,
serving to emphasize the importance of Archbishop Dunstan.
Æthelwold is placed first of the bishops, although only a recent
appointment, likewise emphasizing his status. The florid language used in the first six subscriptions and in those of Bishop
Æthelwold and Abbot Æthelgar (of the New Minster) recalls
that used in the first eight subscriptions in S 690, in favour of
Abingdon Abbey, A.D. 961, written by 'Edgar A' (see above,
p. 15), which subscriptions may have been drafted by Bishop
Oswald of Worcester; see Lapidge 'Æthelwold as Scholar', 92–3.
Many, but not all, of the witnesses also occur in S 739, which
may have been written in the reign of Æthelred (see above,
n. 124); that document, however, has much simpler descriptions
of the important witnesses and different verbs of subscription
and is unlikely to have been copied from **IV**. The exclusion of
Edmund *clito* (who died in 971; see below, n. 128) from the
witnesses in S 739, although given precedence in **IV** over his
half-brother Edward (see below, n. 129) may be additional reason
for thinking that S 739 is later than A.D. 966. The present
witness list was later used in the fabrication of S 746, *BCS* 1191,
which was added to MS. A twice, in the 12th and the 14th
centuries; of those, the first text omits the subscription of

Anglorum basileus hoc priuilegii donum nostro largiens redemtori locoque eius sanctissimo primus omium[z] regum monachorum 'inibi' collegium constituens manu propria signum agiae crucis imprimens confirmaui .

+ Ego DUNSTAN[127] Dorobernensis ęclesię archiepiscopus largifluam beniuoli regis donationem uenerans crucis signaculo corroboraui .

+ Ego Eadmund[128] clito legitimus prefati regis filius crucis signaculum infantili florens etate propria indidi manu .

+ Ego Eadpeard[129] eodem rege clito procreatus prefatam patris munificentiam crucis signo consolidaui [.]

+ Ego Ælfðryð[aa] [130] legitima prefati regis con-

divine grace grants, granting this gift of privilege to our Redeemer and His most holy place, establishing first of all the kings a company of monks in that place, marking the symbol of the Holy Cross with my own hand, have confirmed.

+ I, DUNSTAN,[127] archbishop of the church of Canterbury, respecting the benevolent king's copious donation, have corroborated with the sign of the Cross.

+ I, Edmund[128] Ætheling, the legitimate son of the aforementioned king, flourishing in infantile age, have put the sign of the Cross with my own hand.

+ I, Edward[129] Ætheling, begotten by the same king, have made firm the aforementioned generosity of [my] father with the symbol of the Cross.

+ I, Ælfthryth,[130] the legitimate wife of the

---

[z] MS. error for omnium   [aa] Ælft- altered to Ælfð-

Edmund *clito* and the second changes him into another Edward *clito*.

[126] King Edgar; see above, n. 2. The king's subscription summarises the aims of the document. The identical subscription in S 746 is probably copied from that here. Edgar is also called *Anglorum basileus* in his subscription on an Old Minster diploma, S 806, *CW* 58 and 60 (A.D. 978 for 968).

[127] Archbishop of Canterbury, 959–88. Born in Somerset, *c.*909, Dunstan had been associated with the royal circle since his youth spent at the court of King Æthelstan. He had been ordained as a priest by his kinsman Bishop Ælfheah I of Winchester in *c.*936, on the same day as Æthelwold (see below, n. 134). As abbot of Glastonbury (940–), Dunstan pioneered the revival of Benedictine monasticism in England, with the approval of King Edgar's father King Edmund. While in exile (956–7), in the reign of Eadwig, he stayed at the reformed monastery of St. Peter's, Ghent. On his return, Edgar, as king of Mercia, had made him bishop of Worcester (?957), then of London (957 × 959), before making him primate, once the kingdoms of Mercia (with Northumbria) and Wessex were reunited on the death of Eadwig (cf. below, n. 140). His archiepiscopal corroboration of the *Regularis Concordia* was also sought, and resulted in the addition of a provision prohibiting any monk or other man from entering any of the nunneries; see *RC*, cap. 7. On him, see further N. P. Brooks, 'The Career of St Dunstan', in Nigel Ramsay, Margaret Sparks and Tim Tatton-Brown (ed.), *St Dunstan: His Life, Times and Cult* (Woodbridge, 1992), 1–23; Gretsch *Intellectual Foundations*, 256–7 and 372–6; also J. Armitage Robinson, *The Times of Saint Dunstan* (Oxford 1923, repr. 1969), 81–103. He also subscribes below, **VI, IX**, and **XXII**.

[128] Edmund was the first son of King Edgar and Ælfthryth (see below, n. 130). He died in 971. Although not much more than twelve months old in 966, he is here both called *clito*

legitimus and given precedence over his older half-brother Edward (see below, n. 129). His inclusion is a weighty argument in favour of the genuineness of the present witness list; see John *Orbis Britanniae*, 274–5, and *Councils*, 131, n. 1. The word *clito* is an Anglo-Latin neologism of the 10th cent., a grecism formed from κλυτός 'renowned' / 'distinguished'; see David N. Dumville, 'The Ætheling: a Study in Anglo-Saxon Constitutional History', *ASE* 8 (1979), 1–33, especially 7–10.

[129] Edward, born *c.*962, was the son of King Edgar and his first wife Æthelflæd. He succeeded Edgar as king in 975 but was murdered at Corfe, in Dorset, on 18th March 978. While king, he gave permission to Bishop Æthelwold (see below, n. 134) to make an agreement concerning the acquisition of property in Winchester for part of the Old Minister's precinct; see below, **VIII**.

[130] Ælfthryth, the daughter of Ealdorman Ordgar of Devon (see below, n. 153), was the third wife of King Edgar, whom she married by 964 (see S 725, BCS 1143). She was then the widow of Ealdorman Æthelwold of East Anglia (who had died in 962), whose brother Ealdorman Æthelwine subscribes below, n. 155. In the present document, both Ælfthryth and her son Edmund (see above, n. 128) are described as 'legitimate', stressing their precedence in relation to the future succession of Edgar's children to the throne. This may have been her first subscription as queen; see *Councils*, 131, n. 2. If so, it could have been seen as an opportunity to make her status clear to the whole court. She was a strong supporter of the Benedictine Reform (cf. below, n. 131) and was later designated as the protectress of the nuns by *RC*, cap. 3. On her, see further Hart *ECNE*, 272–4 and Keynes *Diplomas*, 172; and note that the date of her death is assigned to 17 November 999 × 1001 by Keynes ibid. 210, n. 203. She also subscribes below, **VI** and **IX**. In **VII**, below, she is mentioned as acting as a witness, in the company of Bishop Æthelwold (see below, n. 134), to a transaction compensating Nunnaminster for

iuncx mea legatione monachos eodem loco
rege annuente constituens[131] crucem
inpressi .

+ Ego Eadgifu[132] predicti regis aua hoc opus
egregium crucis taumate consolidaui [.]

+ Ego Oscytyl[133] Eboracensis ęclesię archiepiscopus confirmaui .

+ Ego Aðelpold[134] aeclesiae Uuintoniensis
episcopus regis gloriosisimi beniuolentiam
abbatem mea altum mediocritate et alumnos quos educaui[135] illi commendans crucis
signaculo benedixi [.]

+ Ego Ælfstan[136] Lundoniensis ęclesię pontifex
consolidaui .

aforementioned king, with the king's
approval establishing the monks in the
same place, by the sending of my ambassa-
dor,[131] have made the mark of the Cross.

+ I, Eadgifu,[132] the grandmother of the aforesaid king, have made firm this illustrious
work with the symbol of the Cross.

+ I, Oscytel,[133] archbishop of the church of
York, have confirmed.

+ I, Æthelwold,[134] bishop of the church of
Winchester, have blessed with the sign of
the Cross the benevolence of the most
glorious king, entrusting to his protection
the noble abbot and the pupils whom I, in
my insignificance, have educated.[135]

+ I, Ælfstan,[136] pontiff of the church of
London, have made [it] firm.

the loss of their watercourse in Winchester. In another docu-
ment (S 1242, *CW* 61; *AS Writs* 108), her testimony in 995 ×
1001 is recorded concerning the actions of herself and Bishop
Æthelwold taken in support of the repossession, by the Old
Minster, of Ruishton, Somerset, in ?968 (for this date, cf. S 806,
CW 58, 60, *BCS* 1219–20, concerning Taunton, of which
Ruishton was a dependency).

[131] *mea legatione . . . rege annuente constituens*. This would appear
to mean that Ælfthryth had sent someone (or some people) to
support Bishop Æthelwold in his establishment of monks at the
New Minster. This would have paralleled King Edgar's sending in
964 of his thegn Wulfstan of Dalham (cf. below, n. 164) to oversee
the installation of monks at the Old Minster; see Wulfstan *Vita
S. Æthelwoldi*, cap. 18 (ed. Lapidge and Winterbottom, 32–3). The
refoundation of both the Old and the New Minsters is briefly
recorded in *ASC* [A, F], s.a. 964. Either Ælfthryth took her action
in 964 before becoming queen, but as the widow of a powerful
ealdorman and with the king's permission (*rege annuente*: cf.
Wulfstan *Vita S. Æthelwoldi*, cap. 20 (ed. Lapidge and Winterbottom, 36–7), *Ætheluuoldus . . . annuente rege Eadgaro, canonicos de
Nouo expulit Monasterio, illucque monachos introduxit . . .* 'Æthelwold
. . . with the permission of King Edgar drove the canons from the
New Minster, introducing there monks . . .'), or, more likely, the
annal in *ASC* is an over-simplification of the process of refoundation and Ælfthryth's action in support of the monks of the New
Minster occurred in 965 × 966, after her re-marriage. That there
may have been a prolonged period of animosity before the canons
were finally ejected from the New Minster is suggested by **IV, ix**,
and **x**, above, which seek to protect the monks from the
opposition of the canons and their supporters.

[132] Eadgifu was King Edgar's grandmother. She was the
widow (third wife) of King Edward the Elder, the founder of
the New Minster (see above, **II** and **III**) and her presence here
gave continuity to the royal patronage of the same. She was the
beneficiary of S 811, *CW* 80, *BCS* 1319, a grant of 65 hides at
East Meon, Hants, in ?959; she died in 966 or 967. For her
support of Æthelwold (below, n. 134) and other monastic
reformers, see John *Orbis Britanniae*, 193. The thegn Wulfstan
(below, n. 164) may have been her steward..

[133] Oscytel was archbishop of York, 956–71. He was a relative

of Bishop Oswald (below, n. 138), who succeeded him as
archbishop. On him, see Hart *ECNE*, 353–5. He also subscribes
below, **XXII**.

[134] Æthelwold was bishop of Winchester, 963–84. Born at
Winchester, 904/5 × 909, he had been associated with the royal
court since his youth. With Dunstan (above, n. 127) he was
ordained as a priest (in 934/5 × 27 October 939) by Dunstan's
kinsman Bishop Ælfheah I of Winchester, a monk. After a
period as a monk at Glastonbury under Dunstan as abbot,
Æthelwold himself became abbot of Abingdon before 23
November 955 (as such he subscribes below, **XXII**, and is
mentioned in **XXI**) during which time he was responsible for
the education of Edgar; cf. below, n. 135. After becoming bishop
of Winchester (elected 29 November 963) he succeeded in
instigating the reform of both the Old and the New Minsters
and Nunnaminster; cf. below, **V–VIII**, and **XXXIII**. He also
subscribes **IX**, below. For his probable authorship of the present
document and of other related texts, see above, p. 66. On him,
see further Wulfstan *Vita S. Æthelwoldi, passim* (also, ed. Lapidge
and Winterbottom, xxxix–li) ; J. Armitage Robinson, *The Times
of Saint Dunstan* (Oxford, 1921, repr. 1969), 104–22; Hart *ECNE*,
293–4; Barbara Yorke (ed.), *Bishop Æthelwold: His Career and
Influence* (Woodbridge, 1988, repr. 1997); and Gretsch *Intellectual
Foundations*, 235–41 and *passim*.

[135] *abbatem . . . et alumnos quos educaui*. Bishop Æthelwold here
commends a group of his former pupils to another one of them,
King Edgar himself; see above, n. 134. Abbot Æthelgar of the
New Minster (below, n. 149) is described as Æthelwold's
discipulus by both Wulfstan and Ælfric; see above n. 60. Other
of Æthelwold's known pupils amongst the clergy in the present
witness list are Abbots Osgar, Ordbeorht, and Ælfstan; see below,
nn. 146–8. For Æthelwold's role as a teacher, see Lapidge
'Æthelwold as Scholar', 104–17.

[136] Ælfstan was bishop of London, 959 × 964–995 × 996 (in
succession to Dunstan, above, n. 127). On him, see further Hart
ECNE, 269–70. He also subscribes below, **VI**, and **IX**.

+ Ego Osulf[137] episcopus confirmaui

+ Ego Ospold[138] episcopus consignaui

+ Ego Alfpold[139] episcopus consolidaui

+ Ego Byrehtelm[140] episcopus confirmaui

+ Ego Aelfstan[141] episcopus consolidaui

[+] Ego Eadelm[142] episcopus confirmaui

+ Ego Aðulf[143] episcopus consignaui

+ Ego Þynsige[144] episcopus confirmaui

+ Ego Æscpig[145] abbas consolidaui

+ Ego Osgar[146] abbas consignaui

+ Ego Ordbyriht[147] abbas

+ Ego Ælfstan[148] abbas

+ Ego Æðelgar[149] primus huic loco abbas ordinatus[150] Christo gubernante uigui .

+ I, Oswulf,[137] bishop, have confirmed.

+ I, Oswald,[138] bishop, have subscribed.

+ I, Ælfweald,[139] bishop, have made [it] firm.

+ I, Beorhthelm,[140] bishop, have confirmed.

+ I, Ælfstan,[141] bishop, have made [it] firm.

+ I, Eadhelm,[142] bishop, have confirmed.

+ I, Æthulf,[143] bishop, have subscribed.

+ I, Wynsige,[144] bishop, have confirmed.

+ I, Æscwig,[145] abbot, have made [it] firm.

+ I, Osgar,[146] abbot, have subscribed.

+ I, Ordbeorht,[147] abbot.

+ I, Ælfstan,[148] abbot.

+ I, Æthelgar,[149] ordained[150] to this place as the first abbot, have begun to flourish with Christ as guide.

---

[137] Oswulf was bishop of Ramsbury, 949 × 951–970. He also subscribes below, **VI**, and **XXII**.

[138] Oswald was bishop of Worcester, 961–92 (in succession to Dunstan, above, n. 127). He was a monk of Fleury and one of the leading figures of the Benedictine Reform in England. He was the nephew of Archbishop Oda of Canterbury (941–58) and a relative of Archbishop Oscytel of York (above, n. 133), whom he succeeded in 971, holding Worcester and York in plurality. On Oswald, see Nicholas Brooks and Catherine Cubitt (ed.), *St Oswald of Worcester: Life and Influence* (London, 1996); also J. Armitage Robinson, *The Times of Saint Dunstan* (Oxford 1923, repr. 1969), 123–42. He also subscribes below, **IX**, **XXII**, and **XXIV**.

[139] Either Ælfweald I, bishop of Crediton 953–72 (a monk of Glastonbury, see Hart *ECNE*, 279) or Ælfweald I, bishop of Sherborne 958 × (963 × 964)–978 (?previously abbot of Glastonbury; see Hart *ECNE*, 280–1). One or the other also subscribes below, **VI**, and **XXII**.

[140] Beorhthelm was bishop of Wells, 956–73. He was probably the man who was appointed archbishop of Canterbury by King Eadwig in 959 but whom King Edgar replaced with Dunstan (see above, n. 127) in the same year; see D. Whitelock, 'The Appointment of Dunstan as Archbishop of Canterbury', *Otium et Negotium: Studies in Onomatology and Library Science Presented to Olof von Feilitzen*, ed. F. Sandgren (Stockholm, 1973), 232–47. He also subscribes below, **VI**, and perhaps **XXII** (see ibid., n. 46).

[141] Ælfstan was bishop of Rochester, ? × 964–994 × 995. He was a monk of the Old Minster. See Hart *ECNE*, 271–2.

[142] Eadhelm was bishop of Selsey, 956 × 963–979 × 980, being succeeded by Abbot Æthelgar (below, n. 149). He also subscribes below, **VI**.

[143] Æthulf was bishop of Elmham, ? × 955–966 × ? On him, see Hart *ECNE*, 295–6. He also subscribes below, **XXII**.

[144] Wynsige was bishop of Lichfield, 963 × 964–975.

[145] Æscwig was abbot of Bath, *c*.963–?*c*.977. He also subscribes below, **VI**. He may be identical with the Æscwig who was later bishop of Dorchester (cf. below, **IX**, n. 18), but this is not certain; see *HRH*, 28, and cf. Hart *ECNE*, 281–3.

[146] Osgar was abbot of Abingdon, 963–84, in succession to

Æthelwold (above, n. 134) when the latter became bishop of Winchester. He was a monk who had accompanied Æthelwold from Glastonbury to Abingdon *c*.954, and who had subsequently been sent by Æthelwold to the abbey of Fleury in order to study the monastic observances there; see Wulfstan *Vita S. Æthelwoldi*, caps. 11 and 14. On him, see further Hart *ECNE*, 355–6. Osgar was one of the pupils referred to by Æthelwold in the present document; see above, n. 135. He also subscribes below, **VI**.

[147] Ordbeorht was abbot of Chertsey, 964–?988/9. He was probably the same Ordbeorht who later became bishop of Selsey (cf. below, **XXVI**, n. 25); see *HRH*, 38. He may also have been the Ordbeorht, previously a clerk from Winchester, who had accompanied Æthelwold from Glastonbury to Abingdon, *c*.954, see Wulfstan *Vita S. Æthelwoldi*, cap. 11. On him, see further Hart *ECNE*, 350–1. Ordbeorht was one of the pupils referred to by Æthelwold in the present document; see above, n. 135. He also subscribes below, **IX**.

[148] Abbot of ?Glastonbury, 964–70. Ælfstan was probably one of the first monks of the reformed Old Minster but seems to have been promoted almost immediately to take charge of Glastonbury; he was probably later bishop of Ramsbury (after Oswulf, above, n. 137); see *HRH*, 50. He had earlier been a pupil of Æthelwold's at Abingdon (cf. above, n. 135), where he is said to have shown his obedience to him by plunging his hand into a boiling stew-pot; see Wulfstan *Vita S. Æthelwoldi*, cap. 14 (ed. Lapidge and Winterbottom, 28–9). On him, see further Hart *ECNE*, 270–1. He may have acted as abbot of the Old Minster in 964; see Wulfstan, *Vita S. Æthelwoldi*, 28, n. 1, but cf. Keynes *Liber Vitae*, 25–6.

[149] Æthelgar was the first abbot of the reformed New Minster, 964–?988; see above, n. 60. He had previously been a monk at Glastonbury and Abingdon and is referred to in Bishop Æthelwold's subscription as having been educated by him; see above, n. 135. He later held the abbacy in plurality with the see of Selsey (980–8, after Eadhelm, above, n. 142; cf. below, **IX**, n. 4), but gave both up on his succession to Dunstan (see above, n. 127) as archbishop of Canterbury, 988–90; see *HRH*, 80–1, and Hart *ECNE*, 283–4. For his part in the adjustment of the boundaries

+ Ego Ælfhere[151] dux	+ I, Ælfhere,[151] ealdorman.
+ Ego Ælfheah[152] dux	+ I, Ælfheah,[152] ealdorman.
+ Ego Ordgar[153] dux	+ I, Ordgar,[153] ealdorman.
+ Ego Ęðelstan[bb][154] dux	+ I, Æthelstan,[154] ealdorman.
+ Ego Ęþelƿine[cc][155] dux[dd]	+ I, Æthelwine,[155] ealdorman.
+ Ego Beorhtnoð[156] dux	+ I, Beorhtnoth,[156] ealdorman.
+ Ego Ælfƿine[157] minister	+ I, Ælfwine,[157] thegn.
+ Ego Byrhtferþ[158] minister	+ I, Beorhtfrith,[158] thegn.
+ Ego Ospeard[159] minister	+ I, Osweard,[159] thegn.
+ Ego Æþelpeard[160] minister	+ I, Æthelweard,[160] thegn.
+ Ego Ælfpeard[161] minister	+ I, Ælfweard,[161] thegn.

[bb] Æðelstan, *in error*, Councils, *i, 132*   [cc] Æþelwine, *in error* ibid.   [dd] *This subscription and the remainder of the document may be by a different scribe. The writing is smaller than hitherto and in the subscriptions the letter þ is used as well as ð, whereas up to this point only the latter occurs*

---

between the three minsters at Winchester in ?970 × 975, see below, **VII**. He seems to have been the source of the New Minster's ownership of Hyde Moors; see below, **IX**. As abbot, he also subscribes below, **VI**, and is a witness to **VIII (i)** and **(ii)**. As bishop of Selsey, he subscribes below, **XXIV**.

[150] *ordinatus*: 'ordained'. Probably used here in a technical sense, referring to appointment to ecclesiastical office; cf. above, n. 85. Both Ælfric and Wulfstan used *ordinans* when recording his appointment; see above, n. 60.

[151] Ælfhere was ealdorman of Mercia, 956–83. He was the brother both of Ealdorman Ælfheah and of the thegn Ælfwine (see below, nn. 152 and 157); and probably of the thegn Eadric who subscribes below, **XXII** (n. 61). His attestation to the present document may be contrasted to his later anti-monastic activity after King Edgar's death, recorded in the *Vita S. Oswaldi* (see Whitelock *EHD*, 912–13). For his biography and background, see Williams '*Princeps Merciorum gentis*'. He also subscribes below, **VI**, and **XXII**.

[152] Ælfheah was ealdorman of central Wessex, 959–71. He was the brother both of Ealdorman Ælfhere (see above, n. 151) and of the thegn Ælfwine (see below, n. 157); and probably also of the thegn Eadric who subscribes below, **XXII** (n. 61). On him, see Williams '*Princeps Merciorum gentis*', 147–54. For his will, including bequests to his *gefæðeran* Queen Ælfthryth (see above, n. 130) and to her sons by King Edgar, see S 1485, *CW* 185, *AS Wills* 9. He also subscribes below, **XXII**.

[153] Ordgar was ealdorman of Devon, *c*.965–. He was the father of Queen Ælfthryth (see above, n. 130). He was dead by 971; see John *Orbis Britanniae*, 274 and n. 1.

[154] Æthelstan *Rota*, ealdorman of SE. Mercia, 955–70. He was the brother-in-law of Ealdorman Beorhtnoth (see below, n. 156). On him, see further Hart *ECNE*, 299–300, and Williams '*Princeps Merciorum gentis*', 160.

[155] Æthelwine *Dei amicus*, ealdorman of East Anglia, 962–92. He was the son of Ealdorman Æthelstan 'Half-King' of East Anglia and the brother of Ealdorman Æthelwold, the first husband of Queen Ælfthryth (see above, n. 130). His mother

Ælfwen is said to have been King Edgar's foster-mother; see Hart *ECNE*, 231. He was the founder of Ramsey Abbey in 969 and a staunch supporter of the monastic cause. On him, see further C. Hart, 'Athelstan "Half-King" and his Family', *ASE* 2 (1973), 115–44, at 133–8. He also subscribes below, **VI** and **IX**. Cf. also Æthelwine *minister* who subscribes below, **XXII** in 961.

[156] Beorhtnoth was ealdorman of Essex, from 956 until his death in battle at Maldon in 991. He was a benefactor of Ely Abbey and other religious houses. He was the brother-in-law of Ealdorman Æthelstan (see above, n. 154) and a close associate of Ealdorman Æthelwine (see above, n. 155). He is praised as a strong defender of the monks during the period of hostility towards them after King Edgar's death. On him, see D. G. Scragg (ed.), *The Battle of Maldon, A.D. 991* (Oxford, 1991), *passim*; and Janet Cooper (ed.), *The Battle of Maldon: Fiction and Fact* (London and Rio Grande, 1993), *passim*. He also subscribes below, **VI, IX**, and **XXII**.

[157] Ælfwine was a prominent thegn and the brother of Ealdormen Ælfhere and Ælfheah (see above, nn. 151 and 152); as probably also of the thegn Eadric (ibid.). He seems to have become a monk at Glastonbury *c*.970, but was still alive in 975. On him, see Williams '*Princeps Merciorum gentis*', 154–5, and Hart *ECNE*, 277–8. He also subscribes below, **XXII**.

[158] Beorhtfrith was a prominent thegn and a kinsman of King Edgar. On him, see Hart *ECNE*, 301. He subscribes Edgar's diplomas 958 × 975 (including **XXII**, below): Keynes *Atlas*, Table LVII.

[159] This Osweard was probably the thegn of this name who subscribes several of King Edgar's diplomas 959 × 974, usually about sixth or seventh of the *ministri* (see Keynes *Atlas*, ibid.). He is called King Edgar's kinsman in S 803, *CW* 137, *BCS* 1314, by which he was granted 4 hides at South Stoke, Sussex, in 975. He also subscribes below, **XXII**.

[160] Æthelweard was the brother of Ælfweard (see below, n. 161). He is described as *discifer* in 971; see Keynes *Diplomas*, 183 and n. 107. He also subscribes below, **VI**.

[161] Ælfweard subscribes King Edgar's diplomas 959 or 964 × 975 (Keynes *Atlas*, ibid.) and became the most prominent thegn of the early years of the reign of Æthelred II. He was the brother of Æthelweard (see above, n. 160) and is similarly described as *discifer* in 971; see Keynes *Diplomas*, 182–3. He probably subscribes below, **VI** (n. 29), and **IX** (n. 30).

+ Ego Leofƿine[162] minister

+ Ego Ælfƿine[163] minister

+ Ego Þulfstan[164] minister

[165]Omnes qui nominatim hoc[ee] priuilegio regis iussu descripti uidemur . posteritatis nostrę prosapiam subnixe deposcimus ut manuum nostrarum uadimonium Christi cruce firmatum . nequaquam uiolantes irritum faciant . si successorum quispiam temeritatis . usu uiolare presumserit corporis et sanguine[ff] Iesu Christi participatione priuatus . perpetua damnatus perditione anathema sit nisi diuino propitiante respectu ad humilem satisfactionem resipiscens conuersus fuerit [.]

[ee] huic, *in error*, Councils, *i,* 133   [ff] *MS. error for* sanguinis

---

[162] This Leofwine was probably the thegn of this name who subscribes several of King Edgar's diplomas 964 × 975, usually about sixth, seventh or eighth of the *ministri* (see Keynes *Atlas,* ibid.).

[163] This Ælfwine was probably the thegn of this name who usually occurs fairly low among the *ministri* in some of King Edgar's diplomas 958 × 972 (Keynes *Atlas,* ibid.) . He is to be distinguished from his more important namesake (see above, n. 157).

[164] This Wulfstan is perhaps to be identified as the thegn Wulfstan of Dalham, a benefactor of Ely and Bury St. Edmunds. He was a royal reeve, and probably the steward of Queen Eadgifu (see above, n. 132) whom King Edgar sent to supervise

+ I, Leofwine,[162] thegn.

+ I, Ælfwine,[163] thegn.

+ I, Wulfstan,[164] thegn.

[165]We, who are seen described by name in this document by the king's command, all humbly request the family of our posterity that they, violating, should in no way make invalid the recognizance of our hands strengthened with the Cross of Christ; if any successor, by the employment of imprudence should presume to violate [it], let him be cursed, bereft of participation in the body and blood of Jesus Christ, and condemned with perpetual perdition, unless, by the propitiation of divine regard, recovering his senses, he should be turned towards [making] humble reparation.

the installation of monks at the Old Minster (see above, n. 131). See further, Hart *ECNE,* 379; and Wulfstan *Vita S. Æthelwoldi,* cap. 18 (ed. Lapidge and Winterbottom, 32–3 and n. 2). He subscribes 958 × 974 (probably including **VI,** below).

[165] *Omnes . . . conuersus fuerit.* This final clause adds the combined weight of the invocation of Christ by all the witnesses (through their use of the *signum crucis*) to the protection of the terms of the document, and includes a further anathema against violation, to supplement the threats made above, **IV, ix–x** and **xx.** Cf. the additional clause of general consent after the witness-list in **XXVI,** below. For reference to other collective sanctions placed after the witness-list of diplomas, see Keynes *Diplomas,* 103, n. 61.

V

'A.D. 964 × 975', confirmation by King Edgar of the endowment and privileges of the Old Minster

Latin with Old English

(i) **Restoration by King Edgar to Winchester Cathedral of 100 hides at Downton, Wilts., and 30 hides at Calbourne [*et Dreðecumb*], Isle of Wight; and confirmation of the privileged tenure of Chilcomb, Hants, which is to be held by the bishops for the provision of food to the monks of the Old Minster**

S 821, Finberg 109, *CW* 26

(ii) **Confirmation by King Edgar to the monks of the Old Minster of the privileged tenure and beneficial hidation of Chilcomb, Hants; and confirmation by him of the monastic status of the Old Minster**

S 817(1–3), Finberg 110, *CW* 27

(iii) **Old English version of (ii)**

S817(4), Finberg 110, *CW* 28

(iv) **Restoration by King Edgar to Winchester Cathedral of 100 hides at Taunton, Somerset, with 3 hides at Charmouth, Dorset, and 2 at Washford, Somerset**

S 825, Finberg 509, *CW* 29

(v) **Restoration by King Edgar to Winchester Cathedral of 40 hides at Alresford, Hants**

S 814, Finberg 111, *CW* 30

(vi) **Restoration by King Edgar to Winchester Cathedral of 10 hides at Highclere, Hants**

S 819, Finberg 112, *CW* 31

(vii) **Confirmation by King Edgar to Winchester Cathedral of 20 hides at Overton, with woodland at Tadley, 15 hides at North Waltham, and 5 at Bradley, all in Hants**

S 824, Finberg 113, *CW* 32

(viii) **Confirmation by King Edgar to Winchester Cathedral of 60 hides at Tichborne, Beauworth and Ovington, all in Hants**

S 826, Finberg 114, *CW* 33

(ix) Confirmation by King Edgar to Winchester Cathedral of 60 hides at Farnham, Surrey, and 10 hides at Bentley, Hants

S 823, Finberg 115, Gelling 333, *CW* 34

(x) Confirmation by King Edgar to Winchester Cathedral of 70 hides at Beddington, with woodland at Chessington, Tandridge and Lake, all in Surrey

S 815, Gelling 334, *CW* 35

(xi) Confirmation by King Edgar to Winchester Cathedral of 30 hides at Fareham [et *Fearnham*], Hants

S 822, Finberg 116, *CW* 36

(xii) Confirmation by King Edgar to Winchester Cathedral of 38 hides at Bishop's Waltham, Hants

S 816, Finberg 117, *CW* 37

(xiii) Confirmation by King Edgar to Winchester Cathedral of 64 hides in Hants, at Twyford, Crawley, Owslebury, Hensting, Horton, Bishopstoke [*Stoce*], Otterbourne, Chilland, Easton and Hunton.

S 827, Finberg 118, *CW* 38

(xiv) Confirmation by King Edgar to Winchester Cathedral of what he has granted in (i)–(xiii), and also of Downton and Fonthill Bishop, both in Wilts.; Taunton, Somerset; Alresford, Bishopstoke, Highclere, Tichborne and [Headbourne or Martyr] Worthy, all in Hants; and Frensham [*Fermesham*], Surrey. Also provision by him for the government of relations between the bishop and the monks of the Old Minster, whose food is to be provided from Chilcomb, Hants

S 818, Finberg 119, Gelling 335, *CW* 39

V is the nearest equivalent for the Old Minster of the New Minster's re-foundation charter (**IV**, above). It contrasts to the latter, however, both in that it only survives as a cartulary-copy and in that it is much more cadastral in flavour, with references to individual named estates and their supposed tenurial history. More importantly, **V** also differs from **IV** in its degree of authenticity, being generally less reliable than the latter. **V** represents a self-contained textual booklet within the medieval *Codex Wintoniensis*, and consists of an interconnected series of documents (**V, i–xiv**) recording the restoration or confirmation by King Edgar to Winchester Cathedral of its estates in various counties amounting to *c*.670 hides of land.[1] Some of its constituent documents (**V, i–iii, xiv**) also contain provisions relating to the Benedictine Reform at the Old Minster and to the particularly important estate of Chilcomb, Hants, which surrounded the city.[2] All of them lack boundary-descriptions, dating-clauses, and witness-lists, and **V, xiv** lacks details of hidage.

It is likely that **V, i–xiv** already formed a self-contained booklet or file of text before being copied into the *Codex Wintoniensis*.[3] The copying of this file was begun by scribe *a* as the opening part of *Cod. Wint. I* (1129 × 1139), but he seems to have abandoned writing its text after **V, viii**,

---

[1] Or *c*.770 if Chilcomb is counted as 100 hides rather than one. For earlier discussions of these documents, see Finberg, 239–41; and John 'Church of Winchester'.

[2] For Chilcomb, see below, **XXX–XXXII**.

[3] For this MS., see above, pp. 5–9.

leaving space for its completion and not returning to it himself; it was continued later (?*temp.* Henry II), as part of *Cod. Wint. II*, by scribe *c* who also completed the rubrics throughout.[4]

There is internal evidence to suggest that **V, i–xiv** is intended to form a textual unit even though it comprises a number of individual records of grant. This series of texts is preceded in the cartulary by a long Latin rubric which refers to the *cleronomia* or 'inheritance' of the Holy Trinity and SS. Peter and Paul (i.e. of the cathedral church)[5] while most of the constituent documents have introductory vernacular rubrics of a mutually similar type, describing them individually as the *frēolsbōc* 'charter of freedom' relating to such and such an estate. There are also cross references from material in one of the constituent texts to material in another, e.g. to 'the aforementioned Bishop Æthelwold' (**V, viii** and **xi**),[6] 'the aforesaid church of Winchester' (**V, v**),[7] 'the aforesaid bishopric' (**V, xi**),[8] 'the aforesaid Winchester Cathedral' (**V, vii** and **xi**),[9] 'the above-noted estates' (**V, xiv**; some of which (Worthy, Fonthill Bishop, and Frensham) had not in fact mentioned before),[10] and to an Old English version (**V, ii**).[11] In **V, iv** a reference is made to the witness-list being written on the last page (*pada*) of the *scedula* (see below),[12] which would suggest that such a list once existed despite its omission from the cartulary.

The likeliest explanation of the origin of **V** as a unitary text is that it was in effect a form of cartulary drawn up in the late tenth or early eleventh century,[13] probably in small codex form like **IV**, above,[14] or like the original manuscript of the *Regularis Concordia*.[15] Its construction entailed the modification and uniting of various diplomas in the name of King Edgar then extant at the Old Minster into a commemorative text, which calls itself both *scedula* and *sinthama*,[16] intended to perpetuate the Edgarian re-endowment of the reformed Old Minster and see. Some of the diplomas used in its construction would seem to have been genuine and not to have been altered except so far as bounds, date and witness-list have been omitted, others seem at least to have had sections interpolated into them at some time before the booklet was copied into the *Codex Wintoniensis*. The variety of formulae found in the constituent diplomas is noteworthy.[17] It is unlikely that all the constituent diplomas had been issued on the same occasion. All the proems appear to be unique among surviving diplomas of Edgar, except for **V, viii, x** and **xi**,[18] and there is a large variety of royal styles in the superscriptions There are some verbal parallels in **V, i–ii, iv**, and **xiv** with passages in **IV**, above, which was composed by Æthelwold.[19] There is also some wording in **V, xi** comparable with that favoured by the draftsman who worked closely with Æthelwold and who is

[4] For the distinction between *Cod. Wint. I* and *Cod. Wint. II*, see above, pp. 5–6. Scribe *c* also wrote two charters datable to 1144 × 1171 and 1158; ibid. 8. It is possible that scribe *c* omitted the date and witness-list from **V, xiv**, see below.

[5] *HĘC EST CLERONOMIA SVMME TRINITATIS PETRIQVE APOSTOLORVM PRINCIPIS EIUSQVE CO-APOSTOLI PAVLI QVAM EADGARUS REX VENERANDVS CRUCIS SIGNO RENOUARE STUDVIT* .

[6] See below, **V, viii**, n. 144; and **V, xi**, n. 170.

[7] See **V, v**, n. 98.

[8] **V, xi**, n. 169.

[9] **V, vii**, n. 135; and **V, xiii**, n. 197.

[10] **V, xiv**, nn. 224, 230–1, and 233.

[11] **V, ii**, n. 47.   [12] **V, iv**, n. 78.

[13] Had the original MS. survived it might just predate *Tib. I*, the earliest surviving Anglo-Saxon cartulary, from Worcester

cathedral priory (s. xi in., ? *temp.* Archbishop Wulfstan 1000–23); see Davis 1068 (i), and N. R. Ker, 'Hemming's Cartulary: a Description of the Two Worcester Cartularies in Cotton Tiberius A. xiii', in R. W. Hunt, W. A. Pantin, and R. W. Southern (ed.), *Studies in Medieval History Presented to Frederick Maurice Powicke* (Oxford, 1948), 48–75, especially 68–71.

[14] As suggested by John 'Church of Winchester', 407, n. 2.

[15] This was described as an *exiguus codicellus*: *RC*, cap. 5.

[16] For these terms, see **V, iv**, nn. 76 and 78; and **V, i**, n. 21.

[17] There is much more variety than one might think from reading John 'Church of Winchester', 406–7.

[18] See below, **V, viii**, n. 138; **V, x**, n. 151; and **V, xi**, n. 160. There is some degree of similarity between those of **V, viii** and **V, xii**, however; see below, n. 172.

[19] Ibid. **V, i**, nn. 5–6, 12, 24, and 26; **V, ii**, nn. 41–2, and 44; **V, iv**, n. 73; and **V, xiv**, nn. 221, 242, 244, and 250.

known to modern commentators as 'Edgar A'.[20] Certain of these passages are based on formulae previously favoured by the draftsman known as 'Æthelstan A'.[21]

Within **V, i–xiv** there is a significant and uneven distribution of certain textual features, particularly of those passages claiming to give specific references to the tenurial history of an estate and of clauses describing or implementing the Benedictine Reform of the Old Minster:

- such clauses are lacking in **V, vii, ix–xi, xiii**;
- **V, i–vi, viii, xiii** have specific mention of earlier royal grants of an estate,[22] e.g. **V, ii**:

> Hanc quoque renouationem in ipsa eademque libertate . . . perdurare iussi . qua illam ab auis et atauis et ab omnibus regibus antecessoribus meis donatam esse comperi . quorum primi extiterunt . Cynegils rex . et filius eius Cynepalh rex . qui in exordio Christianę fidei sancto Birino episcopo uerbum Dei predicante concesserunt . . . Deinde successores eorum scilicet Ecgbirht rex . Adulf rex . Ælfred rex . Eadpeard rex . et reliqui omnes . . .

- **V, iv** and **vi** make reference to King Æthelwulf's 'decimation' of his lands;[23]
- explicit and implicit references to sections of the Benedictine Rule occur in **V, xiv**,[24] and implicit ones to the *Regularis Concordia*;[25]
- clauses forbidding any secular domination of ecclesiastical estates occur in **V, ii–iii**, and **xiv**;[26]
- **V, vii–xiii** reserve the 'Three Burdens' to the king, but **V, i–vi, xiv** claim full immunity from them, an irregular and suspicious feature.

There is also some variation discernible between the constituent texts as to the frequency of features of Latin prose style of the type favoured by Æthelwold.

- grecisms occur in **V, i–vi**, and **xiv** (e.g. *philargiria* **V, i, iv, vi**, and **xiv**, and *philargirius* **V, v**; and *dyrocheum* **V, xiv**);[27]
- brief passages of rhyming Latin prose occur *passim* but are particularly extensive in **V, xiv**, e.g.

> Certe canonici omni uiciorum neuo *deturpati* . inani gloria *tumidi* . inuidię liuore *tabidi* . philargirię maculis *obcecati* . luxurię facibus *libidi* . gulę omnimodo *dediti* . regi terreno non episcopo *subiecti* . prefati ruris usu ueterano moderno tempore pascebantur alimentis . Ebrietatem siquidem et homicidia *sectantes* . coniuges suas turpiter nimia et inusitata libidine *amplectentes* . . .

- the use of 'envelope patterns' and interlaced word-order, in similar categories to those used in **IV**, above[28] occurs in all of the Latin texts, e.g.

  (i) with noun and adjective separated by a noun or noun phrase in the genitive case:
    V, i: *Altithronus totius creature plasmator*
    V, ii: *predictum sedis episcopalis cęnobium*
    V, viii: *nouis litterarum apicibus*

---

[20] Ibid. **V, xi**, nn. 160–1, 163–5, and 167. Note also the use of the word *cleronomia* in the heading to **V**; see below, **V, i**, n. 1.

[21] Ibid. **V, xi**, nn. 160, 164–5, and 167.

[22] For other such historical passages within the Old Minster archive, see above, p. 17.

[23] **V, iv**, n. 82; and **V, vi**, n. 121.

[24] **V, xiv**, nn. 215, 237, 239, and 241–2.

[25] Ibid. nn. 218, 238–42, and 246.

[26] **V, ii**, n. 41; **V, iii**, n. 61; and **V, xiv**, n. 247.

[27] For *dyrocheum*, see **V, xiv**, n. 212. For other grecisms, see below, Latin word-list, and Lapidge 'Hermeneutic Style'.

[28] For this type of Latin prose style, favoured by Æthelwold, see above, p. 67.

V, xi: *fastidiosam melancolię nausiam*

V, xiv: *unito episcopi fratrumque consilio* and
unanimi regis et monachorum eiusdem monasterii consilio

(ii) with noun and adjective separated by a verb:

V, iv: *ęterna firmatum est dapsilitate* and *uiolenta abstractum est rapina*

V, ix: *noto nuncupatur uocabulo*

V, xi: *humili restituo deuotione*

V, xiv: *actuali degens conuersatione*

(iii) combinations of types (i) and (ii) occur:

V, v: *noua territorii consolidauit cartula*

V, ix: *ad supernam celorum tendens patriam*

V, xii: *incertum futuri temporis statum mutabilitatemque certis dinoscens indiciis*

(iv) pairs of nouns and adjectives are sometimes interlaced:

V, iv: *caducis ęterna perituris mansura*

V, vii: *periculis nimio ingruentibus terrore*

Some of the constituent diplomas (**V, vii–xiii**) can be accepted more readily than others as minimally-edited copies of genuine grants of King Edgar, but the rest have features which point to interpolation if not outright forgery. As suggested by Finberg, the section which concerns Chilcomb in **V, i** is probably an interpolation into a diploma previously only concerned with the hundred of Downton, Wilts.[29] **V, ii–iii**, concerning Chilcomb and its beneficial hidation, may be later than King Æthelred's writ confirming the beneficial hidation (**XXX**, below). Although there are verbal parallels between the vernacular **V, iii** and **XXX**,[30] the latter makes no mention of any document in the name of Edgar (the father of Æthelred) but only refers to a diploma of King Alfred as having being read before Æthelred,[31] whereas **V, ii–iii** do mention an earlier confirmation by Alfred.

There are marked differences in emphasis between **V, ii–iii** and **V, xiv**, which are favourable to the status of the latter, a document which is of great significance in giving details of the reform of the Old Minster and the relations between bishop and monks. This text restores and confirms the lands of the bishopric, while reserving the estate of Chilcomb to the monastic table and certain other estates for the remainder of the needs of the monks with anything over to be given to the poor. It also limits the episcopal succession to monks of the Old Minster or, in exceptional circumstances to monks of other 'well-known' monasteries; these provisions are in accord with both the bull of Pope John XII of ?963 (**XXXIII**, below) and the *Regularis Concordia* of *c.*970 × 973.[32] The monk-bishop's position *in loco abbatis* is here defined perhaps as much for his own benefit as for that of his community, there being no recent precedent for the insular institution of a monastic cathedral. There is no reason to doubt the information in these sections of **V, xiv**, which may well have been formulated by, or for, Bishop Æthelwold. They might once have been part of a genuine grant in the name of Edgar which was later subsumed into **V**. The absence of historical references in **V, xiv**, is a general point in its favour, as is also the lack of any mention of the beneficial hidation of

[29] Finberg, 239.
[30] See below, **V, iii**, nn. 60 and 66.
[31] See below, **XXX**, n. 6. For another reference to a 'charter'

of Alfred, see below, **V, i**, n. 38.
[32] See below, **V, xiv**, nn. 240–1. For the date of *RC*, see *Councils*, 135.

Chilcomb. Although it does include both reference back to the preceding parts of **V**, and a clause claiming full immunity for the estates involved, these parts might be additions made during the construction of **V** from its various sources. **V, xiv** cannot be taken as wholly genuine, yet it seems to contain some believable information and also some formulation that belongs to the Æthelwoldian tradition. It may once have possessed a dating clause and witness-list and it is possible that they were used as the final clauses of **V** in its codex form but that they were omitted by scribe *c* of the *Codex Wintoniensis* who was continuing the copying of **V** into inadequate space left by scribe *a*. One rare grecism in **V, xiv** (*dyrocheum*) appears also in the Tavistock foundation-charter dated 981, a document of uncertain status.[33]

V was probably constructed at the Old Minster at some time in the reign of Æthelred II (978–1016). Passages comparable to the historical sections interpolated into its constituent diplomas also occur in apparently genuine diplomas of Æthelred to the Old Minster dated 979 and 997;[34] others occur in three forged single-sheets, in favour of the Old Minster, in the names of Kings Edward the Elder, Æthelstan, and Eadred and datable on palaeographical grounds to s. x ex. or s. xi[1].[35] There are also verbal connections between the vernacular **V, iii** and Æthelred's writ concerning Chilcomb (**XXX**, below).[36] If from the beginning of Æthelred's reign, then **V** was possibly connected with, and may even have been used in, the ceremony of dedication on 20 October 980 associated with the rebuilding of the Old Minster, when Æthelwold was still alive.[37] Its purpose would have been the commemoration of the Edgarian re-endowment of Winchester's monastic cathedral, and the perpetuation of its new dispensation under Edgar's successors. If from later in Æthelred's reign, then it is to be attributed to one or more of Æthelwold's pupils and probably as a counter to the 'anti-monastic reaction' from after Æthelwold's death in 984 to *c*.993.[38] In either case, the claims of full immunity may already have been present in some of the sources used for **V**, as they do not occur in all of the constituent diplomas; if so, those particular sources were themselves already interpolated or forged.

From the above discussion, it is clear that although **V** must be approached and used with caution as a document of record, it remains significant as a Latin text parts of which were produced either by, or under the influence of, Æthelwold at the reformed Old Minster.[39] It has been remarked that the quotation of historical precedents (some of them suspect) in the constituent documents in **V** is also a feature of documents produced at other monasteries associated with Æthelwold (e.g. Abingdon, Ely, Peterborough) during, or in the wake of, the Benedictine Reform.[40] The purpose

[33] S 838; see below, **V, xiv**, n. 212.

[34] S 835, *CW* 222, *KCD* 622, concerning Long Sutton, Hants, refers to earlier grants by Kings Eadred and Edgar. S 891, *CW* 44, *KCD* 698, concerning the hundred of Downton, Wilts., refers to earlier grants by Kings Cenwealh, Cynewulf, Ecgbeorht, Eadred, and Edgar. Cf. also the historical passages in S 876, *Councils* 39, Æthelred's privilege for Abingdon, dated 993, which is one of the 'Orthodoxorum' group of diplomas; see above, p. 15, n. 4.

[35] S 376 (MS. 1), BL Harl. Ch. 43 C. 1, concerning the beneficial hidation of Chilcomb, Hants; S 443 (MS. 1), BL Cotton Ch. viii. 17, concerning two estates belonging to Taunton, Somerset; and S 540 (MS. 1), BL Cotton Ch. viii. 11, concerning the hundred of Downton, Wilts.

[36] See below, **V, iii**, nn. 60 and 66.

[37] See Daniel J. Sheerin, 'The Dedication of the Old Minster, Winchester, in 980', *Revue Bénédictine* 88 (1978), 261–73. In the

previous month, on 4 September 980, Æthelwold had caused St. Birinus's relics to be translated; see **V, i**, n. 7. Lapidge ('Hermeneutic Style', 127, n. 5) attributes the hermeneutic style in **V** (*BCS* 1147, 1149–59) to Æthelwold's influence 'and possibly his actual authorship'. Note also the use in **V, iii** (see ibid. n. 62) of OE *bearn* for Latin *filius*, apparently a personal preference of Æthelwold.

[38] See Keynes *Diplomas*, 176–86. Cf. ibid. 198–9, for a list of diplomas issued in favour of the church in the following dozen years (including S 889 (**XXVI**, below) and 891 for the Old Minster).

[39] Cf. Lapidge 'Æthelwold as Scholar', *passim*.

[40] See Patrick Wormald, 'Æthelwold and his Continental Counterparts: Contact, Comparison, Contrast', in Barbara Yorke (ed.), *Bishop Æthelwold: His Career and Influence* (Woodbridge, 1988, repr. 1997), 13–42, at 39–40.

of such quotation was to attempt to appeal to a sense of continuity and thereby to help in the retention and fortification of the 'ancient' endowment of a particular church in spite of the changes in personnel and observance introduced by the reformers. It cannot be doubted that such retention and fortification was also the purpose behind the construction of **V**. It is highly significant that in 1129 × 1139 the codex which **V** seems to have formed was the first text to be copied into *Cod. Wint I*, the earliest section of the *Codex Wintoniensis* (MS. B), whose purpose was the retention and restoration of the pre-Norman endowment of Winchester Cathedral. [41] Later medieval and early modern copyists selected only either **V, ii** or **V, xiv** from the series of constituent documents, depending on their interest respectively in the Chilcomb estate and its beneficial hidation (MSS. C, E, G, and H) or the monastic constitution of the Old Minster (MSS. D and F). MS. D is the MS. of Thomas Rudborne's *Historia maior Wintoniensis* and the copy of **V, xiv** which it contains in book ii, cap. xii, has some interpolations added to the text by him, as well as a reference to a papal confirmation (cf. **XXXIII**, below).[42]

---

[41] **V** = *CW* 26–39, at the beginning of the present second quire of the *Codex Wintoniensis* which was Quire I of *Cod. Wint*.   *I*, see Rumble 1982, 153–64. See also above, p. 6.   [42] See below, **V, xiv**, nn. *zz*, *h–j*, and *l*.

MSS.:   B. BL, Add. MS. 15350, fos. 9ʳ–13ᵛ (s. xii¹–xii med.)
        C. WCL, W52/74 [St Swithun's Cartulary], vol. 1, fos. 5ᵛ–6ʳ (s. xiii/xiv) [(**ii**) only]
        D. London, Lambeth Palace 183, fos. 22ʳ–23ʳ (s. xv) [(**xiv**) only], from B, interpolated
        E. BL, Harl. MS. 358, fos. 62ᵛ–63ʳ (s. xvi¹) [(**ii**) part only], from (?copy of) B
        F. CCCC, MS. 350, pp. 43–5 (s. xvi med.) [(**xiv**) only], from D
        G. CCCC, MS. 110, pp. 299–300 (s. xvi med.) [(**ii**) only], from C
        H. Bod, Jones MS. 4 (s. xvii¹) [(**ii**) only], from G

Edited: *Monasticon*, i, 212 (no. 9) [(**ii**) only], from C
        Anglia Sacra, i, 218–20 [(**xiv**) only], from D
        KCD 512 [= (**ii**)], from *Monasticon*, 599–610 [= (**i, iv–xiv**)], from B
        Thorpe, pp. 228–9, 256–7 [= (**ii**) from C], 226–8 [= (**iii**) from B], 257–9 [= (**v**) from B], 259–62 [= (**xiv**) from B]
        BCS 1146–59, from B
        Pierquin, *Recueil*, pt 4, nos. 32–43 [(**i, iv–xiv**)], from B
        Goodman, *Chartulary*, p. 13 (no. 28) [summary of (**ii**)], from C
        AS Ch 38 [(**iii**) only] from B, with translation

Printed from B, with note of significant variants in D

HĘC EST CLERONOMIA SVMME TRINITA-
TIS PETRIQVE APOSTOLORVM PRINCIPIS
EIUSQVE COAPOSTOLI PAVLI QVAM
EADGARUS REX VENERANDVS CRUCIS
SIGNO RENOUARE STUDVIT[.][1]

THIS IS THE INHERITANCE OF THE HOLY
TRINITY AND OF PETER, THE FOREMOST
OF THE APOSTLES, AND OF HIS FELLOW
APOSTLE PAUL WHICH THE WORSHIP-
FUL KING EDGAR DECIDED TO RENEW
WITH THE SIGN OF THE CROSS.[1]

[i][2]

CILTANCVMBES 7 DUNTUNES 7 EBBLES-
BURNAN[3] FREOLSBOC .

[i][2]

CHARTER OF FREEDOM OF CHILCOMB
AND DOWNTON AND BISHOPSTONE[3]

Altithronus totius creature plasmator uniuersa
quę miro ineffabilique condidit ordine per sex
dies[4] luculenter exprimens . formulas distincxit
singulorum . Nam bona a bono edita creatore
cuncta tenorem pulchre seruant[a] naturalem .
excepto homine miseranda seducto cauillatione .
et angelo praeuaricatore superbissimo[5] . per
quem prodolor omnis inrepsit aduersitas in
genus humanum[6] . Nam multis infecatum :
probrosi[b] seculi neuis . cunctis liquido intimatur
sophistis . Inlectum siquidem nefandi neuis[bb]
cosmi . cęlestes ipsius pompas inconsiderate
ambiendo . supernęque patrię emolumenta
amittendo . celsithroni moderatoris[c] gratia
priuatum . barathri incendiis lugubriter
depulsum . iugi miseria puniri merito compul-
sum est . Quod tandem diuina gratia cunctis
succurrens mortalibus gratuite . bonum uidelicet

The high-throned Fashioner of the whole of
Creation, splendidly modelling throughout six
days[4] all things which he produced in marvellous and ineffable order, made distinct the form
of each thing. Indeed all the good things
produced by the good Creator beautifully preserve their natural station, except for Man, who
was seduced by deplorable sophistry and the
very proud transgressor angel,[5] through whom,
alas, all misfortune came upon the human race.[6]
For, it is made clearly known by all learned men,
that is something that has been polluted by the
many blemishes of a shameful world. Having
been seduced indeed by the blemishes of impi-
ety, in rashly seeking to gain the heavenly
splendours of the universe itself and in losing
the benefits of the celestial dwelling-place,
having been deprived by the grace of the
High-Throned Ruler, having been lamentably
cast down into the fires of the Abyss, it was
deservedly forced to be punished with continual
misery. At length, at the end of a pitiable era,
divine grace delivered it with glorious freedom,

---

[a] *Corrected from* aseruant   [b] probosi *'corrected' from*
probo si   [bb] nemis   [c] moderatis

---

[1] *HĘC EST CLERONOMIA . . . RENOUARE STUDVIT.*
The first rubric standing before **V, i** in the *Codex Wintoniensis*
(MS. B) introduces the whole series of edited documents **V, i–
xiv** and was probably borrowed by the cartulary-maker from
the heading to the exemplar. The grecism *cleronomia* (κληρονομία) 'inheritance' provides a link with the work of the draftsman
'Edgar A' who uses the word *cleronomis* (dative pl.) 'heirs' in the
dispositive clause of a number of diplomas (e.g. S 702, 706, 717,
737–8; *BCS* 1085, 1083, 1101, 1189, and 1176) where *heredibus* is
more usually found. On him, see above, p. 15.

[2] **V, i.** A wordy diploma in the name of Edgar, relating
mainly to the hundred of Downton, Wilts., but with an apparent
interpolation concerning the beneficial hidation of Chilcomb
(see below, n. 18). The proem makes use of the story of Creation,
and of the Fall and Redemption of Man, cf. the extensive use of
this in **IV**, above. The first sentence has some similarity to that in
V, vi, below.

[3] *EBBLESBURNAN.* Bishopstone, Wilts., constituted the
detached upland part (45 hides) of Downton Hundred. It is
not elsewhere separately referred to in **V**.

[4] *per sex dies.* As described in Gen. 1. Cf. below, n. 115.

[5] *angelo praeuaricatore superbissimo.* Lucifer, the leader of the
angels who defied the authority of God (cf. 2 Enoch 29: 4–5; and
other references in **IV**, n. 3, above). Their association with the sin
of pride (*superbia*) links them here with the secular canons (see
below, **V, ii**, n. 43).

[6] *per quem . . . omnis inrepsit aduersitas in genus humanum.* Cf.
the link made between the Fall of the Angels and the Fall of
Man at the end of **IV, prol.**, above.

pro malis restituendo . solutis facinorum repagulis . baptismatis regeneratione piando . crucisque gabulum ascendendo . in seculorum fine miserando gloriosa eripuit libertate . Quę uidelicet libertas in totum per apostolos dilata`ta´ orbem . Domini annuente clementia ad Uuest Seaxan sancto predicante Birino[7] directa est . Prefatus equidem pontifex primo regem . Cynegisl[8] . deinde . Cynepealh[9] . nuncupatum . fidei rudimentis imbutum[10] . baptismatis fonte regenerauit . qui uidelicet rex ęcclesiam Uuintonia ilico pulchrę edidit . reuerendeque Trinitati ac indiuiduę Unitati . necnon beato Petro apostolorum principi . eiusque coapostolo Paulo dedicare fecit . cathedramque episcopalem inibi constituens . bonis a Deo sibi collatis locupletans uberrime[d] ditauit[11] . Inde itaque primum copiosa fidei seges[12] paulatim pereunte gentilitatis lolio baptismatis lauacro irrigata . pu`l´lulans secreuit . quę Domini gratia per totam Occidentalem Saxoniam ęcclesię cultoribus sata granaria Domini multiplici reditu repplendo . usque in hodiernum diem incessabiliter accumulat . Hinc ego Eadgar[13] . tocius Brittannię basileus eiusdem letę segetis Christi annuente clementia occa exuberans . primitias Christianę

[d] -imę

gratuitously aiding all mortal things by restoring goodness in place of evil, the restraints of bad deeds having been removed by the atoning rebirth of baptism and by mounting the gallows of the Cross. Which freedom indeed, spread by the apostles through the whole world, was directed by the grant of the Lord's indulgence to the West Saxons through the preaching of St Birinus.[7] The aforementioned bishop indeed first caused the king called Cynegisl[8] to be reborn in the font of baptism, then [the king called] Cenwealh,[9] [each] having been instructed in the rudiments of faith;[10] which [latter] king indeed nobly built a church in the place Wi.. hester and had it dedicated to the venerable Trinity and the indivisible Unity and also to the blessed Peter, the foremost of the apostles, and his fellow apostle Paul; and, founding an episcopal see therein, he enriched it most abundantly,[11] making it rich with goods given to him by God. From that beginning therefore, the plentiful cornfield of faith[12] having been watered by the bathing of baptism, the tares of paganism gradually disappearing, it sprouted and grew; which [faith], swelling as corn in the Lord's granary, accumulates ceaselessly to this day by the grace of the Lord with an extensive return for the Church's labourers throughout Wessex.

Wherefore I, Edgar,[13] ruler of the whole of Britain, making full the same fertile cornfield by the use of a harrow while Christ's mercy allows, give back with most humble devotion to the aforesaid church of Winchester, for the good of my soul and the prosperity of our kingdom, the first-fruits of Christian bounty offered to the Redeemer of the human race by the aforesaid

[7] Birinus, the apostle of the West Saxons, bishop of Dorchester-on-Thames 634–c.650. See Bertram Colgrave and R. A. B. Mynors (ed. and trans.), *Bede's Ecclesiastical History of the English People* (Oxford, 1969), 232–3 (iii. 7). Birinus was held in particular reverence at the Old Minster *temp.* Æthelwold who had his relics translated to the high altar; see Rosalind C. Love, *Three Eleventh-Century Anglo-Latin Saints' Lives* (Oxford, 1996), 44–7 (*Vita Sancti Birini*, cap. 21). See ibid. for a full discussion of his cult.

[8] Cynegisl, king of the West Saxons 611–?642.

[9] Cenwealh, king of the West Saxons 642–72, son of King Cynegisl (see above, n. 8). See below, n. 11.

[10] *fidei rudimentis imbutum.* Cf. *fidei sacramentis imbutum* in **V, v**, below. For the respective conversions of Cynegisl and Cenwealh, see Colgrave and Mynors, *Bede's Ecclesiastical History*, 232–7 (iii. 7).

[11] *bonis . . . ditauit.* Cf. S 229, CW 40, KCD 985, a forged diploma purporting to record a grant by Cenwealh of 100 hides at Downton; and *Winchester ann.*, s.a. 639.

[12] *copiosa fidei seges.* Here begins a series of farming metaphors to describe the growth of Christianity in Wessex. They probably

represent an extension of the metaphor of Birinus's promise 'in the pope's presence that he would scatter the seeds of the holy faith (*sanctae fidei semina*) in the remotest regions of England': Colgrave and Mynors, *Bede's Ecclesiastical History*, 232–3 (iii. 7). Cf. the use of farming metaphors in relation to King Edgar's refoundation of the New Minster; above, **IV, vi**.

[13] Edgar, king of Mercia 957–9, of England 959–75.

dapsilitatis a predicto Cynepalhho[14] . humani generis redemptori oblatas . et a Ceadpalla[15] rege successionis tempore hereditaria consolidatas cartula . et a quibusdam predecessoribus meis iniuste moderno ablatas tempore . ob animę meę remedium regnique nostri prosperitatem . predictę Uuintoniensi ęcclesię humillima reddo deuotione . c . scilicet mansas loco qui celebri et Duntune[16] nuncupatur onomate atque[e] . xxx . in Uecta insula quę noto et Dreðecumb[17] appellantur uocabulo . cum omnibus utensilibus pratis uidelicet siluis salinariis capturis molendinis et omnibus commodis huic ruri pertinentibus reuerende Trinitati predictisque eius apostolis satisfaciendo restituens .

Identidem[f] suburbana eiusdem precipuę ciuitatis Cyltancumb[18] uidelicet cum suis appendiciis benignissime renouare cupiens eadem dito libertate . qua a rege uti dicam primogenito eiusdem ęcclesię neophito[19] . ad usum presulis eidemque loco subiectę familię a catholicis priscis ditatum perhibetur temporibus . Pastus igitur predictę familię nullatenus presumptuose minuatur . sed fideliter ut olim constitutum fuerat a presule dispensando largiatur . Dignum itaque saluberrimo obtimatum meorum utens consilio nostrę mentis duxi archano ut nostrę Occidentalium Saxonum ęcclesię capud . nostręque religionis exordium nullatenus 'aliqua' suę portionis priuaretur substantia . sed redintegrata ad liquidum cuncta clarescerent . ut nobis et presentis uitę iocunda prosperitas . et futurę

[e] adque   [f] It-

Cenwealh[14] and confirmed in following times by King Cædwalla[15] in a charter of inheritance, but unjustly taken away in modern times by certain of my predecessors; restoring with reparation, that is, to the venerable Trinity and its aforesaid apostles, 100 hides in the place which is called by the famous name Downton[16] and 30 in the Isle of Wight which are called by the known name Dreðecumb,[17] with all useful things, namely meadows, woods, saltworks, fisheries, mills and all the advantages belonging to this estate.

Constantly desiring most benevolently to renew, I enrich the areas dependent on the same distinguished city, namely Chilcomb[18] with its appendages, with the same freedom by which the king, [whom] I might call the first-born neophyte of the same church,[19] is said by the orthodox to have enriched [it] in ancient times, to the use of the bishop for the community subject to the same place. Therefore let the food of the aforesaid community not be in any way presumptuously diminished, but let it be given bountifully by being faithfully dispensed by the bishop as was once established. Thus, I, taking the most wholesome advice of my nobles, have brought a worthy thing from the sanctuary of my mind, so that the chief place of our church of the West Saxons and the starting-place of our religion should in no way be deprived of any substance of its share, but all things restored should be made as clear as water so that both the delightful prosperity of present life and the reward of future bliss might

[14] See above, nn. 9 and 11.

[15] Cædwalla, king of the West Saxons 685–8. No diploma of his relating to Downton survives.

[16] Downton belonged to the bishop of Winchester TRE and TRW, apart from 5 hides which had been alienated temp. Cnut: DB, i, fo. 65[v] (DB Wilts. 2: 1). An estate there was bequeathed to the Old Minster by King Eadred in 951 × 955: S 1515; Harmer, SEHD 21. For other diplomas, mostly of doubtful authenticity, granting or confirming Downton to the church of Winchester, see S 229, 275, 393, 540, and 891; CW 40–4; respectively, KCD 985, BCS 391, 690, 862, and KCD 698. See also V, xiv, below.

[17] Dreðecumb. A former name of Calbourne, Isle of Wight, where 32 hides belonged to the bishop of Winchester TRE and

TRW: DB, i, fo. 52[v] (DB Hants IoW 2:1). Compare the bounds of Calbourne in S 274, CW 124, BCS 392 with those of the (unnamed) 30-hide estate on the Isle of Wight said to be appurtenant to Downton in S 1581, CW 120, Finberg 352.

[18] Chilcomb, Hants: see below, V, ii, n. 31; also V, iii and xiv. For the suggestion that the text which mentions Chilcomb here, from Identidem suburbana to dispensando largiatur [i.e. from 'Constantly desiring' to 'once established'] is an interpolation, see Finberg, 239. Note, however, that Chilcomb is also mentioned here in the rubric.

[19] rege . . . primogenito eiusdem ęcclesię neophito. That is Cynegisl; see above, n. 8.

ęternę beatitudinis meritum multiplici fęnore
fiducialiter eueniret Christo largiente qui cum
patre et spiritu sancto cuncta gubernat quę
condidit . Supradictę igitur au`g´mentum ęccle-
się dum nostrę fit prosperitatis supplementum .
nostrę religionis exordia restaurare cupiens .
Nouis quidem cartulis eius territoria partim per
incuriam ueterano[g] usu deleta Adeluuoldo[20]
presule humiliter optinente in hoc presenti
sinthamate[21] distinctis locis semotim non solum
ea quę iniqua ante abstracta rapina a me restituta
sunt . sed etiam illa quę olim a predecessoribus
meis ęternę Trinitati concessa fuerant . pro animę
meę redemptione et regni nostri prosperitate
renouare iubeo . Hoc etenim in nomine Iesu
Christi eiusque genitricis semperque uirginis
Marię et beati Petri apostolorum principis
omniumque sanctorum subnixus precipio ut
nemo successorum meorum hoc nostrum decretum restaurationemque possessionum ęcclesiastici ruris uiolare uel minuere instinctu demonis
presumens audeat . Qui autem hoc nostrum
decretum libertatemque iuris ęcclesiastici[22]
augere munifica uoluerit dapsilitate . augeat
omnipotens Dominus eius et uitam et prosperitatem hic et in futuro seculo . ruantque
aduersarii cuncti ante faciem eius terrore
Domini uelociter prostrati . robustusque uictor
Christi suffragante gratia semper sui cursus stadio
persistens uigeat . omnisque eius successura
posteritas pollens perpetuo proficiat . Qui uero
audax presumptor ausu temerario philargiria[h]
seductus[23] uiolare minuereue temptauerit .
deleatur eius nomen de libro uitę[24] . ac per

---

[g] *Corrected from* ueterono   [h] hpil-

[20] Æthelwold, bishop of Winchester 963–84. See above, **IV**, n. 134.

[21] *in hoc sinthamate.* The grecism *sinthama* [rightly *sinthema*] may refer to the whole of **V**, rather than just to **V, i**. Below, **V** is described as a *scedula*; see **V, iii**, nn. 76 and 78.

[22] *libertatemque iuris ęcclesiastici.* That is, with rights of book-land.

[23] *audax presumptor ausu temerario philargiria seductus.* The grecism *philargiria*, the cardinal vice of avarice, literally 'the love of silver', also occurs in **V, iv, vi**, and **xiv**. Cf. also the adj.

confidently come to us with augmented profit,
by Christ's gift, Who with the Father and the
Holy Spirit governs everything that He created.
Desiring to restore the starting-places of our
religion, may the augmentation of the aforesaid
church therefore be at the same time something
which supplements our good fortune. Its terri-
tories, separated in distinct places, having indeed
partly been abolished by new charters through
neglect of ancient custom, have been reinstated
by me, Bishop Æthelwold[20] humbly acquiring
[them], in this present arrangement of text;[21] I
order to be renewed, for the redemption of my
soul and the good fortune of our kingdom, not
only those [territories] which were taken away
formerly by unjust plundering but also those
which once upon a time had been granted to the
eternal Trinity by our predecessors. This also I
command, supported by and in the name of Jesus
Christ and of his mother, the perpetual Virgin
Mary, and of the blessed Peter the foremost of
the apostles, and of all the saints, that none of my
successors, presuming at the instigation of the
Devil, should dare to violate or diminish this our
decree and the restoration of the possessions of
an ecclesiastical estate. But may the Almighty
Lord enlarge both life and prosperity here and in
a future age for whoever wishes to enlarge with
munificent generosity this our decree and the
freedom of ecclesiastical right;[22] and may all his
enemies tumble down before his face, speedily
overthrown by dread of the Lord; and may he
flourish, continuing as a hardy victor while
Christ's grace always favours the course of his
life; and may all his succeeding posterity advance
forever powerful. But may the name be deleted
from the Book of Life[24] of any daring, presump-
tuous person, having been seduced in an imprudent attempt by avarice,[23] who should try to

philargirius 'avaricious' in **V, v**. The word *philargiria* is also found in diplomas of the 'Orthodoxorum' group (S 658, 673, 786, 788, 812, and 876); see above, p. 15, n. 4.

[24] *libro uitę.* With reference to Rev. See above, **IV**, n. 72; and below, **V, xiv**, n. 250.

beati Petri apostolorum principis regnique cęlorum clauigeri[25] auctoritatem . paradysi ianuis eliminatus . ęternis barathri incendiis iugiter ustulatus . Acharonte putido torridoque suffocatus . cum Iuda Christi proditore eiusque complicibus perhenni calamitate iugi`que´ miseria a Deo et omnibus sanctis iusto dampnatus puniatur iudicio[26] . nisi satisfactione congrua restituerit . quod in Christi possessione minuere presumpsit .

[ii][27]

FREOLSBOC TO CILTANCVMBE .

Mundanę uolubilitatis orbita . numquam in eodem statu permanet . sed cotidiano defectu more fluentis aquę decurrit ob id quę rerum preteritarum effectus obliuioni tradetur . nisi litterarum caracteribus exaretur . quibus quasi quodam anchorę ligamento ne penitus a memoria defluat retinetur . Hoc modo quę[j] olim gesta fuerant posteris innotescit . Quapropter in hac cartula manifeste declaratur . qualiter[28] ego . Eadgar[29] . opitulante gratuita saluatoris mundi clementia Anglorum basileus . Aðelpoldo[30] . michi pontificum dilectissimo suggerente . cum optimatum meorum consilio deuotus renouaui . Cyltancumbes[31] . hereditariam libertatem . quę uallis undique adiacet Wentanę

[j] Hoc quę modo quę

---

[25] regnique cęlorum clauigeri. With reference to Matt. 16: 19 (BSV, ii, 1551) et tibi dabo claves regni caelorum 'And I will give to thee the keys of the kingdom of heaven'. See Addendum.

[26] paradysi ianuis eliminatus. eternis barathri incendiis iugiter ustulatus. Acharonte . . . suffocatus. cum Iuda Christi proditore eiusque complicibus . . . iugi`que´ miseria . . . puniatur iudicio. A similar sanction is used in IV, ix, above; see ibid. n. 65.

[27] V, ii. This diploma confirms the tenure of Chilcomb, said to have been granted to Winchester Cathedral on its foundation. It also confirms its beneficial hidation, or reduced assessment for taxation. There are prohibitions against the leasing out of the estate to secular people and against the reintroduction of 'clerks' at the Old Minster.

[28] in hac cartula manifeste declaratur. qualiter. This is probably a translation of the formulaic vernacular opening clause of V, iii, below: Her is gesputelod on þisum geprite. hu and suggests that the vernacular text was composed first. Cf. the opening of King

violate or diminish [it] and, having been banished from the doors of Paradise by the authority of the Blessed Peter, the foremost of the apostles and the keeper of the keys of the kingdom of Heaven,[25] having been scorched continually by the eternal fires of the Abyss, having been choked in the stinking and torrid Underworld, let him be punished with Judas, the betrayer of Christ, and his accomplices, with continual injury and perpetual misery, condemned in just judgement by God and all the saints,[26] unless he has restored with suitable reparation that which he presumed to diminish in Christ's property.

[ii][27]

CHARTER OF FREEDOM RELATING TO CHILCOMB

The course of earthly mutability never remains in the same state, but by daily default flows out like running water, wherefore the effect of past matters is given to oblivion unless it be set down in the characters of letters, by which it is retained as though by the tie of an anchor lest it flow out from the depths of memory. This action now makes known to posterity those things done once upon a time. Wherefore it is manifestly declared in this charter how[28] I, Edgar,[29] ruler of the English by the aid of the gratuitous forbearance of the Saviour of the world, have piously renewed, as suggested to me by Æthelwold[30] the most beloved of bishops and with the advice of my nobles, the hereditary freedom of Chilcomb,[31] which valley is adjacent on all sides to the city of

---

Edgar's confirmation of Taunton, Somerset, to Winchester Cathedral in ?A.D. 968 (MS. 978), S 806(1), CW 58, BCS 1219: Hac autem cartula liquido declaratur. qualiter, which likewise parallels its vernacular version: Her ys gesputelod on þissum geprite hu S 806 (2), CW 58, BCS 1220.

[29] See above, n. 13.

[30] See above, n. 20.

[31] Chilcomb was held by the bishop of Winchester TRW for the monks of the Old Minster, who owned it TRE: DB, i, fo. 41[r] (DB Hants 3: 1). On the estate, see WS 1, 256–8 and ibid. Fig. 6. See also below, nn. 37–40; V, xiv, and XXX–XXXII.

ciuitati . eandemque renouatam priuilegii libertatem sanctę et indiuiduę Trinitati humillime
commendaui . et in Ueteri Monasterio in
ęcclesia beatorum apostolorum Petri et Pauli
ad usum monachorum Deo inibi regulariter
famulantium . et Christo cotidie pro omni
Christiano populo supplicantium . perpetuo
iure conseruari precepi . Hanc quoque renouationem in ipsa eademque libertate fine tenus
perdurare iussi . qua illam ab auis et atauis et ab
omnibus regibus antecessoribus meis donatam
esse comperi . quorum primi extiterunt . Cynegils[32] rex . et filius eius Cynepalh[33] rex . qui in
exordio Christianę fidei sancto Birino[34] episcopo
uerbum Dei predicante[k][35] concesserunt eiusdem ruris possessionem ad prefatum sancti loci
monasterium . Deinde successores eorum scilicet
Ecgbirht[36] rex . Adulf[37] rex . Ælfred[38] rex .
Eadpeard[39] rex . et reliqui omnes . donec Christi
gratia me quando uoluit . et sicut uoluit super
omne regnum gentis Anglorum regem
constituit . Ideoque precipio in nomine
Domini nostri Iesu Christi . et iuxta priorum
decreta regum tota ipsius telluris quantitas cum
omnibus appendiciis suis : pro una tantummodo
mansa ab omnibus posteris reputetur :[40] Et ut
nullus episcopus eiusdem loci illam terram de
ipso monasterio tradere audeat : nec alicui

Winchester, and have very humbly entrusted
the same renewed freedom of privilege to the
protection of the holy and undivided Trinity;
and have commanded that it be preserved with
perpetual right in the Old Minster in the church
of the blessed apostles Peter and Paul, to the use
of the monks serving God therein according to
the Rule and daily praying to Christ for all
Christian people. I have also ordered that this
renewal should endure to the end in that same
freedom in which I have learnt it was given by
my ancestors and forefathers and by all my
antecedent kings, of whom the first were King
Cynegisl[32] and his son King Cenwealh[33] who
granted possession of the same estate to the
aforesaid monastery of the holy place, when the
holy Bishop Birinus[34] was preaching the word of
God[35] at the beginning of the Christian faith.
Thereafter their successors [granted it]; that is,
King Ecgbeorht,[36] King Æthelwulf,[37] King
Alfred,[38] King Edward[39] and all the rest, until
Christ's grace constituted me as king, as and
when he wills, over the whole kingdom of the
race of the English. Therefore I command, in the
name of our Lord Jesus Christ, and in accordance with the decrees of former kings, that the
whole extent of that estate with all its dependencies should be reckoned by all posterity as
only 1 hide.[40] Also that no bishop of the same
place should dare to transfer that land from that

---

[k] uerbum Dei *underlined for omission after* predicante

[32] See above, n. 8.

[33] Ibid. n. 9.   [34] Ibid. n. 7.

[35] *uerbum Dei predicante*. These words are probably quoted
from the capitulum to Bede's *Historia ecclesiastica*, iii. 7. See
Bertram Colgrave and R. A. B. Mynors (ed. and trans.), *Bede's
Ecclesiastical History of the English People* (Oxford, 1969), 207. I owe
this observation to Martin Biddle. Cf. above, n. 12.

[36] Ecgbeorht, king of the West Saxons 802–39.

[37] Æthelwulf, king of the West Saxons 839–56. For a 13th-
cent. copy of a declaration claiming to record the confirmation
by Æthelwulf, with his son Alfred, of King Cynegisl's grant of
Chilcomb to Bishop Birinus, and its augmentation by Æthelwulf
with a beneficial hidation, see S 325, *CW* 236, *BCS* 493.

[38] Alfred, king of the West Saxons 871–, of the Anglo-Saxons
c.880–99. In **XXX**, below, a copy of a writ of King Æthelred II,
Alfred is said to have renewed the beneficial hidation of
Chilcomb. Cf. above, n. 37, and the reference in 1643 to Alfred's

'charter' concerning Chilcomb in WCL, Book of John Chase,
fo. 18[v] (S 1812).

[39] Edward the Elder, king of the Anglo-Saxons 899–924. BL,
Harl. Ch. 43 C. 1 (S376, MS. 1) is a single-sheet (written ?s.xi[1])
purporting to record Edward's confirmation to Bishop Frithu-
stan of Winchester of the tenure and beneficial hidation of
Chilcomb; it was copied into the *Codex Wintoniensis* as *CW* 190.

[40] *tota ipsius telluris quantitas cum omnibus appendiciis suis : pro
una tantummodo mansa ab omnibus posteris reputetur.* This beneficial
hidation is said elsewhere to have been first granted by King
Æthelwulf; see above n. 37. For later references to it, see below
XXX and **XXXII**, For the OE equivalent of this clause, see
below, **V, iii**, n. 60. As **V, iii** does not refer to the *appendicia* or
'dependencies' it may be that reference to them is an interpolation here in the Latin text; cf. below, **XXXI**.

secularium pro munere quolibet eam dare presumat.[41] Hoc quoque prouida consideratione superaddidi et mandaui . ut nullus filiorum uel nepotum meorum . nec aliquis successorum illorum ad predictum sedis episcopalis cęnobium clericos[42] umquam introducat . sed locus idem semper monachis Christo ibidem seruientibus deputetur . sicut ipse ego cooperante Dei omnipotentis auxilio constitui . quando superbos clericos[43] qui Deo seruire contempserunt . pro nefandis suis actibus et detestandis spurcitiis inde eliminatos expuli .[44] ibique sacram cęnobitarum congregationem qui in hympnis et laudibus Domino uoluntarie seruirent deuotus aggregaui .[45] Prefatę siquidem terrę summa ⸱ centum cassatorum portio est . sed tamen ut dictum est . a cunctis antecessoribus regibus tam pro illorum quam pro omnium successorum illorum ęterna redemptione predicta libertate donata . Deoque omnipotenti et sanctis apostolis eius Petro et Paulo . ęternaliter concessa est .

Quicunque hanc libertatem custodire uoluerit ⸱ custodiat eum Dominus hic et in euum . Si quis autem diabolica suggestione deceptus . hanc libertatem minuere uel infringere presumpserit . ueniant super eum omnia maledictionum genera quę scripta sunt in ueteri et nouo testamento . sitque cęlum ferreum super capud eius . et tellus enea sub pedibus eius[46] . et sit ipse ęterno anathemate separatus a Deo et omnibus sanctis eius . et apostolica beatorum . Petri et Pauli auctoritate ligatus sit quamdiu uixerit . et post maledictum obitum suum gehennalibus flammis cum diabolo et angelis

monastery, nor should presume to give it to any secular person for any type of reward.[41]

This also in prudent consideration I have added and commanded, that none of my sons or grandsons nor any of their successors should ever introduce clerks[42] into the aforesaid monastery of the episcopal see, but that that same place should always be allotted to monks serving Christ there, just as I myself established with the cooperation of Almighty God, when I drove out the proud clerks[43] who disdained to serve God, put out of doors for their criminal deeds and detestable filthinesses,[44] and faithfully gathered there a holy community of monks who might willingly serve the Lord with hymns and praises.[45]

The full assessment indeed of the aforementioned estate is 100 hides; however, it was given as has been said with the aforesaid freedom in eternity to God and his holy apostles Peter and Paul by all the preceding kings, both for their own eternal redemption and for that of all their successors.

May God protect, here and forever, whoever should wish to protect this freedom. But if anyone, deceived by devilish suggestion, should presume to diminish or infringe this freedom, may all the kinds of curse come upon him which are written in the Old and New Testaments, and let there be a sky of iron over his head and a ground of brass under his feet,[46] and let that person be separated by an everlasting curse from God and all his saints and let him be bound by the authority of the blessed apostles Peter and Paul so long as he lives, and after his accursed death let him remain damned and tortured without end in the flames of Hell with the

---

[41] *nec alicui secularium pro munere eam dare presumat.* Cf. below, **V, iii,** n. 61; and **V, xiv,** n. 247. For King Edgar's prohibition of the alienation of the New Minster's property to laymen, see above, **IV, xviii,** and cf. ibid. n. 111.

[42] *clericos.* Members of the secular clergy; see above **IV, vii,** and ibid. n. 44; also below, n. 43.

[43] *superbos clericos.* See above, n. 42. For their association with the sin of pride, see above n. 5, and pp. 17–19. Cf. below, **V, iii,** n. 63.

[44] *pro . . . detestandis spurciiis inde eliminatos.* For similar phraseology, see above, **IV,** n. 11. Cf. below, **V, iii,** n. 64.

[45] *ibique sacram cęnobitarum congregatione . . . aggregaui.* For the Benedictine Reform at the Old Minster, see *ASC* [A, F], s.a. 964; and Wulfstan *Vita S. Æthelwoldi,* caps. 16–18 (ed. Lapidge and Winterbottom, 28–33). See also below, **XXXIII.**

[46] *sitque cęlum ferreum super capud eius . et tellus enea sub pedibus eius.* Cf. Lev. 26: 19 (*BSV,* i, 173) *daboque caelum vobis desuper sicut ferrum et terram aeneam* 'And I will make to you the heaven above as of iron, and the earth as brass'.

eius sine fine dampnatus et cruciatus intereat .
nisi prius emendauerit . quod Deum omnipo-
tentem et sanctos apostolos eius pro nichilo
spernere non timuit .

Huius quoque libertatis renouationem . patria
lingua hoc est Anglica scribere iussi . ne quis
secularium de ignorantia se excusare possit .[47]
quia Latinam sermocinationem forte non
didicit : neque eam quamuis coram se legeretur
intelligere nouit .

Devil and his angels, unless beforehand he has
made amends for not having feared to reject as
nothing Almighty God and his holy apostles.

I have ordered the renewal of this freedom
also to be written in the native, that is English,
tongue lest any secular person might be able to
excuse himself by lack of knowledge[47] because
by chance he has not learnt the Latin language
and would not be able to understand it, however
much it were read in his presence.

[iii][48]

Her is gesputelod on þisum geprite . hu[49]
Aþelpold[50] bisceop begeat æt his leofan cynehla-
forde Eadgare[51] cyninge þæt he mid geþeahte his
pitana¹ genipode . Ciltancumbes[52] freols þære
halgan þrynnesse 7 sancte Petre 7 sancte Paule
into Þintanceastre þan hirede on Ealdan Mynstre .
eal spa his yldran hit ær gefreodon ; ærest
Cynegils[53] cyning 7 his sunu Cynepald[54] cyning .
þe on angynne Cristendomes[55] hit sealdan . eal
spa hit lið on ælche healfe þæs portes into þære
halgan stope . 7 syððan ealle heora æftergengen .
þæt pæs Egcbirt[56] cynincg . and Aþulf[57] cyning . 7
Ælfred[58] cynincg . 7 Eadpeard[59] cynincg . 7 he
geuðe þæt man þæt land on eallum þingon for
ane hide perode . spa spa his yldran hit ær
gesetton 7 gefreodon . pær`e þ´ær mare^m landes .
pær`e þ´ær læsse .[60] 7 he bead on Godes naman
þæt naðer ne þære stope bisceop ne nanes
bisceopes æftergenga þæt land^n næfre of þære

[iii][48]

Here in this writing is declared how[49] Bishop
Æthelwold[50] obtained from his dear royal lord
King Edgar[51] that he, with the advice of his
counsellors, would renew the freedom of Chilcomb[52] to the Holy Trinity and Saint Peter and
Saint Paul at Winchester, for the community at
the Old Minster, just as his forefathers formerly
freed it; first king Cynegisl[53] and his son King
Cenwealh[54] who gave it to that holy place at the
beginning of Christianity,[55] just as it lies on
every side of the city, and afterwards all their
successors [gave it], that was King Ecgbeorht,[56]
and King Æthelwulf,[57] and King Alfred,[58] and
King Edward[59]; and he granted that that land
should be assessed in all things at 1 hide, even as
his forefathers formerly established and freed it,
whether there be more land there or less.[60] And
he commanded in God's name that neither the
bishop of that place nor any of the bishop's
successors should ever alienate that land from

---

¹ p`r´itana *but the interlined letter is later and erroneous*
^m *Corrected from* more   ^n *Corrected from* lond

---

[47] *patria lingua hoc est Anglica scribere iussi ne quis secularium de
ignorantia se excusare possit.* For the English version, see below, **V,
iii**. A similar reason for translating a text from Latin is given, in
relation to Æthelwold's translation of the Rule of St. Benedict
into English, in 'King Edgar's Establishment of Monasteries'; see
Councils 33 (p. 152), and Gretsch *Intellectual Foundations*, 122–3.

[48] **V, iii**. This consists of a vernacular declaration saying
roughly the same as **V, ii**, but probably antecedent to it; see
above, n. 28. This is the first document in the earliest part of the
Codex Wintoniensis written in Old English and scribe *a* at first
had some difficulty with the use of insular minuscule letter-
forms, leading to a number of alterations and corrections.

[49] *Her is gesputelod on þisum geprite hu.* See above, **V, ii**, n. 28.
[50] As above, n. 20.   [51] As above, n. 13.
[52] As above, n. 31.   [53] See above, n. 8.
[54] See above, n. 9.
[55] *on angynne Cristendomes.* That is, in Wessex. This is the
equivalent of *in exordio Christianę fidei* in **V, ii**, above. Cf. below,
XXX, n. 8.
[56] As above, n. 36.   [57] As above, n. 37.
[58] As above, n. 38.   [59] As above, n. 39.
[60] *man þæt land . . . pær`e þ´ær læsse.* See above, n. 40. For the
same OE clause in a writ of Æthelred II, see below, **XXX**, n. 10.
For the verb *werian* 'to be assessed at' and its derivatives, see
Alexander R. Rumble, 'OE *waru*', in Hill and Rumble *Defence of
Wessex*, 178–81.

stope geutode . ne hit nanan portmen[o] pið nanan
sceatte ne pið ceape gesealde .[61] 7 he bead þurh[p]
Godes ælmichtiges myclan mægenþrymm þæt
nan[q] his bearna[62] ne nan heora æftergengcana
þæt menster æfre leng mid preostan gesette . ac
þæt hit efre mid munecan stode . spa spa he hit
mid Godes ælmihtiges[r] fultume gesette . þa þa he
hit þa modigan preostas[63] for heora mandædon
þanan ut adrefde .[64] 7 þerinne munecas gelogode
þæt hi Godes þeopedom æfter sancte Benedictes
tæcinge . 7 dæghpamlice to Gode cleopodon for
ealles Cristenes folces alidsednesse .[65] Ealles þæs
landes is an hund hida . ac þa godan cynegas 7 þa
pisan[66] ælc æfter oþran þ ylce land spa gefreodon
Gode to lofe 7 his þeopan to brycen 7 to
fostorlande . þ hit man æfre on ende for ane
hide perian sceolde .[67] Se þe þysne freols healdan
pille . God ælmihtig hine gehealde her 7 on
ecnesse . Gif hpa þonne[s] þurh ænige dyrstignesse
oðõe þurh deofles lare þisne freols abrecan pille .
oðõe þas gesetednesse on oõer apendan durre . sy[t]
he apyrged mid eallan þan apyrgednessan þe
synd apritene on eallan halgan bocan .[68] 7 sy he
ascyred fram ures drichtnes gemanan 7 ealra his
halgana . 7 sy he gebunden þa hpile þe he libbe
on þisam life mid þan ylcan bendan þe God
ælmihtig þyrh[u] hine sylfne betæchte his halgan
apostolan Petre 7 Paule . 7 æfter his apyrgedan
forõsiõe ligge he efre on healle grundleasan

that holy place, nor should they grant it to any
citizen in return for any money or goods.[61] And
he commanded, by the great power of Almighty
God, that none of his sons[62] nor any of their
successors should ever again establish that monastery with priests, but that it should remain
always as he established it with monks with the
help of Almighty God when he drove out from
there the proud priests[63] because of their evil
deeds[64] and lodged monks therein so that they
might [perform] God's service according to the
teaching of Saint Benedict and might daily call
on God for the salvation of all Christian
people.[65]

The total hidage of this land is 100, but good
and wise kings,[66] each after the other, so freed
that same land, for the love of God and for the
benefit of his servants, as land providing food,
that it should for all time be assessed at 1 hide.[67]
May God protect, here and forever, whoever
should wish to protect this freedom. But if
anyone, through any presumption or through
the Devil's teaching, should wish to destroy this
freedom, or dare to alter this decree, let him be
cursed with all the afflictions which are written
in all the sacred books,[68] and let him be cut off
from the fellowship of our Lord and all his saints,
and let him be bound as long as he lives in this
life with the same bonds that Almighty God
through himself committed to his holy apostles
Peter and Paul, and after his accursed death let
him lie forever in Hell's groundless pit, and let

---

[o] *Corrected from* porõmen   [p] *Corrected from* þurc
[q] *Corrected from* non   [r] ælmilhtiges   [s] freols *added
in the margin at this point by a later hand; BCS includes it in the text*
[t] se   [u] *corrected from* þyrc

---

[61] *ne hit nanan portmen piõ nanan sceatte ne piõ ceape gesealde.*
Note that the Latin *secularis* 'secular person' in **V, ii**, above is
here defined more specifically in OE as *portman* 'citizen'.

[62] *bearna.* Note that the use of OE *bearn* as a translation of
Latin *filius* seems to have been a personal preference of
Æthelwold, contrasting with the use of *sunu* as an item of
standardized 'Winchester' vocabulary. See Helmut Gneuss, 'The
Origin of Standard Old English and Æthelwold's School at
Winchester', *ASE* 1 (1972), 63–83, at 76 and 79; and Mechthild
Gretsch, 'Æthelwold's Translation of the *Regula Sancti Benedicti*
and its Latin Exemplar', *ASE* 3 (1974), 125–51, at 150.

[63] *þa modigan preostas.* The *superbos clericos* of **V, ii**; see ibid.
n. 43. For *mõdig* as a late OE standardized 'Winchester'
translation of *superbus*, see Gneuss, 'Origin of Standard Old

English', 76; and Walter Hofstetter, 'Winchester and the
Standardization of Old English Vocabulary', *ASE* 17 (1988),
139–61, at 150.

[64] *for heora mandædon þanan ut adrefde.* Cf. above, n. 44.

[65] *þerinne munecas gelogode þæt he Godes þeopedom æfter sancte
Benedictes tæcinge dæghpamlice to Gode cleopodon for ealles Cristenes
folces alidsednesse.* See above, n. 45. For St. Benedict (not named in
V, ii), see above, **IV**, n. 93.

[66] *þa godan cynegas 7 þa pisan.* Cf. *se pisa cing Ælfred* in **XXX**,
below; see ibid. n. 9.

[67] *hit man æfre on ende for ane hide perian sceolde.* See above,
n. 60.

[68] *on eallan halgan bocan.* Of the bible; the equivalent of *in
ueteri et nouo testamento* in **V, ii**, above.

pytte . 7 byrne he on þan ecan fyre mid deofle 7
his englan a butan ælcan ende . butan he hit ær
his forðsiðe gebete . Amen .

him burn in the everlasting fire with the Devil
and his angels forever without end, unless he has
made amends for it before his death. Amen.

[iv]⁶⁹

Benigna nos exortatione patientissimus Iob
erumpnose caduci⁰ seculi uitę fragilem conque-
rens calamitatem subtili proclamat indagine
dicens . Nudus egressus sum de utero matris
meę et nudus illuc reuertar .⁷⁰ Et iterum . Nichil
intulimus in hunc mundum . uerum nec auferre
ab eo⁰ quid poterimus .⁷¹ Quapropter ego
Eadgar.⁷² diuina fauente clementia tocius Albionis basileus⁷³ intra mei pectoris . archana˟
superni moderatoris instinctu attactus . obnixe
rimari cęperam . quomodo caducis ęterna .
perituris mansura mercari ualerem . Occurrit
igitur animo deliberanti . ut non solummodo
territoria⁷⁴ Wintoniensis episcopatus ęcclesię
uidelicet consecrate ob reuerentiam agię Trinitatis Unitatisque necnon Petri apostolorum
principis atque Pauli eximii uerbi satoris . pro
redemptione animę meę statuque mei imperii ac
dilectione Adelwoldi⁷⁵ uenerandi antistitis . quę
meis inibi degebant⁷ temporibus renouarem .
atque in una colligerem scedula⁷⁶ . uerum etiam
fundos prefatę basilicę qui iniuste ab aliquibus
marcidulę fastu superbię indomite tumentibus
abstracta uidebantur . intercapedine modici
cromatis⁷⁷ magnopere qualiter olim a meorum

[iv]⁶⁹

Long-suffering Job cries out to us in kindly
exhortation, in distress overcoming the brittle
misfortune of a transitory lifetime, saying
'Naked came I out of my mother's womb, and
naked shall I return thither',⁷⁰ and again 'For we
brought nothing into this world, and certainly
we can carry nothing out'.⁷¹ Wherefore I,
Edgar,⁷² ruler of the whole of Albion while
the divine forbearance allows,⁷³ touched within
the recesses of my breast by the instigation of
the celestial Ruler, had begun strenuously to
investigate how I might be able to trade eternal
lasting things in return for transitory perishable
ones. Thus it occurred to [my] deliberating
mind that not only might I renew and collect
in one document⁷⁶ the landholdings,⁷⁴ as they
existed in my own times, of the church of the
see of Winchester that is consecrated in reverence for the Holy Trinity and Unity and for
Peter the foremost of the apostles and Paul the
distinguished promoter of the Word, in return
for the redemption of my soul and the persis-
tence of my rule and out of regard for the
worshipful Bishop Æthelwold;⁷⁵ but also might
most humbly, observed by the witness of my
nobles whose names are seen written on the last
page of this document,⁷⁸ restore the estates of
the aforementioned cathedral which were seen

ᵛ *Corrected from* casduci   ʷ *Corrected from* habeo
˟ archano   ʸ degebat *but the subject is* territoria *(neuter pl.)*

---

⁶⁹ **V, iv**. This Latin diploma concerning the episcopal estate
of Taunton (see below, n. 79) has verbal similarities in its
exposition to that in **V, xiii**, below. Both refer to Edgar's
mental deliberations about how to restore the possessions of
the Church. Verbal comparison may also be made between **V, iv**
and parts of the exposition and other passages in S 876, *Councils*
39, Æthelred II's diploma in favour of Abingdon Abbey, an
original dated 993 which forms part of the 'Orthodoxorum' group
of 10th-cent. royal diplomas; see above, p. 15, n. 4.

⁷⁰ Job 1: 21.

⁷¹ *Nichil intulimus in hunc mundum . uerum nec auferre ab eo
quid poterimus.* A version of 1 Tim. 6: 7.

⁷² As above, n. 13.

⁷³ *diuina fauente clementia tocius Albionis basileus.* A very similar

royal style appears above in **IV, vi**. Edgar is also said to be ruler
(*basileus*) of the whole of Albion in **V, v** and **V, xiv**.

⁷⁴ *territoria.* From what follows this appears to refer to the
cathedral endowment as it was when Edgar came to power.

⁷⁵ As above, n. 20.

⁷⁶ *in una colligerem scedula.* The same word *scedula* to describe
V as a whole is used again below; see n. 78. Above in **V, i**, the
text is called a *sinthama*; see n. 21.

⁷⁷ *intercapedine modici cromatis.* Literally 'in the interval of a
small chromatic scale'. The grecism *croma* (Lewis and Short, 328,
s.v. *chroma*), more usually used of a chromatic scale in music, is
here used of the measurement of time. See also below, n. 154.

dapsilitate predecessorum benigne cum suis rite sibi pertinentibus dati cessentur . meorum testimonio functus procerum quorum nomina in ultima huius scedulę pada caraxata[78] uidentur humillime restituerem . Hinc Tantun[79] eiusdem quantitatis . c . uidelicet mansis spatiose dilatatum successorumque omnium prosperitate a nobis ęternaliter restituitur ęcclesię . Prefatum etenim rus prius a quadam antiquitus largitum est regina religiosa[80] . ac postea ab Aðulfo[81] rege glorioso tocius sui regni rura decimante[82] copiose augmentatum . renouatisque supradicti territorii cartulis[83] ęterna firmatum est dapsilitate . Rex itidem Eadpeard[84] nouis hereditatum cartis hoc idem rus ęterna consolidauit libertate acceptis uidelicet lx[z] pro eadem libertate mansis[85] . xxx . scilicet æt Banepillan[86] . xx . æt Scealdeburnan . Stoce[87] . x . æt Crapancumbe[88] . quod tamen tot regum[aa] procerumque fixa firmatum donatione instigante

to have been unjustly taken away by some people puffed up with the arrogance of rotten pride, most particularly considering how, in a small interval of time,[77] they have been surrendered, having once upon a time liberally been given by the generosity of my predecessors with all things rightly belonging to them. To this end Taunton[79] is eternally restored by me to the church, at the same extent, that is spaciously dispersed over 100 hides, to the good fortune of all successors. The aforesaid estate was indeed first granted in antiquity by a certain pious queen[80] and afterwards it was enlarged by the glorious King Æthelwulf,[81] when he generously tithed[82] the estates of his whole kingdom, and confirmed with eternal generosity in renewed charters of the abovementioned landholding.[83] King Edward[84] likewise strengthened this same estate with new charters of hereditary rights in eternal freedom, having indeed received 60 hides in return for the same freedom,[85] 30 namely at Banwell,[86] 20 at Stoke by Shalbourne[87] [and] 10 at Crowcombe,[88] all of which, however, having been established by the immovable grant of kings and nobles, was unjustly taken away by

---

[z] *Corrected from* xl   [aa] *Corrected from* regnum

[78] *nomina in ultima huius scedulę pada caraxata.* This is a specific reference to the witness-list which was (or was intended to be) written on the final page (MS. *pada*, ? in error for *pagina*) of the *scedula*, i.e. **V**. For *caraxata*, from the grecism *caraxo*, see above, **IV**, n. 124.

[79] Taunton, Somerset, belonged to the bishop of Winchester *TRE* and *TRW*: *DB* i, fo. 87[v] (*DB Somerset* 2: 1–9). For other diplomas, of varying degrees of authenticity, granting or confirming Taunton to the church of Winchester, see S 254(1), 311(1), 373, 521, 806 (1–3), 1286; respectively, *CW* 119, 117, 118, 57, 58 and 60, and 62; *BCS* 158, 476, 612, 831, 1219–20, and 611. Of these S 806 (1–3) is a bilingual diploma in the name of King Edgar, restoring rights over the estate. It is probable that the Latin part is secondary and is a translation of the OE which may contain some genuine information. Both parts are dated 978, possibly for 968. See also below, **V, xiv**.

[80] *prius a quadam antiquitus largitum est regina religiosa.* Taunton is said to have been first granted to the church of Winchester by Queen Frithugyth, wife of King Æthelheard of the West Saxons (726–?740): *Winchester ann.*, s.a. 721. For related grants in augmentation of Frithugyth's, see S 254(1), *CW* 119, *BCS* 158 and S 310, *CW* 128, *BCS* 475.

[81] See above, n. 37.

[82] *tocius sui regni rura decimante.* For King Æthelwulf's 'decimation', see *ASC* (A,B,D,E) s.a 855, (C,F) s.a. 856. For discussion, see Finberg, chapter 6; and Simon Keynes, 'The West Saxon Charters of King Æthelwulf and his Sons', *EHR* 119 (1994), 1109–49, esp. 1115–16 and 1119–22. See below, n. 83. Cf. also below, **V, vi** (n. 121).

[83] For a diploma claiming to record the grant to the church of Winchester by King Æthelwulf of 133 hides at Taunton, see S 311(1), *CW* 117, *BCS* 476. This was partly based on one of the 'decimation' charters; see Keynes, 'The West Saxon Charters of King Æthelwulf', ibid.

[84] Edward the Elder; see above, n. 39.

[85] *lx . . . mansis.* For a diploma claiming to record a grant by Edward the Elder in 904 to Winchester Cathedral of this 60 hides in exchange for privileges for 'the monastery at Taunton', see S 373, *CW* 118, *BCS* 612. It is also referred to in a separate diploma, bearing the same date, relating to 20 hides at Stoke by Shalbourne alone: S 1286, *CW* 62, *BCS* 611.

[86] Banwell, Somerset, belonged to the bishop of Wells *TRW* and to Earl Harold *TRE*: *DB*, i, fo. 89[v] (*DB Somerset* 6: 9).

[87] Stoke by Shalbourne, Wiltshire, is not separately entered in Domesday Book, but may be represented by Stokke House in Bedwyn; see *VCH Wilts.*, II, 87. See also above, n. 85.

[88] Crowcombe, Somerset. Although apparently granted to Edward the Elder by exchange, it was re-acquired by the Old Minster through the gift of Gytha, the wife of Earl Godwine, according to *Winchester ann.*, s.a. 1053. It belonged to the Old Minster *TRE* but was acquired by the count of Mortain *TRW*: *DB*, i, fo. 91[v] (*DB Somerset* 19: 7). It was restored by King Stephen in 1136: *Regesta*, III, 946; *CW* 7.

diabolo iniuste a quibusdam predecessoribus
meis philargirię uitio seductis[89] uiolenta[bb]
abstractum est rapina . A me iterum Christi
annuente gratia restitutum . perpetua ad usus
predicti pontificatus presulum ditatur[cc] libertate .
Si quis autem hanc nostram uiolare minuereue
munificentiam tyrannica fretus superbia[90] presumpserit anathema sit . et Domini clementia .
sanctorumque omnium priuatus contubernio .
inimicorum omnium persecutione uallatus
depopulatusque intereat . nec in hac uita
ullam obtineat ueniam . sed in futuro perhenni
supplicio deputatus . inferni fauce consumptus .
sine fine persistat cruciatus . nisi satisfaciendo
redintegrauerit quod insipiendus minuendo
deleuit .

Tres mansę in Cearn[91] ad rus prefatum
pertinent et duę æt Þecetforda .[92]

[v][93]

FREOLSBOC TO ALRESFORDA

Cum sacrę auctoritatis doctrina nos ueridica
sedulo ammoneat exortatione . ut non solum
actiuę uisibilibus religiose conuersando . sanc-
tisque proficiendo uirtutibus carismatis dono
perfusi[94] decentissime perfruamur . uerum
etiam contemplatiuę inuisibilia uitę toto
mentis conamine partim a recidiuis semoti
libentissime[dd] cum puro tranquilloque animi
intuitu contemplando amplectemur dicens .
Cuncta quę uidentur temporalia sunt . quę

violent plundering at the instigation of the Devil
by certain of my predecessors who were seduced
by the vice of avarice.[89] Having been restored
again by me with the approving grace of Christ,
it is granted in perpetual freedom for the use of
the bishops of the aforesaid bishopric. But if
anyone, daring with the pride of a tyrant,[90]
should presume to violate or diminish this our
generosity, let him be cursed and, cut off from
the forbearance of the Lord and from the
common dwelling of all the saints, let him die
surrounded and ravaged in the persecution of all
hostile things and let him not receive any mercy
in this life but, destined in the future for
perpetual torment, having been devoured by
the jaws of Hell, let him remain tortured without
end, unless he has restored by giving reparation
for what he foolishly destroyed by diminishing.

3 hides in Charmouth[91] belong to the aforementioned estate, and 2 at Washford.[92]

[v][93]

CHARTER OF FREEDOM RELATING TO ALRESFORD

Since the true teaching of sacred authority
admonishes us with zealous exhortation not
only to properly enjoy passing our lives in the
visible things of practical religion and contributing [to them] with holy virtues, having been
drenched by the gift of grace,[94] but also to love
the invisible things of contemplative life with
complete effort of mind, contemplating most
freely with pure and quiet consideration of the
spirit when partly distant from everyday affairs,
saying 'For the things which are seen, are
temporal; but the things which are not seen,

[bb] *Corrected from* uiolenti   [cc] *Corrected from* ditate
[dd] -issimę

---

[89] *philargirię uitio seductis.* Cf. *philargiria seductus* in **V, i,** above;
V, vi and **xiv,** below.

[90] *tyrannica fretus superbia.* For the perceived dangers of pride,
see above, pp. 17–19. Cf. *tyrannica fretus contumacia* in S 876; see
above, n. 69.

[91] Charmouth, Dorset, appears to have been alienated by
1066: *DB,* i, fo. 80r (*DB Dorset* 26: 67). According to S254(1), *CW*
119, *BCS* 158, these 3 appurtenant hides had been granted in 737
to the church of Winchester by King Æthelwulf for the
construction of salt-works.

[92] Washford, Somerset, is not named in Domesday Book.

Although said to have been granted to the church of Winchester
in 737 (see above, n. 91), it appears to have been alienated by 956
when it was granted by King Eadwig to his thegn Ælfweald; see
S 596, *CW* 40, *BCS* 960.

[93] **V, v.** A Latin diploma restoring the episcopal estate of
Alresford (see below, n. 101). See Addendum.

[94] *carismatis . . . perfusi.* Cf. *carismatum . . . perfusus* in **IV, xv,**
above.

autem non uidentur ęterna .[95] ego Eadgar .[96] Christi annuente clementia tocius Albionis basileus[97] his recidiuis practicę uitę possessiunculis . ęterna theoricę emolumenta lucrando mercari desiderans . quoddam rus a supradicta Wintoniensi ęcclesia[98] iniusta quondam a philargiriis abstractum rapina[99] Aðelwoldo .[100] obtinente presule ab illo qui iniuste possederat iusto arripiens iudicio Trinitati referendę[ee] eiusque apostolis Petro et Paulo humillima reddens restituo deuotione . xl . uidelicet cassatos loco qui cęlebri Alresford .[101] nominatur uocabulo . Nam rex religiosus Cynepalh[102] nuncupatus . a Birino pontifice fidei sacramentis imbutus .[103] idem rus in Christiane religionis exordio prefatę Dei ęcclesię magna animi largitus est[ff] deuotione .[104] Hoc idem Ecgbirct[105] regali fretus stemmate noua territorii consolidauit cartula .[106]

Quidam aliquando predictę pontifex basilicę a notis Denepulf[107] nuncupatus cuidam propinquorum suorum Ælfred uocitato . eatenus cum consensu ęcclesiasticę familię accommodauit . ut annis singulis censum tocius telluris uita comite rite[gg] persolueret .[108] Is equidem insipiens adulterans stuprum propriam religiose pactatam abominans . scortam diligens libidinose commisit . quo reatu omni substantia peculiali

are eternal',[95] I, Edgar,[96] ruler of the whole of Albion while Christ's forbearance allows,[97] desiring to trade these recurring small occupations of practical life in return for winning the eternal benefits of a contemplative [life], restore and give back with most humble devotion to the worshipful Trinity and to its apostles Peter and Paul, Bishop Æthelwold[100] acquiring [it], a certain estate, once taken away from the aforementioned church of Winchester[98] in unlawful plundering by avaricious people,[99] seizing [it] by lawful judgement from he who unlawfully possessed it; that is 40 hides in the place which is called by the famous name Alresford.[101] Indeed the pious king called Cenwealh,[102] having been instructed in the sacraments of faith by Bishop Birinus,[103] granted the same estate with great devotion of spirit to the aforementioned church of God at the beginning of the Christian religion.[104] This same [estate] Ecgbeorht,[105] supported by a royal pedigree, strengthened with a new charter of landholding.[106]

At some time or other a certain bishop of the aforementioned church, called Denewulf[107] by those who know, with the agreement of the ecclesiastical community, granted a lease to one of his kinsmen called Alfred, so that each year while he lived he would pay rent for the whole estate.[108] This foolish man committing adultery, rejecting his own religiously betrothed woman, loving a whore, libidinously committed

---

[ee] *Spelling for* reuerendę   [ff] *The insular abbreviation* ÷ *is used for* est   [gg] ritę

[95] *Cuncta quę uidentur temporalia sunt . quę autem non uidentur ęterna.* A version of 2 Cor. 4: 18.

[96] See above, n. 13.

[97] *Christi annuente clementia tocius Albionis basileus.* See above, n. 73.

[98] *a supradicta Wintoniensi ęcclesia.* This must be a cross-reference to the preceding parts of **V**, as the church of Winchester has not previously been mentioned in **V, v**.

[99] *iniusta quondam a philargiriis abstractum rapina.* For this alienation, see further below.

[100] See above, n. 20.

[101] Alresford, Hants, belonged to the bishop of Winchester *TRE* and *TRW*, see *DB*, i, fo. 40ʳ (*DB Hants* 2: 1). For a diploma claiming to record the grant of Alresford to the church of Winchester by King Ine in 701, see S 242, *CW* 51, *BCS* 102. See also below, **V, xiv**.

[102] See above, n. 9.

[103] *a Birino pontifice fidei sacramentis imbutus.* See above, **V, i**, nn.

7 and 10. The phrasing is Bedan; see, for example, *Historia Ecclesiastica*, ii. 15 (with relation to both Kings Rædwald and Sigeberht of East Anglia): Bertram Colgrave and R. A. B. Mynors (ed. and trans.), *Bede's Ecclesiastical History of the English People* (Oxford, 1969), 190.

[104] *idem rus . . . largitus est deuotione.* For Cenwealh's grant, cf. *Winchester ann.*, s.a. 639.

[105] As above, n. 36.

[106] *noua territorii consolidauit cartula.* For a diploma claiming to record King Ecgbeorht's grant, see S 284, *CW* 54, *BCS* 398.

[107] Denewulf, bishop of Winchester, 878 × 879–908.

[108] *cuidam propinquorum suorum Ælfred . . . accommodauit ut annis singulis censum tocius telluris . . . persolueret.* For this lease, see S 1287, *CW* 121, *AS Ch* 15.

recte priuatus est . et prefatum rus ab eo abstractum rex huius patrię suę ditioni auidus[109] deuenire iniuste optauit . Cuius auiditati presul supradictus minime consentiens . datis centum uiginti auri mancusis[110] . predictam tellurem ad usus presulum[hh] satisfaciendo ęcclesię Dei restituit .[111]

Succedente itaque tempore supradicti adulteri et scelerati filius . falso dicens esse sibi naturale suo iniuste subiciens dominio ab ęcclesia Dei presumptuosus arripuit hereditariamque cartulam nouis litterarum apicibus rege Eadredo[112] cum animę suę consentiente periculo . demonis instinctu fascinatus edidit . Quę igitur cartula et omnes qui ei ausu consenserint temerario in Domini maledictione permaneant et nullo umquam tempore ad aliquam utilitatem perueniat . Uetus nanque et hęc noua quam edidi cartula iugiter Christi omniumque iudicio fidelium incolumis[jj] preualeat adulterina quam predixi cartula ęterna dampnatione ad nichilum redacta . et imperpetuum anathematizata .

Si quis igitur hanc nostram largifluam augere uoluerit donationem . augeat eius Dominus et uitam et prosperitatem hic et in futuro . Qui autem lenocinante diabolo fastu superbię inflatus .[113] nostra uiolare uel minuere presumpserit statuta . in Domini maledictione permaneat . et a sanctę Dei ęcclesię consortio sanctorumque omnium contubernio priuatus . ęterna misellus dampnetur miseria nisi resipiscens satisfaciendo restituerit ⫶ quod in Domini possessione uiolare presumpsit .

debauchery, for which reason he was rightly deprived of all his personal wealth, and the aforementioned estate having been taken away from him, the greedy king[109] of this country unjustly desired that it should become part of his dominion. When the aforesaid bishop opposed his greed, he [the king], when 120 mancuses[110] of gold had been given [to him], made amends to the church of God, and restored the aforesaid estate to the use of the bishops.[111]

At a later time again, the son of the abovesaid adulterer and criminal, falsely saying it was his by reason of his birth [and] unjustly subjecting it to his lordship, presumptuously seized it from the church of God and, bewitched at the instigation of the Devil, brought forth a hereditary charter in new outlines of letters, King Eadred[112] agreeing [to it] in danger to his soul. Let that charter, therefore, and all who have agreed to it in an imprudent attempt, remain under the Lord's curse and let it never at any time come to have any use. Indeed, may the old and this new charter which I have brought about prevail unimpaired in perpetuity in the judgement of Christ and all the faithful, the false charter which I mentioned having been reduced to nothing by eternal damnation and cursed in perpetuity.

Therefore, if anyone should wish to increase this our bountiful donation, may the Lord increase both his life and his good fortune here and in the future. But may he who, puffed up by the enticing Devil with the arrogance of pride,[113] should presume to violate or diminish our decisons, remain under the Lord's curse and, cut off from the fellowship of the holy church of God and from the common dwelling of all the saints, let him be damned as a wretch with eternal misery, unless coming to his senses he has restored with reparation what he presumed to violate in the Lord's possession.

[hh] *Corrected from* presulem   [jj] incolomis

[109] *rex . . . auidus.* From what follows, this refers to Edward the Elder; see below, n. 109. In 899 × 908, Bishop Denewulf and his cathedral community leased Beddington, Surrey, to Edward for life but requested that he would not ask them for further land; see S 1444, *CW* 188–9, *BCS* 618–19.

[110] *mancusis.* For the *mancus*, see above, **III**, n. 6.

[111] *predictam tellurem . . . restituit.* For a diploma claiming to record Edward the Elder's restoration of Alresford, see S 375, *CW* 50, *BCS* 623.

[112] Eadred, king of England 946–55.

[113] *lenocinante diabolo fastu superbię inflatus.* Cf. *BR*, cap. 65.2

maligno spiritu superbiae inflati . . . 'puffed up by the evil spirit of pride'. For the evils of pride, see above, pp. 17–19; also **IV, prol.**, n. 9.

[vi][114]

FREOLSBOC TO CLEARAN

Dominus omnipotens qui uiuit in ęternum creans omnia simul diuino et coęterno uerbo sex diebus[115] formulas rerum distinxit singularum . Ex creatura igitur creatorem agnoscens mirabilem . presentia ad futurorum comparationem bonorum . uelut quisquiliarum peripsema .[116] uel fetidam melancolię nausiam apporiando[117] reprobans . ęternę beatitudinis emolumenta medullitus lucrari desiderans . ego Eadgar[118] diuina largiente gratia totius Brittannię rex ob animę meę salutem regnique nostri ac filiorum successorumque omnium prosperitatem ꞉ quoddam rus . x . uidelicet mansarum quantitate taxatum . usitato æt Clearan .[119] nuncupatum uocabulo . olim ab Aþulfo[120] rege tocius sui regminis rura decimante[121] ad refocillationem pontificum predicte Wintoniensi ęcclesię[122] ęterna largitum est dapsilitate . modernoque tempore a quibusdam perfidis iniuste abstractum raptoribus .[123] reuerende Trinitati Petroque apostolorum principi eiusque coapostolo Paulo ęterna solutum libertate humiliter restituo . Hoc in Christi nomine precipio ut nemo successorum meorum uiolare audacter[kk] presumat quod ego meorum auctoritate

[kk] aucdacter

---

[114] **V, vi**. This Latin diploma concerns the episcopal estate of Highclere (see below, n. 119), which estate is specifically devoted to the supply of food for the bishop; for the monks' food supplies from Chilcomb, see below, **V, xiv**. The proem, like that of **V, i**, above, refers to the Creation. Other phrases are similar to those in **V, xi**, being related to formulae previously used by the draftsman 'Æthelstan A'; see above, p. 15.

[115] *sex diebus*. As above, n. 4.

[116] *quisquiliarum peripsema*. Also below in **V, xi**; see n. 165.

[117] *uel fetidam melancolię nausiam apporiando*. Cf. *uelut fastidiosam melancolię nausiam abominando* in the proem of **V, xi**, below. The combination of *melancolia* with *apporiari* is also used above in **IV, xii**. See Addendum.   [118] As above, n. 13.

[119] Highclere, Hants, was held by the bishop of Winchester *TRW* for the monks of the Old Minster who held it *TRE*: *DB*, i, fo. 41[r] (*DB Hants* 3: 7). See also below, **V, xiv**.

[120] As above, n. 37. No text of Æthelwulf's alleged grant survives.

CHARTER OF FREEDOM RELATING TO HIGHCLERE

When the all-powerful Lord who lives in eternity created, according to the divine and coeternal Word, all things at one time in six days,[115] he made distinct the form of each thing. Recognizing therefore the Creator as marvellous on account of the Creation, condemning things of the present in procuring future benefits, rejecting them as either the offscourings of rubbish[116] or the stinking sickness of melancholy,[117] [and] heartily desiring to gain the benefits of eternal blessedness, I, Edgar,[118] king of the whole of Britain while the divine grace grants, for the salvation of my soul and the good fortune of our kingdom and of all [our] children and successors, humbly restore, emancipated in eternal freedom, to the worshipful Trinity and to Peter the foremost of the apostles and his coapostle Paul, a certain estate taxed at the rate of 10 hides, called by the familiar name Highclere;[119] once upon a time it was granted in eternal generosity to the aforesaid church of Winchester[122] for the feeding of the bishops, by King Æthelwulf[120] when he tithed the estates of his whole kingdom,[121] and in modern times it was unjustly taken away by certain treacherous plunderers.[123] This I command in Christ's name, that none of my successors should audaciously presume to violate what I, with the authority of

---

[121] *tocius sui regminis rura decimante*. For a similar phrase describing Æthelwulf's 'decimation', see above **V, iv**, and n. 82.

[122] *predicte Wintoniensi ęcclesię*. A cross-reference to preceding parts of **V**; cf. above, n. 98.

[123] *modernoque tempore a quibusdam perfidis iniuste abstractum raptoribus*. Note, however, that Edgar himself had granted 10 hides at Highclere to his thegn Ælfwine in 959, according to S 680, *CW* 74, *BCS* 1051. Ælfwine held the estate after Bishop Ælfsige I (died 959), who held it on a lease for four lives from the Old Minster: S 565, *CW* 75, *BCS* 905. He was probably the (unnamed) young kinsman to whom Bishop Ælfsige bequeathed Highclere after its tenure by two other relatives; see S 1491, *AS Wills* 4. If so, he seems to have persuaded or deceived Edgar into converting it to bookland.

procerum Domino recuperando restitui . Si quis autem philargiria seductus[124] aliqua noua et adulterina cartula hanc nostram largifluam a Domino abstrahere uoluerit munificentiam . anathema sit . et inferni incendiis assiduo punitus . iugi miseria cruciatus intereat . Vetus namque et hęc noua quam edidi Domino instigante cartula[125] iugi profectu uigeat . et omnes qui ei iuuamen impenderint peccaminum suorum ueniam consequendo ęternę uitę beatitudinem Christo largiente obtineant . Sit autem hoc rus Adþelpoldo[126] presule obtinente eadem libertate gloriosum . qua priscis fuerat temporibus insignitum . Qui uero eiusdem libertatis gloriam uiolare inique[ll] presumpserit . a Christo reprobatus inferni miseria puniatur nisi satisfaciendo se humiliatum correxerit .

[vii][127]

FREOLSBOC TO VFERANTUNE .

Ecce Christo in ęternum regnante cunctis sophię studium intento mentis conamine sedulo rimantibus liquido patescit . quod huius uitę periculis nimio ingruentibus terrore recidiui terminus cosmi appropinquare dinoscitur . ut ueridica Christi promulgat sententia qua dicit . Surget gens contra gentem . et regnum aduersus regnum .[128] et reliqua . Quamobrem ego Eadgar .[129] Christi conferente gratia tocius Brittannię basileus . Domino nostro Iesu Christo totis uiribus ante futuri tempus iudicii placere desiderans . quandam telluris particulam . xl . uidelicet mansas tribus in locis diremptas . xx . æt Uferantune[130] cum

[ll] inique

---

[124] *philargiria seductus.* See above, n. 89.
[125] *Vetus . . . cartula.* Æthelwulf's; see above, n. 120.
[126] As above, n. 20.
[127] **V, vii**. This Latin diploma grants the episcopal estate of Overton, Hants, with appurtenant woodlands. It is the first subsection of **V** to include immunity and reservation clauses. Some phrases are similar to those in **V, xiii**, below.
[128] Luke 21: 10; also used in **V, xiii**, below.
[129] As above, n. 13.

my nobles, have restored in recovering. But if anyone, seduced by avarice,[124] should wish to take away from the Lord our copious generosity by means of some other new and false charter, let him be cursed and, punished continually in the fires of Hell, let him perish tormented by perpetual misery. Indeed may the old and this new charter,[125] which I have brought about on the Lord's instigation, flourish in perpetual success and may all those who give assistance to it, following forgiveness of their sins, obtain the bliss of eternal life by Christ's grant. Moreover, may this same estate, being acquired by Bishop Æthelwold,[126] be glorious in the same freedom by which it was distinguished in former times. But let anyone who should unjustly presume to violate the glory of the same freedom, having been rejected by Christ, be punished in the misery of Hell unless by making reparation he has reformed himself as one humiliated.

[vii][127]

CHARTER OF FREEDOM RELATING TO OVERTON

Behold! While Christ rules in eternity, it becomes clearly evident to all those who zealously explore the study of wisdom with eager effort of mind that the end of the transient Universe is discerned to approach with excessive terror in the assailing dangers of this life, like the true saying of Christ in which he says, 'Nation shall rise against nation, and kingdom against kingdom',[128] and so forth. Wherefore I Edgar,[129] ruler of the whole of Britain by the conferring of Christ's grace, desiring with all my might to please Our Lord Jesus Christ before the time of future judgement, humbly renew with eternal freedom a certain portion of land, that is 40 hides scattered in three places, 20 at Overton[130] with

[130] 41 hides at Overton, Hants, were held in demesne by the bishop of Winchester *TRE* and *TRW*: *DB*, i, fo. 40ʳ (*DB Hants* 2: 10). This probably included the Tadley and North Waltham land here confirmed.

silua æt Tadanleage[131] huic ruri[mm] pertinente .
xv . æt Þealtam[132] . v . æt Bradanleage .[133] ut a
meis[134] dudum supradictę Wintoniensi basilicę[135] reuerende Trinitati eiusque apostolis
Petro atque Paulo ęterno[nn] largitum fuerat .[136]
ita hac noua cartula cum meorum auctoritate
procerum Aðelpoldo[137] presule obtinente
roboratum . ęterna humilis renouo libertate .
Sint autem omnia hęc supradicta rura omni
terrenę seruitutis iugo libera tribus exceptis .
rata uidelicet expeditione . pontis arcisue
restauratione . Maneat igitur hęc nostra largiflua[nnn] renouata dapsilitas . uti fuerat fixa per
euum . Si quis igitur hanc ęcclesię libertatem
uiolare presumpserit anathema sit ꞉ et inferni
cruciatibus attritus infelix intereat . nisi satisfaciendo ante obitum ueniam optinuerit .

[viii][138]

FR[E]OLSBOC TO TICCEBVRNAN .

Fortuitu seculorum patrimonia incertis nepotum heredibus relinquuntur[oo] . et omnis mundi
gloria appropinquante uitę mortis termino ad
nichilum reducta fatescit . Idcirco terrenis caducarum possessionibus semper mansura supernę
patrię emolumenta adipiscentes Domino patro-
cinante rebus recidiuis lucranda sanctorum
decernimus hortatu . Quamobrem ego

[mm] rure   [nn] ęternę   [nnn] largiflue   [oo] RE-
LINQWNTUR

woodland at Tadley[131] belonging to this estate,
15 at North Waltham[132] [and] 5 at Bradley;[133]
just as formerly it was granted[136] in eternity by
my [relatives][134] to the abovesaid church of
Winchester[135] for the worshipful Trinity and
its apostles Peter and Paul so has it been
strengthened, Bishop Æthelwold[137] acquiring
[it], by this new charter with the authority of
my nobles. Let moreover all these abovementioned estates be free from any yoke of earthly
service except for three, that is in relation to
military service and the repair of bridges and
fortifications. Let then this our renewed generous bounty remain as it was, firmly fixed for ever.
Thus if anyone should presume to violate this
freedom of the church let him be cursed and let
him perish an unhappy person wasted away by
the torments of Hell, unless he has obtained
forgiveness by making amends before [his] death.

[viii][138]

CHARTER OF FREEDOM RELATING TO TICHBORNE

The inheritances of worldly descendants are
casually left to doubtful heirs and all the world's
glory falls apart, reduced to nothing by the
drawing near of the boundary of life and death.
Therefore, while striving with the Lord's support
amongst the earthly possessions of this world for
the perpetually lasting rewards of the celestial
dwelling-place, we determine with the encouragement of the saints that they are to be gained by

[131] Tadley, Hants, is not named in Domesday Book, but see above, n. 130.

[132] North Waltham, Hants, is not named in Domesday Book, but see above, n. 130. The bishop held the manor *temp.* Edward I: PRO, S. C. 12/18/28, dorse.

[133] 5 hides at Bradley, Hants, were held from the bishop by subtenants *TRE* and *TRW*, as part of the manor of Overton: *DB*, i, fo. 40ʳ (*DB Hants* 2: 10).

[134] *ut a meis*. The word *predecessoribus* may have been omitted after *meis* but the same words are used below in **V, xiii**, and *mei* can have the meaning 'my relatives'; see Lewis and Short, 1142.

[135] *supradictę Wintoniensi basilicę*. A cross-reference to preceding parts of **V**; cf. above, n. 98.

[136] *largitum fuerat*. The neuter singular form is used, pre-sumably in agreement with *rus*, although a feminine form agreeing with *particula* might have been expected.

[137] As above, n. 20.

[138] **V, viii**. A Latin diploma confirming the cathedral estates of Tichborne, Beauworth and Ovington, Hants. The proem *Fortuitu . . . hortatu* is a variant of those beginning *Cuncta seculorum patrimonia . . .* occurring in other diplomas of Edgar between 962 and 966: see S 701, 708, 738, and 744, *BCS* 1094, 1124, 1176, and 1186, including two to Abingdon Abbey. Some of the other examples of *Cuncta seculorum patrimonia . . .* are from diplomas of Edward the Martyr and Æthelred II, from 976 and 983: see S 830, 846, and 848; F. Rose-Troup, 'Crediton Charters of the Tenth Century', *Transactions of the Devonshire Association* 74 (1942), 237–61, at 255–56, and *KCD* 638 and 636. Cf. also below, n. 172. **V, viii** is the last sub-section of **V** copied by scribe *a* of the *Codex Wintoniensis*.

Eadgar[139] celsithroni moderatoris annuente
clementia tocius Bryttanię triuiatim potitus
regmine ad ęterni regni beatitudinem toto
mentis conatu largiente Domino uenire
desiderans . lx . telluris cassatos in nostrę
Christianę religionis exordio a Cynewalh[140]
rege catholico Wintoniensi ęcclesię ob reuerentiam summe Trinitatis eiusque apostolorum
Petri et Pauli deuotissime[pp] largitam . nouis
litterarum apicibus Domini instigante gratia
renouare studeo . ne successores futurę prosapię
ignorantes . possessionis Domini quippiam ad
animę suę detrimentum uiolando minuant .
Supradictę igitur telluri ab incolis nomen
inditum uidetur æt Ticceburnan .[141] 7 æt
Beopyrðe .[142] 7 æt Vfinctune .[143] Quam cum
optimatum meorum consilio eadem renouans
libertate munificus ob animę meę remedium
regnique ac successorum futurę posteritatis
prosperitatem libentissime[qq] dito . qua dudum
a predecessoribus meis ditata fuerat . Maneat
igitur ut prefatus pontifex Aðelpold .[144] humiliter deposcit . omni terrenę seruitutis iugo
libera tribus exceptis rata uidelicet expeditione
pontis arcisue restauratione . Si quis hanc nostram munificam renouatamque libertatem
auidus uiolare presumpserit anathema sit et in
Christi omniumque sanctorum maledictione
permaneat nisi cum humili satisfactione peni-
tens emendauerit .

transient things. Wherefore I Edgar,[139] holding
far and wide the kingdom of the whole of Britain
while the forbearance of the heavenly-throned
Ruler allows, desiring with whole effort of mind
to come to the bliss of the eternal kingdom by the
Lord's bounty, determine to renew with new
outlines of letters at the instigation of the
Lord's grace 60 hides of land, very devoutly
granted at the beginning of our Christian religion
by the orthodox King Cenwealh[140] to the church
of Winchester out of reverence for the supreme
Trinity and for its apostles Peter and Paul, lest the
unknowing successors of [my] future kindred
should diminish by violating, to the harm of
their souls, anything of the Lord's possession.
Names seem to have been imposed by the
inhabitants on the abovesaid land thus: Tichborne[141] and Beauworth[142] and Ovington.[143]
Renewing which [land] with the advice of my
nobles, I most benevolently grant it, for the
remedy of my soul and the good fortune of the
kingdom and of [my] successors to come in
posterity, in the same freedom in which it was
once granted by my predecessors. Let it remain
therefore, as the aforementioned Bishop Æthelwold[144] humbly requests, free of any yoke of
earthly service, except for three, that is in relation
to military service and the repair of bridges and
fortifications. If any greedy person should presume to violate this our benevolent and renewed
freedom, let him be cursed and let him remain
under the curse of Christ and all the saints, unless
as a penitent he has made amends with humble
reparation.

[pp] -imę   [qq] -issimo

---

[139] As above, n. 13.
[140] As above, n. 9.
[141] Tichborne, Hants, is not named in Domesday Book, but
was probably included under Chilcomb (DB, i, fo. 41[r]; DB Hants
3: 1), to which it pertained; see below, **XXXI**. See also, below, **V,
xiv.**

[142] 6 hides at Beauworth, Hants, were part of the episcopal
manor of Alresford TRE and TRW: DB, i, fo. 40[r] (DB Hants 2: 1).
[143] Ovington, Hants, is not named in Domesday Book but
was probably included under Chilcomb (DB, i, fo. 41[r]; DB Hants
3: 1), to which it pertained; see below, **XXXI**.
[144] prefatus pontifex Aðelpold. A cross-reference to preceding
parts of **V**; cf. above, n. 98.

[ix]¹⁴⁵

FREOLSBOC TO FEARNHAM .

Gratia Dei cunctis spiritali preditis sapientia qui deificę contemplationis beatitudinem purę mentis intuitu lacrimarum ualle¹⁴⁶ degentes crebro anhelantes suspirio cernere desiderant . manifestissimis scripturarum liquido declaratur indiciis . quod unusquisque fidelium ad supernam celorum tendens patriam potis est imis celestia . caducis ęterna lucrando insegniter promereri . ac mundi huius principem qui uitiorum sectatoribus infestissime dominatur in huius uitę stadio robustissime expugnare . Quapropter ego Eadgar¹⁴⁷ Angligenarum ceterarumque gentium hinc inde persistentium rex a Domino constitutus . non immemor ob hoc mihi transitoria ut his ęterna Christi opitulante gratia lucrarer fore concessa : quoddam rus . lxx . mansis spaciose dilatatum a predecessoribus meis olim Wintoniensi ęcclesię ob alme Trinitatis eiusque apostolorum Petri et Pauli reuerentiam dedicatę . ęterna largiti sunt hereditate . hac hereditaria carta nouis litteris ad prefatam recuperans reduco libertatem . Quod a gnosticis Fearnham¹⁴⁸ noto nuncupatur uocabulo . lx . mansis consistens æt Beonetleh¹⁴⁹ . x . determinatum casatis . Nullus igitur hanc nostram libertatem quam Adelwoldo¹⁵⁰ presule deposcente nuper ut antiquitus fuerat deuotus edidi infringere uel minuere presumat . Sit autem omni terrenę seruitutis solutum . excepta expeditione pontis arcisue recuperatione . Si quis hanc nostram uiolauerit libertatem : anathema sit .

CHARTER OF FREEDOM RELATING TO FARNHAM

By the grace of God it is clearly declared in the very plain evidences of the Scriptures to all those endowed with spiritual wisdom [and] dwelling in the Vale of Tears,¹⁴⁶ who desire, panting from repeated sighing, to comprehend the bliss of sacred contemplation with the attention of a pure mind, that each of the faithful, while striving for the celestial dwelling-place of Heaven, is capable of gaining eternal heavenly things by means of base transient things and is vigorously able to overcome in the course of this life a ruler of this world who governs violently with a train of vices. Wherefore I Edgar,¹⁴⁷ constituted by the Lord as king of the English and other races dwelling hither and thither, not unmindful on account of this that transitory things have been granted to me so that I might in the future acquire eternal things from them while Christ's grace helps, regrant a certain estate, spaciously spread in 70 hides which were once upon a time granted in eternal inheritance by my predecessors to the church of Winchester, dedicated in reverence for the Holy Trinity and for its apostles Peter and Paul, restoring it to the abovementioned freedom with new letters in this charter of inheritance. Which [estate] is called by those who know by the known name Farnham,¹⁴⁸ standing in its boundaries with 60 hides, [together with] 10 hides at Bentley.¹⁴⁹ Let no one therefore presume to infringe or diminish this our freedom which I have faithfully decreed anew as it was in antiquity, on the request of Bishop Æthelwold.¹⁵⁰ Moreover, let it be free of all earthly service except for military service [and] the repair of bridges or fortifications. If anyone should violate this our freedom, let him be cursed.

---

¹⁴⁵ **V, ix**. A Latin diploma confirming the episcopal estate of Farnham, Surrey with its dependency at Bentley, Hants (see below, nn. 148–9). This and the subsequent sections of **V** were copied by scribe *c* of the *Codex Wintoniensis*, probably after an interval of time, but from the same exemplar.

¹⁴⁶ *lacrimarum ualle*. A reference to Ps. 83: 7; also used in **V, xiv**, below.　　　　　¹⁴⁷ As above, n. 13.

¹⁴⁸ Farnham, Surrey, belonged to the bishop of Winchester TRE and TRW: *DB*, i, fo. 31ʳ (*DB Surrey* 3: 1). For 9th-cent. references to its tenure by the bishops, see S 1263, *CW* 115, *BCS* 324 and S 1274, *CW* 224, *BCS* 495.

¹⁴⁹ Bentley, Hants, belonged to the bishop of Winchester

TRE and TRW: *DB*, i, fo. 40ᵛ (*DB Hants* 2: 25).
¹⁵⁰ As above, n. 20.

[x][151]

FREOLSBOC TO BEADDINCTVNE .

Hec autem omnia quę secundum ęcclesiasticam normam iusto decernuntur moderamine quamuis[rr] proprium robur iure obtineant : tamen quia humanę uitę status euidenter incertus agnoscitur . paginis saltem uilibus pro ampliori firmitate roborata signantur . Quapropter ego Eadgar[152] totius Albionis basileus ob amorem celestis patrię et meorum indulgentiam criminum aliquam terrę particulam . lxx . scilicet mansas illic ubi solicolę Beaddinctun[153] dicunt territoria renouando . qualiter ante mei potentatus croma[154] extiterant . uoluntarie perpetualiter permanere concessi . et hac noua rudibus litterarum apicibus edita cartula Wintoniensi pontificum cathedrę Adelwoldo[155] deposcente antistite humiliter restituens[ss] reuerendę Trinitati eiusque apostolis Petro et Paulo ut olim a predecessoribus meis data fuerat . perpetua represento libertate . Ex his . lxx . mansis sunt rura . quę cum siluis sibi pertinentibus his appellantur uocabulis . Cyslesdun .[156] Tenhric .[157] Lace .[158] Sint autem omnia hęc supradicta rura omni terrenę seruitutis iugo libera . tribus exceptis . rata uidelicet expeditione . pontis arcisue restauratione . Si quis igitur hanc ęcclesię libertatem uiolare presumpserit :

[rr] quanuis   [ss] Corrected from instituens

---

[151] **V, x.** A Latin diploma restoring Beddington, Surrey, with its appurtenant woodland (see below, nn. 153, 156–8). The proem *Hec autem omnia . . . roborata signantur* also appears in one version of a diploma claiming to record the grant by Edward the Elder of Overton, Hants, to Winchester Cathedral; see S 377(1), *CW* 112, *BCS* 625.

[152] As above, n. 13.

[153] Beddington, Surrey, is said in *Winchester ann.*, s.a. 828, to have been given to the church of Winchester by King Ecgbeorht, but had apparently been alienated by *TRE*: *DB*, i, fos. 34[v] and 36[v] (*DB Surrey* 19: 15 and 29: 1). It had been leased for life by Bishop Denewulf and his cathedral community to Edward the Elder in 899 × 908; see above, n. 109.

[154] *ante mei potentatus croma*. For *croma*, see above, n. 77. Here it appears to have been taken in error to be a 2nd decl. neuter pl. form, governing the verb *extiterant*.

[x][151]

CHARTER OF FREEDOM RELATING TO BEDDINGTON

All those things indeed which are decreed by just rule according to ecclesiastical precept should by rights maintain their special force; however, because the condition of human life is clearly recognized to be uncertain, they are in any case written down, strengthened for greater firmness by base writings. Wherefore I Edgar,[152] ruler of the whole of Albion, renewing on account of love of the celestial dwelling-place and indulgence of my sins some piece of land, namely 70 hides, in that place where the inhabitants call the district Beddington,[153] have willingly granted that it should remain perpetually how it was before the time[154] of my power existed and, humbly restoring it, at the request of Bishop Æthelwold,[155] to the cathedral of the bishops at Winchester, by this new charter issued in the rude outlines of letters, as it was given once upon a time by my predecessors to the worshipful Trinity and to its apostles Peter and Paul, I grant it with perpetual freedom. Part of these 70 hides are the estates which with the woodlands belonging to them are called by these names: Chessington,[156] Tandridge,[157] Lake.[158] Let moreover all these above-said estates be free from any yoke of earthly service, except for three, that is relating to military service [and] the repair of bridges or fortifications. If anyone therefore should presume to violate this freedom of the church let him be excommunicated, and let him perish an

---

[155] As above, n. 20.

[156] Chessington (*CISEDVNE*), Surrey, was appurtenant to Beddington *TRE*: *DB*, i, fo. 36[v] (*DB Surrey* 29: 2).

[157] Tandridge, Surrey, is not elsewhere recorded as appurtenant to Beddington in the Anglo-Saxon period.

[158] Part of an area of swine-pasture at Lake in Horley, Surrey (*PN Surrey*, 293). In the reign of King Eadred, another part belonged to Merstham, Surrey; see S 528 and A. R. Rumble, 'The Merstham (Surrey) Charter-Bounds, A.D. 947', *JEPNS* 3 (1971), 6–31, at 8 and 19. *Lakelond* in Horley was appurtenant to Beddington in 1544–5: PRO, S. C. 2/204/34.

anathema sit . et inferni cruciatibus attritus infelix intereat . nisi satisfaciendo ante obitum ueniam optinuerit .

unhappy person wasted away by the torments of Hell, unless he has obtained forgiveness by making amends before [his] death.

[xi]¹⁵⁹

FREOLSBOC TO FERNHAMME .

Ineffabili rerum creatore ac moderatore Domino nostro Iesu Christo . in ęternum regnante . Abominabilia¹⁶⁰ titillantis¹⁶¹ seculi piacula diris obscenę horrendeque mortis circumsepta latratibus . quę in huius incolatus patria Christianę religioni subiectos nequaquam securos degere sinunt . sed quasi fetidę corruptelę in uoraginem casuros incitando prouocant libidinoso miserrimoque seculi appetitu . Piaculorum itaque auctorem cum omnibus pompis eius toto mentis conamine non solum despiciendo . sed etiam uelut fastidiosam melancolię nausiam abominando¹⁶² fugiamus . cauentes mundi fragilis prosperum excursum . ne nimio eius amore irretiti apostatando a Domini lugubriter recedamus clementia . illud sedulo rimantes propheticum . Diuitię si affluant . nolite cor apponere .¹⁶³ Quapropter¹⁶⁴ infima quasi peripsima" quisquiliarum¹⁶⁵ abiciens . superna ad instar preciosorum monilium

[xi]¹⁵⁹

CHARTER OF FREEDOM RELATING TO FAREHAM

The ineffable Creator and Ruler Our Lord Jesus Christ rules in eternity! The abominable sins¹⁶⁰ of a titillating¹⁶¹ world, hedged around by the dreadful ragings of repulsive and terrible death, do not allow the servants of the Christian religion to dwell in any way secure in the dwelling-place of this country, but as foul seductions they stimulate those who are going to fall into the Abyss, arousing them with a libidinous and most excessive desire for worldliness. Let us therefore shun the instigator of sins with all his ostentations, not only despising [him] with full effort of mind but also abominating [him] like the loathsome sickness of melancholy,¹⁶² guarding against a successful attack by a weak world, lest we be ensnared by excessive love of it in forsaking our religion and lamentably retreat from the Lord's forbearance; eagerly turning over those words of the prophet, 'If riches abound, set not your heart upon them'.¹⁶³ Wherefore,¹⁶⁴ renouncing the basest things as the offscourings of rubbish,¹⁶⁵ choosing higher things as though they were

---

" Corrected from peripsema

---

¹⁵⁹ **V, xi**. A Latin diploma restoring the episcopal estate of Fareham, Hants (see below, n. 168). It shares several features with S 777 and 781, diplomas of 970, related to the 'Edgar A' type; see below, nn. 160-1, 163-4, 167.

¹⁶⁰ *Abominabilia . . . abominando fugiamus.* The text of the proem from *titillantis* to *fugiamus* is an expansion and adaptation of that beginning *Flebilia fortiter detestanda* favoured earlier in the century by the draftsman known as 'Æthelstan A'; see S 412-13, 416-19, etc., BCS 674-5, 677, 689, 692, 691; and Keynes *Diplomas*, 44. Two diplomas of 'Edgar A' type, dated 970, from the archives of Bath and Ely respectively, also use versions of *Flebilia fortiter*: S 777 and 781, BCS 1257 and 1269; Keynes *Diplomas*, 78-9. See also below, nn. 161, 163-4, 167.

¹⁶¹ *titillantis.* Both S 777 and 781 (see above, n. 159) also use *titillantis* from *titillans* 'titillating', instead of the usual *totillantis* from *totillans* 'tottering', at this point of proems beginning *Flebilia fortiter.* Cf. also below, n. 163.

¹⁶² *uelut fastidiosam melancolię nausiam abominando.* See above, n. 117.

¹⁶³ Ps. 61: 11. Both S 777 and 781 (see above, n. 159) also use this quotation at this point, instead of Luke 6: 38 (*BSV*, ii, 1618) *date et dabitur vobis* 'Give, and it shall be given to you', which is found in other proems of the *Flebilia fortiter* group. Cf. above, n. 160; below, n. 172.

¹⁶⁴ *Quapropter infima . . . iocunditatem.* The text from *infima*, introducing the disposition, is the same as that (but beginning *Qua de re*) used by the draftsman 'Æthelstan A' in S 412, 416, and 418; BCS 674, 677, and 692. It also appears in S 777 and 781, see above, n. 159.

¹⁶⁵ *peripsima quisquiliarum.* These words, here part of the text referred to above in n. 164, are also used in **V, vi**, above. The phrase *peripsema quisquiliarum* derived from Aldhelm, prose *De virginitate*, cap. 10 (ed. R. Ehwald (Berlin, 1919), p. 238). The grecism *peripsema* occurs in 1 Cor. 4: 13.

eligens . animum sempiternis in gaudiis figens .
ad adipiscendam mellifluę dulcedinis misericor-
diam perfruendamque infinite letitię iocunditatem ⁏ ego Eadgar¹⁶⁶ per omnipatrantis dexteram
totius Britannię regni solio sublimatus .¹⁶⁷ quandam ruris particulam id est . xxx . mansas loco
qui celebri ęt Fearnham¹⁶⁸ nuncupatur onomate
predictę episcopatus cathedrę¹⁶⁹ ob sanctę Trinitatis apostolorumque Petri et Pauli reuieren-
tiam ęterna libertate uti priscis data fuerat
temporibus renouando . humili restituo
deuotione . Hanc itaque libertatem prefatus
pontifex Aðelwold¹⁷⁰ Domini cooperante gratia
cum magna optinuit humilitate . Sit igitur""
prefata terra cum omnibus ad se rite pertinentibus omni terrenę seruitutis iugo libera tribus
exceptis . rata uidelicet expeditione pontis arcisue restauratione . Si quis diaboli hortatu hanc
nostram minuere presumpserit libertatem ⁏
anathema sit .

[xii]¹⁷¹

FREOLSBOC TO WEALTHAM .

Kalante diuinę auctoritatis agiographo
commonemur . ut terrena presentis seculi
lucra dantes . cęlestia ęternę beatitudinis emolumenta iugi indefessoque adquiramus labore .¹⁷²
Ideoque incertum futuri temporis statum mutabilitatemque certis dinoscens indiciis totis uiribus prout posse dederit qui cuncta creauit

"" The insular abbreviation ǥ is used for igitur

¹⁶⁶ As above, n. 13.
¹⁶⁷ per omnipatrantis dexteram totius Britannię regni solio sublimatus. This royal style is also used in S 777 and 781 and (with
rex Anglorum) in diplomas drafted earlier in the century by
'Æthelstan A': S 412–13, 416–19, 425; BCS 674–5, 677, 689, 692,
691, and 702. See above, n. 159; and cf. below n. 174.
¹⁶⁸ Fareham, Hants, belonged to the bishop of Winchester
TRE and TRW: DB, i, fo. 40ᵛ (DB Hants 2: 15).
¹⁶⁹ predictę episcopatus cathedrę. A cross-reference to preceding
parts of V; cf. above, n. 98.
¹⁷⁰ prefatus pontifex Aðelwold. A cross-reference to preceding
parts of V; cf. above, n. 98. See also above, n. 20.
¹⁷¹ V, xii. A Latin diploma restoring the episcopal estate of
Bishop's Waltham, Hants (see below, n. 175). The royal style is

precious jewels, [and] focusing my mind on
eternal delights in order to acquire a compassion
of honeyed sweetness and to delight in a joy of
infinite happiness, I Edgar,¹⁶⁶ raised by the right
hand of the Universal Father to the throne of
the kingdom of the whole of Britain,¹⁶⁷ restore
with humble devotion a certain portion of land,
that is 30 hides, in the place which is called by
the famous name Fareham,¹⁶⁸ to the church of
the aforesaid bishopric,¹⁶⁹ in reverence for the
Holy Trinity and for the apostles Peter and Paul,
renewing it with eternal freedom as it was given
in early times. This freedom indeed the aforementioned Bishop Æthelwold¹⁷⁰ acquired with
great humility with the help of the Lord's grace.
Let therefore the aforementioned land, with all
the things rightly belonging to it, be free of any
yoke of earthly service except for three, that is
relating to military service [and] the repair of
bridges or fortifications. If anyone, at the instigation of the Devil, should presume to diminish
this our [grant of] freedom, let him be cursed.

[xii]¹⁷¹

CHARTER OF FREEDOM RELATING TO BISHOPS WALTHAM

We are reminded, as the holy writing of
divine authority urges, that in giving away the
earthly profits of the present world we might
amass by perpetual and unwearied labour the
heavenly benefits of eternal bliss.¹⁷² Therefore,
distinguishing the uncertain and changeable
condition of future time from the certain
proofs [which] He who created everything has
given in the greatest possible abundance, I

related to that in V, xi; see nn. 167 and 174.
¹⁷² terrena presentis seculi dantes . cęlestia ęternę beatitudinis
emolumenta iugi indefessoque adquiramus labore. A general reference
to the sentiments of Luke 6: 38 (BSV, ii, 1618) date et dabitur vobis
'Give, and it shall be given to you'. Cf. above, n. 163. The words
terrena . . . emolumenta have some similarity to terrenis caducarum
possessionibus semper mansura supernę patrię emolumenta in the
proem to V, viii and some other diplomas of the second half
of the 10th century listed above, n. 138.

subnixe delibero . ut redemptoris nostri possessionem ęcclesiis iure delegatam in priorem
sanctę religionis statum sertis roborata litterulis
medullitus consolidarem . Quapropter ego
Eadgar[173] diuina indulgente clementia totius
Britannicę insulę solio sullimatus .[174] quoddam
rus quod prisco Þealtham[175] onomate . xxxviii .
cassatorum olim Wintoniensi Ueteris Monasterii cathedrę commutando concessum nouis
apicum signis renouare Adelwoldo[176] presule
suppliciter deposcente gratanter permitto . Prefatum siquidem rus antecessores nostri sanctę
Dei ęcclesię reuerendę Trinitati eiusque apostolis Petro et Paulo dicatę pro commutatione[177]
illius oppidi quod Porteceaster[178] nuncupatur .
omni mundiali seruicio solutum[179] concesserunt .
Sit igitur prefatum rus cuius ego cum optimatum meorum consilio libertatem fideliter
renouaui . ęterna iocunditate gloriosum cum
omnibus sibi rite pertinentibus . pratis uidelicet .
pascuis . siluis . Expeditionis laborem . pontis
arcisue restaurationem tantummodo persoluat .
alias ęterna iocundetur libertate . Si quis autem
diaboli pellectus instinctu hanc perpetuam
nostrę renouationis libertatem uiolare uel minuere audax presumpserit ⸴ a sancta corporis et
sanguinis Domini nostri Iesu Christi commu-
nione et sancta Dei ecclesia ac sanctorum
omnium contubernio segregatus ęterna inferni
miseria dampnatus intereat . si non satisfactione
congrua humiliter correctus emendauerit . quod
contra nostrum tumidus deliquit decretum .

humbly determine that I should thoroughly
strengthen, as things confirmed by the composition of letters, the property of Our Redeemer
lawfully given to churches in the former circumstances of [our] holy religion. Wherefore I
Edgar,[173] raised to the throne of the whole island
of Britain[174] while divine forbearance allows,
joyfully permit [myself] to renew with new
marks of letter-forms, at the humble request
of Bishop Æthelwold,[176] a certain estate of 38
hides, called from ancient times Bishop's Waltham,[175] which once upon a time was granted by
exchange to the church of the Old Minster at
Winchester. Indeed, our ancestors granted the
aforementioned estate, free of all worldly service,[179] to God's holy church dedicated to the
worshipful Trinity and to its apostles Peter and
Paul, in exchange[177] for the fortification which is
called Portchester.[178] Therefore let the aforementioned estate whose freedom I, with the
advice of my nobles, have faithfully renewed, be
glorious in eternal delight, with all things rightfully belonging to it, that is, meadows, pastures,
[and] woodlands. Let it only render the duty of
military service and that of the repair of bridges
or fortifications, otherwise let it delight in
eternal freedom. But if any audacious person,
enticed at the intigation of the Devil, should
presume to violate or diminish this perpetual
freedom of our renewal, let him perish, damned
in the misery of Hell, having been cut off from
the holy communion of the body and blood of
Our Lord Jesus Christ and from the holy church
of God and from the dwelling-place of all the
saints, unless as one reformed he has humbly
made amends with a fitting reparation for what
he arrogantly committed against our decree.

[173] As above, n. 13.

[174] *totius Britannię insulę solio sullimatus*. This part of the royal
style is a variation on part of that used above in **V, xi**. Cf. above,
n. 167.

[175] Bishop's Waltham, Hants, belonged to the bishop of
Winchester *TRE* and *TRW*: *DB*, i, fo. 40ʳ (*DB Hants* 2: 9).

[176] As above, n. 20.

[177] *pro commutatione*. For a diploma in the name of Edward
the Elder recording this exchange in 904, see S 372, *CW* 131,
BCS 613.

[178] *oppidi . . . Porteceaster*. Portchester, Hants, a Roman Saxon-
shore fort and listed as a fortification in the Burghal Hidage; see
Hill and Rumble *Defence of Wessex*, 24–5, 32, 214–15.

[179] *omni mundiali seruicio solutum*. No such immunity is
included in S 372 (see above, n. 177).

[xiii]¹⁸⁰   [xiii]¹⁸⁰

FREOLSBOC TO TVIFYRDE 7 TO CRAÞANLEA .

CHARTER OF FREEDOM RELATING TO TWYFORD AND CRAWLEY

Luce constat clarius . quod huius uitę terminus uolubili uarie discurrens orbita . iamiamque imminere dinoscitur ut ueridica Christi promulgat sententia . quę altiboando proclamat dicens . Surget gens contra gentem . et regnum aduersus regnum .¹⁸¹ et reliqua . Iccirco ego Eadgar¹⁸² Christi conferente gratia totius Angligenę nationis ceterarumque gentium Brittannica insula degentium rex gloriosus¹⁸³ sancti spiritus carismate partim attactus¹⁸⁴ mentis nostrę archano deliberare cepi . atque optimatum meorum utens consilio . patulo uocum proclamare indicio . quanto inquam simulate transeuntis uitę gloria ut fęni flos uelociter arescens deficit .¹⁸⁵ letalisque huius uitę umbrificę finis imminendo incumbit . tanto etiam catholica Christianę religionis studia totius uirtutis adnisu restauranda . et ęcclesiarum possessione quęcumque obli`t´terata fuerant recuperanda fore nostrę mentis archano assidue rimamur . Hinc igitur . lx . et . iiii . mansas . viii^{to} . locis distinctas quę his usualiter nuncupantur uocabulis . Tuifyrde .¹⁸⁶ Craþanlea .¹⁸⁷ Oselbirig .¹⁸⁸

It is established clearer than light that the end of this life, hastening in various ways in a spinning course, is now already discerned to be imminent, as the true saying of Christ makes known which he proclaims crying from on high, saying, 'Nation shall rise against nation, and kingdom against kingdom',¹⁸¹ and so forth. Wherefore I Edgar,¹⁸² while the grace of Christ grants, glorious¹⁸³ king of the whole of the English nation and of the other peoples dwelling in the island of Britain, touched in part by the grace of the Holy Spirit,¹⁸⁴ have begun to deliberate in the sanctuary of my mind and, making use of the advice of my nobles, to proclaim by the indication of voices open to all; I say that, to whatever degree the pretended glory of transient life is coming to an end, quickly withering like the flower of grass,¹⁸⁵ and the joyful end of this shadowy life oppresses by being imminent, to the same degree should we continually turn over in the sanctuary of our minds that the orthodox study of the Christian religion should be restored by the exertion of all [our] strength and whatever has been obliterated from the possession of churches should be restored from now on. To this end therefore I humbly renew with eternal freedom 64 hides scattered in eight places which are normally called by these names: Twyford,¹⁸⁶ Crawley,¹⁸⁷ Owslebury,¹⁸⁸

---

¹⁸⁰ **V, xiii.** A Latin diploma confirming to Winchester Cathedral a number of small estates in Hampshire, totalling 64 hides. Two of these (Bishopstoke and Easton) had previously been granted for his personal use by King Edgar to Bishop Beorhthelm of Winchester (Æthelwold's predecessor and a kinsman of the king, see below, **XXII**, n. 4); it is possible that some at least of the others had also been so granted, although no record survives. The first biblical quotation links **V, xiii** with **V, vii**, above; see n. 181. For the exposition, cf. above, **V, iv**, n. 69.

¹⁸¹ Luke 21: 10; also used above in **V, vii**.

¹⁸² As above, n. 13.

¹⁸³ *rex gloriosus.* See below, **XXXIII**, n. 5.

¹⁸⁴ *sancti spiritus carismate partim attactus.* Cf. *sancti spiritus actactus flamine*, above, **IV, viii**, and ibid. n. 53. There seems no reason to connect this phrase with Edgar's coronation in 973, as did John 'Church of Winchester', 406–7. The grecism *carisma* occurs also above in **IV, xv** and **V, v**.

¹⁸⁵ *simulate transeuntis uitę gloria ut fęni flos uelociter arescens deficit.* Cf. 1 Pet. 1: 24 (*BSV*, ii, 1865) *quia omnis caro ut faenum et omnis gloria eius tamquam flos faeni exaruit faenum et flos decidit* 'For all flesh is as grass; and all the glory thereof as the flower of grass.

The grass is withered, and the flower thereof is fallen away'.

¹⁸⁶ Twyford, Hants, belonged to the bishop of Winchester *TRE* and *TRW*: *DB*, i, fo. 40^r (*DB Hants* 2: 3–4).

¹⁸⁷ Crawley, Hants, was held by the bishop of Winchester *TRE* and *TRW*: *DB*, i, fo. 40^r (*DB Hants* 2: 8). For a diploma claiming to record the restoration, by Edward the Elder in 909, of 20 hides at Crawley, with 8 at Hunton, see S 381, *CW* 110, BCS 629.

¹⁸⁸ Owslebury in Twyford, Hants, belonged to the bishop of Winchester *TRE* and *TRW*: *DB*, i, fo. 40^r (the second *TVI-FORDE*; *DB Hants* 2: 4).

Hefesylting .[189] Hortun .[190] Stoce .[191] Oterburna .[192] Ceoliglond .[193] Eastun .[194] Hundetun .[195] ut a meis[196] dudum supradictę Wintoniensi basilicę[197] reuerendę Trinitati eiusque apostolis Petro atque Paulo . ęterna largitę fuerant ⫶ ita hac noua cartula cum meorum auctoritate procerum Adelwoldo[198] presule optinente roboratas . eterna humilis renouo libertate . Sint autem omnia hęc supradicta rura omni terrenę seruitutis iugo libera tribus exceptis . rata uidelicet expeditione . pontis arcisue restauratione . Si quis autem hanc recuperatam moderni temporis libertatem uiolare presumpserit ⫶ anathematizatus in Domini persecutione horribiliter deficiat .

[xiv][199]

FREOLSBOC BE ÐARA MVNECA FOSTRE OF CILTANCVMBE .

Ad redemptionis suę augmentum omni conatu cuncti student orthodoxi . ut fidei spei caritatisque[200] alis ueluti uestium fulgore amicti . preciosarumque splendore gemmarum adornati . sanctarum uirtutum copia perspicui . criminum

Hensting,[189] Horton,[190] Bishopstoke,[191] Otterbourne,[192] Chilland,[193] Easton,[194] Hunton;[195] as they were once granted forever by my [relatives][196] to the abovesaid church of Winchester[197] to the worshipful Trinity and to its apostles Peter and Paul, so they are confirmed by this new charter, Bishop Æthelwold[198] acquiring [them], with the authority of my nobles. Let moreover all these abovesaid estates be free from any yoke of earthly service except for three, that is, designated military service [and] the repair of bridges or fortifications. But if anyone should presume to violate this freedom recovered in modern times, let him die horribly, cursed in the Lord's persecution.

[xiv][199]

CHARTER OF FREEDOM CONCERNING THE MONKS' FOOD FROM CHILCOMB

All the orthodox strive with every effort for the enrichment of their redemption as, vested with the wings of faith, hope, and charity[200] as though with the brightness of garments, adorned with the splendour of precious jewels, outstanding in abundance of holy virtues, far

---

[189] Hensting near Owslebury, Hants, is not named in Domesday Book.

[190] Horton, Hants, is not named in Domesday Book, but was probably included under the Bishopstoke entry (see below, n. 191).

[191] Bishopstoke, Hants, belonged to the bishop of Winchester TRE and TRW: DB, i, fo. 40ʳ (DB Hants 2: 6); see also below,**V, xiv**. In 960, King Edgar had granted a life tenure of this estate (Ytingstoce) to Bishop Beorhthelm, with reversion to the Old Minster: S 683 (where wrongly identified as Itchenstoke), CW 216, BCS 1054.

[192] Otterbourne, Hants, was held from the bishop of Winchester by Chiping TRE but was part of 6 hides seized by Ralf of Mortemer TRW; see below, **XXXII**, n. 11.

[193] Chilland, Hants, is not named in Domesday Book, but was probably included under the Old Minster estate of Martyr Worthy (DB, i, fo. 41ᵛ; DB Hants 3: 13).

[194] Easton, Hants; like Bishopstoke (see above, n. 191), Easton had been previously granted to Bishop Beorhthelm; see below, **XXII**.

[195] Hunton, Hants, is not named in Domesday Book. For an alleged earlier restoration, see above, n. 187.

[196] ut a meis. The word predecessoribus may have been omitted after meis, but see above, **V, vii**, and n. 134.

[197] supradictę Wintoniensi basilicę. As above, n. 135.

[198] As above, n. 20.

[199] **V, xiv**. A Latin diploma which contains clauses relating to the effect of the Benedictine Reform on the episcopal community at the Old Minster. Both explicit and implicit allusions are made to the Benedictine Rule; see below, nn. 215, 237, 239, and 242–3. There are also passages which have a connection with the Regularis Concordia; below, nn. 218, 238–42, and 246. Special concern is shown for the safeguarding of the monks' food supplies from the estate of Chilcomb. A full immunity from fiscal obligations is claimed for all the episcopal estates (however, see below, n. 211), but the beneficial hidation of Chilcomb (see above, **V, i–iii**; and below, **XXX–XXXII**) is not mentioned. There are similarities to other charters of the reform period from Abingdon and Ely; see Eric John, 'The King and the Monks in the Tenth-Century Reformation' and 'Some Latin Charters of the Tenth-Century Reformation', in Orbis Britanniae and Other Studies (Leicester, 1966), 154–80 and 181–209; cf. also the Tavistock foundation-charter, see below nn. 209 and 212. **V, xiv** may once have had a date and witness-list (cf. above, n. 78) which may have been omitted from the Codex Wintoniensis for lack of space; see above, p. 100.

[200] fidei spei caritatisque. The three spiritual gifts are grouped together by St. Paul in 1 Cor. 13: 13.

pondere semoti . terreni corporis ergastulo[201]
uersantes . lacrimarum ualle[202] cum nimio
degentes certamine . totius animi cultum celesti
habitatione theorico figunt meditamine . Nostra
inquit apostolus conuersatio in celis est .[203] Hinc
igitur ego Eadgar[204] Domini largiente gratia
totius Albionis basileus[205] sedula procurans
sollicitudine . ne catholicorum quispiam actuali
degens conuersatione . aliqua secularium rerum
uexatione[206] a contemplatiua impeditus uita
incongrue reuocetur . quod olim a predecessoribus nostris ecclesiis Domini ad sui famulatus
obsequium[207] egregia concessum fuerat libertate .
renouando libentissime recupero . Huius rei
gratia rura omnia predicta . et superius distinctis
locis ordinatim nouis litterarum apicibus designata .[208] Christi compunctus spiramine .[209] iusto
utens iudicio . ad usus pontificum supradicte
ecclesie[210] iura[w] religiosa regentium . pro anime
mee salute regnique ac successorum meorum
prosperitate . eterna libertate cum optimatum
meorum consilio deuotus ammodum restitui .
omnique seculari soluta gloriose ditaui
seruitute .[211] ne uexatione mundane afflictionis .
mens presulum pro nostris facinoribus interce-
dentium a diuina contemplatione remota defi-
ciendo lasesceret . In nomine alme Trinitatis ac
indiuidue Unitatis precipio . ut succedentium
temporum episcopi . ita gregem dyrocheo id est

[w] uita D

removed from the burden of evil deeds, dwelling in the prison[201] of an earthly body, [and]
living in the Vale of Tears[202] with exceeding
strife, they direct their whole mind's labour on
the celestial dwelling with contemplative
thought. 'Our abode', says the Apostle, 'is in
Heaven'.[203] Hence therefore, I Edgar,[204] king of
the whole of Albion while the grace of the Lord
grants,[205] taking care with zealous forethought
lest any of the orthodox, living an active existence [but] hindered by some annoyance of
worldly affairs,[206] should be unsuitably drawn
away from the contemplative life, restore most
willingly by renewing what once upon a time
was granted by our predecessors in illustrious
freedom to the Lord's churches in subjugation to
His service.[207] Wherefore I, for the health of my
soul and the good fortune of my kingdom and of
my successors, driven on by the inspiration of
Christ[209] [and] employing righteous judgement,
most faithful, with the advice of my nobles, have
restored with eternal freedom all the aforesaid
estates denoted above in succession in separate
places by the new outlines of letters,[208] to the use
of the bishops of the abovesaid church[210] having
supremacy over [its] religious duties; and I have
gloriously enriched them, freed from all worldly
service[211] lest the minds of the bishops, inter-
ceding for our misdeeds, should be distracted
from divine contemplation and become weary
through exhaustion from the annoyance of
worldly affliction. In the name of the Holy
Trinity and the Indivisible Unity, I command
that the bishops of succeeding times should so

[201] *ergastulo.* The grecism *ergastulum* 'house of correction,
penitentiary' is used in Exod. 6: 6–7 in the context of the slavery
of the Jews in Egypt. Cf. below, n. 207. The word is used
frequently by Aldhelm (*ex inf.* Michael Lapidge).

[202] *lacrimarum ualle.* Ps. 83: 7. Also found in **V, ix**, above.

[203] Phil. 3: 30.

[204] As above, n. 13.

[205] *Domini largiente gratia totius Albionis basileus.* See above,
n. 73.

[206] *actuali degens conuersatione . aliqua secularium rerum uexatione.* Cf. the strictures against worldly distractions made above
in **IV, xii.** The 'active existence' was the fight against temptation,
called *actualis vita* by Cassian; see Owen Chadwick, *John Cassian*
(2nd edn., Cambridge, 1968), 94.

[207] *famulatus obsequium.* This is a pleonastic phrase. Note also
that the word *famulatus* is used in Exod. 1: 14 in a similar context
to *ergastulum*, above, n. 201.

[208] *rura omnia predicta . et superius distinctis locis ordinatim nouis
litterarum apicibus designata.* This can only be a reference to the
preceding content of **V, i–xiii.**

[209] *Christi compunctus spiramine.* Cf. *SANCTI SPIRITUS
GRATIA COMPUNCTUS*, above, **IV, viii**, heading (and ibid.
n. 52), which also occurs in S 838 (cf. below, n. 212).

[210] *supradicte ecclesie.* A reference back to the church of
Winchester as identified fuller in **V, i–xiii.**

[211] *omnique seculari soluta . . . seruitute.* This claim of full
immunity for the episcopal estates is contradicted by the
reservation of the 'Three Burdens' in some of the preceding
texts (**V, vii–ix, xi–xii**).

duplici pastu nutriant monachorum .²¹² ut*ʷʷ* nostris temporibus per sapientium²¹³ ordinatum est prouidentiam . et alimenta ex Ciltan-cumbe*ˣˣ* ²¹⁴ monachis copiose tribuant . et sine ulla retractione*ʸʸ* hilariter subministrent . et nullius nimietatis inquietudine perturbent ⫶ ne a uita theorica uel immoderata superfluitas . uel intolerabilis paupertas cum magno animi detrimento illos amoueat . omnia in uictu et uestitu secundum regulę modificet preceptum .²¹⁵ Certe canonici²¹⁶ omni uiciorum neuo deturpati . inani gloria tumidi . inuidię liuore tabidi . philargirię²¹⁷ maculis obcecati . luxurię facibus libidi . gulę omnimodo dediti . regi terreno non episcopo subiecti .²¹⁸ prefati ruris usu ueterano moderno tempore pascebantur alimentis . Ebrietatem siquidem et homicidia sectantes . coniuges suas turpiter nimia et inusitata libidine amplectentes . ęcclesiam Dei raro et perpauci frequentare uolebant . nec horas celebrare canonicas dignabantur .²¹⁹ Quo reatu eiectis cum preposito²²⁰ canonicis . et eliminata

feed the flock of monks by a division, that is by a bipartite food-rent,²¹² as in our times has been ordained through the foresight of the wise,²¹³ and should plentifully bestow on the monks food from Chilcomb,²¹⁴ and should render it gladly without any hesitation, and should not embarrass [them] with the disquiet of any excess. Lest either immoderate superabundance or intolerable poverty should steal them from the contemplative life with great damage to the spirit, let one moderate all things in food and clothing according to the command of the Rule.²¹⁵ Undoubtedly, the canons,²¹⁶ disfigured by every blemish of vices, exalted with vain glory, putrefying with the malice of envy, blinded by the blemishes of avarice,²¹⁷ taking pleasure in the fires of wantonness, entirely devoted to gluttony, subject to the earthly king not to the bishop,²¹⁸ were wont to feast themselves by ancient custom in modern time on the food of the aforementioned land. Since indeed, following drunkenness with murder, and embracing their wives in an unseemly manner with an excessive and uncommon lust, very few wished to visit God's church, and rarely, they did not deign to keep the canonical hours.²¹⁹ For this guilt, when the canons together with the prior²²⁰ were thrown out and the filth of the impure was put out of

---

ʷʷ id est sicut added (?s.xiii) above ut   *ˣˣ* Chyltancumbe D   *ʸʸ* retractacione D

---

²¹² *gregem dyrocheo id est duplici pastu nutriant monachorum.* Similar wording occurs in Æthelred II's foundation-charter for Tavistock Abbey, dated 981: see S 838, KCD 629 *abbas . . . gregem sibi commissum dirocheo, id est duplici pastu foueat;* cf. above, n. 209. The grecism *dir- dyrocheum* seems to be a ghost-word based on a corrupt reading of *dittocheum* (from δισσός and ὀχή) in manuscripts of Prudentius; see H. P. R. Finberg, *Tavistock Abbey: a Study in the Social and Economic History of Devon* (Newton Abbot, 1969), 281, n. 3). In both the Tavistock and the Old Minster examples, the significance appears to be a division of the food-rents between the bishop or abbot and their respective communities of monks. For the use of *grex* to describe such a community, see above, **IV**, n. 98.

²¹³ *sapientium.* Probably here referring to the *witan.*

²¹⁴ See above, n. 31; also **V, i–iii.** For Chilcomb's dependencies, see below, **XXXI.**

²¹⁵ *in uictu et in uestitu secundum regulę modificet preceptum.* For the monastic diet, see *BR,* caps. 39–40; for clothing, *BR,* cap. 55.

²¹⁶ *canonici.* The pre-Reform secular clergy at the Old Minster. Cf. Wulfstan *Vita S. Æthelwoldi,* cap. 16 (ed. Lapidge and Winterbottom, 30 and n. 3); and above, **IV,** n. 47.

²¹⁷ *philargirię.* See above, n. 23.

²¹⁸ *regi terreno non episcopo subiecti.* Cf. *RC,* cap. 10, which forbids monasteries to acknowledge secular overlordship but provides for petitions to the king or queen for protection.

²¹⁹ *Ebrietatem . . . et homicidia sectantes . coniuges suas turpiter nimia et inusitata libidine amplectentes . ęcclesiam Dei raro et perpauci frequentare uolebant . nec horas celebrare canonicas dignabantur.* Cf. Wulfstan *Vita S. Æthelwoldi,* cap. 16 (ed. Lapidge and Winterbottom, 30–1): *Erant . . . in Veteri Monasterio . . . canonici nefandis scelerum moribus implicati, elatione et insolentia atque luxuria praeuenti, adeo ut nonnulli illorum dedignarentur missas suo ordine celebrare, repudiantes uxores quas inlicite duxerant et alias accipientes, gulae et ebrietati iugiter dediti* '. . . there were in the Old Minster . . . cathedral canons involved in wicked and scandalous behaviour, victims of pride, insolence and riotous living to such a degree that some did not think fit to celebrate mass in due order. They married wives illicitly, divorced them, and took others; they were constantly given to gourmandizing and drunkenness'. Reference to the illicit marriage of cathedral canons is also made at Worcester in S 731, BCS 1135 ('A.D. 964').

²²⁰ *preposito.* On the expected duties of the monastic prior, see below, n. 237.

immundorum spurcicia .²²¹ monachi in sede constituti sunt episcopali .²²² qui sanctis adornati uirtutibus . humilitate²²³ precipui . uigiliis hymnis et orationibus assidui . abstinentia macti . castitate perspicui . legitime uiuerent . et obsequium ęcclesię regulariter implerent . Rura absque dubio superius notata .²²⁴ renouare beniuola studii intentione . et quę iniuste abstracta fuerant .ᶻᶻ Duntunᵃ ²²⁵ uidelicet . Tantun .ᵇ ²²⁶ Alresford .²²⁷ Cleares .ᶜ ²²⁸ Ticceburn .ᵈ ²²⁹ VVordig .ᵉ ²³⁰ Funteal .ᶠ ²³¹ Stoke .²³² Fermesham :²³³ ęcclesię Dei deuotus ammodum ideo restitui . ut tali et tam necessario iocundati additamento ? monachorum Christo humani generis redemptori . fideliter casteque seruientium gregem .²³⁴ facilius libentiusque pascerent . dum prefatis ruribus sublatis . canonici turpiter contra fas inhonesteque degentes .²³⁵ in tam angusti rerum possessione usu pascebantur perpetuo . Alantur igiturᵍ solito monachi . ab huius uitę curis remoti .²³⁶ unde alebantur canoniciʰ ? cum auiditate nimia . curis uitę recidiuę intenti . Rura omnia superius notata episcoporum usui peculiariter ad uotum deseruiant . Illa uero quę canonici olim cum

ᶻᶻ a monachis ab antiquo ecclesiam illam occupantibus 'from the monks who occupied that church from ancient times' *interpolated after* fuerant D   ᵃ Dunton' D
ᵇ Taunton D   ᶜ Cleres D   ᵈ Tycheburn' D
ᵉ Wordy D   ᶠ Funtell' D   ᵍ *As above, note* uu
ʰ ab hiis que a monachis in ipsa ecclesia degentibus olim iniuste abstracta erant 'out of those things which had once upon a time been unjustly taken away from the monks living in the same church' *interpolated after* canonici D

---

²²¹ *eliminata immundorum spurcicia.* See above, **IV**, n. 11
²²² *monachi in sede constituti sunt episcopali.* See above, n. 45.
²²³ *humilitate.* Cf. above, **IV**, n. 77; and above, pp. 17–18.
²²⁴ *Rura . . . superius notata.* A cross-reference to the estates named in **V, i–xiii**.
²²⁵ See above, **V, i**, and n. 16.
²²⁶ See above, **V, iv**, and n. 79.
²²⁷ See above, **V, v**, and n. 101.
²²⁸ See above, **V, vi**, and n. 119.
²²⁹ See above, **V, viii**, and n. 141.
²³⁰ Not previously mentioned in **V**, but to be identified with either Headbourne Worthy or Martyr Worthy, Hants. For the former, see below, **XXXII**, n. 11. Martyr Worthy was held by the bishop of Winchester *TRW*, for the monks of the Old Minster who owned it *TRE: DB*, i, fo. 41ᵛ (*DB Hants* 3: 13). For a

doors,²²¹ and monks were established in the episcopal see²²² who, adorned with holy virtues, distinguished by humility,²²³ constantly occupied in vigils, hymns, and prayers, honoured for their self-restraint, outstanding in chastity, might live properly and fulfil the service of the church according to the Rule. Without doubt I, very devoted to the church of God, have therefore restored the estates noted above,²²⁴ with the benevolent intention of eagerness to renew also those which had been unjustly taken away, namely, Downton,²²⁵ Taunton,²²⁶ Alresford,²²⁷ Highclere,²²⁸ Tichborne,²²⁹ Worthy,²³⁹ Fonthill,²³¹ Bishopstoke,²³² and Frensham,²³³ so that, delighted by so great and so necessary an addition, the flock²³⁴ of monks faithfully and chastely serving Christ, the Redeemer of mankind, might the more easily and freely be maintained, since, during the time that the aforementioned lands had been taken away, the canons, living in an unseemly manner, dishonourably and contrary to the divine law,²³⁵ used to maintain themselves, by unbroken custom, through possession of so small [an amount] of property. Let the monks therefore, removed from the cares of this life,²³⁶ be sustained according to custom whence the canons, intent upon the concerns of this transient life, used to be sustained with excessive greed. Let all the lands noted above be subject to the discipline of the bishops, to their individual wishes. Those indeed which the canons, together

diploma recording its grant in 825 by King Ecgbeorht to SS. Peter and Paul, Winchester, see S 273, *CW* 180, *BCS* 389; and cf. *Winchester ann.*, s.a. 828.
²³¹ Fonthill Bishop, Wilts.; not previously mentioned in **V**, but given to Bishop Denewulf as part of an exchange with Ordlaf, *comes*, in 900: S 1284, *CW* 130, *BCS* 590.
²³² See above, **V, xiii**, n. 191.
²³³ Frensham, Surrey (*PN Surrey*, 177); not previously mentioned in **V**, but perhaps included under Farnham in **V, ix**. It was within the manor of Farnham in 1282: *Reg Pontissara*, 389.
²³⁴ *gregem.* See above, **IV**, n. 98.
²³⁵ *canonici turpiter contra fas inhonesteque degentes.* See above, nn. 216 and 219.
²³⁶ *ab huius uitę curis remoti.* Cf. *á ciuium tumultu remoti*, below, **VI**; and *a secularibus igitur pompis remoti*, above, **V, xii**.

preposito sine peculiari presulis dominio . usu possederant ueterano ⦂ hec eadem monachi communiter ad necessarios usus iure possideant perpetuo . et cum antistitis consilio ac iuuamine bene regant . et per prepositum fratribus cunctis necessarium . episcopoque uti regula precipit . cum omni humilitate subiectum ⦂[237] sapienter disponant .[238] Pastum ex monachorum uillis nequaquam presul diocesim lustrando auidus exquirat . Emptis necessariis fratrum indumentis . quicquid ex lucro uillarum superfuerit . unito episcopi fratrumque consilio ob eternę beatitudinis premium Christi erogetur pauperibus .[j 239] et non loculis episcopi peculiaribus . ad animę detrimentum reclusum custodiatur . Post unius episcopi obitum . alter ex eadem monachorum congregatione qui dignus sit pontificatus ordine fungi . et non aliunde eligatur .[240] Si autem impedientibus peccatis uel imperitia in eodem monasterio talis qui dignus sit inueniri nequiuerit ⦂ ex alio noto monasterio monachus . non autem canonicus . ad tanti gradus dignitatem qui dignus sit secundum meritum atque doctrinam . unanimi regis et monachorum eiusdem monasterii consilio sapienter eligatur .[241] Et non solum in hac pontificis

with the prior, had possessed by ancient custom without the particular rule of the bishop, let the monks now possess communally by perpetual right for their indispensable needs, and let them rule them well, with the advice and help of the bishop, and let them set them wisely in order[238] through an indispensable prior, subject with all humility to all the brothers and to the bishop, as the Rule commands.[237] Let not a greedy bishop, while travelling around the diocese, seek any food-rent from the estates of the monks. When the necessary clothes of the monks have been bought, let whatever is left from the profit of the estates be disbursed to the poor[239] on the joint deliberation of the bishop and the brothers, in return for Christ's reward of eternal bliss, and let not the bishop's private coffers be kept shut to the damage of his soul. After the death of one bishop, let another be chosen from the community of monks, and not from elsewhere, who is worthy to perform the office of bishop.[240] If, however, it should prove impossible to find such a person in the same monastery, either through the hindrance of sins or ignorance, let a monk—but not a canon—be wisely chosen, by the unanimous resolution of the king and the monks of the same monastery, from another well-known monastery, who is worthy of the dignity of such great rank according to his merit and learning.[241] And not only in the election of a

[j] hospitum necessitatibus et ecclesie vsibus omni scrupulacione fideliter expendatur 'for the needs of guests, and faithfully spent with every care on things of use to the church' *replaces text from* ob *to* pauperibus D

[237] *per prepositum fratribus cunctis necessarium . episcopoque uti regula precipit . cum omni humilitate subiectum.* On the duties of the monastic prior (*prepositus*), subordinate to the abbot (here, in a cathedral community, replaced by the bishop), see *BR*, cap. 65. For *humilitas*, cf. above, **IV**, n. 77, and pp. 17–18.

[238] *sapienter disponant.* Cf. the final words of *RC*, cap. 104 (the epilogue): *sapienter disponat.*

[239] *quicquid . . . superfuerit . . . erogetur pauperibus.* Cf. *BR*, cap. 58. 24 *Res . . . eroget . . . pauperibus*, with regard to the entry of a monk into a community. Also *RC*, cap. 104 (epilogue): *rex . . . suasit, ut monasteriorum patres matresque quaecumque super usus necessarios restauerint, per manus pauperum in caelestes . . . recondant thesauros* 'the King . . . exhorted the Fathers and Mothers of monasteries that . . . they should lay up treasure as in heaven, through the hands of the poor, whatever remains over and above necessary use'. This is a reference to Mark 10: 21 (*BSV*, ii, 1592) . . .*quaecumque habes vende et da pauperibus et habebis thesaurum in*

caelo ' . . . sell whatever though hast, and give to the poor, and thou shall have treasure in heaven'. Cf. below, **VI**, n. 2.

[240] *alter ex eadem monachorum congregatione . . . eligatur.* Cf. the provisions for the election of bishops to monastic cathedrals which were laid down in **XXXIII**, below, and *RC*, cap. 9. Cf. below, n. 241.

[241] *Si autem impedientibus peccatis uel imperitia in eodem monasterio talis qui dignus sit inueniri nequiuerit ⦂ ex alio noto monasterio monachus . non autem canonicus . ad tanti gradus dignitatem qui dignus sit . . . unanimi regis et monachorum eiusdem monasterio in consilio sapienter eligatur .* Cf. *RC*, cap. 9: *Si autem imperitia impediente uel peccatis promerentibus talis qui tanti gradus honore dignus sit in eadem congregatione repperiri non potuerit, ex alio noto monachorum monasterio concordi regis et fratrum quibus dedicari debet consilio eligatur* 'But if, owing to their ignorance or sinfulness, there shall not be found in that community one worthy of so high a dignity, let a monk be chosen from another monastery that is well-known,

electione . uerum etiam omnibus rebus regulę usus iugi teneatur custodia . ut in omnibus que egerint uel regulę normam hilariter custodiant . uel maiorum cum omni deuotione imitentur exempla .[242] Electus uero nulla superfluitate monachos perturbet uel inquietet .[243] nec clericos siue laicos in claustra uel refectorium introducat .[244] sed missam celebrans ⁏ monachorum reuerenter fungatur officio .[245] ac in refectorio quotiens uoluerit comedens . eorum et non canonicorum uel laicorum inibi utatur obsequio . Monachos si quoslibet secum suum lustrando episcopium habere uoluerit ⁏ illos sumat qui prouectę etatis sint . quorum profectu et moribus ad Christi roboretur famulatum . et non pueros uel iuuenes lasciuos . quorum leuitate lesus in aliquibus deprauetur .[246] Rura tam a regibus quam a diuersis catholicis ad usus fratrum . Domino largiflue collata . huius seculi militibus siue propinquis carnalibus pro munere quolibet adulando tribuens .[247] ad animę suę detrimentum nequaquam disperdat . Qui predicta statuta beniuola seruare uolontate studuerit ⁏ Domini nostri Iesu Christi benedictione in presenti seculo perfruatur . et post eius obitum ad ęternę beatitudinis uitam Christo opitulante securus perueniat . Si quis autem philargiria seductus[248] aliquid ex his quę

bishop, but also in all matters, let the custom of the Rule be kept with perpetual care, so that in everything which they do they might either gladly observe the precept of the Rule or copy the precedents of their superiors with all devotion.[242] Let the person chosen [as bishop] indeed not upset or disquiet the monks with any excess[243] nor bring clerks or laymen into the cloisters or the refectory,[244] but, in celebrating mass, let him perform the monks' office[245] with veneration and, eating in the refectory as often as he wishes, let him employ their service therein and not that of canons or laymen. If he should wish to have any of the monks with him when travelling around the diocese, let him choose those who are of advanced age, by whose effect and morals he might be strengthened to the service of Christ, and not boys or lascivious youths, through whose levity he might be afflicted in some respects.[246] Let him not in any way despoil, to the damage of his soul, the estates generously bestowed on the Lord, both by kings and by various orthodox persons, for the use of the brothers, by bestowing them for some flattering gift on soldiers of this world or on fleshly kin.[247] May he who has striven with benevolent will to preserve the aforesaid decrees enjoy the blessing of Our Lord Jesus Christ in the present world and, after his death, may he, free from care, attain the life of eternal bliss with Christ's aid. If anyone however, seduced by love of money,[248] should presume to [violate] or diminish any of these things which have been

with the consent of the King and the counsel of the brethren to whom he is to be presented'. The words *non autem canonicus* in **V, xiv** are more specific than the provisions of *RC*. Cf. also below, **XXXIII**, n. 18.

[242] *in omnibus que egerint uel regulę normam . . . custodiant . uel maiorum cum omni deuotione imitentur exempla* . Referring to St Benedict's eighth grade of humility; see *BR*, cap. 7. 55 *nihil agat monachus, nisi quod communis monasterii regula vel maiorum cohortantur exempla* 'a monk does only what is endorsed by the common rule of the monastery and the example set by his superiors'. This was also quoted in *RC*, cap. 8. Cf. above, **IV**, n. 77.

[243] *nulla superfluitate monachos perturbet uel inquietet*. Cf. *BR*, cap. 61.2 *non forte superfluitate sua perturbat monasterium* 'does not make excessive demands that upset the monastery', in relation to a visiting monk.

[244] *nec clericos siue laicos in claustra uel refectorium introducat.* An expansion to cover also secular clergy (see above, **IV**, n. 44) of the decree of the synod of Aachen in 816; see above, **IV**, n. 90.

[245] *missam celebrans ⁏ monachorum . . . fungatur officio.* Presumably at the Principal Mass; see *RC*, cap. 33 [25] (winter) and 83 [55] (summer). For the Morrow Mass, see *RC*, cap. 25 [20].

[246] *non pueros uel iuuenes lasciuos . quorum leuitate lesus in aliquibus deprauetur.* Cf. *RC*, cap. 12 [11] *Iterantes . . . non iuuenculos sed adultos quorum ammonitione meliorentur secum in comitatu ducant* '. . . let the brethren take with them as companions on a journey not youths but grown-up persons from whose conversation they may take profit'.

[247] *huius seculi militibus siue propinquis carnalibus pro munere quolibet . . .* Cf. above, **V, ii**, n. 41.

[248] *philargiria seductus.* Cf. above, **V, i**, n. 23.

cum consilio sapientium[249] precepta sunt[k] uel minuere presumpserit ⁏ deleatur nomen eius de libro uitę .[250] et in Iesu Christi saluatoris mundi eiusque genitricis Marie omniumque sanctorum persecutione maneat . et post uitę suę terminum cum Iuda Christi proditore eiusque complicibus inferni miseria punitus intereat . si non cum satisfactione emendauerit . quod nequiter peiorando deliquit .[l]

commanded with the advice of the wise,[249] let his name be erased from the Book of Life,[250] and let him remain in the persecution of Jesus Christ, the Saviour of the World, and of His mother Mary and of all the saints, and after the term of his life let him perish, punished in the misery of Hell, together with Judas, the betrayer of Christ, and his confederates, unless he has made amends with a reparation for that injury he wretchedly committed.

[k] uiolare *probably omitted here, cf.* **V, v** *and* **xii**   [l] et ista carta auctoritate pape confirmata est. 'and this charter was confirmed by the authority of the pope' *added after* deliquit D; *cf. below,* **XXXIII**

[249] As above, n. 213.
[250] *de libro uitę.* With reference to Rev.; see above, **IV**, n. 72.

VI

*A.D. 984 [? for 970], establishment of the precincts of the three minsters
at Winchester by King Edgar*

Latin

S 807, Finberg 101, *CW* 24

THIS diploma belongs to a small group of documents, also including **VII** and **VIII**, below, which records something of the physical effects of the Benedictine Reformation on the topography of the city of Winchester.[1] Here royal authority is given to the making of separate monastic precincts for the Old Minster, the New Minster, and Nunnaminster, and rights in the extra land obtained by the consequent demolition of citizens' houses are confirmed in the presence of many of those who had subscribed **IV**, above, including Archbishop Dunstan, Bishop Æthelwold, Queen Ælfthryth, and Abbot Æthelgar of the New Minster.

If this is to be accepted as a genuine diploma of King Edgar, and its general diplomatic structure is credible as such, the date given (984) must be taken to be a copying error. The datable subscriptions are of 968 × 970.[2] It may be suggested that the A.D. date should have read 970 (*dcccc.lxx*) and that it was followed by an indiction calculated at 14 (*xiiii*) but that the intervening word *indictione* was omitted at some point, perhaps deliberately (see below).[3]

The text survives as a cartulary copy added to the *Codex Wintoniensis* in the mid twelfth century (by scribe *b*),[4] and has been altered in the course of transcription. It is likely that the subscriptions of some *ministri* were omitted, and that the spellings of some of the personal names in the witness-list were modernized or corrupted (e.g. *Ælfeah, Ealdelm, Ealfric, Ealfpard, Escpig,* and *Wlstan* for *Ælfheah, Ealdhelm, Ælfric, Ælfpeard, Æscpig,* and *Uulfstan* or *Þulfstan,* respectively).[5] The designation of Ælfweard as *minister* has been altered in the cartulary to *dux*.[6] It is also possible that some simplification of the dating-clause was attempted by the cartulary-scribe, causing the error referred to above; the same scribe is known to have made such a simplification in relation to at least one other diploma copied into the *Codex*.[7] The wording of the Latin rubric, however, may have been taken from an endorsement which had been added to the exemplar in the early twelfth century.[8]

---

[1] See above, pp. 23–5.

[2] Or *c*.969 × 970 if Ælfric is abbot of St. Albans; see below, p. 138, n. 18. *HRH* (231) dates the subscriptions to 968 × 974, but this does not fit Bishop Oswulf of Ramsbury (950–70). The date 970 is also given (as a correction to Finberg 101) by Hart *ECNE*, 382.

[3] An indiction of 14 would be acceptable for the latter part of 970 if either the Greek or the Bedan practices of beginning a new cycle in September were used. However, for evidence against these usages and in favour of a change of cycle at 1 January, at least in the later tenth century, see Keynes *Diplomas*, 232.

[4] See above, pp. 7–8.

[5] For evidence of the shortening of witness-lists and the alteration of personal names by this scribe, see Rumble 1980, i, 324, n. 1 and ii, 318.

[6] See below, p. 139, n. 29.

[7] S 1013, MS. 2; *CW* 225. Scribe *b* omitted the indiction, epact, and concurrent, but retained the A.D. date; the first three features are present in BL, Cotton Chart. xii. 76 (S 1013, MS.1), a later medieval copy. See Rumble 1980, ii, 217.

[8] See above, p. 6.

MS.:   B. BL, Add. MS. 15350, fo. 8ᵛ (s. xii med.)

Facsimile: See Pl. IIIa

Edited: *KCD* 582
              BCS 1302
              Pierquin *Recueil*, pt. 4, no. 25

Printed from the manuscript

Diuineᵃ auctoritatis ammonitione pie commonemur . ut recidiuis instantis uisibilisque uitę lucellis ea quę non uidentur et ęterna subsistunt¹ toto mentis annisu assidue indefessi lucremur . iugique animi nostri conamine fidem Trinitatis in Unitatis substantia manentem scrutantes sanctis operibus roborati deuotissime firmemus . The`s´aurum igitur terrene substantię cęlo collocans² ego Eadgar³ totius Brittannię basileus non solum habitaculum Uetusti Monasterii sed etiam Noui . ęque Sanctimonialium . ut cenobite inibi degentes á ciuium tumultu remoti⁴ tranquillius Deo seruirent honorifice magna dilataui cautela . spaciumque⁵ omne prefatis cenobiis contiguum dissipatis secularium domunculis . in honore Domini nostri Iesu Christi eiusque genitricis semperque uirginis Marię . sanctique Petri apostolorum principis et coapostoli eius Pauli . isdem sanctis locis in Wentana ciuitate deifice locatis . eterna largitus sum hereditate . Maneat igitur prefatum donum perpetua libertate iocundum quod ex suis beneficiis ęterno Deo transitorius deuote concessi .

ᵃ *Dilatatio regis Eadgari quam fecit tribus ecclesiis huius ciuitatis.* 'King Edgar's enlargement which he made for the three churches of this city'. *Rubric, probably taken from an earlier 12th cent. endorsement on the exemplar; see above, p. 6.*

---

¹ *ea quę non uidentur et ęterna subsistunt.* Cf. 1 Cor. 2: 9; see above, **IV**, n. 105.

² *The`s´aurum . . . terrene substantię cęlo collocans.* Cf. Matt. 6: 20 (*BSV*, ii, 1534) *Thesaurizate . . . vobis thesauros in caelo* 'Lay up to yourselves treasures in heaven'. Cf. above, **V**, n. 240.

³ King of England, 959–75.

⁴ *á ciuium tumultu remoti.* Cf. above, **IV**, n. 78; and **V**, **xiv**, n. 236.

We are affectionately reminded by the admonition of divine authority that, in the small day to day profits of present and visible life, we might gain, unwearied by the full exertion of an assiduous mind, those things which are not seen and which remain eternal¹ and, strengthened by holy works, we might most faithfully be fortified by the perpetual effort of our spirit examining the enduring faith of the Trinity in the substance of Unity. Therefore, laying up treasure of earthly substance in heaven,² I Edgar,³ king of the whole of Britain, with great prudence have honourably enlarged not only the dwelling-place of the Old Minster, but also that of the New Minster as well as that of Nunnaminster, so that the monks and nuns living therein might serve God more peacefully, removed from the bustle of the citizens. ⁴ I have also granted in eternal heredity, to the same holy places divinely situated in Winchester, in honour of our Lord Jesus Christ and of his mother the everlasting Virgin Mary and of St. Peter the foremost apostle and his co-apostle Paul, all the space⁵ adjacent to the aforesaid monasteries when the small houses of the secular have been demolished. Therefore, let this aforementioned gift which I, a transitory being, have faithfully granted out of His favours remain pleasing to Eternal God in perpetual freedom. I command, in the name of the

---

⁵ *spacium . . . contiguum dissipatis secularium domunculis.* The land to be made available by the clearance referred to below in **VII.**

In nomine alme Trinitatis et indiuidue Unitatis
precipio . ut nemo successorum meorum angu-
stare temere presumat . quod ego amplificans
circa monasteria dilataui . sed spacium omne
muris*b* uel sepibus complexum . uti dedi sanctis
monasteriis perpetualiter deseruiat . Si autem
quispiam altioris uel inferioris ordinis homo
angustando donum nostrum uiolare presumpserit ⸴ anathema sit ⸴ et cum Iuda filii Dei et
Domini nostri Iesu Christi proditore eiusque
complicibus infernali incendio sine fine cruciatus puniatur . nisi ante obitum correctus
emendauerit . quod contra nostrum deliquit
decretum .

Anno dominice incarnationis . dcccc . lxxxiiii .[6]
scripta est hęc carta his testibus consentientibus .
quorum inferius nomina caraxantur .[7]

Ego Eadgar[8] rex prefatam donationem
concessi . Ego Dunstan[9] Dorouernensis archiepiscopus consi`g´naui . Ego Adelwold[10] episco-
pus predictum donum consensi . Ego Ospulf[11]
episcopus adquieui . Ego Ælfstan[12] episcopus
consignaui . Ego Alfwold[13] episcopus
confirmaui . Ego Brihtelm[14] episcopus non
renui . Ego Ealdelm[11] episcopus conscripsi .
Ego Aelfdryd[16] regina hanc donationem
confirmaui .

Ego Escpig[17] abbas[.]
Ego Ealfric [.] [18]
Ego Cynepard[19] abbas[.]
Ego Osgar[20] abbas[.]*c*
Ego Æþelgar[21] abbas[.]
Ego Sideman[22] abbas[.]

bountiful Trinity and of the indivisible Unity,
that none of my successors should presume to
try to diminish what I, extending the monasteries, have enlarged, but that the whole space,
encompassed by walls or hedges, should be
perpetually devoted to the holy monasteries as
I have given it. If moreover, any man, of the
higher or the lower rank, should presume to
violate our gift by diminishing it, let him be
cursed and punished and tormented without
end in the eternal fire with Judas, the betrayer
of Our Lord Jesus Christ, the Son of God, and
his confederates, unless, having been reformed,
he has made amends before his death for what
he has committed against our decree.

This charter was written in the year of the
Lord's Incarnation 984,[6] with these witnesses in
agreement whose names are written[7] below.

I, Edgar,[8] king, have granted the aforesaid
donation. I, Dunstan,[9] archbishop of Canterbury,
have subscribed. I, Æthelwold,[10] bishop, have
agreed to the aforesaid gift. I, Oswulf,[11] bishop,
have acquiesced. I, Ælfstan,[12] bishop, have subscribed. I, Ælfweald,[13] bishop, have confirmed. I,
Beorhthelm,[14] bishop, have not disapproved. I,
Eadhelm,[15] bishop, have written. I, Ælfthryth,[16]
queen, have confirmed this donation.

I, Æscwig,[17] abbot.
I, Ælfric,[18] abbot.
I, Cyneweard,[19] abbot.
I, Osgar,[20] abbot.
I, Æthelgar,[21] abbot.
I, Sideman,[22] abbot.

b Altered from muribus   *c First column of subscriptions ends here*

---

[6] The datable subscriptions are of 968 × 970 or *c.*969 × 970.
However, the true date may be 970; see above, p. 136. In any case,
the text appears to precede the disputes mentioned in **VII**, below.
[7] *caraxantur.* See above, **IV**, n. 124.   [8] As above, n. 3.
[9] Dunstan, archbishop of Canterbury; see above, **IV**, n. 127.
[10] Æthelwold, bishop of Winchester; ibid. n. 134.
[11] Oswulf, bishop of Ramsbury; ibid. n. 137.
[12] Ælfstan, bishop of London; ibid. n. 136.
[13] This Ælfweald was either the bishop of Crediton or of
Sherborne; ibid. n. 139.

[14] Beorhthelm, bishop of Wells; ibid. n. 140.
[15] Eadhelm, bishop of Selsey; ibid. n. 142.
[16] Queen Ælfthryth married King Edgar in 965; ibid.
n. 130.
[17] Æscwig, abbot of Bath; ibid. n. 145. Cf. below, n. 23.
[18] This Ælfric was either the abbot of St. Augustine's,
Canterbury (?955–971) or of Malmesbury (*c.*965–77) or of St.
Albans (*c.*969–?990); see *HRH*, 35, 54, and 65.
[19] Cyneweard, abbot of Milton Abbas, 964–74; ibid. 56.
[20] Osgar, abbot of Abingdon; see above, **IV**, n. 146.
[21] Æthelgar, the first abbot of the reformed New Minster;
ibid. n. 149.
[22] Sideman, abbot of Exeter, 969–?973; see *HRH*, 48.

Ego Ælfeah[23] abbas[.]

Ego Godpine[24] abbas[.][d]

Ego Ælfhere[25] dux .

Ego Bryhtnod[26] dux .

Ego Eðelpine[27] dux .

Ego Oslac[28] dux .

Ego Ealfpard [minister].[e 29]

Ego Eþelpeard[30] minister[.]

Ego Eanulf[31] minister[.]

Ego Wlstan[32] minister[.]

Ego Bryhtric[33] minister[.]

Ego Leofa[34] minister[.][f]

I, Ælfheah,[23] abbot.

I, Godwine,[24] abbot.

I, Ælfhere,[25] ealdorman.

I, Beorhtnoth,[26] ealdorman.

I, Æthelwine,[27] ealdorman.

I, Oslac,[28] ealdorman.

I, Ælfweard, [thegn].[29]

I, Æthelweard,[30] thegn.

I, Eanwulf,[31] thegn.

I, Wulfstan,[32] thegn.

I, Beorhtric,[33] thegn.

I, Leofa,[34] thegn.

---

[d] *Second column of subscriptions ends here*
[e] *dux but see n.*
29. Third column of subscriptions ends here
[f] *Fourth column of subscriptions ends here*

---

[23] Ælfheah was probably abbot of Bath, overlapping with Æscwig (above, n. 17); see *HRH*, 28.

[24] The abbey of which Godwine was abbot has not been identified; ibid. 226.

[25] Ælfhere, ealdorman of Mercia; see above, **IV**, n. 151.

[26] Beorhtnoth, ealdorman of Essex; ibid. n. 156.

[27] Æthelwine, ealdorman of East Anglia; ibid. n. 155.

[28] Oslac, ealdorman of Northumbria from 966; see D. Whitelock, 'The Dealings of the Kings of England with Northumbria in the Tenth and Eleventh Centuries', in

P. Clemoes (ed.), *The Anglo-Saxons* (London, 1959), 70–88, at 78. He subscribes until 975: Keynes *Atlas*, Table LVI.

[29] For Ælfweard, see above, **IV**, n. 161; and below, **IX**, n. 30. His designation as *minister* was changed to *dux* by scribe *b* of the *Codex Wintoniensis*; see above, p. 136.

[30] For Æthelweard, see above, **IV**, n. 160.

[31] Eanwulf signs 958 × 975; see Hart *ECNE*, 329; and Keynes *Atlas*, Table LVII.

[32] For Wulfstan, see above, **IV**, n. 164.

[33] Beorhtric subscribes 962 × 974: Keynes *Atlas*, Table LVII.

[34] Leofa subscribes 959 × 975: ibid. There is no evidence to identify him with the owner of the tenement mentioned below in **XXVI** (see ibid. n. 11).

VII

A.D. ?970 × 975, adjustment of the boundaries and property of the three minsters at Winchester by King Edgar

English

S 1449, Finberg 121, *CW* 25

THIS vernacular record forms part of the group of documents associated with the delimitation of the three monastic precincts at Winchester in the second half of the tenth century.[1] It reveals how intermingled the property of the three minsters had been until then and reflects something of the difficulties involved in isolating the three communities. There is at least the hint of rancour between Nunnaminster and the New Minster over the ruining of Nunnaminster's mill through the diversion of a watercourse, and King Edgar, probably at the request of Queen Ælfthryth and Bishop Æthelwold, may have been acting here as arbitrator to settle a number of disputes at the same time. The leading role apparently played here by Æthelwold in the reorganization of the monastic mills and their watercourses, together with Wulfstan the Cantor's statement about his provision of fresh running water for the Old Minster, and his diversion of part of the R. Thames for the mill of Abingdon Abbey *c.*960, reveals practical skills in landscaping and engineering to be placed beside his undoubted scholarship.[2]

The diplomatic form of the first part of the document is that of a *geswutelung*, or public declaration of the terms of an agreement. The second part, however, takes the form of an injunction by the king that the terms agreed should be permanent. The external form of the exemplar seems to have consisted of one part of a triple chirograph.[3] The document is undoubtedly genuine. It is undated but should probably be placed later than **VI**, above, (?970) and before King Edgar's death in 975.

The text survives as a cartulary copy added to the *Codex Wintoniensis* in the mid twelfth century (by scribe *b*).[4] The exemplar was written in insular minuscule script, some of whose letter-forms were misread by the cartulary-scribe.[5] The wording of the rubric may have been taken from a Latin endorsement added to the exemplar in the early twelfth century.[6]

---

[1] See above, **VI**, and below, **VIII**.
[2] See WS 1, 284 n. 1; and C. J. Bond, 'The Reconstruction of the Medieval Landscape: The Estates of Abingdon Abbey', *Landscape History* 1 (1979), 59–75, at 69. See also, John Crook, 'Winchester's Cleansing Streams', *Winchester Cathedral Record* 53

(1984), 27–34.
[3] See below, p. 143, n. 28.
[4] See above, pp. 7–8.
[5] See below, pp. 141–3, nn. *b-d*, *f-h*, and *k*.
[6] See above, p. 6.

MS.:   B. BL, Add. MS. 15350, fo. 8ᵛ (s.xii med.)

Facsimile: See Pl. III*b*

Edited: *KCD* 594
             Thorpe, 231–3, with translation
             BCS 1163
             Birch *Ancient Manuscript*, appendix D, with translation
             AS Ch 49, with translation

Printed from the manuscript

Her*ᵃ* is gespitulod on ðysum geprite hú Eadgar[1] cining mid rymette[2] gedihligean het þa mynstra on Ƿintancestræ syþþan he hi ðurh godes gyfe to munuclife gedyde .[3] 7 þet asmeagan het þet nan ðera mynstera þær binnan[4] þurh þet rymet piðᵇ oðrum sace næfde . ac gif oðres mynstres ár ʼonʼ oðres mynstres rymette lege þet þes mynstres ealdor ðe to þam rymette fenge ofeode þæs oðres mynstres are mid spilcum þingum spylce ðam hirede ðæ þa are ahte gecpeme pære . For ðy ðonne Aþelpold[5] bisceop on þes cinges gepitnesse 7 ealles þæs hiredes his bisceopstoles[6] gesealde tpa gegrynd butan svðgeateᶜ[7] into Nipan Mynstre ongén ðes mynstres mylne[8] ðe stod on ðam rymette ðe se cing het gerymen into Ealdan Mynstre . 7 se abbod Æþelgar[9] mid geðeahte ures cynelafordes 7 þes bysceopes Aþelpoldes[10] 7 ealles þæs hiredes[11] þa

Here in this writing it is declared how King Edgar[1] ordered that the monasteries in Winchester should be given privacy by means of a clearance,[2] after he, through the grace of God, had turned them to the monastic life,[3] and that he ordered it to be devised that none of the monasteries within that place[4] should have any dispute with another because of the clearance, but if the property of one monastery lay within the space assigned to another then the superior of the monastery which took possession of the space should acquire the other monastery's property by such exchange as might be pleasing to the community which owned the property. For that reason, therefore, Bishop Æthelwold,[5] in the witness of the king and of all his cathedral community,[6] has granted two plots of ground outside South Gate[7] to the New Minster, in exchange for the latter monastery's mill[8] which stood in the space which the king ordered to be made over to the Old Minster. Abbot Æthelgar,[9] moreover, with the advice of our royal lord and of Bishop Æthelwold[10] and of all the community,[11]

ᵃ De aquis et molendinis constitutio regis Eadgari ʼKing Edgar's decree concerning the watercourses and mills' ; *rubric. See above, p. 140*   *ᵇ* ƿid MS.; *a misreading of Anglo-Saxon ð as d. Cf. n. g*   *ᶜ Altered from syð- ; probably a (noticed) scribal misreading of the exemplar's letter u (with a descender) as y. Cf. n. k*

[1] Edgar, king of England, 959–75.

[2] *rymette*. This clearance involved the demolition of houses belonging to some of the citizens; see above, **VI**, n. 5. For Ælfric's use of OE *rȳmet(t)* to describe a space cleared by God for the site of a church, see John C. Pope (ed.), *Homilies of Ælfric: A Supplementary Collection*, i (Early English Text Soc. os 259, Oxford, 1967), 362, lines 112 and 115.

[3] *syþþan he hi . . . to munuclife gedyde*. That is, after 964 when the New Minster was reformed, see WS I, 315. For the reform of the Old Minster, *c*.963, see ibid. 307, and for that of Nunnaminster, in 963–4, ibid. 322.

[4] *þær binnan*. That is, within Winchester.

[5] Æthelwold, bishop of Winchester; see above, **IV**, n. 134.

[6] *þæs hiredes his bisceopstoles*. The community of the Old Minster.

[7] *svðgeate*. This is the earliest surviving reference to South Gate; see WS I, 275. The New Minster appears later to have lost this property, since Hyde Abbey held nothing outside South Gate in 1148: ibid. **II, 900–1067**.

[8] *ðes mynstres mylne*. The site of this mill has not been identified, but was presumably somewhere south of the later Postern Mill. It may have been the same mill as that mentioned below in **XVIII**. Cf. Fig. 1.

[9] Æthelgar, abbot of the New Minster; see above, **IV**, n. 149.

[10] As above, n. 5.

[11] *þæs hiredes*. The community of the New Minster.

ylcan mylne[12] þe se bisceop seolde 7 oðré[13] þæ hi[14] ær ahtun binnan þære byrig to sibbe 7 to sóme[15] gesealde into Nunnan Mynstre . 7 Eadgyfe[16] abbedesse þæs cinges dohter betehte ongen ðone peterscype[17] þe he into Nipan Mynstre be ðes cinges leafan geteah . 7 ær ðes nunhiredes[18] pes . 7 him[19] se tige sume mylne adilgade .[d] 7 he gesealde þam cinge hundtpelftig mancæs[20] reades goldes to ðance beforan Ælf-dryðe[21] þære hlæfdian 7 beforan þam bisceopan Aðelpolde[22] pið þam lande[23] ðæ seo éa ón yrnð . fram ðam norð pealle to þæs mynstres suð pealle an lencge . 7 tpegræ metgyrda[24] brad ðer þet pæter ærest infylð . 7 þær þet land unbradest is þer hit sceol beon eahtatyne fota brad .

Ðyses ic[25] geann Æþelgare[26] abbode. 7 þam hirede into Nipan Mynstre for his gecpemre gehyrsumnesse á on ecnesse . 7 ic halsige ælc ðara ðe eftær me cynerices pealde þurh ða halgan ðrynnesse þet hyra nan næ úndo þet ic to ðam haligum mynstrum binnan þære byrig gedon hebbe . Se þe ðis þonne apendan pylle ðe ic to sibbe 7 to gesehtnesse[27] betpeoh þam

___

[d] Altered from at- ; probably a misreading of insular minuscule d as t

[12] þa ylcan mylne. AS Ch, 103, translates this as 'the aforesaid mill' and (ibid. 348) consequently suggests that some earlier words have been omitted. The present translation obviates the need for such a suggestion. The site of this second mill is unidentified.

[13] oðré. The exact location of this mill is unknown but as it is said specifically to be 'within the city' (binnan þære byrig) it may not have been within the area taken in by the making of the precincts.   [14] As above, n. 11.

[15] to sibbe 7 to sóme. These words form an alliterative doublet of the sort found in Anglo-Saxon writs and formulaic prose; see AS Writs, 85–92. Cf. below, n. 27.

[16] Eadgifu, abbess of Nunnaminster. She may occur again in another vernacular record of 990 × 992 (S 1454, AS Ch 66). On the question whether or not she should be identified with King Edgar's daughter St. Edith (Eadgyth), see HRH, 223, and AS Ch, 348. The latter suggests that the words þæs cinges dohter are an interpolation. If so, they may have been an interlinear addition on the exemplar which was subsumed into the main text in the cartulary.

[17] ðone peterscype. This was perhaps the watercourse associated with the ford and the 'westernmost mill-yair' mentioned above in I (see ibid. nn. 3 and 4; and Fig. 7). It is here associated with a mill; see below, n. 19.

has granted that same mill[12] which the bishop granted [him], and another[13] which they[14] already owned within the city, to Nunnaminster, for the sake of peace and concord,[15] and he has assigned it to Abbess Eadgifu,[16] the king's daughter, in exchange for the watercourse[17] which he, with the king's permission, has diverted into the New Minster, and which formerly belonged to the community of nuns[18]—and the diversion ruined a certain mill of theirs;[19] and he has granted to the king in acknowledgement 120 mancuses[20] of red gold, in front of the Lady Ælfthryth[21] and Bishop Æthelwold,[22] in return for the land[23] through which the water runs, [extending] in length from the north wall to the south wall of the monastery, and 2 'measured yards'[24] broad where the water first flows in, and where the land is narrowest it ought to be 18 feet broad.

This I[25] grant to Abbot Æthelgar,[26] for his pleasing obedience, and to the community at the New Minster in perpetuity, and I beseech through the Holy Trinity each of those who rule the kingdom after me, that none of them ever undo what I have done with respect to the holy monasteries within the city. Should anyone, therefore, desire to change this which I have arranged between the monasteries for the sake of peace and reconciliation,[27] or any of the

[18] ðes nunhiredes. The community of Nunnaminster.

[19] him . . . sume mylne adilgade. AS Ch, 105, translates this as 'destroyed a mill of his', but it seems more likely that the mill affected belonged to the community at Nunnaminster and that him refers back to ðes nunhiredes. This was perhaps the mill which was fed by the 'westernmost mill-yair' mentioned above in I (see ibid. n. 4), which after this diversion became the Postern Stream. See Fig. 1.

[20] mancæs. See above, III, n. 6.

[21] Ælfðryðe. See above, IV, n. 130.   [22] As above, n. 5.

[23] lande. Probably a strip of land between the New Minster and Nunnaminster, here taken into the New Minster precinct.

[24] metgyrda. See above, II, n. 22.

[25] ic. The document here changes from the third to the first person singular. This last paragraph reads in general like a translation into OE from Latin diplomatic formulae of disposition and sanction.   [26] As above, n. 9.

[27] to sibbe 7 to gesehtnesse. These words form an alliterative doublet; cf. above, n. 15.

mynstre*e* geradigod*f* hæbbe oððe*g* þara ðinga þe
on þissan þrim cyrografum*h* 28 ðe on ðissum
þrym mynstrum to spytelungum*j* gesette
syndon . apende hine sé eca drihten fram
heofenan rice . 7 sy*k* his punung æfter his
forðsiðe on hellepite mid þam ðe symle on
ælcre ungeþþærnesse blissiað butan he hit ær
his forðsiðe gebete .

things in these three chirographs[28] which are
placed as evidence in these three monasteries,
may the Eternal Lord turn him away from the
kingdom of Heaven, and let his dwelling after
his death be in the torment of Hell with those
who always exult in every discord, unless he
makes amends for it before his death.

---

e *Error for dat. pl.* mynstrum   *f* pe radi god
MS.; *with misreading of insular minuscule* g *in the exemplar as* p
g odðe *MS.; a misreading as in n.* b   *h* -gafum *MS.;*
a misreading due to the proximity in the exemplar of insular minuscule
g *and* r   *j* *Altered from* -ge   *k* su
MS.; *probably a misreading of* y *in the exemplar as the letter* u *(with a*
descender). Cf. *n.* c

28 *cyrografum.* The text was first written in triplicate on the
same piece of parchment which was then cut to form three
separate documents, one to be kept in the archive of each of the
three communities.

VIII (i and ii)

A.D. 975 × 978, exchange between Bishop Æthelwold and the community at the Old Minster and Ælfwine, son of Ælfsige and Æthelhild; of 12 hides of land æt Mordune [unidentified], for 2 acres of land and a stream in Winchester

(i) English and (ii) Latin

S 1376, Finberg 126, *CW* 22 and 21, respectively

THIS record, which survives in both OE and Latin versions, relates to the later stages of the establishment of the precinct of the Old Minster, legal transactions relative to which were being conducted in the reign of Edgar and apparently continued into that of his successor Edward the Martyr.[1] The transaction here recorded was the exchange of a small but strategically placed area of land and an adjacent stream within the city for a considerably larger rural estate assessed at 12 hides. This exchange was made after the bishop had already had a wall built to enclose the Old Minster precinct. Ælfwine, son of Ælfsige and Æthelhild, the person with whom the bishop and the cathedral community made the exchange, is described as belonging to a family which had previously made benefactions to the Old Minster, where many of its members were buried.

Of the two versions, the OE one is primary and has therefore been so numbered in the present edition. The Latin version is an imperfect translation of the OE one,[2] either contemporary with the latter or made at some time between 975 × 978 and the early twelfth century.[3] Both versions have been translated here into modern English in order to highlight the differences between them. The OE version is called a *gewrit* in its final clause, but in the general sense of 'something written' rather than in the specialised one of 'writ' or formulaic letter.[4] The terms of the transaction were declared before witnesses who included the three monastic communities as well as the citizens of Winchester. The original record was written out four times, one text being given to Ælfwine and one being deposited at each of the three minsters.

The text has survived only as a cartulary copy added to the *Codex Wintoniensis* in the mid twelfth century (by scribe *b*).[5] The exemplar used by the cartulary-scribe probably had both versions of the text written on it, the Latin one first in caroline minuscule script, followed by the OE one in insular minuscule. If, as is possible (see above), the Latin version was a somewhat later translation of the OE one, then it is likely that the exemplar of the cartulary text was written later than the date of the transaction and is not to be identified with the original of one of the four 'writings' mentioned in

---

[1] For those in Edgar's reign, see above, **VI** and **VII**. See also, above, pp. 23–5.

[2] See below, **VIII(ii)**, nn. 4, 7, 14, 18, and 25.

[3] The 'early twelfth century' is the date at which the Latin rubric was probably added to the exemplar; see below.

[4] See BT, s.v. [5] See Pl. II, and above, pp. 7–8.

the record. The wording of the Latin rubric may have been taken from an endorsement added to the exemplar in the early twelfth century.[6]

[6] See above, p. 6.

MS.:   B. BL, Add. MS. 15350, fo. 8[r] (s.xii med.)

Facsimile: See Pl. II

Edited: *KCD* 1347
              Pierquin *Recueil*, pt. 5, no. 56 (Latin version only)
              AS Ch 53 (English version only, with translation)

Printed from the manuscript

(i) [English version]

Her speotelað hu Aðelpold[1] biscop 7 se hired on Þinceastre on Ealdan Mynstre be Eadpardes[2] cyninges leafe gehpyrfdon landa pið Ælfpine Ælfsiges[3] sunu 7 Æðelhilde .[4] þæt is ðonne þet se biscop 7 se hired him sealdon[.] xii . hida landes æt Mordune[5] þe his yldran heora æfter-gengan to ði betehtan[6] þet hi ælce geare of ðan lande geformædon forða þe[7] þa are gestrynden 7 Ælfsige his agen fæder þet ylcæn land[a] æft ðem hyrde on Ealdan Mynstre þær eal his forðfædren

[a] lande *with* e *erased*

Here it is declared how Bishop Æthelwold[1] and the community in the Old Minster in Winchester, with the permission of King Edward,[2] exchanged lands with Ælfwine, the son of Ælfsige[3] and Æthelhild.[4] Namely, that the bishop and the community granted to him the 12-hide estate *æt Mordune*,[5] which his ancestors [had] committed[6] to their successors on the condition that they paid a food-rent every year from the estate on behalf of those[7] who acquired the property, and Ælfsige, his own

[1] Æthelwold, bishop of Winchester; see above, **IV**, n. 134.

[2] King Edward the Martyr, 975–8. For him described as *clito*, see above, **IV**, n. 129.

[3] Possibly the Ælfsige to whom 20 hides at Moredon, Wilts., were granted by King Edmund in 943 (S 486, *CW* 91, *BCS* 788), although that may have been a more distant relative with the same name as Ælfwine's father; however, cf. below, n. 5.

[4] The reference here to Æthelhild is misinterpreted in the Latin version; see below, **VIII(ii)**, n. 4.

[5] *æt Mordune.* The identification by *AS Ch*, 356 of this place as Moredon in Rodbourne Cheney, Wilts., is based on insufficient evidence. The three 10th-cent. diplomas which were preserved at Winchester in the 12th cent. and which are mentioned in favour of the identification in *AS Ch*, ibid., all concerned the 20-hide estate at Moredon, Wilts., but are in favour of laymen (S 486, 638, and 763; *CW* 91, 89–90; *BCS* 788, 983, and 763). There is no unequivocal evidence that land at Moredon was ever held by the Old Minster and it is possible that

the three diplomas mentioned above were copied into the *Codex Wintoniensis* in the 12th cent. because it was thought that they referred to the estate of Steeple Morden, Cambs., which was held by the church of Winchester from 1015 to 1136: S 1503, *CW* 93 and 102, *AS Wills* 20; *Regesta* iii, no. 944. The presence of these diplomas at Winchester may be explained by their having formed part of a family archive deposited for safe-keeping at the Old Minster in the late Anglo-Saxon period; Rumble 1980, i, 157–62. An alternative identification, equally possible on linguistic grounds, would be Morden in Surrey, which was assessed at 12 hides *TRE*: *DB*, i, fo. 32[r] (*DB Surrey* 6: 2). Although Morden was held *TRE* by Westminster Abbey, the allegedly pre-conquest diplomas which include references to the Abbey's tenure of the estate all seem to be forgeries of the 12th cent.: S 774, 1040, and 1043.

[6] *to ði betehtan.* It was presumably bequeathed by will.

[7] *forða þe.* **VIII(ii)**, below, has *pro animabus* here, i.e. on behalf of their souls.

rest⁸ forða feormæ betehte .⁹ 7 he him on þæt
ylcan gerad*ᵇ* ¹⁰ þær togeanes gesealde binnan
Þintanceastre tþegra æcera gepirde landes 7
ðene stream¹¹ þe ðærto ligð binnan ðæm
rymette¹² þe se biscop¹³ mid pealle into¹⁴ ðem
mynstre befangan hæfð to ðan ealdan
portpealle .¹⁵ 7 þa boc¹⁶ þærto agæf ðe
Ælfred¹⁷ cining his yldran gebocode .

Ðonne¹⁸ þes ðises gehþerfes to gepitnesse
Eadþard¹⁹ cining 7 Aðelþold²⁰ biscop 7
Æþælmær²¹ ealdorman 7 Æþelgar²² abbod 7
Æðelhild²³ 7 ða ðry hyredas on Ealdan Mynstre
7 on Nipan Mynstre 7 on Nunnan Mynstre 7 seo
burhþaru²⁴ on Þinceastre .

þonne²⁵ synt ðyses gehþerfes . iiii . geþrytu to
gespitulunge . an is mid Ælfþine . oðer in Ealdan
Mynstre . þridde on Nipan Mynstre . feorðe on
Nunnan Mynstre .

father, [had] later committed⁹ the same estate to
the community in the Old Minster, where all his
forefathers rest,⁸ for [their] subsistence. And he
[Ælfwine], in the same manner,¹⁰ has granted
them in return land amounting to 2 acres within
Winchester and the stream¹¹ which runs next to
it, within the space¹² which the bishop¹³ has
enclosed into¹⁴ the monastery with a wall
extending to the old city-wall;¹⁵ and he gave
[them] the charter¹⁶ relating to it which King
Alfred¹⁷ [had] granted his ancestors.

Further,¹⁸ the witnesses of this exchange were
King Edward,¹⁹ and Bishop Æthelwold,²⁰ and
Ealdorman Æthelmær,²¹ and Abbot Æthelgar,²²
and Æthelhild,²³ and the three communities in
the Old Minster, the New Minster, and Nunnaminster, and the citizens²⁴ in Winchester.

Moreover,²⁵ there are four writings as evidence of this exchange; one is in the possession of
Ælfwine, the second [is] in the Old Minster, the
third in the New Minster, and the fourth in
Nunnaminster.

ᵇ gera *altered in error from* gerad *MS. The phrase* on þæt ylcan
gerad *is equivalent to* eodem tenore *in* **VIII(ii)**. AS Ch 53 *(p. 111)*
misses this equivalence, retains the MS. alteration, and translates 'in the
same year'.

---

⁸ *þær eal his forðfædren rest*. Probably referring to burials in the
cemetery to the NW. of the Old Minster, on which see WS 4.i
(forthcoming).

⁹ *betehte*. As above, n. 6.

¹⁰ *on þæt ylcan gerad*. That is, by exchange. Cf. above, n. *b*.

¹¹ *ðene stream*. One of the two streams which pass through the
south wall of the city (cf. below, n. 15), either a precursor of part
of the Lockburn or the stream which later drove the Floodstock
mill; see WS 1, 283-4. Cf. above, **I**, n. 13, and Fig. 1.

¹² *binnan ðæm rymette*. That is, within the precinct of the Old
Minster, recently enclosed at the command of King Edgar; see
above, **VI**. For other adjustments of property rights consequent
on the enclosure of the three Minsters, see above, **VII**. For the
word *rymet(t)*, see ibid., n. 2.

¹³ As above, n. 1.

¹⁴ *into*. See below, **VIII(ii)**, n. 14.

¹⁵ *to ðan ealdan portpealle*. To the south wall of the city,
between Kingsgate and the Wolvesey enclosure, forming the
southern boundary of the precinct at this point. Cf. below,
XVIII, n. 7; **XXIII**, n. 2; and WS 1, 273.

¹⁶ *boc*. This diploma has unfortunately not survived. Its

transfer safeguarded the Old Minster's title to the urban land
here acquired.

¹⁷ King of the West Saxons 871- , of the Anglo-Saxons
c.880-99.

¹⁸ The order of witnesses given here seems more regular than
the different one found below in **VIII(ii)**.

¹⁹ As above, n. 2.

²⁰ As above, n. 1.

²¹ Æthelmær, ealdorman of Hampshire. He died 18 April 982
and was buried at the New Minster; see Keynes *Diplomas*, 240-1.
For his will, see S 1498, *AS Wills* 10.

²² Æthelgar, abbot of the New Minster; see above, **IV**, n. 149.

²³ Ælfwine's mother; see above.

²⁴ *seo burhparu*. This is the earliest documentary reference to
the citizens of Winchester acting together in an official capacity.
For a reference to them as *þa burhmen* in 1052 × 1053, see below,
XXIX.

²⁵ This final clause does not occur below in **VIII(ii)**. It is not
clear whether the text of the present document was written four
times on separate sheets of parchment or whether it was written
as a quadruple chirograph (cf. above, **VII**, n. 28).

(ii) [Latin version]

In*ᵃ* hac cartula declaratur qualiter Aðelpoldus[1] episcopus et familia Þintaniensis ęcclesię in Uetusto Monasterio cum licentia regis Edwardi[2] commutationem terrarum fecerunt contra Ælfwinum filium Ælfsige[3] et Aðelhildam[4] matrem ipsius . Hoc est quod episcopus et familia eius dederunt . xii . mansas in loco qui dicitur Mordune[5] quod sui antecessores suis posteris ad hoc designauerunt[6] quod omni anno de illa terra pastus familie daretur pro animabus[7] illorum qui hanc scilicet hereditatem adquisierant . Ælfsige denique genitor illius hanc eandem tellurem familię in Uetusto Monasterio ubi omnes sui antecessores requiescunt[8] pro pastu designauit .[9] Et eis eodem tenore[10] é contra concessit intra ciuitatem Wintonie duo iugera ruris et riuum[11] quod terrę adiacet intra amplitudinem[12] quam presul[13] muro usque ad[14] monasterium circumplexus est usque ad murum[15] uetustum predicte ciuitatis . et telligraphium[16] quod Ælfredus[17] basileus suis antecessoribus prescripsit dedit .*ᵇ*

Hic[18] sunt testes huius commutationis . Ego Eadward[19] rex . Ego Æðelgar[20] abbod .*ᶜ* Et tres familię in hac ciuitate hoc est familia in Uetusto Monasterio . Et familia in Nouo Monasterio . Et familia in Monasterio Monialium . Ego Aðelpold[21] episcopus . Ego

In this document it is declared how Bishop Æthelwold[1] and the community of the church of Winchester in the Old Minster, with the permission of King Edward,[2] have made an exchange of lands with Ælfwine, the son of Ælfsige,[3] and with Æthelhild[4] his mother. Namely, that the bishop and his community have given [Ælfwine] 12 hides in the place which is called *Mordune*,[5] which his ancestors committed[6] to their successors on the condition that a food-rent should be given to the community every year from that estate on behalf of the souls[7] of those who had acquired this same inheritance. Ælfsige, this man's father, later committed[9] this same estate to the community in the Old Minster, where all his ancestors lie at rest,[8] for [their] subsistence. And he [Ælfwine], in the same manner,[10] has granted them in return 2 acres of land within the city of Winchester and the stream[11] which is adjacent to that land, within the space[12] which the bishop[13] has enclosed with a wall as far as[14] the monastery, extending to the old wall[15] of the aforesaid city; and he gave [them] the land-charter[16] which King Alfred[17] had granted his ancestors.

These[18] are the witnesses of this exchange: I, Edward, king;[19] I, Æthelgar, abbot;[20] and the three communities in this city, namely, the community in the Old Minster, and the community in the New Minster, and the community in Nunnaminster; I, Æthelwold, bishop;[21] I,

---

ᵃ De escambio terre de Mordun pro aqua Wintonie. 'Concerning the exchange of the land of *Mordun* for water at Winchester'; *rubric*   *ᵇ* ded'e *MS.*, presumably *for* dedere; *here the copyist appears to have assumed an error in the exemplar, which has two adjacent verbs in the same tense and number (but with different subjects), and 'corrected' the second of them to an infinitive*   *ᶜ* Sic MS.; The OE word for 'abbot', although Latin* abbas *would be more consistent here*

[1-3] As above, **VIII(i)**, nn. 1–3.

[4] *Aðelhildam.* The use of the Latin accusative sg. case here associates Æthelhild with the preposition *contra* and shows that the drafter of the Latin version mistakenly took her to be named as an actual party to the exchange here recorded, rather than merely as Ælfwine's mother. In the OE version (**VIII(i)**, above) the name is given in the fem. genitive form.

[5-6] As above, **VIII(i)**, nn. 5–6.

[7] *pro animabus.* There is no specific mention of souls in **VIII(i)**.

[8-13] As above, **VIII(i)**, nn. 8–13.

[14] The Latin *usque ad* used here is not a good equivalent of the OE *into* in **VIII(i)**. The use of *in*, followed by the accusative case, would have conveyed the actual meaning 'into' with better effect.

[15-17] As above, **VIII(i)**, nn. 15–17.

[18] The witnesses are here given in a muddled order, different from that in **VIII(i)**, above.

[19] As above, **VIII(i)**, n. 2.

[20] As above, **VIII(i)**, n. 22.

[21] As above, **VIII(i)**, n. 1.

Æþelmer[22] dux . Ego Æþelhild .[23] Et omnes   Æthelmær, ealdorman;[22] I Æthelhild;[23] and all
ciues[24] istius ciuitatis .[25]   the citizens[24] of this city.[25]

[22] As above, **VIII(i)**, n. 21.

[23-4] As above, **VIII(i)**, nn. 23-4.

[25] *istius ciuitatis.* These words correspond to the more specific

on Pinceastre in **VIII(i)**, above. In the latter, a further clause
follows at this point, referring to four copies of the record having
been made; see ibid. n. 25.

IX

A.D. 983, grant by King Æthelred II to Bishop Æthelgar [of Selsey],
of meadow-land to the north of Winchester

Latin with English

S 845, Finberg 134

THIS royal diploma provides important circumstantial evidence to associate the New Minster with the ownership of land immediately to the north of the city of Winchester in the late tenth century, adjacent to the site at Hyde to which the abbey migrated in the early twelfth century.[1] A measured amount of meadowland on the banks of the River Itchen is here granted by King Æthelred to Bishop Æthelgar [of Selsey] who was also abbot of the New Minster.[2] It is likely that Æthelgar acquired the land on behalf of his abbey but, even if the grant were intended to be personal to him, it is probable that he passed it on to the New Minster, since it was in the abbey's possession at the time of the Domesday Survey.[3] The land concerned had earlier been included in the southern part of the estate of Easton which had been granted to Bishop Beorhthelm of Winchester in 961.[4] Its area was roughly the same as that of the walled area of the city (see Fig. 9).

There is no reason to doubt the authenticity of the basic core of the diploma, once the interpolations to the clause giving the measurements (see below) are removed. The composition of the witness-list is consistent with the date 983 given in the document.[5] Some of the formulae present in the diploma associate it with others of the 980s preserved in the New Minster archive (S 842, 865, and 869).[6] The fact that, of these, S 869 has the same beneficiary as **IX** is particularly worthy of note. It is a diploma of Æthelred II, dated 988, granting 7 hides at South Heighton, Sussex, to Bishop Æthelgar, following an exchange for land at *Lamburna* (unidentified) with Ælfric, ealdorman of Hampshire. It shares aspects of its disposition, sanction and dating clause with **IX**, and may have been drafted by Bishop Æthelgar himself;[7] the core text of **IX** may also have been drafted by him too.

The only complete text of the document that has survived is that copied into MS. D, the late fourteenth- or early fifteenth-century *Liber de Hyda*.[8] In common with the cartulary-scribe's treatment of other Anglo-Saxon texts therein, the present document was interpolated by the addition of both Middle English and Latin translations of its Old English section, that giving the linear measurements of the land granted.[9] In addition, the OE section has itself been given a Latin introductory phrase.[10] The scribe of the *Liber de Hyda* also several times shows his unfamiliarity with the ligature of *r* and *t*, found occasionally in caroline minuscule but not in later scripts, and misreads

---

[1] See below, **XII** and **XIII**.
[2] See below, **IX**, n. 4; and above, **IV**, n. 149.
[3] See below, **IX**, n. 5.
[4] See below, **XXII**.
[5] See below, **IX**, nn. 11–38. The witness-list is to be dated to

that part of 983 after the death of Ealdorman Ælfhere; see Keynes *Diplomas*, 242.   [6] See Keynes *Diplomas*, 92–4.
[7] Ibid. 93.   [8] See above, p. 13.
[9] See below, **IX**, n. 10.   [10] Ibid. n. 8.

the ligature as that of *s* and *t*, which was still in use in the fourteenth century;[11] this may be taken as evidence that the Latin part of the exemplar used by the scribe of the *Liber de Hyda* was written in caroline minuscule script, as one would expect if it were an original document of the year 983.

There are two other surviving texts, both lacking the details of the dimensions of the meadow and the witness-list. One is a copy in MS. B, a cartulary of Hyde Abbey from the second half of the thirteenth century. It is entered there before a diploma of Cnut concerning Drayton, Hants (S 956). The other is in MS. C, the late fourteenth-century revision of B.[12] Its scribe miscopied some Latin words[13] and altered the spelling of others in accordance with French orthographic conventions.[14]

[11] Ibid. n. *p* and examples there cited.
[12] See above, p. 10.

[13] See below, **IX**, nn. *b-e*, etc.
[14] Ibid. nn. *g* and *aa*.

MSS.:   B. BL, Cotton Domitian xiv, fo. 187[rv] (s. xiii[2]; incomplete)
           C. BL, Harl. MS. 1761, fo. 33[rv] (s. xiv ex.; incomplete)
           D. Earl of Macclesfield, Shirburn Castle, *Liber (abbatiae) de Hyda*,
           fos. 32[v]–33[r] (s. xiv/xv; interpolated)

Edited: *KCD* 635, from C
           LH, 228–31, from D collated to C
           LVH, 246–7, from C
           Miller *New Minster* 27, from B, C, and D

Printed from D (*ex* Bod, MS. Film 184) collated to B and C, but variation in the use of *u* and *v* is not usually noted. Interpolations in D are shown in bold type.

Prepollenti[a] cunctitonantis[b] dapsilitate[c] trina fauste rerum machina exstat[d] disposita . ac tam mirifica[e] inexhauste[f] bonitatis clemencia citra aliarum creaturarum uisibilium uidelicet seriem[g] ac[h] materiem protoplaustus luteo[1] confectus tegmine somatis .[2] felici permanet ditatus priuilegio . ut per male suade refrenacionem superbie . ac imitacionem[j] humilitatis limpidissime perque refrigeracionem inopum necne bonorum distribucionem[k] terrestrium .[l] ad nanciscendam Olympice[m] amoenitatis[n] felicitatem . ualeat omuncio terrestris theorice[o] uite percipere gaudia . uirtutum[p] nobiliter decoratus bonarum prerogatiuis . Quapropter ego Ethelredus[q][3] diuina disponente prouidencia industrius Anglorum aliarumque circumiacencium regionum basileos . cuidam michi[r] oppido[s] dilecto antistiti Adelgaro[t][4] uocitamine .[u] ob illius placabilissimam fidelitatem quoddam pratum[5] quod in aquilonali parte iacet[v] famose urbis que scibili appellamine Wyncanceaster[w] uocitatur[x] quodque in orientali parte circumiacet fluuius qui Icene[y] nuncupatur . ad usus sibi

The threefold scheme of things is obvious, favorably arranged by the very remarkable generosity of the All-thundering One and by the equally wonderful forbearance of [His] inexhaustible goodness. The first man, put together with a covering of clay[1] for his body,[2] endures, set apart, that is, from the lineage and stock of other visible creatures, enriched with happy privilege so that, by curbing evil-counselling pride, and by imitating the purest humility, and also by mitigating poverty and distributing earthly goods in order to receive the happiness of Olympian delight he, an earthly dwarf, might know the delights of a contemplative life, nobly adorned with the privileges of good virtues. Wherefore I, Æthelred,[3] by the disposition of divine providence diligent king of the English and of all the surrounding provinces, grant for his own use in perpetual heredity to a certain bishop, named Æthelgar,[4] very dear to me on account of his most pleasing faithfulness, a certain meadow[5] which lies to the north of the renowned city which is called by the well-known name Winchester, and which [meadow] the River Itchen bounds on the east; with

[a] Sequitur donacio regis Etheldredi de pratis quod modo the Hyde Mooris appellamus in Nouum Monasterium Wyntonie quod modo dicitur Hyda anno regni sui quinto ~ 'Here follows King Æthelred's gift concerning the meadows which we now call "the Hyde Moors", to the New Minster, Winchester, which is now called Hyde, in the fifth year of his reign' *rubric D*; Priuilegium regis Ethelredi de moris 'King Æthelred's privilege concerning the Moors' *rubric B and C. This document is number lvi in the Winchester section of C*   [b] cuntitonantis C   [c] dapsaitate C   [d] extat B, C   [e] mrifica C   [f] exhauste D   [g] ceriem C; *a spelling due to the influence of French, cf. note aa*   [h] ac omitted C   [j] limitacionem B; luntatem C, *probably a scribal misreading of imitac'em*   [k] distrubucionem C   [l] terestrium C   [m] Olimpice B, C   [n] amenitatis B, C   [o] teorice C   [p] uistutum D, *a scribal misreading of a caroline minuscule ligature of* r + t *in the exemplar as* s + t; *cf. notes bb, cc, ee, kk, ll, ss*   [q] Adelredus B, C   [r] mihi C   [s] opido C   [t] B, C; Adellaro D   [u] vcitamine C; *cf. note x*   [v] quod iacet in aquilonali parte B, C   [w] Wyntonia B, C   [x] vcatur C; *cf. note u*   [y] Ichene B, C

[1] *protoplaustus luteo confectus tegmine.* For the making of Adam out of clay (*ex limo conditum*), see above, **IV, i,** and ibid. n. 12. Cf. Prudentius, *Liber cathemerinon* 3, 136–8 *Ecce uenit noua progenies, aethere proditus alter homo, non luteus uelut ille prius,* M. P Cunningham (ed.), *Aurelii Prudentii Clementis carmina,* CCSL 126 (Turnh-

out, 1966), 15. ['Behold, a new child comes, the second man has come from Heaven, not made from clay like the first'] Cf. also *protoplastus . . . puluereo confectus tegmine* in the proem to S 858, *KCD* 1283, a diploma from the Abingdon archive, granted by King Æthelred to his thegn Leofwine, dated 985.

[2] *somatis.* From gen. sg. of *soma* (= Greek σῶμα 'body'). Cf. *zomatum,* below, **XXIV,** n. 7.

[3] Æthelred II, king of England, 978–1016.

[4] Æthelgar was bishop of Selsey, 980–8, during which time he retained the abbacy of the New Minster. He resigned both offices on becoming archbishop of Canterbury in 988; see above, **IV,** n. 149. For him as beneficiary of another diploma dated 988, see above, p. 149.

[5] *quoddam pratum.* Hyde Moors, an extensive area of meadow outside the north wall of the city; see Fig. 9. The New Minster's tenure of *pascua quam uocant moram* is recorded in 1086 under Abbots Worthy: *DB,* i, fo. 42[v] (*DB Hants* 6: 17). The 14th-cent. version of this Domesday entry which appears in BL, Harl. MS. 1761, fo. 161[r], refers to *pascua que vocatur moram continentem . xx . acras prati*; however, the words *continentem . . . prati* are an erroneous transcription of the unrelated *quater xx . acre prati* that follow in *DB,* ibid. The area was bounded to the east by the River Itchen and to the west by what was later the Hyde Abbey mill-stream; see WS 1, 266 and Fig. 5; also WS 2.ii, 947.

necessarios in perpetuam concedo hereditatem .
cum omnibus ad illud pertinentibus . tam in[z]
magnis quam in modicis rebus uidelicet aquarum
cursibus . piscium[aa] capcionibus . molendinar-
umque rotacionibus . quatenus ille prospere
perfruatur ac perhenniter possideat . dum laben-
tis eui incolatum artuum[bb] organa pertrahunt .
postque uocante mortalibus notissima morte[cc]
debitum iuris ut soluat cuicumque sibi libuerit
successori iure hereditaria cum Christi benedictione[dd] nostraque libertate[ee] derelinquat . Si quis
autem quod absit hanc donacionem liuore pres-
sus nequissimo euertere studuerit in aliud quam
hic extat insitum . uel si quispiam fortuitu ad hoc
destruendum[ff] scedam aliquam demonstrauerit .
perpetue combustionis[gg] atrocitate[hh] dampnatus
cum Iuda Christi proditore ac Sathanam[jj] pesti-
fero Iuliano .[6] necnon miserimo . Pilatoque[7]
lugubri ac ceteris infernalium claustrorum seuis-
simis commanipularibus . horrifluis sartagini-
bus[kk] perpetue gehenne decoquatur . ac piceis
tenebris miseriisque perhennibus permaneat
addictus . nisi ante mortis articulum[ll] cum
nimia satisfaccione emendare ac tantam pre-
sumpcionem oblitterare toto conamine studuerit .

Huius sane quantitatem prati . longitudinem
necne latitudinem .[mm] hic lector perspiciet legens .
In lingua saxonica[8] ~ þonne is ærest seo
lenge . on pestepeardan . v . furlang . 7 v . gyrda .[9]
on middepeardan . v . furlang . 7 [.] xxvi . gyrda .
on eastepeardan andlang ea . v . furlang . Ðonne
is seo bræd . ærest[nn] on norðhealfe . iii . furlang .
7 i . gyrd . on middeperdan [.] ðreo furlang . 7 .
xxvii . gyrda . on suðepeardan . ðreo furlang . 7 .

everything belonging to it, both in great and
modest matters, that is, with regard to watercourses, the catching of fish, and the turning of
mills, so that he may prosperously enjoy it to the
full and possess it continually while the engines
of [his] strength draw onwards the dwelling of
[his] expiring life, and later, when death, very
familiar to mortals, calls on him to pay [his] just
debt, let him relinquish it in hereditary right to
whichever successor he pleases, with the blessing
of Christ and with our grant of freedom. If
anyone, moreover, which Heaven forbid!, should
strive, driven by the vilest malice, to subvert this
donation into something other than is here
implanted, or if anyone should chance to exhibit
another document in order to destroy this thing,
let him be boiled in the horrific frying-pans of
perpetual Hell and damned in the perpetual
hideousness of burning with Judas the betrayer
of Christ and with Satan and with the noxious
and most miserable Julian[6] and with the lamen-
table Pilate[7] and with the other most barbarous
comrades of the infernal prisons, and let him
remain forever abandoned to the pitch-black
shadows and unceasing miseries, unless before
the moment of death he has striven to make
amends with a very large reparation and to blot
out such great presumption with all his effort.

Here the reader, reading, may truly see the
size of this meadow, the length as well as the
breadth. **In the Saxon tongue:**[8] [This] then
firstly is the length; 5 furlongs and 5 'yards'[9] in
the west, 5 furlongs and 26 'yards' in the middle,
5 furlongs in the east along the river. [This] then
is the breadth; firstly, 3 furlongs and 1 'yard' on
the north side, 3 furlongs and 27 'yards' in the
middle, 3 furlongs and 11 'yards' in the south.

---

[z] in omitted C · [aa] pissium C; a spelling due to the influence
of French, cf. note g · [bb] astuum D, a scribal misreading as in note
p, etc.; arcuum C · [cc] moste D; cf. note p, etc.
[dd] benediccione C · [ee] libestate D; cf. note p, etc.
[ff] B, C; destruendam D · [gg] conbustionis C
[hh] attrocitate C · [jj] Satanam B; Sacanan C
[kk] sastaginibus D; cf. note p, etc. · [ll] asticulum D; cf. note p,
etc. · [mm] B, C which omit matter after latitudinem as far as
Anno; see note rr · [nn] Point after ærest D

---

[6] Julian the Apostate, the pagan emperor of Rome, 360–3. He
is also referred to in the anathema of an interpolated Worcester

diploma of apparent date 964; see S 731, BCS 1135, and Eric
John, *Land Tenure in Early England: A Discussion of Some Problems*
(Leicester, 1964), 99–100.

[7] Pontius Pilate, the Roman procurator of Judea at the time
of the crucifixion of Jesus.

[8] This phrase is an interpolation in MS. D by the cartulary-
scribe. [9] See above, **II**, n. 6.

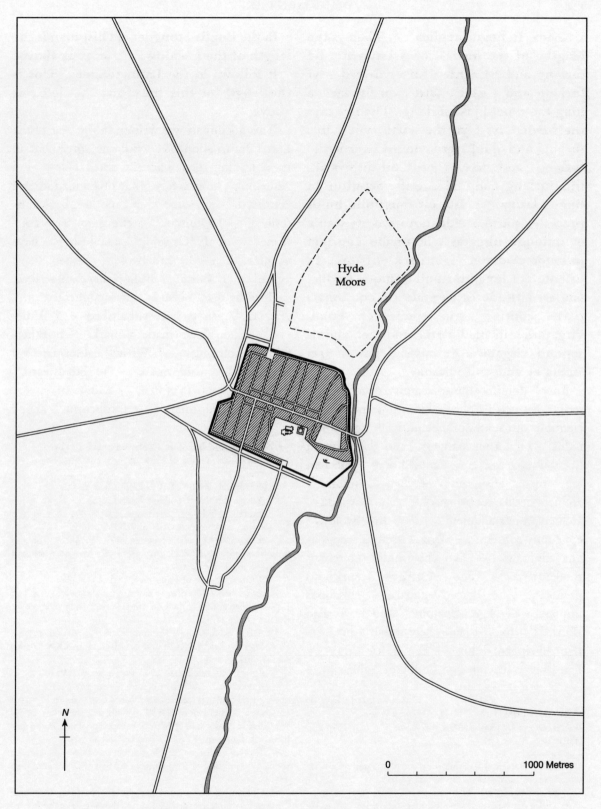

Hyde
Moors

N

0   1000 Metres

Fig. 9. The bounds of Hyde Moors in **IX** (A.D. 983).

xi . gyrda . **In lingua anglica**[10] ~ **Than ys the lengthe of the mede . on westward . fyf furlang and fyf ʒerde . on mydward . fyf furlang and . xxvi . ʒerd . on estward a long the ryuer [.] fyf furlang . Than ys thys the brede . fyrst yn the north syde . iii . furlang and o[un]**[oo]** ʒerd . on mydward . iii . furlang**[pp]** and . xxvii . ʒerd . on suthward . iii . furlang and . xi . ʒerd . Sequitur in lingua latina**[10] ~ Ista est longitudo huius prati . ex parte occidentali quinque stadia et quinque uirgatas . in medio continet quinque stadia et viginti sex virgatas . ex oriente per longum riuuli quinque stadia . Ista est latitudo istius prati . in aquilonari parte continet tria stadia et unam virgatam . in medio tria stadia et viginti septem virgatas . ex australi parte**[qq]** tria stadia et vndecim virgatas.**

Anno**[rr]** dominice incarnacionis . dcccclxxxiii . scripta est cartula**[ss]** hec . his primariis consencientibus qui subter prenotantur . + Ego Ethelredus[11] Anglorum basileos hanc donacionem libenter concessi . + Ego Ælfðryð[12] eiusdem regis mater adsignaui . + Ego Dunstanus[13] archiepiscopus confirmaui . + Ego Oswaldus[14] archiepiscopus adquieui . + Ego Athelwoldus[15] episcopus consensi . + Ego Ælfstanus[16] episcopus adnotaui . + Ego Æþelsinus[17] episcopus roboraui . + Ego Æscpigus[18] episcopus prenotaui . + Ego Wulfgarus[19] episcopus impressi . + Ego Æþelpine[20] dux . + Ego Ælfric**[tt]**[21] dux . + Ego Beorhtnoð[22] dux . + Ego Æþelpeard[23] dux . + Ego Ælfric[24] dux . + Ego þore[25] dux . + Ego Ordbyrht[26] abbas [.] +

[oo] Point before ʒerd D   **[pp]** Point after furlang D
[qq] Point after parte D   **[rr]** B, C begin again here   **[ss]** sic B, C which end here; kastula D, cf. note p, etc.   **[tt]** Point after Ælfric D

---

[10] This phrase and the following set of measurements are interpolations in MS. D by the cartulary-scribe.

[11] As above, n. 3.

[12] Ælfthryth was the widow of King Edgar; see above, **IV**, n. 130.

In the English tongue:[10] **[This] then is the length of the meadow; . . . [etc., as above].**

It follows in the Latin tongue:[10] **This is the length of this meadow; . . . [etc., as above].**

This document was written in the year of the Lord's Incarnation 983, with the agreement of these leading men who are noted below: + I Æthelred,[11] king, freely grant this donation. + I Ælfthryth,[12] the same king's mother, have subscribed. + I Dunstan,[13] archbishop, have confirmed. + I Oswald,[14] archbishop, have acquiesced. + I Æthelwold,[15] bishop, have agreed. + I Ælfstan,[16] bishop, have subscribed. + I Æthelsige,[17] bishop, have confirmed. + I Æscwig,[18] bishop, have subscribed. + I Wulfgar,[19] bishop, have made a mark. + I Æthelwine,[20] ealdorman. + I Ælfric,[21] ealdorman. + I Beorhtnoth,[22] ealdorman. + I Æthelweard,[23] ealdorman. + I Ælfric,[24] ealdorman. + I Thored,[25] ealdorman. + I Ordbeorht,[26] abbot.

---

[13] Dunstan, archbishop of Canterbury; ibid. n. 127.

[14] Oswald, archbishop of York, 971–92. For him as bishop of Worcester, see ibid. n. 138.

[15] Æthelwold, bishop of Winchester; ibid. n. 134.

[16] Ælfstan, bishop of London; ibid. n. 136.

[17] Æthelsige, bishop of Sherborne, 978 × 979–991 × 993. He was one of the beneficiaries of **XXIV**, below.

[18] Æscwig, bishop of Dorchester, 975 × 979–1002; he also subscribes below, **XXIV**. He may previously have been abbot of Bath; see above, **IV**, n. 145.

[19] Wulfgar, bishop of Ramsbury, 981–985 × 986.

[20] Æthelwine, ealdorman of East Anglia; see above, **IV**, n. 155. He subscribed as first of the ealdormen between 983 and 990; see Keynes Diplomas, Table 6.

[21] Ælfric, ealdorman of Hampshire, 982–1016; ibid. 177; he also subscribes below, **XXVI** and is addressed in **XXX**. For his son, see below, n. 31.

[22] Beorhtnoth, ealdorman of Essex; see above, **IV**, n. 156.

[23] Æthelweard, ealdorman of the Western Provinces, c.975–c.998, the chronicler; see Keynes Diplomas, 175, n. 84, and 192. He also subscribes below, **XXVI**. For his son, see below, n. 35.

[24] Ælfric, ealdorman of Mercia; he was appointed in 983 but banished in 985; see Keynes Diplomas, 182, n. 104.

[25] Thored, ealdorman of Northumbria, 975 × 992. He was probably the father of King Æthelred's first wife Ælfgifu; ibid. 187, n. 118.

[26] Ordbeorht, abbot of Chertsey. He may be the same Ordbeorht who succeeded Æthelgar (above, n. 4) as bishop of Selsey. See above, **IV**, n. 147; and below, **XXVI**, n. 25.

Ego Sigeric[27] abbas [.] + Ego Æþelperd[28] abbas [.] + Ego Leofric[29] abbas [.] + Ego Ælfpeard[30] minister . + Ego Ælfgar[31] minister . + Ego Ælfsige[32] minister . + Ego Þulfsige[33] minister . + Ego Þulfric[34] minister . + Ego Æþelmær[35] minister . + Ego Ælfhelm[36] minister . + Ego Ælfpine[37] minister . + Ego Beorhtpold[38] minister .*uu*

+ I Sigeric,[27] abbot. + I Æthelweard,[28] abbot. + I Leofric,[29] abbot. + I Ælfweard,[30] thegn. + I Ælfgar,[31] thegn. + I Ælfsige,[32] thegn. + I Wulfsige,[33] thegn. + I Wulfric,[34] thegn. + I Æthelmær,[35] thegn. + I Ælfhelm,[36] thegn. + I Ælfwine,[37] thegn. + I Beorhtweald,[38] thegn.

uu *There is a punctus simplex* between the name of the witness *and the word* minister *in the subscriptions of the third, fourth, fifth, sixth, seventh, and ninth* ministri *in* D

---

[27] Sigeric, abbot of St. Augustine's, Canterbury, ?980–?985. A monk of Glastonbury, he was later bishop of Ramsbury (985–90) and archbishop of Canterbury (990–4); see *HRH*, 35.

[28] Æthelweard, abbot of Malmesbury, 977 × 993; ibid. 54.

[29] Leofric was abbot either of Exeter (?973 × 993) or of Muchelney (980 × 1005); ibid. 48 and 56.

[30] Ælfweard frequently subscribed at the head of the *ministri* in diplomas of King Æthelred until 986. He had also been prominent in the reigns of Edgar and Edward the Martyr and was described as *discifer* in S 782 (*BCS* 1270; dated 971); see Keynes *Diplomas*, 182–3, and Table 7. He was probably the same as Ælfweard, *minister*, who subscribed above, **IV** (n. 161); and **VI** (n. 29).

[31] Ælfgar occurs consistently as a prominent witness between 982 and 990. He may possibly be identical with Ælfgar, the son of Ealdorman Ælfric (above, n. 21), who was blinded in 993; see Keynes *Diplomas*, 183–4.

[32] Ælfsige was a consistent witness in the reign of Æthelred up to 995, and had been prominent in the reigns of Edgar and Edward the Martyr. He was described as *discifer* in S 782 (*BCS* 1270; dated 971); see Keynes *Diplomas*, 183, and Tables 7 and 8. Two *ministri* of this name subscribe **XXII**, below (nn. 67 and 69), but neither need be identical with the present witness.

[33] Wulfsige was a prominent witness to diplomas between 980 and 988; see Keynes *Diplomas*, 184, and Table 7.

[34] Probably Wulfric Spot, the son of Wulfrun and later the founder of Burton Abbey, who was a consistent and prominent witness during the 990s and until 1002; ibid. 188–9, and Tables 7 and 8. See also Hart *ECNE*, 373–4. For his brother Ælfhelm, see below, n. 36.

[35] Æthelmær was the son of Ealdorman Æthelweard (see above, n. 23) and thus a kinsman of the king. He subscribed 983– , and most prominently 990 × 993–1005, often in close proximity to Beorhtweald (see below, n. 38). He was later ealdorman of the Western Provinces, in succession to his father. On Æthelmær ('the Fat'), see Keynes *Diplomas*, 188, 209–10, and Tables 7 and 8; and Hart *ECNE*, 286. He also subscribes below, **XXVI** (n. 34). He may be identical with Æthelmær, *miles*, one of the beneficiaries of **XXIV**, below.

[36] Ælfhelm was probably the brother of Wulfric Spot (see above, n. 34) who subscribed as *minister* between 982 and 990. He was made ealdorman of Northumbria by 993 and was murdered in 1006. On him, see Keynes *Diplomas*, 189, and Tables 6–8; and Hart *ECNE*, 258–9. See also below, **XXVI**, n. 32.

[37] There are only a few attestations to diplomas by *ministri* called Ælfwine between 981 and *c*.1012, and those may not necessarily all refer to the same individual; cf. Keynes *Diplomas*, Tables 7 and 8.

[38] Beorhtweald was probably a kinsman of the king and subscribed between 980 and 999, often in close proximity to Æthelmær (see above, n. 35). On him, see Keynes *Diplomas*, 188, and Tables 7 and 8.

X

A.D. 1072 × 1086, grant by King William I to the New Minster, of the church of Alton, Hants, with its tithes, rents, and 5 hides of land, and of the church of Kingsclere, Hants, with its tithes, rents, and 4 hides and 1 yardland of land; in exchange for the site of the New Minster cemetery

Latin

Regesta i, no. 37[1]; Bates *Regesta* 344

THIS text records the grant by William I to the New Minster of churches, tithes, rents, and land at Alton and Kingsclere, Hants, in exchange for the abbey's cemetery in Winchester on to which the king wished to extend his palace. It is undated, but the exchange had occurred before the time of the Domesday Survey,[2] while the reference to Abbot Riwallon would place the text after 1072.[3] The date 1070 which was ascribed to the document by both Birch and H. W. C. Davis is dependent upon the testimony of a late medieval memorandum whose chronological data is elsewhere untrustworthy.[4]

The diplomatic form of the document owes more to Norman rather than to English precedent. It lacks invocation, proem or greeting. The form is that of a general notification in the first person (*notum esse uolo*) by William as king of the English (*Dei omnipotentis gratia operante Anglorum rex*) addressed to his subjects in England (*omnibus meis fidelibus intra Anglicas partes commorantibus*). There is a simple verb of disposition in the present tense (*concedo*), but a fairly long sanction with the threat of excommunication (*Si quis autem presumptor . . . cum prophanis puniatur*). There is a clause of corroboration (beginning *Et ut munus istud*) referring to the imposition of the king's *signum*. There is no date and no witness. The document is reminiscent of 'the shorter and more secular type of Norman charter' to which the late Allen Brown drew attention.[5] It may perhaps have been drafted by Abbot Riwallon himself[6] but, since it was not unknown at this time for a royal document to be drafted and written by agents of the beneficiary and then presented to the king for sealing, this would not mean that the text lacked royal approval.[7] As, however, the record was written into a

---

[1] With incorrect reference to BL, Stowe MS. 960, fo. 71.

[2] See below, **X**, nn. 4 and 5.   [3] Ibid. n. 3.

[4] *LVH*, 113 and *Regesta* i, no. 37; see WS 1, 292–3, and Keynes *Liber Vitae*, 80–1. The memorandum recorded a tradition that William I had appropriated the site of the recently-burnt domestic buildings of the New Minster *c.*1070, during the abbacy of Wulfric.

[5] R. Allen Brown, 'Some observations on Norman and Anglo-Norman Charters', in Diana Greenway, Christopher Holdsworth, and Jane Sayers (ed.), *Tradition and Change: Essays in Honour of Marjorie Chibnall Presented by her Friends on the Occasion of her Seventieth Birthday* (Cambridge, 1985), 145–63, at 160–1.

For Norman diplomatic features in general, see Marie Fauroux, *Recueil des Actes des Ducs de Normandie (911–1066)* (Mémoires de la Société des Antiquaires de Normandie 36, Caen, 1961), 47–65; Cassandra Potts, 'The Early Norman Charters: A New Perspective on an Old Debate', in Carola Hicks (ed.), *England in the Eleventh Century* (Harlaxton Medieval Studies 2, Stamford, 1992), 25–40; and Bates *Regesta*, 11–12.

[6] The form of the opening clause is reminiscent of that in **XI**, below.

[7] For example. T. A. M. Bishop and P. Chaplais (ed.), *Facsimiles of English Royal Writs to A.D. 1100 Presented to Vivian Hunter Galbraith* (Oxford, 1957), nos. 9 and 11, and cf. p. xviii.

book, and may perhaps never have been intended to be issued as a single-sheet document, it could not be sealed and the place of the seal has apparently been taken by the roughly inscribed cross which is claimed in the text to be the autograph *signum* of William I. There is no way of disproving this claim, which is integral to the authenticity of the document. Although the *signum* is different in appearance from others which occur on original documents of William I and William II,[8] we do not know the exact circumstances in which it was made, possibly during a public ceremony of exchange in the abbey church. It must be said, however, that the most recent commentators have been doubtful about the originality of the *signum*, while admitting that the text cannot be faulted on diplomatic criteria (or on the facts of the transaction).[9]

In external form the document consists of a late-eleventh-century addition (of 22 lines) to a hitherto almost blank leaf (fo. 41) of the New Minster *Liber Vitae*. This leaf is now misplaced and should follow fo. 49.[10] As Bishop showed, the same scribe not only wrote document **XI**, below, into the *Liber Vitae*, but also made an addition to an eleventh-century collection of astrological tracts associated with Hyde Abbey (*rectius* the New Minster), and another addition to the eleventh-century 'Grimbald Gospels'.[11] He also wrote an addition to a late-eleventh-century psalter from the New Minster.[12] This scribe wrote in a Norman style of caroline minuscule script, with short ascenders and descenders and with diagonal hairline serifs at the base of minims and uprights. A noticeable feature of his hand is the letter *g*, where the head is often not closed at its base. He also used a characteristic comma-like form of the overline, the general mark of abbreviation, as well as the more usual horizontal form. The spelling *Autunę* (MLat. fem. genitive sg.) for Alton, Hants, exhibits the loss of *l* before a consonant found in some place-name spellings in Great Domesday Book.[13] In 1204–5 this document within the *Liber Vitae* was produced in court by the abbot of Hyde as evidence in support of his claim in the Curia Regis to the advowson of the church of Binsted, Hants, although the status of the apparent *signum* of William I was recorded in the enrolment of the case with a certain degree of scepticism.[14]

[8] See *Pal. Soc.* iii, plate 170 (William I); also *New Pal. Soc.* i, Plate 45a, and Bishop and Chaplais, *Facsimiles of English Royal Writs*, Plate XIX (Both William II). Cf. Bates *Regesta*, 20, and comments on the particular documents there listed. Note also that although corroboration by a single ducal cross was a feature of the early 11th cent. Norman charters of Duke Richard II, it had given way to the use of multiple *signa* by the time of William the Conqueror; see Potts, 'Early Norman Charters', 31, and 34.

[9] See Bates *Regesta* 344; and Keynes *Liber Vitae*, 102.

[10] See Keynes *Liber Vitae*, 102–3.

[11] See below, p. 160; Trinity College, Cambridge, MS. R. 15. 32, p. 165; BL, Add. MS. 34890, fos. 158–60; and T. A. M. Bishop, 'Notes on Cambridge Manuscripts, Part II', *Transactions of the Cambridge Bibliographical Society* 2 (1954–8), 189–92.

[12] BL, Arundel MS. 60, fos. 133–42; see Keynes *Liber Vitae*, 102.

[13] Cf. R. E. Zachrisson, 'The French Element', in A. Mawer and F. M. Stenton (ed.), *Introduction to the Survey of English Place-Names* (EPNS 1, Cambridge, 1924) i, 113. Note, however, that the Great

Domesday Book spelling of this Alton is *AVLTONE*: *DB*, i, fo. 43^r (*DB Hants* 6: 1).

[14] See *Curia Regis R* 5–7 *John*, 118–19 (Easter, 5–6 John) '*Et abbas de Hida venit et dicit quod advocacie illius ecclesie* [of Binsted] *spectat ad eum sicut illius quam rex Willelmus conquestor domui de Hida dedit tanquam pertinentem ad ecclesiam de Aulton', quam simul cum pertinenciis ipse dedit predicte domui in escambium cimiterii ubi abbacia de Hida sita prius fuit; et profert quendam librum in quo carta predicti Willelmi notatur cum quodam singno* [sic] *crucis quod idem rex Willelmus, ut abbas dicit, propria manu scripsit*' ['And the abbot of Hyde comes and says that the advowson of this church [of Binsted] belongs to him just like that of another, belonging to the church of Alton, which William the Conqueror gave to the house of Hyde, which together with its appurtenances he gave to the aforesaid house in exchange for the cemetery where the abbey of Hyde was formerly located; and he exhibits a certain book in which the charter of the aforesaid [King] William is marked with a certain sign of the Cross which the same King William, so the abbot says, wrote with his own hand.'] Cf. below, p. 173, n. 7.

MS.:   B. BL, Stowe MS. 944, fo.41ʳ (s.xi ex)

Facsimiles: *LVH*, 110
                 Keynes *Liber Vitae*

Edited: *LVH*, 111–12
                 Bates *Regesta* 344

Printed from the manuscript

Ego . *Willelmus* .[1] Dei omnipotentis gratia operante Anglorum rex: omnibus meis fidelibus intra Anglicas partes[2] commorantibus notum esse uolo quod concedo sancto Petro Noui Monasterii . et Ryuuallono[3] eiusdem cęnobii abbati necnon et monachis inibi diuino seruitio uacantibus ęcclesiam Autunę[4] cum quinque hidis atque decimis et cum aliis redditibus qui ad predictam ęcclesiam pertinent . insuper et ęcclesiam de Clara[5] cum quatuor hidis et una uirgata terrae atque cum decimis et aliis redditibus qui ad predictam ęcclesiam pertinent . Prefatas igitur ęcclesias cum terris et quicquid in eis habetur sancto Petro et abbati. *Ryuuallono* . ita liberas concedo quemadmodum illa terra cimiterii[6] cęnobii iamsemel nominati propria erat sancti Petri suorumque monachorum et ab omni seruitio libera .[7] quam

I, William,[1] king of the English by the effectual grace of almighty God, wish it to be known by all my faithful people dwelling within the English region[2] that I grant to St. Peter of the New Minster, and to Riwallon[3] the abbot of the same monastery, and to the monks freely devoting themselves to divine service therein, the church of Alton,[4] with 5 hides and the tithes together with the other rents which belong to the aforesaid church, and also the church of Kingsclere,[5] with 4 hides and 1 yardland of land together with the tithes and the other rents which belong to the aforesaid church. Therefore I grant the aforementioned churches, with the lands and everybody in them, to St. Peter and Abbot Riwallon, so free as that land of the cemetery[6] of the once-already named monastery belonged to St. Peter and his monks, and free from all service,[7] which [land] I have received in exchange from the abbot so that my hall may be

[1] King William I, 1066–87.

[2] *intra Anglicas partes*. The document is addressed to the king's subjects in his dominion of England as opposed to those in Normandy.

[3] Riwallon, abbot of the New Minster, 1072–88; see *HRH*, 82. He was previously prior of Mont St-Michel; see Keynes *Liber Vitae*, 42, n. 248. For a document in his name, see below, **XI**.

[4] Alton, Hants. It is recorded in *DB* (i, fo. 43ʳ ; *DB Hants* 6: 1) that the abbot of the New Minster held 5 hides here in demesne *TRW* and did not pay geld. Queen Edith had held the manor *TRE*. The county jurors were of the opinion that the abbot had received the manor unjustly by exchange for the *domus regis*, since the latter already belonged to the king (*quia domus erat regis*). This opinion may have stemmed from the fact that one part of the land on to which the king extended the royal palace was already part of the royal fief; see WS 1, 293–4 and **I, 80/1**. For later references to Alton in this context, see below, **XI** and **XIV**. The 5 hides later formed Hyde Abbey's manor of Alton Eastbrook; see *VCH Hants* i, 474.

[5] Kingsclere, Hants. *DB*, i, fo. 43ʳ (*DB Hants* 6: 9) records that

the New Minster held a church, 4 hides, and 1 yardland (*virgata*) here *TRW* and did not pay geld. Queen Edith had formerly held it and King William had given it to the New Minster in exchange for the land in the city (of Winchester) on which the *domus regis* is. For a later reference to the church of Kingsclere in this context, see below, **XIV**.

[6] *terra cimiterii*. For the location of the New Minster's two cemeteries, see WS 1, 315–17. The one acquired by the king appears to have extended across the whole north side of the pre-conquest palace; ibid. 294, and Fig. 9. For reference in 1154 × 1171 to this cemetery, see below, **XVII**, n. 7.

[7] *ab omni seruitio libera*. For a general freeing of the lands of the New Minster from secular dues, see above, **IV, xvii**. Freedom of the lands at Alton and Kingsclere from payment of geld, murder-fine, pleas, and plaints is referred to below in **XIV**, which also states that the land in Winchester for which they were exchanged enjoyed the same privilege.

ego ad aulam[8] meam faciendam mutuo ab abbate accepi: et pro qua ego donum[a] istud sicut iamdictum est concedo . Si quis autem presumptor sancti Petri ęcclesię et nostrę concessioni aduersari . istamque donationem irritam facere uoluerit : excommunicationis supplicio inperpetuum cum prophanis puniatur . Et ut munus istud ratum atque inconuulsum habeatur : signum istud ego ipse manu mea pono: **X**[b]

built [on it],[8] and for which I grant this gift as has already been said. If, moreover, any presumptious person should wish to oppose the church of St. Peter and our grant and to make this donation void, let him be punished forever together with the profane with the penalty of excommunication. And so that this gift may be kept fixed and unshaken, I myself place this symbol with my hand: **X**

---

[a] *don u' MS.*   [b] *A large, roughly-formed cross, perhaps in the same ink as the text, is written in the lower margin of the MS. See above, p. 157.*

[8] *aulam.* For the Norman royal palace, see WS 1, 292–5; WS 2.ii, 573–5, and Fig. 65. See also below, **XIV** and **XV**.

XI

A.D. 1082 × 1087, grant in alms to the poor and to pilgrims by Abbot Riwallon of the New Minster, of the estate of Alton, Hants, which King William I had granted in exchange for the site of the New Minster cemetery

Latin

THE estate of Alton, Hants, having been acquired by the New Minster through the exchange recorded in **X**, above, was later, according to the present record, dedicated to charitable purposes.[1] This gift is to be dated after the appointment of Prior Godfrey of the Old Minster in 1082,[2] and before the death of Abbot Riwallon in 1088.[3] The wording of the references to William I also suggest that the document was composed before his death on 9 September 1087. The church of Alton, with 5 hides of land, was later confirmed to Hyde Abbey by Henry I.[4]

The diplomatic form of the document is that of a general declaration. Its opening clause has similarities to that of **X**, above, which may have been drafted by Riwallon.[5] Unlike **X**, however, the document is corroborated by means of a witness-list. So far as it is possible to say, the individuals named as witnesses appear to be contemporary.[6] Although it is possible that it was never intended that this document be issued as a single-sheet, being a record written into a book (see below), there seems no reason to doubt the authenticity of its text, whose only beneficiaries were the poor and pilgrims.

The text was written into a blank space in the New Minster *Liber Vitae* in the late eleventh century, by the same scribe who added **X**, above, to that book, and who also wrote additions to three other surviving New Minster books.[7]

MS.: B. BL, Stowe MS. 944, fo. 59ʳ (s.xi ex.)

Facsimile: Keynes *Liber Vitae*

Edited: *LVH*, 163–4

Printed from the manuscript

---

[1] For the DB entry, see above, **X**, n. 4.
[2] See below, **XI**, n. 8.
[3] See above, **X**, n. 3.
[4] See below, **XIV**.

[5] See above, p. 156.
[6] See below, **XI**, nn. 6–9, and 12.
[7] See above, p. 157.

Ego Riuuallo¹ gratia dei abbas sancti Petri monasterii quod appellatur Nouum . dedi consentientibus fratribus in elemosina pauperum et peregrinorum terram quae dicitur Auueltona² in perpetuum . quam rex . *Willelmus* .³ nobis dedit in cambiacionem pro terra cimiterii⁴ aecclesiae nostrae . in qua aula⁵ eius constructa est . Inprimis pro anima ipsius regis et uxoris ac filiorum . deinde pro me et pro omnibus fratribus mihi commissis . ad extremum pro omnibus benefactoribus huius loci . Testes autem sunt huius donacionis . Walcel*inus*⁶ episcopus . et Hugo uicecomes .⁷ et Godefredus⁸ prior . et Osbernus de O' .⁹ et Wuill*elmus* de Gimices .¹⁰ et Rod*bertus* Corn' .¹¹ et Teotsel'¹² [.] et Walterius Scot .¹³ et Ioh*annes* . et Will*elmus* . et Bened*ictus* .¹⁴ ceterique homines abbatis . Si quis*ᵃ* autem hanc elemosynam quan*ᵇ* dono subtraxerit de uictu pauperum et peregrinorum excommunicationi subiaceat in aeternum . sitque in inferno dampnatus cum Dathan et Abiron¹⁵ et

ᵃ There is a change of ink at Si quis, *but it and the words that follow are in the same hand as the earlier part of the text*
ᵇ MS. error for quam

¹ Abbot of the New Minster, 1072–88; see above, **X**, n. 3.
² Alton, Hants; ibid. n. 4.   ³ King William I; ibid. n. 1.
⁴ *terra cimiterii*; ibid. n. 6.   ⁵ *aula*; ibid. n. 8.
⁶ Walkelin, bishop of Winchester, 1070–98; see Le Neve, *Fasti, 1066–1300*, ii, *Monastic Cathedrals*, 85.
⁷ *Hugo uicecomes.* Probably Hugh de Port (from Port-en-Bessin, Calvados; see Loyd, 79; Tengvik, 108). He held several estates in Hampshire (including Basing) as tenant-in-chief *TRW* (*DB*, i, fos. 44ᵛ–46ʳ; *DB Hants* 23); others as under-tenant to the bishop of Bayeux (*DB*, i, fo. 46ʳᵛ; *DB Hants* 23: 56–68); Abbotstone as under-tenant to the bishop of Winchester (*DB*, i, fo. 40ᵛ; *DB Hants* 2: 23); 2 hides of the Old Minster's manor of Droxford (*DB*, i, fo. 41ᵛ; *DB Hants* 3: 9); and Bedhampton, Warnford, Lychpit, part of Brown Candover, and part of Micheldever from the New Minster (*DB*, i, fos. 42ʳ–43ʳ; *DB Hants* 6: 4, 6–7, 13, and 16). He was a royal official and in 1096 was described as *vicarius* of Winchester; see *Regesta* i, no. 379 and WS 1, 425. He may, however, be distinct from another contemporary Hugh the sheriff; see *VCH Hants* i, 424, and Judith A. Green, *English Sheriffs to 1154*, Public Record Office Handbooks 24 (London, 1990), 44. He is commemorated in *LVH*, 73. For Hugh de Port's son Henry, see below **XII**, n. 4.
⁸ Godfrey (of Cambrai), prior of the cathedral priory, 1082–1107; see *HRH*, 80.
⁹ From Eu (Seine-Inf.): Loyd, 40; Tengvik, 105. Osbern held the church of Farnham, Surrey, with 1 hide and 1 virgate at

I, Riwallon,¹ by the grace of God abbot of the monastery of St. Peter which is called the New, with the agreement of the brothers, have given in perpetuity, in alms for the poor and for pilgrims, the estate called Alton² which King William³ gave us in exchange for the land of our church's cemetery⁴ on which his hall⁵ has been built. Firstly for the soul of the king himself and that of his wife and children, also for myself and all the brothers entrusted to me, finally for all the benefactors of this place.

The witnesses moreover of this donation are: Bishop Walkelin,⁶ and Hugh the sheriff,⁷ and Prior Godfrey,⁸ and Osbern of Eu,⁹ and William de Gimices,¹⁰ and Robert Corn',¹¹ and Teotsel',¹² and Walter Scot,¹³ and John, and William, and Benedict,¹⁴ and others of the abbot's men.

If anyone moreover should take these alms, which I give, away from the sustenance of the poor and of pilgrims, let him suffer excommunication for all time and let him be damned in Hell with Dathan and Abiron¹⁵

Bentley, Hants, from the bishop of Winchester *TRW*: *DB*, i, fos. 31ʳ and 40ᵛ (*DB Surrey* 3: 1; *DB Hants* 2: 25). He also held the church of Leatherhead, Surrey, from the royal manor of Ewell: *DB*, i, fo. 30ᵛ (*DB Surrey* 1: 9). He was probably identical with Osbern de Auco, a canon of St. Paul's at this time; see Le Neve, *Fasti, 1066–1300*, i, *St. Paul's London*, 69.
¹⁰ *Gimices*. Possibly Jumièges, Seine-Maritime. Cf. the Latin (adjectival) spellings *Gemegiensis, Gimegiensis, Gemeticensis* among those quoted by Bates *Regesta*, 1078.
¹¹ Robert Corn' is otherwise unknown. The byname may be from OFr *corn* 'a musical instrument, horn'; see *DBS*, s.n. Corner.
¹² *Teotsel'*. Probably the same as *Tezelinus*, Hugh de Port's *TRW* tenant at Boarhunt and *Aplestede*, Hants (*DB*, i, fo. 45ᵛ; *DB Hants* 23: 33–4), whose name represents OG *Tetzelin*; see Forssner, 229. He may be the same as *Teotselinus laicus* who, with his wife Ealdgyth, is commemorated in *LVH*, 74.
¹³ Perhaps the same as *Walter . scot* who, with his wife Leofgifu, is commemorated ibid. 72.
¹⁴ *Iohannes . . . Willelmus . . . Benedictus*. It is not possible to identify these remaining witnesses.
¹⁵ Dathan and Abiron, the sons of Eliab, who rebelled against Moses and were swallowed into Hell (Num. 16: 1–33; cf. also Ecclus. 45: 22). They were commonly held up as bad examples in the sanctions of Frankish charters, particularly those of Cluny; see Eric John, *Land Tenure in Early England* (Leicester, 1964), 99 and n. 4. They (with Judas, cf. foll. note) also occur in the sanction of the diploma of A.D. 990 of Duke Richard I of Normandy in favour of the abbey of Fécamp; see Marie Fauroux

Iuda[16] et Nerone .[17] et cum his qui Domino Deo dixerunt . recede a nobis quoniam nolumus scientiam uiarum tuarum[c] .[18] Amen .

and Judas[16] and Nero[17] and with those who have said to the Lord God 'Depart from us, we desire not the knowledge of thy ways'.[18] Amen.

[c] *Corrected in MS. from* situarum

(ed.), *Recueil des Actes des Ducs de Normandie (911–1066)* (Mémoires de la Société des Antiquaires de Normandie, 36, 1961), no. 4. They are referred to in S 201, 731, and 741 (spurious Anglo-Saxon diplomas). In the same period as the present document, they are quoted with reference to Picot, the Norman sheriff of Cambridgeshire, in the *Liber Eliensis*, book II, cap. 131; see E. O. Blake (ed.), *Liber Eliensis* (Camden, 3rd ser. 92, 1962), p. 211. They are also found in the sanction of William the Conqueror's original diploma in favour of St. Denis which was witnessed (*firmatum est*) during mass in Winchester Cathedral (*in monasterio Sancti Swiðun*) on 13 April 1069; see Bishop and Chaplais, plate XXVIII; and Bates *Regesta* 254.

[16] Judas Iscariot, the betrayer of Christ. Also cited in the sanction of the Fécamp diploma of 990 (see prec. note).

[17] The Emperor Nero, A.D. 54–68.

[18] *Deo dixerunt . recede a nobis quoniam nolumus scientiam uiarum tuarum.* Job 21: 14.

XII

Windsor, Berks., [29 May 1110], confirmation of grant by King Henry I to the Old Minster and to Bishop William Giffard of Winchester, of a fair for 8 days at the church of St. Giles on the eastern hill of Winchester and all royal profits in the city during the same period; i.e. for the 3 days which King William II had granted them and for 5 extra days now granted in exchange for the land of the bishopric recently given for the new site of the New Minster outside the north gate of the city

Latin

Regesta ii, no. 947

THIS document and the four that follow (**XIII–XVI**) form a group of texts relating to the period 1110 × 1116 when the New Minster moved to Hyde and established fiscal and judicial rights over its new site.[1] The move entailed a redistribution of land and/or rights at Winchester between the New and Old Minsters, the bishop, and the king. According to the present document (and corroborated by **XIII**, below), the king acquired land for (part of) the new site of the abbey from the bishop in return for an increase to 8 days of the annual duration of St. Giles's Fair at Winchester, with its associated profits, from the 3 days granted to the Old Minster and the bishop's predecessor by William II in 1096.[2]

The text is almost certainly based, with expansions and substitutions, on that of the writ-charter recording William II's grant of St. Giles's Fair, mentioned above.[3] However, the individuals named are consistent with the period 1107 × 1111, while the reference to the confirmation of the transaction at Windsor at Pentecost limits the year to 1110.[4] There is no reason to doubt the authenticity of the document.

The document survives only in two medieval copies, one in a Winchester cathedral cartulary and the other in a royal Charter Roll. Most of the variants are those of punctuation or of the spelling of names; in regard to the latter, MS. C represents a better text.[5]

---

[1] See WS 1, 318, 266–7; and *Winchester ann.*, s.a. 1110.

[2] See *Regesta* i, no. 377, and *Cal Chart R 1300–26*, 351. For later extensions to 14 days by King Stephen and to 16 days by Henry II, see ibid. 352, 355; *Regesta* iii, no. 952; and BL, Add. Chart. 28658. On 5 October 1349, the bishop exhibited at an inquest at Alton the charters concerning the fair which had been issued by William II, Henry I, Stephen, and Henry II; see *Cal Inq Misc 1348–77*, no. 25.

[3] See the edition in *Cal Chart R 1300–26*, 351. Compare, for example, the dating-formula in **XII** with that given for William

II's grant: *Hoc donum confirmatum est apud Hastingas quando rex predictus perrexit in Normanniam pro concordia Rodberti comitis fratris sui euntis Ierosolymam* ['This gift was confirmed at Hastings when the king went to Normandy to make an agreement with his brother Count Robert who was going to Jerusalem']. However, this shows confusion between Count Robert of Flanders and Duke Robert of Normandy, brother of William II.

[4] See *Regesta* ii, no. 947n.

[5] Cf. below, **XII**, nn. *c, h, j, m, r, t,* and *bb.*

MSS.:   B. WCL, W52/74 [St. Swithun's Cartulary], vol. 1, fo. 4ʳ (s.xiii/xiv)
          C. PRO, Chart R 10 Edward II (C53/103), no. 3 (s.xiv¹)

Edited: *Cal Chart R 1300–26*, 351–2, from C
        Goodman *Winchester Chartulary* 21 (calendar) from B

Printed from C collated with B

Henricus*ᵃ* ¹ Dei gratia rex Anglorum Willelmo de Ponte Arc'*ᵇ* ² vicecomiti et Herberto camerario*ᶜ* ³ et Henrico de Portu⁴ et omnibus fidelibus suis Francis et Anglis et*ᵈ* tocius regni Anglie :*ᵉ* salutem . Sciatis me dedisse et concessisse Deo et sancto Petro et sancto Suithuno*ᶠ* Veteris Monasterii et Willelmo Gifardo*ᵍ* ⁵ episcopo et monachis inibi seruientibus vnam feriam⁶ ad ecclesiam sancti Egidii que sita est in monte orientali Winton'*ʰ* et omnes redditus meos et iusticias meas que ad me pertinent in Winton'*ʲ* ciuitate per octo dies integros—*ᵏ*tres videlicet dies quos frater meus rex Willelmus⁷ eis concessit⁸ et post illos tres dies quinque dies⁹ ex mea parte 'in' excambium*ˡ* terre quam ego donaui de terra episcopatus¹⁰ concessu ipsius Willelmi episcopi Gaufrido¹¹ abbati Winton'*ᵐ* in quam

Henry,¹ by the grace of God king of the English, to William of Pont de l'Arche,² sheriff, and Herbert the chamberlain,³ and Henry de Port,⁴ and to all his faithful people, French and English, of the whole kingdom of England, greeting. Know that I have given and granted to God and St. Peter and St. Swithun of the Old Minster, and to Bishop William Giffard⁵ and to the monks serving therein, a fair⁶ at the church of St. Giles which lies on the eastern hill of Winchester and all the rents and profits of justice which belong to me in the city of Winchester for 8 full days, namely the 3 days which my brother King William⁷ granted⁸ them and 5 days after those 3 days,⁹ on my own account, in exchange for the land which I have given from the land of the bishopric,¹⁰ with the consent of the aforesaid Bishop William, to Geoffrey,¹¹ abbot of Winchester, on to which

ᵃ Henricus . B *where the document is introduced by the heading* Carta de feria sancti Egidii per octo dies : 'Charter concerning St Giles's Fair for 8 days'   *ᵇ* Pont'Arch' . B   *ᶜ* Cam' . B
ᵈ et *lacking* B   *ᵉ* : *lacking* B   *ᶠ* Swithuno B
ᵍ Giffardo B   *ʰ* Wynt' B   *ʲ* Wynton' B
ᵏ Point B   *ˡ* escambium B   *ᵐ* Wynton' . B

¹ King Henry I, 1100–35. See also below, **XIII–XVI**.
² From Pont de l'Arche (Eure), see Tengvik, 108. William was sheriff of Hampshire for most of Henry I's reign. He was also sheriff of Berkshire 1129–30 and possibly at another time of Sussex. He purchased the office of chamberlain of the treasury *c.*1130. He was dead by 1148. See WS 1, 33, 390–1; Green, 198–9, 267–8. Note that *Regesta* ii, no. 948 (*CW* 247), in which he is named as sheriff of Wiltshire, seems to be a forgery based on the present document and connected with the cathedral priory's claim to rent at Buttermere, Wilts. He was also the principal addressee of **XV**, below.
³ Herbert was chamberlain of the treasury under William II and royal treasurer under Henry I. He died by 1130, possibly in 1128, according to WS 1, 33, 390; or in 1118, see Green, 32–3.
⁴ Henry was the son of Hugh de Port (see above, **XI**, n. 7); see *Regesta* i, no. 379. He had been sheriff of Hampshire, 1101–?1106; see WS 1, 40. He may have acted as a local justiciar in

Kent 1120 × 1130; see *Regesta* ii, p. xix. He occurs in 1136 as a witness to *Regesta* iii, no. 944, and earlier in **XIII–XIV**, below; cf. also **XVI**. He appears to have been succeeded by his son John by 1148–9; see WS 1, 70.
⁵ William Giffard, bishop of Winchester, 1100–29; see Le Neve, *Fasti, 1066–1300*, ii, *Monastic Cathedrals*, 85. He also occurs below, in **XIII** and **XVII**.
⁶ *feriam*. St. Giles's Fair; see WS 1, 286–8. For the later medieval history of the fair and its site; see WS 2.ii, 1091–1133. See also below, **XIII**. For grants or confirmations of fairs elsewhere by Henry I, see *Regesta* ii, p. xxiv.
⁷ King William II, 1087–1100.
⁸ *tres dies . . . quos frater meus rex Willelmus eis concessit.* See *Regesta* i, no. 377 (A.D. 1096), and above, p. 163.
⁹ *octo dies integros . . . quinque dies ex mea parte.* See *Regesta* ii, no. 949 for a general ratification of Henry I's grant of the 8-day fair which does not refer to the exchange of land.
¹⁰ *terre quam ego donaui de terra episcopatus.* At Hyde, formerly part of the episcopal estate of Easton; see below, **XIII**, n. 4, and **XXII**, n. 3.
¹¹ Geoffrey, abbot of the New Minster, ?1106–1124; see *HRH*, 82. He also occurs below in **XIII**.

ipse Gaufridus abbas remouit ecclesiam suam extra septentrionalem portam ciuitatis et hoc pro anima patris mei et matris et fratris et pro incolumitate corporis mei et coniugis ac heredum meorum et salute animarum nostrarum omniumque^n predecessorum et successorum meorum ita plenarie et quiete cum omnibus consuetudinibus sicut eam haberem si mea propria esset—^{o}Et hoc volo et precipio vt^p omnes ad eam[12] venientes et ibi morantes et inde redeuntes pacem meam habeant—^{q}Hoc donum confirmatum est apud Windresore^r[13] ad Pentecosten^s[14] quando rex reuersus est a Douera^t[15] post colloquium sui^u et Roberti^v[16] comitis Flandrensis^w—^{x}His^y testibus^z Rogero[17] episcopo Salesberie^{aa} et Roberto[18] episcopo Linc'^{bb} et^{cc} Rannulfo cancellario^{dd}[19] et^{ee} Gislberto^{ff} de Aquila^{gg}[20] et^{hh} Haimone dapifero^{ij}[21] et Willelmo de Albinii[.]^{kk}[22]

the said Abbot Geoffrey has removed his church outside the north gate of the city; and this [I have done] for the souls of my father and mother and brother, and for the health of my body and [those] of my wife and heirs, and for the salvation of our souls and [those] of all my predecessors and successors, as fully and [as] quit, with all customary dues, as I would have were it my own. And this I wish and command, that all who come to it[12] and stay there and return thence should have my peace. This gift was confirmed at Windsor,[13] at Pentecost[14] when the king returned from Dover[15] after the discussions between him and Robert,[16] count of Flanders; with these witnesses, Roger,[17] bishop of Salisbury, and Robert,[18] bishop of Lincoln, and Ranulf the chancellor,[19] and Gilbert of Laigle,[20] and Hamo the steward,[21] and William d'Aubigny.[22]

---

^{n} omnique B ^{o} As note k ^{p} ut B ^{q} As note k ^{r} Wydeshores B ^{s} Pentecosten B ^{t} Douoria B ^{u} suum B ^{v} . R . B ^{w} Flandrie B ^{x} As note k ^{y} Hiis B ^{z} Point after testibus B ^{aa} Sar' B ^{bb} Lync' . B ^{cc} As note d ^{dd} Cant' . B ^{ee} As note d ^{ff} Gilb'o B ^{gg} Point after Aquila B ^{hh} As note d ^{ij} Point after dapifero B ^{kk} Albigni . B

---

[12] ad eam. That is, to St. Giles's Fair.

[13] Windsor, Berks. **XIV** and **XV**, below, were also dated there. Regesta ii, nos. 944–5, and probably 946 and 949, were issued on the same occasion. For Regesta ii, no. 948, see above, n. 2. On the dating-clause, see above, p. 163, n. 3.

[14] ad Pentecosten. 29 May 1110.   [15] Dover, Kent.

[16] Count Robert II of Flanders, 1092–1111. The 'discussions' resulted in the renewal, on 17 May 1110, of the treaty of 10 March 1101 concerning the money fief held by the count from King Henry; see Regesta ii, nos. 941 and 515, and Frank Barlow, The Feudal Kingdom of England, 1042–1216 (2nd edn., London, 1961), 175, 194.

[17] Roger, bishop of Salisbury; nominated 1102, consecrated 1107, died 1139. He was King Henry's chief minister; see WS 1,

46; E. J. Kealey, Roger of Salisbury, Viceroy of England (Berkeley, Calif., 1972); and Green, 38–50, 273–4. He is also named as a witness to **XIII–XVI**, below.

[18] Robert Bloet, bishop of Lincoln, 1093–1123; see Le Neve, Fasti, 1066–1300, iii, Lincoln Diocese, 1. He is also named as a witness to **XIII–XIV**, and **XVI**, below.

[19] Ranulf was chancellor, 1107–23; see Regesta ii, p. ix; and Green, 28.

[20] From Laigle (Orne, arr. Mortagne-sur-Huine); see Loyd, 52. Gilbert witnessed documents of Henry I up to 1114 and died in 1118; see Regesta ii, no. 1404 n; and Green, 179. He may be the same as Gilbert son of Richere of Laigle, a tenant-in-chief TRW in both Surrey and Norfolk: DB, i, fo. 36^r, and DB, ii, fo.263^r (DB Surrey 24; and DB Norfolk 42).

[21] Hamo was one of the three stewards of Henry I who had previously served William II. He was both steward and sheriff of Kent in succession to his father of the same name, and died c.1114; see Green, 195, 201.

[22] From Saint-Martin-d'Aubigny (La Manche); see Loyd, 7, and Tengvik, 67. He was the royal master-butler (1101–) and died in 1139; see WS 1, 36, 39, 390; and Green, 169 n, 229–30. He also witnessed **XV**, below. For his brother Nigel, see below, **XIII**, n. 38.

XIII

Westbourne, Sussex, 13 September 1114, declaration by King Henry I of the agreement between Bishop William [Giffard] of Winchester, and Abbot Geoffrey of the New Minster, concerning the removal of the monastery to Hyde, the grant of Worthy [Abbotts Barton], Hants, and the settlement of their dispute about arrangements for the annual Palm Sunday procession; also referring to the grant by the king to the bishop of 5 extra days for St. Giles's Fair

Latin

Regesta ii, no. 1070[1]

THE present document preserves unique information about the complicated series of territorial exchanges associated with the migration of the New Minster to Hyde. It also informs us about alterations in the role of the abbot of New Minster-Hyde in celebration at Winchester of major religious festivals, particularly in connection with the Palm Sunday procession, which in its latter part became in effect subdivided between the cathedral and Hyde Abbey.[2] It further records how the abbot's duties in regard to synods at Winchester were preserved after the move out of the city. It also concerns the division of parochial rights between the abbot and the bishop and the preservation of the citizens' rights of burial in the New Minster. Incidental references are made to property or locations in the city and in the western and northern suburbs. The terms of the agreement between the abbot and the bishop were guaranteed by being recorded in a document issued by Henry I, who seems to have acted as a mediator between the two ecclesiastics and to have contributed to the success of the arrangements himself by augmenting the cathedral's rights at St. Giles's Fair.[3]

The text takes the form of a royal charter declaring the terms of the agreement. The individuals named are consistent with the date given,[4] while the grant relating to St. Giles's Fair is more fully recorded in **XII**, above.

XIII may have been issued as a chirograph, with one part given to the abbot and one to the bishop, and possibly one retained by the king. The surviving MSS. can be divided between those (C and E; whence F and G) stemming from the abbey's original and others (B and D) which stem from the cathedral's. The latter's original appears to have been extant in 1349.[5] MS. C omits some words

---

[1] With incorrect reference to MS. G, m. 4.
[2] See below, **XIII**, nn. 16 and 20.
[3] Cf. above, **XII**.

[4] Cf. the witnesses to *Regesta* ii, nos. 1060–9, 1071–2, documents which were probably issued on the same occasion.
[5] See below, **XIII**, n. 10.

of text and witnesses but these seem to have been present in the abbey's exemplar, as they do occur in MS. E.[6]

<hr>

[6] Ibid., nn. *v*, (second) *x*, and (third) *s*. Both C and E omit *in* on one occasion (first n. *mm*).

MSS.:   B. HRO, Reg Pontissara, fos. 109^v–110^r (s.xiii/xiv)

             C. BL, Cotton MS. Domitian xiv, fo. 22^r (s.xiii^2; incomplete)

             D. PRO, Chart R 10 Edward II (C53/103), no. 9 (s.xiv^1)

             E. PRO, Chart R 4 Edward III (C53/117), no. 85 (s.xiv^1)

             F. *lost*, Letters Patent, 1 November 1 Richard II (s.xiv^2), inspeximus, from E

             G. PRO, Pat R 16 Edward IV, part 2 (C66/539), m. 9 (s.xv^2), from F

Edited: *Monasticon*, ii, 444, from C

             ibid. 444–5, from G (with incorrect reference to Chart R 16 Edward IV)

             Cal Pat R 1476–85, 17, calendar from G

             Cal Chart R 1300–26, 346–7, from D

             Cal Chart R 1327–41, 170–1, from E

             Reg Pontissara, 439–41, from B

Printed from D collated with B, C, and E; G is secondary.

Henricus[a][1]. rex Anglorum archiepiscopis et episcopis et omnibus baronibus Francis et Anglis[b] tocius[c] Anglie salutem . Sciatis quod hanc conuencionem fecit Willelmus[2] Winton'[d] episcopus cum Gaufrido[e][3] abbate sancti Petri Noui Monasterii coram me et baronibus meis . Reddidit ipse episcopus in manu mea Hydam[f][4] in [qua][g] nunc sedet abbatia[h] sancti Petri et preter hanc quandam terram[5] que est ex ea[j] parte in qua abbatia[k] est in qua sunt domus reddentes [.] vii [.][l] solidos .[m] per annum[n] et preter hanc :[o] manerium quod dicitur Wrdie[6] [.][p] Et ego dedi et concessi ipsam Hydam[q] cum predictis [.] vii [.][r] solidatis terre et ipsam terram Wrdie[s] monasterio sancti Petri et abbati et monachis iure perpetuo possidendam[t] ita liberam et quietam sicut quilibet Winton'[u] episcopus melius et liberius ipsam terram[v] vnquam[w] vna die tenuit[x] et sicut abbatia[y] sancti Petri vel[z] abbas quilibet eiusdem loci terram[aa] in qua prius abbatia[bb] in ciuitate sedit[cc][7] melius et liberius vnquam[dd] habuit[ee] et [.] *Willelmus* .[ff] episcopus predictus concessit perenniter[gg] monasterio sancti Petri et abbati parrochiam[hh] harum terrarum et quicquid[jj] pertinebat ad ecclesiam[8] Wrdie[kk] preter episcopalia in uiuis[ll]

Henry,[1] king of the English, to the archbishops and bishops and all the barons, French and English, of the whole of England, greeting. Know that William,[2] bishop of Winchester, has made this agreement with Geoffrey,[3] abbot of St. Peter of the New Minster, in the presence of me and my barons. The said bishop surrendered into my hand Hyde,[4] on which the abbey of St. Peter now stands, as well as that land[5] in the direction of the abbey on which are houses yielding 7 shillings a year, and also the manor which is called Worthy.[6] And I have given and granted the same Hyde, with the aforesaid 7 shillings' worth of land and the said estate of Worthy, to the monastery of St. Peter and the abbot and the monks, to be possessed in perpetual right so free and quit as any bishop of Winchester ever on one day held the said land for the better or the freer, and as the abbey of St. Peter or any abbot of the same place ever had the land on which the abbey formerly stood[7] in the city for the better or the freer. And the aforesaid Bishop William granted to the monastery of St. Peter and the abbot parochial rights in perpetuity (apart from the episcopal dues) over these lands and everybody who used to belong to the church[8] of Worthy,

---

[a] *Henricus* C. *In* B *the document is introduced by the following rubric:* Conuencio facta inter Willelmum episcopum Wynton' et abbatem sancti Petri Noui Monasterii quam inspexit dominus rex . 'Agreement made between William, bishop of Winchester and the abbot of St. Peter's of the New Minster, which the lord king inspected.' *In* C *the rubric is:* Carta de remocione abbacie de Hyda et excambio. 'Charter concerning the removal of the abbey of Hyde and the exchange.'   [b] *Sic* B, C, E; Anglicis D   [c] totius E. *In* B *there is an otiose abbreviation for* -us   [d] Wynton' B   [e] Gaufrido B, Gauf' E   [f] Hidam B, hydam E   [g] *MS. damaged* D; qua B, C, E   [h] abbathia B, C; abbacia E   [j] ea *omitted* E   [k] *As above, n. h*   [l] . vii . B, E; septem C   [m] *Point lacking* B, C, E   [n] *Point after* annum B, C   [o] *Punctuation lacking* B, C, E   [p] Wordie . B, Wordya . C   [q] *As above, n. f*   [r] . vii . B, septem C, E   [s] Wordie B, Word' C   [t] *Point after* possidendam C   [u] Wynton' B, Wintoniensis E   [v] ipsam terram *omitted* C   [w] vmquam B   [x] *Point after* tenuit C   [y] abathia B, abbathia C   [z] uel B, C   [aa] eiusdem terram loci B   [bb] abbathia B, C   [cc] *Point after* sedit C   [dd] nunquam B   [ee] *Point after* habuit B, C   [ff] . W. C; W E   [gg] perhenniter B, C, E   [hh] parochiam B   [jj] quotquot B

[kk] de Wordie B, Word' C   [ll] viuis B, C, E

---

[1] King Henry I, 1100–35.

[2] Bishop William Giffard; see above, **XII**, n. 5.

[3] Ibid. n. 11.

[4] *Hydam*. Land to the north of the city which was to form the precinct of the new site of the abbey; see WS 1, 318, 266. This was formerly part of the episcopal estate of Easton; see below, **XXII** n. 3. The New Minster already held the land called Hyde Moors (see above, **IX**, n. 5) and the abbey church and conventual buildings seem to have been built on its western edge; see WS 1, ibid. See Figs. 2 and 9.

[5] *quandam terram*. Probably in Hyde Street; see WS 1, ibid.

[6] *manerium quod dicitur Wrdie*. Little Worthy, later Abbotts Barton; see ibid. This was formerly part of the episcopal estate of Easton; see below, **XXII**, n. 3.

[7] *terram in qua prius abbatia . . . sedit*. Adjacent and to the north of the Old Minster; see above, **II**; WS 1, 313–17, and ibid. Fig. 9. Cf. below, **XV**, n. 7.

[8] *ecclesiam*. This may have been the church, dedicated to St. Gertrude, in the meadows to the north of Abbotts Barton; see WS 1, 266, n. 5, and 318; cf. WS 2.ii, 954.

et in*mm* mortuis et decimis 'et' sepulturis et oblacionibus sicut ipsam ecclesiam*nn* episcopatus vel*oo* ipsius ecclesie quilibet episcopus ea melius et liberius vnquam*pp* vna die tenuit . Similiter abbas *Gaufridus*qq reddidit*rr* in manu mea ad opus predicti episcopi . *Willelmi* . et ecclesie beatorum apostolorum Petri et Pauli vbi sedes est episcopalis[9] terram intra ciuitatem in qua prius fuit abbatia*ss* [10] cum capellis et domibus et molendinis que sunt infra ambitum ipsius terre [.]*tt* et preterea terram totam de Derleia[11] [.]*uu* Et ego easdem terras eidem episcopo et ecclesie sue concessi et dedi iure perpetuo possidendas*vv* et illam in qua abbatia*ww* erat ita liberam et quietam ab omni consuetudine[12] sicut erat quando abbatia*ww* in ea*xx* sedit et terram*yy* de Durleia*zz* sicut aliquis abbas eam melius vnquam*a* habuit [.]*b* Et ego insuper ex mea parte*c* concessi et dedi ipsi*d* episcopo et episcopali ecclesie . v .*e* dies in feria sancti Egidii[13] super illos tres dies quos prius habebat .*f* et hoc pro escambio illius hyde*g* in qua nunc abbatia*h* sedet*j* Et preter hec*k* ipse abbas concessit episcopo et ecclesie sue corpora mortuorum terre sue proprie quam ipse abbas ea die infra muros ciuitatis habebat .*l* Si qua vero terra post diem facte conuencionis in proprietatem abbatis et monasterii sui uenerit :*m* episcopus Winton'*n* in eius sepulturis vel*o* corporibus nil clamabit .*p* nisi prius ecclesia episcopalis ea per consuetudinem habuit .*q* Illi

concerning both the living and the dead, in tithes and in burial-fees and in oblations, even as the bishopric, or any bishop of the said church, ever on one day held the said church for the better or the freer. Similarly, Abbot Geoffrey surrendered into my hand, to the use of the aforesaid Bishop William and of the church of the blessed apostles Peter and Paul where the episcopal see is,[9] the land within the city on which the abbey formerly was,[10] with the chapels and houses and mills which are within the boundaries of the said land, and, besides, the whole estate of Durley.[11] And I have granted and given the same lands to the same bishop and his church to be possessed in perpetual right; and that on which the abbey was [is to be possessed] free and quit from all customary dues[12] as it was when the abbey stood on it, and the estate of Durley [is to be possessed] as any abbot ever had it for the better. And I in addition, on my own account, have granted and given to the said bishop and to the episcopal church 5 days for St. Giles's Fair[13] in addition to those 3 days which it already had, and this in exchange for that hide on which the abbey now stands. And besides these things, the said abbot granted to the bishop and his church the bodies of the dead of his own land which on that day the said abbot had within the walls of the city. If indeed any land should come into the ownership of the abbot and his monastery after the day on which this agreement was made, the bishop of Winchester shall claim nothing in respect of its burial-fees or corpses unless the episcopal church had them before according to custom.

mm in *omitted* C, E   *nn* ipsa ecclesia C   *oo* As above, n. z   *pp* As above, n. w   *qq* . G . B, C; G . E   *rr* tradidit B   *ss* As above, n. bb   *tt* Point after terre B, C   *uu* Durleia . B, E; Burleia . C   *vv* Point after possidendas B   *ww* As above, n. bb   *xx* mea *for* in ea E   *yy* terra E   *zz* Burleia C   *a* As above, n. w   *b* Point after habuit B, C   *c* ex parte mea E   *d* ipso C   *e* quinque B, C   *f* Point lacking B, C, E   *g* Hyde B, C   *h* abbathia B, C; abbacia E   *j* Point lacking E   *k* hoc C   *l* Point lacking B, C   *m* venerit B, venerit . C, E   *n* Wynton' B   *o* As above, n. z   *p* Point lacking B, E   *q* Point lacking C

[9] *ecclesie . . . vbi sedes est episcopalis.* The Old Minster or cathedral priory.

[10] *terram . . . in qua prius fuit abbatia.* As above, n. 7. In 1349 a

lawsuit over this land occurred between the bishop and the citizens and was settled in the bishop's favour through the production of the cathedral's part of (?the original of) the present document and its confirmation by Edward II (cf. MS. D); see *Cal Pat R 1348–50*, 384–5, 424–6. See also below, n. 15.

[11] Durley, Hants, was a detached part of the New Minster estate which was centred on Micheldever; see above, **III**, n. 29.

[12] *ab omni consuetudine.* Apparently those specified in **XV**, below, as 'gelds and other plaints'.

[13] *feria sancti Egidii.* See above, **XII**, n. 6.

vero*r* qui in terra mea vel*s* baronum[14] meorum in ciuitate manent :*t* libere apud abbatiam*u* Noui Monasterii iacere poterunt*v* si volunt .*w* sicut poterant[15] antequam monasterium transferretur .*x*

De processione Ramispalmarum[16] vnde inter eos fuerat dissensio hoc statutum est :*y* Quod abbas cum duobus vel*z* quot voluerit monachis ad episcopalem ecclesiam veniet ~*aa* si processio ecclesie episcopalis ad sanctum Iacobum[17] sit itura*bb* et cum ipsa processione ad sanctum Iacobum ibit .*cc* Processio vero abbatie*dd* cum priore et reliquis*ee* supra castellum ei obuiam ueniet*ff* ante portam castelli[18] et cum episcopali processione apud*gg* sanctum Iacobum faciet stacionem[19] et reditum vsque ante portam ciuitatis de west ad propinquiorem vicum qui vocatur sancti Walarici*hh* [20] et inde cum suis reuertetur abbas ad monasterium suum . Si me receperit episcopus ueniet*jj* abbas cum toto conuentu ecclesie sue ad processionem illam . Si autem archiepiscopum vel*kk* aliam personam receperit :*ll* adducet abbas . x .*mm* monachos secum ad minus et

Those people, however, who dwell in the city on my land or on that of my barons[14] may be buried freely at the abbey of the New Minster if they wish, as they used to be able[15] before the monastery was moved.

This has been decided concerning the Palm Sunday procession,[16] about which there had been disagreement between them. That, if a procession of the episcopal church should be going to St. James's,[17] the abbot shall come to the episcopal church with two monks, or with as many monks as he wishes, and go with the said procession to St. James's. The abbey's procession, with the prior and relics, shall come above the cas. to meet it before the gate[18] of the castle and shall make a 'station'[19] with the episcopal procession at St. James's and the return to before the west gate of the city, as far as the closest street, which is called St. Valery's,[20] and the abbot with his people shall return from there to his monastery. If the bishop is going to receive me, the abbot shall come, with the whole convent of his church, to that procession. If moreover he [the bishop] is going to receive the archbishop or another personage, the abbot shall bring at least ten monks with him and

---

r uero B   *s* As above, n. z   *t* Punctuation lacking B, E; point C   *u* abbathiam B, C   *v* Point after poterunt B   *w* Point lacking B, E   *x* C omits subsequent material up to note ww below   *y* Punctuation lacking C, D, E   *z* uel B   *aa* Punctuation lacking B, E   *bb* Point after itura B   *cc* Point lacking B   *dd* uero abbathie B   *ee* reliquiis B   *ff* veniet B, E   *gg* ad B   *hh* Walerici B   *jj* veniet B, E   *kk* uel B   *ll* Punctuation lacking B, E   *mm* decem B, E

[14] *terra mea vel baronum meorum.* For the king's fief in Winchester in *c.*1110 and 1148, see WS 1, 350–3; for the *terra baronum* or *terra de . B .*, see ibid. 12, 19–25, 353–5. Rents from the latter in 1148 appear to be associated with the earlier royal fief, including the palace site; ibid. 354.

[15] *iacere . . . poterant.* On the citizens' right of burial in the New Minster, see WS 1, 314; and below, **XVII**. Attempts by the bishop and the monks of the cathedral to bury victims of the Black Death in the former site and graveyard of the New Minster were, however, frustrated by the citizens in 1349 until the bishop won the lawsuit referred to above, n. 10. The citizens at that time were more interested in using the land for purposes of commerce or building. For successive encroachments on to the former precinct of the New Minster in the later medieval period, see WS 2.ii, 547–8, and ibid. Fig. 61.

[16] *processione Ramispalmarum.* For this liturgical procession and its significance, see WS 1, 268–9. For a description of such a procession at Canterbury in the late 11th cent., see David Knowles (ed.), *The Monastic Constitutions of Lanfranc* (London, 1951), 22–6, 151–2. For liturgical processions at Winchester in the later medieval period, see WS 2.i, 128.

[17] *ad sanctum Iacobum.* The church of St. James which stood on the road to Salisbury, just within the outer limit of the suburb outside the west gate of Winchester; see WS 1, 264–5; WS 2.ii, 1036–7. This was probably where the palms were blessed; see WS 1, 268.

[18] *portam castelli.* The principal gate of the castle seems at this time to have been in approximately its later position; see WS 1, 303 and n. 4.

[19] *faciet stationem.* That is, the procession will halt at St. James's and sing relevant parts of the liturgy. Cf. the description of such a *statio* at Canterbury in the late 11th century in Knowles, *Monastic Constitutions*, 24.

[20] *vicum . . . sancti Walarici.* Now Sussex Street, but in the 12th century named by reference to the church of St. Valery, for which see WS 1, **I, 107** and WS 2.ii, 936–7. It would appear that the abbot did not reenter the city with his monks but instead formed with them a separate procession back to his own abbey.

intererit processioni . Secunda vero[nn] die Natiui-
tatis et Pasche et Pentecostes[oo] et in vna festiui-
tate sancti Petri quam episcopus elegerit[pp] abbas
si episcopus eum vocauerit ad episcopalem
ecclesiam veniet cum quot voluerit monachis[qq]
et episcopo[rr] seruiet in celebracione missarum et
cum eo comedet [.][ss] Seruiet eciam[tt] ei abbas
quando missam dicet episcopus ad curiam
meam [.][uu] Ad synodum[vv] quoque veniet si
episcopus eum vocauerit ad danda consilia
episcopo et iudicia facienda ecclesiastica et
audienda precepta episcopi .

Hec[ww] conuencio facta et confirmata est
apud Burnam[xx] [21] anno ab incarnacione
Domini . m . centesimo[yy] . xiiii .[zz] die Idum[a]
Septembrium .[b] presentibus hiis testibus [.][c]
Rad*ulfo*[22] Cantuarie[d] archiepiscopo [.][e] Tur-
stino[23] Eboracensi[f] archiepiscopo . Ric*ardo*[24]
Lundoniensi[g] episcopo .[h] Rogero[25] Salesb'[j]
episcopo . Rodberto[26] Lincolie[k] episcopo [.][l]
Ioh*anne*[27] Batoniensi[m] episcopo [.][n] Will*elmo*[28]
Exonie[o] episcopo . Rann*ulfo*[29] Dunelmensi[p]

enter the procession. On the second day of
Christmas indeed, and at Easter and at Pentecost, and on one of the feast-days of St. Peter
which the bishop shall choose, the abbot, with as
many monks as he wishes, shall come to the
episcopal church, should the bishop summon
him, and shall serve the bishop in the celebration of masses and shall eat with him. The abbot
shall also serve him when the bishop says mass at
my court. He shall also come to a synod, should
the bishop summon him, to give advice to the
bishop and to give ecclesiastical judgements and
to hear the bishop's commands.

This agreement was made and confirmed at
Westbourne[21] on 13 September in the 1114th
year from the Lord's Incarnation, in the
presence of these witnesses: Ralph,[22] archbishop of Canterbury; Thurstan,[23] archbishop
of York; Richard,[24] bishop of London; Roger,[25]
bishop of Salisbury; Robert,[26] bishop of Lincoln; John,[27] bishop of Bath; William,[28] bishop
of Exeter; Ranulf,[29] bishop of Durham;

[nn] uero B   [oo] Pentecost' B   [pp] elegerit : B
[qq] *Point after* monachis B   [rr] *Sic* B, E; ipso D
[ss] com'edet . B; comedet . E   [tt] etiam E. *The word is
represented in* B *by an abbreviation-mark*   [uu] *Point after*
meam B, E   [vv] sinodum B   [ww] C *starts again here*
[xx] Burnham . B, Burnham C   [yy] . m⁰. c⁰ . B; . m⁰ . c . C
[zz] quartodecimo B   [a] Iduu' B, C; Iduum E
[b] Septembr' . B, Septembr' C   [c] *Point after* testibus B, C
[d] Rad'o Cant' B, Rad' Cant' C, Radulfo Cant' E   [e] *Point
after* archiepiscopo C   [f] Thurstino Ebor' B, Thurstino
Ebora's C, Turstano Eboracen' E. *In* E *this witness is an interlined
insertion*   [g] Ric'o London' B, C; Ricardo Lundoniensi E
[h] *Point lacking after this and all subsequent witnesses except the final
one* E   [j] Rog'o Sarr' B, Reg' Salesb' C, Rog'io Salesb'ie E
[k] Rob'to Lincoln' B, Rob'to Lyncoln' C, Rodb'to Lincolie E
[l] *Point after* episcopo C   [m] Ioh'e Bathon' B, C; Ioh'e
Batoniensi E   [n] *Point after this and subsequent witnesses in* B
to end of text; ditto in C *as far as note* s *below*   [o] Will'o
Exonien' B, C; Will'o Exon' E   [p] Ran' Dunelm' B,
Ranulfo Dunelmensi C, E

---

[21] Westbourne, Sussex, on the road from Chichester to
Portsmouth (*PN Sussex*, 55). *Regesta* ii, no. 1071, in favour of
the cathedral priory, was probably issued on the same occasion.
[22] Ralph d'Escures; elected archbishop of Canterbury on 26
April 1114 and died on 19 or 20 October 1122; see Le Neve,
Fasti, 1066–1300, ii, *Monastic Cathedrals*, 3–4.

[23] Although Thurstan was elected archbishop of York at
Winchester on 16 August 1114, he was only ordained as deacon
in September × December 1114, by Bishop William Giffard
(above, n. 2). Due to the dispute between the churches of
Canterbury and York over his profession of obedience, he was
unable to be consecrated in England. He resigned on 19 March
1116, went abroad, and obtained consecration by Pope Calixtus
II at Rheims on 19 October 1119. He resigned finally on 25
January 1140 and died on 5 February. See *HBC*, 281; and Charles
Johnson (ed. and trans.), revised M. Brett, C. N. L. Brooke, and
M. Winterbottom, *Hugh the Chanter: The History of the Church of
York 1066–1127* (Oxford, 1990), 56–9.
[24] Richard of Beaumais (de Belmeis I), bishop of London
1108–27; see Le Neve, *Fasti, 1066–1300*, i, *St. Paul's, London*, 1.
[25] See above, **XII**, n. 17.
[26] Ibid. n. 18.
[27] John de Villula, bishop of Wells 1088–90, of Bath 1090–
1122.
[28] William Warelwast, bishop of Exeter 1107–37. He is also
named below as a witness to **XIV** and **XVI**.
[29] Ranulf Flambard, bishop of Durham 1099–1128; see Le
Neve, *Fasti, 1066–1300*, ii, *Monastic Cathedrals*, 29. He appears to
have been in charge of the New Minster from 1088 to 1090/1
and to have held a tenement outside North Gate before *c*.1110;
see WS 1, **I**, **163** and n. He was commemorated in *LVH*, 67. For
his career, see R. W. Southern, 'Ranulf Flambard', in *Medieval
Humanism and Other Studies* (Oxford, 1984), 183–205.

episcopo . Rodberto[30] comite[q] de Mellent[r] [.] Heanrico[31] comite de Waruuic[s] [.] Waltero constabulario[t] [.][32] Willelmo camerario de Tan-cardeuilla[u] [.][33] Adam de Port[v] [.][34] Nigello de Oillei[w] [.][35] Heanrico de Port[x] [.][36] Radulfo de Limesi[y] [.][37] Nigello de Alb' :[z] [38]

Robert,[30] count of Meulan; Henry,[31] earl of Warwick; Walter the constable;[32] William of Tancarville,[33] the chamberlain; Adam de Port;[34] Nigel d'Oilli;[35] Henry de Port;[36] Ralph of Limésy;[37] Nigel d'Aubigny.[38]

---

[q] Ro'to com' B, Rob'to comite C, Rodb'to comite E   [r] de Meullent C, Demellent E   [s] Henr' comite Warwyk' B, Henr' comite de Warwyk' C, Henrico comite de Waruuic E. *The text in C ends here*   [t] Walt'o constabular' B, Walt'ro constabulario E   [u] Will'o camerar' de Tan-tardiuilla B, Will'o camerario Detancardiuilla E   [v] Ad' de Port B, Adam Deport E   [w] Nigell' de Eielit' B, Nigello Deoillei E   [x] Henr' de Port B, Henrico Deport E   [y] Edmundo (sic) de Lymisy B, Rad'o de Limesi E   [z] Nigell' de Abber . B, Nigello de Albinni . E

---

[30] Robert, count of Meulan, lord of Pontaudemer and Beaumont in Normandy, earl of Leicester in England, died 1118; see WS 1, 33, 56, and 390. He was also named below as a witness to **XIV** and **XVI**, and was the brother of Henry de Beaumont; see below, n. 31. For their careers, see D. B. Crouch, *The Beaumont Twins: The Careers of Waleran Count of Meulan and Robert Earl of Leicester* (Cambridge, 1986).

[31] Henry de Beaumont, earl of Warwick and the brother of Robert, count of Meulan; see above, n. 30. He died in 1119; see WS 1, 67, and 390.

[32] This is the first attestation of Walter of Gloucester as constable. He was also sheriff of Gloucestershire by 1100. He seems to have retired from office in 1126. See Green, 35, 195, and 257.

[33] William was the chamberlain of Normandy. He died in 1129; see *Regesta* ii, p. xv. He came from Tancarville (Seine-Inf.); see Loyd, 100.

[34] Adam son of Hubert, one of the Domesday commissioners for Worcestershire; see *Regesta* i, no. 221; cf. *Regesta* ii, no. 1000. He came from Port-en-Bessin (Calvados) and died c.1138; see Loyd, 79–80. He may have been sheriff of Herefordshire in 1130; see Green, 126. Although he occurs together with Hugh de Port and the latter's son Henry in a document of 1096 (*Regesta* i, no. 379), he seems to have belonged to a different branch of the family, associated with Mapledurwell, Hants, rather than with Basing; see Loyd, ibid.

[35] Perhaps from Ouilly-le-Basset (Calvados); see Tengvik, 103–4; and Green, 265. Nigel was a royal constable and died c.1115; see WS 1, 72; *Regesta* ii, p. xv.   [36] See above, **XII**, n. 4.

[37] Ralph II of Limésy. He died c.1129; see WS 1, 108. He came from Limésy (Seine-Inf.); see Loyd, 54; and Tengvik, 95.

[38] From St. Martin d'Aubigny (La Manche); see Loyd, 7; and Tengvik, 67. Nigel was the brother of William D'Aubigny (see above, **XII**, n. 22). On his death in 1118, he was Henry I's chief minister in the north of England; see Green, 246.

XIV

Windsor, Berks., [?2 February 1116], confirmation by King Henry I to Hyde Abbey, of the churches of Kingsclere and Alton, Hants, with 5 hides of land at Alton, as granted to them by King William I in exchange for the land in Winchester on which he built his hall; the said property to be held free of geld, murder-fine, pleas, and plaints, like the land in Winchester on which the king's house stands

Latin

Regesta ii, no. 1126[1]

THIS document is a confirmation by Henry I of most of the property granted by his father to the New Minster in **X**, above. One important omission, however, is the 4 hides and 1 yardland of land at Kingsclere mentioned both in William I's grant and in Domesday Book.[2] This land appears to have been taken back into royal hands at some time after 1086, since the manor is recorded as being granted in 1121 by Henry I to St. Mary's, Rouen.[3]

The text is that of a writ-charter giving general notification of the king's grant. The witnesses (1107 × 1118) and the place of issue are consistent with a date in 1116.[4] It may have been issued at the same time as **XV**, below. The witness-list was probably used as a source for that in **XVI**, below.[5]

The text has survived only in later transcripts. Of the two thirteenth-century ones, MS. B preserves place-name forms which are probably close to those in the lost original, but is unfortunately incomplete.[6] The original was apparently exhibited in the Curia Regis by the abbot of Hyde in 1204–5 in connection with a dispute over the advowson of the church of Binsted, an appurtenance of the church of Alton.[7] It was also inspected by the prior and convent of the cathedral *c.*1240.[8]

---

[1] With incorrect reference to Chart R, rather than to Pat R, 16 Edward IV.   [2] See above, **X**, n. 5.

[3] See *Regesta* ii, no. 1289. It may be significant that the archbishop of Rouen was in attendance at Windsor on 2 February 1116 when the present document appears to have been granted; see ibid. nos. 1124 and 1127.

[4] See below, **XIV**, n. 15.   [5] See below, p. 178.

[6] Cf. below, **XIV**, nn. *e*, *g*, *h*, *l*, *o*, and *s*.

[7] See *Curia Regis R 5–7 John*, 118–19 (Easter, 5–6 John) '*abbas de Hida . . . profert . . . cartam Henrici regis avi, in qua continentur quod ipse concessit et carta sua confirmavit deo et sancto Petro et abbati et monachis de Hida in liberam et perpetuam elemosinam ecclesias de Kingescler' et Aulton' cum capellis et decimis et omnibus pertinenciis suis et cum v. hidis terre in eadem villa Aulton', sicut rex Willelmus pater suus eis dedit in escambium pro terra illa in qua edificavit aulam suam in urbe Wintonie*'

['The abbot of Hyde . . .brings forth the charter of Henry, the king's grandfather [*rectius* great-grandfather], in which it is claimed that the same [Henry] confirmed in free and perpetual alms to God and St. Peter, and to the abbot and monks of Hyde, the churches of Kingsclere and Alton with their chapels and tithes and all their appurtenances, together with 5 hides of land in the same vill of Alton, even as his father King William gave [them] to them in exchange for their land on which he built his hall in the city of Winchester.'] Cf. above, p. 157, n. 14.

[8] See Goodman, *Chartulary*, no. 392 ('illegible in parts'). That a separate confirmation of **XIV** existed in *c.*1240 in the form of a now-lost *actum* of Bishop William Giffard has been postulated, apparently on the basis of Goodman's calendar entry, by M. J. Franklin (ed.), *English Episcopal Acta VIII: Winchester 1070–1204* (Oxford, 1993), 5 (no. 9).

MSS.: B. PRO, Chart Antiq (C52), 23, document Y (s.xiii)
C. PRO, Chart R 54 Henry III (C53/59), m. 4 (s.xiii^2)
D. PRO, Chart R 4 Edward III (C53/117), no. 85 (s.xiv^I), from C
E. *lost*, Letters Patent, 1 November 1 Richard II (s.xiv^2), inspeximus, from D
F. PRO, Pat R 16 Edward IV, part 2 (C66/539), m. 9 (s.xv^2), from E
G. BL, Harl. MS. 84, fo. 290^v (s.xvi), from B

Edited: *Monasticon*, ii, 444, from B
ibid. 445, from F
LVH, 291, from G
Cal Pat R 1476–85, 18, calendar from F
Cal Chart R 1257–1300, 148, from C
Cal Chart R 1327–41, 172, from D

Printed from B collated to C. B omits the subscriptions and place-date, which are supplied here from C.

Henr*icus*[a][1] rex Angl*orum* .[b] archiepiscopis . episcopis . abbatibus . comitibus . baronibus . vicecomitibus . ministris .[c] et omnibus fidelibus suis Francis et Anglis tocius Anglie salutem . Sciatis quod concessi .[d] et hac carta mea confirmaui Deo et sancto Petro et abbati atque monachis de Hida[e] . in lib[er]am[f] et perpetuam elemosinam ecclesias de Kyngesclera[g][2] et Aweltona[h][3] cum[j] capellis et decimis et omnibus pertinenciis suis . et cum . v . hydis[k] terre in eadem villa Aweltone[l] . sicut rex Will*elmus*[m][4] pater meus eis dedit in escambium[n][5] pro terra[6] illa in qua edificauit aulam[7] suam in urbe Winton'.[o] Et volo et firmiter precipio quod eas habeant et teneant solutas et quietas de geld' .[p] et de murdro[q] et de placitis et de omnibus querelis . sicut terra illa ubi[r] domus[8] mea sedit in

Henry,[1] king of the English, to the archbishops, bishops, abbots, earls, barons, sheriffs, ministers, and all his faithful people, French and English, of the whole of England, greeting. Know that I have granted and by this my charter have confirmed, in free and perpetual alms, to God and to St. Peter and to the abbot and monks of Hyde, the churches of Kingsclere[2] and Alton[3] with their chapels and tithes and all their appurtenances, together with 5 hides of land in the same vill of Alton; even as my father King William[4] gave [them] to them in exchange[5] for that land[6] on which he built his hall[7] in the city of Winchester. And I wish and firmly command that they should have and hold them free from debt, and quit of geld and of the murder-fine and of pleas and of all plaints, even as that land where my house[8] stands in Winchester has ever

[a] H' C; *in B the document is introduced by the heading* Carta abbatie de Hyda. scilicet regis Henrici primi. 'Charter of Hyde Abbey, that is of King Henry I.' [b] *Point lacking after* Anglorum C [c] *Point lacking after* ministris C [d] *Point lacking after* concessi C [e] Hyda C [f] liberam C [g] Kingeclere C [h] Aulton' C [j] cum cum B, *the first instance occurring at the end of a line and being repeated at the start of the next* [k] suis et cum quinque hidis C [l] Aulton' C [m] Will*elmus* C [n] excambium C [o] Wynton' C [p] *Point lacking after* geld' C [q] murdris C [r] vbi C

[1] King Henry I, 1100–35.
[2] Kingsclere, Hants. See above, **X**, n. 5.
[3] Alton, Hants. Ibid. n. 4.
[4] King William I, 1066–87.
[5] *dedit in escambium*. See above, **X**.
[6] *terra*. Ibid. n. 6.
[7] *aulam*. Ibid. n. 8.
[8] *domus*. Henry I's palace, on the same site as his father's; ibid. See also below, **XV**.

Winton'[s] : fuit unquam melius quieta .[9] Testibus[t] . Rogero[10] episcopo Sarr'. R[oberto][11] episcopo
Linc'. W[illelmo][12] episcopo Exon'. R[oberto][13]
comite de Mell'. H[enrico] de Port'.[14] Apud
Wyndes'.[15]

been the better quit.[9] Witnessed by Roger,[10]
bishop of Salisbury; Robert,[11] bishop of Lincoln;
William,[12] bishop of Exeter; Robert,[13] count of
Meulan; Henry de Port.[14] At Windsor.[15]

---

[s] Wynton' C   [t] Testibus C; B *finishes at this point. The
remaining text is supplied here from C*

---

[9] *quieta.* See ibid.
[10] Roger, bishop of Salisbury. See above, **XII**, n. 17.
[11] Robert, bishop of Lincoln. Ibid. n. 18.
[12] William, bishop of Exeter. See above, **XIII**, n. 28.

[13] Robert, count of Meulan. Ibid. n. 30.
[14] Henry de Port. See above, **XII**, n. 4.
[15] Windsor, Berks.; ibid. n. 13. *Regesta* ii, no. 1126, suggests
the date of issue was 2 February 1116; cf. ibid. nos. 1124 and
1127, which (with **XV**, below) may have been issued on the
same occasion. For ibid. no. 1125, see below, **XVI**.

XV

*Windsor, Berks., [?2 February 1116], writ of King Henry I to William of
Pont de l'Arche and the collectors of Winchester, ordering that the land of
Hyde and that taken in exchange by the abbey of Winchester should be as
free from gelds and other plaints as was the land where the abbey used to
stand, and as are the king's own house and the men who dwell in it, and
particularly in regard to the geld of 400 marks and all other gelds*

Latin

Regesta ii, no. 1886

THE present document is consequent upon the exchange recorded in **XIII**, above. It orders the
exemption from taxation of the land acquired by Hyde Abbey in 1114.[1]

The text takes the form of a royal writ-precept addressed to the relevant local officials. Like
XIV, above, it was granted at Windsor and may have been issued on the same occasion.[2] Although
the location of the place-date before the second witness is unusual, it appears to have been thus in
the exemplar since it is the same in both surviving texts.

The text of the document survives in two Hyde Abbey cartularies. In the Winchester section of
MS. B it is numbered *xxv*, in that of C it is *xxvi*.[3]

MSS.:   B. BL, Cotton MS. Domitian xiv, fo. 34[r] (s.xiii[2])
            C. BL, Harl. MS. 1761, fo. 26[v] (s.xiv ex.)

Edited: *Monasticon*, ii, 445, from C

Printed from B collated to C

---

[1] See below, **XV**, n. 4.   [2] Ibid. n. 12.

[3] In B the Winchester section takes up fos. 22[r]–45[v], in C it is
on fos. 23[r]–37[r]. Both cartularies have the same numeration of

Winchester items up to no. xx, after which the charter
numbered *l* in B is inserted in the series in C and thence the
numbers differ by one digit until the overlap of material ceases.

Henricus*a* 1 . rex Anglorum . Willelmo de Pontearcharum2 . et collectoribus3 Wynton' . salutem . Precipio quod terra de Hida*b* . et terra4 de escambio5 abbacie Wynton' . sit ita quieta de geldis et aliis querelis6 . sicut terra abbacie fuit quieta vbi abbacia sedebat7 . et domus mea propria8 . et homines qui in ea manent9 . Et nominatim de geld' de . cccc . marcis10 . et de omnibus aliis geldis . Teste . Rogero11 episcopo Saresbur'*c* . Apud Wyndesor'12 . et teste . Willelmo Albini*d* 13 .

Henry,1 king of the English, to William of Pont de l'Arche2 and the collectors3 of Winchester, greeting. I command that the land of Hyde and the land4 of the abbey of Winchester [acquired] from the exchange5 should be equally quit of gelds and other plaints6 as the land of the abbey where the abbey used to stand7 has been quit, and my own house8 and the men who dwell in it9 [are quit]. And in particular of the geld of 400 marks10 and of all other gelds. Witnessed by Roger,11 bishop of Salisbury, at Windsor.12 Also witnessed by William d'Aubigny.13

a Henr' C. Item de libertatibus abbacie de Hid' et excambio eiusdem. *rubric in B* 'Also concerning the freedoms of Hyde Abbey and its exchange.'; *the same in C but with* Hyda *for* Hid'. *In C the text is not punctuated*   *b* Hyda C   *c* Sar' C
d Abb'e C, *presumably standing for* Abbate *and representing a scribal error influenced by the occurrence of Warner, abbot of Battle (*Warn' Abb'e de Bello*) in the witness-list of the preceding document in C*

1 King Henry I, 1100–35.
2 William of Pont de l'Arche; see above, **XII**, n. 2. Cf. following note.
3 *collectoribus*. The collectors, royal appointees, were also addressed after William of Pont de l'Arche, together with the reeve of Winchester, in *Regesta* ii, no. 1110 (1114 × 1115). See also WS 1, 425.
4 *terra de escambio*. It seems safest to interpret this as referring to the suburban land in Hyde Street acquired in 1114 (see above, **XIII**, n. 5), together with the nearby manor of Little Worthy acquired at the same time (ibid. n. 6; cf. below, **XVII**). There is no

reason to suppose (as does WS 1, 267) that it refers to Alton and Kingsclere, which were elements in the earlier exchange with William I for the New Minster cemetery (see above, **X**, nn. 4 and 5) and whose exemption was confirmed by **XIV**, above.
5 *escambio*. For the record of this exchange, see above, **XIII**.
6 *geldis et aliis querelis*. Referred to as *consuetudo* 'customary dues' in **XIII**, above (see ibid. n. 12).
7 *terra . . . vbi abbacia sedebat*. See ibid. nn. 7 and 10.
8 *domus mea propria*. See above, **XIV**, n. 8.
9 *homines qui in ea manent*. On the possible identity of these *homines*, see WS 1, 302, n. 2 and ibid. addendum, p. 555.
10 *geld' de . cccc . marcis*. That is, £266 13s. 4d. Perhaps the total amount of geld due from the county at this time.
11 Roger, bishop of Salisbury. See above, **XII**, n. 17.
12 Windsor, Berks.; ibid. n. 13. The present document may have been issued at the same time as **XIV**, above (?2 February, 1116 see ibid. n. 15).
13 William d'Aubigny. See above, **XII**, n. 22. For his presence at Windsor on 2 February [1116], see *Regesta* ii, no. 1127.

XVI

A.D. '1107 × 1118', alleged grant by King Henry I to the New Minster, of the 'liberty' of the street outside the north gate of the city of Winchester

Latin

Regesta ii, no. 1125

T HIS text claims to record a grant by Henry I to the New Minster of the 'liberty' (*libertas*) of the street outside the North Gate of Winchester, i.e. Hyde Street.[1] It was doubtless intended to strengthen, and even widen, the exemption of both Hyde and the land in Hyde Street gained in 1114 from royal taxation and other dues.[2] An equally important purpose was to underline the fact of the exclusion of the site of the abbey and its property in the northern suburb from the bishop's soke,[3] at a time when great rivalry still persisted between the abbey and the cathedral.[4]

The document is a forgery based partly on the New Minster Anglo-Saxon diploma concerning the hundred of Micheldever, S 360 (itself a forgery of the first half of the eleventh century[5]), and partly on a witness-list of 1107 × 1118, probably taken from **XIV**, above. It has the same pictorial and verbal invocations, royal style, notification clause, dispositive clause, corroboration clause, prohibition, and anathema as S 360; it also ascribes to the New Minster the same dedication (to the Holy Trinity alone) as in S 360 and 648.[6] It should be noted, however, that **XVI** has some diplomatic clauses in common not only with S 360 and 648, but also with **III**, above.[7] Whereas it is probable that **III** was constructed soon after the move of the New Minster to Hyde, and possibly by 1125;[8] the present document may have been fabricated soon after (by the same person, or an associate), possibly during the reign of Henry I's successor Stephen or grandson Henry II. The additional statement in **XVI** referring to wrongs done by William I to the New Minster may reflect a twelfth-century tradition,[9] while the additional reference to episcopal approval of the grant was probably intended to obviate any challenge to the document by any future bishop.

The text survives written in gold ink on leaves added to the splendid mid tenth-century codex containing **IV**, above, the New Minster refoundation charter. It is in the same twelfth-century hand as the first of two texts of S 746, another spurious New Minster Anglo-Saxon diploma, which are both written in the same quire as **XVI**.[10] Gold ink was used here and in S 746 in deliberate imitation of the refoundation charter, and seems also to have been used in the now-lost exemplar of

---

[1] See below, **XVI**, nn. 5 and 6.
[2] See above, **XIII–XV**.
[3] Cf. WS 1, 267.
[4] As shown by the dispute over the Palm Sunday procession settled in 1114; see above, **XIII**. See also WS 1, 319–20, for further disputes in the 12th century.
[5] See Brooks 'Micheldever Forgery', 193–5, 215–16.

[6] For an edition of S 360, see ibid. 219–22. On the dedication, see below, **XVI**, n. 4.
[7] See above, p. 58.
[8] Ibid.
[9] See below, **XVI**, n. 3.
[10] The first text of S 746 is on fos. 34ʳ–37ʳ of MS. B; the second text, in a later (?s.xii/xiii) hand, is on fos. 39ʳ–43ʳ.

III, above.[11] Two scribal misreadings in **XVI** are due to the peculiarities of the imitative square Anglo-Saxon minuscule script used in S 360.[12]

[11] See above, p. 59.   [12] See below, **XVI**, nn. *d* and *e*.

MS.:   B. BL, Cotton MS. Vespasian A. viii, fos. 37[v]–38[v] (s. xii[I])

Edited: *Rymer's Foedera*, i, 10.

Printed from the manuscript

+ Omnipotentia diutie[a] maiestatis vbique presidente et sine fine cuncta gubernante . Ego Henricus[1] ipso largiente rex Anglorum cuntis[b] gentis nostre fidelibus innotesco quod pro salute anime mee et Þillelmi[2] patris mei qui plura dampna fecit[3] monasterio sancte Trinitatis[4] quod Þentana situm est ciuitate Nouumque apellatur[c] benigne confero eidem ecclesie et monachis ibidem Deo seruientibus libertatem[5] vici[6] extra portam borialem eiusdem ciuitatis in perpetuum possidendis . Huic autem donacioni fuerunt consiliarii mei regni magnates qui assensu et voluntate eiusdem ciuitatis episcopi[7] me ad hanc benignitatem macaueri[d] . qui eciam

+ The omnipotence of divine majesty presides over everywhere and governs all things without end. I, Henry,[1] king of the English while the same [omnipotence] grants, make it known to all the faithful of our people that, for the salvation of my soul and of that of William[2] my father, who did many wrongs[3] to the monastery of the Holy Trinity[4] which is situated in Winchester and is called the New, I liberally give to the same church and to the monks serving God therein the free tenure[5] of the street[6] outside the north gate of the same city so that they may possess it in perpetuity.

Moreover, the ones who advised with regard to this donation were the magnates of my kingdom who, with the approval and desire of the bishop[7] of the same city, urged me on to this liberality, and who all unanimously decided that

---

[a] *Corrected from* diuitie; *for* diuine, *cf.* diuinę *in S 360 (Brooks 'Micheldever Forgery', 219) and* diuine *in* **III**, *above.*   [b] *Sic MS., with correction attempted but not completed; for* cunctis, *cf. S 360 (Brooks, ibid.) and* **III**, *above.*   [c] *A spelling for* appellatur. *The latter occurs in S 360 (Brooks, ibid.) and* **III**, *above.*   [d] *Scribal misreading of* incitauer[unt]. *Cf.* incitauerunt *in S 360 (Brooks, ibid.) and* **III**, *above. The letters* ci *of the correct form have been mistaken for a square* a *of the type used elsewhere by the scribe of S 360; see Brooks 'Micheldever Forgery', Pl. 22. Cf. below, n. e.*

---

[1] King Henry I, 1100–35.

[2] King William I, 1066–87.

[3] *qui plura dampna fecit.* This statement is not adapted from anything in either S 360 or **III**, above. It probably reflects Hyde Abbey tradition in the 12th century and may have been founded on William I's treatment of the New Minster immediately after 1066 when, after Abbot Ælfwig had been killed opposing the Normans at Hastings, he was not replaced for two years, during which time certain estates appear to have been confiscated; see *LVH*, 35, n. 2; *HRH*, 81; and *Monasticon* ii, 428.

[4] *sancte Trinitatis.* This dedication is taken from S 360 (Brooks 'Micheldever Forgery', 219). It also occurs in S 648, which is related to S 360; see above, p. 178. The only dedication of the

New Minster to the Holy Trinity alone in a genuine document appears to be that in the vernacular will of Æthelstan Ætheling of A.D. 1014: S 1503, *CW* 93 and 102 (*AS Wills* 20). Cf. *WS* 1, 313, n. 8 and *LVH*, viii.

[5] *libertatem.* The use here of the word *libertas* was probably suggested by its use to describe the alleged grant of the hundred of Micheldever in S 360 (Brooks, ibid.). There is no independent evidence for the employment of the singular term 'liberty' to describe the abbey's rights in this area. Cf. below, n. 6.

[6] *vici.* Hyde Street; cf. *WS* 2.ii, 946–64. In 1234 the abbot claimed jurisdiction over tenements in Hyde Street, although he cited Henry II's confirmation charter (**XVII**, below) in relation to his *libertates* rather than the present document; see *Curia Regis Rolls 1233–7*, no. 1218. Cf. above, n. 5.

[7] *assensu et voluntate . . . episcopi.* The reference here to the bishop's assent is not adapted from anything in either S 360 or **III**, above. See above, p. 178.

omnes vnanimiter constituerunt vt donacio ista firma et in eternum permaneat . neque a quolibet seu superiore vel inferiore commutetur . Et quisquis violare presumpserit excommuniatur*e* a societate Dei et sanctorum eius . Scripta fuit hec carta subscriptorum testimonio Rogero[8] [.] episcopo Sar' . *Roberto*[9] . episcopo Lincolnie . *Ƿillelmo*[10] . episcopo Exonie . *Roberto*[11] . comite de Mell' . *Henrico* . de Port[12] et aliis .

this donation should remain constant and for all time and should not be changed by anyone, whether of the higher or the lower rank. And let whoever should presume to violate it be excommunicated from the fellowship of God and his saints. This charter was written in the witness of those written below: Roger,[8] bishop of Salisbury; Robert,[9] bishop of Lincoln; William,[10] bishop of Exeter; Robert,[11] count of Meulan; Henry de Port;[12] and others.

e *Scribal misreading of* excommunicetur; *cf. S 360 (Brooks, ibid.) and* **III**, *above. The letters* ce *of the correct form have been mistaken for a square* a *as in n.* d, *above.*

[8] Roger, bishop of Salisbury. See above, **XII**, n. 17.
[9] Robert, bishop of Lincoln. Ibid. n. 18.
[10] William, bishop of Exeter. See above, **XIII**, n. 28.
[11] Robert, count of Meulan. Ibid. n. 30.
[12] Henry de Port. See above, **XII**, n. 4.

XVII

A.D. 1154 × 1171, confirmation by King Henry II to Hyde Abbey of the land of Hyde given by King Henry I and the land of Worthy [Abbotts Barton] given in exchange by Bishop William [Giffard]; to be held as quit and as freely as the abbot and monks used to hold their church and cemetery within the city. Also confirming rights of sanctuary and burial at the abbey church and such freedom of the said lands from service as the king has with regard to his own hall within the city

Latin

ACCORDING to the present document, Henry II confirmed the grants to Hyde Abbey of land and privileges which had been made by his grandfather Henry I and Bishop William Giffard as part of the exchanges associated with the move of the New Minster to Hyde.[1] He seems also to have made more explicit the list of dues from which the lands were exempt, and to have added the right of sanctuary for fugitives in the abbey church.[2]

The document would appear to be genuine although the absence of a witness-list in the surviving copies allows only a bracket-date to be given for its issue.

XVII survives only in two incomplete later copies. One text occurs in the Winchester section of one of the Hyde Abbey cartularies (MS. C) where it is numbered *xxiij*. The other text occurs as part of the evidence quoted in favour of the abbot of Hyde's right to territorial jurisdiction in Hyde Street in a lawsuit in the Curia Regis in 1234.[3]

MSS.: B. PRO, Curia Regis R 18 Henry III (K. B. 26/115B), m. 18[r] (s.xiii[1]; partial text)
    C. BL, Harl. MS. 1761, fo. 26[r] (s.xiv ex.)

Edited: *Monasticon*, ii, 446, from C
    Curia Regis R 1233–7, p. 301, from B

Printed from C collated with B

---

[1] See above, **XII–XIII**, and **XV**; cf. **XVI**.
[2] See below, **XVII**, n. 8.
[3] See *Curia Regis Rolls 1233–7*, no. 1218.

Henricus*a* [1] rex Anglorum et dux Normannorum et Aquitannorum et comes Andegauorum . Henrico[2] episcopo Wynton' et iusticiis vicecomitibus baronibus*b* ministris et omnibus fidelibus suis Francis et Anglis tocius Anglie salutem Sciatis quod ego volo*c* et precipio quod abbas Wynton' et monachi*d* sui habeant et teneant terram quam rex Henricus[3] auus meus dedit sancto Petro que vocatur Hyda*e* [4] et terram de Wordya[5] quam Willelmus[6] episcopus eis dedit in escambio*f* ita bene et in pace libere [et]*g* honorifice et quietam de omnibus placitis et querelis et tallagiis*h* et geldis*j* et scotis et consuetudinibus et omnibus aliis rebus*k* in via et semitis et in campis sicut melius*l* quiecius et liberius tenebant ecclesiam eorum et cimiterium infra ciuitatem[7] Et si quis fugitiuus ad eandem ecclesiam confugerit saluus sit[8] Corpora quoque*m* defunctorum ciuitatis ad ipsam ecclesiam sepeliantur sicut apud aliam mos erat[9] Et sicut ego aulam[10] meam infra ciuitatem ab omni seruicio liberam habeo sic eis has terras predictas liberas perpetualiter confirmo sicut carta regis aui mei testatur etc .[11]

Henry,[1] king of the English, duke of the Normans and of the Aquitainians, and count of the Angevins, to Henry,[2] bishop of Winchester, and to the justices, sheriffs, barons, ministers, and all his faithful people, French and English, of the whole of England, greeting. Know that I will and command that the abbot of Winchester and his monks should have and hold the land which is called Hyde[4] which King Henry[3] my grandfather gave to St. Peter, and the land of Worthy[5] which Bishop William[6] gave them in exchange, so well and in peace, freely [and] honourably and quit of all pleas and plaints and tallages and gelds and scots and customary dues and all other matters on the highway and paths and in fields as the better, the more quit, and the more freely they used to hold their church and cemetery within the city.[7] And if any fugitive flees to the same church let him be safe.[8] Also let the corpses of the city's dead be buried at that church as was the custom at the other.[9] And even as I have my hall[10] within the city free from all service so I confirm to them these aforesaid lands [to be] perpetually free, just as the charter of the king my grandfather bears witness, etc.[11]

---

a Confirmacio regis Henrici . ij . de excambio Hyde 'Confirmation of King Henry II concerning the exchange of Hyde' *rubric in* C   *b* baronii' C   *c* *The text begins here* B
d monach'i C   *e* Hida B   *f* escambium B
g et B   *h* et auxiliis *after* tallagiis B   *j* seldis C
k etc . *after* rebus B *which omits the text from* in via *to* campis
l melius et plenius B *for* melius . . . liberius
m corporaque B

[1] King Henry II, 1154–89.
[2] Henry of Blois, bishop of Winchester, 1129–71.
[3] King Henry I, 1100–35.
[4] *terram quam rex Henricus . . . dedit . . . que vocatur Hyda.* See above, **XIII**, n. 4.
[5] *terram de Wordya.* Ibid. n. 6.
[6] William Giffard, bishop of Winchester, 1100–29; see above, **XII**, n. 5.

[7] *ecclesiam . . . et cimiterium infra ciuitatem.* See above, **X**, n. 6; and **XIII**, nn. 7 and 15.
[8] *si quis fugitiuus . . . confugerit saluus sit.* There is no equivalent to this clause in **XIII**, above. For a general account of the medieval ecclesiastical right of sanctuary, see J. H. Baker, *An Introduction to English Legal History* (3rd edn., London, 1990), 585–6.
[9] *Corpora . . . defunctorum ciuitatis . . . sepeliantur sicut . . . mos erat.* See above, **XIII**, n. 15. In the 15th century, most of the inhabitants of the northern suburb were probably buried at Hyde Abbey or at St. Bartholomew's, Hyde, the parish church within the abbey cemetery; see WS 2.i, 109.
[10] *aulam meam.* By this date this can only refer to residual rights over the site of the royal palace of William I–II and Henry I, near the cathedral, its buildings having been destroyed in 1141 during the reign of Stephen; see WS 1, 297, 299–301, and 326.
[11] *ab omni seruicio . . . liberas . . . confirmo sicut carta regis aui mei testatur.* See above, **XV**.

XVIII–XXIX

ANGLO-SAXON DOCUMENTS
RELEVANT TO THE TOPOGRAPHY
OF THE CITY OF WINCHESTER

XVIII

'A.D. 900', a reference to the southernmost mill in Winchester, pertaining to the 100-hide estate of Micheldever, Hants

English

S 360 (part; MSS 1, 4 only), Finberg 34

THE extract printed below is taken from S 360, a diploma which claims to be the record of Edward the Elder's grant of the 100–hide estate of Micheldever to the New Minster in A.D. 900. The text given occurs at the end of a series of vernacular boundary-descriptions of the constituent parts of the estate. The mill in Winchester is one of three items of real property listed as appurtenant to the estate; it is uncertain where the other two items (a weir on the R. Itchen and half of 'the white cliff') should be located.[1]

Were S 360 a genuine document, the present text would constitute the earliest specific reference to a mill in Winchester.[2] However, as Professor N. P. Brooks has argued, this diploma is a forgery of the first half of the eleventh century and was probably intended to help the abbot of the New Minster to consolidate his authority over several estates, not all of them contiguous, into a private hundred with its centre at Micheldever.[3] Its witness-list is closely related to that in **II**, above. Although, on the sole evidence of S 360, it would be unwise to assert the existence of the mill any earlier than the date proposed for the forgery, it is possible that this part of the diploma was copied from an earlier record relating to the mill in the southern part of the city which is known to have

---

[1] See below, **XVIII**, nn. 4 and 5.
[2] As opposed to the various mill-yairs mentioned in **I**, above.
[3] See Brooks 'Micheldever Forgery', 192–6, 215–18.

belonged to the New Minster before ?970 × 975.[4] Later, probably in the early twelfth century, the Latin part of S 360 was itself used as the base for two other forgeries, **III** and **XVI**, above.[5]

MS. B is a single-sheet document written in an imitation of Anglo-Saxon square minuscule script.[6] MS. C is the copy in the *Liber de Hyda*, and, like other texts in that cartulary, the present extract was supplied with both Middle English and Latin translations by the cartulary-maker. MS. D is the antiquary John Stow's transcript from C, made in 1572.

[4] See below, **XVIII**, n. 6.
[5] See above, pp. 58, 178.
[6] Brooks 'Micheldever Forgery', 192.

MSS.:   B. WCM, 12090 [Cabinet 7, Drawer 2, no.1] (s.xi[1])
              C. Earl of Macclesfield, Shirburn Castle, *Liber (abbatiae) de Hyda*, fos. 14[v]–15[r] (s.xiv/xv)
              D. BL, Lansdowne 717, fos. 31[r]–32[v] (s.xvi[2]), from C

Facsimile: *O. S. Facs.*, ii, Winchester College 1, from B

Edited: *LH*, 95–6, from C collated to B
              BCS 596, from B
              LVH, 207–11, from B
              Brooks 'Micheldever Forgery', 219–22, from B
              Miller *New Minster* 3, from B collated to C, D, and E

Printed from B. C translates the text into both Middle English and Latin, as well as giving the Old English.

7 ða seofan hida æt Þorðige[1] hyrað to þam hund hidan to Myceldefer[2] . eall spa ða landgemæra hit onbutan belicgceað[a 3] . 7 an per on Ycenan[4] 7 healf þæt hpite clif[5] 7 seo syðemyste mylen[6] . on Þinteceastre binnan pealle[7] ;

. . . And the 7 hides at Worthy[1] pertain to the 100 hides belonging to Micheldever,[2] even as the estate-boundaries surround it round about;[3] and one weir on the Itchen,[4] and half the white cliff,[5] and the southernmost mill[6] in Winchester within the wall[7] . . .

[a] Sic *MS.*; *Brooks 'Micheldever Forgery', 221* belicgeað

[1] Abbot's Worthy, Hants. The New Minster held an estate here *TRE* and *TRW*, said to be of 7 hides although it never paid geld: *DB*, i, fo. 42v (*DB Hants* 6: 17).
[2] Micheldever, Hants. See above, **III**, n. 12.
[3] *eall spa ða landgemæra hit onbutan belicgceað*. On the significance of this phrase, see Brooks 'Micheldever Forgery', 214–15.
[4] *on Ycenan*. The R. Itchen, Hants. The location of this particular weir is unknown but its purpose was probably for the capture of fish. In the ME version of the text in MS. C it is stated to lie *at Ychyn be north Wynchester* and in the Latin version *apud Ichyn ex orientali parte Wyntonie*, but neither statement has any standing in relation to the significance of the phrase in MS. B.
[5] *þæt hpite clif*. This place is unidentified but was presumably either a quarry or a landing-place, not too far from Micheldever

or one of its outliers. It is unlikely to be the same as *æt Hwitan clife*, from which the catch of one fishing-boat and the royal toll was granted by King Edgar to Abingdon Abbey in 962: S 701 (*BCS* 1094); cf. Whitecliff Farm, near Swanage, Dorset (*PN Dorset*, ii, 56).
[6] *seo syðemyste mylen*. It is not possible to identify this mill with that of Floodstock just outside the south wall, but it may have been a precursor of it, on the same stream and slightly to the north; cf. WS 1, 283. If the mill referred to here is the same as that given by the New Minster to the bishop in ?970 × 975 (see above, **VII**, n. 8), the 11th-cent. compiler of S 360 may have been using an out of date document as his source here. For the suggestion that the various boundaries in S 360 were taken from different exemplars, see Brooks 'Micheldever Forgery', 215.
[7] *binnan pealle*. In **VIII(i)**, above (975 × 978), the middle part of the south wall is referred to as 'the old city-wall'; see ibid. n. 15. Cf. below, **XXIII**, n.2.

XIX

A.D. 946 × 955, grant by King Eadred to his thegn Æthelgeard, of a mill at the east gate in Winchester and a tenement formerly held by Wulfhun the priest, both of which are to be held as appurtenances of the 12-hide estate at Exton, Hants

English

S 463 (part), Finberg 58, *CW* 203b

ALTHOUGH both the present text and **XX**, below, have been extracted here from the copies of (slightly antecedent) diplomas within which they survive, each is a self-contained vernacular document which can stand on its own. Both texts record the grant of urban property at Winchester by King Eadred to his thegn Æthelgeard, a man known from other sources to have been a benefactor of the New Minster.[1] In each case the urban property was to be held as an appurtenance of a rural estate in Hampshire already held by Æthelgeard through a grant from Eadred's predecessor, his brother King Edmund.

Neither **XIX** nor **XX**, below, is datable except by the outside limits of the reign of Eadred (946 × 955). Both have the diplomatic form of a general declaration, in the vernacular, made by the donor. In view of Æthelgeard's known connection with the New Minster, mentioned above, it is significant to note the survival of two comparable declarations, both by priests in favour of the New Minster, from the reign of Eadred.[2] Æthelgeard also bequeathed Sotwell, Berks., to his wife and then to the New Minster in 957 × *c.* 958 by means of a similar short declaration.[3] Although the authenticity of these three texts has recently been called into question on the basis of unusual linguistic forms,[4] there is no doubt about their New Minster provenance. It is thus possible that **XIX** and **XX** were drafted for Æthelgeard at the New Minster. However, as there is nothing extraordinary about the wording of **XIX** and **XX** and no known connection between the property involved and the New Minster (unless Wulfhun the priest had been a member of its community), there appears to be no reason to doubt their authenticity. Each of these texts records an immediate grant rather than a bequest and each grant is consequent upon a previous royal gift of bookland to the same beneficiary. The use of the first person singular in the wording of these declarations perhaps indicates that these were the actual words spoken by the grantor at a public ceremony of transfer of title. It may be that a list of witnesses to such a ceremony has been omitted from the surviving texts of both **XIX** and **XX**.[5]

---

[1] See below, **XIX**, n. 2.
[2] S 1418–19; *AS Charters* 28–9; Miller *New Minster* 14 and 16.
[3] S 1496; *AS Wills* 6; Miller *New Minster* 21.

[4] Miller *New Minster*, xlvii-li.
[5] S 1418 has such a list, while S 1419 refers to one which appears to have been omitted from the *Liber de Hyda*.

XIX survives only as a copy made by scribe *a* of the *Codex Wintoniensis* in 1129 × 1139.[6] In the *Codex* it is placed immediately after the witness-list of a copy of the diploma (S 463) granted by King Edmund to Æthelgeard in 940 concerning the 12 hides at Exton.[7] The exemplar of the cartulary text of **XIX** may have been in the form of an endorsement added to the earlier diploma when the additional grant was made by King Eadred. The presence of the diploma, and hence of the vernacular document associated with it, in the *Codex*, in spite of the fact that the beneficiary of both documents was a layman, is to be explained by the practice of transferring to the new holder of an estate of bookland any previous documents of title. It is probable that the Old Minster acquired these documents with the estate at Exton shortly after 960;[8] they were thus available for copying at the cathedral in the twelfth century. Like other vernacular documents copied into the *Codex* by scribe *a*, there is a frequent replacement of *e* by *æ*.[9]

[6] *CW* 203b. For the work of scribe *a*, see above, pp. 6–7.

[7] *CW* 203a. This diploma shares many formulae and witnesses with S 461–2, and 464, all of the same year; see Keynes

Diplomas, 44–5.

[8] See below, **XIX**, n. 4.

[9] See Rumble 1980, i, 250.

MS.:   B. BL, Add. MS. 15350, fo. 107[v] (s.xii[1])

Edited: *KCD* 1131

              BCS 758

Printed from the manuscript

[I]c[a] Eadred[1] cyng geaf minum þægnæ Æþel-geardæ[2] to eacan þam þæ min broþor[3] him ær sealde to Eastseaxnatunæ[4] anæ mylnæ[5] æt þam east[b] geate[6] æt Pintanceastræ 7 þonæ hagan þæ Þulfhun preost[7] ær hæfdæ to þære ilcan bocungæ[8] þæ þæt land gæbocod is .

I, King Eadred,[1] give to my thegn Æthel-geard,[2] in augmentation of that which my brother[3] formerly gave him at Exton,[4] a mill[5] at the east gate[6] at Winchester and the tenement which Wulfhun the priest[7] formerly had, in the same privileged tenure[8] as that estate has been granted by diploma.

[a] *Space has been left in the MS. for a decorated initial* I *which was never added* [b] geast *MS., a spelling influenced by the following word* geate

[1] King Eadred, 946–55.
[2] For another grant of property in Winchester by King Eadred to Æthelgeard, see below, **XX**. He is also the beneficiary of some other surviving diplomas relating to estates in Berks., Hants, and the Isle of Wight granted by Kings Æthelstan, Edmund, Eadred, and Eadwig; see S 417, 511, 517, 523, 536, 598, 641, and 1663, BCS 689, 765, 810, 830, 864, 976, 988, and 1025. He may also be the same as the beneficiary of S 599, relating to an estate *æt Nipantune* (unidentified), whom King Eadwig called one of his *kari* in A.D. 956; see Sawyer *Burton* 16. In S 523 (A.D. 947) he is described as *minister ac miles* and in S 598 (A.D. 956) as *princeps*. He occurs as witness to documents of 932 × 958; see Hart *ECNE*, 285. In 957 × *c*. 958 he bequeathed Sotwell, Berks., to the New Minster: S 1496, *AS Wills* 6, Miller *New Minster* 21; hence he is probably to be identified with Æthelgeard *préng* who is mentioned as a benefactor in *LVH*, 22. See also Keynes *Liber Vitae*, 86–7, where it is noted that he was designated *armiger* in the witness-list to S 404, BCS 667; this may be a late addition, however, according to Miller *New Minster*, 89. The vernacular byname may refer to his physical characteristics, but in exactly what respect is not certain; see Tengvik, 330.

[3] King Edmund, 939–46.
[4] Exton, Hants. 12 hides of land here were granted by King Edmund to Æthelgeard in 940, see S 463, *CW* 203a, BCS 758. Later, according to a diploma which was extant at Winchester Cathedral in 1643, Exton was granted in 960 by King Edgar to Ælfwaru with reversion to the church of Winchester: WCL, Book of John Chase, fo. 56[r] (= S 1815), and WCL, MS. 22, p. 98. Ælfwaru is elsewhere said to have granted Exton, with Alver-stoke, and East Woodhay, Hants, to the Old Minster in memory of her husband Leofwine: *Reg Pontissara*, 609–10. Exton was held by the bishop of Winchester *TRW*, for the monks of the Old Minster, to whom it belonged *TRE*: *DB*, i, fo. 41[v] (*DB Hants* 3: 11).
[5] *anæ mylnæ.* Probably a precursor of the mill outside East Gate now known as the City Mill: WS 2.ii, **944**. It seems later to have come into the possession of Wherwell Abbey, ibid.
[6] *æt þam east geate.* This is the first record of this gate. In *c*.900, the urban defence near here was referred to as *cyninges burgheg*; see above, **I**, n. 8.
[7] Wulfhun the priest is otherwise unknown, but may have belonged to the community of either the New Minster or the Old Minster at this time.
[8] *to þære ilcan bocungæ.* That is, it was to be held as bookland. It was thus to be held in perpetuity, to be freely alienable, and to be exempt from customary dues and services apart from the 'Three Burdens'. Cf. below, **XX**, n. 5.

XX

A.D. 946 × 955, grant by King Eadred to his thegn Æthelgeard, of the tenement in Winchester pertaining to the 7-hide estate at West Tisted, Hants

English

S 488 (part), Finberg 61, *CW* 104b

THE present text is similar in purpose and diplomatic nature to **XIX**, above, with which it is contemporary.[1]

Like **XIX**, above, **XX** survives only as a copy made by scribe *a* of the *Codex Wintoniensis* in 1129 × 1139.[2] In the cartulary it is placed after the boundary-clause and before the date and witness-list of a copy of the diploma (S 488) granted in 943 by King Edmund to Æthelgeard, concerning the 7 hides at West Tisted.[3] It is possible that the exemplar of the cartulary-text of **XX** was in the form of an endorsement on the associated diploma, similar to that suggested for the exemplar of **XIX**.[4] Its location in the *Codex* within the main body of the diploma, however, may imply some rearrangement of text by the cartulary-scribe; alternatively, the common exemplar of the *Codex* text of the diploma and **XX** must have been an apograph written some years later than 943, the date of Edmund's grant. The presence of both documents, both in favour of the same layman, in the *Codex* is explicable if they formed part of the back title to the Old Minster's estate at West Tisted.[5]

The surviving text of **XX** exhibits both the replacement of *e* by *æ* characteristic of scribe *a* and a misreading which suggests his unfamiliarity with the Anglo-Saxon letter *ð*.[6]

MS.: B. BL, Add. MS. 15350, fo. 51ᵛ (s.xii¹)

Edited: *KCD* 1144
  BCS 786

Printed from the manuscript

---

[1] See above, pp. 15–16, 185–6.
[2] *CW* 104b. For the work of scribe *a*, see above, pp. 6–7.
[3] *CW* 104a.
[4] See above, p. 186.
[5] See below, **XX**, n. 4.
[6] See Rumble 1980, i, 250, 235–7.

Ic Eadred[1] cyng geaf[a] minum þegne Æðel-
gearde[2] to æcere æhte binnan þære byrig[3] into
Þintanceastre . þa hagan þe to þam seofan
hydum æt Ticcesstede[b][4] gebyriað[c] to þon
ilcan[d] freolsdóme[5] þe he þæt land hæfþ .

I, King Eadred,[1] give to my thegn Æthelgeard[2] in perpetual possession the tenement,
within the city[3] at Winchester, which pertains
to the 7-hide estate at Tisted,[4] in the same free
tenure[5] in which he has that estate.

---

[a] ge eaf *MS.*   [b] TICCESTstede *MS.; a scribal error due to
a change from majuscule to minuscule letters within the word*
[c] gebyriad *MS.*   [d] *Altered from* iccan

[1] King Eadred, 946–55.   [2] See above, **XIX**, n. 2.
[3] *binnan þære byrig.* The significance of OE *burh* here is not so
much a fortified as an urban place, contrasting with the rural
estate to which the tenement pertained. Cf. the common phrase
in OE writs *binnan byrig 7 butan*, e.g. S 986, *AS Writs* 28.

[4] West Tisted, Hants. Both S 488, *CW* 104a, *BCS* 786 (A.D.
943? for 941) and S 511, *CW* 103, *BCS* 765 (A.D. 960 ? for 941)
record a grant of the 7-hide estate here by King Edmund to
Æthelgeard; the former replaced an older diploma which had
been lost. West Tisted belonged to the bishop of Winchester
TRE and *TRW*: *DB*, i, fo. 40[v] (*DB Hants* 2: 22).
[5] *to þon ilcan fréolsdome.* As above, **XIX**, n. 8. Cf. the OE terms
frēols and *frēolsbōc* to denote a diploma: BT, BT *Suppl*, and BT
Addenda, s.vv.

XXI

A.D. 961, a reference to 13 tenements in Winchester pertaining to the 50-hide estate at Hurstbourne Tarrant, Hants

Latin

S 689 (part; MSS 1, 2 only), Finberg 98

THE extract printed below is taken from S 689, a copy of a diploma of King Edgar recording his grant in A.D. 961 to Abingdon Abbey of the important royal estate of Hurstbourne Tarrant, Hants.[1] Unfortunately for the abbey, the estate was taken back into royal possession on the death of Edgar in 975.[2] It is likely that the Winchester tenements, like the other appurtenances, already belonged to the estate in 961[3] and that their later tenurial history continued to follow that of Hurstbourne, at least until the end of the Anglo-Saxon period.

The text of **XXI**, although in the third person singular, may represent a Latin translation of a vernacular document such as **XIX** or **XX**, above.

XXI survives in both of the Abingdon cartularies; of the two, MS. B appears to preserve a slightly better version.

MSS.:   B. BL, Cotton MS. Claud. C. ix, fo. 119ʳ (s.xii med.)
         C. BL, Cotton MS. Claud. B. vi, fo. 78ʳ (s.xiii²)

Edited: *KCD* 1235, from B and C
         Stevenson *Chron. Abingdon*, i, 317, from B
         BCS 1080, from C collated to B
         Pierquin *Recueil*, pt 5, no. 11, from C
         S. E Kelly, *Charters of Abingdon Abbey* (Anglo-Saxon Charters 7–8, Oxford, 2001) 89, from C

Printed from B collated to C

---

[1] See below, **XXI**, n. 2.
[2] Ibid.
[3] Cf. the suggested meaning of *plaudat*; ibid. n. 6.

Predia[1] utique . xiii . que Wintoniensi[a] sita sunt urbe ad rus[2] prefatum pertinentia eadem libertate[3] prefate Dei ęcclesię[b][4] admodum deuoti Æthelwoldo[c][5] optinente[d] eiusdem loci abbate plaudat[e][6] .

. . . Moreover, he confirms[6] 13 tenements[1] situated in Winchester [and] pertaining to the aforementioned estate,[2] in the same freedom,[3] to the aforementioned church[4] of God, the most holy Æthelwold,[5] abbot of the same place, acquiring [them].

[a] uuintoniensi C   [b] ecclesie C   [c] deuoto Aþeluuoldo *altered (by the scribe of the text) from* deuoti Aþeluuoldi C; Æthelwoldo *written in red ink* B   [d] obtinente C
[e] plauda[n]t *KCD and Pierquin*

---

[1] *Predia.* The exact location of the 13 Winchester tenements granted in 961 is not known, nor even whether they were contiguous or scattered through the city. If the former, it is possible, in view of the apparent connection of Hurstbourne with support for the æthelings (see below, n. 2), that they may have been situated in *Athelyngestret* (now Upper High Street), although this street-name is only first recorded in 1227, and may have a derivation from a 12th-cent. byname, rather than from OE **Æðelingastræt* 'street of the æthelings'; see WS 1, 233.

[2] *rus prefatum.* Hurstbourne Tarrant, Hants. 50 hides here were granted in 961 by King Edgar to Abingdon Abbey, as recorded in S 689. However, it seems that Hurstbourne and other estates at Bedwyn and Burbage, Wilts., were wrongfully alienated at this time by Edgar from the land set aside for the support of the æthelings: S 937, *KCD* 1312, Whitelock *EHD* 123. In S 937, a diploma of King Æthelred II, probably of 999, it is also recorded that Edgar's error was rectified on the accession of Edward the Martyr in 975, when the estates were taken back from Abingdon and given to his brother Æthelred; as king, some

twenty years later, Æthelred decided to compensate Abingdon with the gift of other estates. There seems no reason to doubt this story and it is significant that Hurstbourne Tarrant had been one of the estates bequeathed by King Alfred to his eldest son Edward in 873 × 888: S 1507; Harmer *SEHD* 11; and Keynes and Lapidge, 175. Hurstbourne Tarrant was part of the royal demesne *TRE* and *TRW*, contributing with Basingstoke and Kingsclere to the farm of one day: *DB*, i, fo. 39[r] (*DB Hants* 1: 44). There was a royal residence at Hurstbourne in the reign of Henry II; see WS 1, 467. For a possible connected street-name in Winchester, see above, n. 1.

[3] *eadem libertate.* That is, as bookland. Cf. above, **XIX**, n. 8.

[4] *prefate Dei ęcclesię.* Abingdon Abbey, Berks., which had been refounded *c*.954: Knowles and Hadcock, 52, 58.

[5] Æthelwold, abbot of Abingdon, *c*.954–63: *HRH*, 23. He was later bishop of Winchester; see above, **IV**, n. 134.

[6] *plaudat.* The subject of this verb is King Edgar (959–75). Its meaning is less certain. A. Blaise, *Lexicon Latinitatis Medii Ævi*, Corpus Christianorum (Turnhout, 1975), 695, lists *plaudare* as a variant of *plaudere* 'to clap, applaud' [cf. du Cange, vi, 361–2, = *applausum dare*]. However, the particular context here suggests an extended meaning 'to confirm, give approval to' and the king appears to be merely confirming an existing relationship between the tenements and the estate of Hurstbourne Tarrant.

XXII

A.D. 961, grant by King Edgar to Bishop Beorhthelm [of Winchester], of the 7½-hide estate at Easton, Hants

Latin with English

S 695, Finberg 95, *CW* 143

THIS diploma records the grant of an estate centred on Easton, Hants, made by King Edgar to his kinsman, Bishop Beorhthelm, the last bishop of Winchester before the Benedictine reform of the Old Minster.[1] The grant appears to have been one of personal bookland, for Beorhthelm's own benefit and disposal, rather than particularly for the endowment of his church. In the preceding year King Edgar had granted Beorhthelm a life tenure of the Old Minster's estate of Bishopstoke, Hants, and it is possible that he held other cathedral estates for his personal benefit rather than that of the church.[2] The area of the territorial unit delimited by the boundary-clause shows that this particular estate of Easton was much larger than the later parish of the same name.[3] It was also larger than the cathedral estate at Easton earlier leased out by Bishop Ealhfrith of Winchester in 871 × 877,[4] although that could have formed its nucleus. It appears to have been a new unit created for Bishop Beorhthelm, but one which did not survive for long, its constituent parts probably reverting to their previous status soon after Beorhthelm's replacement by Æthelwold in 963.[5]

The diplomatic clauses and the witness-list[6] are consistent with the date A.D. 961 and there is no reason to doubt the authenticity of the document. The witness-list, soon after the reunification of the kingdom (in 959), includes both West Saxon and Mercian elements.

XXII survives only as a copy made by scribes *a* (text) and *b* (rubric) of the *Codex Wintoniensis* in 1129 × 1139.[7] The wording of the rubric in the cartulary was almost certainly taken from that of a vernacular endorsement on the exemplar, contemporary with the main text.[8]

MS.:   B. BL, Add. MS. 15350, fos. 72ᵛ–73ʳ (s.xii¹)

Edited: *KCD* 1230
           BCS 1076

Printed from the manuscript

---

[1] See below, **XXII**, n. 4.
[2] Cf. above, **V, xiii**, nn. 180 and 191.
[3] See below, **XXII**, nn. 3, 5–40. See Fig. 10.
[4] S 1275, *CW* 148a, *AS Ch* 14.
[5] Cf. above, **V, xiii**. For the alienation of Hyde Moors to

Bishop Æthelgar, abbot of the New Minster, in 983, see above, **IX**.
[6] See below, **XXII**, nn. 42–73.
[7] See above, pp. 6–8.
[8] Ibid. 6–7.

Largiflua[a] Christi omnipotentis largiente clementia patenter agnouimus : quod his recidiuis ęterna iugiterque mansura ob perpetuę remunerationis talionem tocius mentis adnisu lucranda sint . Etenim scriptum est . Nichil intulimus in hunc mundum : uerum nec ab eo auferre quid poterimus .[1] Quapropter lubrici potentatus non inmemor ego Eadgar[2] Christo conferente tocius Anglicę regionis basileus : ob maioris premii remunerationem aliquam ruris particulam septem uidelicet mansas et dimidiam in illo loco qui á ruricolis Eastun[3] nuncupatur Byrhtelmo[4] . presuli michi carnalis prosapię nexu copulato ob eius fidele obsequium quod erga me sedulus exibuit perpetua largitus sum hereditate . ut ipse uita comite cum omnibus utensilibus hilaris possideat . et post uitę suę terminum quibuscumque sibi placuerit heredibus inmunem derelinquat . Si`t´ autem predictum rus omni terrene seruitutis iugo liberum tribus exceptis rata uidelicet expeditione pontis arcisue[b] restauratione . Si autem aliquis laruarico inflatus spiritu hoc nostrum decretum discindere temptauerit . nisi satisfactione dignissima in hac uita penituerit . in futura coram Christo et eius angelici agminis collegio pęnis permansuris punitum se sentiat . et in ęternum ligamine sacrilegii strictum agnoscat . His etenim limitibus prefatum rus hic inde gyratur .

[a] Đis is þara ehteðan healfræ hydæ landboc to Eastune þe Eadgar cining gebocode Brihtelm bisceope on éce yrfe 'This is the diploma of the 7½ hides at Easton which King Edgar granted to Bishop Beorhthelm in perpetual inheritance' *rubric*
[b] arcisuę MS., *corrected from* arci suę

[1] A variant of 1 Tim. 6: 7 (*BSV*, ii, 1835) *nihil intulimus in mundum haut dubium quia nec auferre quid possumus*.
[2] Edgar, king of England, 959–75.
[3] Easton, Hants. The estate encompassed by the boundaries given in the present document was rather more extensive than the modern parish. It included not only Abbotts Barton and Hyde Moors (the latter was, however, granted as a separate unit in 983; see above, **IX**), but also Abbots Worthy, Chilland, and part of Kings Worthy; see below, nn. 5–40. An estate of 8 hides, but of smaller actual area than the 7½-hide estate here described, had been granted in 871 × 877 by Bishop Ealhfrith of Winchester to Cuthred, *dux*, and his wife Wulfthryth for the term of three lives: S 1275, *CW* 148a *AS Ch* 14. Although the

We have clearly perceived, by the granting of Almighty Christ's abundant forbearance, that eternal and perpetually lasting things may be gained out of transient affairs by a full effort of mind in return for a reward of perpetual recompense. And indeed it is written, 'we brought nothing into this world: and certainly we will carry nothing out'.[1] Wherefore, not unmindful of fleeting power, I, Edgar,[2] king of the whole English region by Christ's gift, in return for the recompense of a greater profit, have granted in perpetual inheritance a certain small piece of land, namely 7½ hides in that place which by the country people is called Easton,[3] to Bishop Beorhthelm,[4] [who is] related to me by the bond of fleshly kin, in return for his faithful obedience which he has diligently shown towards me, so that he, while living, may possess it blithely, with all its useful things, and after the end of his life he may leave it intact to whichever heirs he pleases. Let moreover the aforesaid land be free from any yoke of earthly service except for three, namely designated military-service and the repair of bridges or fortresses. If moreover anyone, puffed up by a diabolical spirit, should try to tear asunder this our decree, let him feel himself punished for evermore by continuing punishments in the presence of Christ and of the community of his angelic army and let him perceive [himself] tied tight by the bonds of sacrilege for all time, unless he has done penance in this life with a very worthy reparation. And indeed the aforementioned land is encircled on all sides by these bounds.

estate to which the present document relates was the subject of a personal grant to Bishop Beorhthelm, it seems to have been restored to the church of Winchester by King Edgar *c*.964; see above, **V, xiii**. Most of Easton belonged to the bishop of Winchester *TRE* and *TRW*: *DB*, i, fo. 40[r] (*DB Hants* 2: 5). For its connection with the hundred of Chilcomb, see below, **XXXI**.
[4] Beorhthelm was bishop of Winchester 959 × 963. For another grant by King Edgar to him, of a life tenure of Bishopstoke (*Ytingstoce*), Hants, in 960, see S 683 (where wrongly identified as Itchen Stoke; see Rumble 1980, ii, 209), *CW* 216, *BCS* 1054. Cf. above, **V, xiii**, nn. 180 and 191.

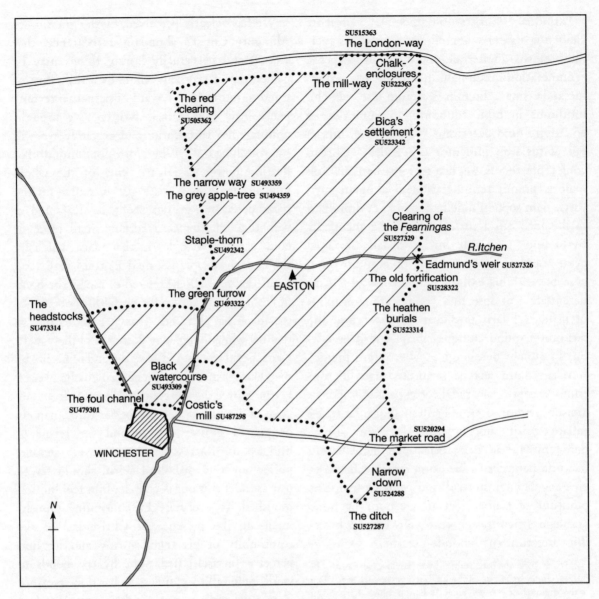

Fɪɢ. 10. The bounds of Easton, Hants, in **XXII** (A.D. 961)

þis synd þa landgemero to Eástune . Ærest ón
Eadmundes pér .[5] óf Eadmundes pere on þa
ealdan byrig .[6] óf þære ealdan byrig upp ꝺlang
díc[7] to þam eþenan byrigelsan .[8] óf þam æþenan
byrigelsan andlang mearce[9] to þære portstrét[10]
ꝺlang smalan dúne[11] úpp to þære díc[12] of þære
díc ꝺlang mearce[13] innan blacan lace .[14] of blaca[c]
lace ꝺlang patæres[15] on Costices mylne .[16] óf
Costices mylne[d] ꝺlang mearce[17] to þære fulan

^c *A spelling for* blacan   ^d *Point after* mylne

These are the estate-boundaries [relating] to
Easton. First to Edmund's weir.[5] From Edmund's
weir to the old fortification.[6] From the old
fortification up along [the] ditch[7] to the heathen
burials.[8] From the heathen burials along [the
marked] boundary[9] to the market-road,[10] along
narrow down[11] up to the ditch,[12] from the ditch
along [the marked] boundary[13] into black watercourse.[14] From black watercourse along [the]
water[15] to Costic's mill.[16] From Costic's mill
along [the marked] boundary[17] to the foul

[5] *ón Eadmundes pér.* 'Edmund's weir' was probably a fish-weir on the R. Itchen (see also below, n. 39), *c.* SU 527326, where the later parishes of Easton, Martyr Worthy, and Itchen Abbas came together; 'Hatches' are marked here on the 1908 edition of the 6″ OS map. The boundary returns to this point at the end of the perambulation; see below, n. 40.

[6] *on þa ealdan byrig.* 'The old fortification' recurs as the first and last point in the boundary of Avington of 961 (12): BL, Add. MS. 15350, fo. 114ᵛ, S 699, *CW* 223 (*Ærest on þa ealdan byrig . . . eft on ða ealdan byrig*). It was probably due S. of 'Edmund's weir' (see above, n. 5), where the later parishes of Easton, Itchen Abbas, and Avington came together and there was a semi-circular projection of the Easton *TA* boundary to the E., *c.* SU 528322. By 1840 this location lay beneath Avington Lake; see Easton *TA*, field no. 117. The word *burh* is here used in its original sense of 'fortification', not in its technical sense of 'borough, city' found in **VII** and **XX**.

[7] *upp ꝺlang díc.* This instruction is probably equivalent to that in the neighbouring Avington boundary (see above, n. 6), running the opposite way: *ꝺlang mearce* (*eft on ða ealdan byrig*). The 1840 Easton *TA* boundary here proceeds SW., part of the way along an embankment shown on the 1908 6″ OS map leading up Beech Hill.

[8] *to þam eþenan byrigelsan.* 'The heathen burials' also occur in the Avington boundary (see above n. 6): *to ðam hæþænan byrigelsan . of þam hæþenan byrigelsan.* They were probably on Beech Hill, *c.* SU 523314, where the Easton and Avington *TA* boundaries made a series of short right-angled turns which may commemorate the burials.

[9] *andlang mearce.* The OE term *mearc* also occurs here in the Avington boundary (see above, n. 6). It refers to the 'marked out' line of the Easton boundary between Beech Hill (see above, n. 8) and the *portstræt* (see below, n. 10). This line was represented by *Turnpike Drive* in the Avington *TA* of 1838 (field no. 105) and appears as Alresford Drive on the 1908 6″ OS map.

[10] *to þære portstrét.* The OE term *portstræt* 'market-road, road leading to or from a market or city' here refers to the medieval road, which may have been Roman in origin, leading from the East Gate of Winchester towards Bishops Sutton; see WS 1, 262. In the Avington boundary (see above, n. 6) it was referred to as a *herepath* or 'army way': *on þone herpað . of þam herpaðe.* The Easton and Avington *TA* boundaries crossed this road at SU 530294. The OE term *port* is also used in relation to Winchester in **V, iii,** above; and in **XXIII**, below (see ibid. n. 1).

[11] *ꝺlang smalan dúne.* The name 'narrow down' occurs here in

the Avington boundary (see above, n. 6): *ꝺlang smalan dune.* It was also mentioned in the earlier Easton boundary of 871 × 877 (12): BL, Add. MS. 15350, fo. 75ᵛ, S 1275, *CW* 148b (*on smalan dune eastepeardne*). It was partially commemorated in the following *TA* field-names: *Down, High Down, Middle Down* (Easton 1840, nos. 272, 270–1), and *Down* (Avington 1838, no. 117). The name refers to the narrow-necked down, *c.* SU 524288, to the N. of Telegraph Hill. The Easton *TA* boundary proceeded SSW. from the road identified in n. 10, above, as the *portstræt*, along the eastern slope of this down.

[12] *úpp to þære díc.* 'The ditch' is probably that referred to in the phrase *on þa hpitan dic . of þære hpitan dic* in the Avington boundary (see above, n. 6). It may have been at SU 527287, where the Easton *TA* boundary turned NW. to proceed over the down referred to above, n. 11. Cf. also, in the earlier Easton boundary (see ibid.) the reference to the *furh ðe Þulfred hét . adrifan* which could describe this ditch.

[13] *ꝺlang mearce.* The OE term *mearc* here refers to the 'marked out' line of the boundary from 'the ditch' (see above, n. 12) to 'black watercourse' (see below, n. 14), descending NW. from high on Chilcomb Down to the R. Itchen. The earlier Easton boundary (see above, n. 11) here goes *of dune on ða dene*: for the *denu*, see below, n. 17.

[14] *innan blacan lace.* The name 'black watercourse' was commemorated by the following *TA* field-names: *Black Lake Field, Upper Black Lake Field* (Easton 1840, nos. 195 and 193), and *Black Lake Field* (Winnall 1838, no. 36). These were adjacent to swampy land along the R. Itchen, *c.* SU 493309. Cf. also *Black Ditch*, W. of the main channel of the river near here in 1753. See WS 1, 236; and John Crook, 'Winchester's Cleansing Streams', *Winchester Cathedral Record* 53 (1984), 27–34, at 27–8, and ibid. Fig. 1.

[15] *ꝺlang patæres.* A short distance S. along the R. Itchen.

[16] *on Costices mylne.* 'Costic's mill' seems to have been a short distance upstream of Durngate, *c.* SU 487298. It was possibly a precursor of Durngate Mill; see WS 1, 236, 283, and WS 2.ii, **972.** Cf. *on ðone mylensteall . . . of ðem mylenstealle* in the earlier Easton boundary (see above, n. 11).

[17] *ꝺlang mearce.* The OE term *mearc* here refers to the 'marked out' line of the boundary E.-W. across the low-lying land to the N. of the city and is commemorated in the second element of the local name Danemark; see WS 1, 236–7, s.n. *Denemarche*, and ibid. 274. The first element is OE *denu*, which seems here to refer to the valley of the R. Itchen between Winchester and Kings Worthy; cf. above, n. 13. Cf. also WS 1, 239, s.n. **(de) Vallo.**

flóde .*e* [18] óf þære fulan flode*e* 7lang strét[19] to
þam eafodstoccan .[20] of þam heafodstoccan
7lang stret[21] innan Icénan .[22] 7lang Icenan to
þæra grenan furh[23] inna*f* þara stræt .[24] 7lang
stræt andlang mearce[25] on stapolþórn .[26] óf
stapolþorne 7lang mearce[27] on þa haran apoldran .[28] óf þara haran apoldran innan þane
smalan peg .[29] of þam smalan pege innan þa

e A spelling *for* flodan, *the oblique case of OE* flode   *f* A
spelling *for* innan

channel.[18] From the foul channel along [the]
road[19] to the head-stocks.[20] From the head-
stocks along [the] road[21] into Itchen.[22] Along
Itchen to the green furrow[23] into the road.[24]
Along [the] road, along [the marked] boundary,[25] to staple-thorn.[26] From staple-thorn along
[the marked] boundary[27] to the grey apple-
tree.[28] From the grey apple-tree into the
narrow way.[29] From the narrow way into the

---

[18] *to þære fulan flóde.* 'The foul channel' is commemorated in
the name Fulflood, a district on the Stockbridge road outside the
NW. of the city; see WS 1, 237, s.n. **(de) Fuleflod'**. The Easton
charter-boundary probably first touched 'the foul channel'
further E. than the modern suburb, at the place where 'the
foul channel', in former times before it was piped, crossed the
Andover road at *c.* SU 479301.

[19] *7lang strét.* This *stræt* is referred to as a *herepath* in the
Chilcomb boundary of at least the early eleventh century; see
BL, Harl. Ch. 43 C.1, S 376 (1): *spá norð 7 east to hearpaðe . a be
hearpaðe.* It represents the Andover road from the NW. of the
city, which is on the line of the Winchester-Mildenhall-
Wanborough Roman road (Margary 43).

[20] *to þam eafodstoccan.* 'The head-stocks' signifies a location
where trees have been pollarded and either where the severed
heads of criminals were displayed (see *EPN,* i, 237, s.v. *hēafod-stocc*)
or where the pollarded tree-stumps themselves look like human
heads. The boundary-point is commemorated in the name of the
modern suburb of Harestock, between the Andover and Stockbridge roads to the N. of Weeke, but the actual location was
probably at a change of direction in the Easton *TA* boundary at SU
473314. The place was also referred to in the boundary of
Headbourne Worthy of 854 (12); see BL, Add. MS. 15350, fo. 90ᵛ;
S 309, *CW* 177: *up to heafodstoccan . of heafodstocca.* It appears in the
Chilcomb boundary too (see above, n. 19): *to heafodstoccum.*

[21] *7lang stret.* The OE term *stræt* here refers to a minor road
linking two, and perhaps three, Roman roads (Margary 42a and
43, and ?45a). To the W. of 'the head-stocks' (see above, n. 20) it
is now known as Salter's Lane, while to the E. it is a footpath
leading towards the R. Itchen (see below, n. 22). The line of the
Easton boundary here is obliquely referred to in the direction *be
Hideburninga gemære* when the later Chilcomb boundary (see
above, n. 19) proceeds along the S. edge of the Headbourne
Worthy estate.

[22] *innan Icénan.* To the R. Itchen at *c.* SU 494318, upstream of,
and on the opposite bank to, 'black watercourse' (see above,
n. 14). The Itchen also formed the boundary here in the earlier
Easton boundary (see above, n. 11) and in the Chilcomb
boundary (see above, n. 19).

[23] *to þæra grenan furh.* 'The green furrow' was probably a
drainage trench between the Itchen (see above, n. 22) and the
stræt (see below, n. 24). The location appears to correspond with
the phrase *þæt spá pið easton Þorðige* in the Chilcomb boundary
(see above, n. 19), which suggests that 'the green furrow' was to
the E. of the settlement at Kings Worthy. There are several side

channels of the Itchen here, including a major one which led
N. from SU 493322, the junction of Easton, Headbourne
Worthy, and Kings Worthy parishes in 1908, but which has
been obscured by part of the A33 road.

[24] *inna þara stræt.* This *stræt* was the Winchester-Silchester
Roman road (Margary 42a), on the line of the modern A33 road.
The Easton charter-boundary probably joined the road a short
distance NE. of Kings Worthy church, *c.* SU 493323.

[25] *7lang stræt andlang mearce.* The boundary followed the *stræt*
(see above, n. 24) NE., probably as far as the cross-roads at SU
496329. It seems then to have left the *stræt* and to have
proceeded along the *mearc,* perhaps taking the same straight
line as the later boundary between Kings Worthy and Abbots
Worthy, represented in 1908 (6" OS) by the road NW. from the
cross-roads referred to above, n. 24; see also below, n. 27. Cf. the
direction *be rihtre mearce* in the Chilcomb boundary (see above,
n. 19).

[26] *on stapolþórn.* 'Staple-thorn' is also mentioned in the
boundary of *Æt Þurðige* (?Abbots Worthy; but, if so, it was
proceeding anti-clockwise, which would be very unusual) of
1026 (12); see BL, Add. MS. 15350, fo. 89ʳ; S 962, *CW* 175: *to
stapolðornæ.* It seems to be identical with 'the boundary-thorn' in
the Chilcomb bounds (see above, n. 19): *to ðæm gemær ðornan.* It
was probably some distance NW. along the *mearc* (see above,
n. 25; below, n. 27), ?c. SU 492342. A 'staple-thorn' was either a
solitary thorn-tree that looked like a staple or pillar, or one
which was supported by a staple or pillar; see *EPN,* ii, 146, and
Brooks 'Micheldever Forgery', 200 (with reference to a similar
name in the Micheldever and Hunton boundaries at SU 505442).

[27] *7lang mearce.* This *mearc* may be a continuation of the line
represented by the *mearc* in n. 25, above.

[28] *on þa haran apoldran.* 'The grey apple-tree' also occurs in the
Æt Þurðige boundary (see above, n. 26): *to þære haran apeldran . fram
þæra haran apeldran.* It may have been at the NW. corner of the
boundary between Kings Worthy and Abbots Worthy, at SU
494359, where there is a sharp turn to E. Cf. William atte
Horeap(p)eldore (*fl.* by 1327, by 1347) who may have come from
near here; see WS 2.ii, 1265.

[29] *innan þane smalan peg.* The charter-boundary seems to have
crossed 'the narrow way', rather than to have proceeded along it,
since the prepositions *innan* and *of,* not *andlang,* are used here. This
route was also mentioned in the *Æt Þurðige* boundary (see above,
n. 26), although in a corrupt form: *to ðam spalan pege.* The location
referred to here may have been at SU 493359, where the later
parish boundaries of Stoke Charity, Weston Colley, and Abbots
Worthy met, the NS. line of the bounds between the first two of
these being continued S. from this place by *TA* field-boundaries.

readan rode .[30] óf þære readan rode andlang þæs mylan peges[g][31] on þone Lunden peg .[32] 7lang þes Lundænes peges innan cealchammæs .[33] of cealchammam 7lang mearce[34] innan Bicasetl .[h][35] of Bicasetle 7lang mearce[36] innan Fearninga lege .[37] of Fearninga lege 7lang dic[38] æft on Icenan[39] innan Eadmundes[j] pér .[40]

Anno dominice incarnationis . dccccclxi . scripta est hęc carta his testibus consentientibus quorum inferius nomina caraxantur .[41]

Ego Eadgar[42] rex Anglorum corroboraui .

Ego Dunstan[43] archiepiscopus concessi .

Ego Oscytel[44] archiepiscopus confirmaui .

red clearing.[30] From the red clearing along the mill-way[31] to the London-way.[32] Along the London-way into chalk-enclosures.[33] From chalk-enclosures along [the marked] boundary[34] into Bica's settlement.[35] From Bica's settlement along [the marked] boundary[36] into clearing of the *Fearningas*.[37] From clearing of the *Fearningas* along [the] ditch[38] again to Itchen[39] into Edmund's weir.[40]

This charter was written in the year of the Lord's Incarnation 961, with these witnesses in agreement whose names are written[41] below.

I, Edgar,[42] king of the English, have corroborated.

I, Dunstan,[43] archbishop, have granted.

I, Oscytel,[44] archbishop, have confirmed.

---

[g] *Point after peges*   [h] *bicafed MS., with scribal misreadings of* s *in the exemplar as* f, *and of* tl *as* d   [j] *Point after* Eadmundes

---

[30] *innan þa readan rode.* 'The red clearing' also occurs in the Chilcomb boundary (see above, n. 19): *þæt to ðære readan rode.* It is probably the same as 'the clearing' in the *Æt Þurðige* boundary (see above, n. 26): *to þære rode . óf þære* [*rode*]. It may have occupied the hollow where Burnt Wood now stands, *c.* SU 505362.

[31] *andlang þæs mylan peges.* 'The mill-way' led from 'the red clearing' (see above, n. 30) to 'the London-way' (see below, n. 32).

[32] *on þone Lunden peg . 7lang þes Lundænes peges.* 'The London-way' was a major W.–E. route in the direction of London. Further W. in the Crawley boundary of 909 (12) it was referred to in the phrase *to Lunden hærpaðe*: BL, Add. MS. 15350, fo. 55ʳ; S 381, *CW* 110. The Easton charter-boundary probably joined it at the point where its crossing of the Winchester-Silchester Roman road (Margary 42a; the modern A33) is commemorated by Lunways Inn, at SU 515363, and which by the early 11th century was the site of the Micheldever hundred moot-house, see Brooks 'Micheldever Forgery', 202–3, 218. The *TA* field-names *Lunways* (1838, Itchen Abbas, nos. 1 and 2), and *Lunways Field* (1840, Martyr Worthy, no.168) adjoined each other a short distance E. of this location.

[33] *innan cealchammæs.* 'Chalk-enclosures' was the name of a place on 'the London-way' (see above, n. 32). It may have been at SU 522363, where the Micheldever, Martyr Worthy, and Itchen Abbas *TA* boundaries came together and where the boundary between the last two parishes made a sharp turn S. The next-but-one field to this location in the Martyr Worthy *TA* of 1840 was *Chalk Dell Field* (field no. 169), while Old Chalk Pit is marked in the same field on the 1908 6" OS map.

[34] *7lang mearce.* The *mearc* is here the northern section of the long stretch of boundary between Martyr Worthy and Itchen Abbas parishes, along Chilland Road, running S. from 'chalk-enclosures' (see above, n. 33). Cf. *be ealdormonnes mearce* in the Chilcomb boundary (see above, n. 19), which probably signifies 'by the marked-out hundred boundary'. Cf. also below, n. 36.

[35] *innan Bicasetl.* If this boundary point has as first element a personal name as here assumed, then the man commemorated in

the name 'Bica's settlement' may have been the same as the one in 'Byca's paddock' which occurs in the Martyr Worthy boundary of 868 (12); see BL, Add. MS. 15350, fo. 91ʳ; S 340, *CW* 178: *on Bycan gærstunes hyrnan.* The two points are not necessarily identical, however. 'Bica's settlement' was probably S. of 'chalk-enclosures' (see above, n. 33) and may have been *c.*SU 523342, high on the ridge S. of Chillingham Farm, whence the end of the perambulation could be seen. An alternative explanation of the first element in both names might be topographical, however, involving in some way or other the OE word **bica* '(?) beak, point'; see *VEPN*, 96.

[36] *7lang mearce.* The *mearc* is here the southern section of the boundary between Martyr Worthy and Itchen Abbas parishes, N. of the B3047 road. Cf. above, n. 34.

[37] *innan Fearninga lege.* The *Fearningas* may have been 'the dwellers at the ferns'; see Christer Johansson, *Old English Place-Names and Field-Names Containing Leah* (Stockholm Studies in English 32, Stockholm, 1975), 74. An alternative derivation, however, might be from the plural of a derivative noun **fearning*, 'ferny place'; the boundary-point would then signify 'clearing with ferny places in it'. The location was at the N. end of a ditch (see below, n. 38) which led to the R. Itchen. It was probably at *c.* SU 527329.

[38] *7lang dic.* This ditch ran N.–S. from 'clearing of the *Fearningas*' (see above, n. 37) into the R. Itchen on the N. side of 'Edmund's weir' (see below, n. 40).

[39] *æft on Icenan.* The R. Itchen at 'Edmund's weir' (see above, n. 5; below, n. 40). The Chilcomb boundary (see above, n. 19) also reached the Itchen at about the same place, before going upstream towards Alresford: *on Icenan . úp be stream to Alresforda.*

[40] *innan Eadmundes pér.* Where the boundary began; see above, n. 5.

[41] *caraxantur.* See above, **IV**, n. 124.

[42] See above, n. 2.

[43] Dunstan, archbishop of Canterbury; see above, **IV**, n. 127.

[44] Oscytel, archbishop of York; ibid. n. 133.

Ego Osulf[45] episcopus subscripsi .	I, Oswulf,[45] bishop, have subscribed.
Ego Brithelm[46] episcopus impressi .	I, Beorhthelm,[46] bishop, have made a mark.
Ego Aþulf[47] episcopus corroboraui .	I, Æthulf,[47] bishop, have corroborated.
Ego Alfþold[48] episcopus consolidaui .	I, Ælfweald,[48] bishop, have made [it] firm.
Ego Ospold[49] episcopus confirmaui .[k]	I, Oswald,[49] bishop, have confirmed.
Ego Aþelpold[50] abbas .	I, Æthelwold,[50] abbot
Ego Ælfhere[51] dux .	I, Ælfhere,[51] ealdorman
Ego Ælfheah[52] dux .	I, Ælfheah,[52] ealdorman
Ego Aþelpold[53] dux .	I, Æthelweald,[53] ealdorman
Ego Brihtnoð[54] dux .	I, Beorhtnoth,[54] ealdorman
Ego Eadmund[55] dux .	I, Edmund,[55] ealdorman
Ego Æþelmund[56] dux .	I, Æthelmund,[56] ealdorman
Ego Ælfgar[57] minister .[l]	I, Ælfgar,[57] thegn
Ego Ælfpine[58] minister .	I, Ælfwine,[58] thegn
Ego Byrtferð[59] minister .	I, Beorhtfrith,[59] thegn
Ego Æþelsige[60] minister .	I, Æthelsige,[60] thegn
Ego Eadric[61] minister .	I, Eadric,[61] thegn
Ego Æþelpine[62] minister .	I, Æthelwine,[62] thegn
Ego Ospeard[63] minister .	I, Osweard,[63] thegn
Ego Osulf[64] minister .	I, Oswulf,[64] thegn
Ego Þulfgar[65] minister .[m]	I, Wulfgar,[65] thegn
Ego Æþelsige[66] minister .	I, Æthelsige,[66] thegn

---

[k] *First column of subscriptions ends here*   [l] *Second column of subscriptions ends here*   [m] *Third column of subscriptions ends here. BCS reads* Þulfstan *for* Þulfgar

---

[45] Oswulf, bishop of Ramsbury; ibid. n. 137.

[46] This Beorhthelm was either the beneficiary, the bishop of Winchester (see above, n. 4), or the bishop of Wells (see above, **IV**, n. 140).

[47] Æthulf, bishop of Elmham; ibid. n. 143.

[48] Either Ælfweald I, bishop of Crediton or Ælfweald I, bishop of Sherborne; ibid. n. 139.

[49] Oswald, bishop of Worcester; ibid. n. 138.

[50] Æthelwold, abbot of Abingdon, c.954 × 963: *HRH*, 23. For him as bishop of Winchester, replacing the beneficiary of the present document, see above, **IV**, n. 134.

[51] Ælfhere, ealdorman of Mercia; ibid. n. 151.

[52] Ælfheah, ealdorman of Hampshire; ibid. n. 152.

[53] Æthelweald, ealdorman of East Anglia, 956 × 962; see Hart *ECNE*, 294.

[54] Beorhtnoth, ealdorman of Essex; see above, **IV**, n. 156.

[55] Edmund, ealdorman of the Western Provinces, 949 × 963; see Hart *ECNE*, 331.

[56] Æthelmund, ealdorman of NW. Mercia, 940 × 965; ibid. 287.

[57] Ælfgar subscribes 951 × 962; ibid. 254, and Keynes *Atlas*, Tables XLVI–VII, LI–II, and LVII. His position advances to that of leading thegn in Wessex by 958. He was a royal kinsman and

the brother of Beorhtfrith (below, n. 59). His death is reported in *ASC* [A], s.a. 962.

[58] For Ælfwine, see above, **IV**, n. 157.

[59] Beorhtfrith was a kinsman of King Edgar, and perhaps also of the beneficiary Bishop Beorhthelm, who is also said to be related to the king, and whose name contains the same prototheme as Beorhtfrith's. His brother, however, was called Ælfgar (see above, n. 57). See further, above, **IV**, n. 158.

[60] One of three thegns called Æthelsige in the present witness-list; see below, nn. 66 and 72. He subscribes 956 × 975: Keynes *Atlas*, Tables XLVII, LI, and LVII. He may be also be the powerful thegn who was an adviser to King Æthelred II in his youth; see Keynes *Diplomas*, 184–5. If so, see also Keynes *Atlas*, Table LXIII.

[61] Eadric subscribes 956 × 963: Keynes *Atlas*, Tables LI and LVII. He was probably the brother of Ealdorman Ælfheah (above, n. 52); see Hart *ECNE*, 318, and S 1292, *AS Ch* 31 (p. 339).

[62] Æthelwine subscribes 958 × 966: Keynes *Atlas*, Table LVII.

[63] For Osweard, see above, **IV**, n. 159.

[64] Oswulf subscribes 959 × 970: Keynes *Atlas*, Table LVII (Osulf 1).

[65] Perhaps the Wulfgar who subscribes 958 × 969, discussed by Hart *ECNE*, 366.

[66] The second Æthelsige; see above, n. 60. He subscribes 959 × 966: Keynes *Atlas*, Tables LI and LVII.

Ego Ælfsige[67] minister .

Ego Þulfhelm[68] minister .

Ego Ælfsige[69] minister .

Ego Ælfred[70] minister .

Ego Ealdred[71] minister .

Ego Æþelsige[72] minister .

Ego Alfþold[73] minister ."

I, Ælfsige,[67] thegn

I, Wulfhelm,[68] thegn

I, Ælfsige,[69] thegn

I, Ælfred,[70] thegn

I, Ealdred,[71] thegn

I, Æthelsige,[72] thegn

I, Ælfweald,[73] thegn

" Fourth column of subscriptions ends here

---

[67] One of two thegns called Ælfsige in the present witness-list; cf. below, n. 70. He subscribes 955 × 973: Keynes *Atlas*, ibid.

[68] Wulfhelm subscribes 958 × 963: Keynes *Atlas*, Table LVII; cf. Hart *ECNE*, 368-9. He was a prominent Mercian thegn, perhaps an ancestor of Wulfric Spot. He received estates in Staffordshire in 951 and 957: S 557, Sawyer *Burton* 11, and S 574, *CW* 147, BCS 987.

[69] The second Ælfsige; see above, n. 67. He subscribes 958 × 973: Keynes *Atlas*, ibid.

[70] Ælfred subscribes 958 × 964: ibid.

[71] Ealdred subscribes 958 × 974: ibid. Tables LI and LVII.

[72] The third Æthelsige; see above, n. 60. He subscribes 959 × 961: Keynes *Atlas*, Table LVII.

[73] Ælfweald subscribes 959 × 968: ibid. Tables LI and LVII (Ælfwold 2).

XXIII

A.D. 961, a reference to a tenement within the south wall at Winchester, pertaining to the 10-hide estate at Kilmeston, Hants

English

S 693a (part), Finberg 96, *CW* 111a

THE extract printed below is taken from S 693, a copy of a diploma of King Edgar which recorded the lease to one of his thegns of an estate belonging to Winchester Cathedral, with the express permission of the bishop and of the religious communities at Winchester.[1] As Dorothy Whitelock observed,[2] this was perhaps the last time that we have a record of the pre-Reform clergy at Winchester acting as a body.

The reference to the urban tenement appurtenant to the said estate occurs at the end of the vernacular boundary-clause in the diploma. There is no reason to doubt its authenticity or that of the diploma itself.

XXIII survives only in the cartulary-copy of S 693 written into the *Codex Wintoniensis* by scribe *a* in 1129 × 1139.[3] It exhibits some of the characteristic misreadings by this particular scribe due to his unfamiliarity with the insular minuscule script of this part, at least, of the now-lost exemplar.[4]

MS.:   B. BL, Add. MS. 15350, fos. 55ᵛ–56ʳ (s.xii¹)

Edited: *KCD* 1231
           BCS 1077

Translated: Whitelock *EHD* 110

Printed from the manuscript

---

[1] See below, **XXIII**, n. 3. S 693b, *CW* 111b, *BCS* 1078, refers to communities (*hiredas*) of both priests and nuns.

[2] Whitelock *EHD*, 110.

[3] See above, pp. 6–7.

[4] See below, **XXIII**, nn. *a-c*, and above, p. 7.

7 se haga on porte*a* *1* bynnan suþ[p]ealla*b* *2* þae to þam lande*3* gebyreð*c* .

... And the tenement in the city,[1] within the south wall,[2] which pertains to the estate[3] ...

a porte *MS., with scribal misreading of* þ *in the exemplar as* p
b suþealla *MS., with scribal confusion of adjacent* þ *and* p *in the exemplar*   *c* gebyred *MS. with scribal misreading of* ð *in the exemplar as* d

[2] *bynnan suþ[p]ealla.* For other references to the south wall, see above **VIII(i)**, n. 15, and **XVIII**, n. 7.

[3] *to þam lande.* Referring to the 10–hide estate of Kilmeston, Hants, which was leased by King Edgar, Bishop Beorhthelm, and the Old Minster to the thegn Æthelwulf (otherwise unknown) in 961 for the term of three lives: S 693ab, *CW* 111ab, BCS 1077–8. The bishop of Winchester held two estates of 5 hides each there TRE and TRW: *DB*, i, fo. 40ʳ (*DB Hants* 2: 2 and 7).

[1] *on porte.* For other references to Winchester using the OE term *port*, see above, **V, iii**, and **XXII**, n. 10.

XXIV

A.D. 988, grant by King Æthelred II to Bishop Æthelsige [of Sherborne],
and Æthelmær, miles, of a tenement in Winchester which Eadgeard
had held

Latin

S 871, Finberg 137

THE tenement granted in **XXIV** is probably identifiable from later references with one situated in the southern suburb of the city. The medieval cartulary in which it is preserved (see below) associates it with the house formerly held by Conan the moneylender which was granted to Glastonbury Abbey *c.*1137 by Henry of Blois, bishop of Winchester;[1] the 1148 Survey of the city places this outside South Gate. [2]

It is unclear why Bishop Æthelsige and Æthelmær are joint beneficiaries. One explanation may be that they were related, perhaps as brothers.

It has been noted by Simon Keynes that the formulae used share some unusual features with those in S 870 and that both documents record the grant of urban tenements, one in Winchester, the other in Wilton.[3] He concludes that 'There can be little doubt that . . . [both texts] were drawn up by a single agency; they may indeed have been produced on the same occasion, for both belong to the period in 988 when there was a vacancy at Canterbury created by Archbishop Dunstan's death . . .' [4]

The text of **XXIV** is only preserved in the Glastonbury cartulary known as the *Secretum abbatis.* Although the *Secretum* is mainly a fair copy, made *c.*1340–2 for the abbot's personal use,[5] of another slightly-earlier cartulary,[6] **XXIV** does not appear in the latter and may have only been discovered when the *Secretum* was being copied. It is probable that the witness-list (here consisting only of the king and five bishops) was truncated by the copyist in order to save space, and it may be that a boundary-description of the property was also omitted by him, since S 870 (see above) does include the bounds of the Wilton tenement.

MS.:   B. Bod, Wood MS. empt. 1, fos. 253ᵛ–254ʳ (s.xiv med.)

Edited: Aelred Watkin (ed.), *The Great Chartulary of Glastonbury,* iii, Somerset Record Soc. 64 (1956), 704 (no. 1303)

Printed from the manuscript

---

[1] See below, **XXIV**, n. *a*
[2] Ibid. n. 4
[3] Keynes *Diplomas,* 91–2. For S 870, see *KCD* 665.
[4] Keynes *Diplomas,* 91.

[5] Davis 435; Aelred Watkin (ed.), *The Great Chartulary of Glastonbury,* i, Somerset Record Soc. 59 (1947), x–xii.
[6] Davis 434; now belonging to the Marquess of Bath (Longleat, MS. 39).

Omnia[a] que uidentur temporalia sunt . et uelud fumalis umbra euanescencia [.] que autem non uidentur eterna[1] sine fine mansura . Ecclesiaste clamante qui ait . quicquid sub sole est uanitas[2] quod uero supra est ethereum et durabile . Precipue uanum et mutabile humanum genus cui quod pulcrum et decorum uidetur placet quod autem asperum renuit et displicet [.] que enim uidimus non uidemus et que non uidemus iam non uisuri sumus . Imagines rerum opes potentum pulcritudines et uarietates camporum diuiciarumque adquisiciones cuncta hec apud homines preciosa et cara . apud uero Deum uilia . Qua de re ego Adelredus[3] tocius Albionis rex inter cetera dapsilia munera que habunde largior . et distribuo . concedo unam curtem Wintonie urbis partem quam habuit Edgeard[4] quodam meo fideli presuli Athelsino[5] et militi meo Adelmaro[b][6]. Vt habeant et possideant hereditario iure perhenniter quamdiu uiuant . Cum autem cognouerint dissolucionem suorum[c] zomatum[7] [.] quod commune est periculum omnium uiuencium commendent heredibus quibuscumque uoluerint in hereditatem propriam post se cum omnibus ad se pertinentibus tam in uiuis quam in mortalibus rebus . Hanc uero meam donacionem volo esse

All 'things which are seen are temporal' and passing away like a smoky shadow, 'but the things which are not seen are eternal'[1] and lasting without end. As Ecclesiastes declares, who says 'Whatever is under the sun is vanity',[2] but what is above it is ethereal and lasting. Mankind is particularly vain and changeable, being pleased by what seems beautiful and decorous, but rejecting and being displeased by what seems austere; for we do not see what we have seen, and what we do not see now we are not going to see. Representations of things, the wealth of powerful men, the beautiful and varied things of the fields, and the acquiring of riches, all these things are precious and dear in the sight of men, vile indeed in the sight of God. Wherefore I, Æthelred,[3] king of all Albion, among the other bountiful gifts which I abundantly give and distribute, grant one curtilege, that part of the city of Winchester which Eadgeard[4] had, to Æthelsige,[5] a certain faithful bishop of mine, and to my soldier Æthelmær,[6] so that they may have and possess it in hereditary right continually for as long as they live. When moreover they perceive their bodies'[7] dissolution, which is the common peril of all living things, let them commit it to whichever heirs they wish in their own heredity after them, with everything belonging to it both in living and in dead things. Indeed I wish this my donation to be

[a] Carta regis Athelredi confirmatoria eiusdem qua supra 'King Æthelred's confirmation-charter of the same [property] as above' rubric. The preceding document in the cartulary is the grant made to Glastonbury Abbey in c.1137 by Bishop Henry of Blois, then also abbot of Glastonbury, of the house in Winchester which Conan the money-lender (fenerator) had held (see below, n. 4) and is introduced by the rubric Carta eiusdem Henrici de domo in Wyntonia data ecclesie. 'Charter of the same Henry concerning a house in Winchester given to the church [of Glastonbury]'.
[b] quam habuit . Edgeard a quodam meo fideli presule Athelsino et militi meo [altered from mee] Adelmaro MS.; the preposition a is probably intrusive here and has caused the alteration of presuli (dative) to presule (ablative). Edgeard may possibly be a misreading of Edpeard but is itself a possible OE dithematic personal name containing the deuterotheme geard (cf. PNDB, 259).   [c] Point after suorum MS.

[1] Omnia que uidentur temporalia sunt . . . que autem non uidentur eterna. Cf. 2 Cor. 4: 18 (BSV, ii, 1793) quae enim videntur temporalia sunt quae autem non videntur aeterna sunt.
[2] quicquid sub sole est uanitas. Cf. Eccles. 1: 14 (BSV, ii, 987) quae fiunt cuncta sub sole et ecce universa vanitas.

[3] Æthelred II, king of England 978–1016.
[4] unam curtem . . . quam habuit Edgeard. The tenement had belonged to Conan the money-lender by c.1137 (see n. a) and is identified as being outside South Gate in 1148; see WS 1, 135 (II, 962–3). For the name Eadgeard (Edgeard), see n. b.
[5] Æthelsige, bishop of Sherborne, 978–990 × 992. He subscribes above, IX.
[6] Æthelmær miles may have been identical with Æthelmær minister, who later became ealdorman of the Western Provinces; see above, IX, n. 35. In 1002 × 1014 the next bishop of Sherborne, Æthelric, appealed to Ealdorman Æthelmær for help in the restoration of ship-scot from estates allotted to his diocese for that purpose: S 1383 (O'Donovan Sherborne 13).
[7] zomatum. From gen. pl. of zoma (= Greek σῶμα 'body'). Cf. somatis, above, IX, n. 2.

liberam ab omni mundiali offendiculo ecceptis[d] tribus . expedicione uidelicet pontis arcisque coedificacione . Si quis sane eam frangere uel mutare uel eciam uoluerit minuere quod absit . sciat se habiturum cum satellitibus Beatmot[8] . in pirflegetonte[e] baratri quibus in ultima examinacione dicetur . discedite a me operarii iniquitatis . non enim noui uos [.] ibi erit fletus oculorum et stridor dencium .[9]

Huius uero donacionis libertatem concessi. ego Adelredus rex anno dominice incarnacionis [.] d . cccc . lxxxviii . istis testibus consencientibus et subnotantibus quorum nomina inferius caraxantur[10] . + Ego Adelredus[11] rex hoc donum concessi . + Ego Oswaldus[12] Eboracensis[f] ecclesie archiepiscopus designando concessi . + Ego Elphian[g] [13] Winton*iensis* ecclesie presul consensiendo[h] designaui . + Ego Athelgar[14] Australium[j] Saxonum subspeculator ascensum[k] prebens subnotaui . `+` Ego Eswi[15] Dorcensis ecclesie episcopus inpressi . + Ego Sirik[16] Coruinensis ecclesie episcopus conclusi .

free from all worldly hinderance except for three, namely military-service and the construction of bridges and fortifications. If anyone however, which Heaven forbid!, should wish to break or change or even to lessen it, let him know that he will be placed with the followers of Behemoth[8] in the conflagration of the Abyss, to whom in the Last Judgement will be said 'Depart from me, workers of iniquity, for I know you not; there shall be weeping of eyes and gnashing of teeth'.[9]

Indeed, I, King Æthelred, have granted the freedom of this donation in the year of the Lord's Incarnation 988, with the agreement and subscription of these witnesses whose names are written[10] below: + I, Æthelred,[11] king, have granted this gift. + I, Oswald,[12] archbishop of the church of York, have granted by indication. + I, Ælfheah,[13] bishop of the church of Winchester, have indicated in agreement. + I, Æthelgar,[14] bishop of the South Saxons, showing approval have subscribed. + I, Æscwig,[15] bishop of the church of Dorchester, have made a mark. + I, Sigeric,[16] bishop of the church of Ramsbury, have concluded.

---

[d] A spelling for exceptis *due either to French influence or to a misreading of* xc *as* cc   [e] pirflegetonte; *Professor Lapidge notes that this is from Gk.* πῦρ φλεγέθων [lit. 'blazing fire'], *a common metaphor for Hell. It was also used by Frithegod,* Breuiloquium Vitae Wilfridi, *line 1353.*   [f] Eboracens' *MS., the final letter over an erasure*   [g] A very corrupt spelling   [h] A spelling for consenciendo < consentiendo   [j] Australus *MS., probably a misreading of* Australiu'   [k] A spelling for assensum

stridor dencium. Cf. Luke 13: 27–8 (*BSV*, ii, 1636, *with* omnes operarii).

[10] caraxantur. As above, **IV**, n. 124.

[11] As above, n. 3.

[12] Oswald, archbishop of York; see above, **IV**, n. 138.

[13] Ælfheah II, bishop of Winchester 984–1006, then archbishop of Canterbury until his murder by vikings at Greenwich on 19 April 1012 (*ASC* [C, D], s.a.). In 996, he obtained for the Old Minster the property restored in **XXVI**, below.

[14] Æthelgar, bishop of Selsey and abbot of the New Minster; see above, **IV**, n. 149, and **IX**, n. 4.

[15] Æscwig, bishop of Dorchester; see above, **IX**, n. 18.

[16] Sigeric, bishop of Ramsbury, 985 × 986–990, then archbishop of Canterbury until his death in 994.

---

[8] Beatmot. Behemoth, *a great or monstrous beast* (OED). *Derived from Hebrew* b'hēmôth, *pl. of* b'hēmāh 'beast', *ultimately from Egyptian* p-ehe-mau 'water-ox'.

[9] discedite a me operarii iniquitatis . . . ibi erit fletus oculorum et

XXV

A.D. 990, a reference to 9 tenements in Tanner Street, Winchester, pertaining to the 15-hide estate at Wootton St. Lawrence, Hants

English

S 874 (part; MS. 1 only), Finberg 138, *CW* 207

THE 9 tenements to which **XXV** refers were located in the Brooks district of Winchester. They were granted by King Æthelred II in 990 as part of the appurtenances of a 15–hide estate at Wootton St. Lawrence, in the country about 15 miles NNW. of the city, which probably later formed part of the Old Minster estate there.[1] The grant is probably indicative of a process of sub-division of the larger urban fiefs in the late Anglo-Saxon period.[2] The tenements do not appear identifiable with any in surviving later records.

The beneficiary of the grant was a thegn called Æthelweard. He may be the same person as one of the addressees of Æthelred's writ concerning Chilcomb in 984 × 1001 and may further have been the high-reeve of Hampshire who was killed in 1001.[3]

The reference to the tenements (as to a meadow at Basingstoke, Hants, and a mill at the unidentified place *æt hines clifæ*) occurs in a separate sentence after the description of the bounds of Wootton itself, in the (authentic) diploma copied into the *Codex Wintoniensis* by scribe *a* in 1129 × 1139.[4] None of the appurtenances are mentioned in the later text recording the bounds of Wootton written on an additional folio of the same cartulary by scribe *l* in the early thirteenth century.[5]

MS.:   B. BL, Add. MS. 15350, fo. 109ᵛ (s.xii¹)

Edited: *KCD* 673

Printed from the manuscript

---

[1] The Old Minster held 20 hides at Wootton *TRE* and *TRW*: *DB*, i, fos. 41ᵛ and 43ʳ (*DB Hants* 3: 24). Another 5 hides there were held *in alodium* by Ælfmær and Ælfgeat from Edward the Confessor: ibid. fo. 46ʳ (23: 58).

[2] See WS 1, 341.

[3] See below, **XXX**, n. 4.

[4] S 874 (1), *CW* 207; see Keynes *Diplomas*, 250. For scribe *a*, see above, pp. 6–7.

[5] *CW* 235, on fo. 117; for an edition of these bounds, see Rumble 1980, ii, 226–7. Sawyer lists them as S 874 (2) but there is no reason to connect them with the diploma of Æthelred; they are quite different from the bounds in the latter and may describe a later medieval estate-unit. For scribe *l*, see Rumble 1980, i, 374–7.

7 [.] ix . hagan on Þintancestre on   . . . And 9 tenements in Winchester, in Tænnerestret[1] .   Tanner Street[1] . . .

---

[1] *Tænnerestret.* Now Lower Brook Street. For the suggestion that the 9 *hagan* perhaps represented the subdivision of a larger tenement, see WS 1, 341.

XXVI

A.D. 996, restoration by King Æthelred II to the Old Minster of a tenement in Winchester bequeathed to them by the noblewoman Ælfswith, and grant of half a fish-weir with adjacent ground at Brentford, Middx.

Latin with English

S 889, Finberg 142, *CW* 17

THE diploma printed below records the grant to the Old Minster, at the request of Bishop Ælfheah II, of two distinct pieces of property with no explicit connection made between them. The first represents the royal enforcement of a right of ownership to a tenement in Winchester, on the north side of High Street,[1] under the terms of a *post obitum* grant formerly made by the noblewoman Ælfswith which was apparently not implemented on her death.[2] The second is the grant of half of a fish-weir, said to be at Brentford (Middx.), with adjacent ground, property which later references in cathedral priory accounts suggest actually to have been the southern half of the weir with land on the Surrey bank of the Thames at Kew.[3] The bounds of the Winchester tenement provide the earliest reference to street-names in the city reflecting occupational specialisation within particular streets, here by the butchers and the shieldmakers.[4]

XXVI is one of a group of apparently authentic diplomas of King Æthelred, dating to 993 × 998, which share similarities of otherwise unusual formulae, suggesting the existence of a single agency behind their drafting.[5] Some of these documents restore property which churches had lost during the period of Æthelred's 'youthful indiscretions', when the progress of the monastic reform had been halted and in places reversed.[6] There are especially close links between XXVI and S 885 (A.D. 995), a grant of land in Kent to the bishopric of Rochester, and S 888 (A.D. 996), a grant of land in and near St. Albans to the abbey there.[7] Features in S 888 comparable with XXVI include the vernacular glossing of the Latin word used for 'tenement';[8] the composite verbs of disposition (*renouando restituo et restituendo . . . praecipio;* cf. *restituendo concedo . et concedendo restituo* in XXVI); and the deliberate employment of a full variety of verbs of attestation for the episcopal subscriptions (including the combination *consentaneus extiti;* also in S 885). The witness-list of S 888 also includes a statement that the grant was made in answer to Bishop Godwine of Rochester's wish (*hoc donum uoti compos optinui*), paralleled by Bishop Ælfheah of Winchester's statement in XXVI (*hanc . . . donationem uoti compos obtinui*).

---

[1] See below, XXVI, n. 12, and Fig. 11.
[2] For Ælfswith, see below, XXVI, n. 6.
[3] Ibid. n. 7.
[4] Ibid. nn. 13 and 14.
[5] See Keynes *Diplomas*, 102–4.

[6] A.D. 984–*c*.993; ibid. 176–86, and cf. 198–9. Note that V may have been constructed in codex form as a response to this unsettled period; see above, pp. 100–4.
[7] Respectively, Campbell *Rochester* 31 and *KCD* 696.
[8] See below, XXVI, n. 5.

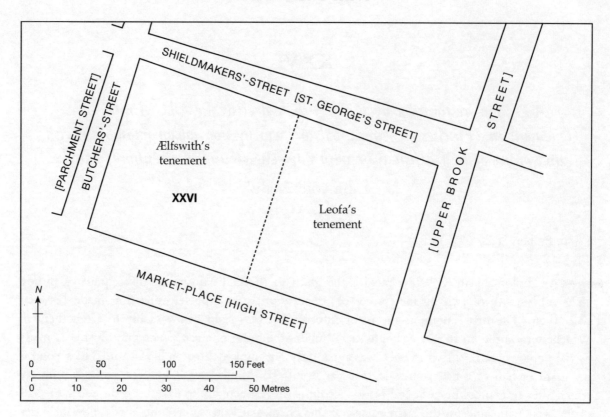

FIG. 11. The bounds of Ælfswith's tenement in **XXVI** (A.D. 996).

S 893 (A.D. 998), another diploma in the group, also in favour of Rochester Cathedral, provides a parallel for the unusual additional clause of general consent added in **XXVI** after the witness-list in the sentence (+ *Nos omnes optimates consensimus*) that appears after its last subscription.[9]

The diploma was added to the *Codex Wintoniensis* by scribe *b* in the mid twelfth century.[10] It is probable that he truncated the witness-list and changed the status of the only three thegns whom he included into that of ealdormen;[11] he also no doubt altered the form of the OE prototheme of the personal-name compounds in Wulf- to *Wlf-* in accordance with contemporary orthography.

[9] Campbell *Rochester* 32. Cf. the final sanction, after the witness-list, in **IV**, above.

[10] See above, pp. 7–8.

[11] See below, **XXVI**, nn. 34–6; and Keynes *Diplomas*, 255.

MS.:   B. BL, Add. MS. 15350, fo. 6^v (s.xii med.)

Edited: *KCD* 1291
            Earle, 364 (bounds only)
            Pierquin *Receuil*, pt 5, no. 38 (without bounds)

Printed from the manuscript

Eterni[a] gubernacula imperii moderante in perpetuum Domino et Saluatore nostro Iesu Christo certissimis pupillarum optutibus quadripartiti[1] mundi cotidie magis ac magis imminere cernitur occasus . Qui quamuis crescendo decrescat et augmentando minuatur . fidelibus tamen diuinitus est concessum . ut nequaquam toti cum deficiente deficiant . sed per umbratilis substantię mercimonium . permanentem sibi thesaurizænt[b] in celis thesaurum . quo iuxta illud dominici promissi fur non appropiat. neque tinea corrumpit .[2] Quapropter superni amoris igniculo succensus ego Æðelred[3] althroni fauente gratia basileus Anglorum ceterarumque gentium in circuitu persistentium sanctę Dei ęcclesię Þentana ciuitate beato Petro apostolorum principi eiusque coapostolo Paulo ob reuerende Trinitatis honorem consecrate . Ælfhego[c][4] eiusdem sedis antistite impetrante . pro meorum expiatione piaculorum meique statu imperii quandam hospicii portionem[5] in prefata ciuitate sitam . quę patria lingua haga solet appellari . uti nobilis matrona Ælfspyð[6] Deo omnipotenti eiusque prenominatis apostolis hereditario iure

While Our Lord and Saviour Jesus Christ guides the government of the eternal dominion in perpetuity, the end of this quadripartite[1] world daily seems more and more imminent in the eyes' surest contemplation. But although it decreases by increasing and lessens by adding, it is however divinely granted to the faithful that in no way will all of them fade away with the fading [world], but through the wealth of shadowy substance they may store up for themselves permanent 'treasure in Heaven, where', according to the Lord's promise, 'no thief approacheth, nor moth corrupteth'.[2] Wherefore I, Æthelred,[3] by the favouring grace of the High-throned One, king of the English and of the other peoples living around, having been set alight by the flame of celestial love, gladly grant by restoring, and restore by granting, to the holy church of God in Winchester consecrated in honour of the venerable Trinity, to the blessed Peter the foremost of the apostles, and to his fellow apostle Paul, at the request of Ælfheah,[4] bishop of the same see, for the expiation of my sins and for the persistance of my dominion, and for the use of the brothers serving Christ in the aforementioned Old Minster, a certain house-plot[5] which is usually called a *haga* in the native tongue, situated in the aforementioned city; just as the noble matron Ælfswith[6] granted it in hereditary right to Almighty God and to his aforenamed apostles,

[a] Ðis is þæs hagan boc on Þinceastre. 7 þes healfan peres æt Brægentforda. 7 ðæs æcersplottes þe þær to lið . þe Æþelred cyning geuðe God⟨e⟩ elmihtigum 7 his halgan apostolan Petre 7 Paule into Ealdan Mynstre on ece inhyrnesse . 'This is the diploma relating to the tenement in Winchester and to half the weir at Brentford, and the acre-plot which belongs to it, which King Æthelred granted to Almighty God and to his apostles Peter and Paul at the Old Minster in perpetual possession.' *rubric, almost certainly copied from an endorsement on the exemplar. For OE æcersplott, 'an acre-plot', see BT Suppt, s.v., and cf. below, n. 8; see also EPN, ii, 139, s.v. splott.* [b] *A spelling for thesaurizant.* [c] *Ælfhego MS., with scribal misreading of insular minuscule f in the exemplar as p; cf. below, n. e*

[1] quadripartiti mundi. For a contemporary reference (by Byrhtferth of Ramsey) to the division of the world into four regions, discussed as part of the mystical properties of the number four, see Peter S. Baker and Michael Lapidge (ed.), *Byrhtferth's Enchiridion* (EETS s.s. 15, Oxford, 1995), 200–1, 342.
[2] *in celis thesaurum . quo . . . fur non appropiat neque tinea corrumpit.* Luke 12: 33.
[3] Æthelred II, king of England 978–1016.
[4] Ælfheah II, bishop of Winchester; see above, **XXIV**, n. 13.
[5] *quandam hospicii portionem . . . quę patria lingua haga solet appellari.* From its bounds (see below, nn. 12–14) part at least of

the tenement appears to have occupied the site of WS 1, **I, 19** on the north side of High Street, at the entry to Parchment Street. For the vernacular gloss, cf. S 888, *KCD* 696, referring to 9 tenements in St. Albans in 996: *habitacula, quae patria lingua Hagan appellari solent.* See above, 207.
[6] Ælfswith, here described as *nobilis matrona*, may possibly be the person of that name who was the sister of Leofric, the former holder of Ruishton, Somerset. Leofric had been induced *temp.* Edgar to surrender to Bishop Æthelwold his title to the estate, which rightfully belonged to the cathedral estate of Taunton, in return for a life-tenancy. In a later memorandum Ælfswith is referred to as having acted with Queen Ælfthryth as an intermediary between Leofric and Bishop Æthelwold to arrange the lease: S 1242, *ASWrits* 108, *CW* 61. She appears to have bequeathed the present tenement to the Old Minster in a *post obitum* grant which had not been executed.

concesserat . quamuis post obitum ipsius eadem possessio ueluti solet á quibusdam personis iniuste possessa fuerit[d] : libens ad usus fratrum in prefato Ueteri Cenobio Christo famulantium eternaliter possidendam restituendo concedo . et concedendo restituo . necnon et dimidium cuiusdam piscarii uadum ad capturam piscium æt Bræge[7] decurrentem . ad Uetus scilicet Monasterium pertinentem . cum unius iugeris sibi adiacentis portione[8] perpetuo iure possidendum concedo . et hoc tam mea quam Dei omnipotentis auctoritate precipio . ut nemo successorum meorum regum . episcoporum . ducum . principumue . aut alicuius superioris seu inferioris dignitatis hoc restitutionis méę donarium uiolare uel mutare presumat . Si quis igitur hęc ausu temerario subuertere et a prefato loco sancto auferre conatus fuerit : ęternę maledictionis sententię subiaceat . et penis ęterne dampnationis inuolutus cum tetre caliginis agminibus sine fine puniatur . nisi digna satisfactione emendauerit quod contra gloriosos apostolorum principes delinquere non timuit . Porro circuitus eiusdem hospicii pro cuius libertatis causa hanc cartam scribere concessi : ita se habere uidetur .

Ðis is þes hagan embegang þe Æþelred[9] cing geuðe into Ealdan Mynstre ofer Þulfsiges dæg preostes .[10] Ærest fram Leofan hagan[11] þest andlang cypstræte[12] oð hit cymð to flæsmangere stræte .[13] andlang flæscmangara stræte þet hit

even though after her death the same possession, as is wont to happen, was to be unjustly possessed by certain persons. And I also grant, to be possessed in perpetual right, half the weir of a certain fishery for the catching of fish, traversing [the river] at Brentford,[7] belonging undoubtedly to the Old Minster, with one acre-plot[8] lying next to it. And this I command, both on my own authority and on that of Almighty God, that none of my successors, kings, bishops, ealdormen, or leading men, or anyone of higher or lower rank, should presume to violate or change this votive offering of my restoration. If anyone, therefore, should try to subvert these things by an imprudent attempt and to take them away from the aforementioned holy place, let him be sentenced to eternal malediction and, enveloped by the penalties of eternal damnation, let him be punished ceaselessly together with the armies of foul darkness, unless he has made amends with a worthy reparation for that which he did not fear to commit against the glorious leaders of the apostles. Moreover, the boundary of the same house[-plot], for whose freedom I have granted that this charter should be written, is seen to be thus:

This is the boundary of the tenement which King Æthelred[9] granted to the Old Minster after Wulfsige the priest's[10] day. First from Leofa's tenement[11] west along market-street[12] until it comes to butchers'-street.[13] Along

---

[d] Corrected from fuerat

[7] æt Bræge. Brentford, Middx., a very important crossing-point over the R. Thames to the west of London. It had been the location of a Mercian synod in 781; see HBC, 587; and Catherine Cubitt, Anglo-Saxon Church Councils, c.650–c.850 (London, 1995), 306–7. The fishery there (Braynford) was confirmed to the cathedral priory by Pope Innocent III in 1205: Goodman Chartulary 45. In c.1356 it belonged to the priory hordarian (ibid. 356) and is represented in medieval account rolls by payments of farm and rent to the hordarian from the fish-weir of Kew (Surrey), on the opposite bank of the river to Brentford, between 1326–7 and 1532–3: ObedR, 253–4, 257, 260–1, 264, 270, 273, 276, 279, 282–3, 285, 290, 293, 296, 299, and 302. The present grant, which probably represents that of the southern half of the weir, is noticed in Winchester ann, s.a. 979.

[8] unius iugeris . . . portio. The Latin phrase translates OE æcersplott in the rubric (see n. a); cf. OE land-splott 'plot of ground' BT, s.v., which occurs as landsplot translated by Latin parva ruris particula in S 964, KCD 746.   [9] As above, n. 3.
[10] Wulfsige the priest seems to have had a life-tenure of the tenement, probably acquired from someone who had usurped the Old Minster's right to the property, bequeathed by Ælfswith; cf. above, n. 6.
[11] Leofan hagan. Leofa's was the adjacent tenement, whose western side formed the whole of the eastern boundary of the present one. For Leofa, cf. above, VI, n. 34.
[12] cypstræte 'market-street'. Now High Street; see WS 1, 234, s.n. (In) Magno Vico. See also above, I, n. 7 and below, XXVIII, n. 16.
[13] flæsmangere stræte 'butchers'-street'. Now Parchment Street; see WS 1, 234.

cymð to scyldpyrhtana stræte .[14] andlang scyldpyrhtana stræte east eft þet hit cymð to Leofan hagan .[15]

Anno dominice incarnationis . dcccc . xcvi . scripta est hęc eadem prefate restaurationis scedula his testibus consentientibus quorum inferius uocabula caraxantur[16].

Ego Æðelred[17] Anglorum basileus prefatum hospicii donum cum dimidio piscario Christo eiusque apostolis concessi .

Ego Ælfric[18] Dorouernensis archiepiscopus prenominate trine[19] donationi consensi et benedixi .

Ego Ealdulf[20] Eboracensis ecclesie archiepiscopus huic regie dapsilitatem sustentationi satis largiter impertiui .

Ego Ælfheah[e] [21] Þintoniensis ęcclesię episcopus hanc prefatam donationem uoti compos obtinui .

Ego Wlfstan[22] Lundoniensis ęcclesię episcopus huic eidem sepe nominate munificentie consentaneus extiti .

Ego Wlfsige[23] episcopus consensi .

Ego Ælfheah[24] episcopus consignaui .

Ego Ordbryht[25] episcopus consolidaui .

Ego Alfpold[26] episcopus corroboraui .

Ego Goduuine[27] episcopus consigillaui .

Ego Aðulf[28] episcopus confirmaui .

Ego Ealdred[29] episcopus conclusi .[f]

butchers'-street so that it comes to shield-makers'-street.[14] Along shieldmakers'-street east so that it comes again to Leofa's tenement.[15]

This same document of the aforementioned restoration was written in the year of the Lord's Incarnation 996, with the agreement of these witnesses whose names are written[16] below:

I, Æthelred,[17] king of the English, have granted the aforementioned gift of a house[-plot] together with half a fishery to Christ and his apostles.

I, Ælfric,[18] archbishop of Canterbury, have agreed and blessed the aforementioned triple[19] donation.

I, Ealdwulf,[20] archbishop of the church of York, have shared very greatly in this royal maintenance of generosity.

I, Ælfheah,[21] bishop of the church of Winchester, have obtained this aforementioned donation, in answer to [my] wish.

I, Wulfstan,[22] bishop of the church of London, have been prominent in agreeing to this same often-mentioned munificence.

I, Wulfsige,[23] bishop, have agreed.

I, Ælfheah,[24] bishop, have subscribed.

I, Ordbeorht,[25] bishop, have made [it] firm.

I, Ælfweald,[26] bishop, have corroborated.

I, Godwine,[27] bishop, have made a mark.

I, Æthulf,[28] bishop, have confirmed.

I, Ealdred,[29] bishop, have concluded.

---

[e] *Ælpheah* MS., *with scribal misreading as above, n. c*
[f] *First column of subscriptions ends here*

acre-plot. The king's subscription, above, omits mention of the acre-plot however.

[20] Ealdwulf, archbishop of York 995–1002.

[21] As above, n. 4.

[22] Wulfstan, bishop of London 996–1002. The homilist and later archbishop of York.

[23] Wulfsige, bishop of Sherborne, ?993–8 January 1002.

[24] Ælfheah, bishop of Lichfield 975–1002 × 1004.

[25] Ordbeorht, bishop of Selsey, 988 × 990–1007 × 1009. Probably identical with Ordbeorht, abbot (of Chertsey), who subscribed **IV**, above (see ibid. n. 147; and **IX**, n. 26).

[26] Ælfweald. bishop of Crediton, 986 × 987–1011 × 1015.

[27] Godwine, bishop of Rochester, 994 × 995–?c.1013 × ?

[28] Æthulf, bishop of Hereford, ? × 971–1013 × ?

[29] Ealdred, bishop of Cornwall, 981 × (988 × 990)–1002 × 1009.

---

[14] *scyldpyrhtana stræte* 'shieldmakers'-street'. In 1148 and later, *Sildwortenestret* or the equivalent was applied to what is now Upper Brook Street; see ibid. 235. In the present document, however, it is applied to that part of the back-street running W.–E. between Parchment Street and Upper Brook Street, to the N. of and parallel to High Street. This is now part of St. George's Street.

[15] *Leofan hagan.* As above, n. 11.

[16] *caraxantur.* As above, **IV**, n. 124.

[17] As above, n. 3.

[18] Ælfric, archbishop of Canterbury 995–1005.

[19] *trine donationi.* That is, the triple grant of the tenement in Winchester, half the fish-weir at Brentford and the adjacent

Ego Æþelþeard .[30] dux .	I, Æthelweard,[30] ealdorman.
Ego Ælfric .[31] dux .	I, Ælfric,[31] ealdorman.
Ego Ælfhelm .[32] dux .	I, Ælfhelm,[32] ealdorman.
Ego Leofsige .[33] dux .	I, Leofsige,[33] ealdorman.
Ego Æðelmer .[34] [minister] .*g*	I, Æthelmær,[34] [thegn].
Ego Ordulf .[35] [minister] *g*	I, Ordwulf,[35] [thegn].
Ego Wlfget .[36] [minister] .*g h*	I, Wulfgeat,[36] [thegn].

Nos uniuersi regis optimates huic regię donationi unanimem*j* consensum alacriter prebuimus .[37]	We, all the king's nobles, have together eagerly shown unanimous agreement to this royal dona-tion.[37]

---

g dux MS., in error for minister; see below, nn. 33–5
h Second column of subscriptions ends here   *j* unanimen MS.

---

[30] Æthelweard, ealdorman of the Western Provinces; see above, **IX**, n. 23. For his son, see below, n. 34.

[31] Ælfric, ealdorman of Hampshire; see above, **IX**, n. 21.

[32] Ælfhelm, ealdorman of Northumbria, 993 × 1006. He was a Mercian who was murdered by Eadric Streona in 1006; see Keynes *Diplomas*, 197, 211. He was the brother of Wulfric Spot, the founder of Burton Abbey. His daughter Ælfgifu of North-ampton became the first wife of King Cnut; see Hart *ECNE*, 258–9. As *minister*, he subscribed **IX**, above, n. 36.

[33] Leofsige, ealdorman of Essex, 994 × 1002. For his banishment, see Keynes *Diplomas*, 108, n. 73.

[34] Æthelmær, *minister*, the son of Ealdorman Æthelweard (above, n. 30); see above, **IX**, n. 35; and **XXIV**, n. 6.

[35] Ordwulf, *minister*, the king's uncle, brother of Queen Ælfthryth. He subscribes 975 × 1005: Hart *ECNE*, 352: Keynes *Diplomas*, 188, 209 and Tables 7 and 8 (Ordulf).

[36] Wulfgeat, *minister*, subscribes 986 × 1005. He was perhaps identical with Wulfgeat, son of Leofeca, who forfeited his estates in 1006; see Keynes *Diplomas*, 188, 210–11 and Tables 7 and 8.

[37] For this additional clause of consent, see above, 208.

XXVII

c. A.D. 1002, a reference to 29 tenements in Winchester pertaining to Wherwell Abbey

Latin and English versions

S 904 (part), Finberg 149

ACCORDING to the Latin version of the short bilingual text printed below as **XXVII**, the 29 tenements to which it refers were 'scattered in different locations' (*uariis disiacentia in locis*) in the city. The text merely records the fact of their existence, it does not give any information about their date of acquisition by Wherwell Abbey, perhaps at varying times since its foundation (*c.* 980); some of them presumably still formed part of the abbey's fief in the city in the post-conquest period.[1]

The text occurs after the witness-list in S 904, an apparently authentic diploma of 1002 which records a composite gift by King Æthelred II to Abbess Heanflæd and the nunnery of Wherwell.[2] This gift comprised a grant of the abbey's privileges; a confirmation of 70 hides previously belonging to the king's mother Ælfthryth[3] in various places (*diuersis disiaceat in locis*) near the abbey; and a grant of 60 hides at Dean, Sussex. In the extant medieval copies the text stands before a note, dated 1008, of an additional grant to Wherwell of 10 hides at Bullington, Hants. Both these additional records may have taken the form of endorsements on the now-lost original diploma but the similarity between the two phrases here quoted suggests that **XXVII** was contemporary with the main body of the diploma of 1002 (and was probably by the same draftsman) rather than connected with the subsequent grant of 1008.

The original diploma has not survived. MS. B is an inspeximus of 44 Henry III. MSS. C and D are copies of the inspeximus, one on to the Charter Roll of the same king, the other into the Wherwell cartulary constructed in the later fourteenth century.[4] E–H are royal enrolments of later inspeximuses from Edward III to Henry VIII. The vernacular version in these MSS. becomes gradually more and more corrupt, until eventually its meaning is unrecognizable.[5]

---

[1] See below, **XXVII**, n. 1.
[2] See Keynes *Diplomas*, 258.
[3] For Ælfthryth, the third wife of King Edgar, see above, **IV**, n. 130.

[4] Davis 1031.
[5] The text in MS. H reads: *Nisan 7 viginti hasena syndon on pintaceastre ye hyrad incoyam menstre mid eallonyam frihtonʒiam pitan yeyar ox arisad.*

MSS.:   B. Oslo and London, The Schøyen Collection, MS. 1354 (s. xiii med.)
             C. PRO, Chart R 44 Henry III (C53/50), m. 1 (s. xiii med.), copy of B
             D. BL, Egerton MS. 2104A, fo. 16ʳ (s. xiv), copy of B
             E. PRO, Pat R 41 Edward III, part 1 (C66/275), m. 33 (s. xiv²)
             F. PRO, Pat R 9 Henry VI, part 1 (C66/429), m. 2 (s. xv¹)
             G. PRO, Pat R 22 Edward IV, part 1 (C66/549), m. 18 (s. xv²)
             H. PRO, Conf R 2 Henry VIII, part 7 (C56/39), no. 9 (s. xvi¹)

Edited: *Monasticon*, ii, 637–8 (no. 3), from C
             KCD 707, from *Monasticon*
             Pierquin *Receuil*, pt 4, no. 75, from *Monasticon*

Printed from B. C–H are secondary.

Viginti uero et nouem predia sunt in urbe Uuentana . uariis disiacentia in locis . que uectigali seruitio prefato subiacent monasterio¹ . omnique alieno permanent extranea dominio . cunctis penalibus causis suprascripto sancto famulantibus loco . quod uulgari usu ita anglice dicitur . Nygan 7 xx . hagena syndon on Þintaceastre þe hyrað into þan menstre¹ mid eallonᵃ þam gerihtonᵇ 7 þam pitan þe þar of arisað .

. . . There are indeed 29 tenements in Winchester, scattered in different locations, which are subject to the aforementioned monastery¹ in the matter of fiscal service and remain outside any other lordship, paying suit in all punishable lawsuits to the above-written holy place. This in common speech is said in English thus: 'there are 29 tenements in Winchester which pertain to the monastery¹ with all the rights and the fines which arise from them' . . .

ᵃ *A late OE form for dative pl.* eallum, *from* eall *'all'*
ᵇ grihton B; gerihton *would be a late OE form of dative pl.* gerihtum, *from* geriht *'right, due'. In the original diploma* gerihton *was probably abbreviated as* ḡrihton

¹ *prefato monasterio; into þan menstre.* Wherwell Abbey, Hants, a Benedictine nunnery, founded *c.*980. The abbey held 31 *masurae* in Winchester TRE and TRW: *DB*, i, fo. 44ʳ (*DB Hants* 16:7). It

also had a mill there *TRW*: ibid. For its 12th-cent. fief, see WS 1, 356 and ibid. Table 11, where its rents in 1148 are shown to have been located in four streets, all in the NW. quarter of the city (*Brudenestret, Scowrtenestret, Alwarnestret,* and *Flesmangerestret*; equivalent respectively to the later Staple Gardens, Jewry Street, St. Peter Street, and Parchment Street). See also WS 2.i, 200, and ii, 1399.

XXVIII

A.D. 1012, grant by King Æthelred II to his queen Ælfgifu, of a tenement in Winchester

Latin with English

S 925, Finberg 150, *CW* 226

THE tenement granted in **XXVIII**, a diploma of Æthelred II in favour of his wife Ælfgifu Emma, included that known as Godbegot which existed in the medieval period as an urban legal and fiscal liberty belonging to the cathedral priory and whose name still survives today as that of a tenement in High Street.[1] The origin of the medieval liberty is probably to be traced to the very unusual grant of full immunity accorded by the king to his wife in **XXVIII** (a privilege confirmed in **XXIX**, below, by Edward the Confessor to the cathedral priory, to whom Ælfgifu Emma had bequeathed the tenement). It should also be noted, however, that at least two of the portreeves of the late Anglo-Saxon city seem to have had an interest in the tenement or neighbouring property, which might suggest that already at the time of Æthelred's grant the tenement could have been privileged as a perquisite of royal office.[2] **XXVIII** is the sole record of the founding of St. Peter in the Fleshambles on the tenement by the portreeve Æthelwine. The text also makes reference to the city's *cyping* or 'market-place', to the north of which the tenement lay.[3]

Although the grant of full immunity caused W. H. Stevenson in 1914 to condemn **XXVIII** as a 'late and clumsy fabrication',[4] there seems reason enough to accept it as the record of an exceptional grant of royal favour by Æthelred to his consort. The reference in the proem to attacks by 'tyrannizing robbers' fits well with the date 1012 when a Danish army murdered the archbishop of Canterbury and threatened the kingdom.[5] The reference to the *Agnus Dei* in the dating clause is also consonant with this period.[6] The elaborate phrasing of other clauses, though not exactly replicated in other surviving documents issued by Æthelred, is not impossible.[7] Although there appears to be an error in the Latin text in relation to the position of the tenement in the NE. as opposed to the NW. of the city, this was probably in the original diploma and may be due to a misunderstanding by the draftsman of the Latin of the significance of *norþ east* in the vernacular boundary-clause (where it is a direction specifically related to the church of St. Peter in the Fleshambles).[8] The large number of grecisms in a relatively short text is notable (*arpago, basilica, catalogus, clyto, cyrographum, epilenticus, griphia, herois, monarches, onoma, parthenalis, rumphea, staurus,*

---

[1] See references given below, **XXVIII**, n. 5; and Goodman *Goodbegot.*

[2] See below, **XXVIII**, n. 10.

[3] Ibid. n. 16; also n. 7.

[4] 'Trinoda Necessitas', *EHR* 29 (1914), 698–703, at 702, and n. 61.

[5] See below, **XXVIII**, n. 1.

[6] Ibid. n. 21.

[7] Cf. Keynes *Diplomas*, 125, n. 135 'a dubious text which grants exemption from the *trimoda necessitas*, but as it is in favour of the queen we might expect some exceptional features'; also, ibid. 265–6 'authenticity uncertain'.

[8] See below, **XXVIII**, n. 6.

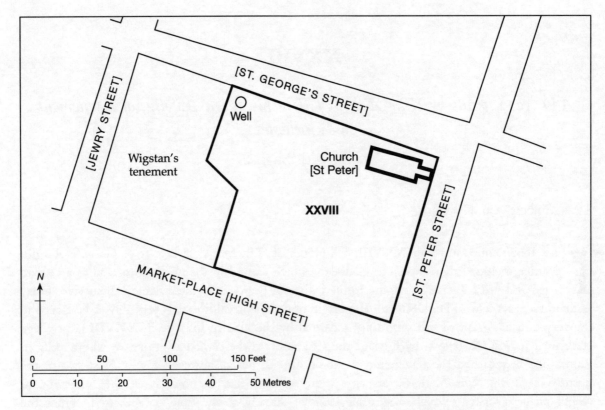

FIG. 12. The bounds of Queen Ælfgifu Emma's tenement in **XXVIII** (A.D. 1012).

theologicum, and *tyrannizo*).[9] That part of the witness-list which survives (it having been curtailed in the MS., see below) shows that at least three of Æthelred's sons by his first marriage witnessed this grant to his second wife.[10]

   XXVIII was added to the *Codex Wintoniensis* by scribe *b* in the mid twelfth century,[11] during the course of which he substantially truncated the witness-list in order to save space. His unfamiliarity with insular minuscule script is reflected in misreadings of the letters *þ* and *g*. [12]

MS.:   B. BL, Add. MS. 15350, fo. 115ʳ (s.xii med.)

Edited: *KCD* 720

Translated: Goodman *Goodbegot,* 2–4

Printed from the manuscript

[9] See below, Latin Word-List, s. vv.
[10] See below, **XXVIII**, nn. 24–5, and 27. The subscription of Eadwig *clyto* might perhaps have been omitted by the cartulary- scribe. He still witnesses in 1014: S 933, O'Donovan *Sherborne* 15.
[11] See above, pp. 7–8.
[12] See below, **XXVIII**, nn. *g–k.*

Contra*a* creatoris ęterni iusticiam dum omnibus ferme in nationibus tyrannizantium uis crudescit raptorum[1] . qui ita aliena tollere sicut lupi cruorem agnorum siciunt bibere . profecto iustitię amatores sunt qui pos`ses´ores quietos . inque propriis contentos priuilegiorum autenticorum cyrographorumue*b* auxiliis sustentatoriis muniunt . pre oculis cordis illud Salomonis ponentes theologicum [.] diligite iustitiam qui iudicatis terram .[2] Quapropter ego Æðelredus[3] egregie opulentęque monarches*c* Brittannie . legitimo iugalitatis uinculo mihi astrictę Ælfgyfæ[4] uocabulo predium[5] quoddam quod infra ciuitatis Þentanę menia ad septemptrionis dextram[6] iuxtaque politanam nundinationis plateam[7] gratulabundus donaui . hocque protestaminis titulo[8] hac inculcare griphia demandaui . Quo quippe predio basilica[9] á quodam ciuitatis eiusdem prefecto nomine Æþelpino[10] sancti Petri honore fabrefacta nitescit . Decretum igitur est ex censoria eminentię nostrę dicione . quo pretaxate conlateranę méé libertas hęc firma et inuiolabilis sed et ab omni seruitii mundialis iugo quamdiu Anglorum patrie facula eluxerit fidei secura

a De terra Godebegeate . 'Concerning the land [called] Godbegot.' rubric. See below, n. 5   *b* Corrected from cyrographorum ue   *c* From Gk. μονάρχης, with the Gk. inflexion retained

___

[1] *dum omnibus ferme in nationibus tyrannizantium uis crudescit raptorum.* No doubt referring to the increase in viking raids on England and its neighbours in the late 10th–early 11th cents. Foremost in the draftsman's mind would have been the activities of the Danish army under Thorkell the Tall which raided southern England between 1009 and 1012. This captured Canterbury in September 1011 and took Archbishop Ælfheah hostage before murdering him at Greenwich on 19 April 1012; see *ASC* [C, D, E], s.aa.

[2] Wisd. 1: 1.

[3] Æthelred II, king of England 978–1016.

[4] Ælfgifu Emma, daughter of Duke Richard I of Normandy. She married King Æthelred in 1002 and, after his death (1016), married King Cnut in 1018. She was the mother of both King Edward the Confessor (cf. below, **XXIX**, n. 5) and King Harthacnut. On her, see Pauline Stafford, *Queen Emma and Queen Edith: Queenship and Women's Power in Eleventh-Century England* (Oxford, 1997), especially 209–54. See also below, n. 22.

[5] *predium.* This urban property was later divided into the tenement called Godbegot, bequeathed to the cathedral by Queen (Ælfgifu) Emma (see below, **XXIX**; WS 1, **I, 23**, n. 1,

While in nearly every nation the strength of tyrannizing robbers increases,[1] who thirst to take other people's things even as wolves thirst to drink the blood of lambs, against the justice of the Eternal Creator, lovers of justice indeed are they who strengthen peaceful and contented possessors in their property with the supporting allies of authentic privileges or writings, putting before the mind's eye that biblical saying of Solomon, 'Love justice, you that are the judges of the earth'.[2] Wherefore I, Æthelred,[3] monarch of eminent and wealthy Britain, have voluntarily given to her called Ælfgifu[4] who is bound to me by the lawful bond of marriage, a certain property[5] within the walls of Winchester, to the north-east,[6] and adjacent to the city marketplace,[7] and I have sought to establish this title[8] of claim with this document. In which property indeed thrives a church,[9] skilfully constructed in honour of St. Peter by a certain reeve of the same city called Æthelwine.[10] Since it has been decreed [to be] outside the taxable authority of our greatness, let this grant of freedom to my aforementioned consort remain constant and inviolable so long as the small torch of faith shall fearlessly shine out on the nation of the English; let it remain [free] even from any yoke of worldly service, and especially from these

and 342), and another tenement retained by her (see WS 1, **I, 75**, n. 1). See ibid. Fig. 12; WS 2.ii, **50–6** (pp. 486–7), and Figs. 52, 54.

[6] *ad septemptrionis dextram.* Literally 'to the right side of north', i.e. NE., but this seems to be in error, as the tenement is to the NW. of the centre of the city. Probably the draftsman of the Latin text was misled by reading the opening of the vernacular boundary-clause (*of þære cyricean norþ east hyrnan*).

[7] *politanam nundinationis plateam.* For the 'city market-place', see below, n. 16.

[8] *hocque . . . titulo.* Professor Lapidge observes that *titulo* is in error for *titulum*, as object of *inculcare.*

[9] *basilica.* St. Peter in the Fleshambles (*in macellis*); see WS 1, **I, 23**, n. 5; WS 2.ii, 493–4; and below, nn. 13 and 20. Although the church is now destroyed, its various ground-plans at different dates, as revealed by excavation, are marked at the site in St. George's Street.

[10] Æthelwine is the first 11th-cent. reeve of the city whose name is known; see WS 1, 424, Table 46. Note that Æthelwold, the reeve *TRE*, was associated with property adjacent to Godbegot; see WS 1, **I, 23**, n. 2.

permaneat . et maxime ab his tribus causis .[11] scilicet pontium murorumque reparatione . ac bellice multitudinis additione . Sitque in predicte auguste arbitro de hoc agere predio uel adhuc ualens uel moriens . quicquid superna gratia suo inspirauerit animo . Quod si cuilibet legirupi rancor multipetax quorumcunque posteritate temporum epilentico illectus spiritu hoc priuilegium autenticum quacunque temeritate quáue frustrare desudabit tergiuersatione . ex obsoleto[d] corpore diaboli extrahatur arpagine[e] et in lebete Sathane decoquatur . sitque infernalium offa carnificum in secula . ni publice penitudinis remedio irę Dei rumpheam[12] super se euaginatam ob contradictionem qua hanc blasphemauit libertatem sedauerit . Presignatum denique prediolum circumquaque sui ambitum habet huiusmodi .

Ærest of þære cyricean[13] norþ east hyrnan nygan girda[14] andlang stræte[15] ut on[f] þa cypinge[16] . spa up anlang cypinge eahta gyrda þet hit cymþ[g] to Pistanes gemære[17] . spa andlang Pistenes gemere nygon girda[h] þet hit cymþ[j] on þone pæterpyt[18] . fram þam pæterpyt . x . gyrda[k] 7lang strete[19] to þære cyrcean[20] norð east[l] hyrnan .

---

[d] *Corrected from* obsolito   [e] *Error for* arpagone, *from the Grecism* (h)arpago   [f] iton *MS.*   [g] cymh *corrected from* cumh *MS., but the* h *is probably a scribal misreading of* þ *in the exemplar; cf. below, n.* j   [h] pirda *MS., a scribal misreading of insular minuscule* g *in the exemplar as* p; *cf. below, n.* k   [j] cymh *MS.; cf. above, n.* g   [k] pyrda *MS.; cf. above, n.* h   [l] *Corrected from* erst

---

[11] *maxime ab his tribus causis.* This immunity from the 'Three Burdens' was an especial favour, these obligations usually being reserved by the king in grants of bookland where other customary rents and services were excused. Note that the Queen's tenement (WS 1, **I, 75**, see above, n. 5) was quit of geld *TRE* and *c.*1110, and that the cathedral priory later claimed extensive privileges for the liberty of Godbegot. Cf. below, **XXIX**, n. 8. For a comparable grant of immunity, by Edward the Confessor in 1060, to Westminster Abbey for the estate of Wheathampstead, Herts., see S 1031; Frank Barlow, *Edward the Confessor* (London, 1970), 333–5.

[12] *rumpheam.* Cf. Ecclus. 26: 27 (*BSV*, ii, 1062) *et qui transgreditur a iustitia ad peccatum Deus parauit eum ad rompheam* 'And he that passeth over from justice to sin, God hath prepared such an one for the sword'.

Three Burdens,[11] namely, the repair of bridges and walls and the assembly of a military host. And let it be up to the judgement of the aforesaid august lady to do with this estate, either during her life or on her death, whatever the celestial grace shall inspire her mind to do. But should at any succeeding time an exceedingly-greedy spite exert itself on any lawbreaker, seduced by a maniacal spirit to frustrate this authentic privilege by whatever imprudence or by whatever subterfuge, let him be drawn out of his worn body by a devil's grappling-hook and be boiled in Satan's cauldron and let him be a morsel for the infernal tormenters for all time, unless he has appeased with the remedy of public repentance the anger of God, the sword[12] unsheathed above him on account of the opposition with which he blasphemed this grant of freedom. Indeed the aforementioned little property has a boundary all around it in this manner:

First, from the north-east corner of the church[13] nine 'yards'[14] along [the] street[15] out into the market-place.[16] Up along [the] market-place eight 'yards' so that it comes to Wigstan's boundary.[17] Along Wigstan's boundary nine 'yards' so that it comes to the well.[18] From the well ten 'yards' along [the] street[19] to the north-east corner of the church.[20]

---

[13] *of þære cyricean.* That is, St. Peter in the Fleshambles; see above, n. 9.

[14] *girda.* See above, **II**, n. 6.

[15] *andlang stræte.* South along what is now St. Peter Street.

[16] *on þa cypinge.* Into the market in High Street; see WS 1, 235, s.n. *(In) Magno Vico.* See also above, n. 7; **I**, n. 7, and **XXVI**, n. 12.

[17] *to Pistanes gemære.* As far as the boundary of Wīgstān who was probably the present or a previous owner of the tenement immediately to the west of the present one.

[18] *on þone pæterpyt.* The use of OE *wæter-pytt* instead of *wiella* 'a spring' reflects its man-made character; cf. BT, s.v. For the archaeological excavation of this well, see Barry Cunliffe (ed.), *Winchester Excavations 1949–60* (Winchester, 1964), i, 43–5.

[19] *7lang strete.* Along the back-street to the north of High Street, now St. George's Street. In 996, part of the street further east seems to have been called *scyldpyrhtana stræt*; see above, **XXVI**, n. 14.

[20] *to þære cyrcean.* As above, n. 13.

Anno igitur . m . xii° . ex quo Agnus Dei[21]de utero parthenali processit incarnatus . postmodum secula stauro affixus saluauit . carta hęc apicum ornatibus uestita est . heroidis[22] unimoda pietate confauentibus[m] . quorum onomata presens inculcat catalogus . Ego Æðelred[23] rex Anglorum huic libertati iugem prerogatiuam contuli . Ego Æðelstan[24] filius regis tranquille mentis fauorem augmentaui . Ego Eadmund[25] clyto[26] libertatem hanc liberam esse uoti compos renuntiaui . Ego Eadred[27] clyto[28] animo hilari assensum beniuolenter accommodaui .

Indeed, in the year 1012 from that in which the Lamb of God[21] came forth incarnate from the Virgin's womb, who fixed to the Cross later saved the world, this charter was dressed in the clothes of letter-forms, with these people, whose names the present list includes, favouring the simple piety of a noble lady:[22] I, Æthelred,[23] king of the English, have conferred perpetual privilege on this grant of freedom. I, Æthelstan,[24] the king's son, have added the approbation of a tranquil mind. I, Edmund,[25] ætheling,[26] in answer to a wish, have declared this grant of freedom to be free. I, Eadred,[27] ætheling,[28] have benevolently adapted myself to approval with a glad mind.

---

[m] *Corrected from* confouentibus

---

[21] *Agnus Dei.* For the extensive interest in the Lamb of God towards the end of the reign of Æthelred, see R. H. M. Dolley, 'The Nummular Brooch from Sulgrave', in Peter Clemoes and Kathleen Hughes (ed.), *England before the Conquest: Studies in Primary Sources presented to Dorothy Whitelock* (Cambridge, 1971), 333–49; also M. K. Lawson, 'Archbishop Wulfstan and the Homiletic Element in the Laws of Æthelred II and Cnut', in Alexander R. Rumble (ed.), *The Reign of Cnut, King of England, Denmark and Norway* (London, 1994), 141–64, at 152–4. For Æthelred's *Agnus Dei* pennies, issued probably in 1009, see Simon Keynes, 'The Vikings in England, *c.*790–1016', in Peter Sawyer (ed.), *The Oxford Illustrated History of the Vikings* (Oxford, 1997), 48–109, at 80–1.

[22] *heroidis.* Queen Ælfgifu Emma (see above, n. 4), here described by the grecism *herois* from ἡρωίς 'demi-goddess, heroine'.   [23] As above, n. 3.

[24] Æthelstan was King Æthelred's eldest son by his first wife Ælfgifu, daughter of Ealdorman Thored. He died 25 June 1014; see Keynes *Diplomas*, 267. For his will, see S 1503, *CW* 93 and 103, *ASWills* 20.

[25] Edmund Ironside, son of King Æthelred by his first wife Ælfgifu; later himself king (April–30 November 1016).

[26] *clyto.* See above, **IV**, n. 128 (*clito*).

[27] Eadred, son of King Æthelred by his first wife Ælfgifu. He died *c.*1012 × 1015.

[28] *clyto.* As above, n. 26.

XXIX

A.D. 1052 × 1053, confirmation by King Edward the Confessor to the Old Minster, of his mother's bequest of the tenement in Winchester called Ælfric's Godbegot; and of the 10-hide estate at Hayling, Hants

English

S 1153, Finberg 169

THE major part of **XXIX** consists of a copy of a genuine vernacular writ of Edward the Confessor confirming his mother Ælfgifu Emma's bequest to the Old Minster of (the greater part of) the tenement in Winchester which **XXVIII**, above, records that King Æthelred had granted to her in 1012. The final clause concerning Hayling, Hants, is a later interpolation, however (see below).

King Edward's confirmation of any bequest made by his mother was of great importance to the Old Minster because in 1043 he had confiscated all of her land and treasure,[1] and although it seems that he may have returned some at least of her land by the time of her death in 1052,[2] the act of confiscation would doubtless have made her heirs and legatees, at either date, feel insecure as to their title.

The writ is constituted in due form and is addressed to Bishop Stigand (of Winchester), Earl Godwine (of Wessex), and all the citizens (*burhmen*) of Winchester. The tenement concerned is designated by the name *Ælfrices gode begeaton* 'Ælfric's good yield', perhaps referring to its rental value.[3] **XXIX** confirms King Æthelred's earlier grant of fiscal and legal immunity for the tenement, recorded in **XXVIII**, above, and transfers its benefit to the cathedral community. The designation of the Old Minster as 'St. Peter and St. Swithun' is the earliest inclusion of Swithun in the dedication in surviving diplomas and writs.[4]

The final clause of the writ as it survives in all the copies concerns a quite different Hampshire estate, that of Hayling, which had also been bequeathed to the Old Minster by Ælfgifu Emma but which was alienated to the abbey of Jumièges *TRW* and which was the subject of a legal dispute between Winchester Cathedral and Jumièges until 1139 × 1141, when Bishop Henry of Blois quitclaimed it to the Norman abbey.[5] This clause has all the appearance of an interpolation, probably added to the now-lost original writ in the early twelfth century in connection with the dispute with Jumièges. F. E. Harmer drew attention to the anachronistic use here of the definite

---

[1] *ASC*[C], s.a.; see further Pauline Stafford, *Queen Emma and Queen Edith: Queenship and Women's Power in Eleventh-Century England* (Oxford, 1997), 248–53.

[2] See Frank Barlow, *Edward the Confessor* (London, 1970), 77.

[3] See below, **XXIX**, n. 6.

[4] It also occurs in a writ in the name of Edward the Confessor concerning Portland, Dorset, but that is probably a forgery of the late 11th or early 12th cent.: S 1154, *CW* 19, *AS Writs* 112.

[5] See below, **XXIX**, n. 11.

article *þe*, as well as the clumsy transition, by the use of 7 and *ge* which have the same meaning in Old English, from the text dealing with the Winchester tenement to that dealing with Hayling.[6]

The large number of surviving copies of **XXIX**, particularly in the form of successive royal enrolments, no doubt reflects the importance accorded by the cathedral priory to maintaining its enjoyment of the 'liberty' of Godbegot in the medieval period.[7] A text of it was included in both the later cartularies (MSS. B and C). Although it was not added to the *Codex Wintoniensis*, it may be noted that the copy in MS. B was written by the scribe who added a text of **II**, above, to the *Codex* in the mid thirteenth century.[8] He appears to have felt that one cartulary copy of **XXIX** would suffice; an opinion apparently not shared with one of the compilers of the later cartulary (MS. C) who, however, substantially modernized the language of the document in the course of copying it therein. The scribe of B produced a linguistically more faithful copy, although he found difficulty with *ð* and *þ* and the insular minuscule form of *r*.

[6] *AS Writs*, 385.

[7] Note also the confirmation to the cathedral priory by William II in 1096 of various houses in Winchester including *Domum . . . Alurici Godebegete* quit of all customary payments and services as held *TRE* and *TRW*: V. H. Galbraith, 'Royal Charters to Winchester', *EHR* 35 (1920), 382–400, no. 11; *Regesta* i, 377a.

For court rolls of the manor of Godbegot, see Goodman *Goodbegot*, 12–37; for a definition of the privileges of the inhabitants of the liberty in 1291, see ibid. 39–40.

[8] Scribe *m* of the *Codex*; see Pl. V, and above, p. 9.

[9] See below, **XXIX**, nn. *b, d–j*.

MSS.:   B. BL, Add. MS. 29436, fo. 10ᵛ (s. xiii med.)
         C. WCL, W52/74 [St. Swithun's cartulary], vol. 1, fo. 6ᵛ (s. xiii/xiv)
         D. PRO, Chart R 10 Edward II (C53/103), no. 7 (s. xivⁱ)
         E. PRO, Chart R 9 Edward III (C53/122), no. 40 (s. xivⁱ), from C
         F. PRO, D. L. 10/291 (s. xiv med.), from E
         G. PRO, E. 32/267, mm. 24–5 (s. xiv med.), from C
         H. PRO, Chart R 4 Richard II (C53/158), no. 10 (s. xiv²), from F
         J. PRO, Chart R 1 Henry IV, part 2 (C53/169), no. 9 (s. xiv/xv), from H
         K. PRO, Chart R 2 Henry V, part 1 (C53/183), m. 39 (s. xvⁱ), from J
         L. PRO, Pat R 2 Henry VI, part 2 (C66/413), m. 11 (s. xvⁱ), from K
         M. PRO, Pat R 2 Edward IV, part 6 (C66/504), m. 6 (s. xv²), from H
         N. ibid. m. 12, from H
         O. PRO, Conf R 4 Henry VII, part 2 (C56/20), no. 13 (s. xv²), from N
         P. ibid. no. 18, from *lost* inspeximus of inspeximus of 16 November 6 Edward IV
         Q. PRO, Conf R 2 Henry VIII, part 2 (C56/34), no. 2 (s. xviⁱ), from O
         R. PRO, Conf R 2 Henry VIII, part 3 (C56/35), m. 3 (s. xviⁱ), from P
         S. Bod, Dodsworth MS. 24, fo. 107ʳᵛ (s. xvii), from D

Facsimile: See Pl. IV, from B

Edited: Goodman *Goodbegot*, 6–7, from B, with translation
         Goodman *Chartulary* 31, (calendar) from C
         AS Writs 111, from B, with translation

Printed from B. C is Middle English

Eadpard*[a][1] cing gret Stigand[2] . bisceop . 7
Godpine[3] eorl. 7 ealle þa burhmen[4] on
Þincestre . frondlice . 7 ic kyðe eop þæt ic
hæbbe geunnen þæt se cpyde stande þe min
moder[5] becpæð*[b] Criste 7 sancte Petre 7 sancte
Spiðune 7 þan hirede into Ealdan Mynstre . þæt
is se haga þe man hæt Ælfrices gode begeaton[6] .
þæne*[c] ic pille þæt hi habban eal spa freo pið*[d]
ealle þa þing þe to me belimpoð*[e] : eal spa he
hire æfter mines fæder gyfe[7] on handan stod . 7
non minra picnera*[f] nane socne nabbe uppon þa
þe þær on uppon sittað*[g][8] . ne nan mann on
nanan þingan : butan se hired*[h][9] . 7 þa þe hi
heom to picneran settað . 7[10] ge þe tene hida æt
Helinge[11] stande al spa*[j] hi hi hem bicpað .

King Edward[1] greets in friendship Bishop
Stigand[2] and Earl Godwine[3] and all the citizens[4]
in Winchester. And I tell you that I have granted
that the bequest shall stand which my mother[5]
bequeathed to Christ and St. Peter and St.
Swithun and the community into [the possession of] the Old Minster, that is the tenement
which is called 'Ælfric's good yield'.[6] I desire also
that they shall have [it] just as freely, in respect
of all the things which pertain to me, as it
belonged to her in accordance with my father's
gift.[7] And none of my officers shall have any
jurisdiction over those who dwell therein,[8] nor
anyone in any matter, except the community[9]
and those whom they shall appoint as their
officers. And[10] also the 10 hides at Hayling[11]
shall stand just as she bequeathed them to them.

---

[a] . Carta sancti Edwardi regis . de Godebiete . 'Charter of St.
Edward the king concerning Godbegot.' *rubric*   [b] becpæd
MS., a scribal misreading of ð *in the exemplar as* d; *cf. below, nn.* d, g
[c] *Altered from* þæt   [d] pid *MS., a scribal misreading, as above,*
n. b   [e] belimpoð *MS., a scribal misreading of* þ *in the*
exemplar as p   [f] *Altered from* picnesa, a *(temporary) scribal*
misreading of insular minuscule r *in the exemplar as insular minuscule*
low s   [g] sittad *MS., a scribal misreading, as above,* n. b
[h] hireð *MS., altered from* hin-; *scribal misreadings of insular*
minuscule r *in the exemplar as* n, *and of* d *as* ð   [j] sya *MS.,*
a scribal misreading of þ *in the exemplar as* y

---

[1] Edward the Confessor, king 1042–66. He was the son of
King Æthelred II and Ælfgifu Emma; cf. above, **XXVIII**, n. 4.

[2] Stigand, bishop of Winchester, 1047–70, also archbishop of
Canterbury 1052–70, and previously (1043, 1044–7) bishop of
Elmham.

[3] Godwine, earl of Wessex 1018 × 1053.

[4] *þa burhmen.* Cf. above, **VIII (i) (ii)**, n. 24.

[5] *min moder.* Ælfgifu Emma; see above, **XXVIII**, n. 4. She
probably died on 7 March 1052; see Simon Keynes, 'The
Crowland psalter and the sons of Edmund Ironside', *Bodleian
Library Record* 11 (1985), 359–70, at 365.

[6] *se haga þe man hæt Ælfrices gode begeaton.* For this tenement,
see above, **XXVIII**, n. 5. For its name, first recorded here, see
WS 1, 158–9, 237 and addendum, ibid. 553. O. Arngart provides
a more recent discussion of the name's meaning in 'Domus
Godebiete', *Studia Neophilologica* 51(1979), 125–6. Ælfric has not
been identified.

[7] *mines fæder gyfe.* For this gift by King Æthelred II, which also

concerned neighbouring property later retained by Ælfgifu
Emma, see above, **XXVIII**.

[8] *non minra picnera nane socne nabbe uppon þa þe þær on uppon
sittað. AS Writs*, 383, quotes a court roll *temp.* Henry VIII which
restates St. Swithun's claim to exemption from the power of any
minister of the king or other lord 'from time immemorial'. The
origin of the liberty probably lay in the privileged tenure under
which Ælfgifu Emma previously enjoyed the property; cf. above,
XXVIII, n. 11. Association with the portreeve may also have
attracted special privileges; see above, p. 215.

[9] *se hired.* That is, the community at the Old Minster.

[10] The last sentence is an interpolation into the writ which
originally concerned Godbegot alone, probably effected in
connection with the dispute with Jumièges over Hayling; see
AS Writs, 384–5, and below, n. 11.

[11] Hayling, Hants. According to S 1476, *AS Ch* 114 (*c.*1053), a
total of 10 hides at Hayling had been bequeathed by Ælfgifu
Emma; 5 of these were left to the Old Minster and 5 to
Wulfweard the White for his lifetime with reversion to the
Old Minster. After Ælfgifu Emma's death, the Old Minster also
leased its 5 hides to Wulfweard for his lifetime. This arrangement was also noted in *DB* (i, fo. 43ᵛ; *DB Hants* 10:1). In 1066 ×
1067, after Wulfweard's death, the estate was granted to the
abbey of Jumièges by William I: Bates *Regesta* 159. William II
confirmed it to Winchester cathedral priory in 1096 × 1100, but
Henry I granted it to Jumièges, to whom Bishop Henry of Blois
quitclaimed in 1139 × 1141: V. H. Galbraith, 'Royal Charters to
Winchester', *EHR* 35 (1920), 382–400, no. 12; *France*, 54–5;
Regesta iii, 417; and M. J. Franklin (ed.), *English Episcopal Acta 8:
Winchester 1070–1204* (Oxford, 1993), no. 58.

XXX–XXXII
LATE ANGLO-SAXON AND EARLY MEDIEVAL DOCUMENTS RELATING TO THE BENEFICIAL HIDATION OF THE ESTATE OF CHILCOMB, HANTS

XXX

A.D. 984 × 1001, confirmation by King Æthelred II to Bishop Ælfheah II [of Winchester] of the beneficial hidation of Chilcomb, Hants, as first granted by his forefathers and previously confirmed by King Alfred

English

S 946, Finberg 141, *CW* 14

THE Chilcomb writ is one of only two extant vernacular writs in the name of Æthelred II.[1] If genuine, its effect would have been to confirm the almost-nil assessment for payment of geld owed to the king from the valuable estate of Chilcomb from which the monks of the Old Minster drew their food supplies.[2] According to Winchester tradition, propagated (and possibly in part invented) by those who drafted the texts commemorating the Edgarian restoration of the cathedral endowment (**V**, above), this fiscal privilege had first been granted in the mid seventh century to St. Birinus by Kings Cynegisl and Cenwealh and was later confirmed to Winchester Cathedral by King Ecgbeorht and his lineal successors Æthelwulf, Alfred, and Edward the Elder.[3] In **XXX**, Æthelred apparently accepted the evidence of a diploma of confirmation in the name of 'the wise' King Alfred but mentioned no other king by name.[4] The tradition of a very early grant is however suggested by the phrase *on angunne Cristendomes*.[5] Although no diploma of Alfred survives,

---

[1] The other is S 945, *AS Writs* 52, relating to St. Paul's, London.
[2] See above, **V, xiv.**

[3] Ibid. **V, ii.**
[4] For the epithet 'wise', see below, **XXX**, n. 9.
[5] Cf. ibid. n. 8.

a 'charter' in his name concerning Chilcomb apparently existed at Winchester in 1643,[6] and it is certain that the question of the hidation of the city (and probably the surrounding estate of Chilcomb) would have been a subject for discussion when Winchester was refortified in the late ninth century.[7] That Chilcomb enjoyed this beneficial hidation *TRE* and *TRW* was accepted as fact by the Domesday commissioners, although no mention of any evidentiary writ was made.[8] Its reality in the earlier part of the eleventh century is suggested by the fact that the hundred of Chilcomb then included 99 hides apart from the estate of Chilcomb itself.[9]

The authenticity of **XXX** has been a topic of debate for more than a century amongst modern commentators interested both in the history of the geld and in the Old English writ-form.[10] No definitive judgement has emerged one way or the other, and Florence Harmer's summarising opinion is still worth quoting in spite of later work by Pierre Chaplais: 'there is at least the chance that we have in this text a copy of an authentic writ of King Æthelred II'.[11] As Harmer demonstrated, although there has probably been a small amount of updating of spellings during copying, the actual formulae are perfectly acceptable so far as diplomatic structure and style are involved.[12] Though it cannot be denied that definite verbal similarities may be pointed out with the vernacular document concerning Chilcomb in the name of King Edgar (**V, iii**, above),[13] it is possible that **XXX** was composed earlier than that text and its Latin counterpart (**V, ii**). It could also be earlier both than the interpolation concerning Chilcomb in **V, i**, above, and than the related forged single-sheet in the name of Edward the Elder.[14] These other documents concerning the beneficial hidation are not mentioned in **XXX** but may belong also to some time in the reign of Æthelred II.[15] If **XXX** were drafted by an agent of the beneficiaries, i.e. the monks of the Old Minster, for approval by the king and subsequent issue as an official royal writ,[16] it is not impossible that elements of the Winchester historical tradition were included in it although they had not yet been written into other texts. Alternatively, as Harmer suggested, it may be that these parts of the writ were borrowed from the diploma of Alfred, whose text we do not now possess.[17]

XXX survives only as a copy written into the *Codex Wintoniensis* by scribe *g* in the mid twelfth century.[18] The same scribe also copied the later list of lands (**XXXI**, below) belonging to (the hundred of) Chilcomb, which might once have been endorsed on the single-sheet MS. of **XXX**. No medieval royal confirmations of **XXX** appear to have been sought, unlike the large number in relation to the Godbegot writ of Edward the Confessor (**XXIX**, above), probably because of the acceptance of the beneficial hidation of Chilcomb in Domesday Book, whose legal status was unassailable.

---

[6] See WCL, Book of John Chase, fo. 18[v] (S 1812): *Alfredus Rex filius Adulfi Regis Carta de Chilcombe, Saxon'*. Cf. also the (fabricated) vernacular declaration in the name of King Æthelwulf, with his son Alfred, which ascribes the beneficial hidation to Æthelwulf as an augmentation of Cynegisl's grant of the estate: S 325, *CW* 236, BCS 493.

[7] See WS 1, 450–3.   [8] See below, **XXXII**.

[9] Ibid. **XXXI**.

[10] For references to the varied opinions of F. W. Maitland, W. H. Stevenson, H. Bresslau, and F. Liebermann, see *AS Writs*, 375–9.

[11] Ibid. 380. Cf. Pierre Chaplais, 'The Anglo-Saxon Chancery: From the Diploma to the Writ', in Felicity Ranger (ed.), *Prisca*

Munimenta: Studies in Archival and Administrative History Presented to Dr. A. E. J. Hollaender (London, 1973), 43–62, at 55–6.

[12] *AS Writs*, 379.   [13] See below, **XXX**, nn. 8–10.

[14] BL, Harl. Ch. 43 C. 1; S 376(1). See above, p. 110, n. 39.

[15] Ibid. 103.

[16] For the writing of some Anglo-Saxon royal writs by the scribe of a beneficiary, see T. A. M. Bishop and P. Chaplais (ed.), *Facsimiles of English Royal Writs to A.D. 1100 Presented to Vivian Hunter Galbraith* (Oxford, 1957), xii–xiii, and xviii. Once the wording of the Anglo-Saxon writ had formalised it should not have been too difficult for a contemporary ecclesiastical draftsman to produce an acceptable text for official approval.

[17] *AS Writs*, 378.   [18] See above, p. 9.

MS.:   B. BL, Add. MS. 15350, fo. 6ʳ (s. xii med.)

Edited: *KCD* 642

BCS 1160

AS Writs 107, with translation

Printed from the manuscript

Æþelred[1] cynig gret Ælfric[2] ealdorman 7 Þulmær[3] . 7 Æþelpeard[4] 7 ealle þa þegenas on Hamtunscire . frunlice . 7 ic cyþe þe 7 eop eallum þ Ælfheah[5] biscop sende to me þæs landes boc[6] æt Ciltancumbe[7] . 7 ic hi let redan ætforan me . þa licode me spyðe þel seo gesetnesse . 7 seo ælmesse þe minne yldran on angunne Cristendomes[8] into þere halgan stope gesetten . 7 se pisa cing Ælfred[9] syððan geednipode on þære bec þe man ætforð me rædde . Nu pille ic þ hit man on eallum þingon for ane hide perige spa spa mine yldran hit ær gesetten . 7 gefreodan . sy þer mare landes sy þer lesse .[10]

King Æthelred[1] greets in a friendly fashion Ealdorman Ælfric[2] and Wulfmær[3] and Æthelweard[4] and all the thegns in Hampshire. And I inform thee and all of you that Bishop Ælfheah[5] sent me the diploma[6] relating to the estate at Chilcomb[7] and I allowed it to be read out in front of me. The decree pleased me very much and the alms which my forefathers gave to the holy place at the start of Christianity[8] and which the wise King Alfred[9] afterwards renewed in the diploma which was read out in front of me. Now I command that it should be assessed at 1 hide in relation to everything even as my forefathers formerly decreed and freed it, whether there be more land or less.[10]

---

[1] Æthelred II, king of England 978–1016.

[2] Ælfric, ealdorman of Hampshire 982–1016: Keynes *Diplomas*, Table 6. He subscribes above, **IX** and **XXVI**. For his death at the battle of *Assandun*, see *ASC* [D, E, F], s.a. 1016.

[3] Wulfmær may be identical with the beneficiary of a lease of the New Minster estate of Barton Stacey, Hants, in 995 × 1006: S1420, *ASCh* 70, Miller *New Minster* 32.

[4] Æthelweard may be identical with the *minister* to whom King Æthelred granted 15 hides at Wootton St. Lawrence, Hants, in 990: S 874, *CW* 207, *KCD* 673. Its appurtenances included 9 tenements in Tanner St; see above, **XXV**. He may also have been the Æthelweard who witnessed S 1420 (see above, n. 3). For the suggestion that he was the high-reeve of Hampshire who was killed at the battle of *Æþelingadene* in 1001 (on 23 May), see A. S. Napier and W. H. Stevenson, *The Crawford Collection of Early Charters and Documents* (Oxford, 1895), 118–20, and further *AS Writs*, 555.

[5] Ælfheah II, bishop of Winchester 984 × 1006. Later archbishop of Canterbury; see above, **XXIV**, n. 13.

[6] *þæs landes boc*. This diploma of King Alfred's has not survived in any form (but cf. S 1812), although a confirmation by him is mentioned in **V, ii** and **iii**, above. Note that Alfred is associated with his father King Æthelwulf in S 325, *CW* 236, *BCS* 493, relating to Chilcomb, but this only survives in a

cartulary-copy of s.xiii med. and is a forgery.

[7] Chilcomb, Hants; see above, **V, ii**, n. 31.

[8] *on angunne Cristendomes*. Cf. *on angynne Cristendomes* in **V, iii**, above; both are equivalent to the Latin *in exordio Christianę fidei* in **V, ii**, *in Christianę religionis exordio* in **V, v**, and *in . . . Christianę religionis exordio* in **V, viii**.

[9] *se pisa cing Ælfred*. Alfred, king of Wessex 871–99. To the epithet *pisa* used here, cf. the phrase *þa godan cynegas 7 þa pisan* in **V, iii**, referring to those (including Alfred) who are said to have confirmed the beneficial hidation of Chilcomb. The description 'wise' is also applied to Alfred in a Middle English boundary of Egham, Surrey, in the Chertsey cartulary (see S 1165, *BCS* 34) and in the Middle English *Proverbs of Alfred*; see Jane Roberts, 'Foreword', in eadem and Janet L. Nelson with Malcolm Godden (ed.), *Alfred the Wise: Studies in Honour of Janet Bately on the occasion of her Sixty-fifth Birthday* (Cambridge, 1997), xiii n. 7, and quotation, ibid. vii.

[10] *hit man on eallum þingon for ane hide perige spa spa mine yldran hit ær gesetten 7 gefreodan . sy þer mare landes sy þer lesse* . Cf. the clause *he geuðe þæt man þæt land on eallum þingon for ane hide perode . spa spa his yldran hit ær gesetton 7 gefreodon . þære þær mare landes . þære þær læsse* in **V, iii**, above, in the name of King Edgar; q.v., n. 60. For the acceptance in Domesday Book of this privilege, see below, **XXXII**.

XXXI

Before A.D. 1086. List of lands [in Hants] belonging to Chilcomb
English

S 1820, Finberg 178, *CW* 15

THE list of lands belonging to Chilcomb that is printed below contains, besides Chilcomb itself, 99 hides in Hampshire, mostly on or near the R. Itchen to the NE. and S. of the city, Chilbolton and its outlier Nursling being notable exceptions on the R. Test to the NW. and SW. respectively.[1] Except in one instance, the dependent settlements are each separately hidated[2] and as a group are distinguished from the parent estate of Chilcomb which enjoyed a reduced or beneficial tax liability of a single hide.[3] It may be no coincidence that the sum total of the hidation of the ancient estate of Chilcomb and these dependencies comes to 100, if it were the case that the number of its dependencies was increased with the purpose of forming a full fiscal hundred of Chilcomb (which existed in 1033 × 1066)[4] at or after the confirmation of the beneficial hidation by King Æthelred II.[5] Such a creation would have been a way of accommodating the anomaly of the beneficial hidation of an ancient estate, perhaps representing the continuation of an an archaic *territorium* around the city, into a more regular late Anglo-Saxon administrative framework based primarily on the hundred.[6] In any case the text would appear to relate to a pre-Domesday situation, as by 1086 the dependent estates were divided between the hundreds of Fawley and Buddlesgate, each of which also contained others not named in **XXXI**, while Chilcomb itself was said to be in 'Falmer' Hundred.[7] The dependent estate of Otterbourne had also been alienated from the Old Minster by then.[8]

The text is an administrative memorandum in the form of a general declaration in Old English. If, as suggested above, it related to the creation of a new but relatively short-lived hundred of Chilcomb, there is no reason to doubt its authenticity.[9] It might perhaps once have been endorsed on the single-sheet MS. of **XXX**, a copy of which it follows in the same cartulary (see below), but this is impossible to prove.

XXXI survives only as a copy written into the *Codex Wintoniensis* by scribe *g* in the mid twelfth century.[10] The same scribe also copied Æthelred II's writ confirming the beneficial hidation of

---

[1] See Fig. 13. Kilmeston is on higher ground ESE. of the city but is not far from the source of the Itchen at SU 5827.

[2] Brambridge and Otterbourne are given a combined hidage of 5 hides, as perhaps in Domesday Book; see below, **XXX**, n. 9.

[3] See above, **XXX**. Note that in **V, ii**, above, the beneficial hidation is said to cover Chilcomb *cum omnibus appendiciis suis* 'with all its dependencies'. However, as there is no equivalent phrase in the vernacular version (**V, iii**), it may be that this is a later interpolation in the Latin text.

[4] See S 1821, *CW* 16, BCS 1161.   [5] See above, **XXX**.

[6] For the possible origins of the Chilcomb estate, see WS 1, 256-7.

[7] See below, **XXXII**. See also *DB Hants*, map of northern hundreds.

[8] See below, **XXXI**, n. 10.

[9] This suggestion would avoid the difficulties listed by Harmer *Writs*, 376-7.

[10] See above, p. 9.

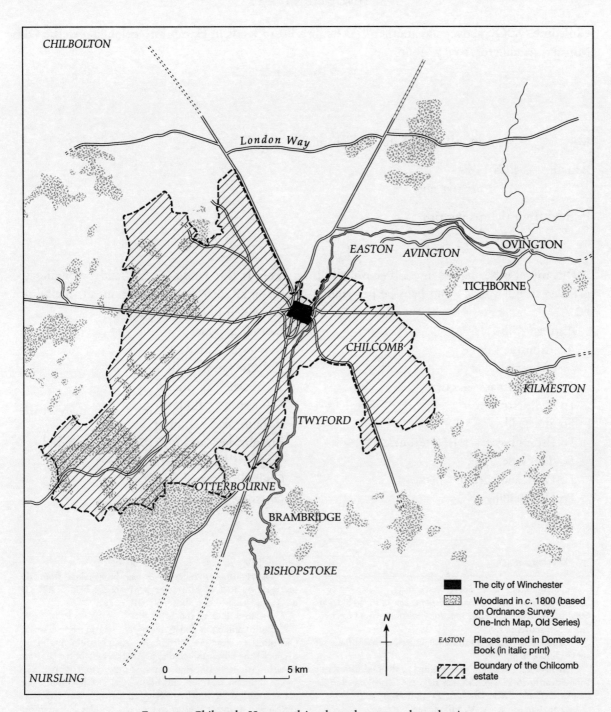

FIG. 13. Chilcomb, Hants, and its eleventh-century dependencies.

Chilcomb (**XXX**, above) and another Old English list of lands in Hampshire belonging to the Old Minster, datable to 1033 × 1066.[11]

[11] As above, n. 4.

MS.:   BL, Add. MS. 15350, fo. 6[r] (s.xii med.)

Edited: *BCS* 1160
                AS Writs 107 note

Printed from the manuscript

Ðus mycel is þæs landes into Ciltecumbe[1][.] þ is ealles an hund hida . mid þam þe þer abutan lið .[2]	This is the extent of the land belonging to Chilcomb:[1] that is 100 hides in all, including those which lie thereabout.[2]
Æstuna[3] . iiii .	Easton[3] 4 [hides]
Æt Afintuna[4] . v .	Avington[4] 5 [hides]
7 æt Ufintuna[5] . v .	and Ovington[5] 5 [hides]
Æt Ticceburnan[a][6] . xxv .	Tichborne[6] 25 [hides]
To Cylmestuna[7] . v .	Kilmeston[7] 5 [hides]
To Stoce[8] [.]v .	Bishopstoke[8] 5 [hides]
To Brombrygce[9] . 7 to Oterburnan[10] . v .	Brambridge[9] and Otterbourne[10] 5 [hides]
To Tpyfyrde[11] . xx .	Twyford[11] 20 [hides]
To Ceolbandingtune[12] [.]xx .	Chilbolton[12] 20 [hides]
To Hnutscillingæ[13] . v .	Nursling[13] 5 [hides]

---

[a] Ticeeburnan *MS.*

[1] Chilcomb, Hants. See above, **V, ii**, n. 31.

[2] *þ is ealles an hund hida . mid þam þe þer abutan lið*. 99 hides are listed below, which with one hide for Chilcomb would total 100 hides. See above, p. 226.

[3] Easton. For various recorded Anglo-Saxon estates here, see above, **XXII**, n. 3.

[4] Avington. 5 hides here were granted to the Old Minster by King Edgar in 961: S 699, *CW* 223, *BCS* 1068. It belonged to the monks *TRE* and *TRW*: *DB*, i, fo. 41[r] (*DB Hants* 3: 4).

[5] Ovington. See above, **V, viii**, n. 143.

[6] Tichborne. Ibid. n. 141.

[7] Kilmeston. The Old Minster estate of 10 hides here was leased, for a term of three lives, to Æthelwulf, *minister*, in 961: S 693ab, *CW* 111ab, *BCS* 1077–8 (cf. above, **XXIII**). The bishop held two estates there, each of 5 hides, *TRE* and *TRW*: *DB*, i, fo. 40[r] (*DB Hants* 2: 2 and 7).

[8] Bishopstoke. See above, **V, xiii**, n. 191.

[9] Brambridge. This place was not named in Domesday Book,

perhaps being included under Otterbourne.

[10] Otterbourne. 4 hides here had been taken from the bishopric by Ralf of Mortemer by 1086; see below, **XXXII**, nn. 11 and 12. See also above, **V, xiii**, n. 192.

[11] Twyford. Ibid. n. 186.

[12] Both Chilbolton and Nursling are said to pertain to the Old Minster estate of Chilcomb in a spurious diploma in the name of King Edward the Elder, probably forged in the late 10th or early 11th cent.: BL, Harl. Ch. 43. C. 1, S 376, *CW* 190, *BCS* 376. A different tradition tells of 10 hides at Chilbolton being granted to the Old Minster by King Æthelstan: S 427, *CW* 183–4, *BCS* 705–6, and *Winchester ann*, s.a. 924. 5 hides and 3 virgates at Chilbolton were held by the bishop *TRW* for the monks of the Old Minster who held 10 hides there *TRE*; the remainder of the 10 hides had been acquired by Richard Sturmy: *DB*, i, fos 41[r], 48[r] (*DB Hants* 3: 3 and 41: 1).

[13] Nursling. 5 hides here were granted to the Old Minster for its refectory by Bishop Tunbeorht in 877: S 1277, *CW* 219, *BCS* 544. It was held by the bishop *TRW* for the monks who held it *TRE*: *DB*, i, fo. 41[r] (*DB Hants* 3: 2), See also above, n. 12.

XXXII

A.D. 1086. The Domesday Book entry for the estate of Chilcomb, Hants

Latin

THE description of Chilcomb in Great Domesday Book stands therein as the first entry of chapter 3 of the Hampshire booklet, containing the account of the land in the county belonging to the monks of Winchester (Cathedral) for their subsistence.[1] Chilcomb, said to be in the otherwise unknown hundred of 'Falmer',[2] rightfully begins the chapter, as one of the largest and most ancient pieces of real property belonging to the monks.[3] Although, like its fellows, the estate was in the hands of the bishop in 1086,[4] the Domesday record, no doubt to the relief of the monks, distinguished its monastic title, even if only as a fact of potential use to future royal administrators. The official acceptance of the beneficial hidation of Chilcomb, which the text also recorded,[5] would have been of equal relief to the monks.

The estate was substantial, but apparently rather over-intensely cultivated, with some 79 ploughs overall working land for 68 ploughs. The holders of 7 *TRW* subtenancies are named in a list which also gives the name of those who held *TRE*; one of the latter subtenants, Chiping, is remarkable as still retaining his holding of land for 1 plough in 1086.[6] A further 6 hides which he had held, 2 of them on leases, had however been appropriated by Ralf of Mortemer by that date.[7]

The general statistics given conform to the expected range and order of information for a major Hampshire manor in Great Domesday Book. The list naming the subtenants (see above) may originally, however, have formed a separate fiscal record. In the MS. it forms a paragraph which has partly been squeezed in over an erasure.[8]

The text of the entry, which is written throughout by scribe *A* of Great Domesday Book,[9] heads the first column of folio 41[r] therein.

---

[1] See below, **XXXII**, n. 1.
[2] Ibid. n. 2.   [3] See WS 1, 256–8.
[4] See below, **XXXII**, n. 1.
[5] On this, see above, **V, ii**, n. 40, and **XXX**.
[6] On him, see below, **XXXII**, n. 8.
[7] Ibid. nn. 11 and 12.

[8] See *DB Hants*, note to 3: 1.
[9] For his handwriting, see Alexander R. Rumble, 'The Domesday Manuscripts: Scribes and Scriptoria', in J. C. Holt (ed.), *Domesday Studies: Papers read at the Novocentenary Conference of the Royal Historical Society and the Institute of British Geographers, Winchester, 1986* (Woodbridge, 1987), 79–99, at 82–6.

MS.:   PRO, E. 31/2, fo. 41^r, col. 1 (s.xi^2)

Facsimiles: *DB*, i (London, 1783: in 'record' type)
              H. James, *Domesday Book . . . Facsimile of the part relating to Hampshire* (Ordnance Survey, Southampton, 1864: photozincograph)
              R. W. H. Erskine (ed.), *Great Domesday: Facsimile* (London, 1986: colour photograph)

Translated: *VCH Hants*, i (Westminster, 1900), 463–4
              DB Hants (Chichester, 1982), section 3: 1
              Ann Williams and R. W. H. Erskine (ed.), *The Hampshire Domesday* (London, 1989)

Printed from the Alecto facsimile. In the edition below, the punctuation of the MS. has been modified by the omission of the points either side of Roman numerals

. . . de uictu monachorum Wint*onie* .[1]

In Fale*mere* Hund*red* .[2]

Walchelinus[3] episcopus tenet Ciltecumbe[4] . T . R . E . et modo se defendit pro una hida .[5] Terra est lxviii carucis . In dominio sunt xii caruce . Et xxx uillani et cxv bordarii cum lvii carucis . Ibi ix ęcclesię[6] et xx serui et iiii molini de iiii libris et xl acre prati . Pro herbagio xxiii solidi et v denarii . Silua ⁊ xxx porci de pasnagio .

De eadem hida tenet Willelmus terram ad iii carucas . Manno[7] tenuit .

Chepingus[8] tenet terram ad unam carucam . Ipsemet tenuit .

Walterus tenet terram ad unam carucam . Ælfer tenuit .

Hugo 'cementarius' tenet terram ad ii carucas . Giraudus tenuit .

. . . for the upkeep of the monks of Winchester[1]

In 'Falmer' Hundred[2]

Bishop Walkelin[3] holds Chilcomb.[4] *TRE* and now it was assessed at 1 hide.[5] There is land for 68 ploughs. In lordship are 12 ploughs. 30 *uillani* and 115 *bordarii* with 57 ploughs. 9 churches[6] there, and 20 slaves, and 4 mills worth £4, and 40 acres of meadow. 23s 5d for grazing. Woodland: 30 pigs from pasturage.

Of the same hide, William holds land for 3 ploughs; Manno[7] held it.

Chiping[8] holds land for 1 plough; he himself held it.

Walter holds land for 1 plough; Ælfhere held it.

Hugh 'the mason' holds land for 2 ploughs; Gerald held it.

---

[1] *de uictu monachorum Wintonie.* Chapter 3 of the Domesday Book account of Hampshire consisted of Old Minster estates which had been given for the upkeep of the monks but which *TRW* were in the hands of the bishop. Like those listed in Wiltshire (*DB*, i, fo. 65^v; *DB Wilts.* 2: 4–12), they probably represented the £300 worth of lands borrowed *c.*1079 by Bishop Walkelin to pay for the rebuilding of the cathedral; see Goodman *Chartulary* 1, and WS 1, 308–9. Cf. *Winchester ann*, s.a. 1098, and *Gesta Pontificum*, 172.

[2] 'Falmer' Hundred is otherwise unknown. It apparently contained only Chilcomb. It is taken to be an error for 'Fawley' Hundred (which later included Chilcomb) by O. S. Anderson, *The English Hundred-Names: The South-Western Counties* (Lund, 1939), 186. See also WS 1, 256.

[3] Walkelin, bishop of Winchester, 1070–98.

[4] Chilcomb, Hants; see above, **V, ii**, n. 31.

[5] *se defendit pro una hida.* See above, **V, ii**, n. 40, and **XXX**.

[6] *ix ęcclesię.* For these, see WS 1, 258.

[7] *Manno.* This form can represent either OE *Manna* or OG *Maino*: *PNDB*, 324.

[8] *Chepingus.* This form represents OE *Cyping*; see WS 1, 153, and *PNDB*, 221. The spelling Chiping used here is that preferred by WS 1, 54–5 (**I, 141–2**) in the first of which entries he is designated as 'of [Headbourne] Worthy'; cf. below, n. 11. He was a royal thegn *TRE* who held estates in Hampshire and the Isle of Wight and tenements in Southampton and Winchester, most of which were acquired *TRW* by Ralf of Mortemer; see below, nn. 11 and 12; WS 1, 54 (**I, 141** n.), and *DB Hants* 29: 1–3, 5–11, 13–14, 16; S2, etc.

Turstinus 'rufus' tenet terram ad unam carucam . Æilmer tenuit .

Osbernus tenet terram ad i carucam . Goduinus tenuit .

Turstinus 'paruus'[9] tenet xxx acras . Ęlfec[10] tenuit .

Qui has terras tenebant T . R . E : non poterant 'cum terra' recedere ad alium dominum . Qui modo tenent : habent in dominio vii carucas et vii uillanos et xxx bordarios cum ii carucis . Ibi xi serui et iiii acre prati .

Totum manerium ualebat T . R . E . lxxiii libras et x solidos et post : tantidem . Modo quod monachi tenent : quater xx libras . Quod homines tenent : xxiiii libras .

Huic manerio adiacuerunt vi hidę[11] T . R . E . quas tenet modo Radulfus de Mortemer[12] . sed ęcclesiæ nullum seruitium facit .

Thurstan 'the red' holds land for 1 plough; Æthelmær held it.

Osbern holds land for 1 plough; Godwine held it.

Thurstan 'the small'[9] holds 30 acres; Ælfheah[10] held it.

Those who held these lands TRE could not withdraw 'with their land' to another lord. Those who hold them now have in lordship 7 ploughs and 7 *uillani* and 30 *bordarii* with 2 ploughs. 11 slaves there and 4 acres of meadow.

The whole manor was worth £73 10s TRE, and the same amount afterwards. Now what the monks hold [is worth] £80, what the men hold [is worth] £24.

6 hides[11] belonged to this manor TRE which Ralf of Mortemer[12] now holds. But he does no service to the church.

---

[9] Thurstan the small may be identical with the Thurstan who held 52 acres from the bishop at Easton TRW, also formerly held (as here) by someone called Ælfheah: DB, i, fo. 40ʳ (DB Hants 2: 5).

[10] For Ælfheah, cf. above, n. 9.

[11] *vi hidę*. These 6 hides consisted of 4 hides at Otterbourne, 1 at Headbourne Worthy (with 8 tenements in Winchester) and 1 at Swampton. All had been held TRE by Chiping (above, n. 8),

the latter two on leases from the Old Minster: DB, i, fos 46ᵛ, 47ʳ (DB Hants 29: 1, 3, and 9). Headbourne Worthy appears to have reverted to the cathedral by 1148; see WS 1, 54 (**I, 141**, n. 1).

[12] Ralf came from Mortemer-sur-Eaulne, arr. and cant. Neufchâtel, Seine-Mᵐᵉ; see WS 1, 54 (**I, 141**, n.2). After 1066 he acquired the 6 hides (above, n. 11) of leasehold land held by his predecessor Chiping, along with most of the latter's other estates; see above, n. 8.

XXXIII

PAPAL LETTER CONCERNING THE REFORM OF THE OLD MINSTER

XXXIII

n.d. [A.D.? 963], letter of Pope John [XII] to King Edgar, giving approval to the replacement of the secular canons at the Old Minster by monks and to new arrangements for the election of the bishop

Latin

P. Jaffé (ed.), *Regesta Pontificum Romanorum . . . ad annum . . . 1198* (2nd edn., eds. W. Wattenbach, S. Loewenfeld, F. Kaltenbrunner, and P. Ewald, Leipzig, 1885–8), no. 3753 (*sub* John XIII). Walther Holtzmann, *Papsturkunden in England* (Berlin, 1931–52), i, p. 127; ii, pp. 39–40, 42.

Tʜɪs is the sole papal document in the present collection. Besides its immediate importance in giving papal authority to the ejection of the secular canons from the Old Minster, it is of great general significance in establishing that a monastic cathedral community should be allowed to elect its bishop,[1] a right subsequently elaborated upon in the *Regularis Concordia*, and in **V, xiv**, above.[2] Although treated by earlier editors as a document of Pope John XIII (1 October 965–6 September 972),[3] surviving copies lack the dating-clause and a convincing case was made by Dom Thomas Symons, followed by Dorothy Whitelock, for its attribution to the earlier pontificate of John XII (16 December 955–14 May 964), and specifically to before early November in the year 963, when he fled from Rome in the face of the army of the emperor Otto I.[4] In Rome in 960 the same pope had given the pallium to Archbishop Dunstan,[5] in answer to whose request on behalf of King

---

[1] On this right, see Dom David Knowles, *The Monastic Order in England: a History of its Development from the Times of St Dunstan to the Fourth Lateran Council 940–1216* (2nd edn., Cambridge, 1963, repr. 1976), 45.

[2] See *RC*, cap. 9; and above, **V, xiv**, nn. 240–1.

[3] E.g. Jaffé 3753 and *BCS* 1275. More recently also by Leo Santifaller, *Liber Diurnus*, Päpste und Papstum 10 (Stuttgart, 1976), 107.

[4] 'Notes on the Life and Work of St Dunstan, II', *Downside Review* n.s. 80 (1962), 355–66, at 357–8; *Councils* 29 (p. 110). For John XII, see J. N. D. Kelly, *The Oxford Dictionary of Popes* (Oxford, 1986), 126–7.

[5] For the papal document recording this, see *Councils* 25; Jaffé 3687. See also Nicholas Brooks, *The Early History of the Church of Canterbury: Christ Church from 597 to 1066* (Leicester, 1984), 244.

Edgar **XXXIII** was issued. John XII is known to have shown interest in monastic reform, at least in Italy,[6] and to have attempted to safeguard free ecclesiastical (papal) elections,[7] both subjects which have some relevance to the concerns of **XXXIII** which deals with monastic reform at the Old Minster and the election of the bishop of Winchester by the monastic community.

Whether issued by John XII or John XIII, **XXXIII** was accepted as 'a genuine papal document' by Wilhelm Levison,[8] and this opinion was noted with respect by Symons and Whitelock.[9] Some of the clauses are formulae from the *Liber Diurnus*,[10] but others may have been influenced by the wording of the now-lost missive apparently received by the pope from Dunstan. The description of Æthelwold as *coepiscopus* was explained by Whitelock as papal anticipation of his consecration (29 November 963),[11] but perhaps Dunstan had already named him in his missive as the intended bishop of Winchester and may himself have described him as his own future *coepiscopus*, a description taken up by the papal draftsman. The absence of any specific reference to **XXXIII** in the *Regularis Concordia* is not surprising as that text set out to deal with all the English monasteries, not just one. A similar absence of reference to it in the earliest manuscript of **V**, above,[12] is explicable by the fact that the latter foregrounds the roles of Edgar and Æthelwold in the reform of the Old Minster and omits mention of Dunstan.

The best surviving text of **XXXIII** is that printed in the first edition of Matthew Parker's *De antiquitate Britannicæ ecclesiæ* (1572); this text was stated to have been copied *ex archiuis*, presumably from a manuscript then extant at Canterbury. Earlier this may have been the source of those parts of **XXXIII** used by Guerno, the draftsman of a forged Canterbury privilege *c.* 1070.[13] A less satisfactory medieval Winchester version is represented by MSS. B–F.

MSS.:   *Lost*, whence Parker (see below)
            B. HRO, Reg Pontissara, fos. 166^v–167^r (s. xiii/xiv)
            C. WCL, W52/74 [St. Swithun's Cartulary], vol. 1, fo. 5^r (s. xiii/xiv)
            D. ibid., vol. 2, fo. 41^r (s. xiv med.)
            E. BL, Harl. MS. 1761, fo. 77^r (s. xiv ex.)
            F. BL, Harl. MS. 358, fos. 63^r–64^r (s. xvi^1)

Edited: Matthew Parker, *De antiquitate Britannicæ ecclesiæ* (1st edn., London, 1572), 66–7; (2nd edn., Hanover, 1605), 91–2, *ex archiuis*
            Michael Alford, *Fides regia Anglicana sive annales ecclesiæ Anglicanæ* (Liège, 1663), iii, 349, from Parker (2nd edn.)
            C. Cocquelines, *Bullarum Romanorum pontificum amplissima collectio* (Rome, 1739–44), i, 262, col. 2, from Parker (2nd edn.)

---

[6] See Kelly, *Oxford Dictionary of Popes*, 126.

[7] Ibid. 127.

[8] *England and the Continent in the Eighth Century* (Oxford, 1946, repr. 1998), 196.

[9] 'Notes on the Life and Work of St Dunstan, II', 357; and *Councils*, 110.

[10] See below, **XXXIII**, nn. 4, 6, 17, and 20–1.

[11] *Councils*, 110.

[12] Although Thomas Rudborne probably alluded to it in his reference to a papal confirmation, added to **V, xiv** (MS. D); q.v., second n. *h*.

[13] See C. N. L. Brooke, 'The Canterbury Forgeries and their Author, I', *Downside Review* n.s. 68 (1950), 462–76, especially 467–9. This particular privilege is seen as distinct from the other Canterbury forgeries (?of 1121–2) by R. W. Southern, 'The Canterbury Forgeries', *EHR* 73 (1958), 193–226, at 194 n. 1.

Giovanni Domenico Mansi *et al.*, *Sacrorum conciliorum nova et amplissima collectio* (Florence, Venice, Paris, 1759–1927), xviii, 483, from Parker (2nd edn.)

Jacques-P. Migne *et al.*, *Patrologia Latina* cxxxv (1879), 986, no. 22, from Parker (2nd edn.)

William Stubbs, *Memorials of Saint Dunstan, Archbishop of Canterbury*, Rolls Series 63 (London, 1874), 364–5, from Parker (2nd edn.)

BCS 1275, from Alford and Cocquelines

Reg Pontissara, 630–1, from B

Goodman *Winchester Chartulary* (calendar) 27 from C, 318 from D

Councils 29, from Parker (1st and 2nd edn.), *Reg Pontissara*, and C, D, and E

Edited from Parker (1st edn.), with some standardization of punctuation, capitals, and orthography [u/v, ii/ij]

Iohannes[1] episcopus, seruus seruorum Dei, Eadgaro[2] regi excellentissimo atque omnibus episcopis, ducibus, comitibus,[3] abbatibus, et cuncto fideli populo Anglicæ gentis, Christianam[a] salutem et apostolicam benedictionem.

Quoniam semper sunt concedenda[b] quæ rationabilibus[c] queruntur desideriis, oportet ut uestræ piæ petitionis studium in priuilegiis minime offendatur præstandis.[4] Scimus enim, gloriose[5] fili, imperii uestri dignitatem zelo diuinæ legis ita undique munitam ut indesinenter pro[d] uenerabilium locorum percogitet stabilitate[e] quatenus proueniente pro[f] labore[6] schola dominici multiplicetur seruitii, et largitori omnium Deo abunde fructus referantur milleni.

Bishop John,[1] servant of the servants of God, to the most excellent King Edgar[2] and to all the bishops, ealdormen, thegns,[3] abbots and the whole faithful people of the English race, Christian greeting and apostolic blessing.

Since the things asked in reasonable petitions should always be granted, it is fitting that the desire of your pious petition should not be rejected in the privileges which are to be given.[4] For we know, O glorious[5] son, that the worthiness of your rule is so strengthened on all sides by zeal for the divine law that it incessantly considers the firm standing of religious places [and] how study of the Lord's service might be increased by pious work in the future,[6] and how thousand-fold fruits might be abundantly repaid to God the Giver of everything.

[a] karissimam *all surviving MSS.*   [b] concedenda sunt *all surviving MSS.*   [c] *Also thus in Liber Diurnus;* rationalibus *all other surviving versions of* **XXXIII**   [d] *Also thus in Liber Diurnus and Parker 2nd edn; all surviving MSS. of* **XXXIII** *omit*   [e] *Also thus in Liber Diurnus and Parker 2nd edn;* stabilitatem *all surviving MSS. of* **XXXIII**   [f] pro; pio *all surviving MSS. and Liber Diurnus*

of the Old Minster in 980 is described.

[4] *Quoniam . . . præstandis.* Cf. *Liber Diurnus*, 23, formula 32: *Quoniam semper sunt concedenda quae rationabilibus congruunt desideriis, oportet ut devotio conditoris pie constructionis oraculi in privilegiis prestandis minime denegetur.*

[5] *gloriose.* Edgar is most prominently described as *gloriosus* in *RC*, cap. 1, where it forms the opening word of the text. The same epithet is used of him in the superscription to **V, xiii**, above; and in Wulfstan *Vita S. Æthelwoldi*, cap. 13 (ed. Lapidge and Winterbottom, 24–5).

[6] *pro uenerabilium locorum percogitet stabilite quatenus proueniente pio labore.* Cf. *Liber Diurnus*, 114, formula 87: *pro venerabilium locorum percogitare stabilitate atque deo servientium securitate, ut hoc proveniente pio labore.*

[1] John XII, pope 16 December 955–14 May 964. Although deposed on 4 December 963 by a synod presided over by the emperor Otto I, he reestablished himself in February 964; see J. N. D. Kelly, *The Oxford Dictionary of Popes* (Oxford, 1986), 126–7.

[2] Edgar, king of Mercia 957–9, of England 959–75.

[3] *comitibus.* Latin *comes* (rather than the more usual *minister*) is also used to mean 'thegn' in Wulfstan *Vita S. Æthelwoldi*, cap. 40 (ed. Lapidge and Winterbottom, 60–1), where the rededication

Quare, rex inclyte ac fili charissime, quid^g uestra excellentia per fratrem et coepiscopum nostrum Dunstanum^7 ab hac apostolica sede, cui licet immeriti præsidemus, exposcit, omnimodis concedimus, authoritate apostolica sancientes ut de monasterio in Wintonia ciuitate in honorem^h sanctæ Trinitatis et beatissimorum apostolorum Petri et Paulo constructo, quod Uetus differentia Noui illius quod iuxta est Coenobii cognominatur, canonici,^{8} Domino^j et episcopo suo, omnibus catholicæ fidei cultoribus^9 ex patentibus culparum suarum turpitudinibus odibiles,^{k} et in eisdem secundum impoenitens cor eorum inuerecunde perdurantes, cum suo præposito,^{10} utpote uasa diaboli, eiiciantur.^{11} Et sicut uestra sublimitas desiderat, dilectissimus frater et coepiscopus noster Ethelwaldus,^{12} regularibus disciplinis apprime imbutus, monachorum secundum præcepta regulæ^{13} uiuentium gregem^{14} enutriat, eisque inibi perpetuam mansionem statuat. Ille igitur^l eorum uitam ita sanctitatis moribus exornet, ut, pastore^{15} ad laboris sui præmium uocato, non aliunde quam ex illa congregatione alter^m in locum regiminis succedat.^{16} Quod si impedientibus, quod absit, peccatis, ad hoc pontificale officium in eadem congregatione idoneum inueniri minime posse contigerit, authoritate apostolorum principis Petri, cui Dominus ac Saluator noster ligandi soluendique potestatem contradidit,$^{n\ 17}$ præcipi-

Wherefore, O illustrious king and dearest son, we grant in all respects that which your excellency requests through our brother and fellow bishop Dunstan,^{7} from this apostolic see over which we undeservedly preside, decreeing with apostolic authority that the canons,^{8} with their prior,^{10} the vessel of the Devil indeed, should be thrown out^{11} from the monastery in the city of Winchester built in honour of the Holy Trinity and of the most blessed apostles Peter and Paul, which is called the Old Minster in contrast to the New one which is adjacent, [each of them] being hateful to the Lord and His bishop and to all cultivators^9 of the true faith because of the open foulness of their crimes and persisting shamelessly in the same according to his impenitent heart. And as your highness requests, let our dearest brother and fellow bishop Æthelwold,^{12} especially imbued with the disciplines of the Rule,^{13} nourish a flock^{14} of monks living according to the commands of the Rule and let him establish a perpetual abode for them in the same place. Let him thus so embellish their life with the practices of sanctity that when the shepherd^{15} has been called to the reward for his work another might succeed to the place of authority only from that community.^{16} If however it should prove, Heaven forbid!, impossible through the hindrance of sins to find a person in the same community suitable for this episcopal office, we command by the authority of Peter the foremost of the apostles, to whom Our Lord and Saviour gave the power of binding and loosing,^{17} that no

---

^{g} quod all surviving MSS. ^{h} honore all surviving MSS.
^{j} Deo all surviving MSS. ^{k} odibilis; odibiles CD
^{l} qui (probably a misreading of the abbreviation ḡ as q̃); igitur all surviving MSS. ^{m} alteri; alter all surviving MSS.

---

^{7} Dunstan, archbishop of Canterbury 959–88; see above, **IV**, n. 127. He received his pallium from Pope John XII (above, n. 1) in 960; see above, p. 233.

^{8} canonici. The secular clergy at the Old Minster; see above, **V, xiv**, nn. 216 and 219.

^{9} catholicæ fidei cultoribus. For the use of cultor in a similar context, see above, **IV, viii**, n. 57.

^{10} præposito. See above, **V, xiv**, n. 220.

^{11} eiiciantur. For the expulsion of the Old Minster clergy, see above, **V, ii** and **xiv**.

^{12} coepiscopus noster Ethelwaldus. Æthelwold, bishop of Winchester 963–84; see above, **IV**, n. 134. For coepiscopus, see

above, p. 234.

^{13} regulæ. The Benedictine Rule in its reformed state; see above, pp. 68–9.

^{14} gregem. Cf. above, **IV**, n. 98, and **V, xiv**, n. 212.

^{15} pastore. That is, the bishop. Cf. above, **IV**, n. 98.

^{16} ex illa congregatione alter in locum regiminis succedat. See above, **V, xiv**, n. 240.

^{17} cui Dominus ac Saluator noster ligandi soluendique potestatem contradidit. With reference to Matt. 16: 18. Cf. Liber Diurnus, 79, formula 75 cui a domino deo potestas ligandi solvendique data est; and ibid. 81, formula 76 cui a domino deo data est potestas ligandi solvendique.

mus ut nemo ex clericorum ordine[18] ad huius regimen ecclesiæ promoueatur, sed potius ex alia qualibet[o] congregatione qui dignus inuentus fuerit monachus assumatur et huic ecclesiæ præficiatur.[19]

Si quis enim interea, quod non credimus, hæc apostolicæ sedis priuilegii decreta irrita facere[p] et ea quæ a nobis pie indulta sunt intaminare præsumpserit, authoritate eiusdem coelestis clauigeri[20] Petri omniumque successorum eius sciat se anathematis uinculo innodatum,[21] et in illo magni[q] iudicii die perpetualiter damnandum.

In Christo ualeas domine fili.[r]

one from the order of clerks[18] should be promoted to rule this church, but that rather a monk who is worthy should be found from some other monastery, adopted, and put in charge of this church.[19]

But if anyone meanwhile, which we do not believe, should presume to invalidate these decrees of the privilege of the apostolic see and to defile those things which have been piously permitted by us, by the authority of the same Peter, the celestial Keeper of the Keys,[20] and of all his successors, let him know that he will be bound by the fetter of anathema[21] and damned in perpetuity on the great Day of Judgement.

Farewell in Christ, O lord son.

---

[n] tradidit *all surviving MSS.*   [o] qualiter *altered in ink to* qualibet *in copy of Parker at CCCC, according to Councils 29, n. bb;* qualibet *most surviving MSS.*   [p] fecerit *all surviving MSS.* [q] *All surviving MSS. omit* magni; mani *Parker 2nd edn (in error)* [r] *All surviving MSS. omit* In . . . fili

---

[18] *nemo ex clericorum ordine.* That is, no secular priest (see above, **IV, vii**, n. 44). Cf. *non autem canonicus* in **V, xiv**, above (see ibid. n. 241).

[19] *Quod si impedientibus ex alia . . . congregatione qui dignus inuentus fuerit monachus . . .* See above, **V, xiv**, n. 241.

[20] *coelestis clauigeri.* Cf. *Liber Diurnus,* 90, formula 83 *beate Petre . . . cui claves regni caelorum ad ligandum atque solvendum . . . dominus Iesus Christus tradidit;* and above, n. 17.

[21] *sciat se anathematis uinculo innodatum.* Also in *Liber Diurnus,* 113, formula 86; 118, formula 89; and 135, formula 101.

LATIN WORD-LIST

THIS word-list includes instances, in the documents edited in the present volume, of words or meanings which are rare, technical, and/or which first appeared in post-Classical Latin. Many of the grecisms have been discussed by Michael Lapidge as part of his study of Anglo-Latin hermeneutic vocabulary; see Lapidge 'Æthelwold as scholar' and *idem*, 'Hermeneutic Style'.

The following abbreviations are used:

n. = noun; v. = verb; adj. = adjective; adv. = adverb; p. p. = past participle; pl. = plural; prep. = preposition; sg. = singular.

accommodo (v.) **V, v**: to lease

Acharon (n., from Greek Ἀχέρων) **IV, ix, V, i**: the Underworld

actualis (adj.) **V, xiv** (note 206): active

adnihilo (v.) **IV, xvi**: to bring to nought, nullify

agiographum (n.) **V, xii**: holy writing

agius (adj., from Greek ἅγιος) **IV, witn.list, V, iv**: holy

altiboo (v.) **V, xiii**: to cry from on high

altithronus (n.) **IV, ii, viii, xxi, XXVI**: the High-throned One, God; (adj.) **V, i**: high-throned

ambitum (n.) **XXVIII**: boundary

anathema (n., from Greek ἀνάθεμα) **IV, ix–x, witn. list, V, ii, iv, vi–xi, VI, XXXIII**: anathema, curse,

anathemizo (v., from ἀνάθεμα + ίζω) **V, v, xiii**: to curse

antistes (n.) **V, iv, x, xiv, IX, XXVI**: bishop

apex (n.) **V, v, viii, x, xiv**: outline; **V, xii, XXVIII**: letter-form

apostato (v.) **V, xi**: to forsake one's religion

aporior (v., from Greek ἀπορέω) **IV, xii, V, vi**: to reject

appropio (v.) **XXVI**: to approach

archanum (n.) **V, i, iv, xiii**: sanctuary

arcisterium (n., from Greek ἀσκητηρίον = asceterion, with

metathesis here as in Abbo of St. Germain's *Bella Parisiacae Urbis*, iii. 81) **IV, viii**: monastery

arpago (n., = *harpago* from Greek ἁρπάγη) **XXVIII**: grappling-hook

baratrum (n., from Greek βάραθρον) **IV, prol., v, ix, xxiii, V, i, XXIV**: the Abyss, Hell

baro (n.) **XIII–XIV, XVII**: baron

basileos, basileus (n., from Greek βασιλεύς) **IV, vi, witn.list, V, i–ii, iv–v, vii, x, xiv, VI, IX, XXII, XXVI**: ruler, king

basilica (n., from Greek βασιλική) **V, iv**: cathedral; **V, v, vii, x–xiii**: [cathedral] church; **XXVIII**: [parish] church

beatmot (n., from Hebrew) **XXIV** note 8: Behemoth, a monstrous beast

bordarius (n.) **XXXII**: 'bordar' [category of rural inhabitant]

brauium (n., from Greek βραβεῖον) **IV, xvi**: reward

caducae (pl. n., fem.; ? for *caduca*, neuter) **V, viii–ix**: this world, transitory things

cambiacio (n.) **XI**: exchange

camerarius (n.) **XII–XIII**: [royal] chamberlain

cancellarius (n.) **XII**: [royal] chancellor

canonicus (n.) **III, IV, vii, ix, V, xiv, XXXIII**: secular canon

caraxo (v., from Greek χαράσσω) **IV, dating clause** (note 124), **V, iv, VI, XXII, XXIV, XXVI**: to write

carisma (n., from Greek χάρισμα) **IV, xv, V, v, xiii**: gift, grace

caritatiuus (adj.) **IV, xii**: charitable

cassatus, casatus (n.) **III, V, ii, v, viii–ix, xii**: hide [fiscal unit of land]

cataclismas (n., from Greek κατακλυσμός) **IV, iv**: the Flood

catalogus (n., from Greek κατάλογος) **XXVIII**: list

catholicus (adj., from Greek καθολικός) **IV, xviii, V, viii, xiii–xiv, XXXIII**: orthodox

celsithronus, cęlsi- (adj.) **V, i, viii**: high-throned

cenobita (n., from following) **V, ii, VI**: monk, nun

cenobium, cęnobium, coenobium (n., from Greek κοινόβιον) **IV, vii, x, xxi, V, ii, VI, X, XXVI, XXXIII**: monastery

circuitus (n.) **XXVI**: boundary

clericus (n., from Greek κλερικός): **IV, vii** (note 44), **viii, V, ii, xiv, XXXIII**: secular clerk

cleronomia (n., from Greek κληρονομία) **V, rubric** (note 1): inheritance

clito, clyto (n., ultimately from Greek κλυτός) **IV**, **witn.list** (note 128), **XXVIII**: ætheling

collector (n.) **XV**: [tax-]collector

comes (n.) **XII, XIV, XVI–XVII**: count; **XIII–XIV**: earl; **XXXIII**: thegn

commanipularis (n.) **IX**: comrade

complex (n.) **IV, prol., ix, V, i, xiv, VI**: confederate

conditor (n.) **IV, prol., iv, xvi**: the Creator

confaueo (v.) **XXVIII**: to favour

congregatio (n.) **IV, xiii, V, ii, xiv, XXXIII**: community

constabularius (n.) **XIII**: [royal] constable

consuetudo (n.) **III, XII, XVII**: customary dues; **XIII**: custom

contubernium (n.) **IV, v–vi, V, iv–v, xii**: common dwelling

conuersatio (n.) **V, iv, xiv**: abode, existence

conuersor (v.) **IV, ii, v, xii, V, v**: to dwell, pass one's life

cosmus (n., from Greek κόσμος) **IV, i, V, i, vii**: the Universe

croma (n., from Greek χρῶμα, a colour) **V, iv, x**: time

cultura (n.) **IV, vi, xviii**: ploughland

cunctitenens (adj.) **IV, xi**: controlling all things

cunctitonans (n.) **IX**: the All-thundering One, God

cuneus (n.) **IV, vii, xv**: troop, throng

curtis (n.) **XXIV**: curtilage

cyrographum (n., from Greek χειρόγραφον) **XXVIII**: writing

dapifer (n.) **XII**: [royal] steward

dapsilitas (n.) **IV, ii, xviii, V, i, iv, vi–vii, xiv, IX, XXVI**: generosity

decimo (v.) **IV, iv, vi**: to tithe, give a tenth part of

se defendere (v.) + *pro* (prep.) **XXXII**: to be assessed at [for taxation]

delinitus (p.p.) **IV, iii**: flattered

demon (n., from Greek δαίμων) **IV, v, x, xxi, V, i**: the Devil

deturpo (v.) **V, xiv**: to disfigure

dux (n.) **IV, VI, VIII(ii), IX, XXII, XXVI, XXXIII**: ealdorman

dyrocheum (n., corruption of Greek διττός and ὀχή) **V, xiv** (note 212): division

elemosina, -yna (n.) **III, XI, XIV**: alms

epilempticus, epilenticus (adj., from Greek ἐπιλεπτικός) **XXVIII**: maniacal

episcopalia (pl. n.) **XIII**: episcopal rights

episcopium (n., from Greek ἐπισκοπειον) **V, xiv**: diocese

ergastulum (n., from Greek ἐργάζομαι) **V, xiv**: prison

erumpnose (adv.) **V, iv**: in distress

escambium (n.) **XIII–XV, XVII**: exchange

exordium **V, i–ii, v, viii**: starting-place, beginning

famulatus (n.) **V, xiv**: service

fascino (v.) **V, v**: to bewitch, enchant

feria (n.) **XII–XIII**: fair

fons (n.) **V, i**: font

gabulus (n.) **IV, v, V, i**: the Cross, gallows

gehennalis (adj.) **V, ii**: of Hell, hellish

geldum or *gelda* (n.) **XIV–XV, XVII**: geld, tax

gradus (n.) **IV, viii**: degree

griphia (n. from Greek γραφή, writing) **XXVIII**: document, writing

harpago, see *arpago*

heiulo (v.) **IV, x**: to bewail

herbagium (n.) **XXXII**: grazing

herois (n., from Greek ἡρωίς) **XXVIII**: noble lady

hida, hyda (n.) **III, X, XIV, XXXII**: hide [fiscal unit of land]

homuncio, see *omuncio*

horrifluus (adj.) **IX**: horrific

hospitium (n.) **XXVI**: house

hundredum (n.) **III**: hundred [territorial unit]

impresentis (adj.) **IV, iv**: present

infeco (v.) **V, i**: to pollute

infernus (n.) **IV, vi, V, iv, vi–vii, x, xii, XI**: Hell

iustitiae (pl. n.) **XII**: profits of justice

iustitius (n.) **XVII**: justice [royal official]

kaleo (n., from Greek καλέω) **V, xii**: to call, summon, urge

largiflua (adj.) **IV, xviii, V, vii**: generous

?*largitor* (v.) **III** (note *b*): to bestow

laruaricus (adj.) **XXII**: diabolical

lauacrum (n.) **V, i**: baptism

lebes (n.) **XXVIII**: cauldron

legirups (n.) **XXVIII**: lawbreaker

libertas (n.) **IV, xvii, xxi, V, i–ii, iv, vi–xii, xiv, VI, IX, XXI, XXIV, XXVI, XXVIII**: freedom; **XVI** (cf. note 5): free tenure

lictor (n.) **IV, ix**: attendant

loetum (n.) **IV, iii**: death

lolium (n.) **V, i**: tares

machina (n.) **IV, prol., IX**: scheme of things, scheme

macrobius (n., from Greek μακρός + βίος) **IV, iii** (note 23): long-lived

malum (n.) **IV, iii**: apple

mancha, mancusa (n.) **III** note 6, **V, v**: mancus [monetary unit]

mansa (n.) **V, i–ii, iv, vi–vii, ix–xi, xiii, VIII(ii), XXII**: hide [fiscal unit of land]

marca (n.) **XV**: mark [monetary unit]

marcidulus (adj.) **V, iv**: rotten

massicus (n.) **IV, ii** (note 17): man-like creature, Adam

mastigia (n., from Greek μαστιγίας) **IV, x**: club

melancolia (n., from Greek μελαγχολία) **IV, xii** (note 81), **V, vi, xi**: melancholy *minister* (n.) **II–IV, VI, IX, XIV, XVII, XXII, XXVI**: thegn

missa (n.) **V, xiv, XIII**: mass

monachicus (adj.) **IV, viii**: monkish

monarches (n., from Greek μονάρχης) **XXVIII**: ruler

multipetax (adj.) **XXVIII**: exceedingly greedy

murdrum (n.) **XIV**: the murder-fine

neophitus (n., from Greek νεόφυτος) **V, i**: neophyte

occa (n.) **V, i**: harrow

odibilis (adj.) **XXXIII**: hateful

offendiculum (n.) **XXIV**: hindrance, obligation

omnipotens (n.) **IV, viii**: the Almighty; (adj.) **IV, prol., X, XXII, XXVI**: almighty, all-powerful

omuncio [for *homuncio*] (n.) **IX**: dwarf

onoma (n., from Greek ὄνομα) **XXVIII**: name

opifex (n.) **IV, xix**: the Maker, God

ordinatus (adj.) **IV, witn.list** (note 150): ordained, appointed to ecclesiastical office

organum (n., from Greek ὄργανον) **IX**: engine

orthodoxi (pl. n., from Greek ὀρθόδοξος) **V, xiv**: the orthodox

pactata (n.) **V, v**: betrothed woman

parrochia (n.) **XIII**: parochial rights

parthenalis (adj., related to Greek παρθένος) **XXVIII**: of the Virgin

pasnagium (n.) **XXXII**: pasture

pastus (n.) **V, i, xiv, VIII(ii)**: food-rent

peculialis (adj., for *peculiaris*) **V, v**: private

peioro (v.) **V, xiv** : to injure

percogito (v.) **XXXIII**: to ponder, consider carefully

perflegeton (= Greek πῦρ φλεγέθων): **XXIV** (note *e*): conflagration, burning

peripsema (n., from Greek περίψημα) **V, vi, xi** (note 165): offscourings, filth

philargiria (n., from Greek φιλαργυρία) **V, i** (note 23), **iv, vi, xiv**: avarice, love of silver / money

philargirius (adj, from preceding) **V, v**: avaricious

piscarium (n.) **XXVI**: fishery

placitum (n.) **XIV, XVII**: [legal] plea

plasmator (n., related to Greek πλάσμα) **V, i**: the Fashioner, Creator

plaudo (v.) **XXI** (cf. note 6): to give with approval

policrates (n., from Greek πολυκρατής): **IV, ii** (note 19): very mighty

politanus (adj.) **XXVIII**: city, urban

pompa (n., from Greek πομπή) **IV, xii, V, i, xi**: pomp, ostentation, splendour

pompaticus (adj., from preceding) **IV, xii**: showy

pontifex (n.) **IV, witn.list, V, i–ii, v–vi, viii, x–xi, xiv**: pontiff, bishop

pontificatus (n.) **V, iv**: bishopric

potentatus (n.) **V, x**: reign

prediolum (n.) **XXVIII**: little property

predium (n.) **IV, xvii, XXI, XXVII–XXVIII**: tenement

prefectus (n.) **XXVIII**: reeve

prepositus (n.) **V, xiv, XXXIII**: prior

presul (n.) **V, iv–vii, ix, xii–xiv, XXII, XXIV**: bishop

primitiae (pl. n.) **V, i**; first fruits

princeps (n.) **XXVI**: leading man

protopla(u)stus (n., from Greek πρωτόπλαστος) **IV, ix, IX**: the first man, Adam

quadripartitus (adj.) **XXVI**: quadripartite, divided into four

querela (n.) **XIV–XV, XVII**: [legal] plaint

quisquiliae (pl. n.) **V, vi, xi** (note 165): rubbish

recidiua (pl. n., from following) **V, v, XXII**: everyday affairs

recidiuus (adj.) **V, vii–viii, xiv, VI**: day to day, recurring

refocillatio (n.) **V, vi**: feeding, refreshment

regmen (n.) **IV, vi–viii, x, xv**: kingdom

rumphea (n., from Greek ῥομφαία) **XXVIII**: sword

sapientes (pl. n.) **V, xiv** (note 213): the *witan*

sartago (n.) **IX**: frying-pan

sceda (n.) **IX**: document

scedula (n., diminutive of preceding) **V, iv, XXVI**: document

scibilis (adj.) **IX**: well-known

scorta (n.) **V, v**: whore

scotum (n.) **XVII**: scot, tax

sedes (n.) **IV, i** : abode, dwelling; **XIII, XXVI, XXXIII**: [episcopal] see

signaculum (n.) **IV, witn.list**: sign

singrapha (n., from Greek συγγραφή) **IV, dating clause** (note 123): document

sinthama (n., from Greek σύνθημα or σύνθεμα) **V, i**: arrangement of text

solidata (n.) **XIII**: a shilling's worth [of land], solidate

solito (adv.) **V, xiv**: according to custom

soma, zoma (n., from Greek σῶμα) **IX, XXIV**: body

sophia (n., from Greek σοφία **V, vii**: wisdom

sophista (n., from Greek σοφιστής) **V, i**: learned man

spurcitia (n.) **IV, i, vi, x, V, ii, xiv**: filth

stadium (n.) **IX**: furlong

statio (n.) **XIII**: 'station' [in a religious procession]

staurus (n., from Greek σταυρός) **XXVIII**: the Cross

stemma (n, from Greek στέμμα) **V, v**: pedigree

Styx (n., from Greek Στύξ) **IV, x** (note 70): the river Styx

subnixe (adv.) **IV, witn.list**: humbly

subspeculator (n.) **XXIV**: bishop

suburbana (pl. n.) **V, i**: suburban area, area dependent on a city

sustentatorius (adj.) **XXVIII**: supporting

tallagium (n.) **XVII**: tallage, tax

tauma (n., ultimately from the Greek letter *tau*) **IV, witn. list**: symbol [of the Cross]

telligraphium (n.) **VIII(ii)**: land-charter

thema (n., from Greek θέμα) **IV, prol.**: theme [of story]

theologicum (n., from Greek θεολογικός) **XXVIII**: biblical saying

theoricus (adj., related to Greek θεωρική) **V, v, xiv, IX**: contemplative

tirannos (n., from Greek τύραννος) **IV, xiv, xviii**: tyrant

tripudio (v.) **IV, xvi**: to rejoice

tripudium (n.) **IV, ii, xii**: jubilation

triuiatim (adv.) **IV, iii, V, viii**: far and wide

typus (n., from Greek τῦφος) **IV, ii**: vanity

tyrannicus (adj., related to Greek τύραννος) **V, iv**: tyrannical, of a tyrant

tyrannizo (v., from Greek τύραννις + ίζω) **XXVIII**: to tyrannize, act like a tyrant towards

umbrificus (adj.) **V, xiii**: shadowy

uadimonium (n.) **IV, witn.list**: recognizance

uicecomes (n.) **XI–XII, XIV, XVII**: sheriff

uillanus (n.) **XXXII**: 'villein' [category of rural inhabitant]

uirgata (n.) **III, X**: yardland, virgate; **IX** rod, 'yard'

uorago (n.) **V, xi**: the Abyss

zabulus (n., from Greek διάβολος) **IV, iii**: the Devil

zelus (n., from Greek ζῆλος) **XXXIII**: zeal

zoma see *soma*

OLD ENGLISH WORD-LIST

THE following list gives references to the occurrence of selected Old English words in the texts, above, and to relevant discussion in the textual notes. Most of the words, or specific senses of them, are part of a technical subset of vernacular vocabulary used in relation to law, topography or administration.

The following abbreviations are used:

acc. = accusative; adj. = adjective; n. = noun; pl. = plural; v. = verb

æcersplott (n.) **XXVI** note 8: acre-plot

bearn (n.) **V, iii** note 62: son
begeat (n.) **XXIX** note 6: yield, return, acquisition
bēodærn (n.) **II** note 15: refectory
*bica (n.) **XXII** note 35: '(?) beak, point'
bisceopstōl (n.) **VII**: cathedral
bōc (n.) **VIII(i), XXVI, XXX**: diploma
(ge)bōcian (v.) **II, VIII(i), XIX**: to grant by diploma
bōcung (n.) **XIX** note 8: privileged tenure
burh (n.) **VII, XX**: city; **XXII** note 6: fortification
burhhecg (n.) **I** note 8: city-hedge
burhmen (pl. n.) **XXIX**: citizens
burhwaru (pl. n.) **VIII(i)** note 24: citizens

cēapstræt, cȳpstræt (n.) **I** note 7, **XXVI** note 12: market-street
cwyde (n.) **XXIX**: bequest
cȳping (n.) **XXVIII** note 16: market-place
cyrograf (n.) **VII** note 28: chirograph

(ge)dīhligean (v.) **VII**: to be given privacy

eāca (n.) **II, XIX**: addition, augmentation
eald (adj.) **I** note 9: former, disused

embegang see *ymbgang*

*fearning (n.) **XXII** note 37: ?ferny place
flæscmangere (n.) **XXVI** note 13: butcher
feorm (n.) **VIII(i)**: subsistence
fostorland (n.) **V, iii**: land providing food
frēols (n.) **V, iii**: freedom
frēolsbōc (n.) **V, i–ii, v–xiv**: charter of freedom
frēolsdōm (n.) **XX** note 5: free tenure
furh (n.) **XXII** note 23: trench, furrow

(ge)grynd (n.) **VII**: plot of ground
gyrd (n.) **II** note 6, **IX** note 9, **XXVIII** note 14: 'yard', rod [5½ modern yards]

haga (n.) **I, XIX–XX, XXIII, XXV–XXVII, XXIX**: [urban] tenement
hēafodstocc (n.) **XXII** note 20: head-stock
hīd, hyd (n.) **V, iii, VIII(i), XVIII, XX, XXX–XXXI**: hide [fiscal unit]
hīrēd (n.) **V, iii, VII, VIII(i), XXIX**: [monastic] community, flock
hīwan (n.) **II** note 3: [the pre-Reform] community [at Winchester Cathedral]
hlæfdige (n.) **VII**: Lady [title of royal consort]

(ge)hwearf (n.) **VIII(i)**: exchange

irfe, yrfe (n.) **II** note 13, **XXII**: inheritance

licgan (v.) **I, VIII(i)**: to run (of boundary or stream); **V, iii**: to lie
līctūn (n.) **II** note 21: cemetery
Lunden-weg (n.) **XXII** note 32: route in the direction of London

mancus [MS. *mancæs*, pl. acc.] (n.) **VII**: mancus [a gold coin, see **III**, note 6]
mearc (n.) **XXII** notes 9, 13, 17: marked boundary
metgyrd (n.) **II** note 22, **VII** note 24: measured 'yard' or rod
mōdig (adj.) **V, iii** note 63: proud
munuclif (n.) **VII** note 3: the monastic life
mylengear (n.) **I** note 4: mill-yair
mylenweg (n.) **XXII** note 31: mill-way

nunhīrēd (n.) **VII** note 18: community of nuns [at Nunnaminster]

ofgān (v.) **VII**: to acquire, exact one's due, obtain an equivalent of

port (n.) **V, iii, XXIII** note 1: city, major market-centre
portmann (n.) **V, iii**: citizen

portstrǣt (n.) **XXII** note 10: road
  leading to a city or market-centre
portweall (n.) **VIII(i)** note 15: city-
  wall
preost (n.) **V, iii**: secular cleric;
  XXVI: priest

rymet(t) (n.) **VII** note 2, **VIII(i)** note
  12: clearance, space

sacu (n.) **VII**: dispute
scyldwyrhta (n.) **XXVI**: shield-maker
(ge)sehtness (n.) **VII** (cf. note 27):
  reconciliation
(ge)setness (n.) **XXX**: decree
sibb (n.) **VII** (cf. notes 15, 27): peace
slāpærn (n.) **II** note 5: dormitory

sōcn (n.) **XXIX**: jurisdiction
sōm (n.) **VII** (cf. note 15): concord
stapolþorn (n.) **XXII** note 26: staple-
  thorn
stician (v.) **I** note 10: to strike, run,
  lie [of boundary]
stōw (n.) **II** note 12, **V, iii, XXX**:
  holy place [Winchester
  Cathedral]
strǣt (n.) **I–II, XXVIII**: urban street;
  XXII note 21: minor road
  linking two Roman roads

(ge)tēon (v.) **VII**: to divert
tige (n.) **VII**: diversion

wæterpytt (n.) **XXVIII** note 18: well

wæterscipe (n.) **VII** note 17:
  watercourse
werian (v.) **V, iii** note 60, **XXX**: to
  be assessed at [for taxation]
westweard (adj.) **I** note 5: western,
  lying to the west
wīcnera (n.) **XXIX**: officer, reeve
windcirice (n.) **II** note 4: 'wound-
  church', ?church made of wattle
witan (pl. n.) **II**: counsellors
worðig (n.) **II** note 11: enclosure,
  estate

ymbgang, embegang (n.) **II, XXVI**:
  circumference, boundary
yrfe see *irfe*

INDEX OF BIBLICAL REFERENCES

The order of the index is that of the Vulgate and of Douai-Rheims

Old Testament
Gen. 1 **V** nn. 4, 115
Gen. 1–3 **IV** n. 3
Gen. 2: 7 **IV** n. 12
Gen. 2: 8 **IV** n. 16
Gen. 2: 15 **IV** n. 16
Gen. 2: 17 **IV** n. 18
Gen. 3: 1–6 **IV** n. 20
Gen. 4–8 **IV** n. 25
Gen. 4: 11–16 **IV** n. 68
Gen. 7: 13 **IV** n. 26
Gen. 8: 18 **IV** n. 26
Gen. 9: 9–17 **IV** n. 27
Exod. 1: 14 **V** n. 207
Exod. 6: 6–7 **V** n. 201
Exod. 23: 8 **IV** n. 64
Lev. 26: 19 **V** n. 46
Num. 16: 1–33 **XI** n. 15
Deut. 4: 31 **IV** n. 27
Deut. 16: 19 **IV** n. 64
Job 1: 21 **V** n. 70
Job 21: 14 **XI** n. 18
Ps. 21: 22 **IV** n. 32
Ps. 61: 11 **V** n. 163

Ps. 83: 7 **V** nn. 146, 202
Eccles. 1: 14 **XXIV** n. 2
Wisd. 1: 1 **XXVIII** n. 2
Wisd. 11: 18 **IV** n. 5
Ecclus. 10: 15 **IV** n. 9
Ecclus. 20: 31 **IV** n. 64
Ecclus. 26: 27 **XXVIII** n. 12
Ecclus. 45: 22 **XI** n. 15
Isa. 14: 12–15 **IV** n. 3
Jer. 1: 10 **IV** n. 40
2 Macc. 7: 28 **IV** n. 4

New Testament
Matt. 6: 20 **VI** n. 2
Matt. 15: 31–43 **IV** n. 114
Matt. 16: 18 **XXXIII** n. 17
Matt. 16: 19 **V** n. 25
Matt. 25: 35–45 **IV** n. 91
Matt. 25: 46 **IV** n. 33
Mark 10: 21 **V** n. 239
Luke 6: 38 **V** nn. 163, 172
Luke 12: 33 **XXVI** n. 2
Luke 13: 27–8 **XXIV** n. 9
Luke 21: 10 **V** nn. 128, 181

John 10: 11–13 **IV** n. 98
Acts 5: 1–11 **IV** n. 69
Rom. 1: 32 **IV** n. 55
Rom. 5: 9–21 **IV** n. 28
1 Cor. 2: 9 **IV** n. 105, **VI** n. 1
1 Cor. 13: 13 **V** n. 200
1 Cor. 15: 21–2 **IV** n. 28
2 Cor. 4: 18 **V** n. 95, **XXIV** n. 1
Phil. 3: 30 **V** n. 203
Ephes. 6: 16–17 **IV** nn. 101–2
1 Tim. 6: 7 **V** n. 71
1 Pet. 1: 24 **V** n. 185
2 Pet. 2: 4 **IV** n. 3
Rev. 12: 9 **IV** n. 3
Rev. 20: 12 **IV** n. 72, **V** nn. 24, 250
Rev. 20: 15 **IV** n. 72, **V** nn. 24, 250
Rev. 21: 27 **IV** n. 72, **V** nn. 24, 250
Rev. 22: 16 **IV** n. 29

Apocalyptica
Jubilees 2: 2 **IV** n. 3
2 Enoch 29: 4–5 **IV** n. 3, **V** n. 5
Testament (Assumption) of Moses
   37 **IV** n. 22

INDEX OF PERSONS NAMED IN THE DOCUMENTS

Abiron **XI**

Adam de Port **XIII**

Ælfgar, thegn **XXII**

Ælfgar, thegn **IX**

Ælfgifu Emma, wife of King
Æthelred II **XXVIII–XXIX**

Ælfheah, abbot (?Bath) **VI**

Ælfheah, bishop (Lichfield) **XXVI**

Ælfheah, bishop (II, Winchester)
XXIV, XXVI, XXX

Ælfheah, ealdorman (Wessex) **IV,
XXII, XXX**

Ælfheah **XXXII**

Ælfhelm, ealdorman (Deira) **XXVI**

Ælfhelm, thegn **IX**

Ælfhere, ealdorman (Mercia) **IV,
VI, XXII**

Ælfhere **XXXII**

Ælfric, abbot **VI**

Ælfric, archbishop (Canterbury)
XXVI

Ælfric, ealdorman (Hants) **IX,
XXVI, XXX**

Ælfric, ealdorman (Mercia) **IX**

Ælfric **XXIX**

Ælfsige, thegn **IX, XXII** (x2)

Ælfsige **VIII(i)(ii)**

Ælfstan, abbot (Glastonbury) **IV**

Ælfstan, bishop (London) **IV, VI,
IX**

Ælfstan, bishop (Rochester) **IV**

Ælfstan **II–III**

Ælfswith, noblewoman **XXVI**

Ælfthryth, wife of King Edgar,
mother of King Æthelred II **IV,
VI–VII, IX**

Ælfweald, bishop (I, Crediton) **IV,
VI, XXII**

Ælfweald, bishop (II, Crediton)
XXVI

Ælfweald, thegn **XXII**

Ælfweard, thegn **IV, VI, IX**

Ælfwine, thegn **IV**(x2), **IX, XXII**

Ælfwine son of Ælfsige and
Æthelhild **VIII(i)(ii)**

Æscwig, abbot (Bath) **IV, VI**

Æscwig, bishop (Dorchester) **IX,
XXIV**

Æthelgar, abbot (New Minster) and
bishop (Selsey) **IV, VI–IX,
XXIV**

Æthelgeard, thegn **XIX–XX**

Æthelhild **VIII(i)(ii)**

Æthelmær, ealdorman (Hants)
VIII(i)(ii)

Æthelmær, *miles* **XXIV**

Æthelmær, thegn **IX**

Æthelmær, [thegn] **XXVI**

Æthelmær **XXXII**

Æthelmund, ealdorman (N. W.
Mercia) **XXII**

Æthelred II, king **IX, XXIII,
XXVI, XXVIII–XXX**

Æthelsige, bishop (Sherborne) **IX,
XXIV**

Æthelsige, thegn **XXII** (x3)

Æthelstan, son of King Æthelred II
XXVIII

Æthelstan, ealdorman (S. E.
Mercia) **IV**

Æthelstan, thegn **II–III**

Æthelstan **II–III** (x2)

Æthelweald, ealdorman (E. Anglia)
XXII

Æthelweard, the king's brother /
son **II–III**

Æthelweard, abbot (Malmesbury)
IX

Æthelweard, ealdorman (Western
Shires) **IX, XXVI**

Æthelweard, thegn **IV, VI**

Æthelweard **XXX**

Æthelwine, ealdorman (E. Anglia)
IV, VI, IX

Æthelwine, thegn **XXII**

Æthelwine, reeve of Winchester
XXVIII

Æthelwold, abbot (Abingdon), then
bishop (Winchester) **IV–IX,
XXI–II, XXXIII**

Æthelwulf, king (W. Saxons) **V,
ii–iv, vi**

Æthulf, bishop (Elmham) **IV,
XXII**

Æthulf, bishop (Hereford) **XXVI**

Alfred, king (W. Saxons) **II–III, V,
ii–iii, VIII(i)(ii), XXX**

Alfred, thegn **XXII**

Alfred, kinsman of Bishop
Denewulf **V, v**

Alla, thegn **II–III**

Ananias **IV, x**

Asser, bishop (Sherborne) **II–III**

Benedict, St. **IV, xiii, V, iii**

Benedict **XI**

Beorhtfrith, thegn **IV, XXII**

Beorhthelm, bishop (Wells) **IV,
VI, XXII**

Beorhthelm, bishop (Winchester)
XXII

Beorhtnoth, ealdorman (Essex) **IV,
VI, IX, XXII**

Beorhtric, thegn **VI**

Beorhtsige, thegn **II–III**

Beorhtweald, thegn **IX**

Beorhtwulf, priest **II- III**

Beornhelm, abbot **II–III**

Beornstan, thegn **II–III** (x2)

Beornstan, priest **II**

Beornwulf, deacon **II–III**

Bica **XXII** (bounds)

Birinus, St. **V, i–ii, v**

Cædwalla, king (W. Saxons) **V, i**

Cenwealh, king (W. Saxons) **V, i–iii, v, viii**

Ceolmund, bishop (Rochester) **II–III**

Chiping **XXXII**

Costic **XXII** (bounds)

Cynegisl, king (W. Saxons) **V, i–iii**

Cyneweard, abbot (Milton) **VI**

Dathan **XI**

Denewulf, bishop (Winchester) **II–III, V, v**

Deormod, thegn **II–III**

Dunstan, archbishop (Canterbury) **IV, VI, IX, XXII, XXXIII**

Eadgeard **XXIV**

Eadgifu, grandmother of King Edgar **IV**

Eadgifu, abbess (Nunnaminster) **VII**

Eadhelm, bishop (Selsey) **IV, VI**

Eadred, king **V, v, XIX–XX**

Eadred, son of King Æthelred II **XXVIII**

Eadric, thegn **XXII**

Eadstan, deacon **II–III**

Eadweald, priest **II**

Eadwulf **II–III** (x2)

Ealdred, bishop (Cornwall) **XXVI**

Ealdred, thegn **XXII**

Ealdwulf, archbishop (York) **XXVI**

Ealhstan **II–III**

Ealhswith, wife of King Alfred **I**

Eanwulf, thegn **VI**

Ecgbeorht, king (W. Saxons) **V, ii–iii, v**

Edgar, king **IV–VII, XXII, XXXIII**

Edgar, bishop (Hereford) **II–III**

Edmund, king (unnamed) **XIX**

Edmund, son of King Edgar **IV**

Edmund (Ironside), son of King Æthelred II **XXVIII**

Edmund, ealdorman (Western Provinces) **XXII**

Edmund **XXII** (bounds)

Edward the Elder, king **II–III, V, ii–iv**

Edward the Martyr, king **VIII(i)(ii)**

Edward the Confessor, king **XXIX**

Edward, son of King Edgar **IV**

Frithugyth, queen (W. Saxons) (unnamed) **V, iv** (n. 80)

Geoffrey, abbot (New Minster) **XII–XIII**

Gerald **XXXII**

Gilbert of Laigle **XII**

Godfrey (of Cambrai), prior (Old Minster) **XI**

Godwine, abbot **VI**

Godwine, bishop (Rochester) **XXVI**

Godwine, earl (Wessex) **XXIX**

Godwine **XXXII**

Gregory, St. **IV, vii**

Hamo the steward **XII**

Henry I, king **XII–XVII**

Henry II, king **XVII**

Henry (of Blois), bishop of Winchester **XVII**

Henry (de Beaumont), earl of Warwick **XIII**

Henry de Port **XII–XIV, XVI**

Herbert the chamberlain **XII**

Hugh the mason **XXXII**

Hugh the sheriff (Hants) **XI**

John [XII], pope **XXXIII**

John (de Villula), bishop (Bath) **XIII**

John **XI**

Judas **XI**

Julian, pope **IX**

Leofa, thegn **VI**

Leofa **XXVI** (bounds)

Leofric, abbot (?Exeter/Muchelney) **IX**

Leofsige, ealdorman (Essex) **XXVI**

Leofwine, thegn **IV**

Manno **XXXII**

Nero, (emperor of Rome) **XI**

Nigel d'Aubigny **XIII**

Nigel d'Oilli **XIII**

Ocea, thegn **II–III**

Ordbeorht, bishop (Selsey) **XXVI**

Ordbeorht, abbot (Chertsey) **IV, IX**

Ordgar, ealdorman (Devon) **IV**

Ordwulf, [thegn] **XXVI**

Osbern of Eu **XI**

Osbern **XXXII**

Oscytel, archbishop (York) **IV, XXII**

Osgar, abbot (Abingdon) **IV, VI**

Oslac, ealdorman (Northumbria) **VI**

Oswald, bishop (Worcester) and archbishop (York) **IV, IX, XXII, XXIV**

Osweard, thegn **IV, XXII**

Oswulf, bishop (Ramsbury) **IV, VI, XXII**

Oswulf, thegn **XXII**

Pilate (Roman procurator) **IX**

Plegmund, archbishop (Canterbury) **II–III**

Ralph (d'Escures), archbishop (Canterbury) **XIII**

Ralph of Limésy **XIII**

Ranulf (Flambard), bishop (Durham) **XIII**

Ranulf the chancellor **XII**

Richard (of Beaumais I), bishop (London) **XIII**

Ralf of Mortemer **XXXII**

Riwallon, abbot (New Minster) **X–XI**

Robert, bishop (Lincoln) **XII–XIV, XVI**

Robert, count of Flanders **XII**

Robert, count of Meulan **XIII–XIV, XVI**

Robert Corn' **XI**

Roger, bishop (Salisbury) **XII–XVI**

Saphira **IV, x**

Sideman, abbot (Exeter) **VI**

Sigeric, bishop (Ramsbury) **XXIV**

Sigeric, abbot (Canterbury) **IX**

Stigand, bishop (Winchester) **XXIX**

Tata, priest **II**

Tata, thegn **III**

Teotsel' **XI**

Thored, ealdorman (Northumbria) **IX**

Thurstan, archbishop (York) **XIII**

Thurstan the red **XXXII**

Thurstan the small **XXXII**

Walkelin, bishop (Winchester) **XI, XXXII**

Walter Scot **XI**

Walter the constable **XIII**

Walter **XXXII**

Wighelm, bishop (Selsey) **II–III**

Wighelm **II–III**

Wigmund, bishop (Lichfield/ Leicester) **II–III**

Wigstan **XXVIII** (bounds)

Wihtbrord, thegn **II–III**

Wilfrith, bishop (?Dorchester/ Lichfield) **II–III**

William I, king **X–XI, XIV, XVI**

William II, king **XII**

William Giffard, bishop (Winchester) **XII–XIII, XVII**

William (Warelwast), bishop (Exeter) **XIII–XIV, XVI**

William d'Aubigny **XII, XV**

William de Gimices **XI**

William of Pont de l'Arche, sheriff (Hants) **XII, XV**

William of Tancarville, the chamberlain **XIII**

William **XI**

William **XXXII**

witan, West Saxon **II**

witan, temp. King Edgar **V, xiv**

Wulfgar, bishop (Ramsbury) **IX**

Wulfgar, thegn **XXII**

Wulfgeat, [thegn] **XXVI**

Wulfhelm, thegn **II–III** (x2), **XXII**

Wulfhelm **II–III**

Wulfhun the priest **XIX**

Wulfmær **XXX**

Wulfnoth, priest **II**

Wulfred, thegn **III**

Wulfred **II**

Wulfric, thegn **IX**

Wulfric **II–III**

Wulfsige, bishop (London) **II–III**

Wulfsige, bishop (Sherborne) **XXVI**

Wulfsige, thegn **IX**

Wulfsige the priest **XXVI**

Wulfsige **II–III**

Wulfstan, bishop (London) **XXVI**

Wulfstan, thegn **IV, VI**

Wulfstan **II–III**

Wynsige, bishop (Lichfield) **IV**

Wynsige **II–III**

INDEX OF PLACES NAMED IN THE DOCUMENTS

References are to pre-1974 counties.
+ = estate with tenement or property in Winchester

Abbots Worthy, Hants **XVIII**
Abbotts Ann, Hants **III**
Abbotts Barton, Hants **XIII, XVII**
Abingdon Abbey, Berks., *see*
     Winchester, tenements
Alresford, Hants **V, v, xiv**
Alton, Hants **X–XI, XIV**
Avington, Hants **XXXI**

Beauworth, Hants **V, viii**
Beddington, Surrey **V, x**
Bentley, Hants **V, ix**
Bishopstoke, Hants **V, xiii–xiv,**
    XXXI
Bishop's Waltham, Hants **V, xii**
Bradley, Hants **V, vii**
Brambridge, Hants **XXXI**
Brentford, Middx. **XXVI**
Brown Candover, Hants **III**
Burcot, Hants **III**

Calbourne, IOW (*et Dreðecumb*) **V, i**
Charmouth, Dorset **V, iv**
Chessington, Surrey **V, x**
Chilbolton, Hants **XXXI**
Chilcomb, Hants **V, i–iii, xiv,**
    XXX–XXXII
Chilland, Hants **V, xiii**
Chisledon, Wilts. **III**
Collingbourne Kingston,Wilts. **III**
Cranbourne, Hants **III**
Crawley, Hants **V, xiii**

Dover, Kent (date) **XII**
Downton, Wilts. **V, i, xiv**
Drayton by Newton, Hants **III**
Dreðecumb, see Calbourne
Durley, Hants **III, XIII**

Easton, Hants **V, xiii, XXII,**
    XXXI
East Stratton, Hants **III**
Exton+, Hants **XIX**

Fareham, Hants **V, xi**
Farnham, Surrey **V, ix**
Fonthill Bishop, Wilts. **V, xiv**
Frensham, Surrey **V, xiv**

Hayling, Hants **XXIX**
Headbourne Worthy, Hants
    XXXII n. 11
Hensting, Hants **V, xiii**
Highclere, Hants **V, vi, xiv**
Horton, Hants **V, xiii**
Hunton, Hants **V, xiii**
Hurstbourne Tarrant+, Hants
    XXI
hwitan clife, æt **XVIII**

Itchen, R., Hants **IX, XVIII, XXII**

Kilmeston+, Hants **XXIII, XXXI**
Kingsclere, Hants **X, XIV**

Lake, Surrey **V, x**

Micheldever+, Hants [Hundred]
    III, XVIII
Mordune, æt **VIII**

Northington, Hants **III**
North Waltham, Hants **V, vii**
Norton by Selborne, Hants **III**
Nursling, Hants **XXXI**

Otterbourne, Hants **V, xiii,**
    XXXI, XXXII n. 11
Overton, Hants **V, vii**
Ovington, Hants **V, viii, XXXI**
Owslebury, Hants **V, xiii**

Popham, Hants **III**

Slackstead, Hants **III**
Southampton, Hants (date) **III**
Swampton, Hants **XXXII** n. 11
Swarraton, Hants **III**

Tadley, Hants **V, vii**
Tandridge, Surrey **V, x**
Tatchbury, Hants **III**
Taunton, Somerset **V, iv, xiv**
Tichborne, Hants **V, viii, xiv,**
    XXXI
Twyford, Hants **V, xiii, XXXI**

Washford, Somerset **V, iv**
Westbourne, Sussex (date) **XIII**
West Tisted+, Hants **XX**
Wherwell Abbey, Hants, *see*
    Winchester, tenements
Winchester
  castle **XIII**
  churches
    Hyde Abbey **XII–XV, XVII**
    New Minster **II–IV, VI–VIII,**
      X–XIII, XVI, XXXIII
     cemetery **X–XI, XVII**
    Nunnaminster **I, VI–VIII**
    Old Minster/cathedral **II,**
     V–VIII, XII–XIII,
     XXVI, XXIX,
     XXXII–III

cemetery **II**

St. Andrew's **II**

St. Gregory's **II**

St. James's **XIII**

St. Peter's in the Fleshambles **XXVIII**

'wound' church **II**

   refectory **II**

   stone dormitory **II**

defences

   'king's city-hedge' **I**

   old city wall **VIII**

   south wall **XVIII, XXIII**

fords **I**

gates

   east **XIX**

   north **XII, XVI**

   west **XIII**

hill, eastern (St Giles's) **XII**

Hyde **XII–XIII, XVII**

Hyde Moors **IX**

Hyde Street, 'liberty' **XVI**

market-place **XXVIII**

mills **VII, XIII**

   Costic's **XXII**

at east gate **XIX**

   southernmost **XVIII**

mill-yairs **I**

monastic enclosures **VI–VIII**

royal palace **XIV–XV, XVII**

St. Giles's Fair **XII–XIII**

streets

   butchers'- **XXVI**

   east **I**

   market- **I, XXVI**

   middle **I**

   north **II**

   St. Valery's **XIII**

   shieldmakers'- **XXVI**

   south **II**

   Tanner- **XXV**

tenements

   Abingdon Abbey's **XXI**

   Ælfgifu Emma's **XXVIII–IX**

   Ælfswith's **XXVI**

   Æthelgeard's **XIX–XX**

   Conan's **XXIV**

   Eadgeard's **XXIV**

   Ealhswith's **I**

   Godbegot **XXVIII–IX**

   Leofa's **XXVI**

   Wherwell Abbey's **XXVII**

   Wigstan's **XXVIII**

   Wulfhun the priest's **XIX**

   Wulfsige the priest's **XXVI**

   see also Exton, Hurstbourne Tarrant, Kilmeston, West Tisted, Wootton St. Lawrence

walls, *see* defences

watercourses **I, VII–VIII, XXII**

Windsor, Berks. (date) **XII, XIV–XV**

Woodmancott, Hants **III**

Wootton St. Lawrence+,Hants **XXV**

porðig, se **II**

Worthy = Abbots

   Worthy, Hants **XVIII**

Worthy = Abbotts

   Barton, Hants **XIII, XVII**

Worthy, Headbourne?, Hants **V, xiv**

Worthy, Martyr?, Hants **V, xiv**

INDEX OF REFERENCES TO
ANGLO-SAXON CHARTERS

The first number is that of the document as listed in Sawyer

201: 162 n. 15

229: 106 n. 11; 107 n. 16

242: 17 n. 16; 117 n. 101

254: 32 n. 29; 115 nn. 79–80; 116 nn. 91–2

273: 132 n. 230

274: 107 n. 17

275: 17 n. 18; 107 n. 16

284: 17 n. 16; 117 n. 106

309: 196 n. 20

310: 17 n. 19; 115 n. 80

311: 17 n. 19; 115 nn. 79 and 83

325: 17 n. 17; 110 n. 37; 224–5 n. 6

340: 197 n. 35

345: 54 nn. 35–6 and 39

348: 54 nn. 36 and 42

350: 56 n. 47

354: 53 n. 24; 62 n. 27

355: 54 n. 36

359: 62 n. 27

360 (part): **XVIII**

360: 14; 50; 57 and n. 8; 58–9; 60 n. a; 63 n. r; 61 nn. 7, 9, 13, and 15–17; 62 nn. 18 and 23; 63 nn. 29, 32, and 36; 178; 179 and nn. 4–5 and 7; 197 n. 32

363: 50

364: 54 n. 35

365: 50; 54 n. 34; 56 n. 46; 62 n. 25

366: 50; 54 n. 34; 56 n. 46; 62 n. 27

369: 54 n. 45

370: **III**

372: 127 nn. 177 and 179

373: 115 nn. 79 and 85

374: 61 n. 7

375: 17 nn. 16 and 18; 53 n. 24; 118 n. 111

376: 17 n. 17; 53 n. 24; 103 n. 35; 110 n. 39; 196 nn. 19–23 and 25–6; 197 nn. 30, 34, and 39; 224 n. 14; 228 n. 12

377: 53 n. 24; 124 n. 151

378: 53 n. 24

379: 62 n. 26

380: 50

381: 128 n. 187; 197 n. 32

383: 53 n. 24

385: 32 n. 35; 56 n. 49

393: 17 n. 18; 107 n. 16

404: 187 n. 2

412: 125 nn. 160 and 164; 126 n. 167

413: 125 n. 160; 126 n. 167

416: 125 nn. 160 and 164; 126 n. 167

417: 125 n. 160; 126 n. 167; 187 n. 2

418: 125 nn. 160 and 164; 126 n. 167

419: 125 n. 160; 126 n. 167

425: 126 n. 167

427: 228 n. 12

443: 17 n. 19; 103 n. 35

461–2: 186 n. 7

463 (part): **XIX**

464: 186 n. 7

471: 84 n. 69

486: 84 n. 69; 145 nn. 3 and 5

487: 84 n. 69

488 (part): **XX**

492: 84 n. 69

495: 47 n. 4

511: 187 n. 2; 189 n. 4

517: 187 n. 2

521: 17 n. 19; 115 n. 79

523: 187 n. 2

526: 32 n. 34

528: 47 n. 5; 124 n. 158

536: 187 n. 2

540: 17 n. 18; 103 n. 35; 107 n. 16

557: 199 n. 68

565: 119 n. 123

596: 116 n. 92

598–9: 187 n. 2

620: 47 n. 4

638: 145 n. 5

641: 187 n. 2

648: 57–8; 178; 179 n. 4

658 and 673: 15 n. 4; 76 n. 16; 84 n. 69; 108 n. 23

680: 119 n. 123

683: 84 n. 65; 129 n. 191; 194 n. 4

687: 68; 84 n. 65; 91 n. 114

689 (part): **XXI**

690: 68 and n. 22; 75 n. 13; 76 n. 16; 84 n. 65; 91 n. 115; 92 n. 125

693a (part): **XXIII**

693b: 200 n. 1; 201 n. 3

693ab: 228 n. 7

695: **XXII**

699: 195 nn. 6–12; 228 n. 4

701: 121 n. 138; 184 n. 5

702: 105 n. 1

703: 68 n. 22; 75 n. 13; 76 n. 16

706: 84 n. 65; 105 n. 1

707: 91 n. 115

708: 121 n. 138

717: 84 n. 65; 91 n. 115; 105 n. 1

725: 93 n. 130

731: 18 n. 23; 75 n. 11; 81 n. 44; 131 n. 219; 153 n. 6; 162 n. 15

737: 92 n. 122; 105 n. 1

738: 105 n. 1; 121 n. 138

739: 92 nn. 122 and 125

741: 162 n. 15
744: 121 n. 138
745: **IV**
746: 62 n. 28; 69 n. 31; 92 n. 125; 93 n. 126; 178
754 and 757-9: 92 n. 122
763: 145 n. 5
773: 92 n. 122
774: 145 n. 5
777 and 781: 125 nn. 159-61 and 163-4; 126 n. 167
782: 91 n. 119; 155 nn. 30 and 32
786 and 788: 15 n. 4; 76 n. 16; 84 n. 69; 92 n. 122; 108 n. 23
792: 87 n. 94; 92 n. 119
803: 96 n. 159
806: 17 n. 19; 93 n. 126; 94 n. 130; 109 n. 28; 115 n. 79
807: **VI**
811: 94 n. 132
812: 15 n. 4; 76 n. 16; 84 n. 69; 108 n. 23
814: **V(v)**
815: **V(x)**
816: **V(xii)**
817: **V(ii)** and **(iii)**
818: **V(xiv)**
819: **V(vi)**
821: **V(i)**
822: **V(xi)**
823: **V(ix)**
824: **V(vii)**
825: **V(iv)**
826: **V(viii)**
827: **V(xiii)**
830: 121 n. 138
835: 17 n. 20; 103 n. 34
838: 103; 129 n. 199; 130 n. 209; 131 n. 212

839: 82 n. 52
842: 149
845: **IX**
846 and 848: 121 n. 138
858: 152 n. 1
865 and 869: 149
870: 202
871: **XXIV**
874 (part): **XXV**
874: 225 n. 4
876: 15 n. 4; 76 n. 16; 87 n. 94; 88 n. 96; 92 n. 122; 103 n. 34; 108 n. 23; 114 n. 69; 116 n. 90
885: 207
888: 207; 209 n. 5
889: **XXVI**
891: 17 nn. 18 and 20; 103 nn. 34 and 38; 107 n. 16
893: 208
904 (part): **XXVII**
911: 87 n. 94
925: **XXVIII**
933: 216 n. 10
937: 191 n. 2
945: 223 n. 1
946: **XXX**
956: 57 n. 4; 62 n. 19; 150
962: 196 nn. 26 and 28-9; 197 n. 30
964: 210 n. 8
986: 189 n. 3
1013: 136 n. 7
1031: 218 n. 11
1040 and 1043: 145 n. 5
1153: **XXIX**
1154: 220 n. 4
1165: 225 n. 9
1242: 94 n. 130; 209 n. 6
1263 and 1274: 123 n. 148

1275: 192 n. 4; 194 n. 3; 195 nn. 11-13 and 22
1277: 33 n. 39; 228 n. 13
1284: 132 n. 231
1285: 50; 52 n. 12
1286: 54 n. 34; 115 nn. 79 and 85
1287: 50; 117 n. 108
1292: 198 n. 61
1376: **VIII**
1383: 203 n. 6
1417: 61 n. 7; 62 n. 27
1418-19: 15 n. 8; 185 nn. 2 and 5
1420: 62 n. 19; 225 nn. 3-4
1428: 9
1443: **II**
1444: 118 n. 109
1449: **VII**
1454: 142 n. 16
1476: 222 n. 11
1484: 33 n. 40
1485: 96 n. 152
1491: 62 n. 25; 119 n. 123
1496: 15 n. 8; 185 n. 3; 187 n. 2
1498: 146 n. 21
1503: 145 n. 5; 179 n. 4; 219 n. 24
1507: 62 n. 27; 191 n. 2
1515: 107 n. 16
1533: 62 n. 25
1560 : **I**
1581: 107 n. 17
1605: 53 n. 24
1663: 187 n. 2
1812: 110 n. 38
1815: 187 n. 4
1820: **XXXI**
1821: 226 n. 4

The following documents are listed only in Sawyer (Kelly)

1428a: 34 n. 56

1451a: 32 n. 26; 34 n. 56

ADDENDA

M. L. = comments by Professor Michael Lapidge

p. 77: **IV**, n. 22.—The Apocalypse of Moses is more correctly called the Testament (Assumption) of Moses, see B. Metzger and M. Coogan (ed.), *The Oxford Companion to the Bible* (Oxford, 1993), 35.

p. 80: **IV**, n. 42.—*inserui* 'inserted' is probably for *inseui* 'sowed' due to confusion between two verbs with the same present tense (M. L.).

p. 82: **IV**, n. 53.—The spellings *actactus, attactus* are for *adtactus* (M. L.).

p. 83: **IV, ix**, line 2.—*contigeret* is probably for *contingeret* (M. L.).

p. 85: **IV, xii**, line 11.—*constringant* is probably for *constringantur* (M. L.).

p. 86: **IV, xii.**—*Ciuium conuiuae . . . utantur cibariis,* cf. *RC*, cap. 11, *Saecularium uero conuiuia, ni forsan itineris hospitalitas inopinate superuenerit, nullo modo ausu temerario nec praelati nec subiecti adire praesumant* 'Neither prelates nor subjects should ever think of presuming to be present at worldly feastings, unless perchance in case of unexpected hospitality when travelling.' The rare adj. *caritativus* found in **IV, xii** also occurs in *RC*, cap. 11 (M. L.).

p. 109: **V, i**, n. 25.—The use of *clauiger* for St. Peter comes from Aldhelm (M. L.).

p. 116: **V, v**, lines 6–7.—*toto mentis conamine* is an Aldhelmian phrase, also used in the (Winchester) *Carmen de libero arbitrio* (line 171), on which see Michael Lapidge, 'Three Latin Poems from Æthelwold's School at Winchester', *ASE* 1 (1972), 85–137; reprinted in *idem, Anglo-Latin Literature 900–1066* (London and Rio Grande, 1993), 225–77 (M. L.).

p. 119: **V, vi**, line 7.—*fetidam melancolię* is also found in Aldhelm, *De virginitate,* cap. 32 (ed. R. Ewald (Berlin, 1919), 274) (M. L.).